THE ANNUAL DIRECTORY OF

Western
Bed & Breakfasts

1999 Edition

THE ANNUAL DIRECTORY OF

Western Bed & Breakfasts

1999 Edition

Tracey Menges, *Compiler*

RUTLEDGE HILL PRESS®
NASHVILLE, TENNESSEE

Published in Nashville, Tennessee, by Rutledge Hill Press®, Inc., 211 Seventh Avenue North, Nashville, Tennessee 37219. Distributed in Canada by H. B. Fenn and Company, Ltd., 34 Nixon Road, Bolton, Ontario L7E 1W2. Distributed in Australia by The Five Mile Press Pty. Ltd., 22 Summit Road, Noble Park, Victoria, 3174. Distributed in New Zeland by Tandem Press, 2 Rugby Road, Birkenhead, Auckland 10. Distributed in the United Kingdom by Verulam Publishing, Ltd., 152a Park Street Lane, Park Street, St. Albans, Hertfordshire AL2 2AU.

Cover design and book design by Harriette Bateman
Page composition by Roger A. DeLiso, Nashville, Tennessee

Printed in the United States of America.

1 2 3 4 5 6—02 01 00 99 98

Contents

Introduction

The 1999 edition of *The Annual Directory of Western Bed & Breakfasts* is one of the most comprehensive directories available today. Whether planning your honeymoon, a family vacation or reunion, or a business trip (many bed and breakfasts provide conference facilities), you will find what you are looking for at a bed and breakfast. They are all here just waiting to be discovered.

Once you know your destination, look for it, or one close by, to see what accommodations are available. Each state has a general map with city locations to help you plan your trip efficiently. There are listings for all 50 states, Canada, Puerto Rico, and the Virgin Islands. Don't be surprised to find a listing in the remote spot you thought only you knew about. Even if your favorite hideaway isn't listed, you're sure to discover a new one.

How to Use This Guide

The sample listing below is typical of the entries in this directory. Each bed and breakfast is listed alphabetically by city and establishment name. The description provides an overview of the bed and breakfast and may include nearby activities and attractions. *Please note that the descriptions have been provided by the hosts. The publisher has not visited these bed and breakfasts and is not responsible for inaccuracies.*

Following the description are notes that have been designed for easy reference. Looking at the sample, a quick glance tells you that this bed and breakfast has four guest rooms, two with private baths (PB) and two that share a bath (SB). The rates are for two people sharing one room. Tax may or may not be included. The specifics of "Credit Cards" and "Notes" are listed at the bottom of each page.

GREAT TOWN

Favorite Bed and Breakfast

123 Main Street, 12345
(800) 555-1234

This quaint bed and breakfast is surrounded by five acres of award-winning landscaping and gardens. There are four guest rooms, each individually decorated with antiques. It is close to antique shops, restaurants, and outdoor activities. Breakfast includes homemade specialties and is served in the formal dining room at guests' leisure. Minimum stay of two nights.

Hosts: Sue and Jim Smith
Rooms: 4 (2 PB; 2 SB) $65-80
Full Breakfast
Credit Cards: A, B
Notes: 2, 5, 8, 10, 11, 12, 13

For example, the letter A means that MasterCard is accepted. The number 10 means that tennis is available on the premises or within 10 to 15 miles.

In many cases, a bed and breakfast is listed with a reservation service that represents several houses in one area. This service is responsible for bookings and can answer other questions you may have. They also inspect each listing and can help you choose the best place for your needs.

Before You Arrive

Now that you have chosen the bed and breakfast that interests you, there are some things you need to find out. You should always make reservations in advance, and while you are doing so you should ask about the local taxes. City taxes can be an unwelcome surprise. Make sure there are accommodations for your children. If you have dietary needs or prefer nonsmoking rooms, find out if these requirements can be met. Ask about check-in times and cancellation policies. Get specific directions. Most bed and breakfasts are readily accessible, but many are a little out of the way.

When You Arrive

In many instances you are visiting someone's home. Be respectful of their property, their schedules, and their requests. Don't smoke if they ask you not to, and don't show up with pets without prior arrangement. Be tidy in shared bathrooms, and be prompt. Most places have small staffs or may be run single-handedly and cannot easily adjust to surprises.

With a little effort and a sense of adventure you will learn firsthand the advantages of bed and breakfast travel. You will rediscover hospitality in a time when kindness seems to have been pushed aside. With the help of this directory, you will find accommodations that are just as exciting as your traveling plans.

We would like to hear from you about any experiences you have had or any inns you wish to recommend. Please write us at the following address:

The Annual Directory of
Western Bed & Breakfasts
211 Seventh Avenue North
Nashville, Tennessee 37219

THE ANNUAL DIRECTORY OF

Western
Bed & Breakfasts

1999 Edition

Alaska

Barrow

Kotzebue

Nenana · Fairbanks
Denali National Park
Delta Junction
Tok
Stephen Lake
Paxson
Talkeetna
Glennallen
Gakona Junction
Copper Center
Sheep Mtn.
Kennicott
Chugiak
Valdez
Palmer
Whittier
Girdwood
Seward
Cooper Landing
Kasilof
Trapper Creek
Willow
Wasilla
Anchorage
Soldotna
Homer
Seldovia

Kodiak

Bethel

Dutch Harbor on Unalaska Island

Whitehorse (Yukon)
Skagway
Haines
Gustavus
Juneau
Sitka
Petersburg
Wrangell
Ketchikan

Alaska

Alaska Private Lodgings: Stay with a Friend

P.O. Box 200047, 99520-0047
(907) 258-1717; FAX (907) 258-6613
e-mail: apl@alaskabandb.com
www.alaskabandb.com

Alpine Woods. Delight in the luxury of the outdoors in this sumptuous, exclusive hillside haven nestled in a natural wooded setting. Guests may choose one of two beautifully decorated rooms, each with a queen-size bed and private bath. Enjoy a full gourmet breakfast overlooking the grandeur of the Denali Mountains, Mount Susitna, and Cook Inlet. Resident pet. No smoking. Winter rates. $96 and up.

Foraker. This home is in a quiet residential area close to the airport and the coastal trail. The hosts are pleased to invite guests to stay in their comfortable queen-size room with private bath. Continental breakfast. No smoking. Winter rates. $66-75.

Garden Quarters. Guests will savor the hostess's breakfast, rated 10 plus by previous guests, on the flower-covered deck or in the sunlit dining room. There are two comfy rooms, one with a queen-size bed, one with a double bed, and a shared bath. Full breakfast. Resident pet. No smoking. $66-75.

"G" Street Bed and Breakfast. These experienced hosts are back in the bed and breakfast business after an absence of a couple of years. They have recently remodeled their home to meet the special needs of their guests. Two rooms each have a private bath and two rooms share a bath and make a comfortable suite for families or couples traveling together. Continental breakfast. No smoking. $66-95.

The Guest Room Bed and Breakfast. This charming two-room guest suite includes a bedroom with a queen-size bed, a country sitting room, and private bath. Take a great opportunity to hike or bike the nearby coastal trail. Continental breakfast. Resident pet. No smoking. $66-75.

Hillcrest Place. This cozy red house offers a small room with a double bed, half-bath, and garden view. A second room with a single bed shares a bath with the host. The hostess offers guests a choice of breakfast. This is an excellent value with wonderful hospitality. Full breakfast. No smoking. Resident pet. $55-65.

Hillside Chalet. This custom chalet, with a view of the city and the mountains, offers two spacious rooms, one with a queen-size bed and one with a king-size bed and each with a private bath. Continental breakfast. No smoking. Winter rates. $76-95.

Homestead Bed and Breakfast. This charming log homestead on an acre of land is hidden in the trees with easy access to city sights. The Country Suite has a double bed, twin beds, a trundle bed, private bath, sitting area, and kitchenette. The separate

NOTES: Credit cards accepted: A MasterCard; B Visa; C American Express; D Discover; E Diner's Club; F Other; 2 Personal checks accepted; 3 Lunch available; 4 Dinner available; 5 Open all year; 6 Pets welcome; 7 No smoking; 8 Children welcome; 9 Social drinking allowed; 10 Tennis nearby; 11 Swimming nearby; 12 Golf nearby; 13 Skiing nearby; 14 May be booked through a travel agent; Handicapped accessible.

cabin offers guests that rustic feeling without leaving the city. Full breakfast. Resident pet. No smoking. Winter rates. $66-95.

Little Rabbit Creek Bed and Breakfast. Experience the real Alaska within the city limits, but nestled in the forest beside a babbling creek. Guests will discover the sounds and wildlife of the creek. The private guest level has two rooms, each with a queen-size bed and private bath. Enjoy the luxury of quiet time in this unique setting. Full and Continental breakfasts. Resident pet. No smoking. $76-95.

The Oscar Gill House. This historic property has three rooms, one with private bath and two that share a bath. Enjoy staying in one of Anchorage's heritage homes. The original house was built in 1913 and was recently renovated by the hosts. Full breakfast. Winter rates available. No smoking. $66-95.

Raven House. Off the coastal trail, overlooking Cook Inlet, this new bed and breakfast has an elegant guest room with a private luxury bath. Or choose one of the two queen-size rooms with shared bath. The Turnagain-by-the-Sea neighborhood is one of the city's nicest. Continental breakfast. No smoking. Resident pet. $66-95.

Sunset Bed and Breakfast. This bed and breakfast offers a cheerful private suite with a queen-size bed and private bath with heart-shaped whirlpool tub. Guests will especially enjoy the adjoining solarium with kitchenette and the views of Turnagain Arm and the Alaska mountain range with its magnificent sunsets. Continental breakfast. No smoking. Winter rates available. $76-95.

Swiss Efficiency. This garden-view private accommodation is in a quiet neighborhood. For guests' comfort the kitchenette is stocked with breakfast makings; a queen-size bed and full futon are available; a sauna and Jacuzzi tub are in the private bath. German, Swiss, Spanish, Italian, and English are spoken by the host. No smoking. $76-95.

Ten Ten on the Green. The Puffin Suite and the Wildflower Room will provide guests with the privacy of their own home away from home. Both have full kitchens and private entrances. These private accommodations are within walking distance to downtown. Private bath. Breakfast provisions provided. No smoking. Winter rates available. $76-95.

Vance Drive Bed and Breakfast. This comfortable home is in a quiet subdivision close to bus lines, universities, and the hospitals. The two rooms, one with queen-size bed and one with twin-size beds, share a bath and are available individually or as a suite for perfect privacy. Continental breakfast. Resident pet. No smoking. Winter rates available. $55-65.

Wilcox Bed and Breakfast. These longtime Alaskan hosts offer a homey atmosphere very close to downtown attractions. Queen-size room and twin room with shared bath. Cook Inlet, Elderberry Park, and the coastal trail right outside the door. Full breakfast. No smoking. Winter rates are available. $66-75.

Alaskan Samovar Inn

720 Gambell Street, 99501
(907) 277-1511; (800) 478-1511
FAX (907) 272-5192

Four speciality suites with designer Jacuzzis. Sixty-one rooms with Jacuzzis. Fifteen minutes from airport (downtown location). Refrigerators and microwaves. Free local calls. Free HBO cable TV. Free airport shuttle. Fine dining and cocktail

NOTES: Credit cards accepted: A MasterCard; B Visa; C American Express; D Discover; E Diner's Club; F Other; 2 Personal checks accepted; 3 Lunch available; 4 Dinner available; 5 Open all year; 6 Pets welcome;

lounge. Room service. A $10 ticket is issued toward bill if full breakfast is taken. In-state personal checks accepted.

Rooms: 68 (PB) $60-99
Continental Breakfast
Credit Cards: A, B, C, D
Notes: 3, 4, 5, 8, 9, 14

Coastal Trail Bed and Breakfast

3100 Iliamna Drive, 99517
(907) 243-5809

Coastal Trail Bed and Breakfast invites guests to a comfortable Alaskan homestay with gardens, featherbeds, and full breakfast. Centrally positioned between airport and downtown. Hunting and fishing tips are provided by traditional Alaskan hosts. Coastal Trail adjoins an urban walking trail where guests may enjoy wildflowers, migratory birds, whales, and views of Denali.

Hosts: Sherry and Derek Tomlinson
Suite: 2 (PB) $75
Full Breakfast
Cards: A, B, C, D
Notes: 2, 5, 7, 8, 9, 10, 13, 14

Elderberry Bed and Breakfast

8340 Elderberry, 99502
(907) 243-6968 (phone/FAX)
e-mail: 103260.3221@compuserve.com

Close to airport, bike and walking trails, bus route, and local restaurants. Beautiful summer flowers. Moose frequently seen. Breakfast done to guests' taste—homemade. Special diets accommodated. Big-screen

ELDERBERRY B&B

TV. Alaska videos. Rooms tastefully decorated in matching decor. Hosts, Norm and Linda, love to talk to guests about their 20 years of Alaskan experiences.

Hosts: Norm and Linda Seitz
Rooms: 3 (2 PB; 1 SB) $70-80s
Full and Continental Breakfasts
Credit Cards: A, B
Notes: 2, 5, 7, 8, 9, 11, 12, 13, 14

A Homestay at Homesteads

807 G Street, Suite 250, 99501
(907) 272-8644; FAX (907) 274-8644

A1. Sit by the big picture window facing the inlet yet be right in the heart of downtown. What could be nicer than a friendly fireplace, good full breakfast, and a knowledgeable naturalist for the cook and host? Most rooms have private baths, yet, for the economy minded, there are a few two rooms that share one bath. Walk to the best restaurants in town, or take to the coastal trail for the evening's stroll or skiing in the winter. $75-160.

A2. Just at the tree line with a great trail across the creek lies this delightful home. In the winter ski from the porch. In the summer climb the mountains surrounding this unique getaway. A wood stove provides the warmth. Homemade quilts. No smoking. Full breakfast. $65-95.

The Lilac House

950 P Street, 99501
(907) 278-2939; FAX (907) 278-4939
e-mail: lilac@pobox.alaska.net

An exceptional bed and breakfast, the Lilac House was designed for the convenience and comfort of all guests and is perfect for both the business and pleasure traveler. In a quiet, prestigious residential neighborhood across the street from Delaney Park and a short walk to downtown Anchorage restaurants, shops, and the beautiful coastal trail. Spacious rooms offer views of Cook Inlet

7 No smoking; 8 Children welcome; 9 Social drinking allowed; 10 Tennis nearby; 11 Swimming nearby; 12 Golf nearby; 13 Skiing nearby; 14 May be booked through a travel agent; 15 Handicapped accessible.

The Lilac House

and the Chugach Mountains. A separate entrance assures guests' privacy.

Host: Debi Shinn
Rooms: 3 (1 PB; 2 SB) $75-120
Continental Breakfast
Credit Cards: A, B, C
Notes: 2, 5, 7, 8, 9, 10, 12, 13, 14

ANCHORAGE—(EAGLE RIVER)

A Homestay at Homesteads

807 G Street, Suite 250, 99501
(907) 272-8644; FAX (907) 274-8644

ER1. Wonderful wood stove and fireplace await travelers after the drive up the seven and one-half tree-lined miles from the main highway. Close to Anchorage, yet surrounded by wilderness, guests can ski from the house or hike across the creek to the Chugach Wilderness trail head. Shared or private half-bath. Full breakfast by the back valley window with a view of two glaciers. Nonsmoking. $65-90.

ER2. One of the most spectacular views in all of Alaska will welcome guests to this log home inside Chugach State Park. The home, in the wilderness, offers a cozy suite, solitude with the friendliness of a bed and breakfast. Hike or ski from the door in a glaciated valley with a rushing river where salmon spawn and the moose, bear, and sheep call home. A suburb of Anchorage, Eagle River is a short commute. Families welcomed. Nonsmoking. $95-115.

ER3. On a clear day guests can see the Alaska Range and Sleeping Lady as they sit by the fire or enjoy the spacious yard at this split-level home. Stay a few days for great hiking, berry picking, fishing, rafting, and cross-country skiing. Two bedrooms, shared or private bath. Continental breakfast. Nonsmoking. $65-85.

ER4. On the north shore of Peters Creek, this newly built bed and breakfast sits in the middle of two and one-half acres of parklike terrain where king salmon spawn in the creek. Designed with the physically challenged in mind, this spacious home is furnished with Victorian antiques and Alaskan memories. Enjoy a full Alaskan breakfast, then hike or ski on the nearby trails. Family-friendly. Nonsmoking. Secluded area set aside for the business traveler. E-mail access and conference room available. $75-85.

ANCHORAGE (PALMER)

A Homestay at Homesteads

807 G Street, Suite 250, 99501
(907) 272-8644; FAX (907) 274-8644

P1. In the Prickley Rose Garden Inn, enjoy the six acres of gardens, lush forestlands, and nature trails. Here is rural Alaska at its best. Hearty Alaskan breakfast served featuring farm-fresh eggs, blueberry pancakes with Alaskan birch syrup, and reindeer sausage. There is also a sunroom; the suite has a private balcony and bath. In the winter, there is cross-country skiing. Open year-round. Nonsmoking. $75-95.

NOTES: Credit cards accepted: A MasterCard; B Visa; C American Express; D Discover; E Diner's Club; F Other; 2 Personal checks accepted; 3 Lunch available; 4 Dinner available; 5 Open all year; 6 Pets welcome;

BARROW

A Homestay at Homesteads

807 G Street, Suite 250, 99501
(907) 272-8644; FAX (907) 274-8644

B1. See the top of the world in the best (and only) hotel in town. One-day or "fly and stay" tours are available from Anchorage. All rooms have private bath. Open all year. Be challenged! Come up in the winter and stay a while. Call for quotes.

BETHEL

Bentley's Bed and Breakfast Inn

624 First Avenue, Box 529, 99559
(907) 543-3552; (907) 543-5923; (907) 543-2257
FAX (907) 543-3561

Experience the warmth of Alaskan hospitality during a stay in southwest Alaska. Bentley's is on the beautiful Kuskokwim River in Bethel. Comfortable rooms, homelike atmosphere, full breakfasts, smoke-free and alcohol-free environment, and reasonable rates are what guests may expect at this home away from home. Connection with kayak and rafting tours June through September. Advance reservations are advisable.

Host: Millie D. Bentley
Rooms: 24 (SB) $95-128
Full Breakfast
Credit Cards: A, B, C, D, E
Notes: 2, 5, 7

CHUGIAK

Peters Creek Inn

22635 Davidson Road, P.O. Box 671487, 99567
(907) 688-2776; (800) 680-2776
FAX (907) 688-5031
www.alaska.net/~pcibnb

A rural, wooded setting that suggests remoteness, yet possesses metropolitan convenience. Only 20 minutes from Anchorage from the bed and breakfast's private entrance. Choose from the five

Peters Creek Inn

Alaskan themed rooms, each with a private bath. Beverage service available 24 hours. A barbecue is available for the one that didn't get away. Walk along the creek's edge or through the woods to see picturesque mountains and Cook Inlet. Nordic ski trails abound in the winter.

Hosts: Martha and Burl Rogers
Rooms: 5 (PB) $75-90
Full Breakfast
Credit Cards: A, B
Notes: 2, 3, 4, 5, 7, 8, 9, 10, 11, 12, 13, 14

COOPER LANDING

Gwin's Lodge, Inc.

Milepost 52–Sterling Highway, HC 64, Box 50, 99572
(907) 595-1266; FAX (907) 595-1681

Built more than 50 years ago, historic Gwin's Lodge is beautifully preserved as one of Alaska's few remaining traditionally built log roadhouses. Centralized

Gwin's Lodge

7 No smoking; 8 Children welcome; 9 Social drinking allowed; 10 Tennis nearby; 11 Swimming nearby; 12 Golf nearby; 13 Skiing nearby; 14 May be booked through a travel agent; 15 Handicapped accessible.

location on Kenai Peninsula. Closest lodge to Kenai and Russian Rivers confluence, the world's most prolific sockeye salmon sportfishery. Comfortable, modern log cabins feature two double beds, bath/shower. Full RV hookups. World renowned restaurant and bar, package store, fishing tackle/licenses, gifts, ice, fish freezing/smoking services, fishing and scenic rafting charters booked.

Hosts: The Siter Family
Rooms: 8 (6 PB) $115
Full Breakfast
Credit Cards: A, B, D
Notes: 2, 3, 4, 8, 9, 12, 14, 15

A Homestay at Homesteads

807 G Street, Suite 250, Anchorage, 99501
(907) 272-8644; FAX (907) 274-8644

CL. This bed and breakfast has a private room, made from logs, large enough for chairs in front of a private fireplace (wood provided), plus two double beds, private bath, and even a private screened-in porch. The hot tub in the garden is shared with other guests. Nearby is a fine restaurant overlooking the Kenai River. Breakfast available, but not included. Coffee maker in room. Winter specials available. $175.

CL1. This rustic inn was originally a log house. It has the best restaurant around. The cabins have two double beds and private baths. The rug is warm, and the place is open year-round. One cabin has a kitchenette. Meals available, but not included. From $65.

COPPER CENTER

A Homestay at Homesteads

807 G Street, Suite 250, Anchorage, 99501
(907) 272-8644; FAX (907) 274-8644

CC1. This homey and historic place is in an original dog team and carriage stop two-story building. Enjoy the "days-gone-by" atmosphere with the gracious living of today. Travelers come from miles around to dine in the formal dining room. Meals available but not included. Some private baths, some shared. A perfect overnight rest stop. Better yet, stay a few days to enjoy the wild and wonderful St. Elias Wilderness. $55-75.

DELTA JUNCTION

Alaska Private Lodgings: Stay with a Friend

P.O. Box 200047, 99520-0047
(907) 258-1717; FAX (907) 258-6613
e-mail: apl@alaskabandb.com
www.alaskabandb.com

Peggy's Alaskan Cabbage Patch Bed and Breakfast. See life in rural Alaska; see this land between the mountains and rivers. Guests might even catch a moose in the cabbage patch. Choose from two rooms, each with a queen-size bed and a shared bath. Continental and full breakfast. Resident pet. No smoking. $60-70.

DENALI NATIONAL PARK

Earth Song Lodge

P.O. Box 89, Healy, 99743
(907) 683-2863; FAX (907) 683-2868
www.akpub.com/akttt/earth.html

North of Denali National Park, close enough for convenience, far enough for peace and quiet. Spectacular views. Charming cabins with handcrafted furniture and private baths. Lodge made with honey-colored Alaskan logs features a fireplace, library, VCR for viewing Alaskan videos, spacious room. There's lots to do: walk, hike, view wildlife, photography, pick berries, visit a working sled dog kennel, dog mushing adventures, and watch evening naturalist slide shows. Gift shop. Pre-packaged lunch may be purchased. Come and share the dream.

NOTES: Credit cards accepted: A MasterCard; B Visa; C American Express; D Discover; E Diner's Club; F Other; 2 Personal checks accepted; 3 Lunch available; 4 Dinner available; 5 Open all year; 6 Pets welcome;

Earth Song Lodge

Hosts: Karin and Jon Nierenberg
Rooms: 10 (PB) $95-115
Continental Breakfast
Credit Cards: A, B
Notes: 2, 5, 6, 7, 8, 9, 13

DENALI NATIONAL PARK AREA

Alaska Private Lodgings: Stay with a Friend
P.O. Box 200047, 99520-0047
(907) 258-1717; FAX (907) 258-6613
e-mail: apl@alaskabandb.com
www.alaskabandb.com

Rock Creek Country Inn. A uniquely Alaskan log home has handcrafted art works and nature crafts. The main house has three guest rooms with private and shared baths. A private suite that is separate from the main house is perfect for couples traveling together. Also available are three log cabins, one with a private bath. There is a modern log shower house and flush toilet convenient for cabin guests. A full breakfast is served in the main house. A winter weekend getaway package is available. No smoking. Rates begin at $66.

At Timberline Bed and Breakfast. Bring the panoramic camera! The view is spectacular. Guests may also catch a glimpse of local wildlife from the viewing deck. All three rooms have queen-size bed, one has private bath, and two share a bath. Continental breakfast. No smoking. Resident pet. $76-95.

A Touch of Wilderness. In this quiet, remote location, there are six nicely decorated rooms, each with two double beds and private or shared baths. A breakfast menu provides choices for a Continental or full breakfast. No smoking. $76-95.

A Homestay at Homesteads
807 G Street, Suite 250, Anchorage, 99501
(907) 272-8644; FAX (907) 274-8644

1. Guests' very own Alaska log cabin overlooking the Nenana River, wildlife, and glaciated mountains. Get away from the usual crowds. Relax on one of the three riverside sun decks, the hot tub, or sauna. The cozy western cedar cabins have private baths, double beds, or one double plus futon sofa. Continental breakfast by the fireplace in the new River Lodge. Cappuccino bar, periodic night programs, exclusive Alaskan art, restaurant next door, outdoor grills on premises. Arriving by train or bus? Shuttle service included, of course. $149-159.

2. Choose the old hotel inside the park. Many hikers and the locals, so dress informally. Most rooms have two double beds and private baths. Walk to park headquarters. Meals available, but not included. Short walk up from the train station. Complimentary shuttles to other hotels. Shoulder season rates available. Call for quotes.

DUTCH HARBOR

A Homestay at Homesteads
807 G Street, Suite 250, Anchorage, 99501
(907) 272-8644; FAX (907) 274-8644

DH. In the heart of Alaska's Aleutians on Unalaska Island, 800 miles southwest of Anchorage, sits a wonderful surprise. This new, elegant facility has more than 100

7 No smoking; 8 Children welcome; 9 Social drinking allowed; 10 Tennis nearby; 11 Swimming nearby; 12 Golf nearby; 13 Skiing nearby; 14 May be booked through a travel agent; 15 Handicapped accessible.

guest rooms and the latest amenities. Works of local artists capture Alaskan landscape and depict its rich culture. Gourmet dining available, but not included. Fly daily from Anchorage or come by ferry (May through September) once a month. Tour prices available. Call for quotes.

FAIRBANKS_____

Alaska Private Lodgings: Stay with a Friend

P.O. Box 200047, 99520-0047
(907) 258-1717; FAX (907) 258-6613
e-mail: apl@alaskabandb.com
www.alaskabandb.com

Beaver Bend Bed and Breakfast. On the Chena River (where beavers can be seen in the summer and skiing and dog-sled racing occurs in the winter) and not far from town, this host offers three guest rooms. A queen-size bed with private bath on the upper level and two rooms, one with a queen-size bed and one with twin beds, on the lower level. They share a bath. Full breakfast. No smoking. Resident pet. Winter rates. $55-75.

By the River Bed and Breakfast. This home is on the bank of the Chena River not far from downtown and the visitor center. The two rooms share a bath and a sitting room, or guests can reserve the whole suite and have a private bath. It is very close to Beaver Bend B&B for folks traveling together. Continental breakfast. No smoking. Winter rates. $55-75.

Cranberry Ridge Bed and Breakfast. A lovely suite with private entrance, quiet relaxed atmosphere, and a panoramic view of Fairbanks and the Alaska Range is hosted by a fifth-generation Alaskan family. It is just minutes from the downtown area and popular attractions. Continental breakfast. No smoking. Winter rates. $76-95.

Jan's Bed and Breakfast. Guests are in central Fairbanks in a residential area with convenient access to all areas of town. Several rooms, as well as a private apartment, are available. Private and shared baths. Full and Continental breakfasts. No smoking. Winter rates. $66-95.

Minnie Street Bed and Breakfast. Choose from several rooms at this bed and breakfast only minutes from the train station and downtown. Many extras are available for guests' comfort. Convenience is a plus at this bed and breakfast. Private and shared baths. Full and Continental breakfasts. No smoking. Resident pet. Winter rates. $66-95.

Mountain View Bed and Breakfast. Guests enjoy an unforgettable stay in a lovely, newly built home high on a hill overlooking the beautiful Alaska Range, Mount McKinley, University of Alaska, and the city of Fairbanks. There is a master suite with queen-size bed and a room with a double bed. Both rooms have a private bath. Full breakfast. No smoking. $76-95.

A Homestay at Homesteads

807 G Street, Suite 250, Anchorage, 99501
(907) 272-8644; FAX (907) 274-8644

F1. This spacious comfortable apartment with a spectacular panoramic view awaits travelers looking for a unique bed and breakfast. This well-known Fairbanks home is nestled on a cliff directly above the beautiful Tanana River where the riverboat *Discovery* cruises. Guests can enjoy breakfast and relax on a large private cliffside deck. Two bedrooms with full bath, kitchen, living room, nature trails, and large yard. Nonsmoking. Children over seven welcome. $60-90.

F2. Elegant home in a surprisingly refreshing riverside niche. Gracious, long-time Alaskan hosts pride themselves on friendly accommo-

NOTES: Credit cards accepted: A MasterCard; B Visa; C American Express; D Discover; E Diner's Club; F Other; 2 Personal checks accepted; 3 Lunch available; 4 Dinner available; 5 Open all year; 6 Pets welcome;

dations with breakfast, of course. Private entrance, private or shared baths, guest kitchenette. Children welcome. Smoking permitted on outside deck and in the yard. Weekly and monthly rates available. $65-90.

F3. Bordering on a small pond, the house with large deck enables guests to enjoy the many hours of summer sun in this lovely residential section of town. Convenient to Alaskaland, University of Alaska, riverboat *Discovery*, airport, and train depot. Four large rooms, shared or private bath, plus an apartment. Enjoy breakfast with this fifth generation Alaskan family. $65-100.

7 Gables Inn

P.O. Box 80488, 99708
(907) 479-0751

Historically, Alaska's 7 Gables Inn was a fraternity house within walking distance to the UAF campus, yet is near the river and airport. This spacious 10,000-square-foot Tudor-style home features a floral solarium, antique stained glass in the foyer with an indoor waterfall, cathedral ceilings, a meeting room, wine cellar, and rooms with dormers. A gourmet breakfast is served daily. Other amenities include cable TV/VCR and telephone in each room, laundry facilities, Jacuzzis, bikes, and canoes.

Hosts: Paul and Leicha Welton
Rooms: 12 (PB) $50-120
Full Breakfast
Credit Cards: A, B, C, D, E, F
Notes: 2, 5, 7, 8, 9, 14

7 Gables Inn

GAKONA JUNCTION (GLENNALLEN)

A Homestay at Homesteads

807 G Street, Suite 250, Anchorage, 99501
(907) 272-8644; FAX (907) 274-8644

GJ. Halfway from everywhere, these gracious accommodations are the perfect rest stop. Motel-style two double beds with private bath. The restaurant is adjacent. Enjoy a full breakfast with the long-time resident hosts. Other meals available, but not included. The perfect place to stay a few days and meander in the shadow of the St. Elias Wilderness mountains. There is a gas station there, too. Seasonal rates. $65-115.

GIRDWOOD

Alaska Private Lodgings: Stay with a Friend

P.O. Box 200047, 99520-0047
(907) 258-1717; FAX (907) 258-6613
e-mail: apl@alaskabandb.com
www.alaskabandb.com

The Glass House. This modern architecturally designed bed and breakfast showcases stained glass by the accomplished artist/owner. Choose from four rooms, each offering a uniquely different experience. Several of the rooms have a clear view of Mount Alyeska. Private and shared baths. Full breakfast. Resident pet. No smoking. $76-95.

Cross Country Meadows Bed and Breakfast

Timberline and Alta Drive, P.O. Box 123, 99587-0123
(907) 783-3333; FAX (907) 783-3335
e-mail: XCountryBB@aol.com
www.AlaskaOne.com/crosscountry

Cross Country Meadows Bed and Breakfast is nestled in the heart of Alaska's prime skiing community of Girdwood. The home was designed and built specifically as a bed

7 No smoking; 8 Children welcome; 9 Social drinking allowed; 10 Tennis nearby; 11 Swimming nearby; 12 Golf nearby; 13 Skiing nearby; 14 May be booked through a travel agent; 15 Handicapped accessible.

and breakfast and furnished for the convenience of all the guests. The hosts cater to those who seek quiet, peaceful accommodations with a luxurious and private atmosphere. The bed and breakfast is a great place for staging day trips to Prince William Sound or the Kenai Peninsula, enjoying a romantic retreat, or just mixing business with pleasure.

Hosts: Brent and Sylvia Stonebraker
Rooms: 2 (PB) $85-125
Continental Breakfast
Credit Cards: A, B, C, D
Notes: 2, 5, 7, 9, 10, 11, 13, 14

Glacier Bay Country Inn

GLENNALLEN

Alaska Private Lodgings: Stay with a Friend

P.O. Box 200047, Anchorage, 99520-0047
(907) 258-1717; FAX (907) 258-6613

Carol's Bed and Breakfast. Welcome to Alaska hospitality with native Alaskans as the hosts. As lifelong residents of the Copper River Valley, they know about the best fishing holes and unique side trips. One room has a king-size bed and one room has a twin bed. Shared bath. Full breakfast. $66-75.

Riverview Bed and Breakfast. Former Alaskan bush teachers welcome guests to enjoy their log home on the bank of the Copper River. Guests have choice of four rooms. Shared and private baths. Full breakfast. No smoking. Resident pet. $71-95.

GUSTAVUS (GLACIER BAY)

Glacier Bay Country Inn

P.O. Box 5-AD, 99826
(907) 697-2288; FAX (907) 697-2289
www.glacierbayalaska.com

Tucked into the rain forest of southeast Alaska, the Country Inn is surrounded by spruce, pine, and hemlock. The atmosphere is elegant, yet informal. Dinner conversa-

tions usually tend toward comment on the cuisine, freshly baked breads, pastries, and desserts. Enjoy fishing, fly-fishing, whale watching, hiking, photography, and Glacier Bay Park boat and plane tours. Rates include three meals, unless otherwise noted, airport transfers, and use of bicycles. Its sister lodge, the Whalesong, offers bed and breakfast rooms, condo rental, and full meal packages.

Hosts: Ponch and Sandi Marchbanks
Rooms: 7 (6 PB; 1 SB) $160-260
Cabins: 3 $276
Full Breakfast
Credit Cards: A, B, C, D
Notes: 2, 3, 4, 7, 8, 9, 14

Gustavus Inn

Box 60, 99826
(800) 649-5220; FAX (907) 697-2255

Glacier Bay's historic homestead, newly renovated, full-service inn accommodates 26. Family-style meals, seafood, garden produce, wild edibles. Boat tours of Glacier

Gustavus Inn

NOTES: Credit cards accepted: A MasterCard; B Visa; C American Express; D Discover; E Diner's Club; F Other; 2 Personal checks accepted; 3 Lunch available; 4 Dinner available; 5 Open all year; 6 Pets welcome;

Bay, charter fishing, and air transportation from Juneau arranged. Kayaking and hiking nearby. Bikes and airport transfers included in the daily rates. Lunch and dinner included. American plan only. Closed September 15 through May 1.

Hosts: David and Jo Ann Lesh
Rooms: 13 (11 PB; 2 SB) $135
Full Breakfast
Credit Cards: A, B, C
Notes: 2, 3, 4, 7, 8, 9, 14, 15

HAINES

Alaska Private Lodgings: Stay with a Friend
P.O. Box 200047, 99520-0047
(907) 258-1717; FAX (907) 258-6613
e-mail: apl@alaskabandb.com
www.alaskabandb.com

Officer's Inn. This bed and breakfast is part of historic Fort William H. Seward, now designated a national historic landmark. Some of their 14 rooms are graced with the original Belgian tile fireplaces and claw-foot bathtubs. Private and shared baths. Continental breakfast. Winter rates. $76-95.

The Summer Inn. This bed and breakfast is a five-bedroom historical house with a live-in innkeeper. The house was built by a member of Skagway's notorious Soapy Smith gang, part of the colorful history of Haines. Private and shared baths. Continental breakfast. $66-95.

A Homestay at Homesteads
807 G Street, Suite 250, Anchorage, 99501
(907) 272-8644; FAX (907) 274-8644

"History is where you find it. Did the notorious Soapy Smith sleep in your bedroom in 1912?" Five bedrooms and a spacious living room welcome the most weary of travelers. Whether going off to watch bald eagles, fish, hike, or laze around with a good book, start the day off with a homemade breakfast.

This place is big enough for privacy, yet small enough for conversation. Views of Lynn Canal and walking distance to the other historical sites. Call for rates.

HOMER

Alaska Private Lodgings: Stay with a Friend
P.O. Box 200047, 99520-0047
(907) 258-1717; FAX (907) 258-6613
e-mail: apl@alaskabandb.com
www.alaskabandb.com

Brass Ring Bed and Breakfast. Near downtown Homer, this log home has six guest bedrooms. The downstairs room has a private bath and the five upstairs rooms share two baths. Each room is individually decorated with many treasures, and in the back yard there is a spa tub. Be very close to downtown Homer and the Homer Spit. Private and shared baths. Full breakfast. No smoking. $66-95.

Halcyon Heights Bed and Breakfast. Guests will be mesmerized as they experience the breathtaking view from this bed and breakfast. Accommodations include six nautical theme rooms, all with private baths. After a long day of sightseeing, gaze out over Kachemak Bay from the hot tub. Continental breakfast. No smoking. Winter rates. Rates begin at $76.

Sara and John's Bed and Breakfast. A lovely home, secluded, yet centrally in the heart of Homer. A large suite with a queen-size bed, private bath with Jacuzzi, and two rooms, each with a queen-size bed and a private bath, are available. Continental breakfast. No smoking. Winter rates. $76-95.

Victorian Heights Bed and Breakfast. Enjoy a bit of Victoria at the end of the road. This new family home offers several rooms with private or shared bath. Some rooms have a Jacuzzi and/or a private deck. Continental breakfast. No smoking. Winter rates. $76-95.

Brass Ring Bed and Breakfast

P.O. Box 2090, 99603
(907) 235-5450; FAX (907) 235-4930
e-mail: vanbrass@ptialaska.net
www.ptialaska.net/~vanbrass

Two-story log home in the heart of Homer. Full breakfasts, freshly ground coffee. Sourdough pancakes are the speciality. Outdoor hot tub for guests' enjoyment. Private cottage with a fantastic view is also available. Great honeymoon spot.

Hosts: Vicki and Dave VanLiere
Rooms: 5 (3 PB; 2 SB) $70-99
Full Breakfast
Credit Cards: A, B, D
Notes: 2, 7, 10, 12, 14

A Homestay at Homesteads

807 G Street, Suite 250, Anchorage, 99501
(907) 272-8644; FAX (907) 274-8644

Come to this spacious log house and a bit of Alaskan nostalgia. Nestled under the tall spruce trees in a quiet neighborhood, walking distance from downtown. A hot tub awaits guests' return from exploring, hiking, skiing, and fishing in this exceptionally beautiful part of Alaska. Private/shared baths. Full Alaskan breakfast. Open May 1 through September 30.

H2. This is the oldest and the only place to stay at the end of the Homer Spit. Walk from here to catch fishing charters, day boat tours, or fish from the beach while watching the boats come and go. Rooms have private baths. Breakfast is not served. When making reservations, please specify smoking or nonsmoking. $75-140.

H3. Come sit by the fire and enjoy this lovely home. Within walking distance of the museum, art galleries, and restaurants. The library/bedroom luxury suite (with Jacuzzi tub) can be divided with a casement door for two couples' sleeping privacy. The garden-view rooms each have queen-size beds. Just the perfect place to enjoy another Alaskan day fishing in beautiful Kachemak Bay or hiking. Hosts will make arrangements for ferry, fishing, dog sledding, and other activities. The Homer Stage picks up and drops off at the door. Nonsmoking. Continental breakfast. $65-110.

H4. What a view! This three-bedroom private cottage overlooks the Kenai Mountains, glaciers, and beautiful Kachemak Bay. A kitchen, full bath, and living room make this the perfect "home away from home." What a honeymoon spot. Open all year.

H5. Use this bed and breakfast as headquarter to enjoy Homer and Kachemak Bay. Within walking distance of art galleries, restaurants, college, and museum, the suite with private bath/Jacuzzi and library (with sofa bed) has windows facing the bay and mountains. There are two other guest rooms, each with private bath and cable TV/VCR. Need reservations for fishing, guided hiking, kayaking, flightseeing, boat tours, and bear watching? The Homer Stage picks up/drops off at door. Nonsmoking. Healthy Continental plus breakfast. $75-110.

Three Moose Meadow Wilderness Bed and Breakfast

P.O. Box 15291, 99603
(907) 235-0755 (phone/FAX)
e-mail: 3moose@xyz.net
www.xyz.net/~3moose

Three Moose Meadow has taken the bed and breakfast to a new level. Understanding that travelers to Alaska want to experience Alaska, the hosts offer guests a newly constructed log cabin in a wilderness setting. The cozy cottage is nestled in the woods

NOTES: Credit cards accepted: A MasterCard; B Visa; C American Express; D Discover; E Diner's Club; F Other; 2 Personal checks accepted; 3 Lunch available; 4 Dinner available; 5 Open all year; 6 Pets welcome;

and overlooks a meadow with snow-capped mountains beyond. Cabins are fully modernized with private baths and cooking facilities. This is the choice for those wanting a real Alaskan experience.

Hosts: Jordan and Jennie Hess
Rooms: 3 (PB) $85-105
Full Breakfast

JUNEAU

Alaska Private Lodgings: Stay with a Friend

P.O. Box 200047, 99520-0047
(907) 258-1717; FAX (907) 258-6613
e-mail: apl@alaskabandb.com
www.alaskabandb.com

Alaska Wolf House. Built on the side of Mount Juneau, this large western red cedar log home is one mile from town. Guests will be within a short walk to glacier hiking, jogging, bicycle trails, public transportation. All six rooms have splendid views. Private and shared baths. Full breakfast. No smoking. Two-night minimum stay required. Rates begin at $76.

Mount Juneau Bed and Breakfast. Enjoy one of the six rooms named after important animals in the native Tlingit culture or the seventh room, the Mount Juneau Room. Walk to historic downtown or borrow a bicycle for a leisurely ride. Private and shared baths. Full breakfast. No smoking. Resident pet. $76-95.

Pearson's Pond. Capture the majestic Mendenhall Glacier as a picturesque backdrop while dining alfresco; enjoy a starlit spa and reflect on life with the healing sounds of nature. Relax in the outdoor hot tub. Inspected, rated, and approved. Excellence awards from AAA and ABBA. Private and shared baths. Continental breakfast. No smoking. Winter rates. Two-night minimum stay required. Rates begin at $76.

A Homestay at Homesteads

807 G Street, Suite 250, Anchorage, 99501
(907) 272-8644; FAX (907) 274-8644

J1. These hosts have the view and know the ferry is a long way out of town. If guests need a rental car, they arrange it; and if guests want to be picked up, they can do that, too! Breakfast is included (most of the time). The inn is booked to assist the legislature when in session; otherwise they will welcome guests. Laundry, cooking, sauna, and picnic area. Nonsmoking. $65-85.

Pearson's Pond Luxury Inn and Garden Spa

4541 Sawa Circle, 99801-8723
(907) 789-3772; FAX (907) 789-6722
e-mail: pearsons.pond@juneau.com
www.juneau.com/pearsons.pond

Award-winning bed and breakfast resort is perfect getaway for nature and privacy lovers. Enjoy a hot tub overlooking Mendenhall Glacier and a massage at this breathtaking waterfront retreat. Photograph wildlife between naps on the dock, or row on the peaceful pond surrounded by gardens and sparkling fountains. Bike or walk

Pearson's Pond Luxury Inn

the adjacent river trail. Garden or water view mini-suites have private entry, kitchens, and every imaginable amenity. Health club access. Frommer's Best B&B of Alaska. Fodor's Best of America. AAA/ABBA Excellence.

Hosts: Steve and Diane Pearson
Rooms: 1 (PB) $89-189
Suite: 2 (PB) $99-429
Continental Breakfast
Credit Cards: A, B, C, D, E, F
Notes: 2, 5, 7, 9, 10, 11, 12, 13, 14

Silverbow Inn

120 Second Street, 99801
(907) 586-4146; (800) 586-4146
FAX (907) 586-4242

In the heart of historic downtown, this unique 1914 building was converted to an inn in 1984. Enjoy modern amenities while being surrounded by beautiful antique furniture. Each room has private bath, telephone, and cable TV. Fresh bagels and bread are served hot for breakfast from the bakery next door. Museums, waterfront, shopping, and hiking are all within walking distance. Continental plus breakfast served.

Hosts: Jill Ramiel and Ken Alper
Rooms: 6 (PB) $69-109
Continental Breakfast
Credit Cards: A, B, C
Notes: 2, 3, 4, 5, 7, 8, 9, 13, 14

KASILOF

Alaska Private Lodgings: Stay with a Friend

P.O. Box 200047, 99520-0047
(907) 258-1717; FAX (907) 258-6613
e-mail: apl@alaskabandb.com
www.alaskabandb.com

Crooked Creek Bed and Breakfast. This bed and breakfast is on the south end of Johnson Lake and has the Lakeview Room with a queen-size bed and the Westside Room with a double bed; they share a bath. Or, if guests wish more privacy, available is one cabin with a queen-size bed and a sofa

couch and one cabin with a double bed and bunks (each cabin has its own bath). Full breakfast. No smoking. Resident pet. Winter rates. $66-75.

Deal's Den Bed and Breakfast. Guests' home away from home on beautiful Cape Kasilof, close to fishing and beachcombing. There are three rooms with shared baths and guests will be served a hearty Alaskan full breakfast with an Irish flair. A new sauna has been added this year. The host is selling fishing licenses and king salmon stamps. No smoking. Resident pet. Winter rates. $76-95.

KENNICOTT

A Homestay at Homesteads

807 G Street, Suite 250, Anchorage, 99501
(907) 272-8644; FAX (907) 274-8644

In the heart of the St. Elias Wilderness lies this "old" newly made antique inn just waiting for adventurous souls to enjoy the gourmet dining and tales of the mining days. Share baths as in the olden times. Plan to spend at least two nights; the hosts and the area are worth it. Most people drive in, but guests may fly in (weather permitting). Public transportation available from Glennallen, Valdez, and Anchorage. Overnight with or without meals available. Day rates vary with the size of the traveling group, but calculate per person with meals at $125.

KETCHIKAN

A Homestay at Homesteads

807 G Street, Suite 250, Anchorage, 99501
(907) 272-8644; FAX (907) 274-8644

K1. In the quiet woods overlooking Knudson Cove marina, guests will feel "almost home" with the privacy and comfort in own apartment. The apartment has a kitchen, linens, washer/dryer, telephone, cable TV, gas barbecue, and deck. Downstairs has three bedrooms and one and one-third baths. Upstairs has a bedroom with private bath. Continental plus breakfast served first morning of stay. Nonsmoking. No pets.

K2. In town in the midst of all the action. Cruise ships, float planes, fishing boats, eagles and whales—on one of Ketchikan's unique stairway streets (not handicapped accessible). Choice of two beautiful rooms with exotic Jacuzzi bathroom; guest bathrobes provided. Also available is a fully outfitted apartment with separate entrance, double bed, futon for two, cot, barbecue, TV, telephone, washer/dryer. Choose Continental or breakfast with hosts. Nonsmoking. Late arrivals OK by arrangement. Open year-round. $50-90.

K3. View Tongass Narrows in the privacy and comfort of own apartment. Kitchen, cable TV, telephone, private baths, gas barbecue. Upstairs has a cathedral ceiling, two double beds, one twin bed and a queen-size sofa bed. Downstairs has two twin and a double bed, a queen-size sofa bed. Knudson Cove marina and Clover Pass resort are just a few minutes north for charters and fine dining. Generous Continental breakfast on arrival. Rates begin at $75.

KODIAK

Alaska Private Lodgings: Stay with a Friend
P.O. Box 200047, 99520-0047
(907) 258-1717; FAX (907) 258-6613
e-mail: apl@alaskabandb.com
www.alaskabandb.com

Wintel's Bed and Breakfast. This bed and breakfast offers the best of Kodiak Island's hospitality. Walk to beaches, shops, fishing, hiking, harbor, and more. Private and shared baths. Full breakfast. No smoking. $66-95.

A Homestay at Homesteads
807 G Street, Suite 250, Anchorage, 99501
(907) 272-8644; FAX (907) 274-8644

KA2. Enjoy the country flavor of this bed and breakfast right in the middle of a wonderful coastal town. Hosts love to cook and plan great breakfasts for all the guests. These long-time Kodiak folks know where to hike, fish, and sightsee. They also know the best pilots in the air and skippers on the sea. Open year-round. Nonsmoking. $65-95.

Kodiak Bed and Breakfast
308 Cope Street, 99616
(907) 486-5367; FAX (907) 486-6567
e-mail: monroe@ptialaska.net
www.ptialaska.net/~monroe

Visitors enjoy a spectacular view of Kodiak's busy fishing fleet in a location just above the boat harbor. Mary's home is easy walking distance from a historic Russian church, art galleries, Baronov Museum, air charters, and Kittiwake Rookery. Enjoy this fishing city with its Russian heritage, stunning beaches, cliffs, and abundant fish and bird life. Fresh local fish is often a breakfast option.

Host: Mary A. Monroe
Rooms: 2 (PB) $70-82
Full Breakfast
Credit Cards: A, B, C
Notes: 2, 5, 6, 7, 8, 9, 14

KOTZEBUE

A Homestay at Homesteads
807 G Street, Suite 250, Anchorage, 99501
(907) 272-8644; FAX (907) 274-8644

Come, enjoy this town right on the ocean so the walk on the street is always refreshing. Tours of one day or overnight stays from Anchorage. There are no roads across Alaska, so a flight is necessary. Private baths, two beds to a room. Restaurant in the two-story hotel. Breakfast is available, but not included. Call for quotes.

7 No smoking; 8 Children welcome; 9 Social drinking allowed; 10 Tennis nearby; 11 Swimming nearby; 12 Golf nearby; 13 Skiing nearby; 14 May be booked through a travel agent; 15 Handicapped accessible.

NENANA

Alaska Private Lodgings: Stay with a Friend

P.O. Box 200047, 99520-0047
(907) 258-1717; FAX (907) 258-6613
e-mail: apl@alaskabandb.com
www.alaskabandb.com

Bed and Maybe Breakfast Bed and Breakfast. Step back in time and be charmed by the atmosphere of the old railroad depot built for President Harding's historic visit in 1923. The Harding Room, Conductor Room, Engineer Room, and the Brakemen Suite share a bath. Continental breakfast. No smoking. Winter rates. $66-75.

PALMER

Alaska Private Lodgings: Stay with a Friend

P.O. Box 200047, 99520-0047
(907) 258-1717; FAX (907) 258-6613
e-mail: apl@alaskabandb.com
www.alaskabandb.com

Prickly Rose Garden Inn Bed and Breakfast. Explore the unique flora, discover mountain vistas, moose, wildflowers, and singing birds that surround this rustic, rural Alaskan home. Two rooms are available, one with queen-size bed and private bath and one with queen-size bed and shared bath. Be close to many of the sights of the famous Matanuska Valley. Full breakfast. Resident pet. No smoking. $76-95.

Timberlings Bed and Breakfast

P.O. Box 732, 99645
(907) 745-4445

A treasure among bed and breakfasts. Log house on 150 acres of wooded hills with panoramic mountain views, exotic birds and plants, alpacas, and a friendly dog. Artists/hosts serve a full gourmet breakfast. Timberlings is the perfect place to return to after a day of hiking, wandering around old gold mines, flying over Mount McKinley, exploring glaciers, river rafting, or shopping and sightseeing in Anchorage.

Hosts: Buz and Alma Blum
Rooms: 1 (SB) $75
Full Breakfast
Credit Cards: D
Notes: 2, 5, 7, 9, 12, 13, 14

PAXSON (DENALI HIGHWAY)

A Homestay at Homesteads

807 G Street, Suite 250, Anchorage, 99501
(907) 272-8644; FAX (907) 274-8644

Old-time Alaskan hospitality awaits guests here. A favorite stage stop in the early 1900s now offers the same warm place to sleep at night plus the restaurant with the best pie around. Stopping for the night before traveling on the most scenic route to Denali National Park? Why not stay a few days to fish, ski, and enjoy peace and quiet. Open year-round. Gas, towing, cocktails, gifts, and rooms with a bath. $80-95.

PETERSBURG

A Homestay at Homesteads

807 G Street, Suite 250, Anchorage, 99501
(907) 272-8644; FAX (907) 274-8644

"We know the Alaska Ferry schedule!" So in the middle of the night, the beds are warm and coffee pots are always on. If guests are traveling light, just walk on over to this lovely home or take a very short taxi ride. Breakfast with the family. Stay a few days on this island and enjoy the change of pace here. $55-90.

NOTES: Credit cards accepted: A MasterCard; B Visa; C American Express; D Discover; E Diner's Club; F Other; 2 Personal checks accepted; 3 Lunch available; 4 Dinner available; 5 Open all year; 6 Pets welcome;

SELDOVIA

Alaska Private Lodgings: Stay with a Friend

P.O. Box 200047, 99520-0047
(907) 258-1717; FAX (907) 258-6613
e-mail: apl@alaskabandb.com
www.alaskabandb.com

Dancing Eagles Lodge. On Seldovia Slough on the circa 1923 Boardwalk, this bed and breakfast has a chalet cabin with living area, kitchen, one bedroom, and a sleeping loft that accommodates six people comfortably. Bed and breakfast lodging is available in the main house. Private and shared baths. Nonhosted. Full breakfast. No smoking. Rates begin at $76.

A Homestay at Homesteads

807 G Street, Suite 250, Anchorage, 99501
(907) 272-8644; FAX (907) 274-8644

SL1. Come dance with the eagles at this lodge over the water where the tides march in and out. The hosts have kayaks to rent, as well as bikes, a nice cozy hot tub (most of the time), and rooms inside the house as well as the self-contained cabin by the hot tub. Flexible and fun-loving hosts. Closed for the winter so as not to freeze the pipes, but the inn plans to be open May 15 through September 15. Rates begin at $50.

SEWARD

Alaska Private Lodgings: Stay with a Friend

P.O. Box 200047, 99520-0047
(907) 258-1717; FAX (907) 258-6613
e-mail: apl@alaskabandb.com
www.alaskabandb.com

Bay Vista Bed and Breakfast. Two private suites are part of this custom-built home. One suite has two bedrooms, each with a private bath and common area. The other suite has two bedrooms that share a bath and the common area. Be close to downtown and enjoy a great view. Continental breakfast. No smoking. $76-95.

Creekside Cabins. Guests will enjoy the quiet, wooded country setting with four guest cabins supplied with electric heat, linens, small refrigerator, coffee maker, and outdoor fire pit. The separate bath house and the toasty log sauna by the creek are shared. Continental breakfast. No smoking. $66-95.

The Farm Bed and Breakfast. This Alaskan "countrified" bed and breakfast is full of character and warmth and is slow paced with a friendly atmosphere. There are four rooms, cottages, and bungalows available. Guests will be just minutes from Seward. Private and shared baths. Continental breakfast. Resident pet. Winter rates. $76-95.

Fjordland Inn. Even though this long-time favorite bed and breakfast has new owners, the Alaskan hospitality and comfort continue to be offered. There are eight rooms to choose from, either in the renovated boat shop or the main house. Private and shared baths. Continental breakfast. No smoking. Winter rates. $66-95.

Harborview Bed and Breakfast. These hosts offer eight rooms, each with a queen-size bed and a private bath. Close to the attractions in Seward, guests are minutes away from all they have planned. A Continental breakfast will be delivered to guests' door each morning. Private bath. No smoking. Winter rates. $76-95.

River Valley Cabins. These newly built cabins offer guests the comfort of home in a

7 No smoking; 8 Children welcome; 9 Social drinking allowed; 10 Tennis nearby; 11 Swimming nearby; 12 Golf nearby; 13 Skiing nearby; 14 May be booked through a travel agent; 15 Handicapped accessible.

rustic outdoors setting. Get away but be 10 minutes from the activities of Seward and close to Exit Glacier. The cabins have a queen-size bed and a private bath. Continental breakfast. No smoking. Winter rates. $76-95.

A Homestay at Homesteads

807 G Street, Suite 250, Anchorage, 99501
(907) 272-8644; FAX (907) 274-8644

S1. Guests' very own log cabin is nestled in the trees next to a rushing salmon spawning stream. Fresh pastries, fruit, and juice are delivered to the door. Lounge in bed and watch the wilderness from the picture windows. So the pipes do not freeze in the winter, there is a year-round heated central bath and shower. There are camping spots available, too. Creekside is a treat worth waiting for. Families are welcome. Just off the highway on the road to Exit Glacier. $65-130.

S2. Surrounded by a panoramic mountain view. This wonderful two-story inn is a bed and breakfast not to be missed. Each room has its own atmosphere sharing a fully equipped kitchen and TV common areas. Private and shared baths. Breakfast is an ample self-serve buffet. In the center for Exit Glacier hiking, fishing, and the Kenai Fjords National Park excursions. Seasonal rates. $60-100.

S3. An eagle's nest is in the tree just outside the upstairs living room wall of windows. This new home is in a rural area but close to town. The hosts love to cook and visit, so plan to join them in the glassed-in formal dining area or out on the upstairs porch. Twin-size beds with shared bath. Nonsmoking. $65-85.

S4. Guests have their own six-room log house with spacious bedrooms, private bath, two double beds covered with hand-made quilts. Hiking and exploring on dirt roads and streams. Close to Seward and the Kenai Fjords National Park but still in the wilds. Rushing stream on both sides of the property hum in the night. Continental breakfast. Nonsmoking. $75-95.

SHEEP MOUNTAIN

A Homestay at Homesteads

807 G Street, Suite 250, Anchorage, 99501
(907) 272-8644; FAX (907) 274-8644

SM. Make these individual log cabins home and stay for a few days away from the crowds. Most have private baths. Dorm rooms are available with central bath. Finest meals around with homemade pastries and pies available, but not included. Explore and hike and enjoy a typical Alaskan experience. $75-110.

SITKA

Alaska Ocean View Bed and Breakfast

1101 Edgecumbe Drive, 99835
(907) 747-8310 (phone/FAX)

Enjoy casual elegance and affordable rates at this superior quality bed and breakfast where guests experience a high degree of personal comfort, privacy, and friendly helpful hosts. Very comfortable king- and queen-size beds. Open the day with the tantalizing aroma of freshly baked breads, freshly ground coffee, and a delicious complimentary buffet-style breakfast. Close the day with a relaxing soak under the stars in the bubbling patio hot tub/spa. Recipient of Alaska's Best award.

Hosts: Carole and Bill Denkinger
Rooms: 3 (PB) $69-129
Full and Continental Breakfast
Credit Cards: A, B, C
Notes: 2, 5, 7, 8, 9, 10, 11, 14

NOTES: Credit cards accepted: A MasterCard; B Visa; C American Express; D Discover; E Diner's Club; F Other; 2 Personal checks accepted; 3 Lunch available; 4 Dinner available; 5 Open all year; 6 Pets welcome;

Alaska Private Lodgings: Stay with a Friend

P.O. Box 200047, 99520-0047
(907) 258-1717; FAX (907) 258-6613
e-mail: apl@alaskabandb.com
www.alaskabandb.com

Alaska Ocean View Bed and Breakfast. Choose from three rooms named after popular Alaska wildflowers and decorated with local artists' work. There is a spectacular view of Sitka Sound with its many islands and Mount Edgecumbe from this large three-level home. Private baths. Full breakfast. No smoking. Winter rates. Rates begin at $76.

A Homestay at Homesteads

807 G Street, Suite 250, Anchorage, 99501
(907) 272-8644; FAX (907) 274-8644

ST1. This home is downtown and up the hill so that the rooms have some of the finest views around. The hosts have been here for years and love to talk about their adventures. Breakfast is included. Shared bath. $55-90.

SKAGWAY

Alaska Private Lodgings: Stay with a Friend

P.O. Box 200047, 99520-0047
(907) 258-1717; FAX (907) 258-6613
e-mail: apl@alaskabandb.com
www.alaskabandb.com

The Skagway Inn. Take heart because snowy sheets, cozy rooms, a delicious breakfast, and great hospitality await guests in this historic bed and breakfast. Turn-of-the-century ambiance will help guests soak in the history, atmosphere, and magic of the great Klondike gold rush. Shared bath. Continental breakfast. Winter rates. $76-95.

A Homestay at Homesteads

807 G Street, Suite 250, Anchorage, 99501
(907) 272-8644; FAX (907) 274-8644

How nice to come home to quiet rooms, fresh sheets, and in the morning to restart the day with a delicious Continental breakfast. Hosts have integrated the old with the new and it's all right downtown. Shared bath. Open year-round. $75-95.

SOLDOTNA

Denise Lake Lodge Bed and Breakfast

41680 Denise Lake Road, P.O. Box 1050, 99669
(907) 262-1789; (800) 478-1789
FAX (907) 262-7184
www.bbonline.com/ak/deniselake

On Denise Lake three miles from Soldotna and the Kenai River. The hosts offer package deals on lodging with fishing or hunting. Fly-out trips are available. The immaculate rooms have private baths and a full breakfast is included. There is a fish-cleaning area and freezer space for fish and an exercise room and coin-operated laundry. Bring warm clothing and rain gear.

Hosts: Elaine and Jim
Rooms: 10 (PB) $89-149
Full Breakfast
Credit Cards: A, B, C, D
Notes: 2, 7, 8, 9, 11, 12, 13, 14, 15

SOLDOTNA (KENAI AREA)

Alaska Private Lodgings: Stay with a Friend

P.O. Box 200047, 99520-0047
(907) 258-1717; FAX (907) 258-6613
e-mail: apl@alaskabandb.com
www.alaskabandb.com

Alaska's Tree Top Bed and Breakfast. Enjoy this Kenai Peninsula bed and breakfast where everyone is treated like a friend. Four comfortable rooms (two with private and two with shared bath). Two cabins also available. In this lakeside setting there is always an opportunity to spot meandering wildlife. Full breakfast. No smoking. Resident pet. Winter rate. Rates begin at $76.

Denise Lake Lodge. This large home on the edge of a small lake offers several rooms with private or shared baths. Great for fisherpersons. Cabins are also available. Full breakfast. Resident pet. $66-95.

Posey's Kenai River Hideaway

A Homestay at Homesteads

807 G Street, Suite 250, Anchorage, 99501
(907) 272-8644; FAX (907) 274-8644

KS1. Enjoy the turn of the tide on this island. This bed and breakfast is more than breakfast as guests will fly in from Kenai in a small plane that lands there at low tide. Guests are welcome to explore this spot where Captain Cook anchored. If guests are so inclined, the hosts' commercially set net site needs crew, too. Rates include meals. Guests pay plane direct (around $380 round trip). Rates per person are: for cabin, $135; for bunkhouse, $125.

KS2. Enjoy the view from the home which is right on the bank of the Kenai River. The captain and host provide early, early breakfast for the fishing and Bidding aficionados. Charters for viewing and/or fishing available (not included). Bring oneself, binoculars, and poles for a truly Alaskan experience. $85-95.

Posey's Kenai River Hideaway Bed and Breakfast Lodge

P.O. Box 4094-ABB, 99669
(907) 262-7430; FAX (907) 262-7430
e-mail: hideaway@alaska.net
www.alaska.net/~hideaway/

On the bank of the Kenai River with its world-record king salmon, guests enjoy good, wholesome breakfast served before fishing. Hosts will arrange guided salmon or halibut charter, also fly-out fishing or sightseeing trips. After catching fish, relax on the sun deck built out over the river and swap fish stories. Hosts will freeze and pack fish for the return trip home. Seasonal rates available.

Hosts: Ray and June Posey
Rooms: 10 (3 PB; 7 SB) $110-130
Full Breakfast
Credit Cards: A, B
Notes: 2, 9, 12, 13, 14

STEPHEN LAKE

A Homestay at Homesteads

807 G Street, Suite 250, Anchorage, 99501
(907) 272-8644; FAX (907) 274-8644

SL. The hosts will pick up guests in their plane and fly them to the dock in front of the main house. Great fishing in the stream nearby. The hosts love to cook gourmet meals; all meals are included. Because of the flight time, guests stay for an unforgettable experience for two or more nights (three or more days). Nonhunting or nonfishing guests may receive reduced rates. Fly-out cabins available; hosts will bring meals out to guests. Call for rates.

NOTES: Credit cards accepted: A MasterCard; B Visa; C American Express; D Discover; E Diner's Club; F Other; 2 Personal checks accepted; 3 Lunch available; 4 Dinner available; 5 Open all year; 6 Pets welcome;

TALKEETNA

Alaska Private Lodgings: Stay with a Friend

P.O. Box 200047, 99520-0047
(907) 258-1717; FAX (907) 258-6613
e-mail: apl@alaskabandb.com
www.alaskabandb.com

Bay's Bed and Breakfast. Just 11 miles off the George Parks Highway into Talkeetna, this log home has three bedrooms that share two baths. Enjoy this truly Alaskan town that is the first stop for climbers getting ready to scale Denali. Continental breakfast. No smoking. Winter rate available. $76-95.

Denali View Bed and Breakfast. This is the life, at this country-style cedar home, complete with a turret, antiques, and Alaskana! Near Talkeetna, it is on 10 acres of a quiet residential area overlooking a valley with a spectacular view of Denali and the Alaska and Talkeetna Ranges. Choose from three Alaskan-style rooms. Private bath. Full breakfast. No smoking. Resident pet. Winter rates. $76-95.

TOK

Alaska Private Lodgings: Stay with a Friend

P.O. Box 200047, 99520-0047
(907) 258-1717; FAX (907) 258-6613
e-mail: apl@alaskabandb.com
www.alaskabandb.com

Cleft of the Rock. This bed and breakfast offers guests clean accommodations and warm, friendly, Christian hospitality. Guests will enjoy the serenity of the rural location. King-size, double, and twin beds are available. Private and shared baths. Full breakfast. No smoking. Winter rates. $66-95.

A Homestay at Homesteads

807 G Street, Suite 250, Anchorage, 99501
(907) 272-8644; FAX (907) 274-8644

Guest rooms are tiny but the host has a big heart in this log home on the highway. Open year-round and has camping places for RVs and tents. One-half mile from the Y in the highway, this hostel offers private baths with double beds or shared baths in the rooms with bunk beds. Warm hospitality is here in the middle of nowhere. Stay awhile and hike, fish, hunt, or enjoy all the winter sports. RV and tent camping $15. Bunk rooms $25. Bed and breakfast $50-75.

TRAPPER CREEK

Alaska Private Lodgings: Stay with a Friend

P.O. Box 200047, 99520-0047
(907) 258-1717; FAX (907) 258-6613
e-mail: apl@alaskabandb.com
www.alaskabandb.com

North Country Bed and Breakfast. Choose from five rooms with private bath and private entrances. Enjoy the lake setting and spectacular view of Denali for those Alaskan photo opportunities. Meet the other guests while relaxing in the recreation room. Paddleboating available on the lake in the summer and snowmobiling in the winter. Full breakfast. Private bath. No smoking. Winter rates. $76-95.

VALDEZ

Alaska Flower Forget-Me-Not Bed and Breakfast

P.O. Box 1153, 99686
(907) 835-2717

Prince William Sound hospitality at its best! Guests will enjoy their visit as they relax in one of the luxurious guest rooms with

7 No smoking; 8 Children welcome; 9 Social drinking allowed; 10 Tennis nearby; 11 Swimming nearby; 12 Golf nearby; 13 Skiing nearby; 14 May be booked through a travel agent; 15 Handicapped accessible.

panoramic views of the Chugach Mountains. A nutritious complimentary breakfast is served from 6 to 8 A.M. Walk to nearby cruise ships, the ferry, and the downtown area. Tour nearby glaciers, the Alaska Pipeline terminal, and pristine waters and mountains. AAA-approved.

Hosts: Betty and John Karinen
Rooms: 4 (2 PB; 2 SB) $75-95
Continental Breakfast
Credit Cards: None
Notes: 2, 5, 6, 7, 8, 9, 11, 12, 14

Alaska Private Lodgings: Stay with a Friend

P.O. Box 200047, 99520-0047
(907) 258-1717; FAX (907) 258-6613
e-mail: apl@alaskabandb.com
www.alaskabandb.com

Because Valdez is a small community and has many summer visitors, this service works closely with a reservation service in Valdez that represents many bed and breakfasts. Please make specific requests and Alaska Private Lodgings will assist guests in finding a comfortable bed and breakfast that meets their needs. There is a 10 percent service charge for Valdez reservations.

A Homestay at Homesteads

807 G Street, Suite 250, Anchorage, 99501
(907) 272-8644; FAX (907) 274-8644

V1. The artistry of bed and breakfast is found in the home. The hosts love travelers. Come stay for a few days in the lovely fjord town to explore the waterways, glaciers, wilderness mountains, white-water rivers. Taking the ferry? The hosts are used to guests leaving at the crack of dawn and/or arriving late. The hospitality door is always open. $75-95.

V4. If guests have a family looking for the perfect stop, the hosts have the right rooms with double and bunk beds. What a joy to find a fun family stop that loves and welcomes well-behaved kids as well as their parents. Families and large groups are welcomed. From $85.

WASILLA

Alaska Private Lodgings: Stay with a Friend

P.O. Box 200047, 99520-0047
(907) 258-1717; FAX (907) 258-6613
e-mail: apl@alaskabandb.com
www.alaskabandb.com

Toller's Timbers. The two chalets are private two-story buildings with spectacular mountain views from guests' own deck. Each has a furnished kitchen available for guests' personal use. The guests' suite has two rooms, kitchenette facilities, and a hot tub room. Private bath. Continental breakfast provisions provided. No smoking. Winter rates. $76-95.

Wasilla Lake Bed and Breakfast. Just minutes from Wasilla center with a view of Wasilla Lake and the mountains, this three-story country home offers a furnished suite on the first level and three bedrooms that share a bath on the third level. Also available is a two-story cabin with two bedrooms and private bath. Full breakfast served. No smoking. Winter rates. $55-95.

Yukon Don's. Enjoy one of four Alaska-decorated rooms as well as the Alaskan Room, a recreation room decorated with 30 years of collectible Alaskana, barrel stove, and log cabin bar. In the heart of the Matanuska Valley with a 270-degree view, this converted barn was once a cow house built on the soil of a one-time homestead/ colony farm. Private and shared baths. Continental breakfast. Resident pets. No smoking. Winter rates. $66-95.

NOTES: Credit cards accepted: A MasterCard; B Visa; C American Express; D Discover; E Diner's Club; F Other; 2 Personal checks accepted; 3 Lunch available; 4 Dinner available; 5 Open all year; 6 Pets welcome;

Yukon Don's Bed and Breakfast Inn

1830 East Parks Highway, Suite 386, 99654 (mail)
2221 Yukon Circle
(907) 376-7472; (800) 478-7472
e-mail: yukondon@alaska.net

All rooms are decorated with authentic Alaskana. Stay in the Iditarod, Fishing, Denali, and Hunting Rooms, or in the Matanuska Suite. Alaska Room offers Alaskan historic library, video library, pool table, cable TV, and gift bar. The all-glass View Room on the second floor offers the grandest view in the Matanuska Valley. Telephones in each room. Continental plus breakfast bar. Sauna and exercise room. Alaska's award-winning bed and breakfast inn: Alaska's Family Business of the Year, 1994; Top 50 Inns in America, 1991; ABBA Award of Excellence; Wasilla's Official Bed and Breakfast Accommodation. AAA-approved 1996, three diamonds. Ask about our oyster farm.

Hosts: Yukon Don and Beverly Tanner
Rooms: 8 (3 PB; 5 SB) $85-135
Continental Breakfast
Credit Cards: A, B, C, D
Notes: 2, 5, 8, 9, 11, 12, 13, 14

WHITEHORSE (YUKON)

Alaska Private Lodgings: Stay with a Friend

P.O. Box 200047, 99520-0047
(907) 258-1717; FAX (907) 258-6613
e-mail: apl@alaskabandb.com
www.alaskabandb.com

Hawkins House Bed and Breakfast. Lavish, spacious, and bright best describe this new Victorian home in downtown. All four guest rooms feature a private bath, queen-size bed, balcony, oak floors, bar sink, refrigerator, cable TV, and VCR. Breakfast is a full feast of northern and international delights. No smoking. Winter rates. Rates begin at $96.

Highland Home Bed and Breakfast. Share this home and the beauty and vastness of the wonderful Yukon. Relax in the sun lounge or in the hot tub/spa in a secluded garden or wander through pine and spruce forest behind the home. Private and shared baths. Continental breakfast. No smoking. Resident pet. $66-95.

WHITTIER

A Homestay at Homesteads

807 G Street, Suite 250, Anchorage, 99501
(907) 272-8644; FAX (907) 274-8644

1. Guests have a world-class view of the spectacular fjord at this warm-water port where two-thirds of the population live in the high rise built for troops during World War II. The ferry and train both leave from the docks below. Enjoy plenty of winter skiing, summer hiking, kayaking, and fishing. Come for overnight or stay a few days. Kitchen, living room in each suite. Continental breakfast and/or early hot meal with the hosts.

2. See Prince William Sound with a retired commercial fisherman and his wife. This very stable boat is available for hire for a great day or overnight on the oceans and around the islands for wilderness hiking, fishing, glacier viewing, and shrimping. Meals and accommodations for up to six lucky folks. They have two boats so could accommodate more. Call early as they book solidly in the summer.

3. Why not try this bed and breakfast on a boat while touring the beautiful Prince William Sound. Captain is the foremost authority on bird habitats in Prince William Sound and is an expert on where to camp as well as the area's forest service cabins and kayaking. The boat is wheel chair and kayak accessible. Come spend a few days

---

7 No smoking; 8 Children welcome; 9 Social drinking allowed; 10 Tennis nearby; 11 Swimming nearby; 12 Golf nearby; 13 Skiing nearby; 14 May be booked through a travel agent; 15 Handicapped accessible.

on the water exploring remote islands in Alaska. Open year-round. Call for quote.

WILLOW

Willow Winter Park Bed and Breakfast

P.O. Box 251, 99688
(907) 495-7547; FAX (907) 495-7638
e-mail: winterpark@matnet.com

An hour and a half north of Anchorage on the Parks Highway. Overlooking Winter Park Lake, this beautiful bed and breakfast is the perfect home base for the Alaskan adventure. Three hours south of Mount McKinley Park, four hours north of Seward. Rooms are furnished with antiques, flannel sheets. Hot tub on outdoor deck. Great salmon and trout fishing, mountain biking, hiking, canoeing in the summer; skiing, dog-sled rides, and snowmobiling in the winter.

Host: Kurt Stenehjem
Rooms: 5 (PB) $75
Full Breakfast
Credit Cards: A, B, C, D, E
Notes: 2, 3, 4, 5, 7, 8, 9, 11, 13, 14

WRANGELL

Grand View Bed and Breakfast

P.O. Box 927, 99929
(907) 874-3225 (phone/FAX)
www.GrandViewBnB.com

Nestled in the woods, quiet, secluded, courtesy transportation. Three guest rooms with private baths and entrances, common dining, living, kitchen area with kitchen privileges. Rooms include cable TV, VCR, touch-tone telephone, extra-long twin or queen-size beds, fruit bowl in room, evening snack, spa, bicycles. Activity planning—i.e., charter fishing, kayaking, jet boat tours, guided walking tours, or car rental. Sack lunches provided on request for an additional fee.

Hosts: Judy and John Baker
Rooms: 3 (PB) $60-90
Full and Continental Breakfast
Credit Cards: None
Notes: 2, 5, 7, 8, 9, 10, 11, 12, 14

Grand View

Arizona

AJO

Mi Casa Su Casa/Old Pueblo Homestays Bed and Breakfast Reservation Service

P.O. Box 950, Tempe, 85280-0950
(602) 990-0682; (800) 456-0682
FAX (602) 990-3390
e-mail: micasa@primenet.com
www.azres.com

4011. Near Organ Pipe Cactus National Monument and 50 minutes from Mexico. Originally built in 1925 to accommodate visiting company officials for Phelps Dodge, this inn has four guest rooms, private baths, a reputation for warm hospitality, and excellent breakfasts. The furnishings reflect the rich traditions of Arizona. There is a guest cottage with living room, kitchen, full hall bath, and three bedrooms. Children welcome. No smoking. Ten dollars for rollaway bed for third person in room. $69-79.

AMADO

Arizona Trails Bed and Breakfast Reservation Service

P.O. Box 18998, Fountain Hills, 85269-8998
(602) 837-4284; (888) 799-4284
FAX (602) 816-4224
e-mail: aztrails@arizonatrails.com
www.arizonatrails.com

AZ 128. Relax in this cozy nine-room western inn just south of Tucson. This inn sits on five acres of riparian habitat with award-winning landscaping, walking trails, and adjacent artists' studios. Just five miles to Tubac and great for hikers and bird watchers. Decorated in a simple but warm Mission style, this inn has rooms with king- or queen-size beds or two oversized twin beds. All rooms have private baths. Breakfast is served each morning in the atrium. Handicapped accessible. $105-135.

BENSON

Mi Casa Su Casa/Old Pueblo Homestays Bed and Breakfast Reservation Service

P.O. Box 950, Tempe, 85280-0950
(602) 990-0682; (800) 456-0682
FAX (602) 990-3390
e-mail: micasa@primenet.com
www.azres.com

4031. Built in 1995 overlooking the San Pedro River Valley near Benson. Adjacent to the Vega-Bray Observatory. Three guest bedrooms, each with a bed, sofa bed, and bathroom. Living room-science studio with a TV/VCR and a kitchenette. Two-mile nature trail that includes the San Pedro River and two large ponds that attract many different species of waterfowl. Guests can make their own full breakfast from the stocked kitchen any time convenient to them, or the hosts can prepare breakfast between 9:00 and 11:00 A.M. No smoking or pets. Five dollars for each additional person. $65-110.

7 No smoking; 8 Children welcome; 9 Social drinking allowed; 10 Tennis nearby; 11 Swimming nearby; 12 Golf nearby; 13 Skiing nearby; 14 May be booked through a travel agent; 15 Handicapped accessible.

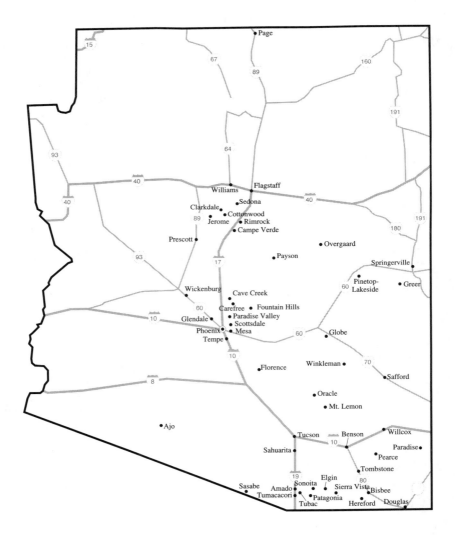

Arizona

BISBEE

Bisbee Grand Hotel

P.O. Box 825, 85603
(602) 452-5900

Capture the ambiance of downtown historic Bisbee by staying at Bisbee's most elegant turn-of-the-century hotel. Each room is individually appointed with antiques featuring Victorian, oriental, and garden suites. Old West bar. Within walking distance to all fine restaurants, shopping, and the famous copper mine tour.

Host: Bill W. Thomas
Rooms: 11 (PB) $55-110
Full Breakfast
Credit Cards: A, B, C, D
Notes: 2, 5, 7, 9, 10, 12, 14

Mi Casa Su Casa/Old Pueblo Homestays Bed and Breakfast Reservation Service

P.O. Box 950, Tempe, 85280-0950
(602) 990-0682; (800) 456-0682
FAX (602) 990-3390
e-mail: micasa@primenet.com
www.azres.com

4041. Cradled in a valley in the Mule Mountains, this two-story red brick house built in 1908 in Warren has been renovated by the host couple. Step back in time while enjoying the art collection and antiques from their lifelong collection. The two guest rooms with private baths are on the second floor. A family room with TV, VCR, many books, and a sunroom decorated in antique wicker are available for relaxing and reading. Full breakfast is served. No small children. Resident dog. Smoking is permitted outside only. $65.

4042. Spanish Mission-style home built in 1906. Spacious rooms with lofty crowned ceilings from which are suspended unusual chandeliers, oak and maple flooring, fireplaces and antique furnishings. Six bedrooms, some with private baths, are available. A generous breakfast offering many homemade items is included. Refreshments are served from 3:00 to 4:00 P.M. Not handicapped accessible. Smoking permitted outside only. No pets. Children are welcome. Fifteen dollars per extra guest. $60-70.

4043. This 1910 two-story Mediterranean-style home, 10 minutes from the quaint shopping district, is in a quiet residential area abounding with excellent restaurants. It boasts spacious bedrooms, balconies, terraces, library, and a sunroom. A variety of roses and fruit trees graces the well-cared-for front and back lawns. Guest rooms include ceiling fans and three are air conditioned. Two guest rooms have private baths. The hosts serve a four-course gourmet breakfast. Smoking permitted outside. Inquire about children and pets. Ten dollars per extra guest. $50-70.

School House Inn

818 Tombstone Canyon, P.O. Box 32, 85603
(520) 432-2996; (800) 537-4333

An old schoolhouse built in 1918 and converted into lovely large rooms and suites with 12-foot ceilings and private baths. High up Tombstone Canyon, the 5,600-foot elevation provides spectacular scenery, clean air, and a relaxing retreat. A full breakfast is served on the shaded patio or in the spacious family room. The inn is close to mine tours, art galleries, antique shops, hiking, bird watching, and much more. Recommended by *Arizona Republic* as "Best Place to Stay in Southern Arizona."

Hosts: Jeff and Bobby Blankenbeckler
Rooms: 9 (PB) $55-75
Full Breakfast

NOTES: Credit cards accepted: A MasterCard; B Visa; C American Express; D Discover; E Diner's Club; F Other; 2 Personal checks accepted; 3 Lunch available; 4 Dinner available; 5 Open all year; 6 Pets welcome; 7 No smoking; 8 Children welcome; 9 Social drinking allowed; 10 Tennis nearby; 11 Swimming nearby; 12 Golf nearby; 13 Skiing nearby; 14 May be booked through a travel agent; 15 Handicapped accessible.

Credit Cards: A, B, C, D, E, F
Notes: 2, 5, 7, 9, 11, 12

CAMP VERDE

Bed and Breakfast Southwest Reservation Service

P.O. Box 51198, Phoenix, 85076-1198
(602) 947-9704; (800) 762-9704
FAX (602) 874-1316

164. Between Cordes Junction and Camp Verde off I-17. Host operates winery on property and has one exquisite room for guests. King-size bed and in-room Jacuzzi make this a special getaway for lovers. Full breakfast. No smoking. No children. $125-150.

Mi Casa Su Casa/Old Pueblo Homestays Bed and Breakfast Reservation Service

P.O. Box 950, Tempe, 85280-0950
(602) 990-0682; (800) 456-0682
FAX (602) 990-3390
e-mail: micasa@primenet.com
www.azres.com

4071. This bed and breakfast was built in 1996 on 20 acres in high chaparral surrounded by forest service land. On the property is an award-winning boutique winery dedicated to the production of fine varietal wines. It is an easy drive to historic Fort Verde, Prescott, Jerome, and Sedona. The large open guest room has a private entrance and is separate from the main house. It has a double whirlpool tub with shower, and sofa bed. Full breakfast.

CAREFREE

Mi Casa Su Casa/Old Pueblo Homestays Bed and Breakfast Reservation Service

P.O. Box 950, Tempe, 85280-0950
(602) 990-0682; (800) 456-0682

FAX (602) 990-3390
e-mail: micasa@primenet.com
www.azres.com

4081. In a secluded valley, this bed and breakfast is minutes from Cave Creek and Carefree restaurants. It has spectacular views of the mountains and great hiking and bird watching along the creek. Across the road is a riding stable where guests can rent horses and ride some of the most beautiful trails in Arizona. The guest accommodations are in the carriage house which has a private entrance, living room with large TV, bedroom, and bath with tub/shower. The full kitchen is stocked with Continental plus breakfast fixings. No smoking. $75-95.

4082. This deluxe executive retreat is on 20 acres surrounded by Tonto National Forest. Convenient to golf, horseback riding, hiking, biking, jeep tours, and fine dining. Each accommodation includes private entrance and private bath. Other amenities include fireplace, stereo with CD, cassette, and radio, TV/VCR, daily paper, iron and board, hair dryers, complimentary laundry service, full concierge services, and afternoon snacks. A heart-healthy breakfast served. Smoking permitted outside. Children not encouraged. No pets. Twelve dollars for each additional guest. $99-199.

CAVE CREEK

Arizona Trails Bed and Breakfast Reservation Service

P.O. Box 18998, Fountain Hills, 85269-8998
(602) 837-4284; (888) 799-4284
FAX (602) 816-4224
e-mail: aztrails@arizonatrails.com
www.arizonatrails.com

AZ 109. Comfort and charm abound at this three-guest-room bed and breakfast. Close to the Phoenix border and only 10 minutes to the freeway, yet nestled in a lush desert landscape that is quiet and

NOTES: Credit cards accepted: A MasterCard; B Visa; C American Express; D Discover; E Diner's Club; F Other; 2 Personal checks accepted; 3 Lunch available; 4 Dinner available; 5 Open all year; 6 Pets welcome;

relaxing. Two guest rooms have TVs and private baths with standup showers. The Dream Catcher suite has sliding glass doors leading to a private patio, private hall bath with standup shower, and private living room with TV, fireplace, and guest refrigerator stocked with cold drinks. An indoor hot tub adjoins the outside deck. Continental breakfast served Monday through Friday, with a full breakfast served on the weekends. $85-95.

AZ 160. Experience the Old West-setting of Arizona at this guest house backing up to Tonto National Forest. The main room features a reproduction antique bed and sitting area with TV/VCR. Full kitchen is stocked daily for a self-serve breakfast and the private bath has both tub and shower. Private entrance and parking. Great views. Stables and trail rides are across the street. Site was once a gold mine. The main house is Victorian and has been featured in a Disney/Mirimax film. $100.

AZ 179. For a true taste of the Southwest, stay at this lovely, new two-guest-room bed and breakfast in the Spur Cross area. One room offers a cowboy theme with queen-size bed and private bath. The upstairs suite has a king-size bed, queen-size sleeper-sofa, full bath with whirlpool tub, kitchenette, and balcony. The grounds are spacious, the views panoramic. Close to town with shops and restaurants. Horse boarding also available. A buffet Continental plus breakfast is served. $95-125.

Bed and Breakfast Southwest Reservation Service

P.O. Box 51198, Phoenix, 85076-1198
(602) 947-9704; (800) 762-9704
FAX (602) 874-1316

131. This new two-story Pueblo-style 4,000-square-foot home is up against the Tonto National Forest and just 18 miles

from central Scottsdale. The El Grande suite is a totally private 600-square-foot upstairs suite with a queen-size bed, sitting room with sleeper sofa, kitchenette, private bath with Jacuzzi tub, TV, and private deck. The Cowboy room offers a king-size bed, private bath with Jacuzzi tub, and southwestern decor. Horseback riding and hiking close by. Four patios, barbecue, and great views. No smoking. Children welcome. $95-125.

Mi Casa Su Casa/Old Pueblo Homestays Bed and Breakfast Reservation Service

P.O. Box 950, Tempe, 85280-0950
(602) 990-0682; (800) 456-0682
FAX (602) 990-3390
e-mail: micasa@primenet.com
www.azres.com

4101. Large rambling home on five acres. Guest accommodations are in one section of the house. Extra-large suite has own living room, TV, large bedroom, connecting full bath. The second bedroom is small and has a hall bath. The compact apartment has a private entrance, bath, kitchenette, and two bedrooms. Pool available for in-season swimming. Spa. Cookouts, barbecues, and hay rides available by appointment. Continental breakfast weekdays; full breakfast on weekends. Resident dog. Smoking outside only. Inquire about accommodations for children. $60-85.

4102. This two-story pueblo-style house constructed in 1997 is on two acres of horse property surrounded by state land and the Tonto National Forest. It offers two luxurious accommodations. On the second floor, the El Grande Suite offers a bedroom with king-size bed and TV, a bathroom with jetted tub and shower, and a separate sitting room with queen-size sofa bed, twin-size rollaway bed, small microwave, and refrigerator. There is also a private deck to view the pristine desert

7 No smoking; 8 Children welcome; 9 Social drinking allowed; 10 Tennis nearby; 11 Swimming nearby; 12 Golf nearby; 13 Skiing nearby; 14 May be booked through a travel agent; 15 Handicapped accessible.

and mountains. The Cowboy Room on the first floor has a queen-size bed, bath with tub/shower, and a small refrigerator. Ten dollars for each additional guest. $95-125.

4103. This seven-acre private horse ranch offers a high desert retreat a few minutes north of Cave Creek's historic Old West center. Guests can relax on their own private patios. Each of the four rooms has a separate entrance and patio, kitchenette, TV, VCR, personal telephone line, and private bathroom. A private outdoor spa is accessible to guests in the Pinto Suite. Supervised horseback riding is available at an additional charge. Horse boarding available. A delectable breakfast is either "serve yourself" or brought to guests' room. No smoking. Small children and pets are considered on an individual basis. $69-119.

CLARKDALE

Arizona Trails Bed and Breakfast Reservation Service

P.O. Box 18998, Fountain Hills, 85269-8998
(602) 837-4284; (888) 799-4284
FAX (602) 816-4224
e-mail: aztrails@arizonatrails.com
www.arizonatrails.com

AZ 145. Relax in this charming two-guest-room homestay on a hillside in Clarkdale, just 12 minutes to Jerome and 20 minutes from Sedona. Spectacular panoramic views take in the surrounding area and red rocks of Sedona. Close to a golf course and shopping, great for hiking. One room features a sitting area, TV, and private hall bath with tub and shower. The guest house has a private bath with shower only, full kitchen, TV, and great views. An outdoor hot tub is great for viewing the stars at night. Cooking class weekends are also available. Full gourmet breakfast is served daily. $79-89.

COTTONWOOD

Arizona Trails Bed and Breakfast Reservation Service

P.O. Box 18998, Fountain Hills, 85269-8998
(602) 837-4284; (888) 799-4284
FAX (602) 816-4224
e-mail: aztrails@arizonatrails.com
www.arizonatrails.com

AZ 159. Relax at this two-room bed and breakfast in a farm setting, close to the Verde River. One room in the main house has a queen-size bed, dressing room, private bath with tub and shower, and private balcony overlooking the pasture. The guest room has a queen-size bed, sitting area, TV, private bath with tub and shower, and is decorated with antiques. Only 20-25 minutes from Sedona and close to the Verde Canyon scenic trail ride. Full breakfast. $85.

Mi Casa Su Casa/Old Pueblo Homestays Bed and Breakfast Reservation Service

P.O. Box 950, Tempe, 85280-0950
(602) 990-0682; (800) 456-0682
FAX (602) 990-3390
e-mail: micasa@primenet.com
www.azres.com

4131. Delightful hostess of Irish descent has pleasant three-bedroom, two-bath stucco house built in 1981 in quiet, residential neighborhood. Landscaped with rock, trees, shrubs, and rose bushes. Large guest room with full bath en suite, TV, radio, coffee maker. Continental plus or full breakfast. Resident parakeet. Two nights preferred. No smoking. No pets. Children six and older welcome. Fifteen dollars for additional person on rollaway. $75.

4132. Large, elegant country home in a serene setting surrounded by mountain views and acres of manicured green pastures. Fourteen miles from Sedona, 15 minutes from Jerome. Spacious 600-square-foot

---

NOTES: Credit cards accepted: A MasterCard; B Visa; C American Express; D Discover; E Diner's Club; F Other; 2 Personal checks accepted; 3 Lunch available; 4 Dinner available; 5 Open all year; 6 Pets welcome;

guest cottage with exterior stairs to private entrance is on the second floor of a building separate from the main house. Queen-size bed, sofa bed, private bath, ample sitting and dining areas, small microwave and refrigerator. In the main house is a spacious master bedroom with queen-size bed, cable TV, dressing room, tub/shower, balcony deck. Refreshments. Sumptuous breakfasts. Third person in cottage $25. Children under two years $10. $85.

DOUGLAS

Mi Casa Su Casa/Old Pueblo Homestays Bed and Breakfast Reservation Service

P.O. Box 950, Tempe, 85280-0950
(602) 990-0682; (800) 456-0682
FAX (602) 990-3390
e-mail: micasa@primenet.com
www.azres.com

4142. This ranch is on the northeastern slope of the Chiricahua Mountains near many historic sites, museums, and Old Mexico. Forty-two miles from Douglas, 150 miles from Tucson. General ranch life offered for the individual and family to take part in. Daily trail rides are available for 4 to 20 people. Bunk houses have one or two rooms and baths and an apartment includes a kitchenette and private patio. Summer ranch riding program. Camper and trailer hook-ups are nearby. A swimming pool and a three-acre catfish pond are on the premises. Rates include room, three daily meals, and horseback riding. $85-160.

ELGIN

Arizona Trails Bed and Breakfast Reservation Service

P.O. Box 18998, Fountain Hills, 85269-8998
(602) 837-4284; (888) 799-4284
FAX (602) 816-4224
e-mail: aztrails@arizonatrails.com
www.arizonatrails.com

AZ 184. This three-room bed and breakfast is in the heart of bird-watching country and the area that claims home to some of Arizona's finest wineries. Each room is appointed with its own full bath, including spa tub and shower, wood-burning stove, private entrance, sitting area, TV/VCR. The 5,000-foot elevation and rolling landscape make for mild summers and sunny winters. Choose from an Old Mexican decor, Native American, or Wild West. Mountain bikes and horse-boarding area available. Full breakfast. $85-100.

Mi Casa Su Casa/Old Pueblo Homestays Bed and Breakfast Reservation Service

P.O. Box 950, Tempe, 85280-0950
(602) 990-0682; (800) 456-0682
FAX (602) 990-3390
e-mail: micasa@primenet.com
www.azres.com

4171. This spacious hacienda was built in 1992 in the middle of 180 acres with a landscape of rolling grasslands and high mountain ranges. In the heart of the Arizona wine country, and in the nation's foremost bird watching area. Fishing and boating are available at two lakes in the vicinity. Endless trails for mountain biking, hiking, and horseback riding are nearby. The three guest rooms each have a private entrance onto the courtyard, a fireplace, sitting area, TV/VCR. Full breakfast. No smoking, no pets. $85.

FLAGSTAFF

Arizona Trails Bed and Breakfast Reservation Service

P.O. Box 18998, Fountain Hills, 85269-8998
(602) 837-4284; (888) 799-4284
FAX (602) 816-4224
e-mail: aztrails@arizonatrails.com
www.arizonatrails.com

AZ 115. Enjoy the quiet atmosphere of the northern pines at this lovely ranch-style bed

7 No smoking; 8 Children welcome; 9 Social drinking allowed; 10 Tennis nearby; 11 Swimming nearby; 12 Golf nearby; 13 Skiing nearby; 14 May be booked through a travel agent; 15 Handicapped accessible.

and breakfast. This ranch house with its large stone fireplace and high ceilings was originally moved from Texas. Close to historic downtown Flagstaff but far enough away to enjoy the peace and relaxation of the pines. Four rooms all with private baths and antiques. The upstairs area can accommodate a family of four and has its own TV. Downstairs suite has a private entrance, sitting room, and kitchenette. Close to parks, a lake, stables, skiing, historic sites, shops, and restaurants. Breakfast and afternoon snacks served in the dining area. Children welcome. $75-100.

AZ 116. Experience this authentic Victorian-style bed and breakfast. Four rooms with antiques and private baths will take guests back in time to a gracious era of charm. Just outside the downtown area in a quiet residential area, guests are only minutes to parks, downtown shops and restaurants, or skiing. Four guest rooms; one with a fireplace and two with porch access. The parlor houses an old-book library. Handmade glycerin soaps in all rooms. Gourmet breakfast served. $95.

AZ 117. Relax in style in this uniquely historic nine-room inn near downtown Flagstaff. Elegantly appointed with antiques and stained glass, mixed with a touch of the Southwest. All rooms have a different theme with private baths; some with Jacuzzi tubs and some with gas fireplaces. All rooms have coffee makers and refrigerators. An elegant experience in the pines of northern Arizona. Walk to shops and restaurants in historic downtown Flagstaff. Full breakfast. Handicapped accessible. $110-155.

AZ 133. This charming two-room apartment-style bed and breakfast offers guests plenty of room to relax in downtown Flagstaff, close to shops and restaurants. Private upstairs entrance leads to one of

two suites, each of which offers a queen-size custom-made western bed, living room with TV and telephone, and private bath with standup shower. Each living area includes a dining table and chairs for guests' in-room breakfast. Each morning a full breakfast will be brought to guests' room. Guests share an area with refrigerator and microwave for midday or late-night snacks. $95.

AZ 177. Stay at this 10-room inn that also offers three- to seven-day adventure packages. Set up lodge style, there are two sitting areas, one with fireplace, board games, and library. Relax in the indoor sauna or the outdoor hot tub. Two suites can sleep up to six. A hearty full breakfast served. Ask about the adventure packages including hiking, rock climbing, mountain biking, dog sledding, and cross-country skiing (in season). Handicapped accessible. $106-164.

Birch Tree Inn

824 West Birch Avenue, 86001-2240
(520) 774-1042; (888) 774-1042
e-mail: birch@flagstaff.az.us

The Birch Tree Inn, circa 1917, offers guests comfortable surroundings in one of the city's finest historic homes. The inviting parlor offers a retreat to read, converse, or relax in front of a warm fire. Each bedroom features its own atmosphere blending antiques and heirloom furnishings or southwestern decor. An outdoor whirlpool tub is great for relaxing the weary hiker or skier. A hearty full breakfast is served in the dining room; in early morning coffee/tea is served upstairs. Afternoon refreshments offer guests a time to acquaint themselves with each other and the hosts.

Hosts: Sandy and Ed Znetko;
   Donna and Rodger Pettinger
Rooms: 5 (3 PB; 2 SB) $59-109
Full Breakfast
Credit Cards: A, B, C, D
Notes: 2, 5, 7, 9, 10, 12, 13, 14

NOTES: Credit cards accepted: A MasterCard; B Visa; C American Express; D Discover; E Diner's Club; F Other; 2 Personal checks accepted; 3 Lunch available; 4 Dinner available; 5 Open all year; 6 Pets welcome;

Comfi Cottages of Flagstaff

1612 North Aztec Street, 86001
(520) 774-0731; (888) 774-0731
www.virtualflagstaff.com/comfi

In historic downtown Flagstaff, cottages are beautifully decorated and furnished with antique pieces having a touch of the Southwest. These one-, two-, and three-bedroom cottages are equipped with everything guests need for comfortable daily living. Breakfast foods are placed in the refrigerator to be prepared at their leisure. All cottages have picnic tables, lawn chairs, and barbecue grills; some have fireplaces. Bicycles are available. Chosen by the *Arizona Republic* as the Best Week-End Getaway.

Hosts: Pat and Ed Wiebe
Cottages: 6 (PB and SB) $95-195
Full Breakfast
Credit Cards: A, B, D
Notes: 2, 5, 7, 8, 10, 11, 12, 13, 14

Dierker House

423 West Cherry, 86001
(502) 774-3249

This lovely, comfortable old house, in the historic registry, offers three large guest rooms on the second floor. Private entrance, guest kitchen, small sitting room, king-size beds with down comforters, antiques, white wine in the refrigerator, and coffee, tea, and cookies all combine to offer guests a quiet homelike atmosphere. An excellent full breakfast is served at 8:00 A.M. in the downstairs dining room. For the early risers, a Continental breakfast is served before 8:00 A.M. A very good value.

Host: Dorothea Dierker
Room: 3 (3 SB) $50
Full and Continental Breakfast
Credit Cards: None
Notes: 2, 5, 7, 9, 10, 11, 12, 13

The Inn at 410

410 North Leroux Street, 86001
(800) 774-2008

The Inn at 410 offers guests four seasons of hospitality in a charming 1907 home. Ele-

The Inn at 410

gantly furnished with antiques, this inn has stained glass and touches of the Southwest. Nine distinctive suites, each with its own private bath, mini-fridge, and coffee maker; some with fireplace and/or Jacuzzi tub. Each guest is pampered with a personal touch that includes oven-fresh cookies, healthy breakfasts, and recommendations about day trips to the Grand Canyon, Indian ruins, hiking, or skiing.

Hosts: Howard and Sally Krueger
Rooms: 9 (PB) $125-165
Full Breakfast
Credit Cards: A, B
Notes: 2, 5, 7, 8, 9, 10, 11, 12, 13, 14, 15

Jeanette's Bed and Breakfast

3380 East Lockett Road, 86004
(520) 527-1912; (800) 752-1912

Wanting a romantic getaway? Ready for a retreat or holiday? Well, "let down your hair" somewhere "inn" time at Jeanette's. Post Victorian architecture recalls Arizona's

Jeanette's

first statehood days. Experience Jeanette's four rooms filled with signs of the time. Private baths reflect the style or the era and a breakfast so devine is served with the flair of a fine Sunday dinner. Jeanette and Ray West cordially invite guests to come and enjoy their home.

Hosts: Jeanette and Ray West
Rooms: 4 (PB) $95-125
Full Breakfast
Credit Cards: A, B
Notes: 2, 5, 7, 9, 13

Lake Mary Bed and Breakfast

5470 South "J" Diamond Road, 86001
(520) 779-7054; (888) 241-9550 (toll free)
FAX (520) 779-7054

Two and one-half miles outside Flagstaff, this country ranch-type house hosts a large wraparound front/side porch. Guest facilities include four large guest rooms with private baths. Start the day with one of the hosts' full home-cooked gourmet breakfasts. Need to unwind before dinner? Relax in one of two common rooms with a good book or by the fireplace with a cup of coffee and a slice of homemade bread or a handful of cookies. Smoking is permitted outside only.

Hosts: Frank and Christine McCollum
Rooms: 4 (PB) $75-100
Full Breakfast
Credit Cards: A, B
Notes: 2, 5, 7, 8, 9, 12, 13, 14

Mi Casa Su Casa/Old Pueblo Homestays Bed and Breakfast Reservation Service

P.O. Box 950, Tempe, 85280-0950
(602) 990-0682; (800) 456-0682
FAX (602) 990-3390
e-mail: micasa@primenet.com
www.azres.com

4181. First a private home, then a fraternity house, this historic two-story house built in 1917 is now a bed and breakfast inn. Five guest rooms on the second floor. The Pella

Room and the Wicker Room share a hall bath. Carol's Room has a private bath. The large Southwest Room has a large private bath. Full breakfast is served. Resident dog. Children 10 and older are welcome. Smoking permitted outside. Free Amtrak pick-up. $69-99.

4182. Rambling five-level home built on a hillside with views of historic downtown, the San Francisco Peaks, and Mars Hill. Within walking distance of shops, restaurants, train, and bus stations. The suite includes a private entrance, deck, living room with sofa bed and cable TV, bath, and fully equipped kitchen stocked for a self-serve Continental plus breakfast. The other guest room has a shared hall bath and is served a Continental plus breakfast. This inn caters to the chemically and environmentally sensitive. Children over eight are welcome. No pets. Smoking is not permitted on premises. Suite has two-night minimum, with $15 for each person over two persons. $65-115.

4183. This three-story house was built in 1915 in the original town site of Flagstaff. There are more than 15 large trees that shade the yard. Five blocks from downtown Flagstaff in quiet residential neighborhood near Thorpe Park. Two suites on the second floor are reached by exterior stairs and they have a private entrance. Each has a sitting room with sofa bed, private bath with shower, cable TV, telephone, small refrigerator, and wet bar. Bicycles and tennis racquets available. Full breakfast is served. Smoking is not permitted on premises. No pets. $95.

4185. The inn has four suites and five guest rooms, all with private bath, refrigerator, and coffee maker. Several have a fireplace and whirlpool tub. Some can accommodate three or four people. One is handicapped accessible. It is close to a variety of both

NOTES: Credit cards accepted: A MasterCard; B Visa; C American Express; D Discover; E Diner's Club; F Other; 2 Personal checks accepted; 3 Lunch available; 4 Dinner available; 5 Open all year; 6 Pets welcome;

winter and summer recreation, sightseeing locations, and is within walking distance of shops, galleries, and restaurants. A full gourmet breakfast is served as well as afternoon snacks. Smoking is not permitted on premises. Children are welcome. No pets. Ten dollars for each additional guest. $110-155.

4186. This 1912 post-Victorian-era bed and breakfast in Flagstaff recalls Arizona's first statehood days. Four bedrooms are filled with signs of the time. Private baths reflect the style of the era and a breakfast is served with the flair and detail of a fine Sunday dinner. Convenient to the Grand Canyon, skiing, Sunset Crater Volcano, Lowell Observatory, Petrified Forest, and Museum of Northern Arizona. Smoking is permitted outside only. No pets. Children under one and over seven are welcome. $65-85.

FLORENCE

Arizona Trails Bed and Breakfast Reservation Service

P.O. Box 18998, Fountain Hills, 85269-8998
(602) 837-4284; (888) 799-4284
FAX (602) 816-4224
e-mail: aztrails@arizonatrails.com
www.arizonatrails.com

AZ 150. This six-room inn built from the original structure of the 1930s is a great midway stopping point between Phoenix and Tucson in the beauty of the Sonoran Desert. The adobe-style inn is centered around a main courtyard with gardens and fountain. Each room has a private bath with standup shower and is decorated in a different decor ranging from western to Victorian. There are also three guest cottages, furnished with one or two bedrooms, living room, kitchen, and bathroom. Outside swimming pool. Continental breakfast. Cottages are rented on a weekly basis. RV park also available next door. $69.

Mi Casa Su Casa/Old Pueblo Homestays Bed and Breakfast Reservation Service

P.O. Box 950, Tempe, 85280-0950
(602) 990-0682; (800) 456-0682
FAX (602) 990-3390
e-mail: micasa@primenet.com
www.azres.com

4201. This 1930s adobe guest ranch was recently renovated to its original charm. Four miles south of Florence, 60 miles from Phoenix or Tucson. Ten golf courses and horseback riding within 30 minutes. Two cottages with kitchens, a pool to use in season, and seven guest rooms with doors opening to the central courtyard with fountain. All have individual heating and air conditioning, private baths, and TVs. Barbecue area. Continental breakfast buffet is available with daily rates only. Smoking is permitted in designated areas only. Children are welcome. Inquire about accommodations for pets. Credit cards are accepted. Weekly and monthly rates are available. $65-85.

FOUNTAIN HILLS

Arizona Trails Bed and Breakfast Reservation Service

P.O. Box 18998, Fountain Hills, 85269-8998
(602) 837-4284; (888) 799-4284
FAX (602) 816-4224
e-mail: aztrails@arizonatrails.com
www.arizonatrails.com

AZ 107. In Fountain Hills, this sprawling Spanish hacienda offers spectacular desert and mountain views. Pool, spa, tennis courts, and hiking trails on the property. The common areas offer a large-screen TV/VCR, fireplace and billiard table. Decorated in southwestern decor, two rooms with private baths and two rooms share a bath. A short distance to Scottsdale and Sky Harbor International Airport. Continental breakfast each morning. $95-165.

7 No smoking; 8 Children welcome; 9 Social drinking allowed; 10 Tennis nearby; 11 Swimming nearby; 12 Golf nearby; 13 Skiing nearby; 14 May be booked through a travel agent; 15 Handicapped accessible.

AZ 125. Nestled in the beautiful desert community of Fountain Hills, just east of Scottsdale, relax at this friendly two-room bed and breakfast. Enjoy views of the surrounding mountains, desert landscapes, and the world's tallest fountain from the deck in the back. Relax in the heated pool or outdoor spa. One room offers a private bath, TV, and telephone. The other suite of rooms can be used as two rooms with a shared bath, or guests can opt for only room with the hall bath being private for a small extra charge. These rooms also have TVs and telephones. All rooms are furnished with plush robes for use in the bath or at the pool. A gourmet breakfast is served. $75-95.

AZ 170. This charming, new, two-guest-room bed and breakfast sits high on a hill with a great mountain view. Both rooms have private entrances, full private baths, TVs, and in-room coffee makers. The downstairs suite is decorated in an antique theme with four-poster bed. The upstairs suite is done in southwestern theme with an outside balcony with swing. Full breakfast. $95.

AZ 181. This 42-room inn/"boutique hotel" offers golf course views and all the amenities guests can imagine. A variety of rooms offers guests the choice of one- and two-room suites, all with southwestern decor, whirlpool jetted tubs in the full private baths, telephones, modem connections, work areas, TV/VCRs, in-room coffee makers, and private patios or decks with up to 50-mile views. Concierge desk available for local information or for arranging tours. Continental plus breakfast buffet served. Pool and spa overlook the 18-hole golf course next door. Three meeting rooms available for groups. Handicapped accessible. $195-345.

Bed and Breakfast Southwest Reservation Service

P.O. Box 51198, Phoenix, 85076-1198
(602) 947-9704; (800) 762-9704
FAX (602) 874-1316

136. High on a hillside with surrounding panoramic views. Four luxurious guest rooms, heated pool with swim-up bar, spa, and tennis courts. Southwestern decor featuring a massive Mexican brick fireplace, big screen TV, and pool table. No smoking. Children over 14 welcome. $75-225.

Mi Casa Su Casa/Old Pueblo Homestays Bed and Breakfast Reservation Service

P.O. Box 950, Tempe, 85280-0950
(602) 990-0682; (800) 456-0682
FAX (602) 990-3390
e-mail: micasa@primenet.com
www.azres.com

4221. This trilevel contemporary home built in 1986 offers panoramic views of the desert, surrounding mountains, and the world's tallest fountain. It offers a great room with fireplace, cable TV, and VCR. A sitting room for reading or relaxing leads outdoors to a heated spa. The two guest rooms share a full hall bath. Guests are welcome to use the two mountain bikes. Scottsdale and Mesa are nearby. Full breakfast served weekends; Continental plus served week days. Smoking permitted. No pets. No children. $85.

4222. As elegant and beautiful as a swan is this large home built on a hill in a scenic area with 50- to 80-mile panoramic mountain views. Luxurious, simple decor with white interior. Ten minutes to Mayo Clinic and Taliesen West; 25 minutes to central Scottsdale; 45 minutes to Phoenix Sky Harbor Airport. Master suite has a king-size

NOTES: Credit cards accepted: A MasterCard; B Visa; C American Express; D Discover; E Diner's Club; F Other; 2 Personal checks accepted; 3 Lunch available; 4 Dinner available; 5 Open all year; 6 Pets welcome;

bed, cable TV, walk-in closet, large bath with large shower, whirlpool tub for two, fireplace. Studio apartment with kitchenette. Other rooms have queen- and twin-size beds. Weekly, monthly rates available. $75-150.

4223. This exquisite bed and breakfast sits on 2.5 acres on a hillside close to Scottsdale. Nearby are three golf courses, casino gambling, horseback riding, jeep tours, and a wildlife park. A private spa, putting green, barbecue grill, and cabana with fireplace and kitchenette, bicycles, and lighted tennis court are also included for guests' enjoyment. Inside is a massive Mexican brick fireplace, a TV connected to a satellite dish, VCR, and pool table. Guests have full access with kitchen privileges. The number of guests has been limited to four, with only two of the four guest rooms rented at any one time. The largest suite has a large sitting area, large bath with a sunken tub and separate shower. The Merry Lane room has a private bath and shower, and a separate entrance. Two smaller rooms share a hall bath. Continental breakfast. On request the hostess can put together a delicious full meal. No smoking or pets. Children are welcome. $95-225.

GLENDALE

Mi Casa Su Casa/Old Pueblo Homestays Bed and Breakfast Reservation Service

P.O. Box 950, Tempe, 85280-0950
(602) 990-0682; (800) 456-0682
FAX (602) 990-3390
e-mail: micasa@primenet.com
www.azres.com

4241. These luxurious casita townhomes, in the Arrowhead Ranch area, overlook the 11th green of the Arnold Palmer-designed championship Arrowhead golf course and offers guests complete use of the country club facilities. Amenities include private full bath, courtesy bath robe, morning newspaper, cable TV, telephone, full kitchen, mini-refrigerator, microwave, living room, and fireplace. Enjoy a welcome fruit basket upon arrival and self-serve Continental plus breakfast daily. Smoking permitted outside. No children or pets allowed. $49-198.

GLOBE

Mi Casa Su Casa/Old Pueblo Homestays Bed and Breakfast Reservation Service

P.O. Box 950, Tempe, 85280-0950
(602) 990-0682; (800) 456-0682
FAX (602) 990-3390
e-mail: micasa@primenet.com
www.azres.com

4252. This bed and breakfast was formerly a schoolhouse, started in 1907 and completed in 1917. The guest rooms are the largest imaginable, as they are former classrooms. There are 12-foot windows with views, comfortable furniture, and private baths. Hearty southwestern or Sonoran-style breakfast. Group rates are available for weddings and small groups. Smoking outside. Possible handicapped accessibility. $65.

GREER

Red Setter Inn

8 Main Street, P.O. Box 133, 85927
(520) 735-7441; FAX (520) 735-7425
www.redsetterinn.com

This 7,000-square-foot log bed and breakfast inn with 13,000-square-foot log annex, is close to skiing, fishing, bird watching,

---

7 No smoking; 8 Children welcome; 9 Social drinking allowed; 10 Tennis nearby; 11 Swimming nearby; 12 Golf nearby; 13 Skiing nearby; 14 May be booked through a travel agent; 15 Handicapped accessible.

and hiking. Some guest rooms have private fireplaces and jetted tubs. The lodge was built in 1995 on the Little Colorado River in a beautiful pine forest and is filled with antiques and an extensive toy collection. The lodge is on the boundary of one million acres of national forest. Picnic lunch included with all guest stays of two nights or longer. Voted Arizona's Best Bed and Breakfast by the *Arizona Republic*. A 3,000-square-foot four-bedroom, three-bath cabin is available on the river.

Hosts: Jim Sankey and Ken Conant
Rooms: 12 (PB) $125-195
Full Breakfast
Credit Cards: A, B, C
Notes: 2, 5, 7, 9, 13, 15

White Mountain Lodge

140 Main Street, P.O. Box 143, 85927
(520) 735-7568; FAX (520) 735-7498

The 1892 farmhouse was residence to the Lund family until 1940. The Basts purchased the farmhouse in 1993 and remodeled during 1994-95. Each bedroom is individually decorated and the common rooms reflect their southwestern country heritage. Overlooking the Greer meadow and Little Colorado River, the Lodge affords guests spectacular scenery and country hospitality. All breakfasts are made-from-scratch and include homemade baked goods. In the afternoon, homemade sweets are provided and hot drinks are always available.

White Mountain Lodge

Hosts: Charles and Mary Bast
Rooms: 7 (PB) $65-100
Full Breakfast
Credit Cards: A, B, D, E
Notes: 2, 5, 6, 7, 8, 9, 13, 14

HEREFORD

Arizona Trails Bed and Breakfast Reservation Service

P.O. Box 18998, Fountain Hills, 85269-8998
(602) 837-4284; (888) 799-4284
FAX (602) 816-4224
e-mail: aztrails@arizonatrails.com
www.arizonatrails.com

AZ 151. In a great central touring spot of southern Arizona, this 10-room inn is a bird-watcher's paradise. On five acres of riparian habitat next to the San Pedro River and the San Pedro Natural Conservation area, the inn is home to more than 100 species of resident birds and over 300 species of migrating birds. All rooms are centered around the courtyard with gardens and fountains. Each room has a private bath with standup shower and hand-carved Mexican furnishings. Also great for group meetings, complete with meeting room and audiovisual screen. The common areas feature a fireplace, work space, telescope, and a computer with bird-watcher's software program. The large, bright dining room is home for a full southwestern breakfast each morning. Handicapped accessible. $115.

JEROME

Bed and Breakfast Southwest Reservation Service

P.O. Box 51198, Phoenix, 85076-1198
(602) 947-9704; (800) 762-9704
FAX (602) 874-1316

156. In the legendary ghost town of Jerome, this bed and breakfast inn was originally built in 1898 and offers a "take your breath away" view. Antique-filled rooms, gourmet breakfast, and afternoon tea will delight guests. No smoking. Children welcome. $75-95.

The Ghost City Inn

541 North Main Street, 86331
(520) 63 GHOST (phone/FAX)

Experience the elegance of days gone by in this unique "living ghost town." The home was originally built in 1898 and has been lovingly restored to include five antique-filled rooms, complete with two common guest areas. Gourmet breakfast and afternoon tea and cookies are served in the dining room or on the spacious veranda with "take-your-breath-away" views.

Host: Joy Beard
Rooms: 5 (1 PB; 4 SB) $75-95
Full Breakfast
Credit Cards: A, B, C, D
Notes: 2, 5, 7, 8, 10, 11, 12, 13, 14

Mi Casa Su Casa/Old Pueblo Homestays Bed and Breakfast Reservation Service

P.O. Box 950, Tempe, 85280-0950
(602) 990-0682; (800) 456-0682
FAX (602) 990-3390
e-mail: micasa@primenet.com
www.azres.com

4281. This historic two-story white stucco inn with red tile roof and arched windows was constructed in 1917 for the chief surgeon of a very large mining company. The three guest rooms are on the second floor; all have private baths. The master suite has a sitting room with oversized day bed, dressing room, and full bath. There is a guest cottage with a full bath, kitchenette, and secluded patio. Complimentary snacks. Smoking outside. Crib and rollaway bed available. Well-behaved children welcome. Twenty-five dollars for each additional person. $85-125.

4282. This inn, built in 1898, continues to offer the legendary hospitality of Jerome—

Arizona's most famous copper ghost town. Just a few steps away are art galleries, clothing, and jewelry boutiques. There are shared baths between two pairs of rooms, and all rooms have TVs, ceiling fans, outside verandas. There are two common areas with telephones and fax, courtyard, and outside spa. Children 10 and older welcome. Additional person in room $15. Refreshments. Full breakfast. Credit cards accepted. $75-95.

4283. This house was built in 1925 of hand-poured concrete (for fire protection), a popular style in 1920s boomtown Jerome. The interior was decorated with the fine built-in cabinetry of the Arts and Crafts fashion of that era. The Copper Suite has two bedrooms with shared bath and a large sitting room. The Jerome View Suite has a large bedroom with private bath, deck, and views. Full breakfast. No smoking. Extra persons $15 each. Children and pets by prior arrangement. $85-125.

LAKESIDE

Arizona Trails Bed and Breakfast Reservation Service

P.O. Box 18998, Fountain Hills, 85269-8998
(602) 837-4284; (888) 799-4284
FAX (602) 816-4224
e-mail: aztrails@arizonatrails.com
www.arizonatrails.com

AZ 999. Charming five-room inn decorated in a country decor. Property backs up to national land with hiking trails and just minutes from one of the many local lakes. All rooms have a private bath with furnished robes and private entrances. All rooms have queen-size beds; two rooms can accommodate an extra person. One room features a fireplace. Picnic lunches can be arranged for an additional cost. Full country breakfast served. $85.

7 No smoking; 8 Children welcome; 9 Social drinking allowed; 10 Tennis nearby; 11 Swimming nearby; 12 Golf nearby; 13 Skiing nearby; 14 May be booked through a travel agent; 15 Handicapped accessible.

Bartram's

Bartram's Bed and Breakfast

Route 1, Box 1014, 85929
(520) 367-1408

Bartram's can be found at the edge of the Apache Indian reservation in a lovely, quiet setting surrounded by two acres of maintained yard. Guests enjoy a wonderful country setting about a mile from town and great restaurants, antique stores, shopping, and a variety of activities, such as horseback riding, golf, hiking, fishing, and more. A full seven-course breakfast is served in a dining room with a large bay window and a great view. Picnic lunches are available at additional cost. Inquire about accommodations for pets.

Hosts: Petie and Ray Bartram
Rooms: 5 (PB) $85
Full Breakfast
Credit Cards: None
Notes: 2, 5, 7, 8, 9, 10, 11, 12, 13, 14

MESA

Mi Casa Su Casa/Old Pueblo Homestays Bed and Breakfast Reservation Service

P.O. Box 950, Tempe, 85280-0950
(602) 990-0682; (800) 456-0682
FAX (602) 990-3390
e-mail: micasa@primenet.com
www.azres.com

4301. Friendly, busy host couple welcome guests to their very large, contemporary Spanish home on one acre. The extra-large guest room has a private entrance, living room, Hide-a-Bed, private bath, dining area, sink, refrigerator, and TV. Continental breakfast furnished the first three days, then self-catering. Unheated swimming pool available. Resident dog. Handicapped facilities possible. A child over 10 years old welcome for additional $10. Smoking outside. Weekly and monthly rates. $45-50.

4302. Friendly, caring Scandinavian host couple from Minnesota welcome guests to a spacious Spanish-style home. In a quiet, handsome neighborhood, it is one mile to the golf course, three miles to baseball spring training, and an easy drive to the Superstition Mountains and Apache Trail. Decor is traditional with some Scandinavian accents. The two guest rooms share a hall bath. Only one party accepted at a time. Full breakfast. Children 12 and older are welcome. No smoking. Seniors 10 percent less. $60.

4303. Spacious stucco Mediterranean home is in well-kept neighborhood within walking distance to a small park. Three guest rooms are available in a private guest wing that has one bath. Only one party at a time. Two rooms have a TV. Guests are welcome to use the family room with stereo and fireplace or living room that has cable TV and VCR. Pool. Small resident dog and parrot. Smoking outside. Fifteen dollars extra for children over 10. Possible handicapped accessibility. $65-89.

4304. In East Mesa, near Apache Junction, the Superstition Mountains, and the Apache Trail, is this contemporary home on an acre of land. Two guest rooms share a hall bath. Guests are welcome to swim in the solar-heated swimming pool or to relax by the living room fireplace. Full breakfast. Children are welcome. Pre-arranged baby-sitting available. Resident cat. Smoking permitted in designated areas only. Special rates are available for longer stays. $50-55.

4305. This ranch-style house was built in the late 1970s with an attached suite. In a residential neighborhood within walking distance of the Mormon Temple or the Genealogy Library. Two guest rooms in the main house have queen-size beds, private baths. The suite has a living room with a sofa bed, bedroom with a king- or twin-size beds, bath, and fully equipped kitchen. Full southwestern breakfast is served. Weekly rates are available. Pets are possible with prior arrangement. $75-125.

MOUNT LEMMON

Mi Casa Su Casa/Old Pueblo Homestays Bed and Breakfast Reservation Service

P.O. Box 950, Tempe, 85280-0950
(602) 990-0682; (800) 456-0682
FAX (602) 990-3390
e-mail: micasa@primenet.com
www.azres.com

5301. Just one hour but a world away from Tucson. Enjoy skiing in winter and hiking, fishing, and bird watching in summer. A conference room that seats 12 is available for special group meetings. There are an elevator and handicapped accommodations. Three romantic bedrooms each provide a fireplace and a two-person spa. A nearby cabin has two bedrooms with living room, kitchen, and two decks. Another nearby cabin has a cozy living room loft, bedroom with a large two-person spa, fireplace, and full kitchen. Breakfast and dinner served. Two-night minimum stay in cabin. Smoking permitted outside. Children are welcome in the cabin only. No pets. $160-200.

ORACLE

Arizona Trails Bed and Breakfast Reservation Service

P.O. Box 18998, Fountain Hills, 85269-8998
(602) 837-4284; (888) 799-4284
FAX (602) 816-4224
e-mail: aztrails@arizonatrails.com
www.arizonatrails.com

AZ 149. Just 30 minutes from Tucson and sitting in the midst of Coronado National Forest, this historic ranch provides six separate adobe casitas. Units have either one or two bedrooms, full kitchens, and a bathroom. One two-bedroom unit has two bathrooms. The main house also offers a guest room with private bath. Meeting room with kitchen available for groups. Just a half-mile from Arizona Trail. Hiking and bird watching are great for this area. The outdoor ramada features an original brick barbecue area great for cowboy cookouts. Hike the trails, then cool off in the swimming pool or ease into one of the relaxing hammocks around the property. Group rental rates are available. Meal plan is available. $95-175.

OVERGAARD (HEBER)

Arizona Trails Bed and Breakfast Reservation Service

P.O. Box 18998, Fountain Hills, 85269-8998
(602) 837-4284; (888) 799-4284
FAX (602) 816-4224
e-mail: aztrails@arizonatrails.com
www.arizonatrails.com

AZ 175. Nestled in the pines of the White Mountains this country inn provides gracious charm to the wilderness area. Three elegantly appointed guest rooms are all upstairs from the restaurant and sitting area which occupy the main level of the inn. All rooms have full baths with garden tubs, TV/VCR with video libraries, mini-refrigerators, coffee makers, and balconies.

7 No smoking; 8 Children welcome; 9 Social drinking allowed; 10 Tennis nearby; 11 Swimming nearby; 12 Golf nearby; 13 Skiing nearby; 14 May be booked through a travel agent; 15 Handicapped accessible.

A full breakfast is included each morning. Hike the area, golf at the nearby golf course, or sit on the grounds and relax around the patio café with outdoor fireplace. $125-150.

PAGE

Mi Casa Su Casa/Old Pueblo Homestays Bed and Breakfast Reservation Service

P.O. Box 950, Tempe, 85280-0950
(602) 990-0682; (800) 456-0682
FAX (602) 990-3390
e-mail: micasa@primenet.com
www.azres.com

4341. This large air-conditioned bed and breakfast is within walking distance of downtown Page. Both guest rooms offer bed, futon, TV/VCR, small refrigerator, and private bath. Guests are welcome to use the patio, barbecue grill, or swimming pool. Refreshments might include salsa and chips or homemade cookies and iced tea. A dog and cat are inside only in the winter time, but not allowed in the guest rooms. Full breakfast is served. Smoking permitted in designated areas only. Sorry, no guest pets. Possible handicapped accessibility, but bathrooms are not specially equipped. Seasonal rates are available. $45-85.

4342. This two-story home overlooks the sheer sandstone of the Vermillion Cliffs beyond a wide expanse of open desert, the blue waters of Lake Powell, and the impressive face of Glen Canyon Dam. The large guest room has a sitting area, private bath, and private upstairs balcony. Double air mattress is available. Continental plus breakfast is served. Smoking permitted in designated areas only. Pets are not welcome. Ten dollars for each additional person. $75.

PARADISE

Mi Casa Su Casa/Old Pueblo Homestays Bed and Breakfast Reservation Service

P.O. Box 950, Tempe, 85280-0950
(602) 990-0682; (800) 456-0682
FAX (602) 990-3390
e-mail: micasa@primenet.com
www.azres.com

4849. This bed and breakfast is a rustic, comfortable two-bedroom guest house in a wooded area with a living room, dining room, kitchen, and full bath. There is an excellent library of regional books, video tapes, field guides, and maps. There is also a screened-in front porch and a patio area with picnic table and a barbecue grill. There is a sofa in the living room. Laundry facilities. The breakfast is stocked in the kitchen and is self-serve. Smoking outside. Possible handicapped accessibility. Very good bird watching area. Inquire about accommodations for pets. $85.

PARADISE VALLEY

Arizona Trails Bed and Breakfast Reservation Service

P.O. Box 18998, Fountain Hills, 85269-8998
(602) 837-4284; (888) 799-4284
FAX (602) 816-4224
e-mail: aztrails@arizonatrails.com
www.arizonatrails.com

AZ 180. This exclusive inn was originally built by one of the famous "cowboy artists." The luxurious grounds encompass 35 combined rooms, casitas and villas, a swimming pool, tennis courts, two in-ground spas, gardens, and a southwestern cuisine restaurant. Choose from a basic room with private bath, private patio, fireplace, and TV/VCR, or go to the top of line with a villa that equals a home with living room, kitchen, two bedrooms, two

---

NOTES: Credit cards accepted: A MasterCard; B Visa; C American Express; D Discover; E Diner's Club; F Other; 2 Personal checks accepted; 3 Lunch available; 4 Dinner available; 5 Open all year; 6 Pets welcome;

baths, fireplace, and wet bar. Two other types of rooms in between offer various levels of amenities including fireplaces, kitchenettes, each with a private patio. Close to both Phoenix and Scottsdale, area golf courses, shops, and restaurants. Continental breakfast. Small meeting room available. Handicapped accessible. Children welcome. $245-595.

PATAGONIA

Mi Casa Su Casa/Old Pueblo Homestays Bed and Breakfast Reservation Service

P.O. Box 950, Tempe, 85280-0950
(602) 990-0682; (800) 456-0682
FAX (602) 990-3390
e-mail: micasa@primenet.com
www.azres.com

4351. This turn-of-the-century adobe home, built as miners' apartment when Patagonia was a thriving mountain town. Each room has a private entrance, sitting room, bedroom, and private bath. Guests enjoy a full breakfast. Smoking permitted outside. Children are welcome. Extra guests are an additional $20. No pets. $70.

PAYSON

Arizona Trails Bed and Breakfast Reservation Service

P.O. Box 18998, Fountain Hills, 85269-8998
(602) 837-4284; (888) 799-4284
FAX (602) 816-4224
e-mail: aztrails@arizonatrails.com
www.arizonatrails.com

AZ 136. Elegance and relaxation in the pines of Payson at this five-room country-style bed and breakfast only minutes to town. All rooms have private baths. Three suites all have private patios or deck, full private baths, gas fireplaces, and sitting areas. The garden room has an entry to and

from the expansive deck that runs along the back of the home. The Mediterranean room is smaller with full bath and deck. There is an outdoor hot tub housed in a separate building with retractable roof. Gourmet breakfast including latte or cappuccino is served. Handicapped accessible. $85-150.

Mi Casa Su Casa/Old Pueblo Homestays Bed and Breakfast Reservation Service

P.O. Box 950, Tempe, 85280-0950
(602) 990-0682; (800) 456-0682
FAX (602) 990-3390
e-mail: micasa@primenet.com
www.azres.com

4361. This inn, which opened in 1997, is an ideal place for a romantic getaway. The Victorian Room has a private entrance, private patio with fountain view, fireplace, and full bath. The Colonial Room has a private entrance, private patio, marble fireplace, and full bath. The Garden Room has a private entrance and wicker accessories. The large hot tub in a gazebo is for guests' scheduled private use. Refreshments. The great room has a TV/VCR, music, games, and a refrigerator for guests' use. Full or Continental plus breakfast. No smoking, pets, or children. Two-night minimum stay on weekends. $85-135.

4362. Set in the pines just below the Mogollon Rim at an elevation of 5,000 feet. Guests at this family-friendly inn have full use of the main lodge and its two-acre grounds. Choose from four theme-oriented bedrooms, each with a queen-size bed, private bath, cable TV. Three of the rooms each have space for two guests; the fourth is a suite for four guests. Full breakfast. Smoking outside. Handicapped possible. Horses and medium-size dogs welcome with prior arrangement. Smoking outside. $69-89.

---

7 No smoking; 8 Children welcome; 9 Social drinking allowed; 10 Tennis nearby; 11 Swimming nearby; 12 Golf nearby; 13 Skiing nearby; 14 May be booked through a travel agent; 15 Handicapped accessible.

4363. In Star Valley, four miles from Payson, guests who like animals are welcome at this large white-brick house with wraparound porch. There are 45 or more barnyard animals and pets. Guests can hike along the creek in the adjacent pine forest or bring their own horses to ride the many area trails. Three comfortable guest room. Children over 10 and pets welcome with prior arrangements. $60-90.

PEARCE

Mi Casa Su Casa/Old Pueblo Homestays Bed and Breakfast Reservation Service

P.O. Box 950, Tempe, 85280-0950
(602) 990-0682; (800) 456-0682
FAX (602) 990-3390
e-mail: micasa@primenet.com
www.azres.com

4370. This working ranch offers luxury accommodations in a casual western setting. Amenities included in the cost are horseback riding, sightseeing, swimming pool, spa, table tennis pool table, TV/VCR, library, guest laundry, hiking, bird watching, rock hounding, and three meals per day. Casitas consist of a bedroom, sitting area , double entry full bathroom, refrigerator, coffee pot, private porch, and sun deck. Cabins offer a spacious single room, sofa bed, bath, coffee pot, private porch, and sun deck. Conference rooms available. Smoking permitted in designated areas. Extra guests are an additional $120-140. Children over 12 are welcome. No pets. $175-340.

PHOENIX

Arizona Trails Bed and Breakfast Reservation Service

P.O. Box 18998, Fountain Hills, 85269-8998
(602) 837-4284; (888) 799-4284
FAX (602) 816-4224
e-mail: aztrails@arizonatrails.com
www.arizonatrails.com

AZ 105. Historic bed and breakfast in a convenient, quiet Phoenix location. Done in Monterey Revival style this inn has five elegant rooms with private baths, imported tile and whirlpool tubs. The living room has a fireplace and grand piano in addition to the TV. Close to shopping, restaurants, galleries, and Scottsdale, yet remote enough to offer private bike paths, a pool, and private courtyard. A gourmet breakfast is served either in the dining room or in the interior courtyard. Evening cappuccino or coffee also available. Handicapped accessible. $165-195.

AZ 131. Enjoy the feel of an English country home in the city at this English Tudor-style bed and breakfast in north-central Phoenix. Lush landscaping and rose gardens surround the inn. Close to public transportation, shops, restaurants, and just minutes to downtown. Five rooms all with private baths. Antiques throughout. Full breakfast. Handicapped accessible. $100-115.

AZ 144. Relax with the at-home feeling of this comfortable and charming homestay in Phoenix on the Paradise Valley border. A private suite of rooms awaits guests in this southwestern home owned by a retired actress from England. The room features a private bath with tub and shower, sliding glass door that leads to a private roof-top patio, and an English country decor. The second room is a private sitting room with cable color TV and the ability to fit in a third guest or child. Full English breakfast served. A high tea is also available with prior notice for $6.50 per person. $85.

AZ 146. Convenience and privacy are featured at this charming cottage guest house on the Phoenix/Paradise Valley border. Decorated in a Ralph Lauren floral pattern, guests will have a sitting area with sleeper-sofa, color cable TV, telephone, a full minikitchen with refrigerator, cook top, microwave, sink, coffee maker, and full array of linens, eating and cooking utensils. Private bath features a

---

NOTES: Credit cards accepted: A MasterCard; B Visa; C American Express; D Discover; E Diner's Club; F Other; 2 Personal checks accepted; 3 Lunch available; 4 Dinner available; 5 Open all year; 6 Pets welcome;

tub and shower. A Continental plus breakfast is delivered to guests' room each morning. Relax by the pool or travel just minutes to area golf courses, restaurants, shops, and museums. $135.

AZ 147. Nothing equals the views from this private bed and breakfast guest house in Phoenix. The private guest suite features a queen-size bed, private bath with tub and shower, TV/VCR, stereo system, mini-kitchen, and fireplace. Unequaled views from the patio, the pool, or spa. Also available is a sports/game room with large screen TV, pool table, and more. Continental breakfast. $175.

AZ 148. This guest house offers quiet, private accommodations close to the Phoenix/Scottsdale border. Close to the Phoenix Mountain Preserve, it's also great for hikers. Decorated in a southwestern decor guests will enjoy the bedroom with a queen-size bed, living room/kitchen area with a TV, telephone, refrigerator, microwave and sink, and private bath with tub and shower. The grounds are surrounded with mature landscaping, a swimming pool, in-ground spa, and badminton/volleyball court. Continental breakfast. $95.

Ashton House

85028
(602) 996-4147

A townhome in private community on the border of Paradise Valley and four minutes from Route 51, Squaw Peak Parkway. The beautifully appointed suite of rooms on the second floor has two twin-size or a king-size bed in large bedroom with sun deck. The sitting room has a day bed for extra guest and contains cable TV, small refrigerator, coffee and tea supplies. Private bathroom, walk-in closets. Private and quiet. Full English breakfast, choice of items served by the Scottish hostess—sorry, no

haggis! Garage parking. Call for brochure. Rates from $60. Special weekend packages. Prefer traveler's checks or currency.

Host: Avis Ashton Baransky
Full Breakfast
Credit Cards: None
Notes: 5, 7, 9, 10, 11, 12, 14

Bed and Breakfast Southwest Reservation Service

P.O. Box 51198, Phoenix, 85076-1198
(602) 947-9704; (800) 762-9704
FAX (602) 874-1316

108. In the heart of the Valley of the Sun, close to fine dining, shopping, musuems, and the convention center. Built in 1934, this Old English Tudor-style bed and breakfast is surrounded by mature trees and offers five rooms, all with private baths and beautifully decorated in Victorian elegance. Large parlor and kitchen welcome guests with their warmth and beauty. Full breakfast served in dining room. No smoking. Older children welcome. $100-115.

135. This historic property is on an acre of lush, verdant land on the Arizona canal with a view of the Squaw Peak and Camelback Mountains. Guest house, decorated with Queen Anne furniture, has a private bath, TV, VCR, and queen-size bed and is canopied by an ancient fig tree. One room in main house with antique double bed and private hall bath with Jacuzzi tub. Hostess serves gourmet breakfast, freshly ground coffee. No smoking. Children welcome. $79-89.

The Harmony House Bed and Breakfast Inn

7202 North 7th Avenue, 85021
(602) 331-9554; FAX (602) 395-8528
e-mail: jfontaine@sprintmail.com

The Harmony House was built in 1934 as a doctor's residence among acres of citrus trees on the outskirts of bustling downtown

---

7 No smoking; 8 Children welcome; 9 Social drinking allowed; 10 Tennis nearby; 11 Swimming nearby; 12 Golf nearby; 13 Skiing nearby; 14 May be booked through a travel agent; 15 Handicapped accessible.

Phoenix. Today, the Harmony House is in the very heart of the Valley of the Sun. Buses offer easy access to downtown, the convention center, and the capitol complex. Theaters, museums, and churches are all close by and the internationally renowned shopping centers and golf courses of the region are all just minutes away.

Hosts: Mike and Jennifer Fontaine
Rooms: 5 (PB) $65-115
Full Breakfast
Credit Cards: A, B
Notes: 2, 5, 7, 8, 9, 10, 11, 12, 13

La Estancia Bed and Breakfast Inn

4979 East Camelback Road, 85018
(602) 808-9924; (800) 410-7655
FAX (602) 808-9925

On two acres of citrus and palms. Built in 1930, renovated in 1996, only Phoenix bed and breakfast in the National Register of Historic Places. Five elegant rooms each with whirlpool tubs, king-size beds with down comforters; gourmet breakfast, in quiet Arcadia residential areas. Pool, bicycles, close to airport, museums, art galleries, shopping, golf.

Hosts: Ruth and Richard Maloblocki
Rooms: 5 (PB) $135-195
Full Breakfast
Credit Cards: A, B, C, D, E
Notes: 2, 7, 9, 10, 11, 12, 14

Maricopa Manor

15 West Pasadena Avenue, 85013
(602) 274-6302; (800) 292-6403

Six luxury suites, spacious public rooms, patios, decks, and the gazebo spa and pool offer an intimate Old World atmosphere in an elegant urban setting. Maricopa Manor is in the heart of the Valley of the Sun, convenient to shops, restaurants, museums, churches, and civic and government centers. The Spanish-style manor house, built in 1928, houses beautiful art, antiques, and a warm southwestern hospitality. Advance reservations required.

Hosts: Mary Ellen and Paul Kelley
Suites: 6 (PB) $89-229
Continental Breakfast
Credit Cards: A, B, C, D
Notes: 2, 5, 7, 8, 9, 10, 12

Mi Casa Su Casa/Old Pueblo Homestays Bed and Breakfast Reservation Service

P.O. Box 950, Tempe, 85280-0950
(602) 990-0682; (800) 456-0682
FAX (602) 990-3390
e-mail: micasa@primenet.com
www.azres.com

4401. Separate guest cottage with its own heat and air conditioning. Bath with shower, sofa bed, small refrigerator, and microwave. The business guest will find a desk, work

La Estancia

table, fax, and private telephone. Near museums, downtown business and government centers, and Encanto Park with its golf courses, tennis courts, and bike paths. One bicycle to loan. Shopping and restaurants are easily accessible. Fifteen dollars for third person. Continental plus breakfast, self-catering. Two-night minimum. No smoking, children, or pets. Possible handicapped accessibility. $85.

4402. The guest cottage is spacious, has a private entrance, living room with TV, full kitchen, two bedrooms, two baths, and an enclosed porch with a double bed. There is a bath with shower, cable TV, a small refrigerator, and microwave. No smoking or pets. Possible handicapped accessibility. Airport pick-up possible. Twenty-five dollars for extra person. $125.

4403. This French Provincial ranch house was built in 1946. The guest room has a bed, sofa, and private hall bath with tub and shower. Guests are welcome in the living room with TV and the back yard. Near the Heard Museum, Phoenix Art Museum, and Encanto Park with golfing, tennis courts, and seasonal swimming. A blue tick hound and the resident cat are restricted from the guest area. No smoking, pets, or children. One block to public transportation. Continental breakfast. $65.

4404. Beautifully landscaped Spanish-style manor house offers six two-room suites and "breakfast in a basket" with homemade specialties. Enjoy the spacious gathering room with outside deck, formal living, dining, and music rooms, patio, gazebo spa, and heated pool. All suites have a TV, telephone, and private bath. Rooms have either full or shower bath. Ten minutes to downtown Phoenix, 15 minutes from the airport. Smoking permitted outside. No pets. Roll-away available. Third person in room $25. Children over seven welcome. Seasonal rates. $89-159.

4405. Ten minutes from airport, near the Heard and Phoenix Art Museums and Phoenix College. Guests welcome in large living room. Walk to bike paths, tennis, park, golf, shopping, and churches or temple. The large guest room has a full bath en suite, cable TV, and a private entrance to an enclosed patio. Continental plus breakfast. A computer/modem and fax are available. Resident cat and dog. Guest's small pet dog possible. Two-night minimum stay. $75.

4451. Handsome, large home near Biltmore has an extra-large yard with pool. Separate guest wing has a large bedroom, private bath with a shower, sitting and writing area, and a private entrance. A full breakfast is served. Three-night minimum stay. $75.

4453. Gracious hostess welcomes guests to a very large southwestern stucco ranch-style home. This house was built beside a golf course in a handsome neighborhood with large trees. One guest room has a full hall bath; another guest room has TV and shares a full hall bath. Only one party is accepted at a time. Guests are welcome to use the large living room with fireplace, cable TV, VCR, or pool. Full breakfast. Smoking allowed outside. No resident pets. Ten-dollar charge for children between 10 and 16. Those 16 and older pay full rate. $65-70.

4454. The main house was built in 1924, and the guest cottage was built in the 1950s. The second-story cottage offers a living room with TV, a kitchenette, a private bath with claw-foot tub, and a porch with a view of the pool. Ten minutes from the Heard Museum, 20 minutes from the airport, and two blocks from Central Avenue. Breakfast is self-catered. Smoking outside only. Guests welcome to use pool in season. Children over five who can swim are welcome. Special rates for longer stays. $75.

7 No smoking; 8 Children welcome; 9 Social drinking allowed; 10 Tennis nearby; 11 Swimming nearby; 12 Golf nearby; 13 Skiing nearby; 14 May be booked through a travel agent; 15 Handicapped accessible.

Mi Casa Su Casa/Old Pueblo Homestays Bed and Breakfast Reservation Service (continued)

4455. Handsome two-story home near the Hilton Pointe Tapatio. Two guest rooms, each with private hall bath. Sofa bed is also available on the second floor on the balcony. Heated pool, tennis, golf course, and stables are nearby. Spanish spoken. Continental breakfast weekdays; full breakfast on weekends. Children nine and older are welcome. Smoking allowed outside. One-night stays an additional $5. Ten-dollar charge per child. $65.

4456. On a mountainside overlooking Phoenix, this stunning home was built to take advantage of the beautiful views. Switchback flagstone stairs take guests up to the spacious house perched on the mountainside. Private, luxurious suite has a fireplace, TV, large bath with double whirlpool tub, and separate shower. Full breakfast. No smoking, children, or pets. $125-150.

4457. This attractive town home is in a very nice small community. Heated swimming pool and spa, tennis courts on grounds. Semiprivate front-door entrance. The guest suite or rooms on the second floor consist of a large, sunny bedroom with private sun deck, private bath with tub and shower, and sitting room. The sitting room has cable TV and a day bed for one additional guest. Coffee and tea fixings in sitting room. Full breakfast. Kitchen privileges. Garage parking. Smoking restricted. No pets. Children 12 and older welcome. Third person $10. Weekly rates. $75-85.

4458. The Spanish-style adobe house has an inviting courtyard with a Mediterranean air. The romantic guest cottage is in the courtyard and has a TV, and private bath with shower. The pool and spa are available for seasonal swimming. Smoking outside. No pets or children. Public transportation one block. Continental plus breakfast. $85-115.

4459. Built in 1934 as a palatial residence, this English Tudor-style manor is convenient to major interstate freeways and the airport. Lush green lawns, fruit orchards, a rose garden, and patios surround it. Beautiful Victorian antiques fill five elegantly furnished bedrooms, each with a private bath. Cable TV. Continental plus breakfast served. On the premises is one outside dog. Smoking permitted outside. No children or pets allowed. $100-115.

4460. Built in 1993, this beautifully appointed studio apartment cottage in prestigious north central Phoenix has a private entrance, living room-bedroom, full kitchen, and private bath. Ten minutes from the Heard Museum, Phoenix Art Museum, theaters, sports facilities. There is a top-quality queen-size wall bed, TV, private telephone. Continental plus breakfast stocked in kitchen. No smoking, pets, children. Weekly and monthly rates. $85.

4501. A contemporary two-story townhouse in a small complex is in a citrus grove near Camelback Mountain, 20 minutes from downtown Phoenix, Scottsdale, or airport. Near public transportation. Guest room is up a spiral staircase on the second floor and has a pleasant southwestern decor, private bath, telephone, and TV. Computer, fax, and Internet available. The unheated community pool is next door. Two nights preferred. Full breakfast. No smoking. Resident cat. $70.

4502. Spacious and comfortable ranch-style house built in 1959 in very quiet, up-scale neighborhood is near everything. Air conditioned. Room one shares full bath with room two. Only one party accepted at a time.

NOTES: Credit cards accepted: A MasterCard; B Visa; C American Express; D Discover; E Diner's Club; F Other; 2 Personal checks accepted; 3 Lunch available; 4 Dinner available; 5 Open all year; 6 Pets welcome;

Guests are welcome to use the pool table in the family room, the TV in the den with fireplace, or the large covered patio. Fenced, unheated diving pool in the nice back yard. No resident pets. Two-night minimum stay. Special rates for children. $85.

4503. This historic adobe house, built in 1916, is on the south side of Camelback Mountain. The separate guest house has two accommodations. The Camelback Suite has a private entrance, living room with sofa bed, fireplace, kitchenette, bedroom, and bath. The Papago Suite has a private entrance, a large room with a bed and sitting area, and private bath. Air conditioned. Continental plus breakfast served in main house. Smoking permitted outside. Children 12 and older welcome. Handicapped accessibility is possible in Papago Suite. Add $10 for one-night stays. $125-175.

4504. The two-story guest house, country club area, has a private entrance, a large living room with cable TV and VCR, and a dining area. Two bedrooms, on the second floor, share a hall bath with shower. Heated swimming pool, barbecue, and lawn furniture. The Library Suite in the main house has a private entrance, a bedroom, and a library/living room with cable TV, VCR, a small refrigerator, and coffee bar. Continental plus breakfast. No smoking, pets, or children. Bath designed for handicapped in suite. Twenty-five dollars for each additional person. $150-200.

4551. This homestay has a large patio where one can observe hummingbirds, an unheated swimming pool, and a view of Camelback Mountain. Award-winning southwestern-design guest room has a TV, telephone, and connecting bath with shower. Full breakfast. Smoking outside. Two-night minimum stay preferred. Five dollars extra for one-night stay. $50.

4601. Built in 1987, this large house is Spanish style with stucco exterior and a tile roof. It is near South Mountain Park, hiking, biking, tennis, and golf. The very private large guest room is separate from the main house. It has a private hall bath with shower, private entrance, cable TV, telephone, small refrigerator, and microwave. Continental breakfast. Two-night minimum. Infants only, no extra charge. Crib, Port-a-crib, and high chair available. Easy drive to Tempe, Gilbert, Chandler, and 15 to 25 minutes from Sky Harbor Airport. Fenced pool. No smoking. Weekly and no-breakfast rates are available. $65.

4602. This extra-large home with an overview of Phoenix is in a quiet rural setting with natural desert landscaping adjacent to the South Mountain Preserve. Bird watching is excellent and an occasional coyote comes to visit. Ten minutes to Sky Harbor Airport. Within 15 to 30 minutes to downtown Phoenix, Tempe, and Mesa. Room one has a TV, ceiling fan, and a private hall full bath. Room two has a TV, ceiling fan, and shares that hall bath with room one. Only one party accepted at a time. Spa on patio that guests are welcome to use. Bicycles to loan. Full breakfast. No smoking. No pets. No children. Two-night minimum. $65-70.

4802. This apartment was built in 1992 and is attached to but separate from the main house. Private entrance, own temperature controls, living room with cable TV, bathroom with roll-in shower, and kitchenette. Continental plus breakfast. Handicapped welcome. Smoking outside only. No pets. Children over eight are welcome. $75.

4803. A one-story home with three guest rooms. One room has private bath and the other two rooms share a bath. Private guest telephone. Continental plus breakfast. No smoking or pets. Public transportation one block away. $50-65.

7 No smoking; 8 Children welcome; 9 Social drinking allowed; 10 Tennis nearby; 11 Swimming nearby; 12 Golf nearby; 13 Skiing nearby; 14 May be booked through a travel agent; 15 Handicapped accessible.

PINETOP

Mi Casa Su Casa/Old Pueblo Homestays Bed and Breakfast Reservation Service

P.O. Box 950, Tempe, 85280-0950
(602) 990-0682; (800) 456-0682
FAX (602) 990-3390
e-mail: micasa@primenet.com
www.azres.com

4804. Nestled in the ponderosa pines of Pinetop with breathtaking scenery, and offers a full-service dining room featuring gourmet foods prepared by an award-winning chef and staff. The inn has seven luxurious rooms with private baths. Several rooms have access to an outside deck. Also one room offers a separate living room with fireplace and TV, and a kitchenette with dining area, microwave, refrigerator, and coffee pot. The downstairs sitting room features a fireplace and antique Victrolla and organ. The upstairs library has more than 300 books, a TV with small video library, games, and puzzles. Minimum stay of two nights; three-night minimum during holidays. Smoking permitted outside in designated areas only. Pets are not permitted. Inquire about accommodations for children. $85-120.

PRESCOTT

Arizona Trails Bed and Breakfast Reservation Service

P.O. Box 18998, Fountain Hills, 85269-8998
(602) 837-4284; (888) 799-4284
FAX (602) 816-4224
e-mail: aztrails@arizonatrails.com
www.arizonatrails.com

AZ 119. Enjoy a peaceful retreat in the beauty of the Granite Dells in Prescott. This four-room rustic log cabin structure will take guests back to a time in western history. Wander the property where old wagon trains used to run, or sit by the pond. At night comtemplate the stars from the outdoor hot tub. The downstairs suite can sleep up to four with a private bath and private patio. Three rooms upstairs all have sitting areas and private baths. One room is furnished with a gas fireplace and skylight over the bed. Only five miles from downtown Prescott. A full country breakfast served. $85-125.

AZ 134. Victorian charm abounds in this cozy two-room bed and breakfast in downtown Prescott. Listed in the National Register of Historic Places. One room in the main house features an antique bed, private bath with claw-foot tub, additional day bed and TV. The suite offers a private bath, with standup shower and full kitchen area. An elegant full breakfast served each morning. Relax in the indoor hot tub or outside on the second-story deck available for guests' enjoyment. $70-90.

AZ 139. Relax in this international country-decor three-guest-room bed and breakfast near downtown Prescott. A private massage therapist is on-call 24-hours for guests' convenience at an extra charge. Professional chefs prepare a wonderful full breakfast and an afternoon social hour. One room is actually a two-room suite that will accommodate up to four. All rooms have private baths with tubs and shower. $90-100.

Hassayampa Inn

122 East Gurley Street, 86301
(520) 778-9434; (800) 322-1927

Locally known as "Prescott's Grand Hotel," the inn offers a full-service restaurant and lounge. Built in 1927 and completely renovated in 1985; its lobby is acknowledged as one of the most beautiful in Arizona. Features tile floors, oriental rugs, oversize easy chairs, and potted palms; the focal point, however, is the beamed ceiling decorated with Spanish

---

NOTES: Credit cards accepted: A MasterCard; B Visa; C American Express; D Discover; E Diner's Club; F Other; 2 Personal checks accepted; 3 Lunch available; 4 Dinner available; 5 Open all year; 6 Pets welcome;

Hassayampa Inn

and Indian motifs. The renowned Peacock Room serves breakfast, lunch, and dinner. Overnight rooms include daily breakfast and an evening cocktail.

Hosts: Bill and Georgia Teich
Rooms: 68 (PB) $89-175
Full Breakfast
Credit Cards: A, B, C, D, E
Notes: 3, 4, 5, 8, 9, 10, 11, 12, 13, 14, 15

Hotel Vendome

230 South Cortez Street, 86303
(520) 776-0900; (888) 468-3583
FAX (520) 771-0395

Hotel Vendome is a historic landmark in the heart of Prescott. Built in 1917, the inn is fully refurbished to an immaculate condition. It is very distinctive with an aura of history and tradition. A cozy, intimate bar, warm, comfortable lobby, and inviting guest rooms all create unique ambiance. Perfect for leisure or corporate travel. Within walking distance to restaurants, antique shops, western shopping, entertainment, museums, etc. Special occasion romance packages available on request. Hiking and picnic packages also available. European-style breakfast. Smoking and nonsmoking rooms available.

Host: Rama Patel
Rooms: 16 (PB) $69-149
Suites: 4
Continental Breakfast
Credit Cards: A, B, C, D, E
Notes: 2, 5, 8, 9, 10, 11, 12, 14

Lynx Creek Farm Bed and Breakfast

P.O. Box 4301, 86302
(520) 778-9573; (888) 778-9573

Secluded country hilltop setting with great views overlooking Lynx Creek, it has spacious suites in separate guest house. Organic garden and orchard supply fresh fruit and produce for full gourmet breakfasts. Hot tub, cold pool, croquet, volleyball, horseshoes, gold-panning, big swing, animals, and exotic birds. Light cocktails and hors d'oeuvres each evening. Also available for weddings and cooking classes. Voted Best Bed and Breakfast in Arizona by the *Arizona Republic* newspaper in November 1994. Smoking is permitted in designated areas only.

Hosts: Greg and Wendy Temple
Rooms: 6 (PB) $75-140
Full Breakfast
Credit Cards: A, B, C, D
Notes: 2, 5, 6, 8, 9, 10, 11, 12, 14

Mi Casa Su Casa/Old Pueblo Homestays Bed and Breakfast Reservation Service

P.O. Box 950, Tempe, 85280-0950
(602) 990-0682; (800) 456-0682
FAX (602) 990-3390
e-mail: micasa@primenet.com
www.azres.com

4871. Join the hosts on the veranda of a magnificently restored turreted Queen Anne Victorian in Arizona's first capital. A short walk to the courthouse, museums, galleries, restaurants, and antiquing. The two-bedroom Ivy Suite on the first floor has a private bath. Three guest rooms are on the second floor. The Tea Rose has a private bath in the hall. The Princess Victoria has a private bath with an 1800s bathhouse-style copper tub. The Queen Anne Suite has a private bath. Rates include afternoon refreshments and a full breakfast. Resident dog. Smoking outside. Credit cards accepted. $75-120.

7 No smoking; 8 Children welcome; 9 Social drinking allowed; 10 Tennis nearby; 11 Swimming nearby; 12 Golf nearby; 13 Skiing nearby; 14 May be booked through a travel agent; 15 Handicapped accessible.

4872. A wonderfully romantic bed and breakfast has rural luxury and scenic views on a 25-acre, wooded, hilly property. The two guest cottages have six suites. The cottages can accommodate up to 18 guests. Amenities include decks, spa, hiking, volleyball, and exotic birds in the large main house. Families welcome. Children enjoy seeing the farm animals. Full country breakfast served in the main house. Smoking is permitted outside only. Twenty dollars for additional adult. Fifteen dollars for children. $85-130.

4873. This two-story bed and breakfast inn, in historic downtown, was built in 1906. On the first floor, the two-room Terrace Suite has a bedroom with private deck. Upstairs, there are three guest rooms. The two-room Pine View Suite has a sitting room with sofa bed, and fireplace. The Garden Room has a private bath. The Coventry has a private bath in the hall. Full breakfast and afternoon refreshments are served. Available for seminars, meetings, and weddings. Smoking is permitted outside only. Inquire about accommodations for children. $85-125.

4875. In Arizona's largest Victorian neighborhood is this restored 1883 two-story Victorian home. The four guest rooms each have a private bath. Guests are welcome to use the cable TV in the parlor or to enjoy games, movies, books, and puzzles. Refreshments. Continental plus or full breakfast. Smoking restricted. No children or pets. Twenty dollars for each additional person. Rates higher during special events. $85-140.

Mount Vernon Inn

204 North Mount Vernon Avenue, 86301
(520) 778-0886; e-mail: mtvrnon@primenet.com
www.prescottlink.com/mtvrnon/index.htm

Built in 1900 and listed in the National Register of Historic Places, the Mount

Mount Vernon Inn

Vernon Inn is one of Prescott's "Victorian Treasures." The four spacious guest rooms with private baths and three beautiful country cottages offer a charming alternative to conventional lodging and are designed for guests' comfort and relaxation. Rated three-diamond by AAA and three-star by Mobil, the Arizona Association of Bed and Breakfast Inns, and the American Hotel and Motel Association, the inn is just a few blocks from the town square. Come and enjoy the hospitality.

Hosts: Michele and Jerry Neumann
Rooms: 7 (PB) $95-125
Full Breakfast
Credit Cards: A, B, D
Notes: 2, 5, 7, 10, 12, 14, 15

Prescott Pines Inn

901 White Spar Road, 86303
(520) 445-7270; (800) 541-5374 (reservations)
FAX (520) 778-3665

Formerly the Haymore Dairy in the 1930s, the inn continues the tradition as a gathering place for family and friends. Eleven guest rooms, each with private bath and entry, are in one of three guest houses around the main house. The 1300-square-foot chalet has three bedrooms, two baths, full kitchen, dining and living room with

Prescott Pines Inn

wood-burning stove, and can sleep up to four couples. Whether for a romantic getaway, a comfortable business stay, or just an escape to rejuvenate, the inn's acre of pines, cedars, roses, and wildflowers will "welcome you home." A full breakfast, optional, is served by reservation, at 8:00 or 10:00 A.M. Only a mile and a third south of the courthouse square and excellent restaurants and shops.

Hosts: Jean Wu and Michael Acton
Rooms: 11 (PB) $75-119
Chalet: 1; $249
Full Breakfast
Credit Cards: A, B
Notes: 5, 7, 12, 14

RIMROCK

Mi Casa Su Casa/Old Pueblo Homestays Bed and Breakfast Reservation Service
P.O. Box 950, Tempe, 85280-0950
(602) 990-0682; (800) 456-0682
FAX (602) 990-3390
e-mail: micasa@primenet.com
www.azres.com

4891. This 1960s spacious, lushly landscaped ranch house is 20 minutes from Sedona. The two large guest rooms are at one end of the house. Both rooms have private baths. Guests are welcome in the living room or may go out and visit the pair of ostriches. Resident cat. Smoking restricted. No pets. Possible handicapped accessibility. Twenty-five dollars for additional person. $75-85.

SAFFORD

Mi Casa Su Casa/Old Pueblo Homestays Bed and Breakfast Reservation Service
P.O. Box 950, Tempe, 85280-0950
(602) 990-0682; (800) 456-0682
FAX (602) 990-3390
e-mail: micasa@primenet.com
www.azres.com

4901. Western Colonial-type brick house built in 1890 has wide verandas that run across the front of the house. Three guest rooms on the second floor share a large hall bath with shower. Guests are welcome to enjoy the sitting room and veranda on the second floor. Two guest cottages are also available, each with a bath with shower. Both cottages have a refrigerator, microwave, cable TV, and telephone. Heated spa. Full breakfast is served. Smoking is not permitted on premises. Ten dollars for each additional person over two people. Children over toddler age and under 12 in guest cottage only. Children 12 and older welcome in main house. Credit cards accepted. $80.

SAHUARITA

Mi Casa Su Casa/Old Pueblo Homestays Bed and Breakfast Reservation Service
P.O. Box 950, Tempe, 85280-0950
(602) 990-0682; (800) 456-0682
FAX (602) 990-3390
e-mail: micasa@primenet.com
www.azres.com

4912. This desert accommodation on four acres features natural landscaping and is just 18 miles from the Tucson airport and 20 miles from downtown Tucson. It is close to San Xavier Mission, Tubac arts district, Madera Canyon, Mexico, and Green Valley with its 126 holes of golf.

7 No smoking; 8 Children welcome; 9 Social drinking allowed; 10 Tennis nearby; 11 Swimming nearby; 12 Golf nearby; 13 Skiing nearby; 14 May be booked through a travel agent; 15 Handicapped accessible.

This spacious home offers two suites, with one suite being larger than the other. Each suite has a private full bath, telephone, TV, microwave, coffee maker, and mini-refrigerator. Continental breakfast served on weekdays; full breakfast on weekends. Smoking is permitted outside only. Children are welcome in the large room only. Cot is $10 extra. Pets are not permitted on premises. $50-85.

Mi Gatita Bed and Breakfast

HCR 70, Box 3401, 85629
(520) 648-6129

Enjoy a pampered respite, sumptuous breakfasts, easy comfort, and abundant wildlife. This adobe-hued, Mexican-style hacienda rests on five acres carved from the historic Navarro Ranch which still runs cattle nearby. Overlooking Tucson, convenient to the city, the high desert setting is wonderful for bird watching, hiking, and stargazing. Spacious rooms and suites, fireplaces, gardens, southwestern arts and antiques, Tarahumara carvings. Pool.

Hosts: Jean and Bentley Pace
Rooms: 3 (PB) $68-100
Full Breakfast
Credit Cards: None
Notes: 2, 3, 4, 5, 7, 9, 11, 12

SASABEE

Mi Casa Su Casa/Old Pueblo Homestays Bed and Breakfast Reservation Service

P.O. Box 950, Tempe, 85280-0950
(602) 990-0682; (800) 456-0682
FAX (602) 990-3390
e-mail: micasa@primenet.com
www.azres.com

4921. Reaching 3,800 feet high in the Sonoran Desert, this fascinating 250-year-old ranch is one of the last great Spanish haciendas still standing in the United States. There are 16 fully modernized guest rooms, each with its own private bath and fireplace. Heated pool, spa, hot tub, and variety of recreational activities on-site, including horseback riding. Three meals are served a day. Horseback riding package. Call for rates.

SCOTTSDALE

Arizona Trails Bed and Breakfast Reservation Service

P.O. Box 18998, Fountain Hills, 85269-8998
(602) 837-4284; (888) 799-4284
FAX (602) 816-4224
e-mail: aztrails@arizonatrails.com
www.arizonatrails.com

AZ 152. Nestled in the lush Sonoran Desert between Scottsdale and Carefree, this "hideout" has combined the best of a luxury resort with all the atmosphere and activities of the finest guest ranches in one spectacular guest house. Sit under a rock waterfall in the pool, or around the campfire zone, play one of many championship golf courses in the area, or relax in the spa. Panoramic views from every direction on guests' private veranda featuring a gas fireplace and outdoor gas grill. The bedroom has a king-size Mountain Man bed, private bath with claw-foot tub, and rock-walled shower. The kitchen features everything guests need for a home away from home including a wagon wheel breakfast bar and washer/dryer. The living room has another gas fireplace and queen-size sleeper-sofa for parties of four. $250.

AZ 156. This charming guest house is close to shops, restaurants, golf, and only minutes to Phoenix or Paradise Valley. Enjoy the views from the sparkling pool or relax on the bed with custom linens and bedding. The guest house has full kitchen that is stocked daily for a self-serve full breakfast. The private bath has a standup shower. No daily maid service is provided unless otherwise requested. $85.

NOTES: Credit cards accepted: A MasterCard; B Visa; C American Express; D Discover; E Diner's Club; F Other; 2 Personal checks accepted; 3 Lunch available; 4 Dinner available; 5 Open all year; 6 Pets welcome;

AZ 162. Convenience and comfort are the key in this well-located bed and breakfast guest house, close to Scottsdale Fashion Square and the Camelback corridor. Private entrance, covered parking, sitting area with TV/VCR and stereo system, large work area with desk and telephone line for business travelers, kitchen, private patio with outdoor fireplace, and swimming pool. Breakfast is stocked in guests' private kitchen so they can help themselves according to their schedule. $135.

AZ 166. Enjoy the resort-like setting combined with the intimate and exclusive atmosphere of this elegant bed and breakfast in north Scottsdale. Two rooms in the main house and two private casitas. Each has an in-room fireplace, private bath, private patio, and TV. One casita offers a full kitchen and the other a sauna with kitchenette. Relax under the covered patio with outdoor fireplace, take a dip in the crystal clear pool, or enjoy a game of tennis on guests' own tennis courts. Continental Breakfast. $175-250.

Bed and Breakfast Southwest Reservation Service

P.O. Box 51198, Phoenix, 85076-1198
(602) 947-9704; (800) 762-9704
FAX (602) 874-1316

115. In prestigious North Scottsdale. A poolside guest cottage with king-size bed, private bath, private entrance, and well-stocked kitchen. Guests may enjoy a day at one of the many fine malls or golf courses that Scottsdale prides itself on or just relax in the sun. No smoking. No children. No pets. $89.

168. This contemporary adobe 8,000-square-foot home is like a sculptured work of art. Palm trees on immaculate lawn surround pool, Jacuzzi, and barbecue area. There is also an exercise room, private tennis court, and beautiful "portal" with a

fireplace and breakfast area for guests. Two guest casitas each with sitting area, fireplace, TV, music system, full bath, and private entrance. Two rooms in the main house each with full bath, TV, and fireplace. Continental breakfast served. No smoking. Older children welcome. $250.

Eagle Mountain—Southwest Inn

9800 North Summer Hill Boulevard,
    Fountain Hills, 85268
(602) 816-3000; (800) 992-8083
FAX (602) 816-3090; e-mail: eminfo@swinn.com
www.southwestinn.com

Beautiful new Santa Fe-style property in Fountain Hills, just one-fourth mile east of Scottsdale, on the Eagle Mountain Golf Course, an 18-hole championship course. This boutique resort bed and breakfast has 42 deluxe rooms and suites (in six building complexes) with fireplaces, private decks, and two-person whirlpool tubs. Every room has a private deck facing the 60-mile views of mountain and desert terrain. The large grounds include a pool, spa, meeting rooms, and a magnificent lobby building known as "The Lodge" which contains the breakfast room.

Hosts: Joel and Sheila Gilguff
Rooms: 42 (PB) $100-400
Continental Breakfast
Credit Cards: A, B, C, D
Notes: 5, 7, 8, 9, 10, 11, 12, 13, 14, 15

Inn at the Citadel

8700 East Pinnacle Peak Road, 85255
(800) 927-8367; FAX (602) 585-3436

A combination of pleasures of distinctive boutiques, galleries, and restaurants surrounding the elegant inn. The inn offers 11 luxurious suites, each appointed with original artwork and antiques. Enjoy a suite with a private Jacuzzi on the terrace overlooking the foothills of the McDowell Mountain Range. Fireplaces, balconies, and terraces combine to form a tapestry of unequaled ambiance.

7 No smoking; 8 Children welcome; 9 Social drinking allowed; 10 Tennis nearby; 11 Swimming nearby; 12 Golf nearby; 13 Skiing nearby; 14 May be booked through a travel agent; 15 Handicapped accessible.

Hosts: Lorraine Irving and staff
Rooms: 11 (PB) $79-335
Continental Breakfast
Credit Cards: A, B, C
Notes: 5, 6, 7, 8, 9, 10, 11, 12, 14, 15

La Paz in Desert Springs

6309 East Ludlow Drive, 85254
(602) 922-5379; (888) 922-0963
FAX (602) 905-0085

Enjoy peace and comfort in this freshly decorated southwestern decor three-room, full bath with private entrance suite. The large master bedroom has a king-size bed with room for a rollaway/crib. The living room has a queen-size sofa bed and entertainment center with cable TV. Kitchenette is equipped with dishes, coffee maker, microwave, and refrigerator. Ideally close to Old Scottsdale, Westworld, Rawhide, and other attractions. Great restaurants, golf, and shopping malls. Near the desert, hiking, rafting, and horseback riding. Within one day's travel to Sedona, the petrified forest, painted desert, meteor and sunset craters, and the Grand Canyon. Available October through April, limited summer. Reservations required. No smoking. Continental plus breakfast served.

Hosts: Luis and Susan Cuevas
Suite: 1 (PB) $95-135
Continental Breakfast
Credit Cards: None
Notes: 2, 7, 8, 9, 10, 11, 12

Mi Casa Su Casa/Old Pueblo Homestays Bed and Breakfast Reservation Service

P.O. Box 950, Tempe, 85280-0950
(602) 990-0682; (800) 456-0682
FAX (602) 990-3390
e-mail: micasa@primenet.com
www.azres.com

5011. This home is in a quiet neighborhood, convenient to downtown Scottsdale, near art galleries, theaters, restaurants, and shopping. There are two guest rooms, each with a private bath. Please reserve outdoor hot tub in advance for heating. Full breakfast. Resident cat. Add $5 for one-night stay. $45-75.

5012. Four-level condominium in a very nice complex one mile from Scottsdale Fashion Square. Extra-large room on the first level has sitting area and private bath up a few steps. Room two on the fourth level has a shared hall full bath. Community pool is heated except December through February. Continental breakfast. Two-night stay preferred. Children over nine. No pets. Smoking outside. $65-75.

5013. Private guest suite with private entrance is attached but separate from the main house. Amenities include climate controls and private telephone. The guest suite has a sitting area, TV, cabinet for hanging clothes, private bath with shower, and kitchenette. AKC Maltese dogs in main part of house. Smoking restricted. Two-night stay preferred. Weekly and monthly rates. $75.

5014. This U-shaped house has two separate bedroom wings. The suite in one of the wings has private entrance, private telephone, living room with cable TV, a complete kitchen, and private patio. There is a hall full bath and the second bathroom has a shower. Pool. A starter Continental breakfast is provided for self-serve breakfast for two mornings. Near public transportation. Weekly and seasonal rates. Three-night minimum. No smoking or pets. Children 11 and olderwelcome. Possible handicapped accessibility. German spoken. $95-125.

5015. A two-bedroom, two-bath condo in quiet complex. The guest bedroom has a bath en suite with shower. Guests welcome in living room with TV. Heated swimming pool. Walking distance to Old Town Scottsdale. Smoking outside. No pets. No children. Public transportation. Add $10 for one-night stays. $80.

NOTES: Credit cards accepted: A MasterCard; B Visa; C American Express; D Discover; E Diner's Club; F Other; 2 Personal checks accepted; 3 Lunch available; 4 Dinner available; 5 Open all year; 6 Pets welcome;

5016. This central Scottsdale bed and breakfast is within walking distance of Old Town Scottsdale. There is a pool for seasonal swimming, a patio, an outdoor beehive fireplace, and redwood deck. The light, airy guest house is attached but separate from the main house. There is a cable TV, stereo, private telephone, full kitchen, and bath with shower. Self-serve Continental plus breakfast. No smoking, pets, or children. Weekly rates. $125.

5051. *Hafod-y-Gwynt* means "shelter from the wind" in Welsh. On 10 acres with mountains in every direction, the guest apartment with private entrance is connected to the main house in a remote scenic area. Air conditioned. Comfortable combined living room and bedroom with TV and traditional decor. Bathroom has shower. Fully equipped kitchen stocked for first few days' breakfasts. Resident pets include horses, dogs, and one cat. Closed May 15 through October 15. Three-night minimum stay is required. $65.

5052. In a handsome neighborhood on an acre in north central Scottsdale is a charming guest house with a bedroom/living room, fully equipped kitchen, full bath, and contemporary furnishings. French doors lead to pool. Guests enjoy jogging or hiking along the nearby scenic canal. Walk to Hilton Village and public transportation. For short stays, breakfast items are stocked in the kitchen. For longer stays, self-catering. Smoking outside. Three-night minimum stay preferred. $85.

5053. Stone-front cozy cottage built in 1985 is opposite the main house with the pool in between. Well-maintained yard with flowering bushes. Cottage has air conditioning, heating, compact living room/ bedroom, small kitchen with all appliances, bath with shower, white tile floors, contemporary furniture, and TV. Kitchen stocked with Continental plus breakfast items. Self-

catering. Telephone, water purifier, and air purifier. Near shopping centers and aquatic center. No smoking. Weekly, monthly, and summer rates are available. $65-85.

5054. A luxurious contemporary adobe home in north Scottsdale. There is also a large outdoor spa and private tennis court. Guest casita one has a living room with TV and kiva fireplace, private bath, and kitchen. Guest casita two has a living room with big screen TV and kiva fireplace, private bath, kitchen, and a sauna. The main house has three bedrooms, two with a private bath. The master bedroom is extra large with a large luxury bath. Continental plus breakfast. No resident pets. Smoking permitted outside. Children 10 or older are welcome in the main house. Two-night minimum stay. $175-275.

5055. Handsome home in the very nice residential area of McCormick Ranch. Guests welcome to use heated pool overlooking a beautiful man-made lake. The three-room suite is separated from the main house. Full bath with a pretty atrium. The separate sitting room has a TV and windows looking out on a small garden. Guests welcome in large living room. Restaurants, shopping, and golf courses nearby. Dog in residence. Smoking restricted. No pets. No children. Full breakfast. Two-night stay preferred. $110.

5056. Two-story Arizona Spanish-style home built in 1995 in the upscale Pinnacle Peak area. Air conditioning. Master bedroom on the first floor has a private full bath, cable TV, and exit to patio. Nearby heated community swimming pool and spa. On the second floor are two guest rooms that each have cable TV and share a full hall bath. Spanish spoken. Smoking restricted. No pets. No children. Full breakfast with "picnic breakfasts" available. Two-night stay preferred. $65-95.

---

7 No smoking; 8 Children welcome; 9 Social drinking allowed; 10 Tennis nearby; 11 Swimming nearby; 12 Golf nearby; 13 Skiing nearby; 14 May be booked through a travel agent; 15 Handicapped accessible.

5058. The guest house has air conditioning and heat controls, a private entrance, private patio, kitchen, separate bathroom with oversized tub and shower, and a private telephone. There is a Hide-a-Bed in the living room, which has cable TV, washer, and dryer. Seasonal pool, outside grill, Arizona fire pit, playground for children, and the sports court. Near Scottsdale and Lincoln Roads, fine shopping, and restaurants as well as McDonald Park and jogging track. Self-serving Continental breakfast replenished every four days. Minimum two nights. No smoking. No pets. Possible handicapped accessibility. $100-150.

5059. This two-bedroom, two-bath guest house has a private entrance, living and dining room, full kitchen, laundry. Room one has a full bath. Room two has a hall full bath. The pool and lounge area are surrounded by majestic palm trees. Continental plus breakfast. Seasonal rates. Weekly and monthly rates. $90-100.

5060. There are two private custom suites, each with a private entrance in this one-story house in a nice residential area. The secluded yard and garden area is made for relaxation with outdoor adobe fireplace, heated whirlpool spa, swimming pool for seasonal swimming, barbecue and Mexican firepits. Each suite has a sitting and dining area, walk-in closet, and bath with shower. In-suite amenities include a wet bar, refrigerator, microwave, cable TV, VCR, and telephone. Continental plus breakfast. Smoking outside. No pets or children. Closed June 1 through October 1. $119-139.

5061. This southwestern home welcomes guests to a tranquil stay. One guest room with TV and private hall bath with tub and shower. Refreshments include kringlas, a delectable Norwegian treat. Special gourmet breakfast. No smoking, pets, or children. Two-night minimum stay. $85.

The Temporary Teepee

Scottsdale, AZ (location)
P.O. Box 24132, Tempe, 85285 (mailing)
(602) 991-6630; FAX (602) 991-9757

Large beautifully decorated suites with private facilities and entrances. Very quiet. Close-in location with magnificent garden area. Pool and spa on grounds. Every conceivable amenity including TV, wet bar, telephone, coffee maker, microwave, and stocked no-charge refrigerator in each suite. Specializing in making the guest feel at home and in providing the highest degree of personalized service, while allowing complete privacy. Smoking permitted in garden area only. Resident cat is not permitted in guest suites. Continental plus breakfast served. Cash, traveler's checks, and personal checks accepted. No children. No pets.

Host: Robert S. Mayer
Rooms: 2 (PB) $139-159
Continental Breakfast
Credit Cards: F
Notes: 2, 7, 10, 11, 12, 14

SEDONA

Apple Orchard Inn

656 Jordan Road, 86336
(800) 663-6968; FAX (520) 204-0044
e-mail: appleorc@sedona.net

Nestled in the heart of Sedona, sitting on the site of the historic Jordan Apple Orchard is the inn. The unparalleled location allows easy access to "uptown" galleries and shops. The secluded setting is on nearly two acres of wooded grounds with spectacular views and hiking to some of Sedona's most magnificent red rocks. The rooms feature king-size beds, whirlpool tubs, TV/VCRs, HBO, 110 complimentary videos, bathrobes and hair dryers, telephones, mini-refrigerators, some rooms with fireplaces, gourmet three-course breakfast, smoke-free environment, and massage room. AAA-rated four diamonds.

Apple Orchard Inn

Hosts: Bob and Paula Glass; Laura Thurlow
Rooms: 7 (PB) $135-195
Full Breakfast
Credit Cards: A, B, C
Notes: 2, 5, 7, 9, 10, 11, 12, 13,1 4, 15

Arizona Trails Bed and Breakfast Reservation Service

P.O. Box 18998, Fountain Hills, 85269-8998
(602) 837-4284; (888) 799-4284
FAX (602) 816-4224
e-mail: aztrails@arizonatrails.com
www.arizonatrails.com

AZ 112. Enjoy the friendly atmosphere of this five-room ranch-style bed and breakfst with spectacular red rock views in Sedona. Property backs up to national forest land for hiking and birding. All rooms have private baths, queen-size beds, each with a different theme. Two rooms share a common kitchen and living room area with fireplace. Close to shops, galleries, and restaurants in the village of Oak Creek and only minutes to uptown Sedona. Full breakfast. $95-115.

AZ 132. Relax in this elegant and special southwestern seven-room inn. Walking distance to shops and restaurants, but in a quiet area with great red rock views and hiking nearby. Each room features a private bath, in-room refrigerator, and TV/VCR with video library. Six of the rooms have whirlpool tubs. Five rooms offer private patios. There is a separate guest massage room with message therapist on call. The inn also has an exclusive tour guide. Full breakfast. Handicapped accessible. $135-195.

AZ 137. Combine bed and breakfast hospitality with hotel-style accommodations and guests will have this wonderful 28-room inn in West Sedona. Continental breakfast. There is a pool and outdoor spa for relaxation. Great red rock views and all rooms are equipped with mini-refrigerators, TV/VCRs, telephones, robes, and fireplaces. Handicapped accessible, children welcome. $115-195.

AZ 138. This elegant Victorian five-room inn sits right on Oak Creek. Wander the grounds down to the creek for a relaxing afternoon. A gourmet breakfast is served. All rooms have private baths with Jacuzzi tubs, private entrances, and some with fireplaces. Authentic 19th-century antiques can be found throughout the inn. Dinner can be arranged on weekends with advance notice. Handicapped accessible. $175-275.

AZ 143. Relax at this southwestern five-room inn in the village of Oak Creek. The inn is adjacent to Sedona Golf Resort with great golf course and red rock views. All rooms have private baths—many with whirlpool tubs and double sinks, private entrances, fireplaces, and queen-size beds with authentic Pendelton blankets. One room is handicapped accessible. Full breakfast. Guests can enjoy swim and tennis privileges at the Sedona Golf Resort. $109-159.

AZ 154. Intimate atmosphere and fantastic views of the red rocks are trademarks of this bed and breakfast homestay in Sedona. The suite offers a private bath with jetted tub and standup shower and private entrance to the redwood deck along the back of the house. Both rooms have TVs and telephones. Full breakfast. Enjoy awe-inspiring views of cathedral rock from the oversized windows. Children welcome. $85-95.

7 No smoking; 8 Children welcome; 9 Social drinking allowed; 10 Tennis nearby; 11 Swimming nearby; 12 Golf nearby; 13 Skiing nearby; 14 May be booked through a travel agent; 15 Handicapped accessible.

Bed and Breakfast Southwest Reservation Service

P.O. Box 51198, Phoenix, 85076-1198
(602) 947-9704; (800) 762-9704
FAX (602) 874-1316

163. A beautiful place to relax and enjoy with room to breathe describes this gracious Sedona inn. Elegantly rustic on two and one-half wooded acres with 12 beautifully appointed guest rooms and suites. Gourmet breakfast served on morning porch. Afternoon tea and late night desserts also served. No smoking. Children welcome. $120-225.

Boots and Saddles Bed and Breakfast

2900 Hopi Drive, 86336
(520) 282-1944; (800) 201-1944
FAX (520) 204-2230

Boots and Saddles Bed and Breakfast offers the charm of the Old West in a magnificent setting among Sedona's spectacular red rock country. Each room is distinctly furnished with cowboy decor to take guests back to those thrilling days of yesteryear. Full breakfast is served in the dining room with beautiful red rock views. All private baths. Rooms with deck or balcony access. Area orientation provided.

Hosts: John and Linda Steele
Rooms: 4 (PB) $65-125
Full Breakfast
Credit Cards: A, B, C, D
Notes: 2, 5, 7, 8, 9, 10, 11, 12, 13, 14

Briar Patch Inn

3190 North Highway 89A, 86336
(520) 282-2342; (888) 809-3030
FAX (520) 282-2399
e-mail: briarpatch@sedona.net
www.bbhost.com/briarpatch

Nestled in Oak Creek Canyon on nine lush creekside acres, this oasis is described by guests as a paradise. Summer mornings guests can breakfast by the creek with Bach and Mozart played by resident musicians.

In the winter, cozy up to a favorite fireplace with a good book. Handcrafted cabins, southwestern furnishings, and Native American crafts create relaxing and memorable moments. Discover Sedona's unique beauty: Indian ruins, hiking, galleries, and vortex energy. Close to the Grand Canyon and Navajo and Hopi Indians. A real gem! No smoking in cabins. Inquire about accommodations for children.

Host: Rob Olson
Rooms: 17 (PB) $149-295
Full Breakfast
Credit Cards: A, B, C
Notes: 2, 5, 9, 10, 11, 12, 13, 14

The Canyon Wren— Cabins for Two

6425 North HWY 89A, 86336
(520) 282-6900; (800) 437-WREN (9736)
e-mail: cnynwren@sedona.net
www.sedona.net/hotel/canyonwren

Six miles north of Sedona, four cabins are set against the parklike frame of red rock cliffs and green canyon landscape. Specializing in one to two adults only for private retreats or romantic getaways. The cabins offer kitchens, fireplaces, whirlpool bathtubs, decks, and patios. Gas grills. No TVs or telephones. Continental plus breakfast. Away from bustle of Sedona, yet close enough to enjoy town benefits. Personal, friendly service. Nonsmoking property inside and outside. Creek swimming, hiking, and fishing are a stone's throw away.

Hosts: Milena Pfeifer and Mike Smith
Cabins: 4 (PB) $125-140
Continental Breakfast
Credit Cards: A, B, D
Notes: 2, 5, 7, 9, 10, 11, 12, 13, 14

Casa Sedona

55 Hozoni Drive, 86336
(520) 282-2938; (800) 525-3756

Casa Sedona offers fabulous red rock views from an acre of wooded property. The rooms are spacious, luxurious, and include

private baths, spa tubs, and a delightful fireplace. Guests are served a hearty southwestern breakfast and afternoon appetizers in a smoke-free environment (inside and out). Casa Sedona offers a tranquil, serene experience. Enjoy a soak in the outdoor hot tub. Children over 10 are welcome.

Hosts: John and Nancy True
Rooms: 16 (PB) $125-205
Full Breakfast
Credit Cards: A, B,
Notes: 2, 5, 7, 9, 10, 11, 12, 13, 14, 15

The Graham Bed and Breakfast Inn

150 Canyon Circle Drive, 86351
(520) 284-1425; (800) 228-1425
FAX (520) 284-0767; e-mail: graham@sedona.net

The Graham Inn is an impressive, award-winning southwestern inn with huge windows providing views of Sedona's famous red rock formations. Six guest rooms with private baths, TV/VCRs, balconies with red rock views, fireplaces, and whirlpool tubs. Four new luxury casitas with waterfall showers and bath fireplaces. Enjoy wonderful breakfasts, afternoon refreshments, and

The Graham Bed and Breakfast Inn

videos. Pool, Jacuzzi, and bicycles are available for guests' use.

Hosts: Roger and Carol Redenbaugh
Rooms: 6 (PB) $109-369
Casitas: 4
Full Breakfast
Cards: A, B, D
Notes: 2, 5, 7, 9, 10, 11, 12, 14

The Inn on Oak Creek

556 Highway 179, 86336
(520) 282-7896; (800) 499-7896
FAX (520) 282-0696

The Inn on Oak Creek is a luxurious 11-room bed and breakfast overlooking beautiful Oak Creek. All 11 rooms have private baths, gas fireplaces, whirlpool tubs, TVs, and VCRs. Most rooms have private decks overlooking the water and scenic red rocks. Within walking distance of Tlaquepaque shopping village, art galleries, and fine restaurants. A creekside park, full gourmet breakfast, and afternoon refreshments all serve to pamper the guests. Smoking is not permitted.

Hosts: Pam Harrison and Rick Morris
Rooms: 11 (PB) $150-235
Full Breakfast
Credit Cards: A, B, D
Notes: 2, 5, 7, 9, 11, 12, 13, 14, 15

The Lodge at Sedona

125 Kallof Place, 86336
(800) 619-4467; FAX (520) 204-2128
e-mail: lodge@sedona.net
www.lodgeatsedona.com

"It's the nearest to heaven you'll come at 4,500 feet," wrote the *Arizona Republic* when naming the Lodge "Arizona's Best Bed and Breakfast Inn." Elegantly rustic, it offers secluded privacy on three wooded acres of gardens, lawns, and labyrinth. Thirteen guest rooms and large, elegant common rooms with country pine antiques provide a comfortable and nurturing experience. Some rooms have private decks, fireplaces, and Jacuzzi tubs. A full gourmet breakfast is served on the morning porch.

7 No smoking; 8 Children welcome; 9 Social drinking allowed; 10 Tennis nearby; 11 Swimming nearby; 12 Golf nearby; 13 Skiing nearby; 14 May be booked through a travel agent; 15 Handicapped accessible.

Refreshments, appetizers, and dessert are served every afternoon and evening. Romantic dinners are available.

Hosts: Barb and Mark Dinunzio
Rooms: 13 (PB) $120-225
Full Breakfast
Credit Cards: A, B, C, D
Notes: 2, 4, 5, 7, 9, 10, 11, 12, 13, 14, 15

Mi Casa Su Casa/Old Pueblo Homestays Bed and Breakfast Reservation Service

P.O. Box 950, Tempe, 85280-0950
(602) 990-0682; (800) 456-0682
FAX (602) 990-3390
e-mail: micasa@primenet.com
www.azres.com

5151. This five-bedroom inn, built in 1983, is a triplex ranch-style house at the foot of Castle Rock. All bedrooms have private baths. Each pair of bedrooms shares a sitting room featuring a fireplace and small kitchen. The fifth bedroom is in the main part of the triplex. Full breakfasts served. Resident dogs. Children welcome. Smoking outside. Handicapped accessible. $95-115.

5152. Large contemporary home built in 1993 with breathtaking views of the red rock formations. Separate suite has a private entrance and patio. The sitting/bedroom has a luxurious bath with whirlpool tub and shower, cable TV, and private telephone. Two-night minimum stay preferred. Self-catering Continental plus breakfast. No children. No pets. No smoking. Additional $5 charge for one-night stay. $85.

5153. Placed along the spring-fed waters of Oak Creek is this delightful inn with 16 separate and private cottages. These hand-crafted, delightful cabins all have private baths. Many of the cabins have sitting areas, fireplaces, and kitchens. Full breakfast. Smoking restricted. No pets. Possible handicapped accessibility. Add $25 for each additional person. $149-225.

5154. Chosen as Arizona's Best Bed and Breakfast Inn by the *Arizona Republic* in 1993 and 1994, this inn is known for its "wealth of creature comforts, beautiful surroundings, and gracious reception and attention from the innkeepers." Enjoy 13 beautifully appointed guest accommodations, of which three are luxury suites. Several have private outdoor decks with brick fireplaces, mountain or wooded views, Jacuzzi tubs. Afternoon appetizers. Sumptuous breakfasts. $120-225.

5155. Bordering the Sedona Golf Resort, this is a new (1996) adobe hacienda with verandas and a fountain. It has red rock and golf course views. Each spacious room has telephones, gas-log fireplaces, outside entrances, Saltillo tile floors, and private baths with showers. Four of the rooms have jetted tubs. Southwestern-style breakfasts. No smoking. No pets. $99-159.

5156. This bed and breakfast offers fabulous red rock views from each of its 15 terrace guest rooms. Each luxurious room is individually appointed to please and pamper with a private bath including whirlpool tub, fireplace, refrigerator, and telephone. A hearty southwestern breakfast is served outside most of the year. Appetizers are served in the afternoon. Children over 10 are welcome. An additional $25 for each extra guest. No smoking or pets. $110-185.

5157. This bed and breakfast is convenient to hiking, shops, art galleries, and restaurants. Guests enjoy private tennis club privileges and by special arrangement may use the facilities. All accommodations feature ground-level rooms, private bath, secured entry, and TV. Two rooms share a private deck with a view. Five minutes away is one-bedroom apartment. Full breakfast . Italian and English spoken. Children over 10 welcome. Fifteen dollars for each additional guest. No smoking or pets. $85-135.

NOTES: Credit cards accepted: A MasterCard; B Visa; C American Express; D Discover; E Diner's Club; F Other; 2 Personal checks accepted; 3 Lunch available; 4 Dinner available; 5 Open all year; 6 Pets welcome;

5158. Enjoy incredible red rock formations and Cathedral Rock in Sedona on a redwood deck from guest suite. The luxurious suite has an adjoining bath with a large Jacuzzi tub and marble shower. Another room has a private hall bath. Special dietary requirements must be specified at the time of reservation. Two-night minimum on weekends. Smoking outside. No pets. Inquire about accommodations for children. $85-95.

Southwest Inn at Sedona

Southwest Inn at Sedona

3250 West Highway 89A, 86336
(520) 282-3344; (800) 483-7422
FAX (520) 282-0267; e-mail: info@swinn.com
www.swinn.com

The Southwest Inn is a wonderful combination of a small luxury hotel and a bed and breakfast. The inn has large, beautifully decorated rooms with king- or queen-size beds, fireplaces, and decks or patios facing dramatic red rock views. The inn has a swimming pool and spa and is close to all the varied activities Sedona has to offer, including hiking, horseback riding, jeep tours, hot-air balloon rides, and helicopter rides. Several restaurants, galleries, and theaters are within walking distance. AAA four-diamond rating.

Hosts: Joel and Sheila Gilguff
Rooms: 28 (PB) $99-195
Continental Breakfast
Credit Cards: A, B, C, D
Notes: 5, 7, 8, 9, 10, 11, 12, 13, 14. 15

Territorial House: An Old West Bed and Breakfast

65 Piki Drive, 86336
(520) 204-2737; (800) 801-2737
FAX (520) 204-2230

The Territorial House is built of native stone and cedar. Each unique room is comfortably decorated with a theme depicting Sedona's territorial history. Guests enjoy western hospitality as they relax around the large native-stone fireplace, watch numerous birds from the veranda, soak in the hot tub, or just rest in the peaceful, serene setting. Rooms available with fireplace, balcony, deck, whirlpool tub, and TV. Full gourmet breakfasts are served in the Saltillo-tiled dining room. Late afternoon snacks are available after a full day of exploring Sedona's red rock country.

Hosts: John and Linda Steele
Rooms: 4 (PB) $109-159
Full Breakfast
Credit Cards: A, B, C, D
Notes: 2, 5, 7, 8, 9, 10, 11, 12, 13, 14

A Touch of Sedona Bed and Breakfast

595 Jordan Road, 86336
(602) 282-6462; (800) 600-6462
FAX (602) 282-1534
www.touchsedona.com

In historic uptown, this California ranch-style inn is within easy walking distance of shops, galleries, restaurants, the Sedona Art Center, and playhouse. The quiet, intimate inn is designed for guests' comfort and convenience. Panoramic red-rock views and sensational stargazing from the deck. Private baths. Generous hospitality, multicourse gourmet breakfasts with home-baked goodies. Quiet residential area is also near forest service trails. Smoke-free environment. No pets. AAA-, ABBA-, and Mobil-rated.

Hosts: Bill and Sharon Larsen
Rooms: 5 (PB) $99-159
Full Breakfast
Credit Cards: A, B, C, D
Notes: 2, 5, 7, 9, 10, 11, 12, 14

7 No smoking; 8 Children welcome; 9 Social drinking allowed; 10 Tennis nearby; 11 Swimming nearby; 12 Golf nearby; 13 Skiing nearby; 14 May be booked through a travel agent; 15 Handicapped accessible.

SIERRA VISTA

Mi Casa Su Casa/Old Pueblo Homestays Bed and Breakfast Reservation Service

P.O. Box 950, Tempe, 85280-0950
(602) 990-0682; (800) 456-0682
FAX (602) 990-3390
e-mail: micasa@primenet.com
www.azres.com

5181. Guests will enjoy this secluded two-story ranch house and separate guest casita in a peaceful river valley amid the San Pedro Riparian National Conservation Area. Both guest rooms have private baths, microwaves, and refrigerators. The casita has a private entrance, sitting area, and gas fireplace. It is quiet, cozy, and romantic. The common room provides a TV, pool table, and small library. Enjoy the shaded courtyard and walled patio area with swimming pool (in season) and hot tub. Outside dog in residence. Two-night minimum stay. Smoking restricted. No pets. Children over 12 welcome. Full breakfast. Ten dollars extra for a one-night stay. $70-80.

SONOITA

Mi Casa Su Casa/Old Pueblo Homestays Bed and Breakfast Reservation Service

P.O. Box 950, Tempe, 85280-0950
(602) 990-0682; (800) 456-0682
FAX (602) 990-3390
e-mail: micasa@primenet.com
www.azres.com

5192. The main house, built in 1916, has been updated but maintains the ambiance of the original hacienda while providing three attractive bedrooms with private baths and private entrances. The attached guest house has sitting room, bedroom, bath, and private entrance. Full breakfast.

Smoking outside. No pets. Children 12 and older welcome. $85-95.

SPRINGERVILLE

Mi Casa Su Casa/Old Pueblo Homestays Bed and Breakfast Reservation Service

P.O. Box 950, Tempe, 85280-0950
(602) 990-0682; (800) 456-0682
FAX (602) 990-3390
e-mail: micasa@primenet.com
www.azres.com

4161. Carefully restored Colonial Revival home, circa 1910, allows a visitor to step back in time to the Victorian era. Four bedrooms with private baths are furnished with antiques, handmade quilts, and goosedown pillows. Full breakfast is served. Seventeen miles from Sunrise, Arizona's largest ski resort, and 13 miles from Lyman Lake. Two miles from Casa Malpais Pueblo, prehistoric Indian structures. Smoking is permitted outside only. $65-75.

TEMPE

Arizona Trails Bed and Breakfast Reservation Service

P.O. Box 18998, Fountain Hills, 85269-8998
(602) 837-4284; (888) 799-4284
FAX (602) 816-4224
e-mail: aztrails@arizonatrails.com
www.arizonatrails.com

AZ 158. This charming homestay is conveniently close to ASU, Scottsdale, and Phoenix Sky Harbor Airport. A suite with two rooms and private entrance. Relax in the country antique bedroom with brass bed. The bath has both tub and shower. An additional room is available for small children and includes a sleeper sofa and crib. Outside enjoy the pool and patio area. Full breakfast. $80.

Mi Casa Su Casa/Old Pueblo Homestays Bed and Breakfast Reservation Service

P.O. Box 950, Tempe, 85280-0950
(602) 990-0682; (800) 456-0682
FAX (602) 990-3390
e-mail: micasa@primenet.com
www.azres.com

5201. This bed and breakfast is in an older, quiet, well-kept neighborhood two blocks from ASU and downtown Tempe. The main house was built in 1939. A new addition with a private entrance onto the patio blends well with the old house. This area consists of large open space with sitting room/bedroom with TV, VCR, microwave, and small refrigerator. The private bath has a whirlpool tub. Resident dog. Smoking outside. Infants welcome; Port-a-crib available. Minimum stay is two nights. Ten dollars each additional person. $75.

5202. This homey one-story bed and breakfast is in a nicely maintained, quiet neighborhood which is near everything. One guest room has a TV. Guests have private full hall bath. There is also a private half-bath available. Guests are welcome to watch TV in the living room or the family room. Refreshments. Full country-style breakfast. Smoking outside. No pets. Infants only. Minimum stay two nights. $55-70.

5203. This private guest suite has two bedrooms and private full bath; private living room has TV and a sofa bed to accommodate children. Private entrance available if needed. Full breakfast. Resident cat. Minimum two nights. Only one party at a time. Three blocks from public transportation. Airport pick-up available. Additional persons $10 each. $90-110.

5204. Large ranch-style home in a quiet neighborhood in south Tempe. The guest suite has a private entrance, sitting room

with a sofa, TV, VCR, microwave, small refrigerator. The private bath has tub and shower. A second room next door to the suite has a baby room with a crib and double futon. Pool available for seasonal swimming. Possible handicapped accessibility. Prize-winning breakfasts. Infants stay free. Each additional person $10. Weekly rates. $80.

Valley O' the Sun Bed and Breakfast

P.O. Box 2214, 85252
(602) 941-1281; (800) 689-1281 (phone/FAX)

This bed and breakfast is in the college district of Tempe but still close enough to Scottsdale for guests to enjoy the glamour of its shops, restaurants, and theaters. Valley O' the Sun Bed and Breakfast offers clean, comfortable rooms at reasonable and affordable rates. Continental plus breakfast is served. Personal checks accepted on second visit.

Host: Kathleen Curtis
Rooms: 3 (1 PB; 2 SB) $40-50
Continental Breakfast
Credit Cards: None
Notes: 5, 9, 10, 11, 12, 13, 14

TOMBSTONE_____

Mi Casa Su Casa/Old Pueblo Homestays Bed and Breakfast Reservation Service

P.O. Box 950, Tempe, 85280-0950
(602) 990-0682; (800) 456-0682
FAX (602) 990-3390
e-mail: micasa@primenet.com
www.azres.com

5241. Originally Emily Morton's Boarding House, this house was totally renovated in 1994-95 to become a charming bed and breakfast. It is next door to the famous 1880 county courthouse, now a museum. Three guest rooms each have private bath and cable TV. Outside cat and dog, three birds in

7 No smoking; 8 Children welcome; 9 Social drinking allowed; 10 Tennis nearby; 11 Swimming nearby; 12 Golf nearby; 13 Skiing nearby; 14 May be booked through a travel agent; 15 Handicapped accessible.

parlor. Smoking outside. No children or pets. Arrangements can be made for stage coach weddings, desert trail horseback rides, mine tours, train trip to the San Pedro River, Kartchner Caverns tours. $55-75.

5242. This accommodation consists of two 1880s adobe houses surrounded by a picket fence. An artist's studio is also available A hearty breakfast is served. Each of the seven rooms, plus a small miner's cabin, has a private entrance and private bath. Smoking outside. Children welcome. Ten dollars for each additional guest. Inquire about accommodations for pets. $50-80.

5243. This 1904 home was restored and retains all the original wood, some of the gas lighting fixtures, and a large oak staircase. It is the only remaining two-story clapboard Victorian house in the county. The three rooms upstairs share the shower bath on the same floor. A guest room downstairs has a private bath and TV. Smoking permitted outside. Children welcome. No pets. $40-100.

5244. This 1880 adobe home, listed in the National Register of Historic Places, was originally built as a boarding house. The common room is filled with antiques, memorabilia, puzzles, games, and books. A barbecue area is available. Each guest room is filled with antiques of various themes and provides a sink and vanity. Full breakfast. Smoking permitted outside. Children over six welcome. Ten dollars for each additional guest. No pets. $65-85.

5245. This newly remodeled, two-story building has a balcony and homey atmosphere. On the second floor are four bedrooms. The largest room has a private entrance onto the balcony and a private bath. Three rooms share a large hall bath. Only two are rented at a time, unless it is group traveling together. Smoking outside. No pets. Children are welcome. $65-85.

5246. This newly remodeled 1927 homestead and working cattle ranch that has retained its Old West atmosphere is in the San Pedro Riparian National Conservation Area. Its newly constructed western town consists of 14 buildings, each filled with antiques and memorabilia. Horseback tours, wagon rides, and chuck wagon suppers with musical western stage shows entertain guests. The "hotel" offers six large rooms, private shower baths, and sleeping porch. There are also four themed cottages. Prices include three meals per day and 15 percent gratuity will be added. Smoking permitted in designated areas. Children over 12 welcome. No pets. $140-280.

TUBAC

Mi Casa Su Casa/Old Pueblo Homestays Bed and Breakfast Reservation Service

P.O. Box 950, Tempe, 85280-0950
(602) 990-0682; (800) 456-0682
FAX (602) 990-3390
e-mail: micasa@primenet.com
www.azres.com

5262. This bed and breakfast is in the historic district of Tubac within easy walking distance to all shops and galleries. There are two units, each with refrigerator, wet bar, and coffee maker. The Queen's Wreath unit has a private bath, patio, a fireplace, microwave oven, electric range. The Jasmine unit has a private bath. Continental breakfast. No smoking or pets. Children welcome. Ten dollars per each additional guest. $80.

Tubac Country Inn

Corner Plaza and Burruel, P.O. Box 1540, 85646
(520) 398-3178

Visit the 75 art galleries, boutiques, and restaurants all within walking distance of the inn. Or drive a few minutes to shop in Mexico, or visit missions, museums, national parks, or play golf at one of seven

---

NOTES: Credit cards accepted: A MasterCard; B Visa; C American Express; D Discover; E Diner's Club; F Other; 2 Personal checks accepted; 3 Lunch available; 4 Dinner available; 5 Open all year; 6 Pets welcome;

courses within easy access. Or if quiet relaxation is what is desired, then sit on the patio and enjoy the sounds of the birds singing while the sun sets in the west. "Since we do not sell drinks you are encouraged to bring your own favorites."

Hosts: Jim and Ruth Goebel
Rooms: 4 (PB) $75-95
Continental Breakfast
Credit Cards: None
Notes: 2, 5, 7, 8, 9, 10, 11, 12

TUCSON

Adobe Rose Inn

940 North Olsen Avenue, 85719
(520) 318-4644; (800) 328-4122
FAX (520) 325-0055

Causal comfort best describes the atmosphere of this beautifully restored 1933 adobe home in a prestigious older neighborhood just two blocks from the University of Arizona. There are three charming, lodge-pole-furnished rooms in the main house, two which have cozy beehive fireplaces and stained-glass windows. There are also two private cottages that are ideally suited for the longer stay. All the rooms have cable TV and access to the very private bougainvillaea-draped swimming pool and hot tub.

Host: Diana Graham
Rooms: 5 (PB) $55-125
Full Breakfast
Credit Cards: A, B, C, D, F
Notes: 2, 5, 7, 9, 10, 11, 12, 13, 14

Arizona Trails Bed and Breakfast Reservation Service

P.O. Box 18998, Fountain Hills, 85269-8998
(602) 837-4284; (888) 799-4284
FAX (602) 816-4224
e-mail: aztrails@arizonatrails.com
www.arizonatrails.com

AZ 102. Enjoy the Spanish hacienda on 16 acres in the beautiful Tucson desert with spectacular views. Hiking trails and bird watching are favorites. Two suites and one private two-bedroom casita all with private baths, antique stoves/fireplaces, and kitchenettes. Decorated with Mexican influence and southwestern decor. Private courtyard with fountain and flowers. Two therapeutic outdoor hot tubs. Close to parks, attractions, restaurants, and shopping. Breakfast is served in the dining room each morning. Outdoor cats wander the property along with other desert wildlife. $95-135.

AZ 103. Southwestern home in a quiet desert neighborhood nestled on the threshold of the Catalina Mountains. Four rooms all with private baths and contemporary southwestern decor. All the rooms can sleep up to four comfortably. Enjoy the pool or spa and keep favorite snacks in the separate guest refrigerator that is available. Minutes to Tucson shops, restaurants, and other area attractions. Full breakfast. Children welcome. $100.

AZ 104. Enjoy the convenience of this downtown Tucson location in a nice neighborhood close to the bus line. One room with private bath and one suite which sleeps up to four with private bath; washer/dryer privileges for extended stays. An eclectic collection of art and artifacts from South America and Africa adds to the southwestern decor. Minutes to the university, shopping, and restaurants. Continental breakfast. $65.

AZ 118. Enjoy this lovely six-room inn built in 1933 and in the historic Sam Hughes neighborhood of Tucson. Just two blocks to the University of Arizona, shops, and restaurants. Three rooms all with private baths in the main house and three guest cottages with telephones and kitchenettes. Enjoy the pool and enclosed patio area, or watch color TV with cable in the privacy of own room. Some rooms include fireplaces. Southwestern breakfast served. $95-125.

7 No smoking; 8 Children welcome; 9 Social drinking allowed; 10 Tennis nearby; 11 Swimming nearby; 12 Golf nearby; 13 Skiing nearby; 14 May be booked through a travel agent; 15 Handicapped accessible.

AZ 120. This 1940s ranch-style home in central Tucson hosts three lovely guest rooms. This private setting is only minutes to shopping and restaurants and a neighboring small city park. Two rooms share one bath and the separate guest house has its own bath. Specialty of the house is breakfast with a southwestern twist and homemade mesquite-flour baked goods when available. $75-100.

AZ 126. Two-room bed and breakfast ideal for those who appreciate the outdoors and are train enthusiasts. Nestled in the desert of northwest Tucson, this bed and breakfast sits on a beautiful site with hiking trails and Indian ruins on the property. One room has a private bath across the hall. The other is a separate guest cottage across from the main house. There is a private patio, microwave, and Ben Franklin stove in the cottage. Full breakfast is served. $65-85.

AZ 140. Relax in the area of northwest Tucson at this lovely four-room bed and breakfast nestled in the glorious Tucson desert. All rooms have a private entrance, in-room refrigerators, cable TV, telephone, and private baths. The master suite also has a large sitting area and a two-person jetted tub. Cool off with a dip in the pool. Continental plus breakfast buffet is included in the rates. $80-100.

AZ 163. The main house features two rooms that combine for a family unit with hall bath featuring a sunken tub and shower. One room features a private bath and color cable TV. The Sonoran Suite (handicapped accessible) has a sitting area with sleeper sofa, microwave and mini-refrigerator, cable TV, and large bath area. The Eastlake Suite has a sitting area, two-person jetted tub and standup shower, microwave, refrigerator, and cable TV. Full breakfast. Relax by the pool, the spa, or try out the putting green. $95-165.

AZ 164. Guests will fall in love with this elegantly appointed bed and breakfast in central Tucson. It is near the center of town, but in a quiet residential area where guests feel away from it all surrounded by an acre plus of natural desert landscaping. Built in the 1940s, this house once belonged to a famous Western movie star. Four rooms all with separate guest entrances, color cable TV, private patio or balcony. Two suites also have sitting areas, microwaves, and mini-refrigerators. Enjoy the outdoor hot tub or linger in the sunny breakfast room. $85-135.

AZ 165. Relax in quiet and solitude at this four-room bed and breakfast. Great views of the Tucson Mounatins provide a perfect backdrop to the pool and spa area. Two rooms have fireplaces, private baths, and sitting areas with TV/VCR. Two rooms share a bath. Full breakfast is served. Close to Sonoran Desert Museum and Old Tucson Studios. $65-125.

AZ 168. This four-room bed and breakfst is close to shops, restaurants, and not far from the downtown historic district. Each room has a private bath. Two rooms upstairs share a common sitting room with TV/VCR and guest refrigerator. The two suites downstairs both have sitting areas with sleeper-sofas and TV/VCRs, and private baths. Relax by the pool or make use of the exercise room. A guest kitchen is also available for guests staying five nights or more. Full breakfast is served. Children of all ages are welcome. $85-105.

AZ 176. Escape the world and retreat to this two-room bed and breakfast overlooking Saguaro National Park Annex. Owned by an artist and photographer, original works of art decorate the rooms. Two guest rooms with full private baths. Relax in the common area with TV/VCR, library, wet bar, and great views. Full breakfast. $85-95.

NOTES: Credit cards accepted: A MasterCard; B Visa; C American Express; D Discover; E Diner's Club; F Other; 2 Personal checks accepted; 3 Lunch available; 4 Dinner available; 5 Open all year; 6 Pets welcome;

Bed and Breakfast Southwest Reservation Service

P.O. Box 51198, Phoenix, 85076-1198
(602) 947-9704; (800) 762-9704
FAX (602) 874-1316

133. Guest ranch with 16 spacious and intimate casitas, some with fireplaces and patios with views. Activities include swimming, croquet, shuffleboard, horseback riding, hiking, mountain biking, star gazing, and shopping Tubac and Nogales. Spa with hot tub, sauna, and massages. Restaurant serves lunch, dinner, and complimentary breakfast. Conference room available. Several golf courses are nearby. Smoking permitted. Children welcome. $85-175.

Casa Alegre Bed and Breakfast Inn

316 East Speedway, 85705
(520) 628-1800

This charming 1915 Craftsman-style home is between the University of Arizona and downtown Tucson. A scrumptious full breakfast is served in the formal dining room or poolside on the serene patio. Casa Alegre allows easy access to Tucson's many historical, cultural, and recreational attractions, state and national parks, as well as great shopping and fantastic eateries.

Host: Phyllis Florek
Rooms: 5 (PB) $70-105
Full Breakfast
Credit Cards: A, B, D
Notes: 2, 5, 7, 9, 10, 11, 12, 14

Car-Mar's Southwest Bed and Breakfast

6766 West Oklahoma, 85735
(520) 578-1730; (888) 578-1730
e-mail: CarMarBB@aol.com
www.members.aol.com/carmarbb/carmarbb.htm

Southwestern by design, close to popular attractions, such as Arizona-Sonora Desert Museum and Old Tucson Movie Studios.

Each room is uniquely decorated with lodgepole and saguaro rib furniture. Hot tub under the stars, poolside refreshments, and luxurious robes may be relished during guests' stay. Freshly baked treats at turndown. Full, scrumptious breakfast served in dining room or garden by request. Super Summer special in effect May 15 through August 31. (Buy two nights and get the third consecutive night free.)

Host: Carole Martinez
Rooms: 4 (2 PB; 2 SB) $65-125
Full Breakfast
Credit Cards: A, B
Notes: 2, 5, 7, 9, 10, 11, 12, 14

Casa Tierra Adobe Bed and Breakfast Inn

11155 West Calle Pima, 85743
(520) 578-3058; FAX (520) 578-8445
e-mail: casatier@azstarnet.com

Casa Tierra is on five acres of beautiful Sonoran Desert 30 minutes west of Tucson. This secluded area has hundreds of saguaro cacti, spectacular mountain views, and brilliant sunsets. The rustic adobe house features entryways with vaulted brick ceilings, an interior arched courtyard, Mexican furnishings, and a Jacuzzi overlooking the desert. Great hiking and bird watching. Near Arizona-Sonora Desert Museum, Saguaro National Park. Vegetarian breakfasts are served. Eco-sensitive. Rental house available.

Hosts: Karen and Lyle Hymer-Thompson
Rooms: 3 (PB) $85-95
Full Breakfast
Credit Cards: None
Notes: 2, 7, 8, 9

Catalina Park Inn

309 East First Street, 85705
(520) 792-4541; (800) 792-4885
FAX (502) 792-0838
www.catalinaparkinn.com

Exceptional architectural details abound in this elegant 1927 historic district jewel. Six guest rooms are smartly appointed sanctu-

Catalina Park Inn

Host: Gertrude M. Eich
Rooms: 6 (4 PB; 2 SB) $79-95
Full Breakfast
Credit Cards: None
Notes: 2, 5, 7, 10, 11, 12, 14

El Presidio Bed and Breakfast

297 North Main Street, 85701
(520) 623-6151; (800) 349-6151

A Victorian adobe, this inn is a splendid example of American-Territorial style and is listed in the National Register of Historic Places. In El Presidio historic district. Walk to the best restaurants, museums, and shopping. Guests enjoy true southwestern charm in spacious suites, two with kitchens that open onto large courtyards and gardens, fountains, and lush floral displays. A tranquil oasis with the ambiance of Old Mexico. Three-star rating from Mobil and AAA.

Host: Patti Toci
Rooms: 3 (PB) $95-115
Full Breakfast
Credit Cards: None
Notes: 2, 5, 7, 9, 10, 11, 12, 14

aries of privacy that combine time-tested comforts and modern conveniences. Savor the day while relaxing on own private porch or in the fragrant lush gardens. Each morning enjoy a glorious breakfast prepared and garnished with herbs and flowers from the garden. The superb central location is handy to many of Tucson's attractions. Recommended by Fodor's and Frommer's guidebook.

Hosts: Mark Hall and Paul Richard
Rooms: 6 (PB) $95-115
Full Breakfast
Credit Cards: A, B, D
Notes: 2, 5, 7, 9, 10, 11, 12, 14

Copper-Bell Bed and Breakfast

25 North Westmoreland Avenue, 85745
(520) 629-9229 (phone/FAX)

Copper Bell is a unique turn-of-the-century lava stone home which was built from 1907 to 1920 providing a unique blend of architectural styles. The owner, relocated here from Germany, has created the inn by combining the Old World with the New. Four of the six guest rooms have a private ground-level entry and are in separate guest houses. Each has a private bath and climate control. A private honeymoon suite is also available. Guests will enjoy the homemade German breakfast in the large and sunny dining room with beautiful stained-glass windows.

Hacienda Bed and Breakfast

5704 East Grant Road, 85712-2235
(520) 290-2224; (888) 236-4421 (outside Tucson)
FAX (520) 721-9066; e-mail: Hacienda97@aol.com
www.members.aol.com/hacienda97/index.html

Four quiet, air-conditioned rooms with private baths. Two rooms have TV/VCR, refrigerator, full-size Hide-a-Bed, and outside entrance. One is handicapped accessible with coffee maker and microwave. Two bedrooms share a sitting room with TV/VCR, private courtyard, barbecue, solar pool, spa, exercise room. Computer, fax, copier, fireproof file for valuables. No smoking. Supervised children are welcome. AAA-rated. Member of the Tucson Convention Bureau, the Chamber of Commerce, and AABBI.

Hosts: Barbara and Fred Shamseldin
Rooms: 4 (PB) $85-105
Full Breakfast
Credit Cards: A, B, C, D
Notes: 2, 5, 7, 9, 12, 14

NOTES: Credit cards accepted: A MasterCard; B Visa; C American Express; D Discover; E Diner's Club; F Other; 2 Personal checks accepted; 3 Lunch available; 4 Dinner available; 5 Open all year; 6 Pets welcome;

June's Bed and Breakfast

3212 West Holladay Street, 85746
(520) 578-0857

This Tucson mountain hideaway features a magnificent view and a friendly hostess who is an artist.

Host: June Henderson
Rooms: 3 (1 PB; 2 SB) $45-55
Continental Breakfast
Credit Cards: None
Notes: 2, 5, 7, 11, 12

La Posada Del Valle

1640 North Campbell Avenue, 85719
(520) 795-3840 (phone/FAX)

An elegant 1920s inn nestled in the heart of the city has five guest rooms with private baths and private entrances. Mature orange trees perfume the air as guests enjoy a gourmet breakfast and sip tea each afternoon on the patio overlooking the Santa Catalina Mountains. Children over eight are welcome. *Wir sprechen Deutsch.* Private off-street parking is available.

Hosts: Tom and Karin Dennen
Rooms: 5 (PB) $90-135
Full Breakfast
Credit Cards: A, B
Notes: 2, 5, 7, 9, 10, 11, 12, 13, 14

La Tierra Linda Guest Ranch Resort

7501 North Wade Road, 85743
(520) 744-7700; FAX (520) 579-9742

La Tierra Linda Guest Ranch Resort is in Tucson's picturesque western mountains, nestled at the base of Sombrero Peak. Originally built in the 1930s, this scenic 30-acre ranch is surrounded by an abundance of centuries old saguaro cacti, wildflowers, and lush desert vegetation. La Tierra Linda is adjacent to the 24,000-acre Saguaro National Park and near many of Tucson's popular attractions. The Wolfe family invites guests to step back in time and

La Tierra Linda Guest Ranch Resorrt

experience western hospitality and atmosphere at this family-run ranch. Continental plus breakfast.

Hosts: Mark and Francie Wolfe
Rooms: 16 (PB) $100-250
Continental Breakfast
Credit Cards: A, B, C, D
Notes: 2, 5, 7, 8, 9, 10, 11, 12, 13, 14, 15

Mi Casa Su Casa/Old Pueblo Homestays Bed and Breakfast Reservation Service

P.O. Box 950, Tempe, 85280-0950
(602) 990-0682; (800) 456-0682
FAX (602) 990-3390
e-mail: micasa@primenet.com
www.azres.com

5351. Built in 1886, this inn is convenient to shops, theaters, museums, and restaurants. The Carriage House has a living room/kitchen and private bath. In the main house, the Gate House suite has a living room/bedroom, Pullman kitchen, private bath, and private entrance. Two other guest rooms have private baths. Full gourmet breakfasts. Smoking outside. No resident pets. Children age 15 and older welcome. Two-night minimum stay with exception of the Carriage House, which has a three-night minimum stay. Weekly and monthly rates. $75-120.

7 No smoking; 8 Children welcome; 9 Social drinking allowed; 10 Tennis nearby; 11 Swimming nearby; 12 Golf nearby; 13 Skiing nearby; 14 May be booked through a travel agent; 15 Handicapped accessible.

Mi Casa Su Casa/Old Pueblo Homestays Bed and Breakfast Reservation Service (continued)

5352. Guests enjoy the private guest area in this Santa Fe-style patio home, built in 1993, in a quiet north central area with unobstructed views of the Catalina Mountains. Landscaped back yard with desert plantings and access to community pool. The guest room has a private hall bath. Guests are welcome in the living room with fireplace. Laundry privileges. Enclosed garage. Full breakfast. Smoking outside. Children over three welcome. $65.

5353. Warm, outgoing hostess welcomes guests to a delightfully restored Spanish Colonial two-story home built around 1900 in a quiet, well-kept neighborhood near the University of Arizona. On the first floor, room one has a private entrance, sitting area, and a private bath. Room two on the second floor shares the hall bath. Light kitchen privileges available. Near public transportation. Continental plus breakfast. No resident pets. Children welcome. $65-75.

5354. Near the University of Arizona is a 1915 Craftsman-style bungalow. The Hacienda Room and the Saguaro Room have en suite baths, and the Amethyst Room has a private hall bath. The Arizona Room offers a TV/VCR and opens onto the patio, swimming pool, and spa. The Buchanan House, next door, has two guest rooms with private baths. These can be individually occupied or rented as a suite. For the guests occupying the suite, there are a kitchen, dining room, and living room. Full breakfast. Inquire about accommodations for children. Smoking outside. $80-150.

5355. Built in 1928, this pre-Santa Fe home is in an older quiet neighborhood with a view of the Catalina Mountains. It is in a midtown location, three blocks north of the University of Arizona Medical Center and near shopping and theaters. The cottage has a private entrance, is decorated in eclectic Southwest, has one bedroom, bath with shower, living room, fully equipped kitchen, TV, private telephone, and small patio. Double futon in living room can be used for third person. Off-street parking. Weekly and monthly rates. $85.

5356. This adobe southwestern-style home with antiques, stained glass, tile, attractive gardens, patios, and pool surrounded by a six-foot wall in a quiet neighborhood east of the University of Arizona. Five guest rooms with private baths. Each room has cable TV. The hostess takes pride in her gourmet breakfast. Smoking permitted outside. Children over 12 are welcome. No pets. Prices included tax. $105.03-126.93.

5357. Built in the 1920s as a corner market, the adobe structure, in one of Tucson's historic barrios, is furnished with antiques and folk art. The great room has a fireplace, books, and music. Guests are invited to relax outside in an enclosed garden with well-established desert plants. The downtown arts district, Tucson Museum of Art, shops, restaurants, and the convention center are just blocks away. Two suites each have two bedrooms and each suite has a shared bath. The larger suite has a kitchen. Continental breakfast. Smoking permitted outside. Children welcome. No pets. Rates quoted are per bedroom occupancy. $65-75.

5359. This gracious southwestern inn in the early Santa Fe style was built in 1929. It is within walking distance of the University of Arizona and its medical center. All rooms offer a private outside entrance and private bath. Two suites are available, one with kitchenette. A gourmet breakfast and afternoon tea are served. Hosts speak English and German. Children welcome. No smoking or pets. $90-125.

5360. Just minutes from downtown, the University of Arizona, and the medical center is this beautifully restored Victorian home built in 1905. Three beautifully decorated rooms (one in the main house, and two in a 1917 bungalow adjacent to it which includes a living room) have private baths. Each of two two-bedroom guest houses has a living room, dining area, full kitchen, laundry, private patio, telephone, and TV. A one-bedroom apartment for monthly rental does not include breakfast. A gourmet breakfast is served, but special dietary needs can be provided with advance notice. Smoking permitted outside. Children welcome. No pets. $78-165.

5361. A warm welcome is provided at this quiet home filled with period antiques. The guest room has an antique vanity, TV, radio, telephone, air conditioning, rocking chair, and private hall bath with whirlpool tub. Delight in a tastefully prepared breakfast in a charming dining area or on the front patio with mountain view. High tea can be served in the late afternoon, if desired. No smoking, children, or pets. $65-70.

5362. This 1940s family ranch, with Saltillo tile throughout, is convenient to sightseeing, restaurants, shopping, and recreation. A spacious living room with fireplace offers relaxing diversions. Two guest rooms share a Mexican tiled bath. A guest house offers a yard, patio, and Mexican tiled private shower bath. Full gourmet breakfast served. Picnics can be arranged on request. Cat in residence. Open September through May and by special arrangement in the summer. Discount stays of three or more nights. No smoking or pets. Inquire about accommodations for children. Ten dollars for extra guests. $65-100.

5401. Guests are welcome to use common room with cable TV, VCR, and fireplace. Light kitchen privileges, grill, outside spa, laundry facilities, and cordless telephones in rooms. The Quail's Nest honeymoon suite has views, private patio, TV, fireplace, and private bath with double tub. The Cactus Wren has views, private hall bath with whirlpool tub, and TV. Rollaway and cot available for small additional fee. Continental plus and full breakfasts. Inquire about accommodations for children. Smoking outside. Resident pets. Handicapped accessible. Two-night minimum. $75-95.

5402. Delightful, gracious hostess welcomes guests to this beautiful, spacious adobe-style home in fashionable north Tucson. Very private extra-large room has a private entrance, a sofa, TV, and a small refrigerator. Bath with shower. Sliding glass doors lead to private patio and unheated pool. Continental plus breakfast provided. Two-night stay preferred. A child over 10 welcome. Maximum number: two guests. No pets. Smoking outside. $80.

5403. This handsome two-level home in the Catalina foothills is in a quiet neighborhood which has views of majestic mountains and the city. Guests have a private entrance from the large pool/patio area into a large guest living room, dining and kitchen area. In the living room is a private telephone, TV/VCR, fireplace, and small library with books and brochures. On each side of the living room are two guest rooms with private baths. For guests' use, there is a large refrigerator, microwave, toaster, coffee maker, and dishes. Smoking restricted. No pets. Children over eight who can swim welcome. Full breakfast. $70.

5404. A getaway in a quiet northwest neighborhood below the Catalina Mountain cliffs. Nearby are golf, a state park, restaurants, and a health club. Guests can relax on the patio, in the spa, or in the solar-heated pool. This Territorial home provides a large entryway living room with fireplace and cable TV. Private and shared baths. Full

Mi Casa Su Casa/Old Pueblo Homestays Bed and Breakfast Reservation Service (continued)

breakfast served. Smoking permitted outside. Inquire about accommodations for children. No pets. $65-85.

5405. A spectacular view of the mountains and the city can be enjoyed from a quiet patio at this accommodation. Three rooms, all light and cheerful, are tastefully furnished with cherry and walnut antiques, oriental rugs, telephones, a TV on request, and private baths. Two bedrooms have a private entrance and Jacuzzi. A full gourmet breakfast served. Open September through June. Smoking outside. Children 12 and older welcome. Pets welcome. $50-95.

5406. This ranch home is five miles north of Tucson. The bunkhouse room has a loft that can sleep four and has a private hall bath with tub, shower, and double sinks. Two other rooms share a bath with a whirlpool tub. All rooms feature ceiling fans and cable TV/VCR. Guests have choice of a Continental or a full sit-down special breakfast served between 8:30 and 9:30 A.M. Hosts speak Spanish and will pick guests up at the airport. Smoking permitted outside. Children over 12 welcome. No pets. $95-110.

5409. At the base of the Catalina Mountains, this cozy suite has easy access to shops, restaurants, and the University of Arizona. The suite consists of a TV, private bath, private entrance, and a kitchenette that includes a microwave, toaster oven, and mini-refrigerator. Enjoy the views of the mountains from the front patio with a fountain or the city lights at night while relaxing in the pool or spa. The refrigerator is stocked with ingredients for a Continental plus breakfast. Resident dog. No smoking.

Inquire about accommodations for pets and children. $75-80.

5451. Large stucco home built in 1990 in a resort community north of Tucson. Available are a club house with its own restaurant, tennis courts, 9- and 18-hole golf course, two heated swimming pools, driving range, and health club with spa. Guests have private use of the living room with fireplace, dining room, and den. Room one has a private full bath in the hall. Room two has a sofa bed for additional members of the party and shares the hall bath. Full breakfast. Children welcome with children's rates. Guest pets welcome by arrangement. Smoking permitted. Weekly rates available. Closed May 1 through October 1. $75.

5452. This guest house has mountain and city views. On the porch of the guest house, guests overlook a beautifully landscaped tropical yard with a pool, Jacuzzi, and waterfall. One hour to skiing on Mount Lemmon in season. The guest house has air conditioning and heating, a living room with cable TV, bath with shower, telephone, and kitchen. An outside gas grill is available. A mountain bike and a 10-speed bike available. Continental plus breakfast. Smoking restricted. No pets. Infants welcome and children who are swimmers. Three-night minimum. Weekly rates. $95.

5454. Casual southwestern Territorial-style home in a natural desert setting on four acres. The main house and guest cottage are separated by a patio. The guest cottage has a private entrance, private bath, refrigerator, TV, telephone, library of bird and western lore, private patio, pool, and spa. There is a smaller room in the main house with a private full bath in the hall. Full ranch breakfast. Children two and older welcome. Smoking outside. Ten dollars additional for children. Horses boarded. $55-75.

5455. This spacious Territorial adobe home is on three acres on the far northeast side of Tucson. Two guest rooms are in a private wing of the house. Each has a private hall bath, and a sitting room with TV, writing desk, and reading material is shared by both. Pool. Washer/dryer. The breakfast menu caters to low-cholesterol, low-fat, and gluten-free diets, but not exclusively. By special request, a picnic lunch is available as well as a quiet, romantic dinner. No smoking. Children welcome. Inquire about pets. $65-75.

5456. This modern adobe brick home has a large nonsmoking suite that can either be a one- or a two-bedroom accommodation with a living room and private bath. Both rooms have private entrances. Relax by the pool, in a large hammock, or enjoy walking, hiking, and bird watching. For guests' convenience there is a microwave oven, barbecue grill, TV, a theater organ, and lots of books. Continental breakfast served, plus complimentary fresh fruit, coffee, and tea are available 24 hours a day. No smoking. Children over 12 welcome. Inquire about accommodations for pets. $70-90.

5460. This brick home with Mexican and oriental influence is in a quiet neighborhood. Enjoy the mountain and desert views, private walled gardens, hammock, pool, and spa. The oversized recreational room has a Ping-Pong table, minitrampoline, TV/VCR, dumbbells, and recliner and sectional sofa which opens into a queen-size bed. Two bedrooms share a hall bath with double sink, tub, and shower. Terry-cloth robes for adult guests. Telephone in each room and TV/VCR upon request. No smoking. Inquire about accommodations for children. Pets are welcome. $75-80.

5461. This newly constructed air-conditioned home is nestled on the threshold of the Catalina Mountains. It offers two large rooms with sleeper-sofas, a sitting area, cable TV, telephone, private bath, and private entrance. A smaller room has cable TV, telephone, and private bath. All rooms share a refrigerator in the hall. Relax by the pool and spa. Full breakfast. Add $10 per day to heat the pool. No smoking or pets. Children welcome for an additional charge. $70-100.

5462. This spacious new southwestern contemporary home sits on six acres of beautiful Sonoran Desert. The guest suite has a private bath, a sitting room with TV, telephone, and opens onto a private adjoining patio. The Sabino Canyon recreation area is minutes away, as are hiking and riding trails, golf courses, and many exceptional restaurants. Stereo, TV, and VCR. A full or Continental breakfast catering to guests' special dietary needs is served. No children, pets, or smoking. $55-75.

5464. A miniranch on five acres in a quiet, safe neighborhood is just minutes away from Sabino Canyon. This solid adobe brick Mission-tiled ranch house with unheated pool has two guest suites. One room is a spacious two-room suite with fireplace and private full bath. The other room has a sleigh bed and large full bath. Full breakfast. Smoking outside. Inquire about accommodations for children. Pets welcome. $75-85.

5501. Quiet neighborhood is within walking distance of park mall, restaurants, theaters. Two guest rooms both have double beds, one with bath and shower en suite, the other with shared full hall bath. Guests welcome to watch cable TV in den or use the living room or back yard. Dog and cat in residence. Hostess offers choice of breakfast. Public transportation nearby. Two-night minimum stay. No smoking. No pets. Children over 12 welcome. $60.

5502. This bed and breakfast is in a quiet eastside neighborhood within walking distance of a supermarket, bus stop, and

7 No smoking; 8 Children welcome; 9 Social drinking allowed; 10 Tennis nearby; 11 Swimming nearby; 12 Golf nearby; 13 Skiing nearby; 14 May be booked through a travel agent; 15 Handicapped accessible.

Mi Casa Su Casa/Old Pueblo Homestays Bed and Breakfast Reservation Service (continued)

restaurants. The predominantly southwestern decor includes African and American Indian carvings. The air-conditioned suite has a private entrance, private bath, an off-the-wall bed, microwave, refrigerator, washer/dryer, and sitting room with a trundle bed. Another room in the main residence includes a private bath. Continental plus breakfast served. Open October through May. No smoking. Children over four welcome. Small pets welcome. Rates are slightly higher during the Tucson International Gem and Mineral Show. $65-85.

5503. Two-story inn has many extras which include a heated pool, spa, patio, exercise room, covered parking, fax, copier, computer, and telephones. On the first floor are two rooms, one of which is handicapped accessible. They have private baths and entrances. four guest rooms are on the second floor and each pair of rooms has its own living room. One pair of rooms has a shared bath. In the first great room there are a fireplace and areas for visiting, reading, or TV/VCR. In the second great room, a patio and kitchen are available for small weddings and conferences. Full breakfasts included in rates for short stays. No smoking or pets. Infants and children over 10 who can swim are welcome. Seasonal, weekly, and monthly rates available. $65-105.

5504. This bed and breakfast is near Saguaro National Park East. Amenities include a lighted tennis practice area, nature trail, garden courtyard, patio with fire pot, and pool (summer only). A private casita nesting near the main house offers an off-the-wall bed with desk, sofa bed, TV, telephone, radio, full bath, full kitchen, and private entrance. The refrigerator is stocked

with ingredients for a full breakfast. Also in the main house is a room with a private bath. Smoking permitted outside. Inquire about accommodations for children and pets. Ten dollars for each additional guest. $70-85.

5551. This trilevel French chateau-style home is a mile from Saguaro National Park East on three acres. It offers unobstructed views of the beautiful Sonoran Desert, a private courtyard, and convenience to shopping, restaurants, and local points of interest. A separate apartment offers a living room with sofa bed, TV/VCR, radio, telephone, private dining area, full kitchen stocked for a Continental plus breakfast, and full bath. A room in the main house offers a TV/VCR, radio, and private hall full bath. English, French, German, and Spanish spoken. Smoking permitted on the patio only. Children over 12 welcome. Ten dollars for each additional guest. No pets. $60-85.

5552. An adobe hideaway providing the flavor of Old Mexico near Saguaro National Park East. Its restful environment is perfect for bird watchers, hikers, and nature lovers. Both guest rooms have an informal country-Territorial flavor, ornate antique heating stoves, kitchenettes, TV/VCR, private entrances, private baths, and shared spa. A two-bedroom casita has a full kitchen with washer/dryer, saguaro-ribbed ceiling, Saltillo tile floors in the living room, kitchen, full bath, a wood-burning stove, TV/VCR, air conditioning, and a spa. Continental plus breakfast. Smoking permitted outside. Children welcome. Fifteen dollars per extra guest. No pets. $80-130.

5553. This lovely hacienda is on six acres of Sonoran Desert near Saguaro National Park East. High tea is served by the pool or in the great room by a roaring fire. In the library is a cable TV, stereo, and a baby grand piano that overlooks the pool and spa. The suite features a bedroom with fireplace, a sitting room with TV and stereo system and fireplace, large bath, and private entrance to both the pool and the courtyard. Another room has a private hall bath. Full breakfast with natural whole foods. Available for special occasions, business meetings, and retreats. Complimentary horse facilities are also available. Arrangements can be made for a licensed massage therapist. Children over 10 are welcome. No smoking or pets. $65-125.

5651. This bed and breakfast lies amidst the quiet Sonoran Desert with courtyards and pathways accentuated by native landscaping and wildlife feeders. It offers the perfect setting for small weddings and parties as well as a retreat from a fast-paced life. Amenities include a pool, spa, TV/VCR, refrigerator, microwave, barbecue, and patio. Four suites are each uniquely decorated using saguaro rib furniture designed and built by the hostess. A special heart-healthy full breakfast is provided on request. Smoking permitted outside. Inquire about accommodations for children. No pets. $65-125.

5702. This working ranch was originally built in the early 1900s. Heated pool and indoor redwood hot tub. Children enjoy the petting zoo. Rates include three meals, hayrides, and all ranch activities per person. There are 29 units, all with private baths and air conditioning. Some deluxe suites have fireplaces and whirlpool tubs. Rollaway beds available. Laundry facilities. Families are welcome. No smoking in dining room. Free airport transportation. Closed May 1 through October 1. Four-night minimum. Weekly rates. Children welcome. Seventy-nine dollars for third person in room. $97-159.

5703. This adobe house offers three guest rooms with private baths. All guests have access to a small refrigerator, barbecue, and microwave oven. Each room has its own private entrance, private patio, and opens into the common courtyard. Enjoy relaxing in the spa under the desert sky. The area is great for hiking and bird watching. Mornings begin with freshly ground coffee, a variety of teas, and a full breakfast, including home-baked goods. Two resident cats, two dogs, and one tortoise live outside on property. Two-night minimum. Smoking permitted outside. Children welcome. No pets. $75-95.

5704. This comfortable home is on a cul-de-sac in a quiet neighborhood three miles from the University of Arizona and close to a bus stop, a beautiful park, golf, and driving range. The attractive guest room has a TV, radio, telephone, and private hall bath. There are limited kitchen and laundry privileges. Continental breakfast served, although a full breakfast can be requested for an additional $5 per person. Smoking permitted outside. No children or pets. $45-55.

5705. This southwestern-style home is on 10 acres in the heart of the Tucson Mountains and on the edge of Saguaro National Park West, 30 minutes from downtown Tucson. The home has high ceilings, tile floors, a large Arizona room, satellite TV, and several fireplaces to create an inviting environment. Both guest rooms have private entrances, share a large shower bath, and have coffee makers. The second room can be blocked to have a private bath. Continental plus breakfast served. A full breakfast can be requested for an additional $5 per person. Smoking permitted outside. Inquire about accommodations for children. $70-80.

5751. Attached but separate architect-designed, very large, charming guest cottage with private patio is in the Catalina Mountain foothills. Living room/bedroom

Mi Casa Su Casa/Old Pueblo Homestays Bed and Breakfast Reservation Service (continued)

has fireplace and large private bath. Private telephone. Full kitchen. For short stays, the kitchen is stocked, and guests serve themselves during the week. Full breakfasts are served on the weekends. Inquire about accommodations for children. Two-night minimum on weekends. Resident dog in main house. Smoking outside. Add $10 for one-night stay. Weekly rate available. Possible handicapped accessibility. Swedish spoken. $90.

5752. Guests experience living in a Santa Fe-style, environmentally designed, passive solar, rammed earth and adobe home with walls 27-inches thick, offering a panoramic view of the ever-changing Catalina Mountains in a quiet desert setting where wildlife abounds. Amenities include use of the laundry facilities, swim stream hot tub, TV, VCR, and CD. Light snacks can be kept in the home kitchen. Two rooms share a bath. Another room includes a fireplace, private bath, and private entrance. Continental breakfast. Hostess has two small dogs. Smoking permitted outside. No children. No pets. $65-85.

5753. This luxurious Spanish hacienda is nestled on six acres in the Tucson Mountains and is close to Saguaro National Park West, Sanctuary Cove, and hiking and walking trails. Amenities include a pool, spa, and use of the Arizona room with fireplace and baby grand piano. A horse corral is available. The main house has three guest rooms with private baths. A large separate apartment is also available. Continental plus breakfast served. Add $10 per day to heat spa. Smoking permitted outside. Inquire about accommodations for pets. Children welcome. $65-175.

5754. One of the original properties in the Orange Grove homes built in the 1930s, the guest cottage was refurbished by the architect-owner and his wife. Air conditioning and heat. The cottage has Saltillo-tile floors with inset carpet in the living room and bedroom. The roomy living room has a fireplace, cable TV, and private telephone. Private bath with shower. A roll-away bed and crib available. The Pullman-style kitchen is completely equipped. Kitchen stocked with Continental plus breakfast. Guests are welcome to swim in the pool in season. Ten dollars for third person. One-night stay add $10. Special summer rates. $95.

5755. Hacienda de Raphael is a spacious, southwestern-style home. The guest wing has a large bedroom, separate den, and private hall bath with tub and shower. The separate den has cable TV, VCR, telephone, and writing desk. Near restaurants, two shopping malls, golf, tennis, hiking trails, horseback riding, and bird watching trails. Gourmet breakfast. No smoking, pets, or children. $85.

5756. This spacious three-story home, 10 miles from downtown Tucson, features antiques and has a cable TV. It boasts tile floors, attractive desert landscaping, patio, spa, and solar-heated pool. A separate guest house has two bedrooms that share a bath, a spacious living room with a sofa bed, and full kitchen. Main house has four guest rooms with private and shared baths. Full breakfast. Smoking permitted outside. Inquire about accommodations for children. No pets. $45-125.

5757. This secluded two-story adobe and rock ranch house, built in 1931, is on 30 acres. The house contains a library, baby grand piano, fireplace, TV, telephone, dining room, three guest rooms, and a suite on the top level. Separate from the main

NOTES: Credit cards accepted: A MasterCard; B Visa; C American Express; D Discover; E Diner's Club; F Other; 2 Personal checks accepted; 3 Lunch available; 4 Dinner available; 5 Open all year; 6 Pets welcome;

house is a large casita containing seven rooms all with private baths and entrances. There is also a back-to-back casita containing two suites; both have private baths and entrances. Other amenities include a heated swimming pool and spa, large patio, shaded hammocks, and hiking and walking trails. Full breakfast. Lunch and dinner also available at an additional cost. A variety of meeting rooms is available for seminars, as well as indoor and outdoor locations for reunions and weddings. Arrangements for additional meals for group events may be made. Smoking permitted outside. Children welcome. No pets. $100-150.

5758. This ranch-style home with desert landscaping is 10 miles from downtown Tucson. The spacious home has a patio, spa, pool, and Arizona room with guest kitchen facilities. The living room warms guests with a fireplace and entertains with cable TV. The suite has a private entrance with outside sitting area, cable TV, and a large two-person sunken tub with shower. One guest room boasts a private entrance, tile floor, cable TV, and full bath. Three other rooms share two full hall baths. A self-served Continental breakfast is provided. Dog on premises. Open October through June. Smoking permitted outside. Inquire about accommodations for children. No pets. Add $10 per day to heat spa. $55-80.

5759. This bed and breakfast is nestled deep in the Tucson Mountains. It is within walking distance of Saguaro National Park West in an area known for its vegetation, mountains, and desert landscapes, 20 minutes from downtown Tucson, and 18 miles from the airport. Outdoors is a pavilion and barbecue area (which can accommodate reunions or gatherings), hiking and walking trails, and horse facilities. Five private adobe casitas each offer covered parking space, either complete kitchens or kitchenettes, fireplaces, air conditioning,

TV/VCR, stereo, and a refrigerator stocked with ingredients for a Continental breakfast. Hosts speak English and Greek. Smoking is permitted outside only. Children welcome. Inquire about accommodations for pets. $175.

5760. This ranch home on a secluded acre surrounded by citrus, pine, and desert trees is in what used to be an orange grove estate and is convenient to the University of Arizona, downtown, shops, and restaurants. Amenities include a pool, spa, barbecue, cable TV, newspaper, and piano. The guest room has a private bath, radio, and refrigerator and opens onto a patio/pool area. Continental plus breakfast. A dachshund and a cat are owned by the host. Smoking permitted outside. No children or pets. $85.

5761. A large adobe ranch-style home at the foothills on four desert landscaped acres in the Tucson Mountains, yet just minutes from shopping, dining, and sights rich in history and culture. Three rooms with private entrances, private bath, cable TV, small refrigerator, and coffee maker. The master room can be combined with a twin-size room to make a suite. Relax in the spacious Grand Room, on the patio, or by the pool. A high energy Continental breakfast served. Smoking permitted outside. Inquire about accommodations for children and pets. $70-95.

5762. This bed and breakfast in Tucson's northwestern area is convenient to restaurants, shops, and excellent golf courses. All guest rooms share a sitting room with fireplace and TV/VCR. A refrigerator, coffee pot, and exercise bicycle are available in the Arizona rooms. A large room offers a private shower bath, TV, telephone, radio alarm clock, and dresser. One other room shares a bath. Also a guest house with two guest rooms and private baths share a sitting room and kitchenette. Full breakfast.

7 No smoking; 8 Children welcome; 9 Social drinking allowed; 10 Tennis nearby; 11 Swimming nearby; 12 Golf nearby; 13 Skiing nearby; 14 May be booked through a travel agent; 15 Handicapped accessible.

Smoking is permitted outside. Children over 10 are welcome. No pets. $55-85.

5763. This 1996 southwestern hacienda-style home with center courtyard brings back the flavor of Old Mexico. Each of the spacious rooms has a private outside entrance, covered patio, TV, telephone, and full bath. Guests have access to a library, games, and laundry facilities. A full or Continental breakfast at guests' request, plus a snack bar with drinks, fruits, and goodies are available. Will cater to vegetarian diets. Smoking is permitted outside only. Sorry, pets and children cannot be accommodated. $75-85.

5764. This working miniature horse operation is only minutes away from the Arizona-Sedona Desert Museum, Avra Valley Airport and Skydiving Center, Saguaro National Park West, and a photo-op astride Pecos, a 2,400-pound Brahma bull. Relax in a mobile home with a private bath, a kitchen/dining/living room with air conditioning, cable TV, and sofa bed. Continental breakfast provided, or for $8 a full cowboy steak breakfast. A real cook-out with campfire and cowboy yarns available for $16. English and Spanish spoken. No smoking or pets. Children over 12 welcome. $75-85.

5765. An intimate ranch nestled in the mountains offers 23 rooms, all with individual air conditioning and private full bath. Rates include three meals, horseback riding daily, airport transfers, and use of ranch facilities, such as the swimming pool and spa, lighted tennis courts, shuffleboard, horseshoe courts, Ping-Pong, billiards, library, bar, piano, and TV/VCR. Activities include cookouts, hayrides, picnic rides, western dancing, and sightseeing. Golf courses are nearby. Fifteen percent gratuity will be added. Three-night minimum stay required. Smoking permitted. Children are

welcome. Extra guest $25-85. No pets. Seasonal rates. $115-300.

Natural Bed and Breakfast

3150 East Presidio Road, 85716
(520) 881-4582

At Natural Bed and Breakfast, the word "natural" is true in all senses of the word. Attention is paid to a natural, non-toxic, and non-allergenic environment. For example, this home is water cooled rather than air conditioned, and only natural foods are served. Shoes are not worn inside. The natural home environment is very nurturing. Professional massages are available. Guests are invited to share the large, homey living room with fireplace. "You'll feel at home."

Host: Marc Haberman
Rooms: 3 (2 PB; 1 SB) $55-65
Full Breakfast
Credit Cards: None
Notes: 2, 3, 4, 5, 7, 8, 10, 11, 12, 13, 14

Rincon Valley

Rincon Valley Bed and Breakfast

7080 South Camino Loma Alta, 85747
(520) 647-3335; e-mail: valleyretreat@theriver.com
www.personal.riverusers.com/~valleyretreat/

Retreat to the two and one-half acres where the stars at night are unbelievably vivid, and the howl of coyotes can be heard on the rise, then greet the morning with the tunes of wonderful birds of many types. Enjoy the sight of the abundant wildlife, where even an occasional bobcat can add extra spice to the stay. A visit here includes hearty breakfasts with good health in mind. Sharon cooks with organic produce, whole grains, and eggs from cage-free chickens. Homemade treats with coffee and tea are served in the afternoon.

Hosts: Larry and Sharon Wilson
Rooms: 2 (PB) $85-95
Full Breakfast
Credit Cards: A, B
Notes: 2, 5, 7, 9

The Swedish Guest House Bed and Breakfast

941 West Calle Dadivoso, 85704
(520) 742-6490; FAX (520) 544-9382
e-mail: swhouse941@aol.com

At the beginning of the Catalina foothills, this spacious guest house offers 1,100-square-foot quarters. Amenities include fireplace, telephone with private number, TV, radio, air conditioning, parking in garage, private patio overlooking the swimming pool. Plush bathroom has bathtub and an extra-large shower. Nearby are golf courses, hiking, horseback riding. Eighteen minutes from the University of Arizona. Hosts are transplanted Swedes from Stockholm and Tucson residents since 1977. Full breakfast served on weekends only. Breakfast is self-serve during the week. *Välkommen*!

Hosts: Lars and Florence Ejrup
Guest house: 1 (PB) $90
Full Breakfast
Credit Cards: None
Notes: 5, 7, 9, 11, 12, 14

The Swedish Guest House

TUMACACORI

Mi Casa Su Casa/Old Pueblo Homestays Bed and Breakfast Reservation Service

P.O. Box 950, Tempe, 85280-0950
(602) 990-0682; (800) 456-0682
FAX (602) 990-3390
e-mail: micasa@primenet.com
www.azres.com

5261. This bed and breakfast was constructed in the 1920s and served as a grocery store, post office, and gathering place until the 1960s. It is adjacent to a design studio featuring work by regional artists and is near Tumacacori National Historical Park and the ruins of an old Spanish colonial mission. The south wing consists of a breakfast/sitting room with small refrigerator, bedroom, TV, sleeping alcove, private shower bath, private entrance, and patio. A full breakfast is served. Host owns a cat. Children are welcome. Extra guest an additional $20. No smoking. Sorry, not guest pets. $50-65.

WICKENBURG

Mi Casa Su Casa/Old Pueblo Homestays Bed and Breakfast Reservation Service

P.O. Box 950, Tempe, 85280-0950
(602) 990-0682; (800) 456-0682
FAX (602) 990-3390
e-mail: micasa@primenet.com
www.azres.com

5801. This ranch, circa 1926, is listed in both the state and national historic registers. The handmade adobe buildings are snuggled near the Hassayampa River, and the food is worth a letter home. Three meals a day are included, and guests can choose from a variety of lodging choices. Horseback riding and heated pool. Accommodations for 20 guests. Open October 15 through April 30.

7 No smoking; 8 Children welcome; 9 Social drinking allowed; 10 Tennis nearby; 11 Swimming nearby; 12 Golf nearby; 13 Skiing nearby; 14 May be booked through a travel agent; 15 Handicapped accessible.

Two-night minimum stay is required until February 15. Four-night minimum after February 15. $225-240.

WILLCOX

Mi Casa Su Casa/Old Pueblo Homestays Bed and Breakfast Reservation Service

P.O. Box 950, Tempe, 85280-0950
(602) 990-0682; (800) 456-0682
FAX (602) 990-3390
e-mail: micasa@primenet.com
www.azres.com

5811. This bed and breakfast is a large eastern Colonial-style home near Willcox on 70 acres. The guest suite offers a private bath, private entrance, air conditioning, TV, and kitchenette with hot plate, coffee maker, and refrigerator. Two rooms each have a bed and sofa bed in bedroom and share a bathroom and sitting room with TV, books, and magazines. Continental plus breakfast. No smoking or pets. Children over two welcome. Ten dollars per each additional guest. $60-80.

WILLIAMS

Arizona Trails Bed and Breakfast Reservation Service

P.O. Box 18998, Fountain Hills, 85269-8998
(602) 837-4284; (888) 799-4284
FAX (602) 816-4224
e-mail: aztrails@arizonatrails.com
www.arizonatrails.com

AZ 141. Treat oneself to a grand experience at this five-room inn in Williams—the town closest to the Grand Canyon. Luxury abounds at this great hillside retreat. Work out in the exercise room, then take a dip in the outdoor patio spa. Relax with dinner in the dining room (extra charge) and play billiards after dinner in the entertainment room. Each morning guests will be treated to a gourmet breakfast and fantastic views of the surrounding landscape. All rooms have cable TV/VCR, CD players, and private baths. $85-165.

AZ 178. Visit this log-cabin-style bed and breakfast with four guest rooms in the pines of historic Williams. Just minutes to the Grand Canyon Railroad and area shopping. Two rooms have a fireplace, one has a whirlpool jetted tub, and all four have private baths. Socialize in the parlor area and enjoy a delicious full breakfast each morning. Sit on the front porch and watch the stars from one of the rockers or relax out back in the barbecue gazebo. $90-120.

Bed and Breakfast Southwest Reservation Service

P.O. Box 51198, Phoenix, 85076-1198
(602) 947-9704; (800) 762-9704
FAX (602) 874-1316

165. On two secluded acres in the historic mountain town of Williams and surrounded by tall pines, this beautiful bed and breakfast offers four guest rooms and one family suite, all with private baths. All rooms are elegantly decorated and have a TV, VCR, and CD player/stereo. Complimentary happy hour in the entertainment room. Delicious gourmet breakfast served. Hot tub, patio, several decks, billiards, and work-out rooms. Close to Grand Canyon and Grand Canyon Railroad. No smoking. Children welcome. $85-185.

Mi Casa Su Casa/Old Pueblo Homestays Bed and Breakfast Reservation Service

P.O. Box 950, Tempe, 85280-0950
(602) 990-0682; (800) 456-0682
FAX (602) 990-3390
e-mail: micasa@primenet.com
www.azres.com

NOTES: Credit cards accepted: A MasterCard; B Visa; C American Express; D Discover; E Diner's Club; F Other; 2 Personal checks accepted; 3 Lunch available; 4 Dinner available; 5 Open all year; 6 Pets welcome;

4187. This bed and breakfast is in a town where a steam train travels to the Grand Canyon every day of the year. Other areas to visit are Sunset and Meteor Craters, Oak Creek Canyon, and ski slopes. This two-story host-built log home has four elegantly and individually furnished rooms on the first floor with private baths featuring claw-foot tubs, antiques, and country furniture. One room has a day bed, which can accommodate two extra persons and another has a fireplace. A full breakfast is served in the dining room. Handicapped accessible. Smoking permitted outside. Children are welcome. Extra guests are an additional $15. No pets. $60-110.

5821. Built in 1988, this three-story home is in the pines within walking distance of downtown. On the first floor is the Juniper Room with private full bath. For a family, it can be combined with the Ponderosa Room. The Oakwood Room has a private entrance and bath with shower. On the second floor is the Rosewood Room with a large marble bath with soaking tub and separate shower, fireplace, and wet bar. The Cottonwood Room has a marble bath with tub/shower. Hot tub on patio. Full breakfast. Smoking outside. Inquire about accommodations for children and pets. $85-185.

5822. There are four sizable guest rooms, all on the first floor, with comfortable country-Victorian decor and private baths. Full breakfast. Cat in residence. No smoking, no alcohol, no pets. Children welcome. Possible handicapped accessibility. Less in winter season. Additional persons $15 each. $110.

WINKELMAN

Arizona Trails Bed and Breakfast Reservation Service

P.O. Box 18998, Fountain Hills, 85269-8998
(602) 837-4284; (888) 799-4284
FAX (602) 816-4224
e-mail: aztrails@arizonatrails.com
www.arizonatrails.com

AZ 167. Escape to the solitude and beauty of this natural setting just outside Arvaipa Canyon Wilderness area. Two rooms with private entrances, kitchenettes, and fireplaces. Outdoor patios and barbecue areas. The package includes all three meals with breakfast served in the room, a picnic lunch and dinner in the main house. Great for bird watching, hiking, or just relaxing. $200.

Mi Casa Su Casa/Old Pueblo Homestays Bed and Breakfast Reservation Service

P.O. Box 950, Tempe, 85280-0950
(602) 990-0682; (800) 456-0682
FAX (602) 990-3390
e-mail: micasa@primenet.com
www.azres.com

5831. Perfect for the traveler seeking a rural regenerative experience abundant with wildlife and absent the modern conveniences. Each of the two guest houses have a private shower bath, and rustic, country furnishings. Outdoor barbecue and sitting area. Rates include three delicious meals with local organically grown produce. A dog and flock of sheep share the farm. Smoking outside. Inquire about children being welcome. No pets. $200.

---

7 No smoking; 8 Children welcome; 9 Social drinking allowed; 10 Tennis nearby; 11 Swimming nearby; 12 Golf nearby; 13 Skiing nearby; 14 May be booked through a travel agent; 15 Handicapped accessible.

California

California

Silver Spur Bed and Breakfast

44625 Silver Spur Trail, 93601
(559) 683-2896

The Silver Spur Bed and Breakfast is nestled in the Sierra Nevadas of California, just off historic Highway 49. Key to the California gold country and the south and west gates of famed Yosemite National Park, it is only minutes from many outdoor sports. It features beautiful, clean rooms with private baths and entrances and comfortable beds and is tastefully decorated in American Southwest. Outdoor rest and dining areas boast outstanding Sierra views. Come enjoy Yosemite, and be treated to old-fashioned hospitality and great value.

Hosts: Patty and Bryan Hays
Rooms: 2 (PB) $60
Continental Breakfast
Credit Cards: A, B, D
Notes: 2, 5, 7, 8, 9, 11, 12, 13

ALBION

Albion River Inn

P.O. Box 100, 95410
(707) 937-1919; (800) 479-7944
e-mail: ari@mcn.org; www.albionriverinn.com

On the ocean, six miles south of the historic town of Mendocino, this romantic clifftop inn, on 10 acres of coastal bluffs, offers beauty, serenity, and luxury in New England-style cottages with stunning ocean views, garden entrances, fireplaces, decks, and spa tubs. Complimentary wine, morning newspaper, fresh coffee, and full breakfast are included in the rates. The restaurant is open nightly serving the celebrated coastal cuisine of Chef Stephen Smith and an award-winning wine list. Weddings welcome!

Hosts: Flurry Healy and Peter Wells
Rooms: 20 (PB) $170-260
Full Breakfast
Credit Cards: A, B, C
Notes: 2, 4, 5, 7, 8, 9, 10, 11, 12, 15

Fensalden Inn

P.O. Box 99, 95410
(707) 937-4042; (800) 959-3850
FAX (707) 937-2416; e-mail: ehamby@mcn.org

This restored 1860s stagecoach way station has antique furnishings; all units have fireplaces. Quiet country setting with pastoral and ocean views. Enjoy strolling country lanes where grazing deer share the crisp morning air, or relish the evening panorama of the setting sun over a crimson-stained ocean. Minimum-stay requirements weekends and holidays.

Host: Lyn Hamby
Rooms: 8 (PB) $120-175
Full Breakfast
Credit Cards: A, B
Notes: 2, 5, 7, 9, 10, 11, 12, 14, 15

AMADOR CITY

Imperial Hotel

Box 195, 95601
(209) 267-9172

"There is a rich, almost seductive opulence to this brick 1879 hostelry that

---

NOTES: Credit cards accepted: A MasterCard; B Visa; C American Express; D Discover; E Diner's Club; F Other; 2 Personal checks accepted; 3 Lunch available; 4 Dinner available; 5 Open all year; 6 Pets welcome; 7 No smoking; 8 Children welcome; 9 Social drinking allowed; 10 Tennis nearby; 11 Swimming nearby; 12 Golf nearby; 13 Skiing nearby; 14 May be booked through a travel agent; 15 Handicapped accessible.

comes at you in whispers and peeks"—
Sunset magazine, April 1997. The restored
Imperial Hotel offers six handsome guest
rooms with full breakfast, air conditioning, and modern private baths. The original bar has a large selection of spirits and
California wines. The elegant, nationally
acclaimed dining room is open for dinner
nightly from 5:00 to 9:00 P.M. Skiing is
one hour away.

Hosts: Bruce Sherrill and Dale Martin
Rooms: 6 (PB) $75-105
Full Breakfast
Credit Cards: A, B, C, D
Notes: 2, 4, 5, 7, 9, 10, 11, 12, 14, 15

ANAHEIM

Bed and Breakfast International

P.O. Box 282910, San Francisco, 94128-2910
(650) 696-1690; (800) 872-4500
FAX (650) 696-1699; e-mail: info@bbintl.com
www.bbintl.com

GG-04. Convenient to Orange County
attractions, this home features large comfortable rooms, full breakfast, and TV room
with fireplace. Four guest rooms with private and shared baths. $50-65.

SA-W1. This 1930s Renaissance cottage
with antiques and country French decor features one guest room with French doors that
open onto a deck overlooking a garden and
pond. Choice of breakfast, queen-size bed,
and private bath. Near South Coast Plaza,
Orange County Airport, and major freeways. No smoking. $75.

APTOS

Apple Lane Inn

6265 Soquel Drive, 95003-3117
(408) 475-6868

Apple Lane Inn is a historic Victorian farmhouse restored to the charm and tranquility
of an earlier age. It is just south of Santa

Cruz on two and one-half acres of grounds,
with gardens, a romantic gazebo, and fields.
Explore the many miles of beaches within
walking distance. Golf, hiking, fishing,
shopping, and dining are all nearby.

Hosts: Doug and Diana Groom
Rooms: 5 (PB) $70-175
Full Breakfast
Credit Cards: A, B, D
Notes: 2, 5, 6, 7, 8, 9, 10, 11, 12, 14

Bayview Hotel

8041 Soquel Drive, 95003
(800) 422-9843; FAX (831) 688-5128
e-mail: lodging@bayviewhotel.com
www.bayviewhotel.com

An 1878 beautiful Victorian hotel. Each
room was renovated and refurbished during
1992-1995, in keeping with its historic
grandeur. The tastefully appointed rooms
provide charming antiques, cozy beds with
feather mattresses, comfortable sitting
areas, and fireplaces as well as private baths
(some with two-person jet tubs), telephones
with modem capacity, some built-in TVs
(other TVs and business conveniences are
available upon request). Complimentary
breakfast served in the Vintage Room or
brought to guests' room. Restaurant on-site.
Adjacent to the Forest of Nisene Marks
State Park.

Host: Gwen Burkard
Rooms: 11 (PB) $90-150
Continental Breakfast
Credit Cards: A, B, C
Notes: 2, 3, 4, 5, 7, 8, 9, 10, 11, 12, 14

Mangels House

570 Aptos Creek Road, Box 302, 95001
(408) 688-7982

A large Southern Colonial, on four acres of
lawn and orchard and bounded by a 10,000-
acre redwood forest, is less than a mile
from the beach. The five large, airy rooms
are eclectic in decor and European in feel,
reflecting the owners' background. Closed
December 24 through 26. Inquire about
accommodations for pets. Limited smoking

NOTES: Credit cards accepted: A MasterCard; B Visa; C American Express; D Discover; E Diner's Club;
F Other; 2 Personal checks accepted; 3 Lunch available; 4 Dinner available; 5 Open all year; 6 Pets welcome;

Mangels House

allowed on outside porch. Inquire about accommodations for children.

Hosts: Jacqueline and Ronald Fisher
Rooms: 6 (PB) $115-160
Full Breakfast
Credit Cards: A, B, C
Notes: 2, 7, 9, 10, 11, 12, 14

ARROYO GRANDE

Arroyo Village Inn

407 El Camino Real, 93420
(805) 489-5926; (800) 563-7762
FAX (805) 543-9075
www.centralcoast.com/arroyovillageinn

Romantic, award-winning English country-style inn offering a delightful blend of yesterday's charm and hospitality with today's comforts and conveniences. Spacious suites are decorated with Laura Ashley prints and antiques with private baths, spas, fireplaces, window seats, and skylights. In the heart of California's central coast, halfway between Los Angeles and San Francisco. Near beaches, wineries, San Luis Obispo; less than one hour to Hearst Castle. "The greatest little secret on the Central Coast," says the *Los Angeles Times.*

Host: Gina Glass
Rooms: 7 (PB) $125-350
Full Breakfast
Credit Cards: A, B, C, D, E
Notes: 2, 5, 7, 9, 12, 14

House of Another Tyme Bed and Breakfast

227 Le Point Street, 93420
(805) 489-6313

On a quarter-acre of hillside with gardens to allow sunlight in and create a tranquil area containing natural rock wall, exotic finches, and 70-year-old palms, the House of Another Tyme reflects its name. Circa 1916, the single-walled-construction home was renovated by upgrading bathrooms and kitchen. All bedrooms have queen-size beds and private baths and are furnished in antiques. A full country breakfast is served. One block from historic village with antique shops and fine restaurants.

Hosts: Jack and Judy
Rooms: 3 (PB) $95
Full Breakfast
Credit Cards: A, B, D
Notes: 5, 7, 11, 12

AUBURN

Power's Mansion Inn

164 Cleveland Avenue, 95603
(916) 885-1166; FAX (916) 885-1386

This magnificent mansion was built from a gold fortune in the late 1800s. It has easy access to I-80 and off-street parking. Close to gold country, antiquing, water sports, hiking, horseback riding, skiing, and restaurants. Smoking outside only.

Owners: Arno and Jean Lejnieks
Rooms: 13 (PB) $79-149

Power's Mansion Inn

7 No smoking; 8 Children welcome; 9 Social drinking allowed; 10 Tennis nearby; 11 Swimming nearby; 12 Golf nearby; 13 Skiing nearby; 14 May be booked through a travel agent; 15 Handicapped accessible.

Full Breakfast
Credit Cards: A, B, C
Notes: 2, 5, 7, 8, 9, 10, 11, 12, 13, 14

AVALON

Zane Grey Pueblo Hotel

199 Chimes Tower Road, P.O. Box 216, 90704
(310) 510-0966

If one rode a horse or hiked up into the hills overlooking Avalon Canyon and took in the beautiful vista of blue ocean, rolling grass-lands, and the yacht-spotted harbor below, one would have some idea of just why this island appealed to Zane Grey as a haven from the literary bustle surrounding a best-selling author. On the cactus-covered hillside above the Avalon casino is the sprawling Hopi Indian-style pueblo that Grey built in 1926. It is now a hotel for guests to enjoy. Continental breakfast consists of coffee, tea, and toast.

Host: Karen Baker
Rooms: 17 (PB) $85-155
Continental Breakfast
Credit Cards: A, B, C
Notes: 5, 7, 8, 9, 10, 11, 12, 14

BALLARD

The Ballard Inn

2436 Baseline Avenue, 93463
(805) 688-7770; (800) 638-2466
FAX (805) 688-9560

Comfortably elegant accommodations in the heart of the Santa Barbara wine country. Just 40 minutes from Santa Barbara, yet nestled in country orchards and vineyards, the Bal-lard Inn offers an intimate retreat. Each of the 15 guest rooms possesses its own special charm and character reflecting local history. Visit Fess Parker at his winery, or drop by any of the award-winning wineries nearby. Personal checks accepted with identification.

Host: Kelly Robinson
Rooms: 15 (PB) $150-220
Full Breakfast
Credit Cards: A, B, C
Notes: 4, 5, 7, 10, 11, 12, 14, 15

BENICIA

Bed and Breakfast California

P.O. Box 282910, San Francisco, 94128-2910
(650) 696-1690; (800) 872-4500
FAX (650) 696-1699; e-mail: info@bbintl.com
www.bbintl.com

Charming Victorian in Benicia's historic dis-trict filled with antiques. Amenities include quilts and comforters, a lovely garden avail-able for dining in good weather, port and sherry in rooms in the evenings. Peace and serenity are the key factors at work at this inn. Just a short drive to Napa. $75-90.

Captain Walsh House

235 East L Street, 94510
(707) 747-5653; FAX (707) 747-6265

The Captain Walsh House commands a dis-tinguished place in California history. Designed by prominent architect Andrew Jackson Downing, the house was built in Boston, dismantled, shipped around the Horn, and erected in Benicia in 1849. The house has been featured in numerous books and is con-sidered one of the "most important pieces of residential architecture in Northern Califor-nia." Captain Walsh House stands only two blocks from Benicia's charming First Street, where guests can choose to shop for antiques, rent a windsurfing rig, take a vintage carriage ride, or visit California's first state capitol.

Hosts: Mrs. Reed and Mr. Steve Robbins
Rooms: 5 (PB) $125-150
Full Breakfast
Credit Cards: B, C
Notes: 2, 5, 7, 9, 10, 11, 12

BERKELEY

Bed and Breakfast California

P.O. Box 282910, San Francisco, 94128-2910
(650) 696-1690; (800) 872-4500
FAX (650) 696-1699; e-mail: info@bbintl.com
www.bbintl.com

A. Ideal for the single woman traveler! Completed in 1936, this home is a well-

NOTES: Credit cards accepted: A MasterCard; B Visa; C American Express; D Discover; E Diner's Club; F Other; 2 Personal checks accepted; 3 Lunch available; 4 Dinner available; 5 Open all year; 6 Pets welcome;

architected ranch-style house with spacious rooms in a well defined setting which separates bedrooms from living and dining areas. It is in a quiet neighborhood of well-kept homes. $60-75.

B. A spacious Mediterranean-style home, with a pool and a hot tub in a landscaped setting, which has been featured in *Los Angeles Times Home* magazine. The home is beautifully furnished and has floor-to-ceiling bookcases and views of the bay. The Casablanca Suite on the first floor is adjacent to the front door and includes a sitting room plus an en suite bath. The Spinnaker Room on the second floor has a view of the bay and twin beds. $75-85.

Bed and Breakfast International

P.O. Box 282910, San Francisco, 94128-2910
(650) 696-1690; (800) 872-4500
FAX (650) 696-1699; e-mail: info@bbintl.com
www.bbintl.com

BE-H51. This 1904 Craftsman-style inn is close to the university campus, restaurants, hiking, and public transportation. Relax in the parlors or patio areas on the lovely grounds. Five guest rooms with private baths and king- or queen-size or twin beds. No smoking. Continental plus breakfast. $65-105.

BIG BEAR LAKE

Gold Mountain Manor Historic Bed and Breakfast

117 Anita, P.O. Box 2027, 92314
(800) 509-2604

Gold Mountain Manor is Big Bear's only historic 1928 log mansion bed and breakfast. At the end of the 1920s, on Northshore, Alexander Buchanan Barret, a wealthy Los Angeles movie investor, built Gold Mountain Manor. Set in a forest of pine trees, the house is three stories high with birds-eye

Gold Mountain Manor

maple floors and beamed ceilings. Eight fireplaces, antiques, and romantic ambiance. Mentioned in *The Best Places to Kiss* and *Fifty Most Romantic Places* books. Hiking nearby.

Rooms: 6 (PB) $120-190
Full Breakfast
Credit Cards: A, B, C, D
Notes: 5, 7, 11, 12, 13, 14

The Inn at Fawnskin Bed and Breakfast

880 Canyon Road, P.O. Box 378, Fawnskin, 92333
(909) 866-3200

The Inn at Fawnskin, on the quiet north shore of Big Bear Lake, is a beautiful custom-built log home nestled in its own pine forest only steps from the lake and forest trails. Living room has big stone fireplace, decks with lake and forest views. Enjoy a gourmet breakfast next to fireplace in dining room. Game room has wide-screen TV, video library, pool and game table. Breathtaking master suite with fireplace and balcony. Handmade quilts and terry-cloth robes.

Hosts: Kathy and Todd Murphy
Rooms: 4 (2 PB: 2 SB) $85-175
Full Breakfast
Credit Cards: A, B, C
Notes: 2, 5, 7, 9, 10, 11, 12, 13, 14

7 No smoking; 8 Children welcome; 9 Social drinking allowed; 10 Tennis nearby; 11 Swimming nearby; 12 Golf nearby; 13 Skiing nearby; 14 May be booked through a travel agent; 15 Handicapped accessible.

Truffles

Truffles Bed and Breakfast

43591 Bow Canyon Drive, P.O. Box 130649, 92315
(909) 585-2772

Gracious hospitality in peaceful surroundings describes this country manor home in a mountain resort with lake, golf, and ski facilities nearby. Attention to detail is evident with five individually appointed bedrooms with private baths and featherbeds, full breakfast, afternoon appetizers, and truffles on bedtime pillows. This spacious facility is traditionally furnished and includes large, comfortable gathering room with piano, TV, video library, and fireplace. Large outside decks also available. Children over 10 welcome.

Hosts: Marilyn Kane and Carol Bracey
Rooms: 5 (PB) $115-150
Full Breakfast
Credit Cards: A, B, C, D
Notes: 2, 5, 7, 9, 12, 13, 14

BODEGA

Bed and Breakfast California

P.O. Box 282910, San Francisco, 94128-2910
(650) 696-1690; (800) 872-4500
FAX (650) 696-1699; e-mail: info@bbintl.com
www.bbintl.com

The Villa. Guests eager to experience the simple elegance of country living will enjoy the quiet peacefulness of the Villa. Terraced grounds, terra-cotta stucco, red-tiled roofs, and an expansive veranda give the inn a distinct Mediterranean atmosphere. Twelve beautifully appointed guest rooms offer beamed ceilings and wood-burning fireplaces. A landscaped courtyard with a swimming pool and a large indoor Jacuzzi are just steps from guests' room. $185-295.

BOONVILLE

Anderson Creek Inn

12050 Anderson Valley Way, P.O. Box 217, 95415
(707) 895-3091; (800) LLAMA-02
www.andersoncreekinn.com

Elegant and secluded, this spacious inn is on 16 lovely acres with views from every room. Guests are treated to wine and appetizers in the evenings, and a memorable breakfast is served in the dining room, the patio, or in a basket brought to the room. Lazy days can be spent walking the grounds, visiting the animals, or lounging around the Olympic-size pool. Wine tasting, shopping, restaurants, hiking, and the Mendocino coast are just minutes away.

Hosts: Rod and Nancy Graham
Rooms: 5 (PB) $110-170
Full Breakfast
Credit Cards: A, B
Notes: 2, 5, 7, 9, 10, 11, 12

BURLINGAME

Burlingame Bed and Breakfast

1021 Balboa Avenue, 94010
(650) 344-5815

Boating, swimming, fishing (bay and ocean), running, golf, hiking, art, entertainment, sports. Near Stanford, other colleges, and transportation. Ten dollars for each additional person.

Hosts: Joe and Elnora Fernandez
Room: 1 (PB) $60
Continental Breakfast
Credit Cards: None
Notes: 2, 5, 7, 8, 10, 11, 12

NOTES: Credit cards accepted: A MasterCard; B Visa; C American Express; D Discover; E Diner's Club;
F Other; 2 Personal checks accepted; 3 Lunch available; 4 Dinner available; 5 Open all year; 6 Pets welcome;

CALISTOGA

Bear Flag Inn

2653 Foothill Boulevard, 94515
(707) 942-5423; FAX (707) 942-1509
e-mail: bearflagginn@ap.net
www.bearflaginn.com

This historical turn-of-the-century farmhouse
has fabulous views. Luxuriate in period furnishings, queen-size beds, and restored private baths. Enjoy a gourmet breakfast served
on the sun porch or in the marvelous dining
room. Complimentary wine and hors d'oeuvres served poolside or fireside. Experience
local wine tasting, hiking, or biking, and top
off the day with one of the award-winning
local restaurants close by.

Rooms: 5 (PB) $150-200
Full and Continental Breakfast
Credit Cards: A, B, D
Notes: 2, 5, 7, 8, 9, 10, 11, 12, 14, 15

Bed and Breakfast International

P.O. Box 282910, San Francisco, 94128-2910
(650) 696-1690; (800) 872-4500
FAX (650) 696-1699; e-mail: info@bbintl.com
www.bbintl.com

CA-S31. Very close to Napa Valley wineries,
1900 country farmhouse on several acres
offers quiet and comfort. Each of the guest
accommodations have a private entrance.
Full breakfast and afternoon refreshments
are served in guests' room, suite, or on the
tree-shaded pool deck. One guest room and
two suites have private baths and queen-size
beds. No smoking. $95-150.

CA-S71. Seven suites with private
entrances are featured at this California-
style bungalow inn in town. Within walking
distance to shopping and spas. Wineries,
golf, bicycling, tennis, and hiking are
nearby. A full breakfast and afternoon
refreshments are served daily. $125-145.

CA-S91. Uniquely decorated rooms, some
with fireplaces and whirlpool tubs, and a

pool fed by the inn's own hot springs are
some of the special offerings at this wine
country estate. A Continental plus breakfast
and afternoon refreshments are provided.
Nine guest rooms with private baths and
king- or queen-size beds. No smoking.
$125-210.

"Culvers," A Country Inn

1805 Foothill Boulevard, 94515
(707) 942-4535

A lovely Victorian residence built in
1875, filled with antiques and offering a
full country breakfast. Jacuzzi and seasonal pool available for guests' enjoyment. Within minutes of wineries, mud
baths, and downtown Calistoga. Lovely
view of St. Helena mountain range from
the veranda. Sherry and hors d'oeuvres
are offered in the afternoon, with an afternoon beverage and baked treats offered
upon arrival. Closed December through
January, and Thanksgiving and New
Year's. Reservations are held for seven
days on a credit card, with payment by
personal or traveler's check. Children 16
and older are welcome.

Hosts: Meg and Tony Wheatley
Rooms: 6 (PB) $156.80-179.20
Full Breakfast
Credit Cards: None
Notes: 2, 7, 9, 10, 11, 14, 15

The Elms Bed and Breakfast Inn

1300 Cedar Street, 94515
(707) 942-9476; (800) 235-4316

This 1871 French three-story Victorian is
one-half block from town next to a park
on the Napa River. It is very quiet and
peaceful, yet within walking distance of
restaurants, spas, gliders, bike rentals,
golf, and tennis. The rooms are very
romantic—decorated with antiques. All
have coffee makers, bathrobes, chocolates, and port for after dinner. The feather
beds are piled high with pillows and down

---

7 No smoking; 8 Children welcome; 9 Social drinking allowed; 10 Tennis nearby; 11 Swimming nearby;
12 Golf nearby; 13 Skiing nearby; 14 May be booked through a travel agent; 15 Handicapped accessible.

The Elms

House offers spacious suites individually decorated with antiques, each with private bath and entrance, fireplace, and small refrigerator. Three suites offer Jacuzzi tubs. Complimentary wine and hors d'oeuvres each evening. Elegant private cottage is also available.

Hosts: Doris and Gus Beckert
Rooms: 3 (PB) $150-300
Full Breakfast
Credit Cards: A, B, C, D
Notes: 2, 5, 7, 9, 10, 11, 12, 14

Hillcrest

comforters. Most rooms have fireplaces, TV, and some have spa tubs. A huge gourmet breakfast is served, and wine and cheese are served in the afternoon. Limited handicapped accessibility.

Hosts: Stephen and Karla Wyle
Rooms: 7 (PB) $110-180
Full Breakfast
Credit Cards: A, B
Notes: 2, 5, 7, 10, 11, 12, 14

Hillcrest

3225 Lake County Highway, 94515
(707) 942-6334

Foothill House

3037 Foothill Boulevard, 94515
(707) 942-6933; (800) 942-6933

"The most romantic inn of the Napa Valley," according to the *Chicago Tribune* travel editor. In a country setting, Foothill

Breathtaking view of Napa Valley countryside. Hiking, swimming, and fishing on 40 acres. Family-owned property since 1860. Hilltop modern country home decorated with heirlooms from family mansion. Rooms have balconies. Fireplace and grand piano, rare artwork, silver, crystal, china, and oriental rugs. Family photo albums date back to 1870s. Breakfast is served weekends on a 12-foot antique table fit for a king. Enjoy the outdoor spa and large pool. Water skiing is a 45-minute drive away.

Host: Debbie O'Gorman
Rooms: 4 (1 PB; 3 SB) $50-98
Continental Breakfast
Credit Cards: None
Notes: 2, 5, 6, 7, 9, 10, 11, 12, 14

Foothill House

NOTES: Credit cards accepted: A MasterCard; B Visa; C American Express; D Discover; E Diner's Club; F Other; 2 Personal checks accepted; 3 Lunch available; 4 Dinner available; 5 Open all year; 6 Pets welcome;

La Chaumière, Bed and Breakfast

1301 Cedar Street, 94515
(707) 942-5139; (800) 474-6800
FAX (707) 942-5199

An abundance of flowers greets guests at the entrance of La Chaumière, Bed and Breakfast; a 1910 Cotswald-style home, reflecting an attention to detail and environment of warmth, vitality, and charm. Two rooms in the main house have their own baths. The upstairs suite offers a private sitting room and the downstairs room features French doors that lead to a private deck. The third is a cozy separate cottage, a quiet "getaway" providing a wonderful country atmosphere. Wine and cheese are served in the late afternoon, port in the rooms for a nightcap. Just one-half block from downtown Calistoga.

Host: Gary Venturi
Rooms: 3 (PB) $125-175
Full Breakfast
Credit Cards: A, B
Notes: 2, 5, 7, 9, 10, 11, 12, 14

Quail Mountain

Mount View Hotel

1457 Lincoln Avenue, 94515
(707) 942-6877; (800) 816-6877
FAX (707) 942-6904

A national historic landmark, the hotel is set like a gem in the heart of Calistoga. A warm fire greets guests as they enter the lobby. A private courtyard, hot mineral whirlpool, and large pool invite guests to ease back or dive in. Lovely guest rooms, elegant suites, and private cottages await. Fresh flowers and Calistoga bottled water in each individually appointed room. The hotel is also home to Catahoula Restaurant and Saloon, one of the valley's finest, and Calistoga's only world-class spa.

Rooms: 32 (PB) $110-225
Continental Breakfast
Credit Cards: A, B, C, D
Notes: 4, 7, 9, 10, 12, 14

Quail Mountain Bed and Breakfast Inn

4455 North St. Helena Highway., 94558
(707) 942-0316

A secluded luxury bed and breakfast on 26 heavily wooded idyllic acres on a mountain top between St. Helena and Calistoga. Three guest rooms, each with king-size bed, private bath, and private deck. Cabernet vineyard and fruit orchard on property. Full breakfast and complimentary wine with gracious, personalized hospitality. Close to world-class restaurants, wineries, and golf. A two-night minimum stay on weekends and holidays. Advance reservations recommended.

Hosts: Alma and Don Swiers
Rooms: 3 (PB) $120-150
Full Breakfast
Credit Cards: A, B, C, D
Notes: 2, 5, 7, 9, 10, 11, 12, 14

7 No smoking; 8 Children welcome; 9 Social drinking allowed; 10 Tennis nearby; 11 Swimming nearby; 12 Golf nearby; 13 Skiing nearby; 14 May be booked through a travel agent; 15 Handicapped accessible.

Trailside Inn

4201 Silverado Trail, 94515
(707) 942-4106; FAX (707) 942-4702

A charming 1930s farmhouse in the country with three very private suites. Each suite has its own entrance, porch with vineyard view, bedroom, bath, fireplace, and air conditioning. Fresh home-baked breads provided in guests' fully equipped kitchen. Complimentary wine, lovely pool and spa, soft terry-cloth robes. Close to all major wineries and restaurants.

Hosts: Randy and Lani Gray
Suites: 3 (PB) $165-185
Continental Breakfast
Credit Cards: A, B, C, D
Notes: 2, 5, 7, 9, 10, 12, 14

Zinfandel House

1253 Summit Drive, 94515
(707) 942-0733

Zinfandel House is in a wooded setting on a western hillside with a spectacular view of the famous Napa Valley vineyards. Halfway between St. Helena and Calistoga. Choose from three tastefully decorated rooms with a private or shared bath. Breakfast is served on the deck or in the solarium.

Hosts: Bette and George Starke
Rooms: 3 (PB or SB) $75-100
Full Breakfast
Credit Cards: A, B, D
Notes: 2, 5, 7, 9, 10, 11, 12

Zinfandel House

CAMARILLO

Bed and Breakfast California

P.O. Box 282910, San Francisco, 94128-2910
(650) 696-1690; (800) 872-4500
FAX (650) 696-1699; e-mail: info@bbintl.com
www.bbintl.com

Pick oranges and avocados at this three-acre ranch just 15 minutes south of Ventura or 30 minutes to Santa Barbara. There are two guest wings surrounded by orchards with rooms with balconies, from which guests can see the ocean on a clear day. A huge deck offers a hot tub for relaxing. $65.

CAMBRIA

Bed and Breakfast California

P.O. Box 282910, San Francisco, 94128-2910
(650) 696-1690; (800) 872-4500
FAX (650) 696-1699; e-mail: info@bbintl.com
www.bbintl.com

Watch the ocean from the hot tub. The entire lower level of this luxury home in Cambria is designed for bed and breakfast pampering. There is a bedroom with queen-size bed, living room with fireplace, stereo and TV systems, dining area, fully equipped kitchen (including goodies), and two decks—both with ocean view and one with guests' own hot tub. British hostess bakes fresh scones as part of every gourmet breakfast. Walking distance to town. There is even a secret, private entrance. $110.

J. Patrick House

2990 Burton Drive, 93428
(800) 341-5258; FAX (805) 927-6759
e-mail: jph@jpatrickhouse.com
www.jpatrickhouse.com

Discover the charming and romantic hidden secret of the central coast. The J. Patrick House is a beautiful log home that blends with its wooded setting above the old village of Cambria. The inn overlooks a forest of tall Monterey pines and yet the ocean is only minutes away. All rooms have wood-burning fireplaces and private baths. Home-made hors d'oeuvres are served and complemented by fine wines. A lovely breakfast is served in the garden room. Inquire about accommodations for children.

Hosts: Barbara and Mel Schwimmer
Rooms: 8 (PB) $115-180
Full Breakfast
Credit Cards: A, B, C, D
Notes: 2, 5, 7, 10, 12, 14

The Pickford House Bed and Breakfast

2555 Macleod Way, 93428
(805) 927-8619

Only eight miles from Hearst Castle, Pickford House is decorated with antiques reminiscent of the golden age of film. Eight rooms have king- or queen-size beds, private baths, fireplaces, and views of the mountains. Parlor with an 1860 bar is used for wine and tea bread at 5:00 P.M. TV in rooms. All baths have claw-foot tubs and showers. Enjoy wine tasting nearby or rock collecting on the beach. Twenty dollars for each additional person any age. Plenty of off-street parking.

Host: Anna Larsen
Rooms: 8 (PB) $89-140
Full Breakfast
Credit Cards: A, B
Notes: 2, 5, 7, 8, 9, 10, 11, 12

A Summer Place

P.O. Box 1516, 93428
(805) 927-8145

Two-story Cape Cod-style home done in country interior. View of Pacific Ocean through the pine. In the woods, away from the traffic. Birds. Dear privacy. No traffic noise. Fireplace, living room with TV. Minutes from village shops.

Hosts: Don and Desiree D'Urbano
Rooms: 2 (PB) $65

Continental Breakfast
Credit Cards: None
Notes: 2, 5, 9, 10, 11, 12

CAPITOLA BY THE SEA

Inn at Depot Hill

250 Monterey Avenue, 95010
(831) 462-3376; (800) 572-2632
FAX (831) 462-3697
e-mail: lodging@innatdepothill.com
www.innatdepothill.com

Near a sandy beach in a quaint Mediterranean-style resort, this award-winning inn was named one of the top 10 inns in the country. A decorator's delight, upscale rooms resemble different parts of the world: Côte d'Azur, a chic auberge in St. Tropez; Paris, a romantic French hideaway; Portofino, an Italian coastal villa; and a traditional English garden named Sissinghurst. All rooms have fireplaces, TV/VCR, stereo systems, telephones, modems, robes, featherbeds, flowers. Most have private hot tubs in garden patios.

Hosts: Suzie Lankes and Dan Floyd
Rooms: 12 (PB) $190-275
Full Breakfast
Credit Cards: A, B, C, D
Notes: 2, 5, 7, 9, 10, 11, 12, 14, 15

CARDIFF BY THE SEA

Bed and Breakfast International

P.O. Box 282910, San Francisco, 94128-2910
(650) 696-1690; (800) 872-4500
FAX (650) 696-1699; e-mail: info@bbintl.com
www.bbintl.com

CA-B1. Charming couple host an elegant bed and breakfast with a relaxed atmosphere near Hearst Castle and midcoast beaches. First floor is guests' domain with large bedroom/sitting room in English country decor. A gourmet breakfast and afternoon refreshments are provided. Private bath and twin or king-size bed. No smoking. $90.

7 No smoking; 8 Children welcome; 9 Social drinking allowed; 10 Tennis nearby; 11 Swimming nearby; 12 Golf nearby; 13 Skiing nearby; 14 May be booked through a travel agent; 15 Handicapped accessible.

CA-B71. Contemporary oceanfront bed and breakfast inn on the beach has antique furnishings, ocean views, and outdoor decks. Afternoon refreshments and a full breakfast are served. No smoking. Seven guest rooms. Private bath. $120-150.

CA-D2. Friendly, comfortable bed and breakfast in wooded area offers a peek at the ocean in quiet surroundings. Two guest rooms with double and twin beds. Private bath. No smoking. Full breakfast. $40-60.

CA-061. Each guest room at this 1873 Greek Revival-style historic inn, in the village, is decorated differently, but all have antiques from the 1800s. The innkeeper's cottage, suite, and two new guest rooms are also available. A full breakfast and afternoon refreshments are served. Walk to shops and restaurants. $85-165.

CA-P31. Just south of Hearst Castle at the ocean, this bed and breakfast features rooms with fireplaces, private patios, and baths en suite. A full breakfast is served with an ocean view. No smoking. Three guest rooms. Private bath. $85.

CA-S2. Set on three wooded acres five minutes from the ocean, this bed and breakfast has one quiet suite and another guest room, each with a private deck. Host is docent at the Hearst Castle. A Continental breakfast is served. $95.

CB-P8I. Private entrance and fireplace in individually decorated room can be found at Cape Cod-style bed and breakfast in quiet seaside village 100 yards from the beach. Full breakfast served. $85-150.

CS-C17I. Individually decorated guest rooms at family-run inn, one block from the beach in a serene seaside village. An easy commute to San Diego and most tourist attractions in San Diego and Orange Counties. Continental plus breakfast served. $105-250.

CARMEL

Absolutely Accommodations

P.O. Box 641471, San Francisco, 94164-1471
(415) 677-9789; (888) 982-2632
FAX (415) 982-9580
e-mail: travelinfo@iname.com

This is a free reservation service committed to assisting travelers in finding the best possible accommodations in California. It offers access to private homestay bed and breakfasts and inns. It can help guests find the proper accommodations that meet their individual needs. The service's goal is to provide both its clients and hosts with the best possible customer service.

Carmel 101. This inn is convenient in the heart of Carmel-by-the-Sea. Within walking distance to shops, restaurants, and art galleries. Each one of the 24 rooms features a fireplace, refrigerator, and TV. All private baths. $95-180.

Carmel 102. This inn features a collection of cottages among lush gardens. Eighteen rooms with each room appointed in a unique country style with a private bath and private entrance. Some rooms feature fireplaces. Four blocks away from the beach and a few blocks from downtown Carmel. $105-225.

Bed and Breakfast California

P.O. Box 282910, San Francisco, 94128-2910
(650) 696-1690; (800) 872-4500
FAX (650) 696-1699; e-mail: info@bbintl.com
www.bbintl.com

Snug within the heart of Carmel, this family of inns gives guests Old World ser-

NOTES: Credit cards accepted: A MasterCard; B Visa; C American Express; D Discover; E Diner's Club; F Other; 2 Personal checks accepted; 3 Lunch available; 4 Dinner available; 5 Open all year; 6 Pets welcome;

vice and a charming setting. Spacious rooms and suites are designed to accommodate the whole family, and one inn even takes pets! Many rooms have full kitchens and wood-burning fireplaces, and some have Jacuzzis. A short stroll to the shops, restaurants, and galleries of downtown Carmel, including the famous Hog's Breath Restaurant where one might catch a glimpse of owner Clint Eastwood. A Continental breakfast and complimentary newspaper are delivered to the door each morning. With rates ranging from affordable to luxury, these inns have something to offer everyone.

Bed and Breakfast International

P.O. Box 282910, San Francisco, 94128-2910
(650) 696-1690; (800) 872-4500
FAX (650) 696-1699; e-mail: info@bbintl.com
www.bbintl.com

CA-251. This country inn offers large, lovely decorated guest rooms, each with a fireplace. Full breakfast and afternoon refreshments are served. Convenient to all Carmel area attractions. $105-175.

CA-V11I. Fireplace and mini-refrigerator are available in all rooms of this lovely English Tudor-style inn built around a courtyard. Within walking distance to beaches, shops, and restaurants. Several suites have a kitchenette. Continental breakfast is served. $85-145.

CA-D12I. Rustic bed and breakfast near Carmel shops offers 12 rooms and suites with fireplaces. Private baths. Continental breakfast. $80-135.

CA-H201. Contemporary inn has spacious, attractive rooms, some with view, balconies, and fireplace. Continental breakfast. $80-160.

CA-S131. Very close to beach, 1929 European-style inn has some ocean-view rooms

and others with fireplace. Near tennis, golf, hiking, and restaurants. Continental breakfast. $100-180.

Carriage House Inn

Junipero between 7th and 8th, 93921
(800) 433-4732

Fresh flowers and country inn flavor. Continental breakfast and newspaper delivered to the room each morning. Wood-burning fireplaces, down comforters. Spacious rooms, many with open-beam ceilings and whirlpools or soaking tubs. Wine and hors d'oeuvres each evening in the library. Carmel's AAA four-diamond inn. A romantic getaway! Two-night minimum stay required for weekends and holidays.

Host: Cathy Lewis
Rooms: 13 (PB) $179-299
Continental Breakfast
Credit Cards: A, B, C, D
Notes: 2, 5, 9, 11, 12, 14

Cypress Inn

Lincoln and 7th Streets, P.O. Box Y, 93921
(408) 624-3871

Built in 1929, this classic Spanish-Mediterranean-style inn in the heart of Carmel by the Sea, within walking distance to all shops, restaurants, galleries, and the beautiful Carmel beach. The spacious living room lobby with fireplace and the garden courtyard are ideal for enjoying

Cypress Inn

a complimentary Continental breakfast or a cocktail from the full-service Library Lounge. A variety of rooms are available, all with private baths, TVs, and telephones, and some with gas-burning fireplaces, sitting areas, wet bars, verandas, and ocean views. Smoking permitted in designated areas only. Limited handicapped accessibility.

Innkeeper: Hollace Thompson
Owners: Doris Day, Terry Melcher, and
   Dennis Levett
Rooms: 33 (PB) $110-285
Continental Breakfast
Credit Cards: A, B, C, D
Notes: 2, 5, 6, 8, 9, 10, 11, 12, 14

Green Lantern Inn

Cassanova and Seventh, (P.O. Box 1114), 93921
(408) 624-4392; FAX (408) 624-9591
e-mail: info@greenlanterninn.com

Eighteen charming rooms all with private baths nestled among beautiful terraced and landscaped gardens. Buffet breakfast and afternoon refreshments. Four short blocks to sandy beach, shops, and restaurants. All rooms have refrigerator and hair dryer. Some fireplaced units. Children welcome. No pets. No smoking

Host: Cathy Matthews
Rooms: 18 (PB) $85-195
Continental Breakfast
Credit Cards: A, B, C, D
Notes: 5, 7, 8, 11, 12, 14

Happy Landing Inn

Monte Verde between 5th and 6th Avenues
   (location)
P.O. Box 2619, 93921 (mailing)
(408) 624-7917

Built as a family retreat in 1926, this early-Comstock-design inn has evolved into one of Carmel's most romantic places to stay. The Hansel and Gretel look is accentuated by a central garden and gazebo, pond, and flagstone paths. There are cathedral ceilings and the rooms are filled with antiques. Breakfast is taken to guests' rooms.

Hosts: Robert Ballard and Dick Stewart
Rooms: 7 (PB) $90-170
Continental Breakfast
Credit Cards: A, B
Notes: 2, 5, 7, 10, 12, 14, 15

The Sandpiper Inn-at-the-Beach

2408 Bay View Avenue, 93923
(408) 624-6433; (800) 633-6433
FAX (408) 624-5964

The inn closest to Carmel beach with views across the bay to Pebble Beach. Rooms and cottage rooms are filled with country antiques and fresh flowers. Some have glorious ocean views, others have gas  fireplaces. Beautiful buffet breakfast and afternoon tea and sherry served in the parlor area. Perfect for special occasions and anniversaries. Children over 12 welcome.

Host: Graeme Mackenzie
Rooms: 16 (PB) $95-195
Continental Breakfast
Credit Cards: A, B, C, D
Notes: 2, 5, 7, 9, 10, 11, 12, 14

Sea View Inn

P.O. Box 4138, 93921
(408) 624-8778

The Sea View Inn, a simple country Victorian, has been welcoming guests for more than 70 years. A quiet, cozy bed and breakfast, the Sea View has eight individually decorated rooms, six with private baths. Near the village and the beach, the Sea View provides a welcoming retreat. A generous Continental breakfast and afternoon tea are complimentary. Children over 12 welcome.

Hosts: Diane and Marshall Hydorn
Rooms: 8 (6 PB; 2 SB) $85-140
Continental Breakfast
Credit Cards: A, B, C
Notes: 2, 5, 7, 9, 10, 11, 12, 14

NOTES: Credit cards accepted: A MasterCard; B Visa; C American Express; D Discover; E Diner's Club;
F Other; 2 Personal checks accepted; 3 Lunch available; 4 Dinner available; 5 Open all year; 6 Pets welcome;

The Stonehouse Inn

8th below Monte Verde, P.O. Box 2517, 93921
(408) 624-4569; (800) 748-6618

Experience this luxurious country house in a quiet neighborhood setting. All one hears at night is the ocean! The Stonehouse Inn offers a tastefully restored turn-of-the-century vacation retreat. Superior accommodations and attention await guests' pleasure on the Monterey Peninsula by beautiful Carmel Bay. A generous home-cooked breakfast is served each morning in the sunny dining room. Carmel's world-famous shops and restaurants are only two blocks away.

Hosts: Kevin and Terri Navaille
Rooms: 6 (PB) $110-199
Full Breakfast
Credit Cards: A, B
Notes: 2, 5, 7, 9, 10, 11, 12, 14

Vagabond's House Inn

4th and Dolores, P.O. Box 2747, 93921
(408) 624-7738; (800) 262-1262 (US)
(800) 221-1262 (Canada); FAX (408) 626-1243

In the heart of the village, this inn surrounds a Carmel-stone courtyard dominated by large oak trees, plants, ferns, and flowers in profusion. The 11 unique guest rooms are appointed with a combination of collectibles and antiques in a mixture of European elegance and country tradition.

Host: Sally Goss (innkeeper)
Rooms: 11 (PB) $85-165
Continental Breakfast
Credit Cards: A, B, C
Notes: 2, 5, 6, 7, 9, 10, 11, 12, 14

CARMEL VALLEY

The Valley Lodge

Carmel Valley Road and Ford Road, P.O. Box 93, 93924
(408) 659-2261; (800) 641-4646

A warm Carmel Valley welcome awaits the individual guest, a couple, or a small conference. Relax in a garden patio room or a cozy one- or two-bedroom cottage with fireplace

and kitchen. Enjoy a sumptuous Continental plus breakfast, the heated swimming pool, sauna, hot spa, and exercise room. Tennis and golf are nearby. Walk to fine restaurants and quaint shops, or the Carmel Valley village. Or just relax and vegetate. Inquire about accommodations for pets. Smoking and nonsmoking rooms available.

Host: Peter Coakley
Rooms: 31 (PB) $99-269
Continental Breakfast
Credit Cards: A, B, C
Notes: 2, 5, 8, 9, 10, 11, 12, 14, 15

COLOMA

The Coloma Country Inn

345 High Street, P.O. Box 502, 95613
(530) 622-6919

Charming 1852 farmhouse inside 300-acre historic gold rush park and one block from American River. Includes five guest rooms in main inn and two deluxe suites in carriage house. Decorated throughout with American antiques and treasures. Recreational packages include hot-air ballooning and white-water rafting. Grounds include five acres of gardens and lily pond. Featured in *Country Living* and *Country Inns* magazines. Walk to Sutter's Mill, museums, and visitor center. Families welcome.

Hosts: Alan and Cindi Ehrgott
Rooms: 7 (5 PB: 2 SB) $90-130
Full Breakfast
Credit Cards: None
Notes: 2, 5, 7, 8, 9, 11, 12, 13, 14

COLUMBIA

Columbia City Hotel

Box 1870, 95310
(209) 532-1479; e-mail: info@cityhotel.com
www.cityhotel.com

In the heart of a historic gold rush town that is preserved and protected by the state of California, this impeccable inn is surrounded by relics of the past. All rooms

7 No smoking; 8 Children welcome; 9 Social drinking allowed; 10 Tennis nearby; 11 Swimming nearby; 12 Golf nearby; 13 Skiing nearby; 14 May be booked through a travel agent; 15 Handicapped accessible.

have been restored to reflect the 1850s. Downstairs, the highly acclaimed restaurant and always inviting What Cheer Saloon provide a haven for travelers seeking comfort and gracious hospitality. All rooms have half-baths; hall showers. Buffet-style breakfast served. Closed Christmas Eve and Christmas Day.

Host: Tom Bender
Rooms: 10 (PB) $85-105
Continental Breakfast
Credit Cards: A, B, C, D
Notes: 2, 4, 7, 8, 9, 10, 11, 12, 13, 14

Fallon Hotel

Washington Street, 95310
(209) 532-1470; e-mail: info@cityhotel.com
www.cityhotel.com

Since 1857, the historic Fallon Hotel has provided a home away from home to countless visitors. Authentically restored to its Victorian grandeur, most of the furnishings are original to the inn. Several rooms have private balconies, and all rooms have half-baths. Baskets of toiletries, robes, and slippers are provided for the showers off the hallway. One handicapped room available. In the heart of a state-restored gold rush town. Adjacent to the Fallon Theatre, which provides year-round productions. Call or write for price information.

Host: Tom Bender
Rooms: 14 (SB) $50-105
Continental Breakfast
Credit Cards: A, B, C, D
Notes: 2, 4, 5, 7, 8, 9, 10, 11, 12, 13, 14

CROWLEY LAKE

Rainbow Tarns

Rainbow Tarns Bed and Breakfast at Crowley Lake

HC 79, Box 1053, 93546
(760) 935-4556; (888) 588-6269

Near Mammoth Lakes, at an altitude of 7,000 feet, Rainbow Tarns is a secluded retreat amid three acres of ponds, open meadows, and the Sierra Nevada mountains. Country-style lodge includes luxury touches, such as double Jacuzzi tub, queen-size beds, down pillows and comforters, and a skylight for star-gazing. Afternoon hors d'oeuvres and wine. Gourmet restaurants nearby. The area provides excellent fishing, hiking, horseback riding, and winter skiing. Rainbow Tarns Road, off Crowley Lake Drive near Tom's Place. Closed March. Children 12 and older welcome.

Hosts: Brock and Diane Thoman
Rooms: 3 (PB) $90-140
Full Breakfast
Credit Cards: None
Notes: 2, 3, 7, 9, 11, 12, 13, 14, 15

NOTES: Credit cards accepted: A MasterCard; B Visa; C American Express; D Discover; E Diner's Club; F Other; 2 Personal checks accepted; 3 Lunch available; 4 Dinner available; 5 Open all year; 6 Pets welcome;

CUPERTINO

Bed and Breakfast International

P.O. Box 282910, San Francisco, 94128-2910
(650) 696-1690; (800) 872-4500
FAX (650) 696-1699; e-mail: info@bbintl.com
www.bbintl.com

CU-M2. Townhouse with pool within commuting distance to San Jose, Stanford, and San Francisco offers a guest room with country French decor and a choice of breakfast. $80-85.

DAVENPORT

Davenport Bed & Breakfast Inn

31 Davenport Avenue, 95017
(408) 425-1818; (800) 870-1817
FAX (408) 423-1160; e-mail: inn@swanton.com
www.swanton.com/BnB

Halfway between Carmel-Monterey and San Francisco, on Coast Highway 1. Small rural coastal town noted for whale watching, windsurfing, Ano Nuevo Elephant Seal State Reserve, hiking, bicycling, and beach access. Wonderful restaurant and gift store with unusual treasures and jewelry. Personal checks accepted two weeks prior to stay.

Hosts: Bruce and Marcia McDougal
Rooms: 12 (PB) $85-130
Full Breakfast
Credit Cards: A, B, C
Notes: 3, 4, 5, 8, 9, 11, 12, 14

DAVIS

University Inn Bed and Breakfast

340 "A" Street, 95616-4103
(530) 756-8648; (800) 756-8648
FAX (530) 753-6920; e-mail: yancher@aol.com

Adjacent to the University of California at Davis, this country inn offers a charming escape from a busy college town in a home-like setting. Each room has a private bath,

telephone, refrigerator, cable TV; off-street parking; a microwave oven is available. A generous Continental plus breakfast is served. Complimentary chocolates, beverages, and flowers. Inquire to see what type of pets accepted. Smoking permitted outside only. Special university events rates.

Hosts: Lynda and Ross Yancher
Rooms: 4 (PB) $55-135
Continental Breakfast
Credit Cards: A, B, C, D, E
Notes: 2, 5, 6, 7, 8, 9, 10, 11, 12, 14, 15

DEL MAR

The Blue Door

13707 Durango Drive, 92014
(619) 755-3819

Enjoy New England charm in a quiet southern California setting. Lower-level two-room suite with king-size bed, private bath, and cozy sitting room opening onto bougainvillaea-splashed patio with open vista of Torrey Pines Reserve Canyon. Only 20 miles north of San Diego. Creative full breakfast. Children over 16 welcome.

Hosts: Bob and Anna Belle Schock
Suite: 1 (PB) $60-70
Full Breakfast
Credit Cards: F
Notes: 2, 5, 7, 9, 10, 11, 12

DESERT HOT SPRINGS

Travellers Repose

66920 First Street, P.O. Box 655, 92240
(760) 329-9584

Bay windows, gingerbread trim, and stained glass decorate this two-story Victorian home. The interior is color coordinated throughout, blending natural woods and wallpapers. The three individually decorated bedrooms are spacious and all have queen-size beds. Guests enjoy the view of desert floor and mountains rising to 11,000 feet. Amenities include a patio, gardens, and spa. Desert Hot Springs is famous for its natural hot mineral

7 No smoking; 8 Children welcome; 9 Social drinking allowed; 10 Tennis nearby; 11 Swimming nearby; 12 Golf nearby; 13 Skiing nearby; 14 May be booked through a travel agent; 15 Handicapped accessible.

waters. Palm Springs is only minutes away, with its museums, shopping, famous restaurants, celebrities, golf tournaments, tennis tournaments, theaters, and stage shows. Closed July and August.

Host: Marian Relkoff
Rooms: 3 (PB) $65-85
Continental Breakfast
Credit Cards: None
Notes: 2, 7, 9, 10, 11, 12, 14

DULZURA

Brookside Farm
Bed and Breakfast Inn

1373 Marron Valley Road, 91917
(619) 468-3043; FAX (619) 468-9145

A country farmhouse furnished with collectibles, handmade quilts, and stained glass. Tree-shaded terraces by a stream, farm animals, gardens, hot tub in the grape arbor. Perfect for country walks. Close to Tecate, Mexico, and 35 minutes from San Diego. Two-night minimum stay required for holidays and some rooms. Many guests come for the gourmet country weekend.

Rooms: 10 (PB) $80-115
Full Breakfast
Credit Cards: A, B, C, D
Notes: 2, 4, 5, 7, 9, 12, 14, 15

Brookside Farm

ELK

Elk Cove Inn

6300 South Highway 1, P.O. Box 367, 95432
(707) 877-3321; (800) 275-2967
FAX (707) 877-1808; www.elkcoveinn.com

The Elk Cove Inn is an 1883 lumber baron's oceanfront estate on the Mendocino Coast, with gardens, gazebo, roof deck, and private steps down to the beach. Antique-filled rooms, cottages and suites all offer private baths, fireplaces, bathrobes, coffee makers. All have either dramatic ocean views or lovely garden views. House has common room with TV/VCR, refrigerator, microwave, books, and games. A cocktail bar is also in the house. A huge, multicourse gourmet breakfast is served in the oceanfront dining room. Wineries, redwoods, whale watching, unique shops, and gourmet restaurants are just minutes away. Dinner is available Tuesdays and Wednesdays during the winter.

Hosts: Elaine Bryant and Jim Carr
Rooms: 15 (PB) $108-278
Full Breakfast
Credit Cards: A, B, C
Notes: 2, 5, 7, 9, 10, 12, 14, 15

Greenwood Pier Inn

5928 South Highway One, 95432
(707) 877-9997; FAX (707) 877-3439
e-mail: gwpier@mcn.org
www.elkcoast.com/greenwoodpier

On edge of the bluff with stunning views of rock formations in Ocean Cove. Abundance of flower gardens. Next door to state park with beach. Cliffhouse and Seacastles feature second-story double-size tub looking down on the cove. Gourmet restaurant on premises—the inn grows own herbs and 15 kinds of salad greens. Also a gift shop, the Country Store, and a garden shop for inside and outside decor. Inquire about accommodations for pets and children.

Host: Kendrick Petty
Rooms: 12 (PB) $110-235
Continental Breakfast
Credit Cards: A, B, C
Notes: 2, 3, 4, 5, 7, 9, 10, 12

NOTES: Credit cards accepted: A MasterCard; B Visa; C American Express; D Discover; E Diner's Club; F Other; 2 Personal checks accepted; 3 Lunch available; 4 Dinner available; 5 Open all year; 6 Pets welcome;

Sandpiper House Inn

5520 South Highway One, P.O. Box 149, 95432
(707) 877-3587; (800) 894-9016

Built in 1916 on the bluffs of the rugged
Mendocino Coast, this inn boasts rich redwood paneling and beamed ceilings in the
living and dining rooms. It is tastefully furnished in the style of a European country
inn and offers stunning ocean views over
perennial gardens and private beach access.
The guest rooms are all beautifully
appointed with antiques and comfortable,
traditional furnishings.

Hosts: Claire and Richard Melrose
Rooms: 5 (PB) $110-220
Full Breakfast
Credit Cards: A, B, C, D
Notes: 2, 5, 7, 9, 10, 12

ENCINITAS

Bed and Breakfast International

P.O. Box 282910, San Francisco, 94128-2910
(650) 696-1690; (800) 872-4500
FAX (650) 696-1699; e-mail: info@bbintl.com
www.bbintl.com

EN-S4I. In a renowned flower-growing
area in southern California, this bed and
breakfast has ocean views, a southwestern
decor, and a relaxed atmosphere with large
rooms, an apartment, and penthouse with
Jacuzzi. All baths are private and rooms
have a queen- or king-size bed. A Continental plus breakfast and afternoon refreshments are served. Walking distance to the
ocean. $75-150.

SeaBreeze Bed and Breakfast

121 North Vulcan Avenue, 92024
(760) 944-0318
www.compuvar.com/internet/seabreeze

Encinitas's first bed and breakfast. "An
absolute treasure," said KABC talk radio.
Features in this contemporary two-story
ocean-view home are three bedrooms, a
common sitting room with a fireplace, and

kitchenette. A new addition to the inn is
the penthouse, a true "boudoir," with
cable TV, VCR, whirlpool tub and shower,
plus an eight-foot spa on an ocean-view
balcony. Also, an upstairs one-bedroom
apartment with fireplace, kitchen, and
double soaking tub. Sun deck in the front
yard with a waterfall and fish pond. Intimate wedding grotto available. Make
reservations early.

Host: Kirsten Richter
Rooms: 5 (PB) $75-150
Continental Breakfast
Credit Cards: A, B, D
Notes: 2, 5, 8, 9, 10, 11, 12, 14

EUREKA

Abigail's Elegant Victorian Mansion

1406 C Street, 95501
(707) 444-3144; FAX (707) 442-5594
www.bnbcity.com/inns/20016

An award-winning 1888 national historic
landmark featuring spectacular gingerbread
exteriors, opulent Victorian interiors,
antique furnishings, and an acclaimed
French-gourmet breakfast. Breathtakingly
authentic, with all the nostalgic trimmings
of a century ago, this meticulously restored
Victorian masterpiece offers both history
and hospitality, combined with romance
and pampering. With "the most stunningly
spectacular interiors in the state," *World
Traveler* magazine calls it "the best lodging

Abigail's Elegant Victorian Mansion

7 No smoking; 8 Children welcome; 9 Social drinking allowed; 10 Tennis nearby; 11 Swimming nearby;
12 Golf nearby; 13 Skiing nearby; 14 May be booked through a travel agent; 15 Handicapped accessible.

value in California." Ocean views, beaches, Redwood National Park nearby.

Hosts: Doug and Lily Vieyra
Rooms: 4 (2 PB; 2 SB) $75-185
Full Breakfast
Credit Cards: A, B
Notes: 3, 5, 7, 9, 10, 12, 14

Bed and Breakfast International

P.O. Box 282910, San Francisco, 94128-2910
(650) 696-1690; (800) 872-4500
FAX (650) 696-1699; e-mail: info@bbintl.com
www.bbintl.com

EU-W4I. This 1883 Victorian offers old-fashioned hospitality, wonderful gardens, and features a studio of a fiber artist. Full breakfast is served. Four guest rooms have king- or queen-size, or twin beds. Private and shared baths. No smoking. $65-110.

EU-C30I. These charming 1981 and 1986 re-creations of 1880 Victorian mansions offer superb hospitality and excellent full breakfasts. This seaport town offers many recreational activities, including fishing, hiking, golf, biking, and museums. One site has seven guest rooms and the other has 23 guest rooms with private and shared baths. King- or queen-size or double beds available. No smoking. $115-295.

Carter House Victorians

301 L Street, 95501
(707) 444-8062; (800) 404-1390
FAX (707) 444-8067
e-mail: carter52@carterhouse.com
www.carterhouse.com

The Carter House Victorians consists of four properties: The Original Carter House, the Hotel Carter, and the Bell Cottage. Each inn is distinctively designed and graciously appointed and unites contemporary good taste with the timeless elegance of a bygone era. This perfect synthesis of style is sure to delight the most discriminating, and the affable hospitality remains constant throughout one's stay. Room rates include a full breakfast, evening wine and

hors d'oeuvres, and homemade cookies and tea at turndown.

Hosts: Mark and Christi Carter
Rooms: 31 (PB) $152-500
Full Breakfast
Credit Cards: A, B, C, D, E, F
Notes: 2, 4, 5, 6, 7, 8, 9, 10, 11, 12, 14, 15

Old Town Bed and Breakfast Inn

1521 Third Street, 95501
(707) 445-3951; (800) 331-5098
FAX (707) 268-0231
www.dreamwalkerusa.com/otb-b

The uniquely Victorian seaport of Eureka is the setting for this 1871 Greek Revival Italianate two-story Victorian. A short stroll to Humboldt Bay brings nostalgic memories of the great fleets of sailing ships that once carried loads of redwood lumber to San Francisco and the world and brought the bounty of the fishing fleets home. Only two blocks from lumber baron William Carson's famous mansion. Teak hot tub, evening tea, and award-winning breakfast treats. Bring cameras and appetites. Single and corporate rates available. Children under 10, please pre-arrange.

Hosts: Leigh and Diane Benson
Rooms: 6 (4 PB; 2 SB) $80-140
Full Breakfast
Credit Cards: A, B, C, D, E
Notes: 2, 5, 7, 9, 10, 11, 12, 14

A Weaver's Inn

1440 B Street, 95501
(707) 443-8119; (800) 992-8119
FAX (707) 443-7923
e-mail: weavrinn@humboldt1.com
www.humboldt1.com/~weavrinn

Circa 1883. A stately Queen Anne with beautiful gardens and spacious lawn. Four lovely guest rooms furnished in antiques, with down comforters and fresh flowers from the garden. The charm of the Victorian parlor and elegant dining room, fireplaces, and delicious full breakfasts reflect the genteel elegance of a bygone era. The

NOTES: Credit cards accepted: A MasterCard; B Visa; C American Express; D Discover; E Diner's Club; F Other; 2 Personal checks accepted; 3 Lunch available; 4 Dinner available; 5 Open all year; 6 Pets welcome;

Eureka area offers many fine restaurants, antique and speciality import stores, and the special treat of the Victorian era ambiance in Old Town—fish from a boat, enjoy a tour of the harbor, or comb a beach. Inquire about accommodations for pets and children. Smoking is permitted outside only.

Hosts: Lea L. Montgomery, Shoshana McAvoy, and
Lee Montgomery
Rooms: 4 (2 PB; 2 SB) $75-125
Full Breakfast
Credit Cards: A, B, C, D, E
Notes: 2, 5, 7, 9, 12, 14

FAIRFAX

Bed and Breakfast Exchange of Marin County— Referral Service

45 Entrata, San Anselmo, 94960
(415) 485-1971; FAX (415) 454-7179

Scenic Homestay Bed and Breakfast. This bed and breakfast apartment is like a true house in the woods. Lovely, quiet setting and view of forest and creek. Great for extended stays because it has a full kitchen. Self-catered breakfast. No smoking. $85.

FALLBROOK

Bed and Breakfast International

P.O. Box 282910, San Francisco, 94128-2910
(650) 696-1690; (800) 872-4500
FAX (650) 696-1699; e-mail: info@bbintl.com
www.bbintl.com

FB-B2. Relax and unwind poolside in peaceful, rural hilltop setting at large country French chateau nestled on a working avocado ranch. Bed and breakfast offers antique-accented guest suite with queen-size bed, dressing room, and private bath that overlooks the garden. Wineries, antique shops, golf courses are nearby. Dogs and cats in residence. Full breakfast. $75.

FERNDALE

The Gingerbread Mansion

400 Berding Street, P.O. Box 40, 95536
(707) 786-4000; (800) 952-4136

The Gingerbread Mansion inn is well known as one of America's most photographed homes. Its striking Victorian architecture trimmed with gingerbread, its colorful peach and yellow paint, and its surrounding English gardens all make the Gingerbread Mansion a photographer's delight. It is an understatement to say that the interiors are also spectacular. AAA-rated four diamonds. Rates are subject to change.

Host: Ken Torbert
Rooms: 5 (PB) $140-180
Suites: 5 (PB) $150-350
Full Breakfast
Credit Cards: A, B, C
Notes: 2, 5, 7, 8, 9, 14

The Gingerbread Mansion

FORT BRAGG

Bed and Breakfast International

P.O. Box 282910, San Francisco, 94128-2910
(650) 696-1690; (800) 872-4500
FAX (650) 696-1699; e-mail: info@bbintl.com
www.bbintl.com

FB-G14I. Landmark redwood building has 14 guest rooms, all with private baths.

---

7 No smoking; 8 Children welcome; 9 Social drinking allowed; 10 Tennis nearby; 11 Swimming nearby; 12 Golf nearby; 13 Skiing nearby; 14 May be booked through a travel agent; 15 Handicapped accessible.

King, queen, double, and twin beds are available. Near scenic railway, state parks, beaches, fishing, and hiking, and within walking distance to shops and galleries. Full breakfast. No smoking. $85-180.

Glass Beach Bed and Breakfast Inn

726 North Main Street, 95437
(707) 964-6774; www.glassbeachinn.com

In the tradition of inns of early days, Glass Beach Inn is a gracious guest house where hosts offer guests elegance, relaxation, and all the comforts of home. On the beautiful Mendocino Coast. Access to beaches, shops, restaurants, museums, and the famous Skunk Train. "If you have tired of today's commercialism, you will appreciate the ambiance of this beautifully restored home, built in 1920." Anniversaries and honeymoons.

Host: Nancy Cardenas
Rooms: 9 (PB) $95-140
Full Breakfast
Credit Cards: A, B, C, D
Notes: 5, 7, 8, 9, 10, 11, 12, 14, 15

Grey Whale Inn

615 North Main Street, 95437
(707) 964-0640; (800) 382-7244 (reservations)
e-mail: stay@greywhaleinn.com
www.greywhaleinn.com

Handsome Mendocino Coast landmark since 1915. Cozy rooms to expansive suites, all private baths, telephones, and TVs. Ocean, garden, or hill and city views. Some have fireplaces; one has whirlpool tub. Recreation area: pool table, fireside lounge, TV/VCR room. Conference room seats 16 people. Friendly, helpful staff. Full buffet breakfast. Walk to beach, Skunk train, restaurants, shops, microbrewery. Three-star rating from Mobil. ABBA-rated three crowns. AAA three-diamond-rated. Inquire about accommodations for children.

Host: Colette Bailey
Rooms: 14 (PB) $100-170

Grey Whale Inn

Full Breakfast
Credit Cards: A, B, C, D, F
Notes: 2, 5, 7, 9, 10, 11, 12, 14, 15

FREMONT

Lord Bradley's Inn

43344 Mission Boulevard, 94539
(510) 490-0520

This Victorian is nestled below Mission Peak, adjacent to the Mission San Jose. Numerous olive trees on the property were planted by the Ohlone Indians. Common room, garden, patio. Parking in rear. Take the bus or Bay Area Rapid Transit to San Francisco for a day. Close to San Jose airport.

Hosts: Susie and Steve Wilson
Rooms: 8 (PB) $75-125
Continental Breakfast
Credit Cards: A, B, C, D
Notes: 2, 5, 7, 9, 10, 12

GEORGETOWN

American River Inn

Main at Orleans Streets, P.O. Box 43, 95634
(800) 245-6566; FAX (916) 333-9253
e-mail: ari@pcweb.net

In the heart of gold country nine miles off Highway 49 between I-80 and I-50, this "Jewel of the Mother Lode" is a totally restored 1853 miners' boarding house. Each room is individually decorated with Victorian and turn-of-the-century antiques.

NOTES: Credit cards accepted: A MasterCard; B Visa; C American Express; D Discover; E Diner's Club; F Other; 2 Personal checks accepted; 3 Lunch available; 4 Dinner available; 5 Open all year; 6 Pets welcome;

Gorgeous natural gardens, a refreshing mountain stream pool and Jacuzzi, a dove aviary, and mountain bikes. Enjoy a full breakfast in the morning, local wines and treats in the evening. Antique shop on the premises. Other amenities include a croquet field, putting green, and minidriving range. Georgetown is a Sierra foothills village with real flavor and only six miles from Gold Discovery Park in Coloma. Retreat and conference facility.

Hosts: Will and Maria
Rooms: 17 (6 PB; 11 SB) $85-115
Suites: 8 (PB)
Full Breakfast
Credit Cards: A, B, C, D, E
Notes: 2, 5, 8, 9, 10, 11, 12, 13, 14, 15

GEYSERVILLE

Campbell Ranch Inn

1475 Canyon Road, 95441
(707) 857-3476; (800) 959-3878
FAX (707) 857-3239
www.campbellranchinn.com

A 35-acre country setting in the heart of Sonoma County wine country. Spectacular view, beautiful gardens, tennis court, swimming pool, hot tub, and bicycles. Four spacious rooms, one private cottage with fireplace and hot tub. All rooms have private baths, king-size beds, balconies, fresh flowers, and fruit. Air conditioned. Refreshments and homemade evening dessert. Full breakfast served on the terrace. Teenagers welcome. Color brochure available. Minimum stay requirements for weekends.

Hosts: Mary Jane and Jerry Campbell
Rooms: 5 (PB) $125-225

Campbell Ranch Inn

Full Breakfast
Credit Cards: A, B, C
Notes: 2, 5, 7, 9, 12, 14

GILROY

Country Rose Inn Bed and Breakfast

P.O. Box 2500, 95021
(408) 842-0441; FAX (408) 842-6646

Country Rose Inn Bed and Breakfast is nestled in San Martin between Morgan Hill and Gilroy in the original California wine region in south Santa Clara Valley. Is is just minutes from historic San Juan Baulita boasting the only California mission with its original plaza. The heart of Silicon Valley, San Jose, is just 25 miles north. Its rural setting and gracious hostess create a warm hospitable feeling to be remembered. "Every window is a living postcard. It is beautifully simple."

Host: Rose Hernandez
Rooms: 5 (PB) $129-189
Full Breakfast
Credit Cards: A, B, C, D, E
Notes: 2, 5, 7, 12, 14

GLEN ALLEN

Gaige House Inn

13540 Arnold Drive, 95442
(707) 935-0237; (800) 935-0237
FAX (707) 935-6411; e-mail: gaige@sprynet.com
www.gaige.com

Central for all wine country explorations, the spacious and stylish Gaige House Inn is just a short walk to "hip" and delicious restaurants. Thirteen stylish rooms and suites recently redesigned with Plantation/Indonesian influences feature fireplaces, telephones, and luxurious linens as well as Jacuzzi baths and oversized showers in the suites. A pool, spa, lush landscaping, and creekside setting all make for a rare and enjoyable find. Gourmet breakfast. $175-350.

7 No smoking; 8 Children welcome; 9 Social drinking allowed; 10 Tennis nearby; 11 Swimming nearby; 12 Golf nearby; 13 Skiing nearby; 14 May be booked through a travel agent; 15 Handicapped accessible.

Glenelly Inn

5131 Warm Springs Road, 95442
(707) 996-6720; e-mail: glenelly@vom.com
www.glenelly.com

Built in 1916 as an inn, Glenelly offers country hospitality with modern comforts. All eight rooms open to verandas or decks, have private entrances, private baths, down comforters, terry-cloth robes, and country and antique furnishings. Full gourmet breakfast is served in cozy common room or outside. Large garden with outdoor spa and spacious grounds with chairs, tables, swing, and hammock allow enjoyment of beautiful views of surrounding hillsides. Close to fine wineries, restaurants, shops, state parks, horseback riding, biking, and ballooning.

Host: Kristi Hallamore Jeppesen
Rooms: 8 (PB) $115-150
Full Breakfast
Credit Cards: A, B
Notes: 2, 5, 7, 8, 9, 10, 11, 12

Glenelly Inn

GRASS VALLEY

Murphy's Inn

318 Neal Street, 95945
(916) 273-6873; (800) 895-2488
FAX (916) 272-1716

Manicured ivy trims the 1866 Colonial Revival classic built by one of the gold barons as a wedding present for his wife. Eight rooms, four with fireplaces and four with dual shower heads, are decorated in

Murphy's Inn

Victorian elegance. Large outside deck and wraparound porch. Inquire about accommodations for children.

Hosts: Ted and Nancy Daus
Rooms: 8 (PB) $95-150
Full Breakfast
Credit Cards: A, B, C
Notes: 2, 5, 7, 9, 10, 11, 12, 13, 14

GUALALA

North Coast Country Inn

34591 South Highway 1, 95445
(707) 884-4537; (800) 959-4537

A cluster of rustic redwood buildings with ocean views. Rooms feature king- and queen-size beds, fireplaces, private baths, decks, and private entries. The inn has a hot tub and gazebo. Full breakfast is served in common room. Golf, hiking, horseback riding, fishing, and beaches are nearby. Minimum stay requirements for weekends and holidays.

Hosts: Loren and Nancy Flanagan
Rooms: 6 (PB) $150-195

North Coast Country Inn

NOTES: Credit cards accepted: A MasterCard; B Visa; C American Express; D Discover; E Diner's Club; F Other; 2 Personal checks accepted; 3 Lunch available; 4 Dinner available; 5 Open all year; 6 Pets welcome;

Full Breakfast
Credit Cards: A, B, C
Notes: 2, 5, 7, 9, 10, 12, 14

GUERNEVILLE

Bed and Breakfast California

P.O. Box 282910, San Francisco, 94128-2910
(650) 696-1690; (800) 872-4500
FAX (650) 696-1699; e-mail: info@bbintl.com
www.bbintl.com

A vacation home in one of northern California's most beautiful wine country areas. Very peaceful atmosphere, high quality decor, fireplace, and hot tub. Sleeps six. Walk to the Russian River. $150-250.

Ridenhour Ranch House Inn

12850 River Road, 95446
(707) 887-1033

A 1906 inn on two and one-quarter acres of trees, gardens, and meadow in the Russian River area of northern California. Each room is decorated in country English and American antiques, quilts, plants, and fresh flowers. The area has many restaurants, and dinner can be arranged at the inn.

Hosts: Diane and Fritz Rechberger
Rooms: 8 (PB) $95-130
Full Breakfast
Credit Cards: A, B, C
Notes: 2, 4, 5, 7, 8, 9, 11, 12, 14

Santa Nella House

Pocket Creek Canyon, 12130 Highway 16, 95446
(707) 869-9488

Santa Nella is nestled in a redwood forest a short walk to the Russian River and Korbel Champagne Cellars when the summer bridge is in. The house is a country Victorian, circa 1870, with a grand wraparound veranda and restored turn-of-the-century guest rooms—all with wood-burning fireplaces. A well-stocked library is available and a large country kitchen with wood-burning stove and a bay window. Enjoy the hot tub under the redwoods. Large country breakfasts consisting of fresh fruits, juices, freshly ground and brewed coffee, various egg dishes, waffles, and homemade cake are served in the dining room or on the veranda and gazebo on warm mornings.

Hosts: Ed and Joyce Ferrington
Rooms: 4 (PB) $100-110
Full Breakfast
Credit Cards: A, B
Notes: 2, 9, 10, 11, 12, 14

HALF MOON BAY

Bed and Breakfast California

P.O. Box 282910, San Francisco, 94128-2910
(650) 696-1690; (800) 872-4500
FAX (650) 696-1699; e-mail: info@bbintl.com
www.bbintl.com

Old Thyme Inn. A beautifully restored, charming 1899 Queen Anne Victorian, this inn offers guest rooms named for familiar herbs. All of the rooms are unique, with lovely antiques, stuffed animals, fresh flowers, and private baths. Cozy fireplaces and whirlpool baths are in most of the rooms. Full breakfasts are served each morning in the parlor, with a background of classical music. The inn, on historic Main Street, is near shops, restaurants, and galleries. Call for rates.

Cypress Inn on Miramar Beach

407 Mirada Road, 94019
(650) 726-6002; (800) 83-BEACH
FAX (650) 712-0380
e-mail: lodging@cypressinn.com
www.cypressinn.com

Ten steps to the sand. The Bay area's only oceanfront bed and breakfast on five miles of sandy beach 30 minutes south of San Francisco. Private decks, most with unobstructed, breathtaking views of the ocean; all with fireplaces, private baths, telephones. Natural pine and wicker furniture and sky lights. A palette of nature's colors from the sea, sky, and earth, and colorful folk art capture the essence of California contemporary

7 No smoking; 8 Children welcome; 9 Social drinking allowed; 10 Tennis nearby; 11 Swimming nearby; 12 Golf nearby; 13 Skiing nearby; 14 May be booked through a travel agent; 15 Handicapped accessible.

beachside living. Complimentary wine and hors d'oeuvres, and evening dessert. In-house massage therapist. Conference room.

Hosts: Suzie Lankes and Dan Floyd
Rooms: 12 (PB) $165-275
Full Breakfast
Credit Cards: A, B, C, D
Notes: 2, 5, 7, 9, 10, 11, 12, 14, 15

The Farallone Inn Bed and Breakfast

1410 Main Street, Montara, 94037
(415) 728-8200; FAX (415) 728-8740

A gracious bed and breakfast built in 1906. This turn-of-the-century roadside hotel still echoes the unique coastal heritage. From the old red brick used in landscaping to the high ceilings of the spacious rooms, the modernized rooms welcome guests. Enjoy the ocean view or walk to the beach, a quarter-mile away. All guest rooms have private entrances with decks. Short drive to restaurants and San Francisco.

Host: Nina
Rooms: 9 (PB) $95-160
Full Breakfast
Credit Cards: A, B, C, D, E, F
Notes: 5, 6, 7, 8, 9, 10, 11, 12, 14

The Goose and Turrets

835 George Street, Box 937, Montara, 94037-0937
(650) 728-5451; e-mail: rhmgt@montara.com
www.montara.com/goose.html

A quiet, historic bed and breakfast catering to readers, nature lovers, pilots—and

The Goose and Turrets

enthusiastic eaters who appreciate after-noon tea and four-course breakfasts. Only 30 minutes from San Francisco airport and 5 minutes from the beach, this makes a convenient headquarters for visits to San Francisco, Berkeley, Silicon Valley, Monterey, and Carmel. Nearby are tidal pools, bird watching, elephant seals, whale watching, aerotours, fishing, and horse-back riding, as well as restaurants, shops, and galleries. French spoken.

Hosts: Raymond and Emily Hoche-Mong
Rooms: 5 (PB) $85-120
Full Breakfast
Credit Cards: A, B, C, D, E
Notes: 2, 5, 7, 8, 9, 10, 11, 12, 14

Zaballa House

324 Main Street, 94019
(415) 726-9123; FAX (415) 726-3921

The first house built in Half Moon Bay (1859), standing at the entrance to historic Main Street, has been carefully restored into a bed and breakfast. The inn is close to the beach, shopping, and two fine restaurants. Guests enjoy the Victorian decor in rooms with high ceilings and antiques, some with double-wide whirlpool tubs and fireplaces. The friendly innkeeper provides wine and cheese in the evening and a wonderful breakfast in the morning.

Host: Kerry Pendergast
Rooms: 12 (PB) $75-250
Full Breakfast
Credit Cards: A, B, C, D
Notes: 2, 5, 6, 7, 9, 10, 12, 14

NOTES: Credit cards accepted: A MasterCard; B Visa; C American Express; D Discover; E Diner's Club; F Other; 2 Personal checks accepted; 3 Lunch available; 4 Dinner available; 5 Open all year; 6 Pets welcome;

HEALDSBURG

Bed and Breakfast California

P.O. Box 282910, San Francisco, 94128-2910
(650) 696-1690; (800) 872-4500
FAX (650) 696-1699; e-mail: info@bbintl.com
www.bbintl.com

B. This contemporary architect-designed home has a lovely guest suite with a private entrance. It is on the site of an old winery and boasts a 1908 wine cellar in the garden. The suite is attractively furnished in a mix of modern and antique styles and the walls are covered with handmade wallpaper. The home is surrounded by beautiful hills and vineyards with private deck and Jacuzzi for guests. $125.

Bed and Breakfast International

P.O. Box 282910, San Francisco, 94128-2910
(650) 696-1690; (800) 872-4500
FAX (650) 696-1699; e-mail: info@bbintl.com
www.bbintl.com

HE-F2. This 70-acre grape ranch in Sonoma County's spectacular Dry Creek Valley is a family-run bed and breakfast. Enjoy charming antique-decorated guest rooms, tranquil vineyard setting and walks, swimming pool, garden terrace, and wildlife pond. Two guest rooms have queen-size beds and private baths. Full breakfast. No smoking. $90-100.

HE-C91. An 1869 Italianate Victorian townhouse on one-half acre has landscaped grounds with pool and large antique-filled guest rooms. Breakfast with freshly baked breads and afternoon refreshments are served. Nine guest rooms. Shared and private baths. $75-135.

HE-G71. This 1902 Queen Anne Victorian offers an elegant return to a bygone era. Upstairs rooms have roof windows and view of the lovely grounds. Full country breakfast. Seven guest rooms. Private bath. No smoking. $85-130.

Bed and Breakfast San Francisco

P.O. Box 420009, San Francisco, 94142
(415) 931-3083; FAX (415) 921-BBSF (2273)
e-mail: bbsf@linex.com; www.bbsf.com

24. A wonderful bed and breakfast hideaway near the center of town. The owners grow their own grapes and bottle their own wines. The beautiful accommodation has a private entrance and a private bath. Full breakfast. Enjoy the deck and hot tub. $100-125.

Sonoma County Wine and River Country. Jane's place is in rustic Healdsburg in the heart of the wine country, just minutes from some of California's finest wineries, close to the Russian River beaches and resorts, and only one-half hour from the Pacific Coast. There are three quaintly furnished rooms on an estate overlooking vineyards. All the bedrooms have private baths. If guests are lucky, they will be entertained by the wild turkeys while enjoying a home-cooked full breakfast in the morning. $85.

Calderwood Inn

25 West Grant Street, 95448
(707) 431-1110; (800) 600-5444

A romantic 1902 Victorian Inn, just blocks from the plaza and renowned wineries. Grand porches, fountains, koi ponds, and gardens in a lush forested estate. Full breakfast with gourmet coffees and teas is served at 9:00 A.M. Appetizers and port are served in the evenings. Beautiful yet comfortable antiques throughout. Hand-stenciled Victorian wall and ceiling papers. Private baths in each room with either whirlpool, claw-foot tub/showers, or tiled showers. Air conditioned. Walk to plaza and wine tastings.

Hosts: Jennifer and Paul Zawodny
Rooms: 6 (PB) $110-185
Full Breakfast
Credit Cards: None
Notes: 2, 5, 7, 8, 9, 10, 11, 12, 14

7 No smoking; 8 Children welcome; 9 Social drinking allowed; 10 Tennis nearby; 11 Swimming nearby; 12 Golf nearby; 13 Skiing nearby; 14 May be booked through a travel agent; 15 Handicapped accessible.

Camellia Inn

211 North Street, 95448
(707) 433-8182; (800) 727-8182
FAX (707) 433-8130
e-mail: info@camelliainn.com
www.camelliainn.com

Italianate Victorian townhouse, built in 1869, elegantly decorated with antiques. Nine rooms with private baths, several with double whirlpools and gas fireplaces. Full buffet breakfast is served in the dining room beneath massive mahogany mantel. Fifty camellia varieties plus roses on half-acre. Afternoon refreshments in double parlors or by swimming pool. Forty-five-minute drive to coast through redwoods. Walking distance to town square for shopping, restaurants, wineries.

Hosts: Ray, Del, and Lucy Lewand
Rooms: 9 (PB) $75-155
Full Breakfast
Credit Cards: A, B, C
Notes: 2, 5, 7, 8, 9, 10, 11, 12, 14

Haydon Street Inn

321 Haydon Street, 95448
(707) 433-5228; FAX (707) 433-6637

Turn-of-the-century Queen Anne home in old, quiet neighborhood within walking distance of downtown historic plaza and a short drive to many fine wineries. The main house has six comfortable and tastefully decorated guest rooms, all with private baths. A Victorian Gothic-style two-story cottage with two luxurious rooms with private baths and double whirlpool tubs. Abundant, delicious, home-cooked breakfasts served in the sunlit dining room. Air conditioned. Special midweek rates. Canine greeter.

Haydon Street Inn

Rooms: 8 (PB) $95-165
Full Breakfast
Credit Cards: A, B
Notes: 2, 5, 7, 9, 10, 11, 12, 14

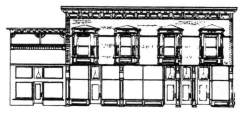

Healdsburg Inn on the Plaza

Healdsburg Inn on the Plaza

110 Matheson Street, P.O. Box 1196, 95448
(707) 433-6991; (800) 431-8663
www.healdsburginn.com

This 1900 brick Victorian, formerly a Wells Fargo stagecoach express station, has been restored and is now elegantly furnished as a bed and breakfast. Features include bay windows with a view of the plaza or open balconies, fireplaces, and central heat/air. Solarium for afternoon tea, snacks, popcorn, wine, music. Coffee and cookies available all day. Champagne breakfasts on weekends. TV, VCR, telephone, and gift certificates. Family owned and operated; close to everything. Midweek and winter rates are discounted 20 to 30 percent.

Hosts: Genny Jenkins and LeRoy Steck
Rooms: 10 (PB) $165-245
Full Breakfast
Credit Cards: A, B
Notes: 2, 5, 7, 10, 11, 12, 14

The Raford House

10630 Wohler Road, 95448
(707) 887-9573; (800) 887-9503
FAX (707) 887-9597
www.rafordhouse.com

This charming landmark Victorian summer house overlooks award-winning vineyards and is surrounded by towering palm trees and old-fashioned flower gardens. Guest rooms are furnished with turn-of-the-century antiques. A full breakfast is served in

NOTES: Credit cards accepted: A MasterCard; B Visa; C American Express; D Discover; E Diner's Club; F Other; 2 Personal checks accepted; 3 Lunch available; 4 Dinner available; 5 Open all year; 6 Pets welcome;

the dining room. The sunroom and front porch entice guests to enjoy the splendid view and complimentary evening wine and hors d'oeuvres. Near many fine wineries, restaurants, the Russian River, and the rugged northern California coast.

Hosts: Carole and Jack Vore
Rooms: 5 (PB) $100-155
Suite: 1 (PB) $180-220
Full Breakfast
Credit Cards: A, B, C, D
Notes: 2, 7, 9, 11, 12, 14

HOLLYWOOD

Bed and Breakfast International

P.O. Box 282910, San Francisco, 94128-2910
(650) 696-1690; (800) 872-4500
FAX (650) 696-1699; e-mail: info@bbintl.com
www.bbintl.com

HH-G2. Savor a panoramic view of the Los Angeles basin from this Hollywood Hills bed and breakfast. Ten minutes from Westwood or Beverly Hills. Full breakfast. $75-90.

HO-N1. Historic West Hollywood neighborhood is the setting for very private self-hosted one-bedroom guest house with kitchen, living room, private bath, double bed, and pool. Central to most tourist attractions, and good public transportation is available. No smoking. $90-100.

LA-G2. A 1910 California bungalow on a quiet palm-tree-lined street close to Hollywood's well-known attractions. There are two second-floor guest rooms, both with private bath and one with a sun deck. Well-traveled hosts speak several languages. Good public transportation. Resident dog. Continental breakfast. $40-50.

HOPE VALLEY

Sorensen's

14255 Highway 88, 96120
(916) 694-2203; (800) 423-9949

Three bed and breakfast cabins are available at this resort for all seasons in the Sierra Nevada. One cabin has a small sitting area with comfortable rockers, an old-fashioned tub in the bath. The other two cabins are side-by-side (robes provided) and can be rented together or separately. They share a small sitting area and full bath. Guests can enjoy cross-country skiing, backpacking, hiking, fishing, bicycling, or just plain relaxing. Close to skiing, mineral hot springs, horseback riding, river rafting, and the delights of Lake Tahoe. Also available are one- or two-person cabins, group cabins, log cabins, and homes. Pets and children are welcome. No smoking.

Hosts: John and Patty Brissenden
Cabins: 3 (1 PB; 2 SB) $70-120
Full Breakfast
Credit Cards: A, B, C, D
Notes: 2, 3, 4, 5, 6, 7, 8, 9, 10, 11, 12, 13, 14, 15

HOPLAND

Fetzer Bed and Breakfast Inn at Valley Oaks Ranch

13601 East Side Road, 95449
(707) 744-1250; FAX (707) 744-7488

Nestled in the vineyards of historic Valley Oaks Ranch is the charming six-room bed and breakfast inn at the Fetzer Visitor Center. Beautifully furnished, the rooms feature patios with stunning views of the surrounding vineyards. Several rooms feature a kitchenette and/or whirlpool tub. The rooms include Continental breakfast, telephones, TV, and seasonal access to the pool. Three additional rooms are in the historic Haas House. The Hopland location makes it ideal for day-trips throughout the Redwood Empire. No smoking. Children are welcome.

Hosts: Jo Gennaso and Ines Guevara
Rooms: 9 (PB) $120-200
Continental Breakfast
Credit Cards: A, B, C, D
Notes: 3, 5, 7, 8, 9, 11, 12, 14, 15

---

7 No smoking; 8 Children welcome; 9 Social drinking allowed; 10 Tennis nearby; 11 Swimming nearby; 12 Golf nearby; 13 Skiing nearby; 14 May be booked through a travel agent; 15 Handicapped accessible.

IDYLLWILD

The Pine Cove Inn

23481 Highway 243, P.O. Box 2181, 92549
(888) 659-5033; FAX (909) 659-5034

A unique bed and breakfast experience. Ten units available, all with private entrance and bath. Nine units have microwaves and refrigerators; one unit has a full kitchen. Four units have wood-burning fireplaces and three have electric fireplaces. Six units have mountain views. Families are encouraged. Midweek rates are available. Two-night minimum stay required on weekends.

Hosts: Bob and Michelle Bollmann
Rooms: 10 (PB) $70-100
Full Breakfast
Credit Cards: A, B, C, D
Notes: 2, 5, 8, 9, 14

Strawberry Creek Inn

26370 Highway 243, P.O. Box 1818, 92549
(909) 659-3202; (800) 262-8969

Award-winning bed and breakfast inn is in a rambling large home and courtyard wing in the San Jacinto Mountains. Its cedar-shingled exterior blends in quietly with the surrounding pines and oaks. Comfort mixes with nostalgia in the glassed-in porch where guests enjoy a full breakfast, the specially decorated bedrooms, a spacious living room with fireplace, and the inviting outdoor decks and hammocks.

Strawberry Creek Inn

Hosts: Diana Dugan and Jim Goff
Rooms: 10 (PB) $79-150
Full Breakfast
Credit Cards: A, B, D
Notes: 2, 5, 7, 9, 14, 15

INVERNESS

Bed and Breakfast California

P.O. Box 282910, San Francisco, 94128-2910
(650) 696-1690; (800) 872-4500
FAX (650) 696-1699; e-mail: info@bbintl.com
www.bbintl.com

A long driveway takes guests to one of the most beautiful and romantic original Inverness homes. Perched on a hill just beyond the village of Inverness, this inn is a Craftsman-style home built in 1916 offering decks with sweeping views overlooking Tomales Bay and the Marin Hills beyond. The guest rooms feature claw-foot tubs, pedestal sinks, and French showers. Guests are invited to plunk on the upright piano or relax in front of the massive river rock fireplace or in the hot tub. Weekends a delicious and hearty breakfast awaits, and on weekdays a Continental breakfast served. $98-167.

Fairwinds Farm Bed and Breakfast Cottage and Dan's En Suite Room

82 Drake's Summit, P.O. Box 581, 94937
(415) 663-9454; FAX (415) 663-1787
e-mail: fairwinds9@aol.com

Overlooking 75,000 acres of national seashore with direct access. Only visible light is the lighthouse on Farallon Islands. Over 100-square-foot private cottage, fully equipped kitchen, full bath, fireplace, TV/stereo/VCR (500-plus movies), library, beach umbrella, toys, playhouse, barnyard animals, garden with ponds, waterfalls, giant swing. Hot tub on private deck. Queen-size bed, two doubles, crib, and two futons. Dan's En Suite Room has a private entrance, wraparound decks, fireplace, TV/VCR, movies, microwave, refrigerator, deck-top hot tub with ocean view. Continental breakfast and evening treats.

Cottage: 1 (PB) $148.50
En Suite Room: 1 (PB) $100
Full Breakfast/Continental Breakfast
Credit Cards: None
Notes: 2, 5, 7, 8, 9, 10, 11, 12

Ten Inverness Way

10 Inverness Way, P.O. Box 63, 94937-0063
(415) 669-1648; FAX (415) 669-7403
e-mail: inn@teninvernessway.com

Built in 1904, this handsome redwood-shingled bed and breakfast features a stone fireplace, sunny library with many good books, gourmet breakfasts, picnic lunches, and access to a diverse recreational area. Enjoy a relaxing soak in the garden hot tub after an afternoon hike. Just 45 minutes from San Francisco's Golden Gate Bridge, the inn is nestled in a nostalgic waterfront village abutting the Point Reyes National Seashore.

Hosts: Scott and Teri Moweny
Rooms: 5 (PB) $145-180
Full Breakfast
Credit Cards: None
Notes: 2, 3, 5, 7, 11, 12, 14

IONE

The Heirloom

214 Shakeley Lane, 95640
(209) 274-4468

The Heirloom

Travel down a country lane into a romantic English garden where a petite Colonial mansion (circa 1863) is shaded by century-old trees and scented by magnolias and gardenias. Fireplaces and balconies. Breakfast has a French flair. Enjoy gracious hospitality. Closed Thanksgiving, Christmas Eve, and Christmas Day. Children over 10 welcome.

Hosts: Patricia Cross and Melisande Hubbs
Rooms: 6 (4 PB; 2 SB) $65-98
Full Breakfast
Credit Cards: A, B, C
Notes: 2, 7, 9, 11, 12, 14

JACKSON

Bed and Breakfast International

P.O. Box 282910, San Francisco, 94128-2910
(650) 696-1690; (800) 872-4500
FAX (650) 696-1699; e-mail: info@bbintl.com
www.bbintl.com

JA-C8I. Walking distance to gold rush town's historic area and near wineries, 1872 Victorian inn with a lovely rose garden and spa serves a full breakfast. Private or shared baths. $90-130.

JAMESTOWN

Jamestown Hotel

18153 Main Street, P.O. Box 539, 95327
(209) 984-3902; (800) 205-4901
FAX (209) 984-4149; e-mail: jthotel@sonnet.com

The Jamestown Hotel lets guests sample the flavor of life in the gold rush days. From the old brick exterior and wooden veranda-style balcony, to the exquisitely furnished suites, the hotel has been carefully restored to the elegance of the mid-1800s. Here is the perfect place for city-weary people seeking a country retreat. Seven of the guest rooms feature furnishings indicative of the gold rush era, with antiques and private Victorian bath with brass shower. The other three guest rooms have whirlpool tubs, TVs, and VCRs. The hosts offer the charm of a small country inn, friendly staff,

7 No smoking; 8 Children welcome; 9 Social drinking allowed; 10 Tennis nearby; 11 Swimming nearby; 12 Golf nearby; 13 Skiing nearby; 14 May be booked through a travel agent; 15 Handicapped accessible.

full-service dining room, and bar. Skiing is one hour away.

Hosts: Janet and Lee Hammond
Rooms: 10 (PB) $70-135
Continental Breakfast
Credit Cards: A, B, C, D, E
Notes: 2, 3, 4, 5, 7, 8, 9, 10, 11, 12, 14

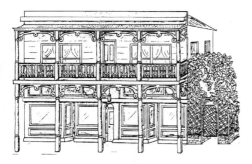

Jamestown National Hotel

Jamestown National Hotel, A Country Inn

18183 Main Street, 95327
(209) 984-3446; (800) 894-3446
FAX (209) 984-5620
e-mail: info@national-hotel.com
www.national-hotel.com

This historic hotel (bed and breakfast) is in the heart of the gold country, near Yosemite and numerous outdoor activities. The 1800s authentic decor will take guests back to a simpler and romantic time, while the warm and congenial staff will tend to every need. The restaurant and original saloon wide range of menu options. Continental plus breakfast.

Host: Stephen Willey
Rooms: 9 (PB) $80-120
Continental Breakfast
Credit Cards: A, B, C, D, E, F
Notes: 3, 4, 5, 6, 7, 9, 10, 11, 12, 13, 14

The Palm Hotel Bed and Breakfast

10382 Willow Street, 95327
(209) 984-3429; FAX (209) 984-4929
e-mail: innkeeper@palmhotel.com
www.palmhotel.com

This 100-year-old Victorian, off Main Street, graces Jamestown with its rare arched windows and five-story tower. Eight unique rooms have private baths. Relax in a bubble bath in a claw-foot tub or enjoy double-headed marble showers. High vaulted ceilings and sunny sitting areas recall days past. Walk to antique shops, gourmet restaurants, and Railtown 1897 State Historic Park.

Hosts: Rick and Sandy Allen
Rooms: 8 (PB) $85-145
Full Breakfast
Credit Cards: A, B, C
Notes: 5, 7, 8, 9, 11, 12, 13, 14, 15

Royal Hotel

18239 Main Street, P.O. Box 219, 95327
(209) 984-5271; FAX (209) 984-1675
www.ameri-land.com

Gold rush Victorian theme, English antiques, Axminster carpeting, honeymoon cottage in second oldest gold mining town in the West. Silent movies and cliffhangers shown daily. Ninety exhibit frames of movies and TV productions in county since 1916. Two-story, on one-half acre, four cottages, and four-unit miner's shack. Impeccably clean. Town of 1,200 people and one long block of restaurants, antique shops, and memorabilia.

Hosts: Robert and Nancy Bosich
Rooms: 20 (16 PB; 4 SB) $55-85
Continental Breakfast
Credit Cards: A, B, C
Notes: 5, 7, 8, 9, 10, 11, 12, 13, 14

JENNER

Bed and Breakfast California

P.O. Box 282910, San Francisco, 94128-2910
(650) 696-1690; (800) 872-4500
FAX (650) 696-1699; e-mail: info@bbintl.com
www.bbintl.com

Jenner is a little town just north of Point Reyes. Guests may rent one of the 11 rooms or a whole beachfront house. The inn has some of the furnishings of the house's original owners from the 1890s. Try snuggling

NOTES: Credit cards accepted: A MasterCard; B Visa; C American Express; D Discover; E Diner's Club; F Other; 2 Personal checks accepted; 3 Lunch available; 4 Dinner available; 5 Open all year; 6 Pets welcome;

down on a chesterfield in the main room with a good book. Full breakfast is provided. House rentals include linens and firewood but no breakfast. Groups as large as 10 may be accommodated. Call for rates.

JULIAN

Bed and Breakfast California

P.O. Box 282910, San Francisco, 94128-2910
(650) 696-1690; (800) 872-4500
FAX (650) 696-1699; e-mail: info@bbintl.com
www.bbintl.com

Julian White House. This intimate, petite Colonial mansion sits among tree-lined country roads just a few miles from town. Four guest rooms are appointed with antiques, each with private bath. The honeymoon suite is spacious with mountain views, a claw-foot slipper tub, and white canopied bed. Full breakfast served in the dining room or in room upon request. Freshly baked cookies are a terrific tuck-in treat. $90-165.

Eden Creek Orchard Bed and Breakfast

1052 Julian Orchards Drive, 92036
(760) 765-2102; (800) 916-2739
FAX (760) 943-7959
e-mail: eden_bb@ramonamall.com
www.ramonamall.com/eden_bb.html

Two romantic cottage suites on a 10-acre apple orchard. In historic Julian, a gold mining town in the mountains one hour east of San Diego. Eden Creek Suite has two lavishly furnished fireplaces, kitchenette, two patios, fountain, and swing. The Orchard Suite is luxurious with a private deck, fireplace, kitchenette, queen-size canopied bed, and claw-foot tub. Both suites have TV, VCR, and CD player. Jacuzzi overlooks mountains. Winery next door, carriage ride, hiking, horseshoes, large cozy barn for weddings and reunions. Horses welcome.

Hosts: Gary and Lee Simons
Rooms: 3 (PB) $95-125
Full and Continental Breakfast

Credit Cards: A, B, C, D
Notes: 2, 5, 7, 8, 9, 10, 11, 12, 14

Orchard Hill Country Inn

2502 Washington Street, P.O. Box 425, 92036-0425
(619) 765-1700

A winding, tree-lined drive leads to the hilltop home of Orchard Hill Country Inn, an award-winning, traditional country inn offering 22 guest rooms and four-diamond dining, in the mountain hamlet town of San Diego County's historic Julian. The inn is comprised of four cottages, each containing three plush suites. Still higher on the hill is a two-story lodge with 10 more guest rooms, dining room, club room, and great room with massive stone fireplace. Suites and lodge rooms offer deluxe amenities. Rates include full breakfast and afternoon hors d'oeuvres. Reservations required.

Hosts: Pat and Darrell Straube
Rooms: 22 (PB) $132-225
Full Breakfast
Credit Cards: A, B, C
Notes: 2, 3, 4, 5, 7, 9, 10, 11, 12, 14, 15

KERNVILLE

Kern River Inn Bed and Breakfast

119 Kern River Drive, P.O. Box 1725, 93238
(760) 376-6750; (800) 986-4382

Charming, classic country riverfront bed and breakfast on the Wild and Scenic Kern River in the southern Sierra Nevada three hours north of Los Angeles. All bedrooms have private baths and feature river views; most have whirlpool tubs or fireplaces. Full breakfast. Walk to shops, restaurants, parks, museum. Short drive to giant sequoias. An all-year vacation area with white-water rafting, fishing, and kayaking; golf, skiing, hiking, and biking; water skiing, boating, wind surfing, and fishing.

Hosts: Jack and Carita
Rooms: 6 (PB) $79-99
Full Breakfast

7 No smoking; 8 Children welcome; 9 Social drinking allowed; 10 Tennis nearby; 11 Swimming nearby; 12 Golf nearby; 13 Skiing nearby; 14 May be booked through a travel agent; 15 Handicapped accessible.

Kern River Inn

Credit Cards: A, B, C
Notes: 2, 5, 7, 8, 9, 11, 12, 13, 14, 15

KLAMATH

Historic Requa Inn

451 Requa Road, 95548
(707) 482-8205; (888) 788-1706

Historic 1914 inn with easy access to Redwood National Park. Nearby activities include
hiking in the Redwoods, beaches, whale and
bird watching, salmon and steelhead fishing.
Nearby attractions include Klamath River Jet
Boat tours, Trees of Mystery, and the Tour-
thru-Tree. The lobby offers a stunning Klamath River view, comfortable chairs, and a
cozy fireplace. The guest rooms are quaint
and comfortable. Choose between claw-foot
tub or shower. Fabulous dinners served.

Host: Susie Reese
Rooms: 10 (PB) $59.50-97.50
Full Breakfast
Credit Cards: A, B, D
Notes: 2, 3, 4, 5, 6, 7, 8, 9, 14

LAGUNA BEACH

Bed and Breakfast California

P.O. Box 282910, San Francisco, 94128-2910
(650) 696-1690; (800) 872-4500
FAX (650) 696-1699; e-mail: info@bbintl.com
www.bbintl.com

Originally built in 1946, this newly renovated property is in quintessential beach
style, with open rafters and Mexican tile
floors. The upstairs guest apartment sleeps

four. French doors open to a deck looking
towards the ocean, and guests are only one-
half block from the beach. A private tiled
patio provides a perfect place to enjoy a
meal or relax with a book. The downstairs
studio has a private entrance and offers
double bed and private bath. $100-200.

Bed and Breakfast International

P.O. Box 282910, San Francisco, 94128-2910
(650) 696-1690; (800) 872-4500
FAX (650) 696-1699; e-mail: info@bbintl.com
www.bbintl.com

DP-B291. Romantic Cape Cod-style inn at
water's edge is renowned for its hospitality
and gourmet breakfasts. A fireplace and
Jacuzzi tub and robes are featured in each
room as is a view of the ocean, harbor, or
hills. Excellent restaurants and shops
nearby. $135-150.

LA-C6I. This New Orleans-style Colonial
inn with central courtyard and subtropical
plants is two blocks from the beach. It is in
the heart of the village and within walking
distance to shops and galleries. The six guest
rooms have private baths and queen-size
beds. Continental plus breakfast. $95-150.

LG-C201. Charming Spanish-style bed and
breakfast inn with unique guest rooms and
suites provides a generous buffet breakfast
and evening refreshments in the library or
poolside. Nineteen guest rooms and one
cottage. Private bath. $95-155.

LG-E121. Rooms in lovely Continental-
style bed and breakfast in the heart of Laguna
are set around a courtyard. Guests may enjoy
breakfast and lounging near the fountain,
flowers, and tables. The beach is just outside
the back gate. No smoking. Eleven guest
rooms and one suite. Private bath. $100-175.

SA-C81. Imaginatively decorated rooms with
Paradise Island themes are featured in unique

NOTES: Credit cards accepted: A MasterCard; B Visa; C American Express; D Discover; E Diner's Club;
F Other; 2 Personal checks accepted; 3 Lunch available; 4 Dinner available; 5 Open all year; 6 Pets welcome;

bed and breakfast at the ocean. Several rooms have Jacuzzis, fireplaces, and ocean views. Honeymoon suites available. Midweek rates available. Full breakfast. $120-350.

The Carriage House

The Carriage House of Laguna Beach

1322 Catalina Street, 92651
(714) 494-8945

The Carriage House features all private suites with living room, bedroom, bath, and some kitchen facilities. Two-bedroom suites available. All surround a courtyard of plants and flowers, two blocks from the ocean. Close to art galleries, restaurants, and shops. Minimum-stay requirements for weekends and holidays. Inquire about accommodations for pets.

Hosts: Lesley and Andy Kettley
Suites: 6 (PB) $95-150
Continental Breakfast
Credit Cards: A, B, C
Notes: 2, 5, 7, 8, 9, 10, 11, 12, 14

LA JOLLA

Bed and Breakfast California

P.O. Box 282910, San Francisco, 94128-2910
(650) 696-1690; (800) 872-4500
FAX (650) 696-1699; e-mail: info@bbintl.com
www.bbintl.com

This Mediterranean-style home is set in an exclusive area with a stunning view of the Pacific. Hosts have two rooms with private baths. Hosts are an architect and a retired teacher who also collect modern art. Full breakfast on the terrace by the pool. $95.

The Bed and Breakfast Inn at La Jolla

7753 Draper Avenue, 92037
(619) 456-2066

Offering deluxe accommodations in 15 charmingly decorated rooms, one block from the beach in the heart of La Jolla by the Sea, the Bed and Breakfast Inn at La Jolla is listed as Historical Site 179 on the San Diego registry. Fireplaces and ocean views are featured in many rooms. Fresh fruit, sherry, fresh flowers, and terry-cloth robes await in each guest room. Savor a large breakfast in the dining room, on the patio, or in the bedroom. A picnic basket to add the finishing touch to the day is also available. Children 12 and older welcome. Limited handicapped accessibility.

Rooms: 15 (PB) $110-250
Full Breakfast
Credit Cards: A, B, C
Notes: 2, 5, 7, 9, 10, 11, 12, 14

Bed and Breakfast International

P.O. Box 282910, San Francisco, 94128-2910
(650) 696-1690; (800) 872-4500
FAX (650) 696-1699; e-mail: info@bbintl.com
www.bbintl.com

LJ-S2. Tastefully decorated contemporary bed and breakfast designed by the architect/host in La Jolla features views of San Diego and beaches from the pool and Jacuzzi. Two guest rooms with private baths and private entrances. No smoking. Full breakfast. $85-95.

LJ-MS1. Guest suite with private balcony in mountaintop home in gated community. Beautiful antiques throughout. View of Mount Soledad and ocean below. $115.

LJ-B16I. Beautifully decorated bed and breakfast inn with ocean views and attractive gardens offers an elegant, comfortable way to enjoy this seaside paradise. Private bathrooms have queen-size or twin beds and some rooms have a fireplace. Continental plus breakfast and afternoon refreshments served. $85-225.

Prospect Park Inn

1110 Prospect Street, 92037
(619) 454-0133; (800) 433-1609
FAX (619) 454-2056

Twenty-two-room inn in the heart of La Jolla, one block from the beach. Most rooms offer ocean views. Decor is contemporary with queen-size bed, cable TV, air conditioning, and private bath. Rooms rates include Continental breakfast and parking. Two beautiful penthouse suites available. Nonsmoking property.

Rooms: 22 (PB) $110-400
Continental Breakfast
Credit Cards: A, B, C, D, E, F
Notes: 5, 7, 8, 9, 10, 11, 12, 14

LAKE ARROWHEAD

The Carriage House Bed and Breakfast

472 Emerald Drive, P.O. Box 982, 92352
(909) 336-1400; (800) 526-5070
FAX (909) 336-6092

New England-style house hidden in the woods, with views of Lake Arrowhead. Country decor, with feather beds and down comforters. Three rooms, each with private bath. Fireplace in suite. Beverages and snacks in afternoon. Large sunroom and deck. Close to lake and wonderful walking trails. Returning guests rave about the warmth and hospitality of the hosts and the great breakfasts. Personal checks accepted seven days prior to arrival. May be booked through a travel agent Monday through Thursday only.

Hosts: Lee and Johan Karstens
Rooms: 3 (PB) $95-135.

Full Breakfast
Credit Cards: A, B, C, D
Notes: 5, 7, 9, 10, 11, 13

Eagle's Landing

12406 Cedarwood, 92317
P.O. Box 1510, Blue Jay, 92317 (mail)
(909) 336-2642; (800) 835-5085
www.southerncalonline.com

The interesting Mountain Gothic architecture, tower, stained glass, 26-foot ceilings, and walls of glass with grand views of Lake Arrowhead make Eagle's Landing a landmark; but the warmth, fun, and hospitality of the hosts are what guests return for. The three beautiful rooms are decorated with art, antiques, and crafts collected from around the world. The suite is cabin-like and done in Early California style.

Hosts: Dorothy Stone and Jack
Rooms: 4 (PB) $95-195
Full Breakfast
Credit Cards: A, B, C, D
Notes: 2, 5, 7, 9, 11, 13, 14

LAKEPORT

Forbestown Inn

825 Forbes Street, 95453
(707) 263-7858; FAX (707) 263-7878
e-mail: forbestowninn@zapcom.net
www.innaccess.com/fti

A charming Civil War-era Victorian farmhouse with four bedrooms and a separate carriage house all furnished with oak antiques. Lovely, secluded garden with pool. Afternoon treats as well as wine and cheese are served daily. Enjoy beautiful Clear Lake for water sports and fishing, and downtown Lakeport for shopping and dining, both within easy walking distance. Many fun local events throughout the year, as well as big name entertainers in concert at nearby Konocti Harbor Resort. Listed in many publications including "North California Best Places."

Hosts: Wally and Pat Kelley
Rooms: 5 (3 PB; 2 SB) $85-150
Full Breakfast

NOTES: Credit cards accepted: A MasterCard; B Visa; C American Express; D Discover; E Diner's Club; F Other; 2 Personal checks accepted; 3 Lunch available; 4 Dinner available; 5 Open all year; 6 Pets welcome;

Credit Cards: A, B, C, D
Notes: 2, 5, 7, 9, 10, 11, 12, 14

LAKE TAHOE

Bed and Breakfast International

P.O. Box 282910, San Francisco, 94128-2910
(650) 696-1690; (800) 872-4500
FAX (650) 696-1699; e-mail: info@bbintl.com
www.bbintl.com

LT-C4. Lakefront historic Tahoe stone house with private beach and pier has contemporary decor with antique accents and full breakfast. Queen- and king-size beds and private baths. Bicycle and paddle boat rentals are available and skiing is nearby. Pet dog. $110-135.

LT-C71. A 1938 Old Tahoe-style house with European pine furniture offers cottage suites and large rooms, full breakfast, afternoon refreshments, private beach with a dock, and winter ski packages. Private bath. No smoking. $100-160.

LT-F5. This 1934 Old Tahoe-style house with French country decor has private beach privileges, terry-cloth robes, guest refrigerator, dining area, and Continental plus breakfast. Choice of queen- or king-size bed and private or shared baths. Additional accommodations nearby include a guest cottage with a lake view. $95-155.

LT-R41. Lakefront bed and breakfast decorated with Laura Ashley fabrics has pine walls and lake view. Four guest rooms with private and shared baths. Full breakfast. $100-200.

LONG BEACH

Bed and Breakfast California

P.O. Box 282910, San Francisco, 94128-2910
(650) 696-1690; (800) 872-4500
FAX (650) 696-1699; e-mail: info@bbintl.com
www.bbintl.com

Bluff Park. This perfectly restored 1912 Craftsman home has two big guest rooms and one smaller one: perfect for a family. On a quiet residential street, just two blocks from the beach. Antique furnishings are simple and serene. Breakfast is sumptuous on weekends, self-serve during the week. $65.

Kennebec Corner. Private retreat in a 1920s California Craftsman home. Enjoy the entire second floor in guests' own private suite. The bedroom adjoins the sitting room and includes the most comfortable king-size bed guests will ever sleep on. The bath is equipped with a glass-enclosed shower as well as a double-size bathtub sunken in marble. If guests must work, there is an office area off the sitting room which features a magnificent wood-burning fireplace. Guests may use an outdoor spa at any time. $95-140.

Bed and Breakfast International

P.O. Box 282910, San Francisco, 94128-2910
(650) 696-1690; (800) 872-4500
FAX (650) 696-1699; e-mail: info@bbintl.com
www.bbintl.com

LB-L5I. Former mayor's home is now a bed and breakfast inn with spacious rooms. Convenient for the tourist or business traveler. The five guest rooms have private baths and queen or twin beds. Full breakfast served. No smoking. $95.

LB-M1. This bed and breakfast is three short blocks from the beach, with a second-floor guest room and suite with kitchen. Private bath. Weekly rates available. Continental breakfast. $50-75.

LB-G1. This 1920s California Craftsman, in historic Bluff Park features a very private guest suite that is the entire second story. Amenities include a fireplace, sitting room, balcony, king-size bed, large bath/dressing room, and full breakfast on weekends. A patio and hot tub are available. Hosts can

7 No smoking; 8 Children welcome; 9 Social drinking allowed; 10 Tennis nearby; 11 Swimming nearby; 12 Golf nearby; 13 Skiing nearby; 14 May be booked through a travel agent; 15 Handicapped accessible.

assist with arrangements for a unique gondola cruise through the canals of nearby Naples, tickets to Civic Light Opera, and other events. Convenient for business people weekdays, as suite offers a small office with fax and telephone. $80-140.

Bed and Breakfast Southwest Reservation Service

P.O. Box 51198, Phoenix, AZ 85076-1198
(602) 947-9704; (800) 762-9704
FAX (602) 874-1316

303. In Long Beach's historic Bluff Park, two blocks from the beach, this circa 1920s home offers a private four-room romantic suite with cozy sitting room with fireplace, and private bath with sunken double-size marble tub. French doors lead to courtyard and Jacuzzi spa. Gourmet breakfast on weekends; Continental or California health breakfast weekdays. No smoking. No pets or children. $85-140.

Lord Mayor's Indn Bed and Breakfast

435 Cedar Avenue, 90802
(562) 436-0324 (phone/FAX)
e-mail: innkeepers@lordmayors.com
www.lordmayors.com

This elegantly restored 1904 home of the first mayor of Long Beach invites guests to enjoy the ambiance of years gone by. Recipient of awards in 1991 for restoration and beautification. The inn's rooms have ten-foot ceilings and are all tastefully decorated with period antiques. Each unique bedroom has a private bath and access to a large sun deck. A full breakfast is prepared by the hosts and served in the dining room or on the deck overlooking the garden area. Convenient to beaches, the convention center, civic center, and theaters.

Rooms: 11 (PB) $80-125
Full Breakfast
Credit Cards: A, B, C, E
Notes: 2, 5, 7, 8, 9, 10, 11, 12, 14

LOS ANGELES

Bed and Breakfast California

P.O. Box 282910, San Francisco, 94128-2910
(650) 696-1690; (800) 872-4500
FAX (650) 696-1699; e-mail: info@bbintl.com
www.bbintl.com

Art Nouveau in Old LA. This 1930s custom home is on manicured grounds in prestigious Hancock Park. Elegant guest suite has sitting area, king-size bed, and huge original tile bath. Full breakfast in the formal dining room on weekends; Continental on weekdays. Very, very beautiful architecture. $85.

California Classic Near Sunset Boulevard. This stunning California Spanish mansion is on a residential street one block from Sunset Boulevard and has four guest rooms, two with private bath and two sharing a bath. Telephones and TVs available. Amenities include terraced garden, gazebo, hot tub, and gated parking. The host is a gourmet chef and can provide meals in addition to the full breakfast upon arrangement. $65-75.

Country in the City. Just a few minutes from the airport, this condo is shared with the interior decorator hostess. The bedroom has a private bath and is appointed with bent-willow furniture and country charm. The hostess can pick up guests at the airport and help with other arrangements. Full breakfast. $65.

Country Manor in Westwood. This elegant mansion was built when Los Angeles still had rolling hills and UCLA was a budding university. Just a block from Wilshire Boulevard and a mile from the campus, two bedrooms are impeccably decorated, including the original hand-painted bathroom tile. Full breakfast in the dining room or in the country garden. $75.

NOTES: Credit cards accepted: A MasterCard; B Visa; C American Express; D Discover; E Diner's Club; F Other; 2 Personal checks accepted; 3 Lunch available; 4 Dinner available; 5 Open all year; 6 Pets welcome;

Gail's House. A 1927 completely restored Spanish-style building with European interior. This 3,000-square-foot home is on the second floor. The dining room opens onto a small patio on one side and a large gourmet kitchen on the other side. Guest room has a king-size bed which converts to twins and a private bath; second room with king-size bed sometimes available as well. Very high quality. Close to Century City, downtown, Beverly Hills. Fifteen minutes to the ocean. $85.

Historic Ambiance. Close to the USC campus, this 1910 Craftsman historic registry home has two upstairs guest rooms, with a bath between them. There's a shaded porch in front, a sunny deck in the rear, and a small sun porch off one guest room. Close to the freeways and Music Center, and very close to the convention center. $50-60.

Moon Villa in Washington Heights. Enjoy 360-degree views from the multilevel deck/patio of this spacious hillside house. The Western Room can accommodate a family of four; the other comes with sunken double tub. Start the day with a full gourmet breakfast and then enjoy the attractions of Los Angeles, Pasadena, and the San Gabriel Mountains. $75-80.

Bed and Breakfast International

P.O. Box 282910, San Francisco, 94128-2910
(650) 696-1690; (800) 872-4500
FAX (650) 696-1699; e-mail: info@bbintl.com
www.bbintl.com

LA-AU3. This stately bed and breakfast once owned by a studio mogul is on a private cul-de-sac. Guests may enjoy music, billiards room, Olympic-size swimming pool and spa, as well as living room and sunroom. Bedrooms with private bath are beautifully appointed with period antiques. Conveniently near Sunset Strip with easy freeway access to downtown or studio attractions. Continental breakfast served. $75-85.

LA-B4. At the foot of the Hollywood Hills near West Hollywood restaurants and attractions, this Mediterranean-style house with a music room, interesting artifacts, and antiques offers four guest rooms with queen-size, double, or twin beds and private or shared baths. Amenities include a full breakfast, patio areas, hot tub, and off-street parking. Good public transportation is available. No smoking. $50-85.

LA-C2. Beautifully restored Craftsman-style house in the National Register of Historic Places is close to USC and civic and convention centers. Two comfortable guest rooms, lovely gardens, and patio are available for guests to enjoy. Shared and private baths. No smoking. $45-50.

LA-D2. Spacious apartment, on the border of Westwood and Century City, offers convenience and homey comfort. Just minutes from the Getty Museum, Santa Monica, and Beverly Hills. Well-traveled host makes a wonderful built-in concierge. Continental breakfast. $65.

LA-S1. This convenient and spacious 800-square-foot, three-room apartment with patios is a good location for vacationing sightseers, business people, and people interested in relocating to the Los Angeles area. Breakfast is self-catered. No smoking. $65-75.

LA-S3. Two-story, Art Deco-style, architect-designed bed and breakfast nestled in the beautiful Los Feliz Hills of Los Angeles near Griffith Park and the Greek Theatre offers a quiet, comfortable setting convenient to fine restaurants, entertainment, and tourist attractions. Two guest rooms have private bath. Public transportation available. $60-65.

---

7 No smoking; 8 Children welcome; 9 Social drinking allowed; 10 Tennis nearby; 11 Swimming nearby; 12 Golf nearby; 13 Skiing nearby; 14 May be booked through a travel agent; 15 Handicapped accessible.

LA-S1B. Very private suite in the Hollywood Hills with grand views of Los Angeles offers a large living room with kitchen area. Guest suite has a private bath. No smoking. $100-135.

WLA-C1. French country decor and collectibles throughout this lovely, spacious apartment hosted by interior decorator. Queen-size bed with private bath. Convenient to LAX, beach cities, freeways, and many tourist attractions. Continental plus breakfast. Garage parking. $60-65.

Inn at Playa del Rey

435 Culver Boulevard, Playa del Rey, 90293
(310) 574-1920; FAX (310) 574-9920
e-mail: playainn@aol.com

The Inn at Playa del Rey is close to the beach and overlooks both the main channel of Marina del Rey and a 200-acre bird sanctuary. The inn was the only California bed and breakfast inn featured on America Online's "Inn of the Week." All 21 rooms are just as refreshing as the views, with distinctive decor. Rooms facing the wetlands have fireplaces, decks, marina sailboat views, and Jacuzzi tubs. Two "romance suites" feature a fireplace in the bathroom next to a bubbling oversized Jacuzzi tub for two. Recently pictured in *Country Inns* as an "Urban Oasis." The village of Playa del Rey offers a variety of restaurants and shops and is just five minutes from Los Angeles International Airport.

Hosts: Susan Zolla and Donna Donnelly
Rooms: 21 (PB) $125-245
Full Breakfast
Credit Cards: A, B, C
Notes: 2, 3, 5, 8, 9, 10, 11, 12, 13, 14, 15

MALIBU

Bed and Breakfast California

P.O. Box 282910, San Francisco, 94128-2910
(650) 696-1690; (800) 872-4500
FAX (650) 696-1699; e-mail: info@bbintl.com
www.bbintl.com

Bella Vista. Nestled in the Santa Monica Mountains with a beautiful view of Malibu Canyon, this spacious ranch-style home is just five miles from Malibu Beach. With access to local hiking trails as well, this is a perfect location for guests who love the out-of-doors. The guest room is furnished in antiques and offers a king-size bed and a large wood-burning fireplace. $85.

Casa Larronde

Box 86, 90265
(213) 456-9333

This is the area of the "famous," so the locals call this beach "Millionaires' Row." The Ocean Suite has 40 feet of windows adjoining its deck. Features include TV, telephone, fireplace, kitchenette, ceiling fan over a king-size bed, floor-to-ceiling three-way mirrors in the dressing room, and a large bathroom with twin basins. Cocktails are offered in the evening, and a full American breakfast is served leisurely in the morning. Closed July through mid-October. Inquire about arrangements for children.

Host: Charlou Larronde
Rooms: 2 (PB) $115-150
Full Breakfast
Credit Cards: None
Notes: 2, 7, 9, 10, 11, 12, 15

MAMMOTH

Absolutely Accommodations

P.O. Box 641471, San Francisco, 94164-1471
(415) 677-9789; (888) 982-2632
FAX (415) 982-9580
e-mail: travelinfo@iname.com

This is a free reservation service committed to assisting travelers in finding the best possible accommodations in California. It offers access to private homestay bed and breakfasts and inns. It can help guests find the proper accommodations that meet their individual needs. The service's goal is to provide both its clients and hosts with the best possible customer service.

NOTES: Credit cards accepted: A MasterCard; B Visa; C American Express; D Discover; E Diner's Club; F Other; 2 Personal checks accepted; 3 Lunch available; 4 Dinner available; 5 Open all year; 6 Pets welcome;

Mammoth 101. A perfect location for visiting Mammoth Lakes. Walk to shops and restaurants. All individually decorated rooms with antiques, quilts, and private baths. Some have fireplaces and kitchens. $63-98.

MANHATTAN BEACH

Bed and Breakfast International

P.O. Box 282910, San Francisco, 94128-2910
(650) 696-1690; (800) 872-4500
FAX (650) 696-1699; e-mail: info@bbintl.com
www.bbintl.com

MB-L2. Beachfront bed and breakfast is the entire first floor of this lovely home on the Strand. Two guest rooms with private baths. Private entrance, living/dining room area with fireplace, wet bar, and guest parking are some of the amenities offered. Continental breakfast. No smoking. $75-85.

MARINA DEL REY

Deluxe 129-159   Std. room $119-$149

Bed and Breakfast International

P.O. Box 282910, San Francisco, 94128-2910
(650) 696-1690; (800) 872-4500
FAX (650) 696-1699; e-mail: info@bbintl.com
www.bbintl.com

MB-P1. Ocean and mountain views are spectacular from contemporary Malibu bed and breakfast with interesting art work. Very large guest suite has private entrance and Jacuzzi tub. Continental plus breakfast. $80-150.

MR-M40I. French country decor is featured in this large bed and breakfast inn close to the beach, good restaurants, and shopping. Forty guest rooms with private baths. No smoking. Continental breakfast. $70-125.

PL-D2. Designed and built by hosts, this four-story bed and breakfast exudes Old World charm. Set on a hillside at the beach, the guest quarters are on first floor and include living room and courtyard. Gourmet Continental plus breakfast served.

PL-I23I. A few blocks from the marina and beach and five minutes from the airport, this new bed and breakfast inn offers rooms with fireplace, Jacuzzi, deck, queen- or king-size beds, and private bath. Additional amenities include a full breakfast, afternoon refreshments, and the attention to needs from a romantic getaway to a business trip. $85-200.

MARINA DEL REY (VENICE BEACH)

The Mansion Inn

327 Washington Boulevard, 90291
(310) 821-2557; (800) 828-0688 (reservations)
FAX (310) 827-0289

A charming European-style hotel just two blocks from Venice Beach. The hotel has queen-size and twin-bedded standard rooms and five bilevel loft suites. All rooms have air conditioning, refrigerators, hair dryers in the vanity areas, full baths and showers, telephones, TVs, and in-room movies each night. All rooms have been completely renovated and are decorated in an upbeat, cheerful, fun beach decor. A very generous Continental plus breakfast is included each morning in the café in the cobblestone courtyard. Nonsmoking rooms available. Four rooms handicapped accessible.

Rooms: 43 (PB) $69-139
Continental Breakfast
Credit Cards: A, B, C, D, E
Notes: 5, 8, 11, 14

MARIPOSA

Bed and Breakfast International

P.O. Box 282910, San Francisco, 94128-2910
(650) 696-1690; (800) 872-4500
FAX (650) 696-1699; e-mail: info@bbintl.com
www.bbintl.com

MA-L3I. Contemporary bed and breakfast on an old stagecoach route, hosted by

---

7 No smoking; 8 Children welcome; 9 Social drinking allowed; 10 Tennis nearby; 11 Swimming nearby; 12 Golf nearby; 13 Skiing nearby; 14 May be booked through a travel agent; 15 Handicapped accessible.

long-time residents, is on four acres and offers gold panning and hiking on the inn's property. Three guest rooms have private baths. Mini-refrigerator, TV, VCR, and many other amenities are available. The inn is near museums, wineries, and Yosemite National Park. Handicapped accessible. Continental breakfast is served. $80-100.

MS-GG2I. An 1896 Victorian farmhouse en route to Yosemite. Outdoor spa, gazebo, and farm animals. Full breakfast. $75-85.

The Pelennor Bed and Breakfast

3871 Highway 49 South, 95338
(209) 966-2832; e-mail: pelennor@yosemite.net

Country atmosphere about 45 minutes from Yosemite National Park. Four guest rooms, featuring twin, double, and queen-size beds. After a day of sightseeing, guests may want to take a few laps in the pool, unwind in the spa, enjoy the available games, relax in the sauna, and listen to an occasional tune played on the bagpipes. Smoking permitted outside. Golf within 15-mile drive, and skiing within a 60-mile drive.

Hosts: Dick and Gwen Foster
Rooms: 4 (4 S2B) $45
Full Breakfast
Credit Cards: None
Notes: 2, 5, 6, 8, 9, 11

MCCLOUD

McCloud River Inn

325 Lawndale Court, P.O. Box 1560, 96057
(916) 964-2130; (800) 261-7831
e-mail: mort@snowcrest.net
www.riverinn.com

Circa 1900. This beautiful country Victorian inn is within the wonder of the Shasta National Forest and is listed in the National Register of Historic Places. The inn is on

five acres of rolling lawns and woodland. The interior has been lovingly restored and each guest room is filled with the charm of Old World antiques. Private Jacuzzi tub available. Guests wake each morning to the aroma of a home-cooked breakfast being served in the parlor.

Hosts: Ron and Marina Mort
Rooms: 5 (PB) $65-135
Full Breakfast
Credit Cards: A, B, C, D
Notes: 2, 3, 5, 7, 8, 9, 12, 13, 14, 15

MENDOCINO

Bed and Breakfast California

P.O. Box 282910, San Francisco, 94128-2910
(650) 696-1690; (800) 872-4500
FAX (650) 696-1699; e-mail: info@bbintl.com
www.bbintl.com

Huckleberry House. Four suites are available, three designed for families of up to four people, with queen-size beds, lofts, and lots of gardens and hiking trails. Guests enjoy a full, fresh breakfast and are just a short walk from the ocean. $100-150.

At Jughandle Beach. Offering views of the ocean and the country, this classic little bed and breakfast inn is run by devoted owner-occupants who take satisfaction in making a stay memorable. There are four bedrooms, all with private baths, two with ocean views. In the little town of Fort Bragg, near Mendocino. Try whale watching from December through March, or charter a boat at Noyo Harbor. Hiking, beachcombing, riding, canoeing, cycling, or just relaxing to the sound of the ocean. Full breakfast. $70-100.

Bed and Breakfast International

P.O. Box 282910, San Francisco, 94128-2910
(650) 696-1690; (800) 872-4500
FAX (650) 696-1699; e-mail: info@bbintl.com
www.bbintl.com

ME-M20I. These 1882 Victorian inn and garden cottages are furnished with Persian

NOTES: Credit cards accepted: A MasterCard; B Visa; C American Express; D Discover; E Diner's Club; F Other; 2 Personal checks accepted; 3 Lunch available; 4 Dinner available; 5 Open all year; 6 Pets welcome;

rugs and Tiffany lamps and offer a true bed and breakfast experience. Adjacent barn has contemporary accommodations. Several rooms have a fireplace, others a wood-burning stove. $75-201.

ME-J10I. This 1879 Victorian farmhouse, cottage, and water tower are near the ocean, golf, shops, wineries, hiking, and fishing. Rooms have private baths. Full breakfast. $90-165.

Brewery Gulch Inn

9350 Coast Highway 1, 95460
(707) 937-4752; (800) 578-4454
www.virtualcities.com

An authentic country bed and breakfast farm on the rugged coast, just one mile from the village of Mendocino. The lovely old white farmhouse is furnished in the Victorian style with antiques, fireplaces, and private baths. Each guest room window provides a view of the gardens and meadows beyond. Gourmet breakfasts feature the bed and breakfast's own chicken eggs. Ben and Cindy (resident dogs) will greet guests with love and enthusiasm. Smoking permitted outside. Inquire about accommodations for children only.

Host: Anne Saunders
Rooms: 5 (3 PB; 2 SB) $85-135
Full Breakfast
Credit Cards: A, B
Notes: 2, 5, 7, 9, 10, 12, 14

Captain's Cove Inn

44781 Main Street, P.O. Box 803, 95460
(707) 937-5150; (800) 780-7905

This oceanfront bed and breakfast is on Main Street in the village, two blocks from all activity, yet still very secluded with private parking and private path to the beach. The rooms have private decks, fireplaces, private baths, and great ocean and beach views. Coffee pots and newspaper are delivered to all guest rooms. Enjoy the full breakfasts which are served in the oceanfront dining room.

Hosts: Bob and Linda Blum
Rooms: 5 (PB) $129-199
Full Breakfast
Credit Cards: A, B
Notes: 2, 5, 10, 11, 12, 14

Joshua Grindle Inn

44800 Little Lake Road, P.O. Box 647, 95460
(707) 937-4143; (800) GRINDLE
e-mail: info@joshgrin.com
www.joshgrin.com

On two acres in a historic village over-looking the ocean, the Joshua Grindle Inn is a short walk to the beach, art center, shops, and fine restaurants. Stay in the lovely two-story Victorian farmhouse, a New England-style cottage, or a three-story water tower. Six rooms have fire-places; all have private baths, antiques, and comfortable reading areas. Enjoy a

Brewery Gulch Inn

Joshua Grindle Inn

7 No smoking; 8 Children welcome; 9 Social drinking allowed; 10 Tennis nearby; 11 Swimming nearby; 12 Golf nearby; 13 Skiing nearby; 14 May be booked through a travel agent; 15 Handicapped accessible.

full breakfast served around a 10-foot 1830s harvest table. Off-street parking.

Hosts: Jim and Arlene Moorehead
Rooms: 10 (PB) $100-185
Full Breakfast
Credit Cards: A, B
Notes: 2, 5, 7, 9, 10, 12, 14

Mendocino Farmhouse

Box 247, 95460
(707) 937-0241; (800) 475-1536
www.innaccess.com/mfh/

Mendocino Farmhouse is a small bed and breakfast with all the comforts of home, surrounded by redwood forest, beautiful gardens, a pond, and meadow. Choose from comfortable rooms decorated with country antiques for a quiet night's rest and enjoy a farmhouse breakfast in the morning. Mid-week discounts available. Children welcome by prior arrangements.

Hosts: Margie and Bud Kamb
Rooms: 5 (PB) $85-130
Full Breakfast
Credit Cards: A, B
Notes: 2, 5, 7, 9, 11, 12

Mendocino Village Inn

44860 Main Street, P.O. Box 626, 95460
(707) 937-0246; (800) 882-7029

The inn was built for the first physician and his family in 1882 and is in the heart of the historic district. The building was lovingly restored in the early 1980s and is filled with

Mendocino Village Inn

antiques and some contemporary pieces. The three-story watertower was built in 1992. The house is surrounded by lush flower and herb gardens. There is a frog pond with waterfall in the southeast portion of the garden. Everything in town is within an easy walk. A full two-course breakfast is served 8:30-10:30 A.M. Guests may help themselves to afternoon tea in the parlor from 4:00 P.M. Evening refreshments in the common room are served 5:00-7:00 P.M.

Rooms: 10 (8 PB; 2 SB) $75-175
Full Breakfast
Credit Cards: None
Notes: 2, 5, 7, 9, 10, 12, 15

Rachel's Inn

P.O. Box 134, 95460
(707) 937-0088; (800) 347-9252
FAX (707) 937-3620

Comfort with style in an elegantly restored 1860s home and new barn with ocean, garden, and meadow views. Nine rooms, all with private baths; six with fireplaces; three luxury suites with private sitting room and fireplace. Wheelchair accessible. Adjoining 320-acre state park with beach, deer meadow, woodlands, and ocean bluffs for seal and whale watching. Hiking and golf nearby. Lavish full breakfast included. Two miles south of Mendocino village.

Host: Rachel Binah
Rooms: 9 (PB) $96-215
Full Breakfast
Credit Cards: A, B
Notes: 2, 5, 8, 9, 10, 12, 14, 15

Sea Rock Bed and Breakfast Inn

11101 Lansing Street, P.O. Box 906, 95460
(707) 937-0926; (800) 906-0926 (reservations)

Country cottages on a hillside overlooking the ocean—spectacular white-water ocean views. All units have fireplaces, cable TV, and VCRs. Feather beds in many rooms and all rooms furnished with fine linens, down comforters, and pillows. The cozy cottages are surrounded by cypress trees, beautifully landscaped gardens, and spacious lawns. Continental plus breakfast.

Hosts: Susie and Andy Plocher
Rooms: 14 (PB) $85-225
Continental Breakfast
Credit Cards: A, B, C, D
Notes: 2, 5, 7, 8, 10, 12

MILL VALLEY

Bed and Breakfast Exchange of Marin County— Referral Service

45 Entrata, San Anselmo, 94960
(415) 485-1971; FAX (415) 454-7179

3. Private guest suite with king- or twin-size beds. Extra bed for families traveling with children. Private entrance. Walk to lovely old-fashioned village of Mill Valley. Refrigerator and small kitchen. $85.

4. Private cottage in the redwoods. Full kitchen and fireplace. Garden view. Walk to town. Great value. Suitable for short or longer stays. No smoking. $110 per night.

Mountain Home Inn

810 Panoramic Highway, 94941
(415) 381-9000

A romantic country inn high atop Mount Tamalpais, offering spectacular views of the Marin Hills and San Francisco Bay. Ten guest rooms, some offering Jacuzzi baths, private decks, and fireplaces. Just outside the front door is Mount Tamalpais State Park, offering miles of hiking trails. Muir Woods National Monument, Muir Beach, and Stinson Beach are a short drive away, with downtown San Francisco only 45 minutes away. Restaurant on premises. Smoking permitted in designated areas only.

Rooms: 10 (PB) $139-249
Full Breakfast
Credit Cards: A, B, C
Notes: 2, 3, 4, 5, 8, 9, 10, 11, 12, 14, 15

MILL VALLEY (MARIN COUNTY)

Bed and Breakfast San Francisco

P.O. Box 420009, San Francisco, 94142
(415) 931-3083; FAX (415) 921-BBSF (2273)
e-mail: bbsf@linex.com; www.bbsf.com

Tree Top Bed and Breakfast. The charming town of Mill Valley, nestled beneath Mount Tamalpais in Marin County, is the location of this bed and breakfast. The three guest rooms designed by the hostess, an interior designer, offer all the amenities such as private baths, private decks, TVs, a large living room with fireplace, and a full breakfast. $125-250.

MONTEREY (CARMEL)

Bed and Breakfast San Francisco

P.O. Box 420009, San Francisco, 94142
(415) 931-3083; FAX (415) 921-BBSF (2273)
e-mail: bbsf@linex.com; www.bbsf.com

Barlockers Rustling Oaks Ranch. Stay on a beautiful horse ranch in the picturesque Salinas Valley, a 25-minute ride east of Monterey. The hostess offers her three guest rooms, each with private bath, and a big country breakfast each morning. The views and surrounding area are beautiful. The ranch has chickens, dogs, cats, pigs, goats, and lots of horses. Horseback riding is available. This is a wonderful place for a family. There is even a pool for summertime use. $90-150.

MONTEREY (CARMEL)

The Jabberwock

598 Laine Street, 93940
(408) 372-4777; (888) 428-7253
FAX (408) 655-2946

Alice's Wonderland just four blocks above Cannery Row and Monterey Bay Aquarium.

7 No smoking; 8 Children welcome; 9 Social drinking allowed; 10 Tennis nearby; 11 Swimming nearby; 12 Golf nearby; 13 Skiing nearby; 14 May be booked through a travel agent; 15 Handicapped accessible.

The Jabberwock has one-half acre of lush gardens, waterfall, and is overlooking the bay. Each room has down pillows and comforters. Hors d'oeuvres at 5:00 P.M. and cookies and milk at bedtime.

Hosts: Joan and John Kiliany
Rooms: 7 (5 PB; 2 SB)
Full Breakfast
Credit Cards: A, B
Notes: 2, 5, 7, 9, 10, 11, 12, 14

MONTE RIO

Huckleberry Springs Country Inn and Spa

8105 Old Beedle Road, P.O. Box 400, 95462
(800) 822-2683
e-mail: mail@huckleberrysprings.com
www.huckleberrysprings.com

On 56 acres of redwoods in the Russian River region offering private cottage accommodations in an intimate and peaceful setting. Four modern cottages offer guests amenities, including VCR, stereo, and wood-burning stoves. The lodge boasts dramatic views. Swimming pool and spa. Massage cottage. Full breakfast is served each morning and a four-course gourmet dinner is available on Wednesdays and Saturdays. Canoeing the Russian River, wine tasting, and exploring the Sonoma coast are favorite activities.

Host: Suzanne Greene
Rooms: 4 (PB) $145
Full Breakfast
Credit Cards: A, B
Notes: 2, 4, 7, 9, 10, 11, 12, 14

MORAGA

Hallman Bed and Breakfast

309 Constance Place, 94556
(925) 376-4318

Bed and breakfast on a quiet cul-de-sac in the beautiful Moraga Valley. Bed down in one of the tastefully appointed rooms.

Awake refreshed with breakfast in the comfortable dining room. Take off and "do" San Francisco or any other Bay Area attractions. There are two guest rooms with queen-size beds and shared bath available. Both rooms are used only when guests are in the same party.

Host: Virginia Hallman
Rooms: 2 (SB) $60
Full Breakfast
Credit Cards: None
Notes: 2, 5, 7, 9, 11

MORRO BAY

Bed and Breakfast California

P.O. Box 282910, San Francisco, 94128-2910
(650) 696-1690; (800) 872-4500
FAX (650) 696-1699; e-mail: info@bbintl.com
www.bbintl.com

The Howell House. This incredible mansion on the coast has a guest suite with bedroom, full private bath, ocean-view deck, and a full English-style pub sitting room. Coffee service is delivered by dumbwaiter, and a refrigerator is available. The Scottish hostess makes a great, gracious breakfast. $100-120.

Bed and Breakfast International

P.O. Box 282910, San Francisco, 94128-2910
(650) 696-1690; (800) 872-4500
FAX (650) 696-1699; e-mail: info@bbintl.com
www.bbintl.com

MO-H2. Hillside bed and breakfast with view of Morro Rock offers a first-floor guest room with private bath, private entrance, and a pub-style common room featuring a touch of Scotland. Convenient to midcoast beaches and attractions. Full breakfast. $120.

MOSS BEACH

Seal Cove Inn

221 Cypress Avenue, 94038
(415) 728-4114; FAX (415) 728-4116
e-mail: sealcove@coastside.net

NOTES: Credit cards accepted: A MasterCard; B Visa; C American Express; D Discover; E Diner's Club; F Other; 2 Personal checks accepted; 3 Lunch available; 4 Dinner available; 5 Open all year; 6 Pets welcome;

Set among wildflowers, Seal Cove Inn looks out to the ocean over acres of parkland. Paths lead to secluded beaches, tidal pools, and windswept ocean bluffs. The inn is decorated with antiques and each guest room has private bath, wood-burning fireplace, and views of park and ocean. This four-star and four-diamond inn is set in the quiet coastal town of Moss Beach, just 30 minutes south of San Francisco.

Hosts: Karen Brown and Rick Herbert
Rooms: 10 (PB) $180-260
Full Breakfast
Credit Cards: A, B, C, D
Notes: 2, 5, 7, 8, 12, 14, 15

MOUNT SHASTA

Bed and Breakfast International
P.O. Box 282910, San Francisco, 94128-2910
(650) 696-1690; (800) 872-4500
FAX (650) 696-1699; e-mail: info@bbintl.com
www.bbintl.com

MS-M9I. This 1923 two-story ranch house is near fishing, hiking, boating, and skiing areas. Full breakfast and afternoon refreshments served. Hot tub. Nine guest rooms with queen-size and twin beds and private and shared baths. No smoking. $70-85.

MS-W2I. Small ranch in a mountain sanctuary near skiing, boating, fishing, golf, and hiking. Enjoy a wonderful full breakfast, large deck with spectacular views, ranch animals, and walking trails. Two guest rooms with private baths. No smoking. $65-80.

MOUNT SHASTA

Mount Shasta Ranch
1008 W. A. Barr Road, 96067
(530) 926-3870; e-mail: alpinere@snowcrest.net

This northern California historic two-story ranch house offers affordable elegance. There are four spacious guest rooms in the main house, each with private bath. Car-

riage house accommodations include five rooms. Two-bedroom vacation cottage available year-round. Guests are invited to enjoy the rec room with Ping-Pong, pool table, and piano. Relax in the hot-spring spa. Close to lake, town, and ski slopes. Full country-style breakfasts each morning.

Hosts: Bill and Mary Larsen
Rooms: 9 (4 PB; 5 SB) $55-95
Cottage: 1
Full Breakfast
Credit Cards: A, B, C, D
Notes: 2, 5, 6, 7, 8, 9, 10, 11, 12, 13, 14

MUIR BEACH

Bed and Breakfast California
P.O. Box 282910, San Francisco, 94128-2910
(650) 696-1690; (800) 872-4500
FAX (650) 696-1699; e-mail: info@bbintl.com
www.bbintl.com

Architecturally interesting contemporary home with panoramic views of the Pacific Ocean. On Muir Overlook, a bluff overlooking Muir Beach and near Muir Woods. Just over the hill from charming Sausalito and the Golden Gate Bridge. Stinson Beach is nearby in the other direction. The guest unit is on the second floor and has a private entrance. The guest suite is a spacious, light room with a fireplace and a spectacular view of the ocean. $120.

Bed and Breakfast Exchange of Marin County— Referral Service
45 Entrata, San Anselmo, 94960
(415) 485-1971; FAX (415) 454-7179

See the ocean from the bedroom. This carefully crafted cottage is totally surrounded by the Golden Gate National Recreation Area. Private entrance. Includes separate Japanese tatami meditation room. Loll in front of the fire in the large hammock and see the rolling hills across the valley and the whitecaps of the surf. Walk

7 No smoking; 8 Children welcome; 9 Social drinking allowed; 10 Tennis nearby; 11 Swimming nearby; 12 Golf nearby; 13 Skiing nearby; 14 May be booked through a travel agent; 15 Handicapped accessible.

to dinner at an English inn. Twenty minutes from the Golden Gate Bridge. $165.

Pelican Inn

10 Pacific Way, 94965
(415) 383-6000; FAX (415) 383-3424

The romantic getaway over the hills to the beach, a country inn capturing the spirit of 16th-century England's west country awaits. The hospitable Pelican nestles among pines and alders surrounded by open countryside—a refuge between the ocean and redwoods of Golden Gate National Recreation Area. The Pelican opens its doors for the fellowship of its Tudor Bar, British ales, carefree feasting, and relaxation. On Highway 1, scarcely 20 minutes north of the Golden Gate Bridge.

Hosts: Katrinka McKay
Rooms: 7 (PB) $158-180
Full Breakfast
Credit Cards: A, B
Notes: 2, 3, 4, 5, 7, 8, 9,

MURPHYS

Dunbar House, 1880

271 Jones Street, 95247
(209) 728-2897; (800) 692-6006
e-mail: dunbarhs@goldrush.com
www.dunbarhouse.com

Explore gold country during the day and enjoy a glass of lemonade or local wine on the wide porches in the afternoon. Inviting fireplaces and down comforters in antique-filled rooms. The Cedar Room has a two-person whirlpool bath. All rooms have TVs, VCRs, and a classic video library. Breakfast may be served in the room, in the dining room, or out in the century-old gardens. Two-night minimum stay required for weekends. Children over 10 welcome.

Hosts: Bob and Barbara Costa
Rooms: 4 (PB) $125-170
Full Breakfast
Credit Cards: A, B, C
Notes: 2, 5, 7, 9, 10, 11, 12, 13, 14

NAPA

Absolutely Accommodations

P.O. Box 641471, San Francisco, 94164-1471
(415) 677-9789; (888) 982-2632
FAX (415) 982-9580
e-mail: travelinfo@iname.com

This is a free reservation service committed to assisting travelers in finding the best possible accommodations in California. It offers access to private homestay bed and breakfasts and inns. It can help guests find the proper accommodations that meet their individual needs. The service's goal is to provide both its clients and hosts with the best possible customer service.

Napa 111. This 1889 three-story grand mansion stands on an acre of well-cared-for lawns and rose gardens. Each of the 11 rooms feature luxurious private baths. Full breakfast. $115-189.

Napa 112. This elegant 1886 Queen Anne mansion is in walking distance to the historic district of Napa. It has been lovingly restored and offers guests a blend of romance and Victorian elegance. Relax in one of the parlors or by the pool and outdoor spa. Fourteen rooms. $159-289.

Napa 113. This luxury inn is just north of Napa where the vineyards begin. Twenty rooms are individually decorated with quality antiques, fine designer linens, some with working fireplaces, patios, or verandas. Relax by the pool and spa. Charming and convenient to all the splendors of the valley, this inn is the best choice for the discriminating traveler. Full breakfast. $165-235.

Napa 114. Start the day with a gourmet breakfast served in an elegant candlelit dining room. This landmark Queen Anne-style inn is one of the finest examples of Victorian architecture in Napa. Elegantly appointed accommodations, including a

NOTES: Credit cards accepted: A MasterCard; B Visa; C American Express; D Discover; E Diner's Club; F Other; 2 Personal checks accepted; 3 Lunch available; 4 Dinner available; 5 Open all year; 6 Pets welcome;

magnifient collection of fine period antiques, oriental carpets, and beautiful stained-glass windows. Within walking distance of Old Town Napa and a variety of restaurants and shops. Excellent location to explore the wine country.

Beazley House

Beazley House

1910 First Street, 94559
(800) 559-1649; FAX (707) 257-1518
e-mail: jbeaz@aol.com

Guests sense the hospitality as they stroll the walk past verdant lawns and bright flowers. The landmark 1902 mansion is a chocolate brown masterpiece. Visitors feel instantly welcome as they are greeted by a smiling innkeeper. The view from each room reveals beautiful gardens. All rooms have a private bath; some have a private spa and a fireplace. Napa's first bed and breakfast and still its best!

Hosts: Carol and Jim Beazley
Rooms: 11 (PB) $115-225
Full Breakfast
Credit Cards: A, B, C
Notes: 2, 5, 7, 8, 9, 10, 11, 12, 14, 15

Bed and Breakfast California

P.O. Box 282910, San Francisco, 94128-2910
(650) 696-1690; (800) 872-4500
FAX (650) 696-1699; e-mail: info@bbintl.com
www.bbintl.com

The Gables. Architect-designed English country manor, over 10,000 square feet. All rooms have private baths and a full breakfast is served, as well as wine and hors d'oeuvres in the evening. There is a fireplace in the living and family rooms, and a large-screen TV for the guests' use. The house has been lovingly restored and is beautifully furnished with antiques and Victoriana. Guest rooms are spacious. Conveniently three blocks from downtown Napa with many shops and restaurants and close to many wineries. Call for rates.

McClellan House. Experience the stately elegance of this historic landmark taking guests back to 1879. Four large elegantly decorated bedroom suites with private baths offer guests comfort in a classic ambiance. Fine European antiques and authentic chandeliers. This is wine country at its finest. A full breakfast is served in the formal dining room with handcrafted ornate ceilings. Complimentary wine and hors d'oeuvres in the early evening. Call for rates.

Bed and Breakfast International

P.O. Box 282910, San Francisco, 94128-2910
(650) 696-1690; (800) 872-4500
FAX (650) 696-1699; e-mail: info@bbintl.com
www.bbintl.com

NA-B11. This 1902 Napa landmark is a striking, elegant mansion on one-half acre of lawns and gardens. Eleven guest rooms have private baths. The Carriage House hosts five large rooms with private spas and fireplaces. Full buffet breakfast. No smoking. $110-190.

NA-C91. Bed and breakfast in the heart of wine country is offered in the 1889 mansion that has been designated a national historic landmark. The nine guest rooms are individually decorated and have private baths. Enjoy a Continental plus breakfast, and relax on the veranda with evening refreshments. No smoking. $75-160.

7 No smoking; 8 Children welcome; 9 Social drinking allowed; 10 Tennis nearby; 11 Swimming nearby; 12 Golf nearby; 13 Skiing nearby; 14 May be booked through a travel agent; 15 Handicapped accessible.

The Blue Violet Mansion

443 Brown Street, 94559-3348
(800) 959-2583; FAX (707) 257-8205

This 1886 Victorian mansion, in the National Register of Historic Places, was awarded the 1996 gold award for Best Bed and Breakfast in North America. Rooms with spas. Balconies, fireplaces, antique furnishings, and oriental carpets. Deluxe Camelot-theme floor; faux- and mural-painted stained glass. Hot beverages bar, ice, wine, and snacks available. Fountains. Enjoy the swimming pool and spa. Picnic baskets available. In-room candlelight dinner and massage services. Evening wine service and late-night desserts and dancing in the Conservatory. In historic Old Town near shops, the Napa Valley Wine Train, hot-air balloons, and wine tastings.

Hosts: Bob and Kathy Morris
Rooms: 14 (PB) $145-285
Suites: 3
Full Breakfast
Credit Cards: A, B, C, D, E, F
Notes: 2, 4, 5, 7, 8, 9, 10, 11, 12, 14

Candlelight Inn

1045 Easum Drive, 94558
(707) 257-3717

The Candlelight Inn is a lovely English Tudor built in 1929 on a quiet parklike one acre garden setting. The elegant inn is nestled beneath redwood groves and towering

trees along the banks of the Napa Creek. The suites feature in-room two-person marble Jacuzzis and marble fireplaces with private decks or balconies, each done in its own special decor. The inn is conveniently five minutes west of downtown and only minutes away from all the attractions the wine country has to offer.

Hosts: Johanna and Wolfgang Brox
Rooms: 10 (PB) $95-225
Full Breakfast
Credit Cards: A, B, C, D
Notes: 5, 7, 9, 12, 14, 15

Cedar Gables Inn

Cedar Gables Inn

486 Coombs Street, 94559
(707) 224-7939; (800) 309-7969
www.cedargablesinn.com

In Old Town Napa, this 106-year-old home is styled after English country manors of the 16th century. Antique furnishings are throughout the house. Some rooms have fireplaces and whirlpool tubs. Huge family room with large fireplace and big-screen TV are also available for guests. Minutes from wineries, restaurants, and the Napa Valley Wine Train.

Hosts: Margaret and Craig Snasdell
Rooms: 6 (PB) $139-189
Full Breakfast
Credit Cards: A, B, C, D
Notes: 2, 7, 12

NOTES: Credit cards accepted: A MasterCard; B Visa; C American Express; D Discover; E Diner's Club; F Other; 2 Personal checks accepted; 3 Lunch available; 4 Dinner available; 5 Open all year; 6 Pets welcome;

Churchill Manor

Churchill Manor Bed and Breakfast Inn

485 Brown Street, 94559
(707) 253-7733

Churchill Manor, an 1889 mansion, is listed in the National Register of Historic Places. Elegant parlors boast carved-wood ceilings and columns, leaded-glass windows, oriental rugs, brass and crystal chandeliers, four fireplaces, and a grand piano. Guest rooms are individually decorated with gorgeous antiques; five of the guest rooms have fireplaces. Enjoy freshly baked cookies and refreshments in the afternoon, complimentary wines and cheeses in the evening, and a delicious gourmet breakfast. Complimentary tandem bicycles and croquet.

Hosts: Joanna Guidotti and Brian Jensen
Rooms: 10 (PB) $95-195
Full Breakfast
Credit Cards: A, B, D
Notes: 2, 5, 7, 9, 10, 11, 12, 14, 15

La Belle Epoque Bed and Breakfast

1386 Calistoga Avenue, 94559
(707) 257-2161; FAX (707) 226-6314

This 1893 Queen Anne features an extensive display of vintage and contemporary stained glass. Fine Victorian antiques grace each of the six guest rooms and extend into the common areas. A full gourmet breakfast is served in the elegant formal dining room or on the plant-filled sun porch. Complimentary wine and appetizers are served nightly in the on-premises wine-tasting parlor. The inn is within an easy walk of Old Town Napa and the Napa Valley Wine Train.

Host: Georgia Jump
Rooms: 6 (PB) $149-209
Full Breakfast
Credit Cards: A, B, C, D
Notes: 2, 5, 7, 9, 10, 11, 12, 14

La Belle Epoque

Napa Inn

1137 Warren Street, 94559
(707) 257-1444; (800) 435-1144

This beautiful Queen Anne Victorian is in the historic section of Napa. Furnished with turn-of-the-century antiques, the inn features a large parlor and a formal dining room. Each bedroom has its own private bath, and two suites feature fireplaces. Convenient to the Napa, Sonoma, and Carneros wine regions, hot-air ballooning, gliding, biking, hiking, many fine restaurants, and the Napa Valley Wine Train. Sorry, the inn is closed Christmas Day.

Hosts: Ann and Denny Mahoney
Rooms: 6 (PB) $130-190
Full Breakfast
Credit Cards: A, B, C, D, E
Notes: 2, 7, 9, 10, 11, 12, 13, 14

---

7 No smoking; 8 Children welcome; 9 Social drinking allowed; 10 Tennis nearby; 11 Swimming nearby; 12 Golf nearby; 13 Skiing nearby; 14 May be booked through a travel agent; 15 Handicapped accessible.

Oak Knoll Inn

Oak Knoll Inn

2200 East Oak Knoll Avenue, Napa Valley, 94558
(707) 255-2200

Tall French windows, rustic stone walls, and vaulted ceilings distinguish the four spacious guest rooms at this luxurious inn, set well off the bustle of the main roads and surrounded by 600 acres of Chardonnay vineyards. The rooms have king-size beds, marble fireplaces, private baths, and sitting areas with overstuffed chairs and sofas. A full breakfast is served at guests' leisure in the room, dining room, or on the veranda surrounding the heated pool, spa, and magnificent views. In-state personal checks accepted.

Hosts: Barbara Passino and John Kuhlmann
Rooms: 4 (PB) $250-385
Full Breakfast
Credit Cards: A, B
Notes: 5, 7, 9, 10, 11, 12, 14

The Old World Inn

1301 Jefferson Street, 94559
(707) 257-0112

For a holiday of romance and plentiful gourmet delights, plan a stay at this charming Victorian inn. Relax in the outdoor spa or choose a room with a sunken spa tub. Guests are pampered with home-baked treats throughout their stay: savor afternoon tea and cookies when one arrives, unwind during the wine and cheese social,

treat oneself to a chocolate lover's dessert buffet before retiring, and awaken to a gourmet breakfast.

Host: Sam VanHoeve
Rooms: 8 (PB) $115-150
Cottage: 1-$205
Full Breakfast
Credit Cards: A, B, C, D
Notes: 2, 5, 7, 9, 10, 11, 12, 14

NAPA VALLEY

La Residence Country Inn

4066 St. Helena Highway, Napa, 94558
(707) 253-0337

Accommodations, most with fireplaces, are in two structures: a Gothic Revival home, decorated in traditional American antiques, and the "French barn," decorated with European pine antiques. Two acres of grounds with large spa and a heated swimming pool include a gazebo and trellis. Complimentary wine is served each evening.

Hosts: David Jackson and Craig Claussen
Rooms: 20 (PB) $175-275
Full Breakfast
Credit Cards: A, B, C, E
Notes: 5, 7, 8, 12, 14, 15

NEVADA CITY

Deer Creek Inn

116 Nevada Street, 95959
(530) 265-0363; (800) 655-0363
FAX (530) 265-0980; e-mail: deercreek@gv.net

At the edge of downtown Nevada City guests will find Deer Creek Inn. A spectacular Queen Anne Victorian, it sits majestically high above historic Deer Creek. As guests wander among the romantic rose gardens and creekside setting, one's mind will release itself of present day concerns. A kiss on the hand, a glance of the eye, can say it all...Romance and elegance...Deer Creek Inn. The gourmet breakfasts and evening hors

Deer Creek Inn

d'oeuvres that await guests are only a sampling of the treats in store. Smoking is permitted on balcony only. Inquire about accommodations for children.

Hosts: Elaine and Chuck Matroni
Rooms: 5 (PB) $90-145
Full Breakfast
Credit Cards: A, B
Notes: 2, 5, 9, 10, 11, 12, 13, 14

National Hotel

211 Broad Street, 95959
(530) 265-4551; (888) 265-4551
FAX (530) 265-2445

The National Hotel is a registered historical landmark listed in the National Register of Historic Places. Enjoy old-fashioned comfort and luxury at the oldest continuously operated hotel west of the Rocky Mountains. The sumptuous suites are furnished with antiques from the gold rush days. Most rooms have private baths. Enjoy swimming and sunny afternoons in the secluded swimming pool filled with cool, clear mountain water. One hour from Sacramento, two and one-half hours from San Francisco, and 90 minutes from Reno.

Host: Thomas A. Coleman
Rooms: 42 (30 PB; 12 SB) $75-120
Full Breakfast
Credit Cards: A, B, C
Notes: 2, 3, 4, 5, 7, 8, 9, 10, 11, 12, 13, 14, 15

NEWPORT BEACH

Bed and Breakfast California

P.O. Box 282910, San Francisco, 94128-2910
(650) 696-1690; (800) 872-4500
FAX (650) 696-1699; e-mail: info@bbintl.com
www.bbintl.com

On Newport Peninsula. This charming home in a quiet neighborhood on the Balboa Peninsula of Newport Beach features stained glass, used bricks, and natural wood surroundings. Upstairs loft room has a private bath and access to a large sun deck with ocean and beach views. Downstairs brass bedroom offers a large private bath. Just steps from the beach and bay. Bicycles and beach chairs are available. Full breakfast. $60-85.

Bed and Breakfast International

P.O. Box 282910, San Francisco, 94128-2910
(650) 696-1690; (800) 872-4500
FAX (650) 696-1699; e-mail: info@bbintl.com
www.bbintl.com

NP-D2. Crow's nest with 360-degree view tops this trilevel beach home. Two guest rooms. Private baths. The third level is a large guest deck with barbecue and refrigerator. Stained glass is featured throughout the house. Perfect for beach and bay activities; bicycle and beach chairs available. Full or Continental breakfast and afternoon refreshments. $50-85.

NP-D101. A very special beachfront bed and breakfast inn has spacious antique-filled guest rooms, each with its own fireplace and some with ocean views and Jacuzzis. Ten guest rooms. Private baths. Full breakfast. $135-275.

NP-W2. Stunning, well-decorated bed and breakfast on the water's edge has two guest rooms, private baths, a guest den with retractable roof, lounge chairs, refrigerator, and grassy yard for sunbathing. Take the

7 No smoking; 8 Children welcome; 9 Social drinking allowed; 10 Tennis nearby; 11 Swimming nearby; 12 Golf nearby; 13 Skiing nearby; 14 May be booked through a travel agent; 15 Handicapped accessible.

shuttle or bike to unique shops and restaurants. Minimum stay is two nights. Resident dog. Continental breakfast. $80-85.

Portofino Beach Hotel

2306 West Oceanfront, 92663
(714) 673-7030; FAX (714) 723-4370

On the oceanfront and boardwalk of this fashionable beach town which is just south of Los Angeles and 15 minutes from the Orange County Airport. Fifteen guest rooms are available, each with telephone, TV, private bath, and individual decor. Several rooms include marble baths with Jacuzzis, private sun decks, and fireplaces. Walk the boardwalk to visit nearby art galleries, bookstores, boutiques, and historical sites. Disneyland is a short 30-minute drive and sailing is available nearby. Continental breakfast buffet includes fresh fruit and homemade muffins. Private parking provided. Bar and restaurant on premises.

Host: Kathryn Reider
Rooms: 15 (PB) $150-275
Continental Breakfast
Credit Cards: A, B, C, D, E
Notes: 4, 5, 7, 9, 10, 11, 12, 14

NICE

Featherbed Railroad Company

2870 Lakeshore Boulevard, P.O. Box 4016, 95464
(707) 274-4434; (800) 966-6322

Nine lovingly refurbished theme cabooses reflect the Casablanca Orient Express. Most have Jacuzzi tubs for two. All have small refrigerators, cable TV (all with VCRs). Small sitting areas, coffee pot, assorted complimentary beverages, private pool, and spa are available. Full breakfast. Year-round fishing. Enjoy serene country setting.

Host: Len and Lorraine Bassignani
Rooms: 9 (PB) $90-140
Full Breakfast

Credit Cards: A, B, C, D
Notes: 2, 5, 7, 8, 9, 10, 11, 12, 14

NIPTON

Hotel Nipton

107355 Nipton Road, 92364
(760) 856-2335; e-mail: hotel@nipton.com
www.nipton.com

Hotel Nipton, originally built in 1904, was restored in 1986. In the Mojave National Preserve, 1.4 million acres of California desert, 65 miles southwest of Las Vegas between the Grand Canyon and Death Valley. Enjoy the beautiful panoramic views of Ivanpah Valley and New York Mountains. Outside Jacuzzi for star gazing. Only bed and breakfast in the preserve. Historic mining town has a population of 60.

Hosts: Jerry and Roxanne Freeman
Rooms: 4 (SB) $59.95
Continental Breakfast
Credit Cards: A, B, D
Notes: 5, 7, 8, 9, 11, 12, 14

OAKLAND

Dean's Bed and Breakfast

480 Pedestrian Way, 94618
(510) 652-5024; FAX (510) 597-0280
e-mail: dimped@aol.com

Set in a beautiful Japanese garden, the cottage has a private telephone line, remote

Dean's

control TV, and a very comfortable, customized full-size bed. Also, it has a private bath with tub and shower. It is very close to College Avenue with its many restaurants and chic retail shops. The Rockridge BART station, just a five-minute walk, offers 20-minute train service to San Francisco.

Host: Dean Manheimer
Rooms: 1 (PB) $75-90
Continental Breakfast
Credit Cards: A, B
Notes: 2, 5, 6, 7, 9, 10, 11

OJAI

Bed and Breakfast International

P.O. Box 282910, San Francisco, 94128-2910
(650) 696-1690; (800) 872-4500
FAX (650) 696-1699; e-mail: info@bbintl.com
www.bbintl.com

OJ-M2. Contemporary home on 10 acres with separate guest entrance features gardens, a stream, quiet, and serenity. Guest sitting room and kitchen, pool, and Continental breakfast are additional amenities. $100-150.

OLEMA

Olema Inn

10000 Sir Francis Drake Boulevard, 94950
(415) 663-9559; FAX (415) 663-8783

Olema Inn opened in 1876 as a gathering place for loggers, ranchers, and stage coach passengers. It is one of a few buildings that survived the 1906 earthquake. Restored in 1988, the Olema Inn offers first-class accommodations and a full-service restaurant. Ideal for hiking, whale watching, beaches, horseback riding, and more. Olema is also available for special parties and weddings.

Rooms: 6 (PB) $95-115
Continental Breakfast
Credit Cards: A, B
Notes: 3, 4, 5, 7, 9

ORLAND

The Inn at Shallow Creek Farm

4712 Road DD, 95963
(530) 865-4093; (800) 865-4093

A gracious two-story farmhouse offering spacious rooms furnished with antiques— a blend of nostalgia and comfortable country living. Three miles off I-5. The inn is surrounded by an orange grove. Breakfast features old-fashioned baked goods and fruits and juices from the family orchard.

Hosts: Kurt and Mary Glaeseman
Rooms: 4 (2 PB; 2 SB) $65-85
Full Breakfast
Credit Cards: A, B
Notes: 2, 5, 7, 9, 11, 12, 14

PACIFIC GROVE

Absolutely Accommodations

P.O. Box 641471, San Francisco, 94164-1471
(415) 677-9789; (888) 982-2632
FAX (415) 982-9580
e-mail: travelinfo@iname.com

This is a free reservation service committed to assisting travelers in finding the best possible accommodations in California. It offers access to private homestay bed and breakfasts and inns. It can help guests find the proper accommodations that meet their individual needs. The service's goal is to provide both its clients and hosts with the best possible customer service.

7 No smoking; 8 Children welcome; 9 Social drinking allowed; 10 Tennis nearby; 11 Swimming nearby; 12 Golf nearby; 13 Skiing nearby; 14 May be booked through a travel agent; 15 Handicapped accessible.

Pacific Grove 101. A charming Victorian designated as a historical landmark is within walking distance from Lover's Point in Pacific Grove. All of the 20 rooms are tastefully decorated and have private baths.

Bed and Breakfast California

P.O. Box 282910, San Francisco, 94128-2910
(650) 696-1690; (800) 872-4500
FAX (650) 696-1699; e-mail: info@bbintl.com
www.bbintl.com

1. Cozy, private cottages with fireplaces, claw-foot tubs, and wet bars...airy attic suites...elegant rooms...intimate hide-aways with Jacuzzi tubs...for more than 100 years, this award-winning inn has been the destination of choice for charm and romance. Stroll down to Lover's Point or over to Cannery Row, or visit the historic town of Pacific Grove, famous for its annual migration of monarch butterflies. $89-219.

2. The suites offer comfort and luxury at its finest. This boutique Cape Cod-style village is the Monterey Peninsula's best kept secret. Each suite offers a king- or queen-size bed with down pillows, fireplace, Jacuzzi tub, and plush robes. Awaken each morning to a chef-prepared breakfast, cooked to order and served in the elegant dining room. Complimentary wine and hors d'oeuvres are offered in the afternoon. $169-575.

Bed and Breakfast International

P.O. Box 282910, San Francisco, 94128-2910
(650) 696-1690; (800) 872-4500
FAX (650) 696-1699; e-mail: info@bbintl.com
www.bbintl.com

PG-C20I. Century-old Victorian boarding house is now a refurbished award-winning bed and breakfast inn. Beautifully decorated rooms, private baths, delicious breakfast, and afternoon refreshments. $90-185.

PG-G08I. This 1884 Victorian with ocean view was renovated and opened its doors in 1990 to become a Pacific Grove bed and breakfast inn close to the beach. Each room is uniquely decorated and features views or sun decks and private baths. Delicious full breakfast and afternoon refreshments are provided. No smoking. $110-150.

PG-G11I. This 1888 Queen Anne-style mansion-by-the-sea has a panoramic view of Monterey Bay. Delicious breakfast and afternoon refreshments. Shared and private baths. $100-160.

PG-G21I. Beautifully preserved 1887 Victorian in the National Register of Historic Places can now be enjoyed as a bed and breakfast inn. Wonderful breakfast, afternoon hors d'oeuvres, and wine or tea served. $85-185.

PG-09I. Four rooms in this 1910 Cape Cod-style inn have ocean views. Convenient to the aquarium, beaches, and most local attractions. Full breakfast served. $90-150.

Centrella Inn

612 Central Avenue, 93950
(800) 433-4732

Historic bed and breakfast inn built in 1889. Victorian guest rooms, parlor rooms, attic suites, cottages with fireplaces, and a garden suite with Jacuzzi. All rooms have private bath. Continental plus breakfast buffet; afternoon wine, sherry, and hors d'oeuvres. Walking distance to Lover's Point, Asilomar Beach, Cannery Row, and Monterey Bay Aquarium. Two-night minimum stay on weekends.

Host: Larry Hoover
Rooms: 26 (PB) $109-219
Continental Breakfast
Credit Cards: A, B, C, D
Notes: 2, 5, 7, 9, 12, 14

NOTES: Credit cards accepted: A MasterCard; B Visa; C American Express; D Discover; E Diner's Club; F Other; 2 Personal checks accepted; 3 Lunch available; 4 Dinner available; 5 Open all year; 6 Pets welcome;

Gatehouse Inn

225 Central Avenue, 93950
(408) 649-8436; (800) 753-1881
FAX (408) 648-8044

This historic home, built in 1884, was the summer residence of Senator Langford. Each of the nine guest rooms is individually decorated in grand Victorian style. Many of the rooms have ocean views, fireplaces, and claw-foot tubs. Enjoy the gourmet full breakfast or relax on the garden patio at teatime while soaking in the view of Monterey. Near excellent restaurants, shopping, and activities. Just 100 yards away from the ocean.

Hosts: Lois DeFord, Lewis Shaefer, and
 Susan Kuslis
Rooms: 9 (PB) $110-165
Full Breakfast
Credit Cards: A, B, C, D
Notes: 2, 5, 7, 9, 10, 11, 12, 14, 15

Gatehouse Inn

Grand View Inn

557 Ocean View Boulevard, 93950
(831) 372-4341

Built in 1910, the Grand View Inn is at the edge of Monterey Bay. The inn was completely restored in 1994 by the Flatley family, owners of the Seven Gables Inn, which is next door. Guests are welcomed to a tradition of warm personal service, spectacular natural surroundings, comfortably

appointed accommodations, irresistible breakfasts, and sociable gatherings at afternoon tea. A feeling of quiet elegance encompasses the inn. Along with unsurpassed views of Monterey Bay from each room, guests enjoy the comfort of marble tiled private baths, patterned hardwood floors, beautiful antique furnishings, and lovely grounds.

Hosts: Susan Flatley and Ed Flatley
Rooms: 10 (PB) $155-285
Full Breakfast
Credit Cards: A, B
Notes: 2, 5, 7, 9, 10, 11, 12, 15

The Martine Inn

255 Ocean View Boulevard, 93950
(408) 373-3388; (800) 852-5588
FAX (408) 373-3896
www.martineinn.com

The Martine Inn is a grand 1890s home overlooking the rocky coastline of Pacific Grove on Monterey Bay. All 19 rooms have private bathroom, authentic museum-quality antiques, a fresh rose, a silver Victorian bridal basket with fresh fruit, and a telephone. Some rooms overlook the waves crashing against the rocks and/or have a wood-burning fireplace. Breakfast is served on Old Sheffield silver, Victorian-style china, crystal, and lace. Play pool in the game room, lounge in the spa, or view vintage cars from the Martine's collection.

Hosts: Don Martine and Tracy Harris
Rooms: 19 (PB) $150-295
Full Breakfast
Credit Cards: A, B, C, D
Notes: 2, 5, 9, 10, 11, 12, 14, 15

The Old St. Angela Inn

321 Central Avenue, 93950
(408) 372-3246; (800) 748-6306

The Old St. Angela's Inn, built as a country home in 1910, was converted to a rectory and convent in 1920. Within this Cape Cod home, overlooking Monterey Bay, are rooms of distinctive individuality and warmth to provide guests with comfort and serenity. Enjoy afternoon wine and teatime

7 No smoking; 8 Children welcome; 9 Social drinking allowed; 10 Tennis nearby; 11 Swimming nearby;
12 Golf nearby; 13 Skiing nearby; 14 May be booked through a travel agent; 15 Handicapped accessible.

by the fireplace. Relax on the garden patio amidst flowers, butterflies, and sunshine. Just 100 yards from the ocean and only minutes from excellent restaurants, shopping areas, and activities. Inquire about accommodations for pets.

Hosts: Lewis Shaefer and Susan Kuslis
Rooms: 8 (PB) $110-165
Full Breakfast
Credit Cards: A, B, D
Notes: 2, 5, 7, 8, 9, 10, 11, 12, 14

Seven Gables Inn

555 Ocean View Boulevard, 93950
(831) 372-4341

It's hard to imagine a more picturesque and romantic location than that of Seven Gables. The waves crashing along the rocky shoreline, the sea otters frolicking just offshore, the whales spouting, the surrounding mountains lit up by the sunset…these are the images seen from each guest room of this century-old Victorian inn. Such natural beauty is complemented on the inside by an unmatched array of museum-quality European, Asian, and American antiques. A bountiful breakfast, enjoyable afternoon tea, outstanding guest service, and the comfort of all private baths combine to make Seven Gables, truly, one of the most outstanding inns in California.

Rooms: 14 (PB) $155-350
Full Breakfast
Credit Cards: A, B
Notes: 2, 5, 7, 10, 11, 12

PACIFIC PALISADES

Bed and Breakfast International

P.O. Box 282910, San Francisco, 94128-2910
(650) 696-1690; (800) 872-4500
FAX (650) 696-1699; e-mail: info@bbintl.com
www.bbintl.com

PP-H1. Large, sunny condominium one-half mile from the ocean offers a good location, friendly hospitality, and pool. Private bath. Continental breakfast. No smoking. Resident cat. $50-55.

PALM DESERT

Bed and Breakfast International

P.O. Box 282910, San Francisco, 94128-2910
(650) 696-1690; (800) 872-4500
FAX (650) 696-1699; e-mail: info@bbintl.com
www.bbintl.com

PD-B4. New contemporary-style bed and breakfast features southwestern decor, a welcoming delightful atmosphere, many amenities, pool, and spa. Four guest rooms. Private baths. A Continental plus breakfast is served, and refreshments are available during the day. Within walking distance to El Paseo with its boutiques, galleries, and restaurants and to other entertainment areas. No smoking. $100-160.

Tres Palmas

Tres Palmas Bed and Breakfast

73135 Tumbleweed Lane, 92260
(760) 773-9858; (800) 770-9858
www.innformation.com/ca/trespalmas

Tres Palmas is one block south of El Paseo, the "Rodeo Drive of the Desert," where guests will find boutiques, art galleries, and restaurants. Or stay "home" to enjoy the desert sun in and around the pool and spa. Guest rooms, featuring queen- or king-size beds, color cable TVs, are decorated in southwestern style. Lemonade and iced tea are always available. Snacks are provided in the late afternoons. Rated A-plus by ABBA and three diamonds by AAA.

Hosts: Terry and Karen Bennett
Rooms: 4 (PB) $110-170

NOTES: Credit cards accepted: A MasterCard; B Visa; C American Express; D Discover; E Diner's Club; F Other; 2 Personal checks accepted; 3 Lunch available; 4 Dinner available; 5 Open all year; 6 Pets welcome;

Continental Breakfast
Credit Cards: A, B, C
Notes: 2, 5, 7, 9, 10, 11, 12, 14

PALM SPRINGS

Bed and Breakfast International

P.O. Box 282910, San Francisco, 94128-2910
(650) 696-1690; (800) 872-4500
FAX (650) 696-1699; e-mail: info@bbintl.com
www.bbintl.com

PA-C3. Japanese-style inn and decor create a relaxed bed and breakfast stay. Shoji windows open to the pool. Three guest rooms have private baths. Shiatsu massage, kimonos, and additional amenities available. Choice of American or Japanese breakfast. No smoking. $65-75.

PS-B2. Self-hosted two-bedroom condo with living room, dining room, patios, full kitchen, and laundry room offers privacy and comfort for a relaxed sun-filled holiday. Private baths, pool, and spa. $100.

PS-H3. This former home of a glamorous 1930s and 1940s movie star is now a unique bed and breakfast with a suite and two additional guest rooms. Private baths. Wonderfully decorated with period pieces and antiques, this bed and breakfast has warm and gracious hospitality. Full breakfast served. No smoking. $90-125.

Casa Cody Bed and Breakfast Country Inn

175 South Cahuilla, 92262
(760) 320-9346

This romantic and historic hideaway is in the heart of the village of Palm Springs. Beautifully redecorated in Santa Fe style, with kitchens, wood-burning fireplaces, patios, two pools, and a spa. Close to the Desert Museum, Heritage Center, and Moorten Botanical Garden. Nearby hiking in Indian canyons, horseback riding, tennis, golf, polo, ballooning, helicopter and desert Jeep tours. Near celebrity homes, date gardens, and Joshua Tree National Monument.

Hosts: Therese Hayes and Frank Tysen
Rooms: 23 (PB) $79-299
Continental Breakfast
Credit Cards: A, B, C, D, E
Notes: 2, 5, 6, 8, 9, 10, 11, 12, 13, 14, 15

L'Horizon Garden Hotel

1050 East Palm Canyon, 92264
(760) 323-1858; (800) 377-7855
FAX (760) 327-2933

The serenity of gentler times lives on at L'Horizon Garden Hotel, a secluded resort at the foot of the spectacular Mount San Jacinto. Twenty-two luxurious rooms and suites decorated to reflect the pastel beauty of the desert surround the refreshing pool and Jacuzzi. Amenities include complimentary Continental breakfast, an extensive library, table games, afternoon refreshments by the pool, and a hotel staff dedicated to guests' comfort. Experience a true oasis in the desert at L'Horizon Garden Hotel.

Host: Sandi Howell
Rooms: 22 (PB) $95-140
Continental Breakfast
Credit Cards: A, B, C, D, E
Notes: 7, 9, 10, 11, 12, 14

Villa Royale Inn

1620 Indian Trail, 92264
(760) 327-2314; (800) 245-2314
FAX (760) 322-3794; e-mail: info@villaroyale.com
www.villaroyale.com

This romantic European-style country inn is an oasis in the desert, with a series of interior courtyards framed with pillars, cascading bougainvillaea, and hovering shade trees. Many rooms have wood-burning fireplaces and private spas. Each accommodation represents a different

---

7 No smoking; 8 Children welcome; 9 Social drinking allowed; 10 Tennis nearby; 11 Swimming nearby; 12 Golf nearby; 13 Skiing nearby; 14 May be booked through a travel agent; 15 Handicapped accessible.

Villa Royale Inn

European country. There are two pools and a spa. The main courtyard has a terrace for the complimentary Continental breakfast served daily, and in the evening, dinner is served outside or in the romantic, internationally renowned Europa Restaurant. Brunch is available.

Rooms: 33 (PB) $75-295
Continental Breakfast
Credit Cards: A, B, C, E
Notes: 4, 5, 9, 10, 11, 12, 13, 14

The Willows Historic Palm Springs Inn

412 West Tahquitz Canyon Way, 92262
(760) 320-0771; FAX (760) 320-0780
e-mail: innkeeper@thewillowspalmsprings.com

AAA four-diamond, Mobil four-star small luxury hotel, the Willows recreates the ambiance and elegance of Palm Springs in the 1930s. Albert Einstein, Marion Davies, Clark Gable, and Carole Lombard slept here. Accommodations feature luxurious linens, fine antique furnishings, sumptuous bathrooms with handmade tiles and claw-foot tubs, hardwood floors, fireplaces, private patios, pool, and spa. Lush gardens with spectacular views and fine cuisine complete the magic.

Rooms: 8 (PB) $250-500
Full Breakfast
Credit Cards: A, B, C, D, E
Notes: 2, 3, 4, 5, 7, 9, 10, 11, 12, 14

PALO ALTO

Bed and Breakfast International

P.O. Box 282910, San Francisco, 94128-2910
(650) 696-1690; (800) 872-4500
FAX (650) 696-1699; e-mail: info@bbintl.com
www.bbintl.com

ST-Y4. This 1920-vintage house on a one-acre estate, 30 miles south of San Francisco near the Stanford College community, offers privacy and tranquility in a parklike setting. Amenities include solar heated pool, bicycles, afternoon refreshments, and superb hospitality. Four guest rooms with private baths. Smoking is not permitted. $110.

The Victorian on Lytton

555 Lytton Avenue, 94301
(650) 322-8555

Special amenities include down comforters, Battenberg lace canopies, botanical prints, Blue Willow china, and claw-foot tubs. Wander through the English country garden with over 900 perennial plants. Five king-size and five queen-size beds are available. Relax in the parlor with a picture book or a novel and a cup of tea while listening to classical music. One room is handicapped accessible.

Hosts: Maxwell and Susan Hall
Rooms: 10 (PB) $138-225
Continental Breakfast
Credit Cards: A, B, C
Notes: 5, 7, 10, 11, 12, 14, 15

PALOS VERDES

Bed and Breakfast International

P.O. Box 282910, San Francisco, 94128-2910
(650) 696-1690; (800) 872-4500
FAX (650) 696-1699; e-mail: info@bbintl.com
www.bbintl.com

PV-B2. Ocean breezes, a panoramic view of the Pacific, and private beach facilities are offered by this homey bed and break-

NOTES: Credit cards accepted: A MasterCard; B Visa; C American Express; D Discover; E Diner's Club; F Other; 2 Personal checks accepted; 3 Lunch available; 4 Dinner available; 5 Open all year; 6 Pets welcome;

fast with two guest rooms and a private bath. Continental plus breakfasts are served in the dining area or on the deck by well-traveled host.Sorry, smoking is not permitted. $50-60.

PASADENA

Bed and Breakfast California

P.O. Box 282910, San Francisco, 94128-2910
(650) 696-1690; (800) 872-4500
FAX (650) 696-1699; e-mail: info@bbintl.com
www.bbintl.com

Three-story Victorian Mansion. Wake up to the smell of freshly baked bread as a part of a full breakfast on weekends. Enjoy hearty Continental breakfast during the week. Elegantly restored Victorian house on a half-acre corner lot; four warmly decorated guest rooms, each with private bath. Conveniently near Old Town Pasadena, museums, and the renowned Huntington Library. $100-150.

Bed and Breakfast International

P.O. Box 282910, San Francisco, 94128-2910
(650) 696-1690; (800) 872-4500
FAX (650) 696-1699; e-mail: info@bbintl.com
www.bbintl.com

AL-J1. This pool house with a small kitchen, queen-size sleeper sofa, twin bed, and private bath offers privacy and comfort on a cul-de-sac across from golf course. Good local hiking, but only 15- to 20-minute drive to LA Civic Center or to Hollywood. Continental breakfast is served. Smoking is not permitted. $45-55.

AL-M2. Large Mediterranean-style home with mountain views offers two large guest rooms with private baths. Beautiful neighborhood with good hiking areas, yet 7 minutes to Old Town and 20 minutes to Los Angeles. Resident dog and cat. Smoking is not permitted. $50-55.

AL-R2. Large contemporary home with Old World wine cellar has Angeles National Forest as its back yard. Two guest rooms with private baths. Host teaches wine classes and is a gourmet cook. Wine dinners and wine tastings available upon request. Continental or full breakfast served. No smoking. $55-65.

AL-S1. This large well-landscaped yard in a quiet residential community is a wonderful retreat at the end of the day. One guest room with private bath. Continental breakfast is served. Smoking is not permitted. $50-60.

AL-SC2. Spacious Colonial-style home surrounded by an acre of well-tended garden. Guest rooms are beautifully appointed with period antiques. Common room available for small conferences. Continental breakfast is served. $65-75.

AL-W2. Cape Cod-style bed and breakfast, appointed with Early American antiques on one of Altadena's loveliest streets, is hosted by horse enthusiasts. Two guest rooms with private baths. Large yard with pool. Resident dogs. Continental breakfast is served. Smoking is not permitted. $50-55.

AR-W2. This home sits on a quiet cul-de-sac near the Santa Anita Racetrack, Los Angeles County Arboretum, golf courses, and the beautiful San Gabriel Mountains. Private bath. Weekly rates are available. Continental breakfast is served. $35-40.

PA-G1. In walking distance to convention center, Old Town, and museums, uniquely decorated condominium offers privacy and wonderful sitting areas. One guest room has twin beds and private bath. Garage parking. Continental breakfast served weekdays; full

---

7 No smoking; 8 Children welcome; 9 Social drinking allowed; 10 Tennis nearby; 11 Swimming nearby;
12 Golf nearby; 13 Skiing nearby; 14 May be booked through a travel agent; 15 Handicapped accessible.

breakfast served on weekends. Smoking is not permitted. $55-65.

PA-L1. Dramatic contemporary bed and breakfast within walking distance of the Rose Bowl offers a quiet setting near most tourist attractions. The guest room has queen-size bed and a private bath. Continental breakfast is served. Smoking is not permitted. $85-95.

PA-P2A. Sprawling ranch-style house in Colonial style has a large living room and book-lined library, both with a fireplace. Two guest rooms are available. Private and shared baths. Close to Los Angeles and most tourist attractions. Full scrumptious breakfast is served. Smoking is not permitted. $65.

PA-P2B. This Craftsman-style house near Orange Grove's historic Millionaire's row offers gracious surroundings and friendly well-traveled hosts. Guest room has king-size beds, private bath. Walk to Old Town, restaurants, and museums. Continental breakfast is served. Smoking is not permitted. $75-90.

PA-R3. Only a short walk to Pasadena Civic and Convention Center, this bed and breakfast is an older, well-kept California bungalow with first-floor guest accommodations, as well as a separate, private apartment. Private and shared baths. Hosts who enjoy travel have lived abroad and speak Swedish. Continental or full breakfast served. Smoking is not permitted. $35-75.

PA-S9. Gracious hosts interested in art offer very private guest quarters, which make up the entire first floor of this contemporary hillside home, with guest living room and patio. Garden and pool lend an

oriental atmosphere. Delicious full breakfast, along with a view of the city, makes this bed and breakfast a special place for guests to stay. Two guest rooms; shared bath. Smoking is not permitted. $55-75.

PA-W2. Half-timbered Tudor-style home was designed and built by the host, who is a magician, yoga enthusiast, and vegetarian gourmet cook. One guest room with private bath. Lovely community with good hiking is close to museums and tourist attractions. Smoking is not permitted. $55-65.

SP-A5I. This 1895 Victorian farmhouse has been refurbished and decorated to recall the heritage of the home and city. Four guest rooms with double, queen- or king-size beds and private baths. Full breakfast is served and afternoon refreshments are available. Smoking is not permitted. $100-120.

SP-B4I. Restored elegant Victorian in the National Register of Historic Places close to Old Town, museums, and restaurants offers gracious hospitality, lovely grounds, and a full or Continental breakfast served in the dining room or patio areas. The three guest rooms on the top floor each have a queen-size bed, sitting area, and private bath en suite. Two additional guest rooms have twin beds and shared bath. A short commute to Los Angeles Civic Center, Hollywood, beaches, and most tourist destinations. $90-150.

SP-P1. A 400-square-foot redwood guest house shares patio and Jacuzzi with host's home, which faces Arroyo Seco natural recreation area. Horse stable, par three golf course, racquetball, and tennis courts are within walking distance. Cottage has cooking facilities and TV. Private bath. Twelve-minute drive to Los Angeles. Smoking is not permitted. $55-75.

NOTES: Credit cards accepted: A MasterCard; B Visa; C American Express; D Discover; E Diner's Club; F Other; 2 Personal checks accepted; 3 Lunch available; 4 Dinner available; 5 Open all year; 6 Pets welcome;

Bissell House

Bissell House

201 Orange Grove Avenue, South Pasadena, 91030
(626) 441-3535; (800) 441-3530
FAX (626) 441-3671

The historical landmark Bissell House was built in 1887 and offers quiet, intimate accommodations. It is on the southwestern anchor of Pasadena's Millionaires Row and just a whisper's distance from Old Town Pasadena, Wrigley Mansion, the Rose Bowl, Norton Simon Museum, Pacific Asian Museum, Gamble House, and the Huntington Library. Twelve minutes from downtown Los Angeles, the Bissell House offers convenience and pleasure to the business and vacation traveler alike. Inquire about accommodations for children. Two-night minimum stay on weekends if Saturday is included.

Hosts: Russ and Leonore Butcher
Rooms: 5 (PB) $115-160
Full and Continental Breakfast
Credit Cards: A, B, C
Notes: 2, 5, 7, 9, 10, 11, 12

PESCADERO

Bed and Breakfast California

P.O. Box 282910, San Francisco, 94128-2910
(650) 696-1690; (800) 872-4500
FAX (650) 696-1699; e-mail: info@bbintl.com
www.bbintl.com

Halfway between Half Moon Bay and Santa Cruz, this romantic retreat provides an atmosphere of rustic elegance and historic interest. It is on one of many old saw mill sites dating back to the late 1800s and early 1900s. A full gourmet buffet breakfast and afternoon wine and hors d'oeuvres are included in the room rate. $105-175.

PETALUMA

Bed and Breakfast California

P.O. Box 282910, San Francisco, 94128-2910
(650) 696-1690; (800) 872-4500
FAX (650) 696-1699; e-mail: info@bbintl.com
www.bbintl.com

Step back in time in this charming riverfront Victorian town. Weary travelers can unwind and forget about their cares at this inn, which is in walking distance from historic downtown Petaluma. The elegant main home, built in 1902, is paneled with rare heart redwood. Climb the beautiful staircase to a stunning octagonal landing which opens into four lovely guest rooms. The three-room cottage next door has a more casual garden cottage theme, complete with a lush garden mural. A luscious gourmet breakfast is served. Afternoon wine and sweets at bedtime provide the finishing touches. $75-125.

Cavanagh Inn

10 Keller Street, 94952
(707) 765-4657; (888) 765-4658
FAX (707) 769-0466

Step back into the romantic past and enjoy the warmth and charm of Petaluma's first bed and breakfast. Appreciate the rare redwood-heart paneling in both the 1902 Georgian Revival home and the 1912 California Craftsman cottage. Award-winning chef Jeanne Farris prepares a gourmet breakfast guests will long remember. Local wines are served in the evening. Cavanagh Inn is in the historic downtown area and within walking distance of restaurants, shops, and the riverfront. San Francisco is 42 miles south across the Golden Gate Bridge. Se habla español.

7 No smoking; 8 Children welcome; 9 Social drinking allowed; 10 Tennis nearby; 11 Swimming nearby; 12 Golf nearby; 13 Skiing nearby; 14 May be booked through a travel agent; 15 Handicapped accessible.

Cavanagh Inn

Hosts: Ray and Jeanne Farris
Rooms: 7 (5 PB; 2 SB) $75-125
Full Breakfast
Credit Cards: A, B, C
Notes: 2, 5, 7, 12, 14

PLACERVILLE

The Chichester-McKee House

800 Spring Street, 95667
(530) 626-1882; (800) 831-4008
www.innacess.com/cmh/ orel-dorado.ca.us/~inn

This elegant home was built in 1892 by the lumber baron D. W. Chichester. Enjoy the fireplaces, fretwork, stained glass, antiques, and relaxing hospitality. A "special" full breakfast is served in the dining room. Four air-conditioned guest rooms, two with private baths and two with private half-baths. Robes are available. Downtown near Apple Hill, Gold Discovery Site, and white-water rafting. Subject of artist Thomas Kinkade's *Victorian Christmas III.*

Hosts: Doreen and Bill Thornhill
Rooms: 4 (PB) $90-125
Full Breakfast

Credit Cards: A, B, C, D
Notes: 2, 5, 7, 8, 9, 10, 11, 12, 13, 14

POINT REYES STATION

Bed and Breakfast California

P.O. Box 282910, San Francisco, 94128-2910
(650) 696-1690; (800) 872-4500
FAX (650) 696-1699; e-mail: info@bbintl.com
www.bbintl.com

The Country House. This three-bedroom, two-bath inn, in the picturesque Point Reyes Station, features a huge country kitchen fireplace. All linens, dishes, cooking utensils, and firewood are provided. An acre of orchards and gardens overlooks Inverness Ridge. Full breakfast. $125-200.

Cricket Cottage

Box 627, 94956
(415) 663-9139; FAX (415) 663-9090
e-mail: pinc@nbn.com; www.nbn.com/people/pinc

A cozy, romantic country cottage set in an intimate garden overlooking a meadow, surrounded by elegant cypress and eucalyptus trees. The cottage is furnished with antique furniture, original art, library, Franklin fireplace, and just outside the front door, a private redwood hot tub under the stars. A stay at the cottage also provides an opportunity to explore the permaculture garden including an earthen bread oven, orchard, pond, ducks, and beds of herbs, vegetables, and berries.

Hosts: James Stark and Penny Livingston
Cottage: 1 (PB) $115-145
Full Breakfast
Credit Cards: None
Notes: 2, 5, 7, 8,9, 11, 12

Gray's Retreat

P.O. Box 56, 94956
(415) 663-1166; FAX (415) 663-1343

Private cottage quarters on the ground floor of a classic barn converted to elegant living—floor to ceiling windows for a view of the Inverness Ridge and sunset, two garden

---

NOTES: Credit cards accepted: A MasterCard; B Visa; C American Express; D Discover; E Diner's Club;
F Other; 2 Personal checks accepted; 3 Lunch available; 4 Dinner available; 5 Open all year; 6 Pets welcome;

patios, Franklin fireplace, full tile kitchen with gas stove, dishwasher, microwave, and service for eight. Four-poster queen-size bed in bedroom, double and trundle in living room sleep six. High chair, crib, and stroller available. Tub and shower in bath. Secluded garden spa. Cable TV with VCR available. Private telephone. Walk to town. Large nature library; laundry. Stocked kitchen. Pets welcome by prior arrangements. Partially handicapped accessible.

Jasmine Cottage

Host: Karen Gray
Cottage: $185
Credit Cards: A, B, C
Notes: 2, 4, 5, 7, 8, 9, 14

Holly Tree Inn and Cottages

3 Silverhills Road, P.O. Box 642, 94956
(415) 663-1554; FAX (415) 663-8566
www.hollytreeinn.com

This inn's setting is a 19-acre valley of lawns, herbs, and wooded hillsides with a gazebo and garden hot tub. Spacious living and dining rooms decorated in flowery prints and antiques have vast couches, French doors, and fireplaces. Two cottages, the Sea Star Cottage on Tomales Bay and Vision Cottage in the Bishop pine forest, each have queen-size beds, hot tub, and fireplace. The Cottage-in-the-Woods is a magical two-room getaway, with fireplace and claw-foot soaking tub. Outstanding breakfasts, afternoon tea.

Hosts: Diane and Tom Balogh
Rooms: 4 (PB) $120-230
Cottages: 3 (PB)
Full Breakfast
Credit Cards: A, B, C
Notes: 2, 5, 7, 8, 9, 11, 12, 14

Jasmine Cottage

P.O. Box 56, 94956
(415) 663-1166; FAX (415) 663-1343

A complete garden cottage all for guests: full kitchen, fireplace, secluded flower gardens furnished with barbecue, large nature library, garden spa under the stars, and lots of sunshine. Full breakfast is provided as well as a stocked kitchen with coffees, teas, herbs, spices, and lots of cooking gear. An equipped picnic basket, beach chairs, and beach barbecue included. TV with cable and VCR by request. A Jasmine Cottage stay always includes bouquets of fresh flowers. High chair, crib, and stroller available. Walk to town. Dogs welcome with prior arrangements. Partially handicapped accessible.

Host: Karen Gray
Cottage: $185
Full Breakfast
Credit Cards: A, B, C
Notes: 2, 5, 7, 8, 9, 14

The Tree House

73 Drake Summit, P.O. Box 1075, 94956
(800) 495-8720; FAX (415) 663-8720
www.treehousebnb.com

A secluded, peaceful getaway in legendary West Marin on top of Inverness Ridge. Enjoy breathtaking views of the surrounding countryside while relaxing on the deck. Fireplace. TV. Spa/hot tub. Continental plus breakfast served. Hiking and bike trails on-site. A bird watchers' paradise year-round. Nearby are the ocean, mountains, Point Reyes National Seashore, and Golden Gate National Recreation Area. Horseback riding. Whale watching from December through April. Midweek and winter rates available. Two-night minimum stay on weekends.

Host: Lisa P. Patsel
Rooms: 3 (PB) $100-125

---

7 No smoking; 8 Children welcome; 9 Social drinking allowed; 10 Tennis nearby; 11 Swimming nearby; 12 Golf nearby; 13 Skiing nearby; 14 May be booked through a travel agent; 15 Handicapped accessible.

Continental Breakfast
Credit Cards: A, B, C
Notes: 2, 5, 6, 7, 8, 9, 12, 14

POINT RICHMOND

East Brother Light Station, Inc.
117 Park Place, 94801
(510) 233-2385

Perched atop an island in the straits that separate San Francisco and San Pablo Bays. This bed and breakfast, while only minutes from shore and less than an hour from San Francisco, is close enough for a weekend jaunt and yet a world away. Listed in the National Register of Historic Places. Rates include transportation from Point San Pablo Yacht Harbor, hors d'oeuvres and beverages upon arrival, dinner with wines, and hot breakfast the following morning. Lunch available upon prior arrangement. Smoking is permitted outside only. Open year-round.

Hosts: Julie Robinson; Gary Sullivan
Rooms: 4 (2 PB; 2 SB) $295
Full Breakfast
Credit Cards: A, B, C
Notes: 2, 4, 5, 7, 9

PORTOLA

Pullman House Inn
256 Commercial, 96122
(916) 832-0107

Built in 1910 as a boarding house, it again is serving people needing sleeping accommodations. Newly remodeled reflecting a railroad theme, it is within walking distance to the Portola Railroad Museum, restaurants, shops, and recreation. If guests like the outdoors and fresh mountain air, they will love Plumas County.

Hosts: Jan and George Breitwieser
Rooms: 6 (PB) $58-95
Full Breakfast
Credit Cards: A, B, C, D
Notes: 5, 7, 8, 9, 10, 11, 12, 13

QUINCY

The Feather Bed
542 Jackson Street, P.O. Box 3200, 95971
(530) 283-0102; (800) 696-8624

The Feather Bed is a country Victorian, circa 1893, in a small community in the Plumas National Forest. All five guest rooms and two cottages have private baths, queen-size beds, and private entrances. An abundant country breakfast is served in the charming dining room and on the Victorian porch. Enjoy hiking, swimming, and fishing. Stroll through historic downtown, dine in one of the fine restaurants, or relax on the front porch.

Hosts: Bob and Jan Janowski
Rooms: 7 (PB) $80-130
Full Breakfast
Credit Cards: A, B, C, D, E
Notes: 2, 5, 7, 8, 9, 10, 11, 12, 14, 15

The Feather Bed

REDDING

Palisades Paradise Bed and Breakfast
1200 Palisades Avenue, 96003
(530) 223-5305

Guests will love the breathtaking view of the Sacramento River, the city, and surrounding mountains from this beautiful contemporary home with its spa, fireplace, in-room TV, and homelike atmosphere. Palisades Paradise is a serene setting for a

---

NOTES: Credit cards accepted: A MasterCard; B Visa; C American Express; D Discover; E Diner's Club; F Other; 2 Personal checks accepted; 3 Lunch available; 4 Dinner available; 5 Open all year; 6 Pets welcome;

quiet hideaway, yet one mile from shopping and I-5, with water skiing and river rafting nearby. Inspected and approved by the CABBI. Inquire about accommodations for pets. Smoking permitted outside only. Children welcome when booking both rooms.

Host: Gail Goetz
Rooms: 2 (SB) $65-100
Continental and Full Breakfasts
Credit Cards: A, B, C
Notes: 2, 5, 7, 9, 10, 11, 12, 13, 14

REDLANDS

Morey Mansion Bed and Breakfast Inn

190 Terracina Boulevard, 92373
(909) 793-7970

Built in 1890 by David Morey, a retired shipbuilder, this Queen Anne Victorian with a Russian dome is a landmark in historical Redlands. There are five guest rooms available, four with a private bath, and a Continental breakfast is served in the morning. The downstairs area, as well as the veranda and lawn, is available for weddings, receptions, and teas.

Host: Larry Armijo
Rooms: 5 (3 PB; 2 SB) $110-185
Continental Breakfast
Credit Cards: A, B, C, F
Notes: 2, 5, 7, 8, 9, 10, 11, 12, 13, 14

REDONDO BEACH

Bed and Breakfast California

P.O. Box 282910, San Francisco, 94128-2910
(650) 696-1690; (800) 872-4500
FAX (650) 696-1699; e-mail: info@bbintl.com
www.bbintl.com

Egan House. Hosts have remodeled their home to include a guest suite with private bath. Quiet, residential neighborhood, close to LA International Airport and not far from the beach or tourist attractions. Hosts are both teachers and, in the summer, guests

may have breakfast served at the Jacuzzi on their deck. $75-85.

Breezy Inn

122 South Juanita Avenue, 90277-3435
(310) 316-5123

In a quiet upscale neighborhood. Large suite with private entrance, private bath with spa, oriental carpet, California king-size bed. Breakfast area with microwave, toaster oven, and stocked refrigerator. Good ventilation with skylight and ceiling fan. Also other guest room with twin beds, private bath, TV, and refrigerator.

Host: Betty Binding
Rooms: 2 (PB)
Continental Breakfast
Credit Cards: None
Notes: 2, 5, 7, 8, 9, 10, 11

Bed and Breakfast International

P.O. Box 282910, San Francisco, 94128-2910
(650) 696-1690; (800) 872-4500
FAX (650) 696-1699; e-mail: info@bbintl.com
www.bbintl.com

RE-E2. Walk to Redondo Beach from this cozy, comfortable bed and breakfast in quiet, residential neighborhood. Sunny guest room has private entrance, private bath, deck, and hot tub. Continental plus breakfast. $65-75.

RUNNING SPRINGS

Bed and Breakfast California

P.O. Box 282910, San Francisco, 94128-2910
(650) 696-1690; (800) 872-4500
FAX (650) 696-1699; e-mail: info@bbintl.com
www.bbintl.com

Running Springs Hideaway. In the middle of the San Bernadino Mountains, this country bed and breakfast was originally part of a sawmill. Open for winter skiing and summer sunning. Three guest rooms feature antique furnishings and quilts. Enjoy a full breakfast served by the fireplace or on the deck. Enjoy wine and cheese in the after-

7 No smoking; 8 Children welcome; 9 Social drinking allowed; 10 Tennis nearby; 11 Swimming nearby; 12 Golf nearby; 13 Skiing nearby; 14 May be booked through a travel agent; 15 Handicapped accessible.

noon, brandy in the evening, and maybe a song from the host. $95-130.

RUTHERFORD

Rancho Caymus Inn

1140 Rutherford Road, 94573
(707) 963-1777; FAX (707) 963-5387

An Early California hacienda-style inn. All 26 rooms are suites and encircle an award-winning garden courtyard. All rooms feature black-walnut-framed queen-size beds, air conditioning, color TV, telephone, refrigerator, and wet bar. The inn is in the heart of the Napa Valley, minutes away from dozens of world-famous wineries and gourmet restaurants.

Rooms: 26 (PB) $145-295
Continental Breakfast
Credit Cards: A, B, C, E
Notes: 4, 5, 9, 14, 15

SACRAMENTO

Bed and Breakfast California

P.O. Box 282910, San Francisco, 94128-2910
(650) 696-1690; (800) 872-4500
FAX (650) 696-1699; e-mail: info@bbintl.com
www.bbintl.com

Spacious two-story traditional home in Sacramento's finest neighborhood, convenient to the capitol, Sacramento State University, and other places of interest. It has a swimming pool and lovely garden which includes a bonsai collection. Two guest rooms share one bath. $75-85.

Bed and Breakfast International

P.O. Box 282910, San Francisco, 94128-2910
(650) 696-1690; (800) 872-4500
FAX (650) 696-1699; e-mail: info@bbintl.com
www.bbintl.com

SA-A5I. In the historic district, this 1912 Colonial Revival offers spacious, airy rooms with antiques. Walk to the capitol or

restaurants, relax in the hot tub, enjoy gourmet full breakfasts and afternoon refreshments. Five guest rooms have private baths and king- or queen-size beds. No smoking. $80-155.

SA-A9I. Just eight blocks from the capitol, this inn is on a quiet tree-lined street of historic homes. Cozy rooms or elegant suites have private baths, double, king- or queen-size beds. Full breakfast; afternoon refreshments help guests relax after a day of business or sightseeing. No smoking allowed. $85-195.

SA-I7I. The 1936 grand mansion is the former home of an ambassador to the United States and is across from South Side Park in the state capitol area. Seven guest rooms have private baths. Amenities include a full breakfast, hot tub room, and guest kitchenette. No smoking. $70-185.

Hartley House Bed and Breakfast Inn

700 22nd Street, 95816
(916) 447-7829; (800) 831-5806
FAX (916) 447-1820

A stunning turn-of-the-century mansion with the sophisticated elegance of a small European hotel in historic Boulevard Park in midtown. Offering exquisitely appointed rooms, the inn is near the capitol, Old

Hartley House

NOTES: Credit cards accepted: A MasterCard; B Visa; C American Express; D Discover; E Diner's Club; F Other; 2 Personal checks accepted; 3 Lunch available; 4 Dinner available; 5 Open all year; 6 Pets welcome;

Town, the convention center, the city's finest restaurants, and coffee and dessert cafés. Step back in time and ride a horse and carriage to a restaurant and back to the inn. The host also has a cookie jar filled with freshly baked cookies!

Host: Randy Hartley
Rooms: 5 (PB) $110-160
Full Breakfast
Credit Cards: A, B, C, D, E, F
Notes: 2, 5, 7, 9, 10, 11, 12, 13, 14

ST. HELENA

Bartels Ranch and Country Inn

1200 Conn Valley Road, St. Helena, 94574
(707) 963-4001; FAX (707) 963-5100
e-mail: Bartelsranch@WEBTV.net
www.innformation.com/ca/bartels

In the heart of Napa Valley, a peaceful 60-acre estate overlooks oak hillsides and vineyards. Six minutes east of St. Helena. In *Best Places to Stay in California.* Three uniquely decorated rooms and honeymoon suite. Amenities: fireplaces, music, movies, coffee, robes, bubble bath, bicycles, library, living room with baby grand piano, entertainment room. Breakfast served until noon. Telephone and fax. ABBA Award of Excellence. Dinner catered. Designated smoking areas. Limited handicapped accessibility.

Host: Jami Bartels
Rooms: 4 (PB) $165-425
Full Breakfast
Credit Cards: A, B, C, D, E, F
Notes: 2, 3, 5, 8, 9, 10, 11, 12, 14

Bartels Ranch

Bed and Breakfast California

P.O. Box 282910, San Francisco, 94128-2910
(650) 696-1690; (800) 872-4500
FAX (650) 696-1699; e-mail: info@bbintl.com
www.bbintl.com

A 1950s home surrounded by vineyards and fruit trees. Enclosed pool and spa. Extensive rose, vegetable, and herb gardens for use by guests. Fireplace, ceiling fans, barbecue, stunning views. Two comfortable bedrooms with designer touches make guests' stay in the wine country more enjoyable. The whole house is for guests to enjoy! $200-250.

Bed and Breakfast International

P.O. Box 282910, San Francisco, 94128-2910
(650) 696-1690; (800) 872-4500
FAX (650) 696-1699; e-mail: info@bbintl.com
www.bbintl.com

SH-C3I. This 1904 Craftsman-style inn with 1920-vintage furnishings is within walking distance of shopping areas and restaurants. Three spacious, comfortable rooms have private baths. Full breakfasts and afternoon refreshments are provided. Self-hosted cottages also available just outside town. No smoking. $90-155.

SH-D3I. Secluded in a forest above vineyards, yet near town, this small bed and breakfast offers a peaceful, rustic retreat. Guest room has private entrance and fireplace. Carriage Room, studio, and two-room cottage are decorated with antiques and are very private. Private baths. Full breakfast is served.Sorry, smoking is not permitted. $125-140.

SH-W20I. This New England-style inn offers large, comfortable rooms and elegant hospitality. There are 20 guest rooms and suites, many with a fireplace, whirlpool, patio, balcony, and beautiful view. Private baths. Continental plus buffet breakfast is served. No smoking. $140-210.

7 No smoking; 8 Children welcome; 9 Social drinking allowed; 10 Tennis nearby; 11 Swimming nearby; 12 Golf nearby; 13 Skiing nearby; 14 May be booked through a travel agent; 15 Handicapped accessible.

Cinnamon Bear

Cinnamon Bear
Bed and Breakfast

1407 Kearney Street, 94574
(707) 963-4653; (888) 963-4600
FAX (707) 963-0251

Historic Craftsman bungalow, circa 1904,
the Metzner Estate is now a cozy, inviting
bed and breakfast. Two blocks from Main
Street, discover the best wineries, shopping,
and restaurants in Napa Valley. The guest
rooms are filled with antiques, king- or
queen-size beds, all with private baths. Relax
after a day of tasting and touring on the spacious front porch or by the fireplace in the
sitting room. Great hospitality. A wonderful
breakfast awaits guests in the morning.

Host: Cathye Ranieri
Rooms: 3 (PB) $115-190
Full Breakfast
Credit Cards: A, B, C
Notes: 2, 5, 7, 9, 10, 11, 12, 14

Deer Run Inn

P.O. Box 311, 94574
(707) 963-3794; (800) 843-3408
FAX (707) 963-9026

Old World hospitality awaits guests at
Deer Run Inn tucked away in the forest on
Spring Mountain Road in the wine country of Napa Valley. A cedar-shingled bungalow on four lush acres, lovingly
restored, offers comfort, friendly
ambiance, and gracious personal service.

Rooms are fully carpeted, decorated with
family antiques and heirlooms. Feather
beds, fine linens, decks, fireplaces, private
baths, down quilts, evening brandy, mints,
coffee and tea service, air conditioning,
refrigerators, robes, and hair dryers.
Dinner available by local delivery service.
Heated swimming pool.

Hosts: Tom and Carol Wilson
Rooms: 4 (PB) $130-175
Full Breakfast
Credit Cards: A, B, C
Notes: 2, 5, 7, 9, 10, 11, 12, 14

Hilltop House
Bed and Breakfast

9550 St. Helena Road, P.O. Box 726, 94574
(707) 944-0880; FAX (707) 571-0263

Poised at the very top of a ridge that separates the famous wine regions of Napa and
Sonoma, Hilltop House is a country retreat
with all the comforts of home, with a view
that must be seen to be believed. The host
built this contemporary home with this
mountain panorama in mind, and the vast
deck allows guests to enjoy it at leisure
with a glass of wine in the afternoon, with
breakfast in the morning, or with a long
soak in the hot tub. From this vantage point
sunrises and sunsets are simply amazing.
Guests will cherish the natural setting,
caring hospitality, and prize location.

Host: Annette Gevarter
Rooms: 4 (PB) $120-175
Full Breakfast
Credit Cards: A, B, C
Notes: 2, 5, 7, 8, 9, 10, 11, 12, 14

La Fleur Bed and Breakfast

1475 Inglewood Avenue, 94574
(707) 963-0233; www.lafleurinn.com

A charming 1882 Queen Anne Victorian
nestled in the heart of Napa Valley is on a
quiet country lane. The guest rooms are
custom decorated and beautifully appointed,
featuring spectacular views, private baths,
and queen-size beds. Some rooms have bal-

conies and fireplaces. A breakfast of gourmet delights is served in the solarium overlooking St. Helena's beautiful vineyards. Join the hosts for a private tour of the award-winning Villa Helena Winery.

Host: Ms. Kay Murphy and staff
Rooms: 3 (PB) $150-200
Continental Breakfast
Credit Cards: F
Notes: 2, 7, 9, 10, 11, 12, 14

Shady Oaks Country Inn

399 Zinfandel Lane, 94574
(707) 963-1190

Secluded and romantic on two acres, nestled among the finest wineries and restaurants in Napa Valley. Wine and cheese are served each evening, and the full gourmet champagne breakfast is known as "the best in the valley." The inn's reputation has been built on warm, sincere hospitality with all comforts in mind. Each immaculate room is spacious and furnished with antiques; elegant ambiance and country tranquility. Two rooms with private entrances and three rooms with fireplaces. Off-season and midweek rates available. Not suitable for children.

Hosts: John and Lisa Wild-Runnells
Rooms: 5 (PB) $155-179
Full Breakfast
Credit Cards: A, B
Notes: 2, 5, 7, 9, 10, 11, 12, 14

Spanish Villa Inn

474 Glass Mountain Road, 94574
(707) 963-7483; FAX (707) 967-9401
www.napavalley.com/spanishvilla

Experience the quiet splendor of this spacious two-story Spanish villa during a visit to the Napa wine country. Nestled in a wooded valley on Glass Mountain Road, the villa is a short drive from downtown St. Helena, mud baths, and glider rides in Calistoga, and world-famous wineries. The surrounding country roads are perfect for jogging and cycling. The Culinary Institute of America is nearby. Gourmet Continental breakfast. Cancellation notice of seven days is required.

Spanish Villa Inn

Hosts: Roy and Barbara Bissenber
Rooms: 3 (PB) $125-175
Continental Breakfast
Credit Cards: A, B
Notes: 2, 5, 7, 10, 11, 12, 14

Villa St. Helena

2727 Sulphur Springs Avenue, 94574
(707) 963-2514
www.napavalley.com/villasthelena

This secluded hilltop Tuscan villa combines quiet country elegance with panoramic views of Napa Valley. Romantic antique-filled rooms, private baths, entrances, and fireplaces in some. A private world on a wooded 20-acre estate; walking trails, spacious courtyard. World-class wine tasting, dining, and shopping nearby. Convenient to tennis and golf. Complimentary wine in the cozy library and an exclusive Continental breakfast in the solarium.

Villa St. Helena

7 No smoking; 8 Children welcome; 9 Social drinking allowed; 10 Tennis nearby; 11 Swimming nearby; 12 Golf nearby; 13 Skiing nearby; 14 May be booked through a travel agent; 15 Handicapped accessible.

Rooms: 3 (PB) $195-275
Continental Breakfast
Credit Cards: A, B
Notes: 2, 5, 9, 10, 11, 12, 14

The Wine Country Inn

1152 Lodi Lane, 94574
(707) 963-7077; FAX (707) 963-9018
e-mail: romance@winecountryinn.com
www.winecountryinn.com

Perched on a knoll overlooking manicured vineyards and the nearby hills, this country inn offers 24 individually decorated guest rooms. The host used family-made quilts, local antiques, fireplaces, and balconies to create an atmosphere of unparalled comfort. Closed Christmas.

Host: Jim Smith
Rooms: 24 (PB) $145-275
Full Breakfast
Credit Cards: A, B
Notes: 2, 7, 9, 10, 11, 12, 14

SAN ANDREAS

The Robin's Nest

247 West St. Charles Street, P.O. Box 1408, 95249
(209) 754-1076; (888) 214-9202
FAX (209) 754-3975
www.touristguide.com/b&b/ca/robinsnest

A homey 1895 Queen Anne Victorian mansion. Traditional yet informal. Gourmet five-course breakfast. Hot tub. Central to seven wineries, three caverns, four golf

The Robin's Nest

courses, eight public lakes, historic gold-mining towns, giant redwoods, and more.

Hosts: Karen and William Konietzny
Rooms: 9 (7 PB; 2 SB) $60-110
Full Breakfast
Credit Cards: A, B, C, D
Notes: 2, 4, 5, 7, 8, 9, 10, 11, 12, 13, 14

SAN ANSELMO

Bed and Breakfast Exchange of Marin County— Referral Service

45 Entrata, 94960
(415) 485-1971; FAX (415) 454-7179

The Lamortes San Anselmo Bed and Breakfast. Be the exclusive guests at this charming bed and breakfast apartment. Within walking distance to town, shops, fine restaurants, and even a lake. This is a great spot for visiting anywhere in Marin County—it is only 15 miles north of San Francisco and one hour to the wine country. Sleeps up to four people. Full kitchen. Discount for longer stays. Full breakfast. No smoking. Children welcome. $85.

San Anselmo Village Cottage. Private cottage on a tree-lined street close to town. Completely self-contained. Off-street parking. Full kitchen, including dishwasher and bath. Queen-size bed. Walk to restaurants and parks. $110.

SAN DIEGO

Bed and Breakfast Southwest Reservation Service

P.O. Box 51198, Phoenix, AZ 85076-1198
(602) 947-9704; (800) 762-9704
FAX (602) 874-1316

301. A 1948 cottage-style home on the north bluffs overlooking hotel circle and Fashion Valley Mall. Warm and cozy with easy freeway access and magnificent views, only minutes from beaches and local attractions. Two guest rooms and one family suite all with private baths, cable TV, VCR, refrigerators, and queen-size beds. Jacuzzi spa and deck. Hostess serves full breakfast. No smoking. Children welcome. $95-115.

The Balboa Park Inn

The Balboa Park Inn

3402 Park Boulevard, 92103
(619) 298-0823; (800) 938-8181
FAX (619) 294-8070

One of San Diego's most romantic settings—a guest house in the heart of the city. The affordable difference is a suite for the price of a room. Within easy walking distance of the San Diego Zoo, Old Globe Theatre, museums, and restaurants, and only 10 minutes to the beach.

Host: Ed Wilcox
Suites: 26 (PB) $80-200
Continental Breakfast
Credit Cards: A, B, C, D, E
Notes: 5, 8, 9, 10, 11, 12, 14, 15

Bed and Breakfast California

P.O. Box 282910, San Francisco, 94128-2910
(650) 696-1690; (800) 872-4500
FAX (650) 696-1699; e-mail: info@bbintl.com
www.bbintl.com

San Diego does not get any better than this. A gorgeous plantation-style home with ocean views from the pool and spa. Lots of art work, European decor, and hospitality. Classy and inviting. $95.

Blom House. This charming cottage in a quiet residential neighborhood is on a bluff less than 10 minutes from downtown, the beach, and all local tourist attractions. The 65-foot deck features a spa and a superb view of Hotel Circle below. All accommodations have 14-foot ceilings, antique furnishings, color TV/VCR, telephones, refrigerators, and bathrobes. $95-120.

Carole's House. Designated a historical site in 1984, this charming inn has eight bedrooms and five baths. There is a pool and Jacuzzi for guests' use; some of the rooms are at poolside. The home is furnished in antiques and with oriental rugs. A Continental breakfast is served in the morning. There are also two studios and a two-bedroom apartment across the street. The inn is less than one mile from the zoo and also within walking distance of Balboa Park. $65-150.

Bed and Breakfast International

P.O. Box 282910, San Francisco, 94128-2910
(650) 696-1690; (800) 872-4500
FAX (650) 696-1699; e-mail: info@bbintl.com
www.bbintl.com

SD-B2. Pacific Beach bed and breakfast is a short walk to the ocean or to Mission Bay. The two guest rooms have queen-size and double beds with a shared bath. Enjoy the relaxed beach atmosphere and the homemade full breakfast served in the dining room or on the private, walled patio. No smoking. $75-100.

SD-B4. Ten minutes from downtown, beaches, and local tourist attractions. Relax and enjoy views from the 75-foot deck with spa. Four guest rooms with private baths. Robes, mini-refrigerator, TV, and VCR are provided. Gourmet breakfast

7 No smoking; 8 Children welcome; 9 Social drinking allowed; 10 Tennis nearby; 11 Swimming nearby; 12 Golf nearby; 13 Skiing nearby; 14 May be booked through a travel agent; 15 Handicapped accessible.

and afternoon refreshments. Smoking is not permitted. $75-95.

SD-C2. Restored 1914 Craftsman bungalow in the national register is in a quiet residential neighborhood minutes from downtown attractions. Guest rooms are appointed with fine antiques including four-poster and brass beds. Scenic walk to the park and local shops. Continental breakfast. $75.

SD-E1. Separate guest house with turn-of-the-century furnishings assures privacy in central San Diego and offers a bedroom, sitting room with wood-burning stove, and dining area where a delicious Continental breakfast is served. Additional guest room with private entrance is available. Private bath. $55-75.

SD-E21. Newly built bed and breakfast less than a block from the beach offers friendly hospitality and a wonderfully convenient location. Cape Cod-style architecture. Seven guest rooms with private baths. A Continental plus breakfast is served. No smoking. $85.

SD-H91. This 1889 Victorian antique-furnished bed and breakfast inn is in a restored village convenient to tourist attractions. Nine guest rooms with private baths. Full breakfasts, candlelight dinners, and special amenities available. No smoking. $85-265.

SD-KH2. Enchanted cottage nestled away on quiet cul-de-sac is just minutes away from zoo, Balboa Park, and golf course. Bed and breakfast is also convenient to downtown and many tourist attractions. Suites have a private entrance and patios overlooking a wooded canyon and a fragrant herb garden. Full breakfast is served. $75-95.

SD-S2. Just a 5-minute drive from Harbor Island Convention Center and 10 minutes from the Downtown Convention Center, beaches, and other attractions, this beautiful Mediterranean-style bed and breakfast is in the Point Loma neighborhood. Two suites have private baths. Full breakfast is served. Pool, Jacuzzi, and kitchen for guests. $95.

SD-Y1. Pacific Beach cottage includes pool and garden. It has a double bed and private bath. Walk tomany area tourist attractions along the Mission Bay. Public transportation is nearby. Self-hosted full breakfast is available for guests. Smoking is not permitted. Weekly rates are available. $85.

Blom House Bed and Breakfast

1372 Minden Drive, 92111
(619) 467-0890
www.virtualcities.com/ons/ca/x/cax4701.htm

Blom House is a charming cottage in a quiet residential neighborhood less than 10 minutes from downtown, the zoo, airport, beach, and all local tourist attractions. The 65-foot deck features a spa and a superb view of Hotel Circle lights and the I-163 and I-8 interchange below. All accommodations have 14-foot ceilings, antique furnishings, TV, VCR, air conditioning, telephones, refrigerators with complimentary wine and cheese, bathrobes, and private baths. A two-bedroom suite with private bath is also available for families or two couples. Guest lounge offers after-dinner drinks, cookies, and a video library. The hostess also has a luxury condo in San Diego and one in Palm Desert on the 10th tee.

Host: Bette Blom
Rooms: 3 (PB) $75-130
Full Breakfast
Credit Cards: A, B, C, D
Notes: 2, 5, 7, 8, 9, 10, 11, 12, 14

NOTES: Credit cards accepted: A MasterCard; B Visa; C American Express; D Discover; E Diner's Club; F Other; 2 Personal checks accepted; 3 Lunch available; 4 Dinner available; 5 Open all year; 6 Pets welcome;

Carole's Bed and Breakfast Inn

short blocks from the business district with restaurants and wonderful antique shops. Ten to 15-minutes' drive from Sea World, airport, San Diego Zoo, Seaport Village, and downtown. Each of the rooms features queen-size bed, full private bath, balcony or patio area immediately off bedroom, and private entrance. Continental plus breakfast.

Hosts: Katie and Phil Elsbree
Rooms: 6 (PB) $95
Continental Breakfast
Credit Cards: A, B
Notes: 2, 5, 7, 9, 10, 11, 12, 13, 14

Carole's Bed and Breakfast Inn

3227 Grim Avenue, 92104
(619) 280-5258

Historic 1904 two-story Craftsman home built by the city's mayor is furnished with antiques and a piano; a rose garden is on the grounds. Swimming pool, hot tub, and gas barbecue. Less than one mile to zoo. Close to all major attractions. Continental plus breakfast is served in guest room or dining area. Refreshments served in the evening. A garden studio apartment and a two-bedroom apartment are available across the street. Dinner is available but not included in the rate. Smoking on designated patio only. Senior rates are available. Reservation deposit is required. Traveler's checks are accepted.

Hosts: Carole Dugdale and Michael O'Brien
Rooms: 6 (2 PB; 4 SB) $65-85
Apartments: 2 (PB) $95-150
Continental Breakfast
Credit Cards: A, B, C, D
Notes: 5, 8, 9, 10, 11, 12, 14

The Elsbree House Bed and Breakfast

5054 Narragansett Avenue, 92107
(619) 226-4133; e-mail: ktelsbree@juno.com
www.oceanbeach-online.com/elsbree/b&b

This recently constructed Cape Cod-style house has intimate and lush garden landscaping. It is a short half-block from the Ocean Beach pier and public beach. Two

Harbor Hill Guest House

2330 Albatross Street, 92101
(619) 233-0638

Overlooking the San Diego Harbor is the ideal location for business, weekend getaways, honeymoons, and family reunions. Accommodates 16 adults. The Carriage House is a separate hideaway for two. Private baths. Continental breakfast. Each level has a semiprivate entry. A kitchen is on each level.

Rooms: 6 (PB) $65-90
Continental Breakfast
Credit Cards: A, B
Notes: 2, 5, 8, 9, 10, 11, 12, 14

Mi Casa Su Casa/Old Pueblo Homestays Bed and Breakfast Reservation Service

P.O. Box 950, Tempe, AZ 85280-0950
(602) 990-0682; (800) 456-0682
FAX (602) 990-3390
e-mail: micasa@primenet.com; www.azres.com

7551. Don't go boatless in San Diego! The boat and breakfast at Cabrillo Isle Marina offers boat and breakfast accommodations as well as harbor tours, custom charter, sunset cruises all under the supervision of licensed captains. The 42-foot Carver motor yacht and the 33-foot Sea Ray are attractively furnished including kitchenette, lounge, and sleeping areas. Off-season. November 1 to May 1. Can rent boats by

---

7 No smoking; 8 Children welcome; 9 Social drinking allowed; 10 Tennis nearby; 11 Swimming nearby; 12 Golf nearby; 13 Skiing nearby; 14 May be booked through a travel agent; 15 Handicapped accessible.

the hour, with a two-hour minimum. Rates for boat and breakfast are $150-200.

7552. On the North Bluffs overlooking Hotel Circle and Fashion Valley Mall in a modest San Diego neighborhood is this charming 1948 cottage-style home with antique and contemporary furnishings. The guests have exclusive use of a sitting room with cozy antique gas fireplace and an extensive video library. There are two guest rooms and one two-couple or family suite, all with private baths. Each room has a refrigerator with complimentary cold beverages, snacks, coffee and tea, air conditioning, TV, VCR, terry-cloth robes, and hair dryer. Smoking is permitted outside. No pets. Children are welcome. Fifteen dollars extra per additional guest. $79-120.

Park Manor Suites

525 Spruce Street, 92103
(619) 291-0999; (800) 874-2649
FAX (619) 291-8844

Come and experience Old World charm across from the world famous Balboa Park, home of the San Diego Zoo. There are 80 suites, most with breathtaking views of the San Diego skyline. Inn at the Park restaurant and piano bar. Meeting and banquet space available. Complimentary Continental breakfast served in the penthouse each morning from 7:00 until 10:00 A.M.

Suites: 80 (PB) $69-159
Continental Breakfast
Credit Cards: A, B, C, D
Notes: 3, 4, 5, 6, 7, 8, 9, 10, 11, 12, 13, 14, 15

SAN FRANCISCO

Absolutely Accommodations

P.O. Box 641471, San Francisco, 94164-1471
(415) 677-9789; (888) 982-2632
FAX (415) 982-9580
e-mail: travelinfo@iname.com

This is a free reservation service committed to assisting travelers in finding the best possible accommodations in California. It offers access to private homestay bed and breakfasts and inns. It can help guests find the proper accommodations that meet their individual needs. The service's goal is to provide both its clients and hosts with the best possible customer service.

San Francisco 101. Built in 1907 as a private home, this inn has been lovingly restored and is furnished with hand-picked antiques. Convenient to Union Square, cable cars, and Chinatown. Twenty-one rooms with private baths. $99-249.

San Francisco 102. Restored to its true Victorian elegance, this home was built in the late 1800s and is furnished with heirloom antiques. Convenient to all tourist attractions. Walk to the cable cars or dine at fine restaurants within a short walk from this bed and breakfast. Two shared baths and two private baths. $88-125.

San Francisco 103. Stay in own private suite in downtown San Francisco. Walk to Union Square and the cable cars. Easily accessible to all tourist attractions. Fully furnished in a true San Francisco style. Three rooms with private baths. $150-175.

The Andrews Hotel

624 Post Street, 94109
(415) 563-6877; (800) 926-3739
FAX (415) 928-6919

Two blocks west of Union Square, the Andrews Hotel is at the heart of the shopping and theater districts. Built as the Sultan Turkish Baths in 1905 and converted into a hotel in the 1920s, this Queen Anne structure features bay windows in 10 of the 48 guest rooms. Continental breakfast is served buffet style in the hallways. Complimentary wine and 24-hour coffee and tea service are

NOTES: Credit cards accepted: A MasterCard; B Visa; C American Express; D Discover; E Diner's Club; F Other; 2 Personal checks accepted; 3 Lunch available; 4 Dinner available; 5 Open all year; 6 Pets welcome;

also available. Additional charge for parking. Smoking in designated areas only.

Hosts: Erwin, Lisa, Nick, and Tatiana
Rooms: 48 (PB) $89-129
Continental Breakfast
Credit Cards: A, B, C, E, F
Notes: 4, 5, 8, 9, 10, 11, 12, 14

Archbishop's Mansion

1000 Fulton Street, 94117
(415) 563-7872; (800) 543-5820
FAX (415) 885-3193

On a beautiful park surrounded by much-photographed Victorian homes. All the interesting areas of the city are only minutes away. Every guest room is custom designed to create a personalized atmosphere reminiscent of the last century. Amenities include exquisite antiques, embroidered linens, and comfortable sitting area. Most rooms have fireplaces. Lovely private baths, stacks of towels, and French-milled soaps. Complimentary evening wine service. No smoking allowed in rooms.

Host: Rick Janvier
Rooms: 15 (PB) $129-385
Continental Breakfast
Credit Cards: A, B, C, E
Notes: 5, 8, 9, 10, 11, 12, 14

Art Center and Bed and Breakfast Suites, Wamsley

1902 Filbert Street, 94123
(415) 567-1526; (800) 821-3877
www.citysearch7.com

The best residential area—Marina, Cow Hollow—where history stands still. Just a 20-minute walk to Fisherman's Wharf. A French New Orleans inn with community kitchen, canopied queen-size beds, fireplaces, and whirlpool. Shopping on Union Street and jogging at the marina. Day tours of northern California's charms, nearby theater, music, cruising, and dancing on the bay—all within easy reach. Business travelers and families welcome. Art classes arranged.

Host: Helvi Wamsley
Rooms: 5 (PB) $105-145

Continental Breakfast
Credit Cards: A, B, C, D
Notes: 5, 7, 8, 14

Bed and Breakfast California

P.O. Box 282910, San Francisco, 94128-2910
(650) 696-1690; (800) 872-4500
FAX (650) 696-1699; e-mail: info@bbintl.com
www.bbintl.com

1. Three-story turn-of-the-century home that has been pictured in *Sunset* magazine. Favorite spot for many returning guests. Only 15 minutes from Union Square and an equal distance to an ocean beach. Within walking distance to Golden Gate Park, the Presidio, and the many shops and restaurants on Clement Street. One room with sitting area and private bath. Two rooms with shared bath. $70-80.

2. This 1876 Victorian is "eccentrically, eclectically, and very tastefully decorated." This home is truly San Francisco and is close to shops and restaurants in popular Pacific Heights. There is a guest room with private bath, minikitchen, and sitting room. In the back garden, a guest cottage affords privacy and opens onto the patio. $105.

4. This quintessential 1896 Victorian in Pacific Heights has been lovingly restored and is close to downtown and within walking distance to shops and restaurants on popular Fillmore Street. High quality antiques and linens are used in four guest rooms. One guest room has a private bath and two guest rooms share a bath. A suite with a private entrance and private bath was added last year. $88-120.

6. Fabulous location! This cozy one-bedroom apartment is in a 1926 Moorish-style building covered in wisteria vines. Large windows make it bright and airy, and it has been recently redecorated in cool blues and greens with chintz fabrics. There is a kitch-

7 No smoking; 8 Children welcome; 9 Social drinking allowed; 10 Tennis nearby; 11 Swimming nearby; 12 Golf nearby; 13 Skiing nearby; 14 May be booked through a travel agent; 15 Handicapped accessible.

enette hidden off of the living/dining room with a sink, microwave, and refrigerator. The bed and breakfast is within walking distance of Chinatown and Fisherman's Wharf. $135.

7. A secluded retreat furnished in American country style in hues of teal and peach. A brick path through a lovely private garden leads guests to their own private entrance and into a spacious guest room with a sitting area and kitchenette. Enjoy breakfast on the sunny deck overlooking another garden. Guests are just steps from a cable car line which can take them one way to Fisherman's Wharf, and the other to Union Square. $135.

8. Built in 1910, this home was built in the Craftsman style and has been remodeled to give it a very spacious and open feeling. The apartments are individually decorated and are open and sunny, with a parlor, vanity area, and separate entrances. The host prepares luscious gourmet breakfasts served in his dining room, which has a panoramic view of the city including the Bay Bridge. $110.

9. Recently renovated large Queen Anne Victorian within walking distance of Golden Gate Park, close to good public transportation and restaurants in the "Greenwich Village" of San Francisco. Its six guest rooms are spacious, sunny, and include kitchenettes; two also have fireplaces. Guests are pampered with robes and slippers provided for their use. $69-99.

10. In a quiet residential neighborhood, this pleasant home was built in 1923 and is just three blocks from Golden Gate Park and six blocks from Ocean Beach with its famous Cliff House restaurant. The home has a fireplace, ocean view, and a deck, and there are always homemade cookies in the cookie jar.

The guest rooms are inviting and cozy, with antique beds, down comforters, and plush robes. $95-115.

11. Stately 1862 Italianate Victorian home with lovely city views. This is the oldest Victorian in the neighborhood and has been very well kept over the years. The house is tastefully furnished in a classic style with oriental rugs, heirloom quality antiques, and fine art. There are high ceilings and crown moldings throughout this charming house. The guest room has tall leaded-glass doors that lead out to the host's plant-filled garden and patio area. $90.

12. This elegant, contemporary, two-bedroom flat is part of a Mediterranean-style building built in the mid-1900s. It includes a kitchen, a front room with fireplace, cable TV, VCR, a cozy deck with a garden, and a wonderful bay view. The flat is decorated with original and unusual artwork. The building is in a quiet residential neighborhood, ideally within walking distance of the crooked part of Lombard Street, Fisherman's Wharf, the Marina, Chinatown, and downtown. $150.

Fuchsia Tree. Lovely studio apartment on the ground floor of an attractive 1879 Victorian built by Charles Eastridge. Looks out onto a private patio and garden. The charming, contemporary suite has a private entrance, is furnished with a sleigh bed, and has a full kitchen and dining area. In the sunny heart of San Francisco, guests are minutes from many restaurants and shops. $110.

Shannon-Kavanaugh. This spectacular home is the anchor of the famous "Postcard Row" in San Francisco's historic Alamo Square district. Built in 1892 by carpenter-builder Matthew Kavanaugh for his family, it has been meticulously

NOTES: Credit cards accepted: A MasterCard; B Visa; C American Express; D Discover; E Diner's Club; F Other; 2 Personal checks accepted; 3 Lunch available; 4 Dinner available; 5 Open all year; 6 Pets welcome;

restored and has appeared in numerous films and TV shows. The guest apartment is large and beautifully decorated in contemporary style, with a sunken living room that looks out over the garden, a large kitchenette, and a large bedroom with a canopied bed. A wonderful two-bedroom house with garden next door is also available. $175-300.

Tenth Avenue Inn. Guests will find plenty of peace and quiet at this lovely 1910 Edwardian home only two blocks from Golden Gate Park. Walk to the De Young Museum, the Steinhart Aquarium, and the Strybing Arboretum. The home is tastefully furnished with antiques and chandeliers, and guests will be delighted by their host's collection of fine silver and stemware. Two roomy guest rooms with private baths have brass beds, and bathrobes are provided for their comfort. $85.

Bed and Breakfast International

P.O. Box 282910, San Francisco, 94128-2910
(650) 696-1690; (800) 872-4500
FAX (650) 696-1699; e-mail: info@bbintl.com
www.bbintl.com

SF-A1. One-half block from Marina Green in the Marina District, this bed and breakfast features views of Golden Gate Bridge and Alcatraz. Well-traveled host serves as a docent for the San Francisco Art Museum. Full breakfast is served. $70.

SF-A3. Victorian with Old World decor offers friendly hospitality and excellent location in the Marina District. Good public transportation. Three guest rooms with shared baths. Continental breakfast is served. $65-85.

SF-B1. Unique small cottage to the rear of the host home atop one of San Francisco's highest points near Golden Gate Park. Fire-place and kitchen. Private bath. Car essential. Three-night minimum stay. Continental breakfast is self-catered. $95-100.

SF-G23I. This 1913 turn-of-the-century Edwardian family-run bed and breakfast with antique furnishings is two blocks from Union Square and the cable cars. Twenty-three guest rooms with private and shared baths offered. Continental breakfast is served. $60-90.

SF-K51. Victorian bed and breakfast in Alamo Square area is convenient to tourist attractions, theater, opera, the business district, and public transportation. Guest rooms have a queen-size or double bed and private or shared bath. A two-bedroom suite with fireplace is available. Enjoy the hot tub in the patio area and a full breakfast in the dining area or on the patio. $75-125.

SF-M1. Comfortable guest room with queen-size bed and shared bath in a well-maintained garden apartment has parking and a generous breakfast. Safe, convenient location close to Golden Gate Park, music, art, gardens, golf course, and ocean. Call for rates.

SF-M301. This four-story Victorian hotel, now a Marina District bed and breakfast inn, features four-poster beds and modern amenities. Thirty guest rooms with private baths. Continental breakfast is served. $65-85.

SF-P261. Two unique bed and breakfast inns, one country French and the other formal English, are two blocks from Union Square and offer beautifully appointed rooms, hospitality, afternoon refreshments, and wonderful breakfasts. Twenty-six guest rooms with private baths. $110-250.

7 No smoking; 8 Children welcome; 9 Social drinking allowed; 10 Tennis nearby; 11 Swimming nearby; 12 Golf nearby; 13 Skiing nearby; 14 May be booked through a travel agent; 15 Handicapped accessible.

SF-P3. Hilltop home in Diamond Heights area has glorious view of the bay and city from the two-story living room. Enjoy a full breakfast in the Scandinavian dining area. Each of three guest rooms has a balcony. Two baths. $40-50.

Bed and Breakfast San Francisco

P.O. Box 420009, 94142
(415) 931-3083; FAX (415) 921-BBSF (2273)
e-mail: bbsf@linex.com; www.bbsf.com

3. A cozy country-style bed and breakfast in the heart of San Francisco has four guest rooms that are comfortably furnished with country antiques and brass beds. The house is at the end of a quiet street, away from the city noise. There is a small patio with trees and birds for the guests to enjoy. A full breakfast is served in the sunny kitchen each morning, and complimentary wine is always available. Four guest rooms share two full baths. $59-69.

4. In one of the most photographed areas of San Francisco, the historic district of Alamo Square, the bed and breakfast is close to the Civic Center, Opera House, Davies Symphony Hall, Union Square, and all of the sights that make the city famous. Most of the guest rooms feature fireplaces, and private baths have been tastefully decorated to show the charm of old San Francisco homes. One room features an antique Chinese wedding bed. In the evening guests can help themselves to wine, relax in the hot tub, and perhaps enjoy a surprise visit from Nosey, the neighborhood resident raccoon. Two-bedroom family apartment with fireplace and kitchen is also available. Full breakfast. $65-125.

5. In one of San Francisco's most beautiful neighborhoods, Jay's place is atop the Broadway tunnel. Walk down the steps to North Beach Italian restaurants, Fisherman's Wharf, and Chinatown. Cable cars are only one block away. This exclusive, quiet location offers San Francisco sights just minutes away. Jay's one bed-and-breakfast guest room is traditionally furnished and has a private bath. Full breakfast. $100.

10. A million-dollar panoramic view of San Francisco Bay and the Golden Gate Bridge plays host to this upscale Presidio Heights bed and breakfast. This prestigious area offers a wealth of wonderful restaurants, interesting walks, and the historic Presidio. Two rooms with private baths are available. Full breakfast. $85-125.

11. A scenic location in San Francisco with a panoramic view. Two bathrooms are available. Each room is equipped with a TV. The spacious family room also has a sitting area and a piano. Guests have ample on-street parking in a quiet neighborhood. Public transportation is nearby. Crib available. Full breakfast. $70-95.

12. High atop charming Russian Hill, a two-bedroom Victorian apartment has a spectacular view of the bay. A great place for two couples or a family includes a living room, sunny solarium, a full kitchen, and bath. A futon is also available. The living room has TV, fireplace, and telephone. The area is great for walking. Cable cars are on the corner, and the wharf is just a short distance away. Special rates for stays over seven days. Full breakfast. $150-200.

13. A wonderful, charming, recently renovated Victorian bed and breakfast. Three guest rooms, two with bay views. At the bottom of world-famous crooked Lombard Street, guests are within walking distance of Fisherman's Wharf, North Beach restaurants,

NOTES: Credit cards accepted: A MasterCard; B Visa; C American Express; D Discover; E Diner's Club; F Other; 2 Personal checks accepted; 3 Lunch available; 4 Dinner available; 5 Open all year; 6 Pets welcome;

San Francisco, CA   167

and cable cars. Excellent parking. All rooms have private baths. Full breakfast. $85-125.

14. One of San Francisco's most enjoyable neighborhoods, Noe Valley is a local treasure of restaurants and shops. This beautifully renovated, charming San Francisco home offers a bed and breakfast suite. Private entrance, king-size bed, and full kitchen. Transportation to the center of downtown (15 minutes away) is excellent. Full breakfast. $95.

15. A wonderful bed and breakfast penthouse with a panoramic view of the city, the bay, and Alcatraz in San Francisco's nicest neighborhood. It's a full flat with kitchen, full bath, balcony, and private entrance. There is a queen-size bed in one room and a set of twin beds in a separate room. The hosts offer TV, VCR, and stereo. All of this within walking distance of the famous sites of San Francisco. Full breakfast. Ten dollars for each additional person. $150.

Cole Valley/Golden Gate Park Bed and Breakfast. This is a 1922 Edwardian home, with original fixtures and an Italianate garden atrium. It is style that Robert offers, mostly, as well as wall-to-wall books, art work, charm, and warmth. There are four guest rooms; one room boasts a panoramic view of Golden Gate Park, the Golden Gate Bridge, and the bay. Cole Valley is adjacent to the Haight Ashbury district and close to the Castro and to the UCSF Med Center. It takes only about 10 to 15 minutes to get to the center of downtown. Full breakfast. $65-75.

Luxurious Pacific Heights Victorian. In one of San Francisco's most upscale neighborhoods, this Victorian offers three fabulously furnished guest rooms. Room one is a master suite with a queen-size poster bed, private bath with claw-foot tub, a sitting area with fireplace, and a private deck. There are also two additional guest rooms,

each with fireplace, TV, and VCR. One room has a deck overlooking the back garden. Cable cars are only four blocks away and the center of downtown is just 10 minutes away. Full breakfast. $85-125.

Noe Valley Garden Studio. The hostess offers a beautiful and peaceful garden studio with a private entrance and private bath. Guests sleep in a cozy queen-size bed, and prepare breakfast at their own leisure. French doors lead to quiet garden. One block from the streetcar in the quaint Noe Valley area where there are restaurants and shops within walking distance. Only a 15-minute ride to Moscone Center and downtown sights. Full breakfast provided. $85.

Richmond District. Still in the heart of San Francisco, the Richmond District offers a wealth of wonderful things to do from bike riding and walking trails to excellent restaurants. Two guest rooms with TVs, VCRs, and private baths. One room offers an ocean view and accommodates a third person. The living room has a fireplace and ocean view. The world-famous Cliff House restaurant, Seal Rocks, and Ocean Beach are just a few blocks away. Transportation to downtown is excellent. Express bus to Union Square in 15 minutes. Full breakfast. $95-115.

Romantic Garden Cottage. A beautifully decorated, romantic cottage with a private entrance and patio. It's furnished with queen-size bed, stereo, TV, and small kitchen. The location on Sacramento Street offers many wonderful shops and restaurants. Full breakfast. $125.

Russian Hill Victorian Cottage. Enjoy the privacy of a large cottage suite with private bath and queen-size bed. The living room has a fireplace, skylight, TV, and stereo. French doors lead out to a deck and garden. Cable cars are only one-half block away. The Wharf, North Beach, and Chi-

7 No smoking; 8 Children welcome; 9 Social drinking allowed; 10 Tennis nearby; 11 Swimming nearby; 12 Golf nearby; 13 Skiing nearby; 14 May be booked through a travel agent; 15 Handicapped accessible.

natown are within walking distance. Full breakfast. $125.

Brady Acres

649 Jones Street, 94102
(415) 929-8033; (800) 6 BRADY 6 (627-2396)
FAX (415) 441-8033; e-mail: staff@bradyacres

Small hotel in theater district three blocks northwest of Union Square. Close to shopping and cable car. Fully accessorized with kitchenware, all rooms have wet bar with microwave, refrigerator, coffee maker, and toaster. Six very sunny rooms with bay windows are decorated with antiques. All rooms are fully furnished with kitchenettes and have private baths with tub and shower. All have private-line telephone with answering machine, color TV, and cassette player. Laundry facilities available. Weekly rates are also available.

Host: Deborah Brady
Rooms: 25 (PB) $75-95
Credit Cards: A, B
Notes: 2, 5, 8, 14

The Chateau Tivoli

1057 Steiner Street, 94115
(415) 776-5462; FAX (415) 776-0505

The Chateau Tivoli

This prize-winning restored Victorian townhouse is in the Alamo Square historic district near the center of San Francisco. The ornate gold-leaf trim and 22 colors of the exterior are prelude to the grandeur inside. Elaborate woodwork, a grand oak staircase, and period antique furnishings return guests to the opulence and comfort of San Francisco's golden age. Continental plus breakfast weekdays; champagne brunches on weekends. Dinners available by request.

Hosts: Chris Clarke, Sonny Coatar, and Victoria Funestig
Rooms: 9 (5 PB; 4 SB) $90-220
Continental Breakfast
Credit Cards: A, B, C
Notes: 2, 4, 5, 7, 8, 9, 14

Country Cottage Bed and Breakfast

5 Dolores Terrace, 94110
(415) 479-1913; (800) 452-8249
FAX (415) 921-2273

A cozy country-style bed and breakfast in the heart of San Francisco. The four guest rooms are comfortably furnished with antiques and brass beds. The house is at the end of a quiet street, away from the city noise. There is a small patio with trees and birds. A full breakfast is served in the sunny kitchen.

Hosts: Susan and Richard Kreibich
Rooms: 4 (S2B) $69
Full Breakfast
Credit Cards: A, B, C
Notes: 2, 5, 7, 8, 9, 10

Golden Bear Bed and Breakfast

P.O. Box 641081, 94164-1081
(415) 362-4936 (phone/FAX)
e-mail: goldencub@unforgettable.com

Come stay in an elegant Edwardian or Victorian home in true San Francisco style. Choose one of three wonderful neighborhoods, North Beach, Upper Buena Vista Park, and Pacific Heights.

NOTES: Credit cards accepted: A MasterCard; B Visa; C American Express; D Discover; E Diner's Club; F Other; 2 Personal checks accepted; 3 Lunch available; 4 Dinner available; 5 Open all year; 6 Pets welcome;

The homes are warm, private, and distinctly San Franciscan and are often compared to the Irish/English tradition of bed and breakfast. Furnished in heirloom antiques and designer linens. Catering to the tourist, business traveler, and Broadway national touring companies.

Rooms: 10 (6 PB: 4 SB) $88-250
Continental Breakfast
Credit Cards: None
Notes: 5, 7, 10, 11, 12

The Golden Gate Hotel

775 Bush Street, 94108
(415) 392-3702; (800) 835-1118
FAX (415) 392-6202

The ambiance, location, and price make the Golden Gate Hotel an extraordinary find in the heart of San Francisco. Dedicated to a high standard of quality and personal attention, the hosts keep fresh flowers in all the rooms. Rates include a Continental breakfast of fresh croissants and the city's strongest coffee and afternoon tea. Personal checks and pets welcome by prior arrangements.

Hosts: John and Renate Kenaston
Rooms: 23 (14 PB; 9 SB) $65-115
Continental Breakfast
Credit Cards: A, B, C, E
Notes: 5, 8, 9, 11, 14

The Grove Inn

890 Grove Street, 94117
(415) 929-0780; (800) 829-0780

The Grove Inn

The Grove Inn is a charming, intimate, and affordable Victorian bed and breakfast. Close to public transportation. The owners and managers are always available for information, help in renting cars, booking shuttles to the airport, and city tours. Free parking is available. Closed December. No smoking.

Hosts: Klaus and Rosetta Zimmermann
Rooms: 18 (14 PB; 4 SB) $70-100
Continental Breakfast
Credit Cards: A, B, C
Notes: 2, 7, 8, 9, 10, 11, 12, 14

The Inn at Union Square

440 Post Street, 94102
(415) 397-3510; (800) 288-4346
www.unionsquare.com

An elegant, small European-style hotel in the heart of San Francisco's financial, theater, and shopping districts. Each floor has an intimate lobby and fireplace where guests enjoy complimentary afternoon tea and wine and hors d'oeuvres in the evening. Rooms are individually decorated with beautiful fabrics and comfortable Georgian furniture, and soft terry-cloth robes are provided. Penthouse accommodations include a cozy sauna, whirlpool bath, fireplace, and wet bar. Personalized service and attention to detail. "We are a nonsmoking and a nontipping hotel." Open year-round.

Host: Brooks Bayly
Rooms: 30 (PB) $165-350
Penthouse: 1 (PB) $350
Continental Breakfast
Credit Cards: A, B, C, D, E
Notes: 2, 5, 7, 9, 11, 14, 15

Moffatt House

431 Hugo Street, 94122
(415) 661-6210; FAX (415) 564-2480

Vacation in a vibrant San Francisco neighborhood. Guests will find the Inner Sunset a safe delight, boasting 30 restaurants and

7 No smoking; 8 Children welcome; 9 Social drinking allowed; 10 Tennis nearby; 11 Swimming nearby; 12 Golf nearby; 13 Skiing nearby; 14 May be booked through a travel agent; 15 Handicapped accessible.

sidewalf cafés near Ninth Avenue and Irving Street. Walk to major attractions in Golden Gate Park or hop the MUNI to downtown San Francisco or ocean beaches. Guest rooms in two 1900s homes. Ask about exercise and weekly discounts. A complimentary Continental plus breakfast is included in the rated. Open year-round. No smoking. Children are welcome.

Host: Ruth Moffatt
Rooms: 8 (2 PB: 6 SB) $41-91
Continental Breakfast
Credit Cards: A, B, C
Notes: 2, 5, 7, 8, 10, 12, 14

The Monte Cristo

600 Presidio Avenue, 94115
(415) 931-1875; FAX (415) 931-6005

The elegantly restored Monte Cristo was originally built in 1875 as a saloon and hotel. It has served as a bordello, a refuge after the 1906 earthquake, and a speakeasy. Only two blocks from Victorian shops, restaurants, and antique stores on Sacramento Street; 10 minutes to any other point in the city. Buffet breakfast served. Two-night minimum stay required for weekends and holidays. Smoking in designated areas only.

Host: George
Rooms: 14 (11 PB; 3 SB) $73-118
Continental Breakfast
Credit Cards: A, B, C, D, E
Notes: 5, 8, 14

No Name Victorian

847 Fillmore Street, 94117
(415) 479-1913; FAX (415) 921-2273
e-mail: bbsf@linex.com
www.bbsf.com

In one of the most photographed areas of San Francisco, the historic district of Alamo Square, the bed and breakfast sits close to all the sights that make this city famous. Most of the guest rooms feature fireplaces and private baths. All the rooms have been tastefully decorated to show the charm of old San Francisco homes. One room features an antique Chinese wedding bed. In the evening, guests are encouraged to help themselves to wine and relax in the hot tub where many a guest has had a surprise visit from Nosey, the neighborhood resident raccoon. Open year-round. Also, a two-room family apartment with kitchen is available. Children are welcome. This is a nonsmoking establishment.

Hosts: Susan and Richard Kreibich
Rooms: 6 (4 PB; 2 SB) $79-125
Full Breakfast
Credit Cards: A, B, C
Notes: 2, 5, 7, 8, 9, 10, 14

The Queen Anne Hotel

1590 Sutter Street, 94109
(415) 441-2828

This 1890 landmark has been beautifully restored with 48 individually designed rooms and suites, many of which include bay windows, fireplaces, and turn-of-the-century antiques. The Queen Anne Hotel is on the corner of Sutter and Octavia Streets in lower Pacific Heights. Easy access to downtown, civic center, and Fisherman's Wharf. Complimentary Continental breakfast, morning limousine to downtown (weekdays), and nightly tea and sherry are only a few of the amenities provided. The Queen Anne Hotel is open year-round. Nonsmoking rooms are available. Children are welcome.

Host: Steven L. Bobb
Rooms: 48 (PB) $130-295
Continental Breakfast
Credit Cards: A, B, C, D, E, F
Notes: 5, 8, 9, 10, 11, 12, 14, 15

NOTES: Credit cards accepted: A MasterCard; B Visa; C American Express; D Discover; E Diner's Club; F Other; 2 Personal checks accepted; 3 Lunch available; 4 Dinner available; 5 Open all year; 6 Pets welcome;

Red Victorian Bed, Breakfast and Art

1665 Haight Street, 94117
(415) 864-1978; FAX (415) 863-3293
e-mail: redvic@linex.com

The Red Victorian is dedicated to a peaceful world. In the geographic heart of San Francisco, on famous Haight Street, near Golden Gate Park, it welcomes creative people from everywhere. Breakfast is served family style around a big table. Beloved for its 18 lighthearted and fanciful guest rooms, some meditative, like the Japanese Tea Garden Room and the Redwood Forest Room, some funny, like the Playground or Friends, some romantic, some historic. All celebrate the Summer of Love (1967 peace and ecology movement) and Golden Gate Park. The most friendly small hotel in San Francisco. Plan to stay awhile. Open year-round. No smoking. Children are welcome.

Host: Sami Sunchild
Rooms: 18 (6 PB; 12 SB) $86-200
Continental Breakfast
Credit Cards: A, B, C
Notes: 2, 5, 7, 8, 10, 11, 12, 14

Stanyan Park Hotel

750 Stanyan Street, 94117
(415) 751-1000; FAX (415) 668-5454
e-mail: info@stanyanpark.com
www.stanyanpark.com

The Stanyan Park Hotel is an elegant, thoroughly restored Victorian hotel, across the street from San Francisco's Golden Gate Park, which will take guests back to a bygone era of style, grace, and comfort. The 36 romantic rooms and suites are equipped with color cable TVs, direct dial telephones, and full, modern tiled baths. The suites have full kitchens, dining rooms, and living rooms. The hotel offers a complimentary Continental breakfast and evening tea service. No smoking. Children are welcome.

Rooms: 36 (PB) $109-250
Continental Breakfast
Credit Cards: A, B, C, D, E
Notes: 5, 7, 8, 10, 11, 12, 14, 15

Victorian Inn on the Park

301 Lyon Street, 94117
(415) 931-1830; (800) 435-1967

Queen Anne Victorian near Golden Gate Park, decorated with Victorian antiques. Many rooms have fireplaces, and the Belvedere Room features a private balcony overlooking the park. The inn features fireplaces, dining room with oak paneling, and a parlor with fireplace. Complimentary wine served are nightly. Parking is available. Continental plus breakfast including fresh breads served daily. No smoking. Children are welcome.

Hosts: Lisa and William Benau
Rooms: 12 (PB) $124-174
Continental Breakfast
Credit Cards: A, B, C, D, E
Notes: 2, 5, 7, 8, 9, 10, 11, 12, 14

Victorian Inn on the Park

Rancho San Gregorio

hand-painted beam ceilings and walls, 10-foot fireplace, antique crystal and brass chandeliers, and hand-painted and gilded walls and ceilings. Queen-size beds, TV, VCR, telephones, voice mail, air conditioning, whirlpools, fireplace, and gourmet breakfasts. Refreshments are served in the afternoon. In downtown historical district, with restaurants, museums, and theaters also close.

Innkeepers: Ron Evans and Tony Contreras
Rooms: 8 (PB) $115-225
Full Breakfast
Credit Cards: A, B, C, D, E
Notes: 2, 3, 4, 5, 7, 9, 10, 11, 12, 14

SAN GREGORIO

Rancho San Gregorio
Route 1, Box 54 (Highway 84), 94074
(650) 747-0810; FAX (650) 747-0184
e-mail: rsgleebud@aol.com

Five miles inland from the Pacific off SR 1 in a rural valley, Rancho San Gregorio welcomes travelers to share relaxed hospitality. This country getaway has 15 acres, an old barn, creek, gardens, decks, and gazebo. Full country breakfast features home-grown specialties. Only 45 minutes from San Francisco, Santa Cruz, and the Bay Area. Smoking is permitted outside only. Children are welcome.

Hosts: Bud and Lee Raynor
Rooms: 4 (PB) $75-115
Suite: $145
Full Breakfast
Credit Cards: A, B, C, D
Notes: 2, 5, 8, 9, 11, 12

SAN JOSE

The Hensley House
456 North Third Street, 95112
(408) 298-3537; (800) 498-3537
FAX (408) 298-4676; e-mail: henhouse@ix.com

Three-story Queen Anne with square witch's cap tower, 40-foot living room with

The Hensley House

SAN JUAN CAPISTRANO

Bed and Breakfast International
P.O. Box 282910, San Francisco, 94128-2910
(650) 696-1690; (800) 872-4500
FAX (650) 696-1699; e-mail: info@bbintl.com
www.bbintl.com

SJ-V2. Set in the heart of historic San Juan, across from the train station and near the mission, restaurants, and shopping, new western-style bed and breakfast with Victorian decor and antiques offers friendly hospitality, a full breakfast, and a great location. Use the bicycles to visit nearby beaches and marina. Two guest rooms with double beds and shared bath. No smoking. $65-75.

NOTES: Credit cards accepted: A MasterCard; B Visa; C American Express; D Discover; E Diner's Club; F Other; 2 Personal checks accepted; 3 Lunch available; 4 Dinner available; 5 Open all year; 6 Pets welcome;

SAN LUIS OBISPO _____

Baywood Bed and Breakfast Inn

1370 2nd Street, Baywood Park, Baywood, 93402
(805) 528-8888; FAX (805) 528-8887
e-mail: innkeeper@baywoodinn.com
www.baywoodinn.com

This inn is on Morro Bay, 12 miles west of
San Luis Obispo in a small neighborhood
on a tiny peninsula. The inn is close to
kayaking, golfing, hiking, bicycling, and
picnicking. Beautiful Montana de Oro State
Park and Hearst Castle are minutes away.
The inn features 15 suites which have
lovely bay views, cozy seating areas, fireplaces, and private baths. Guests are treated
to afternoon wine and cheese, room tours,
and breakfast in bed.

Hosts: Margaret Bennett; Pat and Alex Benson
Rooms: 15 (PB) $90-160
Full Breakfast
Credit Cards: A, B
Notes: 2, 5, 7, 8, 9, 12, 14, 15

SAN LUIS OBISPO (ARROYO GRANDE) ____

Bed and Breakfast International

P.O. Box 282910, San Francisco, 94128-2910
(650) 696-1690; (800) 872-4500
FAX (650) 696-1699; e-mail: info@bbintl.com
www.bbintl.com

LO-03. Well-traveled, multilingual host
offers comfortable accommodations. The
guest room has a king-size bed and private
bath en suite. Living room has a view of
Morro Rock. A delicious breakfast is
served. No smoking. $40-50.

PB-S301. Contemporary inn on the beach
in the midst of 23 miles of unspoiled sand
and surf. Twenty-five guest rooms with private baths. Continental breakfast delivered
to the guest room. $75-175.

SL-G9I. One block from the 1772 San
Luis Mission, this restored 1887 Italianate

Queen Anne home is near shops and
restaurants. Spacious rooms, some with
gas fireplace and whirlpool tub, individually decorated. Eleven guest rooms and
four suites. Private baths. A full breakfast
and afternoon refreshments are served in
the dining room or patio areas. No smoking. $90-160.

SAN MATEO _____

Bed and Breakfast California

P.O. Box 282910, San Francisco, 94128-2910
(650) 696-1690; (800) 872-4500
FAX (650) 696-1699; e-mail: info@bbintl.com
www.bbintl.com

Hidden quietly in the San Francisco
peninsula's reflective past, guests will
find this Tudor Revival bed and breakfast
that offers rustic pleasures of days gone
by. Built in 1891 by noted English architect Ernest Coxhead, it brings to life a bit
of England in a leisurely atmosphere with
gardens to enjoy and comfortably elegant
accommodations. The beautifully furnished guest rooms offer antiques, period
furnishings, and hand-painted murals.
Full breakfast. Every evening refreshments are served in the great room, inviting guests to relax after a long day of
work or play. $119-149.

The Palm House

1216 Palm Avenue, 94402
(650) 573-7256

Built in 1907, this Craftsman-style home
is in a quiet residential area within walking distance of public transportation,
restaurants, and shops. San Francisco
International Airport is eight miles to the
north. Stanford University to the south
and the Pacific Ocean to the west are each
30 minutes by car. The Palm House is one
block east of Highway 82 between 12th
and 13th Avenues.

---

7 No smoking; 8 Children welcome; 9 Social drinking allowed; 10 Tennis nearby; 11 Swimming nearby;
12 Golf nearby; 13 Skiing nearby; 14 May be booked through a travel agent; 15 Handicapped accessible.

Hosts: Alan and Marian Brooks
Rooms: 3 (1 PB; 2 SB) $75-80
Continental Breakfast
Credit Cards: F
Notes: 2, 5, 8, 9, 10

SAN RAFAEL

Bed and Breakfast Exchange of Marin County— Referral Service

45 Entrata, San Anselmo, 94960
(415) 485-1971; FAX (415) 454-7179

1. Barr Mansion Bed and Breakfast. Be the exclusive guests in this historic Victorian in a lovely leafy area of San Rafael. Guest will have a private hot tub in the private bath. Full breakfast is served. Swimming pool is available. Lovely garden setting. $125.

2. This Victorian bed and breakfast has four guest rooms and a hot tub. Gourmet full breakfasts are served. Kitchen is available. Great location near Dominican College. $110.

SANTA ANA

Bed and Breakfast California

P.O. Box 282910, San Francisco, 94128-2910
(650) 696-1690; (800) 872-4500
FAX (650) 696-1699; e-mail: info@bbintl.com
www.bbintl.com

Built in the early 1920s, this registered historic home has been decorated for beauty and romance. One private guest suite features private bath, French doors to the deck, garden, and koi pond. A wonderful full gourmet breakfast is served in the guests' room or on the deck. Host is an artist with an eye for sunshine and perfection. $85.

Bath Street Inn

SANTA BARBARA

Bath Street Inn

1720 Bath Street, 93101
(805) 682-9680; (800) 341-2284
FAX (805) 569-1281

An 1890 Queen Anne Victorian in the heart of historic Santa Barbara. Scenic downtown is within walking distance. Rooms have views, balconies, and private baths, and three feature fireplaces and Jacuzzis. Breakfast is served in the dining room or in the garden; evening wine and afternoon tea.

Host: Susan Brown
Rooms: 12 (PB) $75-190
Full Breakfast
Credit Cards: A, B, C
Notes: 2, 5, 7, 8, 9, 10, 11, 12, 14, 15

Bed and Breakfast California

P.O. Box 282910, San Francisco, 94128-2910
(650) 696-1690; (800) 872-4500
FAX (650) 696-1699; e-mail: info@bbintl.com
www.bbintl.com

Riviera Rendezvous. This Santa Barbara mid-twenties estate sits on a hilltop in the middle of town. The guest room has a private entrance and the intimacy of a cottage. Cozy guest suite has a private bathroom, art-

NOTES: Credit cards accepted: A MasterCard; B Visa; C American Express; D Discover; E Diner's Club; F Other; 2 Personal checks accepted; 3 Lunch available; 4 Dinner available; 5 Open all year; 6 Pets welcome;

work, and its own romantic patio overlooking terraced gardens. Full gourmet breakfasts are served with a spectacular view of the city and harbor. Off-street parking. $95-120.

Bed and Breakfast International

P.O. Box 282910, San Francisco, 94128-2910
(650) 696-1690; (800) 872-4500
FAX (650) 696-1699; e-mail: info@bbintl.com
www.bbintl.com

SB-B1. Hosts designed this home in the hills above Santa Barbara. The setting brings guests close to nature, but the center of town is a 10-minute drive away. The guest room has a queen-size bed and private bath. Full breakfast. No smoking. $85.

SB-C110. Luxurious Victorian inn with a wide choice of uniquely decorated guest rooms is convenient and offers an excellent breakfast. Eleven rooms. Private bath. No smoking. $90-250.

SB-O61. Delicious, elegant breakfasts, comfortable rooms, and friendly hospitality can be found at this convenient inn near beaches and mission. This 1904 Craftsman-style bungalow has individually decorated rooms, several with private decks. Beach towels and chairs provided. Six rooms with private baths. Full breakfast. $105-175.

SB-R1. This architect-designed contemporary home is nestled among oaks near Mission Santa Barbara and five minutes to the beach and shopping. One room with private bath. Choice of full or Continental breakfast. Smoking is not permitted. $45-55.

SB-S8. Convenient and filled with country charm, the beautiful grounds of this inn provide a feeling of seclusion. Eight rooms with private and shared baths. Bicycles available. Delicious full breakfast and evening refreshments. No smoking. $95-195.

Casa Del Mar Inn

18 Bath Street, 93101
(805) 963-4418; (800) 433-3097
FAX (805) 966-4240
www.casadelmar.com

Walk to all beach activities, sailing, shopping, and fine restaurants from this beautiful Mediterranean-style inn. Lush gardens year-round. Twenty rooms offer a variety of accommodation options. One room is newly remodeled for full wheelchair access. All rooms feature private baths, telephones, and color remote-control TV. Amenities include a garden courtyard spa and sun deck, buffet-style breakfast, evening wine and cheese social hour. Newly decorated in 1996. All rooms are nonsmoking.

Hosts: Yun and Yessy Kim
Rooms: 20 (PB) $59-219
Continental Breakfast
Credit Cards: A, B, C, D, E
Notes: 5, 6, 7, 8, 9, 10, 11, 12, 14, 15

Cheshire Cat Inn

36 West Valerio Street, 93101
(805) 569-1610; FAX (805) 682-1876
e-mail: cheshire@cheshirecat.com
www.cheshirecat.com

Two elegant Victorian Queen Anne houses and a coach house surrounded by flower-filled gardens, brick patios, decks, and fountains house the Cheshire Cat. Wedgewood china, English antiques, Chinese rugs, and Laura Ashley furnishings add to the sophisticated ambiance. Enjoy a delicious gourmet breakfast which includes

7 No smoking; 8 Children welcome; 9 Social drinking allowed; 10 Tennis nearby; 11 Swimming nearby; 12 Golf nearby; 13 Skiing nearby; 14 May be booked through a travel agent; 15 Handicapped accessible.

Cheshire Cat Inn

coddled eggs, seasonal fruits, yogurt, freshly baked breads and pastries, cereal, and fresh fruit juices. Afternoon wine hour with brie, hors d'oeuvres, and crudités. Seventeen guest rooms, cottages, and suites, some with Jacuzzi tubs, fireplaces, TV/VCRs, and private balconies. Only four blocks from shops, restaurants, and theaters. No smoking.

Hosts: Christine Dunstan (owner); Amy Taylor (manager)
Rooms: 17 (PB) $140-300
Full Breakfast
Credit Cards: A, B, C
Notes: 2, 5, 7, 8, 9, 10, 11, 12, 14

Glenborough Inn

1327 Bath Street, 93101
(805) 966-0589; (800) 962-0589

Experience the ultimate in romance. Three Victorian/California Craftsman-era homes, each featuring gardens and sitting areas for guests' enjoyment. Full hot breakfast served in guest rooms. Secluded spa for private use. All rooms with private baths, coffee makers, robes, and telephones; many with private entrances and mini-refrigerators; some with fireplaces, Jacuzzi tubs, and hot tubs. Daily evening cookies and beverages; weekend evening social hour including hors d'oeuvres. Walk three blocks to fine shops, restaurants, and theaters. In-state personal checks accepted. .No smoking. Children are welcome.

Hosts: Michael and Steve
Rooms: 11 (PB) $110-400
Full Breakfast
Credit Cards: A, B, C, D, E
Notes: 5, 7, 8, 9, 10, 11, 12, 14

Long's Seaview Bed and Breakfast

317 Piedmont Road, 93105
(805) 687-2947

Relax and recharge in this lovely ranch-style home overlooking the ocean and Channel Islands. Prestigious, quiet neighborhood. Gardens and family orchard. Huge patio offers fantastic views. Large bedroom with king-size bed, private bath, and private entrance. Carefully prepared breakfast featuring the bed and breakfast's own fresh fruits. Local information and maps. Warm hospitality.

Host: LaVerne Long
Room: 1 (PB) $80
Full Breakfast
Credit Cards: None
Notes: 2, 7, 9, 10, 11, 12

The Mary Ma y Inn

111 West Valerio Street, 93101
(805) 569-3398
www.silcom.com/nricky/mary.htm

Perhaps Santa Barbara's best-kept secret. The Mary May Inn has two historical properties dating back to the 1800s and has been warmly welcoming guests since 1981. Rooms with Jacuzzis or fireplaces are available. A quiet haven from the excitement and bustle of the West Coast's most popular resort city. The Mary May Inn is the perfect departure point for a tour to the wine country, a sunny day at the beach, or a walking tour of the unique shops that have made this town a shopping mecca. Rates subject to change.

Host: Kathleen M. Pohring
Rooms: 12 (PB) $100-180
Full Breakfast
Credit Cards: A, B, C, D
Notes: 2, 5, 6, 7, 8, 9, 10, 11, 12, 14

NOTES: Credit cards accepted: A MasterCard; B Visa; C American Express; D Discover; E Diner's Club; F Other; 2 Personal checks accepted; 3 Lunch available; 4 Dinner available; 5 Open all year; 6 Pets welcome;

The Old Yacht Club Inn

431 Corona Del Mar Drive, 93103
(805) 962-1277; (800) 549-1676 (CA)
(800) 676-1676 (US)

The Old Yacht Club Inn has 12 guest rooms in two houses: a 1912 California Craftsman and a 1920s Early California-style building. The inn opened as Santa Barbara's first bed and breakfast in 1980 and is now world renowned for its hospitality and warmth in comfortable surroundings and for its fine food. Within a block of the beach, the inn is close to tennis, swimming, boating, fishing, and golf. Evening wine, bikes, and beach chairs. Dinner available Saturdays.

Hosts: Nancy Donaldson and Sandy Hunt
Rooms: 12 (PB) $105-190
Full Breakfast
Credit Cards: A, B, C, D, E
Notes: 2, 5, 7, 8, 9, 10, 11, 12, 14

Olive House Inn

1604 Olive Street, 93101
(805) 962-4902; (800)786-6422
FAX (805) 899-2754; e-mail: olivehse@aol.com

Enjoy the quiet comfort and gracious hospitality at this restored 1904 Craftsman-style house in a quiet residential neighborhood near the mission and downtown. Ocean and mountain views, terraced garden, large sun deck, off-street parking. Gracious living room replete with bay windows, redwood paneling, fireplace. Private decks, hot tubs. Afternoon wine, evening tea, sherry, and treats. Credit card is required for reservations.

Host: Ellen Schaub
Rooms: 6 (PB) $110-180
Full Breakfast
Credit Card: A, B, C, D
Notes: 2, 5, 7, 9, 10, 11, 12, 14

Secret Garden Inn and Cottages

1908 Bath Street, 93101
(805) 687-2300; (800) 676-1622
FAX (805) 687-4576

Relax and enjoy the quiet garden that surrounds the main house and cottages. Linger over a delicious full breakfast, including home-baked goods, served on the patio or in the main house dining room. Some rooms have private outdoor hot tubs. Take the inn's bicycles for a day of adventure, then return for afternoon wine and light hors d'oeuvres. Sip hot spiced apple cider in the evening before enjoying a restful sleep in a cottage, suite, or guest room. Near town and beaches.

Host: Jack C. Greenwald
Rooms: 11 (PB) $110-215
Full Breakfast
Credit Cards: A, B, C, D
Notes: 2, 5, 7, 9, 10, 11, 14

Simpson House Inn

121 East Arrellaga, 93101
(805) 963-7067; (800) 676-1280
www.simpsonhouseinn

Beautifully restored 1874 Victorian estate secluded on an acre of English gardens. Only a five-minute walk to historic downtown, restaurants, and shopping. Cottages, suites, and rooms elegantly furnished with antiques and oriental rugs feature private patios with fountains, fireplaces, and Jacuzzis. Full spa service and health club with pool available. Rates include concierge services, afternoon beverages, lavish Mediterranean hors d'oeuvres buffet, evening wine, bicycles, and croquet. Minimum-stay requirements for weekends and holidays. North America's only five-diamond AAA bed and breakfast. No smoking.

Hosts: Glyn and Linda Davies; Dixie Budke
Rooms: 14 (PB) $160-375
Full Breakfast
Credit Cards: A, B, C, D
Notes: 2, 5, 7, 9, 10, 11, 12, 14, 15

Tiffany Inn

1323 De La Vina Street, 93101
(805) 963-2283; (800) 999-5672
FAX (805) 963-0994; e-mail: tiffanyinn@aol.com
www.sbinns.com/tiffany

A charming 1898 Victorian home filled with classic antiques and period furnishings. All

7 No smoking; 8 Children welcome; 9 Social drinking allowed; 10 Tennis nearby; 11 Swimming nearby; 12 Golf nearby; 13 Skiing nearby; 14 May be booked through a travel agent; 15 Handicapped accessible.

seven guest rooms are individually decorated and feature queen-size beds, private bathrooms, choice of fireplaces, whirlpool spas, and garden or mountain views. A short walk to downtown shops and restaurants. Full breakfast served on veranda overlooking garden. No smoking.

Hosts: Carol and Larry MacDonald (owners)
Janice Hawkins (manager)
Rooms: 7 (PB) $125-250
Full Breakfast
Credit Cards: A, B, C, D
Notes: 5, 7, 9, 11, 12, 14

The Upham Hotel

The Upham Hotel and Garden Cottages

1404 de la Vina Street, 93101
(800) 727-0876

Established 1871, this beautifully restored Victorian hotel is on an acre of gardens. Guest rooms and suites feature period furnishings and antiques. Continental breakfast and afternoon wine and cheese. Walk to museums, galleries, historic attractions, shops, and restaurants downtown. No smoking. Children are welcome.

Host: Jan Martin Winn
Rooms: 50 (PB) $130-375
Continental Breakfast
Credit Cards: A, B, C, D, E
Notes: 3, 4, 5, 7, 8, 9, 10, 11, 12, 14

SANTA BARBARA AREA

Carpinteria Beach Condo

1825 Cravens Lane, Carpinteria, 93013
(805) 684-1579

In a lush flower-growing valley and across the street from "the world's safest beach." Unit has mountain view. Tropical island decor has a sunset wall mural. Fully furnished kitchen, queen-size bed, and color cable TV. Pool, spa, and gas barbecue on complex. Self-catering with beverage provided and fruit from host's ranch. Sleeps four. Eleven miles south of Santa Barbara. Hosts available for tennis, bridge, or tour of their semitropical fruit ranch.

Hosts: Bev and Don Schroeder
Suite: 1 (PB) $75-85
Continental Breakfast
Credit Cards: None
Notes: 2, 5, 7, 8, 9, 10, 11, 12

D&B Schroeder Ranch Bed and Breakfast

1825 Cravens Lane, Carpinteria, 93013
(805) 684-1579

Nestled in the foothills of Carpinteria one mile from Highway 101 with an ocean view, the Schroeder ranch produces avocados and semitropical fruit. The guest accommodation has a separate entrance, color TV, small refrigerator, and private bath. There are decks for viewing the Pacific Ocean, Channel Islands, and gorgeous sunsets. Guests may enjoy strolling around the 10 acres, discovering fruit trees and a year-round creek. There is a spa in a lush tropical setting to soothe weary travelers. The world's safest beach is 2 miles away. Santa Barbara is 12 miles away. Inquire about accommodations for children. No smoking.

Hosts: Bev and Don Schroeder
Room: 1 (PB) $75-85
Full Breakfast
Credit Cards: None
Notes: 2, 5, 7, 9, 10, 11, 12

NOTES: Credit cards accepted: A MasterCard; B Visa; C American Express; D Discover; E Diner's Club; F Other; 2 Personal checks accepted; 3 Lunch available; 4 Dinner available; 5 Open all year; 6 Pets welcome;

Babbling Brook Inn

SANTA CRUZ

Babbling Brook Inn

1025 Laurel Street, 95060
(800) 866-1131; FAX (831) 427-2457
e-mail: lodging@babblingbrookinn.com
www.babblingbrookinn.com

Waterfalls, brook, 16-foot historic water-wheel, garden gazebo in an acre of red-woods, gardens, and pines, yet close to downtown, restaurants, beaches, board-walk, and wineries. Four chalets in country French decor offer privacy with separate entrances, French doors, decks, fireplaces, cable TV, telephones, brook and garden views. All private baths, some with jet tubs for two. Complimentary tea and "irresistible" cookies, evening wine and cheese. Site of California's first flour mill, built in 1796.

Hosts: Dan Floyd and Suzie Lankes
Rooms: 14 (PB) $145-195
Full Breakfast
Credit Cards: A, B, C, D, E
Notes: 2, 5, 7, 9, 10, 11, 12, 14, 15

Bed and Breakfast California

P.O. Box 282910, San Francisco, 94128-2910
(650) 696-1690; (800) 872-4500
FAX (650) 696-1699; e-mail: info@bbintl.com
www.bbintl.com

1. Vacation home in the redwoods. This 1,600-square-foot home in a breathtaking natural environment is just 10 minutes from the Santa Cruz beaches. Two bedrooms, both with private bath and spa robes, a fully equipped kitchen, cable TV, VCR, stone fireplace, and redwood deck with hot tub—even a piano. The hosts stock the refrigerator with breakfast supplies and a welcoming bottle of wine for guests. $195.

2. This inn lies nestled between spectacular beaches and lush green strawberry fields just 10 minutes from the Santa Cruz Beach Boardwalk . The beautifully furnished guest rooms all offer fireplaces, private baths, and two-line telephones, and some have double Jacuzzi tubs. Resort activities include two clay tennis courts, volleyball, croquet, and badminton; a driving net awaits the golfer prepping for a round at one of the local championship golf courses. $140-270.

Sanctuary—created to provide guests the serene environment they deserve. This spectacular retreat with sweeping views of Monterey Bay and redwood forests is the perfect gateway to the Monterey Peninsula. Hike through redwood forests or enjoy a peaceful time on the deck with a favorite book. Art work and antiques from around the world create a warm and inviting atmosphere. $150-250.

Bed and Breakfast International

P.O. Box 282910, San Francisco, 94128-2910
(650) 696-1690; (800) 872-4500
FAX (650) 696-1699; e-mail: info@bbintl.com
www.bbintl.com

SC-B12I. Most rooms at this charming, unique inn with French country decor have a fireplace and private entrance. Several rooms also have a whirlpool tub. All have a private bath and a king- or queen-size bed. A great breakfast and afternoon refreshments are served. The inn is close to the beach and boardwalk. A garden stream and gazebo serve as a picturesque place for a wedding. $85-165.

7 No smoking; 8 Children welcome; 9 Social drinking allowed; 10 Tennis nearby; 11 Swimming nearby; 12 Golf nearby; 13 Skiing nearby; 14 May be booked through a travel agent; 15 Handicapped accessible.

Chateau Victorian

Chateau Victorian,
A Bed and Breakfast Inn

118 First Street, 95060
(408) 458-9458

Chateau Victorian was built in the 1880s as a family home. Only one block from the beach and Monterey Bay. The house was opened in June 1983 as an elegant bed and breakfast inn. Each room has a private bath, fireplace, queen-size bed, carpeting, and individual heating system. A Continental plus breakfast is served each morning. Each room is furnished in Victorian style. Within walking distance of downtown, the municipal wharf, the Boardwalk amusement park, and fine dining. No smoking.

Hostess: Alice June
Rooms: 7 (PB) $110-140
Continental Breakfast
Credit Cards: A, B, C, F
Notes: 2, 5, 7, 9, 10, 11, 12

Pleasure Point Inn
Bed and Breakfast

2-3665 East Cliff Drive, 95062
(408) 475-4657

This beachfront home overlooks the beautiful Monterey Bay. Guest rooms have ocean views, private baths, whirlpool tubs, and fireplaces. Forty-foot motor yacht for fishing or cruising daily. Within walking distance of Capitola Beach and three miles to the Santa Cruz Beach boardwalk. Innkeepers love to share their inn with guests.

Hosts: Margaret and Sal Margo
Rooms: 4 (PB) $125-155
Continental Breakfast
Credit Cards: A, B
Notes: 5, 7, 10, 11, 12, 14, 15

Valley View

P.O. Box 67438, 95067
(650) 321-5195; FAX (650) 325-5121
www.valleyviewinn.com

Romantic, secluded, fabulous view overlooking 20,000 acres of redwoods. Ten minutes to Santa Cruz and beaches. This unhosted bed and breakfast can make a guest's fantasy a reality. Walls of glass reflect the gorgeous view. Large viewing deck features Jacuzzi spa. Interior features luxury furnishings, white carpet, fully equipped kitchen, and stone fireplace for elegant evenings. Continental breakfast and wine are left in the refrigerator. Read, hike, or head for the beach. No smoking indoors. Rate includes entire house.

Host: Tricia Young
Rooms: 2 (PB) $195
Continental Breakfast
Credit Cards: A, B, C, E
Notes: 2, 5, 7, 9, 10, 11, 12, 14

SANTA MONICA

Bed and Breakfast California

P.O. Box 282910, San Francisco, 94128-2910
(650) 696-1690; (800) 872-4500
FAX (650) 696-1699; e-mail: info@bbintl.com
www.bbintl.com

This is a designer-built addition to the second floor of a renovated 1920 California bungalow. There is a nice deck and the apartment has contemporary furnishings with natural wood, as well as a kitchenette. It is close to the Venice Boardwalk and one mile from Santa Monica Pier. It is within two blocks of the beach. $85.

NOTES: Credit cards accepted: A MasterCard; B Visa; C American Express; D Discover; E Diner's Club; F Other; 2 Personal checks accepted; 3 Lunch available; 4 Dinner available; 5 Open all year; 6 Pets welcome;

Bed and Breakfast International

P.O. Box 282910, San Francisco, 94128-2910
(650) 696-1690; (800) 872-4500
FAX (650) 696-1699; e-mail: info@bbintl.com
www.bbintl.com

SM-C14I. Near Santa Monica Canyon and the beach, this 1910 shingle-clad Colonial Revival inn offers gracious hospitality and an excellent location. Fourteen guest rooms withprivate baths. Some of the amenities provided are a spa, bicycles, and a full breakfast. No smoking. $95-210.

VE-V101. This turn-of-the-century beach estate is now a lovely bed and breakfast inn. Guest rooms and suites are individually decorated with antiques and hand-detailed furnishings. Ten guest rooms have shared and private baths. Large Continental breakfast and evening refreshments are served. No smoking. $85-165.

Channel Road Inn

219 West Channel Road, 90402
(310) 459-1920; FAX (310) 454-9920
e-mail: channellinn@aol.com

Named by the readers of *Sunset* magazine as one of the best bed and breakfast inns in the West and recently featured in *Country Inns*, the Channel Road Inn is just one block from the beach. All 14 rooms are richly decorated and all have private baths. Some rooms have blue ocean views and fireplaces; some have sun-warmed decks; all offer telephones, TV, fine linens, and a respite from the outside world. A flowering garden Jacuzzi and bicycles for exploring the 30-mile oceanside bike path are available. Several of the city's well-known restaurants are within walking distance; fashionable shops along Montana Avenue, and the new Getty Center are both close by.

Host: Heather Suskin
Rooms: 14 (PB) $125-245
Full Breakfast
Credit Cards: A, B
Notes: 2, 3, 5, 8, 9, 10, 11, 12, 14, 15

SANTA ROSA

The Gables Inn

4257 Petaluma Hill Inn, 95404
(707) 585-7777

A beautifully restored Victorian mansion sits grandly on three and one-half acres in the center of Sonoma wine country. Elegant guest rooms feature fluffy goose-down comforters, antiques, and private bathrooms. A separate cozy creekside cottage features a whirlpool tub for two. Sumptuous four-course gourmet breakfast is included. Easy access to 140 premium wineries, the giant redwoods, the Russian River Resort, the craggy north coastline, and just one hour north of San Francisco.

Hosts: Mike and Judy Ogne
Rooms: 8 (PB) $135-225
Full Breakfast
Credit Cards: A, B, C, D, E
Notes: 2, 5, 7, 10, 11, 12, 14, 15

The Gables Inn

Melitta Station Inn

5850 Melita Road, 95409
(707) 538-7712; (800) 504-3099

Late 1800s restored railroad station, this American country bed and breakfast is on a country road in the Valley of the Moon and the center of wine country. Decorated with

7 No smoking; 8 Children welcome; 9 Social drinking allowed; 10 Tennis nearby; 11 Swimming nearby; 12 Golf nearby; 13 Skiing nearby; 14 May be booked through a travel agent; 15 Handicapped accessible.

Melitta Station Inn

antiques and country collectibles. Within minutes of many fine restaurants and wineries. Next to two major parks offering hiking, biking, and jogging. Only 12 miles from Calistoga.

Hosts: Diane Crandon and Vic Amstadter
Rooms: 6 (5 PB; 1 SB) $95-109
Full Breakfast
Credit Cards: A, B, C
Notes: 2, 5, 7, 9, 10, 11, 12, 14

Vintners Inn

4350 Barnes Road, 95403
(707) 575-7350; (800) 421-2584
www.vintnersinn.com

Amid a 45-acre vineyard in the Sonoma wine country, this four-diamond, 44-room, European-style inn features antique furnishings, modern private baths, fireplaces if desired, balconies or patios, vineyard and plaza views, along with a complimentary breakfast. Beautiful sun deck and Jacuzzi. Also the home of the nationally acclaimed John Ash & Co. restaurant.

Hosts: John and Cindy Duffy
Rooms: 44 (PB) $161.32-245.25
Continental Breakfast
Credit Cards: A, B, C, E
Notes: 3, 4, 5, 7, 8, 9, 10, 11, 12, 14, 15

SAUSALITO

Bed and Breakfast California

P.O. Box 282910, San Francisco, 94128-2910
(650) 696-1690; (800) 872-4500
FAX (650) 696-1699; e-mail: info@bbintl.com
www.bbintl.com

Cottage by the Bay. This charming home is a piece of Bay Area history known as one of the "arks," a summer home for a wealthy San Francisco resident before the Golden Gate Bridge was built. The delightful cottage in back is bordered by a large deck with an expansive, water's edge view across Richardson's Bay. Bright and sunny, it is furnished in summer cottage antiques and has a white wroughtiron bed. If privacy, peace, and quiet are wanted, then this is the place! $155.

Little Harbor View. Charming separate guest unit adjacent to host's home up on a hill above the town of Sausalito. The unit consists of a bedroom/living room with an alcove, free-standing fireplace, and queen-size bed. There is also a fully equipped kitchen and lovely deck filled with flowers and views of Richardson's Bay. It is light, sunny, and offers complete privacy. $135.

Bed and Breakfast Exchange of Marin County— Referral Service

45 Entrata, San Anselmo, 94960
(415) 485-1971; FAX (415) 454-7179

Bed and Breakfast on the Bay. Stay in a private cottage built on a pier with a peaceful water view. Separate entrance, private bath, and deck. Guests may feel as if they are far away from the hustle and bustle of town but they are actually within walking distance to all the sights and the ferry boat to San Francisco. $125.

NOTES: Credit cards accepted: A MasterCard; B Visa; C American Express; D Discover; E Diner's Club; F Other; 2 Personal checks accepted; 3 Lunch available; 4 Dinner available; 5 Open all year; 6 Pets welcome;

Patchwork Dragon Houseboat. This houseboat is small but it has a great berth and view of San Francisco and the city lights. This non-hosted bed and breakfast is booked to one group at a time. Self-catered breakfast supplied. Full kitchen. Suitable for one or two adults only. A great value. $85.

Bed and Breakfast International

P.O. Box 282910, San Francisco, 94128-2910
(650) 696-1690; (800) 872-4500
FAX (650) 696-1699; e-mail: info@bbintl.com
www.bbintl.com

SA-C35I. This 1885 Victorian-style inn with restaurant can be found in the hills. There are 35 guest rooms with private baths, some with fireplaces. Continental breakfast is served. Smoking is not permitted. $105-225.

Bed and Breakfast San Francisco

P.O. Box 420009, San Francisco, 94142
(415) 931-3083; FAX (415) 921-BBSF (2273)
e-mail: bbsf@linex.com; www.bbsf.com

17. The Marin County picturesque village of Sausalito offers wonderful restaurants, quaint shops, and a romantic view of San Francisco. Stay aboard a houseboat, a permanently moored home on the bay. There are decks on three sides, living room with fireplace, full kitchen, and a full bath. The home is unhosted but all items for a full breakfast are supplied. Enjoy the view as the city lights come on and the sun slips behind Mount Tamalpais. $125.

The Butterfly Tree

P.O. Box 790, 94966
(415) 383-8447

Guests are staying at the home of Karla Andersdatter, local poet, novelist, author, and artist. Walking distance to the beach,

ocean views, surrounded by the Golden Gate National Recreation Area, and Muir Woods. The monarch butterflies return here each year. This is a secluded, fragile environment, a perfect hideaway for lovers, friends, and "time out!" Only 30 minutes from San Francisco, 15 minutes to Sausalito shopping, an hour to Sonoma wineries, a coastal paradise.

Host: Karla Andersdatter
Rooms: 1 (PB) $135
Full Breakfast
Credit Cards: None
Notes: 2, 5, 7, 9, 14

Hotel Sausalito

16 El Portal, 94963
(415) 332-0700; (888) 442-0700
FAX (415) 332-8788

Just across the Golden Gate Bridge, this 1920s hotel is Sausalito's new gem. Evocative of a boutique hotel along the French Riviera, the hotel recently underwent a massive renovation. Sixteen rooms and suites now feature park and harbor views, in-room dataports, private voice mail, cable TV, luxurious beds, and stylish decor. Rarely will guests find the kind of attention to design and comfort combined with affordability that is now found at the Hotel Sausalito. Rates include morning coffee and pastry. $125-265.

SEAL BEACH

Bed and Breakfast International

P.O. Box 282910, San Francisco, 94128-2910
(650) 696-1690; (800) 872-4500
FAX (650) 696-1699; e-mail: info@bbintl.com
www.bbintl.com

SB-S241. A bed and breakfast inn with the look and ambiance of an elegant European inn is surrounded by lovely gardens. Inn has a brick courtyard, pool, library, and a gracious dining room for large Continental breakfasts and evening refreshments. Twenty-four guest rooms all have individual decor

7 No smoking; 8 Children welcome; 9 Social drinking allowed; 10 Tennis nearby; 11 Swimming nearby; 12 Golf nearby; 13 Skiing nearby; 14 May be booked through a travel agent; 15 Handicapped accessible.

and private baths. This lovely, quiet beach community is a well-kept secret. $120-225.

The Seal Beach Inn and Gardens

212 5th Street, 90740-6115
(562) 493-2416; (800) HIDEAWAY (443-3292)
FAX (562) 799-0483
e-mail: hideaway@sealbeachinn.com
www.sealbeachinn.com

Designated as one of America's top inns by *Country Inns* magazine. An elegant country inn by the sea, with a classic French Mediterranean appearance. The accommodations are appointed in handsome antique furnishings. Many have sitting areas and kitchens. This is a full-service country inn with all the conveniences, activities, and amenities of a fine hotel. The inn is surrounded by small, lush, colorful gardens, French sculpture, fountains, and ancient garden art. Disneyland, Hollywood, LAX, ocean beaches nearby. Personal checks accepted two weeks in advance for deposit only. Smoking limited to designated outside area. Children are welcome. Limited facilities for handicapped guests.

Host: Marjorie Bettenhausen Schmaehl
and Marty Schmaehl
Rooms: 23 (PB) $125-275
Full Breakfast
Credit Cards: A, B, C, D, E, F
Notes: 3, 4, 5, 7, 9, 10, 11, 12, 13, 14

Seal Beach Inn

SEQUOIA NATIONAL PARK

Bed and Breakfast California

P.O. Box 282910, San Francisco, 94128-2910
(650) 696-1690; (800) 872-4500
FAX (650) 696-1699; e-mail: info@bbintl.com
www.bbintl.com

Built in 1876, this Victorian inn is constructed of redwood from the Sequoias. Guests enjoy the ambiance of the Victorian era along with the comforts of in-room cable TV, private telephones with computer connections, refrigerators, and other amenities. Swimming pool/spa. Full breakfast. Sequoia National Park is only 40 minutes away. $75-85.

Bed and Breakfast International

P.O. Box 282910, San Francisco, 94128-2910
(650) 696-1690; (800) 872-4500
FAX (650) 696-1699; e-mail: info@bbintl.com
www.bbintl.com

LE-M9I. Family-run inn near entrance to Sequoia National Park offers gorgeous scenery and friendly hospitality. Ten guest rooms. Private or shared baths. Full breakfast. No smoking. $55-95.

TR-R1. Sequoia National Park is very near this lovely, quiet, rural community. Self-contained cottage adjacent to hosts' home offers fireplace and private bath. Continental breakfast served. No smoking. $75.

Mesa Verde Plantation Bed and Breakfast

33038 Highway 198, Lemoncove, 93244
(800) 240-1466

Only 16 miles from Sequoia National Park. Nestled in the foothills of the Sierra Nevada among acres of orange groves. Heated swimming pool, hot tub, fireplaces, gazebos, and verandas. Rooms are named after characters from *Gone With the Wind* and

---

NOTES: Credit cards accepted: A MasterCard; B Visa; C American Express; D Discover; E Diner's Club; F Other; 2 Personal checks accepted; 3 Lunch available; 4 Dinner available; 5 Open all year; 6 Pets welcome;

decorated accordingly. Full gourmet breakfast served in the formal dining room or outside on the 5,000-square-foot brick courtyard. Freshly squeezed orange juice served every morning, picked from bed and breakfast's own orchard.

Hosts: Scott and Marie Munger
Rooms: 8 (6 PB; 2 SB) $70-155
Full Breakfast
Credit Cards: A, B, C, D, E
Notes: 2, 5, 7, 9, 11, 12, 13, 14

SOLVANG

The Alisal Guest Ranch and Resort

1054 Alisal Road, 93463
(805) 688-6411; (800) 425-4725
FAX (805) 688-2510

Enjoy a journey back to the Old West. Tucked away among 10,000 acres of picturesque countryside, the Alisal is California's only full-service guest ranch. The rustic charm of a historic cattle ranch combines with first-class accommodations, fine conference facilities, horseback riding, boating, and fishing. Fireplaced cottages. Amenities include two championship golf courses, 100-acre private lake, supervised activities for children, 6,000 square feet of meeting space, theme parties, western barbecues, and group rodeos. Breakfast and dinner are included in the room rates. No smoking. Children are welcome.

Host: David S. Lautensack, general manager
Rooms: 73 (PB) $335-415 MAP
Full Breakfast
Credit Cards: A, B, C
Notes: 2, 3, 4, 5, 7, 8, 9, 10, 11, 12, 14, 15

Bed and Breakfast California

P.O. Box 282910, San Francisco, 94128-2910
(650) 696-1690; (800) 872-4500
FAX (650) 696-1699; e-mail: info@bbintl.com
www.bbintl.com

Charming Cannon Home. This lovely nonsmoking home has a guest room with a

view of the mountains. Full breakfast served. Guests may sit and relax on the screened porch in good weather. Just a short walk to the little Danish town of Solvang. $85.

Bed and Breakfast International

P.O. Box 282910, San Francisco, 94128-2910
(650) 696-1690; (800) 872-4500
FAX (650) 696-1699; e-mail: info@bbintl.com
www.bbintl.com

SO-C1. In the rolling hills above Solvang, this spacious home is on one acre. A lovely guest room with large bath en suite is available. Relax in the living room or on the screened patio surrounded by 100-year-old oak trees. Walk a mile into town or bicycle or drive to nearby Lake Cachuma and Santa Ynez wineries. Horseback riding, golf, and boating are all nearby. $85-95.

SO-S9I. This English Tudor is decorated with Hans Christian Andersen story themes and antique furnishings. Many rooms have fireplaces, and several have whirlpool tubs. Nine guest rooms are available. Each of hte guest rooms have a private baths. Full breakfast is served. Smoking is not permitted. $90-180.

SONOMA

Bed and Breakfast International

P.O. Box 282910, San Francisco, 94128-2910
(650) 696-1690; (800) 872-4500
FAX (650) 696-1699; e-mail: info@bbintl.com
www.bbintl.com

SO-T6I. These 1900 Victorian vintage houses furnished with antiques circa 1910 and Arts and Crafts furniture are very close to the plaza. Some rooms have a fireplace and Jacuzzi tub. A full breakfast, afternoon refreshments, garden hot tub, and complimentary bicycles are available. Wineries are nearby. $100-160.

7 No smoking; 8 Children welcome; 9 Social drinking allowed; 10 Tennis nearby; 11 Swimming nearby; 12 Golf nearby; 13 Skiing nearby; 14 May be booked through a travel agent; 15 Handicapped accessible.

SO-C7I. Chalet-style farmhouse and cottages convenient to town plaza and wineries provide the relaxed atmosphere of a rural getaway. Rooms have shared baths. Cottages have private baths. Hot tub and bicycles are available. Golf and hiking trails are nearby. Continental plus breakfast. $75-135.

Sonoma Hotel

Sonoma Hotel

110 West Spain Street, 95476
(707) 996-2996; (800) 468-6016
FAX (707) 996-7014

This beautiful vintage hotel offers accommodations and dining to the discriminating seeker of relaxation and respite from the urban hustle. To spend an evening here is to step back into a romantic period of history. Each antique bedroom evokes a distinct feel of early California; the emphasis on comfort is European. On a tree-lined plaza, it is within walking distance of famous wineries, beautiful picnic spots, distinctive art galleries, unique shops, and historic landmarks. Guests receive wine upon arrival. Children 13 and older welcome.

Hosts: John and Dorene Musilli
Rooms: 17 (5 PB; 12 SB) $75-130
Continental Breakfast
Credit Cards: A, B, C,
Notes: 2, 3, 4, 5, 9, 10, 11, 12, 14

Sonoma Vineyard Cottage

600 Peru Road, 95476
(707) 996-4668; FAX (707) 935-1762

SONOMA VINEYARD COTTAGE

Private hideaway in the Sonoma wine country. Relax and enjoy the quiet and tranquility of 35 acres in the beautiful Valley of the Moon. The cottage has a living/sitting room with secluded deck, a bedroom with king-size bed, and a full bath. Many amenities including a TV, VCR, stereo, mini-refrigerator, toaster, and microwave are provided for guests' comfort and convenience. Breakfast is provided in cottage. No smoking.

Host: Ingrid Sandbach
Cottage: 1 (PB) $100-125
Continental Breakfast
Credit Cards: None
Notes: 2, 5, 7, 9, 10, 12, 14

Trojan Horse Inn

19455 Sonoma Highway, 95476
(707) 996-2430; FAX (707) 996-9185
e-mail: trojaninn@aol.com

Enjoy a wine country getaway at the Trojan Horse Inn, an 1887 Victorian home that sits on the banks of Sonoma Creek. The inn is furnished with antiques and its six rooms, all with private baths, offer queen-size beds, plush linens, ceiling fans, and air conditioners. A delicious full breakfast is prepared each day; beverages and hors d'oeuvres are offered each evening. The lower patio offers a spa for guest use and bicycles are available. No smoking. Open year-round

Hosts: Joe and Sandy Miccio
Rooms: 6 (PB) $125-155
Full Breakfast
Credit Cards: A, B, C, D
Notes: 2, 5, 7, 12, 14, 15

NOTES: Credit cards accepted: A MasterCard; B Visa; C American Express; D Discover; E Diner's Club;
F Other; 2 Personal checks accepted; 3 Lunch available; 4 Dinner available; 5 Open all year; 6 Pets welcome;

Victorian Garden Inn

316 East Napa Street, 95476
(707) 996-5339; (800) 543-5339
FAX (707) 996-1689
www.victoriangardeninn.com

Nestled beside Nathanson Creek on an acre of beautiful gardens with private patios and winding paths, this lovely and historic (1870) farmhouse is just one and one-half blocks from Sonoma's historic plaza and the Sebastiani Winery. The comfortable and artfully decorated rooms are designed for comfort. A gourmet California breakfast is served in garden, guests' room, or dining room. A therapeutic spa and full-size swimming pool in the gardens are available for guests' enjoyment. Concierge services are provided. Inquire about accommodations for children.

Host: Donna Lewis
Rooms: 4 (3 PB; 1 SB) $99-175
Full Breakfast
Credit Cards: A, B, C, E, F
Notes: 2, 5, 7, 9, 10, 11, 12, 14

SONORA _____

Barretta Gardens Bed and Breakfast Inn

700 South Barretta Street, 95370
(209) 532-6039; (800) 206-3333
FAX (209) 532-8257

The inn is an elegantly restored Victorian home, fully air conditioned, and well-known for its special warm atmosphere and gold country charm. Guests enjoy relaxing in the three open-air porches, plant-filled solarium, living room with fireplace, formal dining room, first- and second-floor parlors, and cheery breakfast room. Barretta Gardens is the only Sonora bed and breakfast with a hilltop acre of gardens and lawns overlooking town and the sunset. Acclaimed by "Best of the Gold Country" and Mobil Travel Guide.

Host: Nancy Brandt
Rooms: 5 (PB) $95-105
Full Breakfast

Credit Cards: A, B, C
Notes: 2, 5, 7, 8, 9, 11, 12, 13, 14

Lavender Hill

683 South Barretta, 95370
(209) 532-9024; (800) 446-1333 ext. 290
e-mail: lavender@sonnet.com
www.lavenderhill.com

Delightfully restored 1900 Victorian with four lovely guest rooms, all with private baths. Full hearty breakfast served in antique dining room. Formal parlor, sitting room with TV, wraparound porch with swing, beautiful gardens. Walking distance of shops, restaurants, live repertory theater, and historical Highway 49. Close to golf, gold panning, white-water rafting, and steam train rides. Dinner/theater packages available.

Hosts: Charlie and Jean Marinelli
Rooms: 4 (PB) $75-95
Full Breakfast
Credit Cards: A, B, C
Notes: 2, 5, 7, 8, 9, 10, 11, 12, 13, 14

SOQUEL _____

Blue Spruce Inn

2815 Main Street, 95073
(408) 464-1137; (800) 559-1137
FAX (408) 475-0608
e-mail: pobrien@bluespruce.com

Spa tubs, fireplaces, and quiet gardens foster relaxation for guests. The Blue Spruce is four miles south of Santa Cruz, one mile

Blue Spruce Inn

7 No smoking; 8 Children welcome; 9 Social drinking allowed; 10 Tennis nearby; 11 Swimming nearby; 12 Golf nearby; 13 Skiing nearby; 14 May be booked through a travel agent; 15 Handicapped accessible.

inland from Capitola Beach—an ideal location for a romantic getaway, special celebration, business travel, or an important business meeting. Hike in the redwoods. Bike through country fields. Walk to fine dining. Relax in the outdoor hot tub. Professional, personal attention is the hallmark of this inn. Visit soon!

Hosts: Pat and Tom O'Brien
Rooms: 6 (PB) $85-150
Full Breakfast
Credit Cards: A, B, C, D
Notes: 2, 5, 7, 9, 10, 11, 12, 14

SPRINGVILLE

Annie's Bed and Breakfast

33024 Globe Drive, 93265
(209) 539-3827
e-mail: bozanich@lightspeed.net

On five acres in the beautiful Sierra foothills, this inn is beautifully furnished with antiques, feather beds, and handmade quilts. Full country breakfast is prepared on an antique wood cookstove. The host has a custom saddle and custom golf shop and horse training facility on the property. Close to redwoods, golf, tennis, fishing, hiking, and boating. Enjoy a great place to relax and enjoy the peace and quiet of country life. Members of CABBI and PAII.

Hosts: John and Annie Bozanich
Rooms: 3 (PB) $95
Full Breakfast
Credit Cards: A, B, C, D, E
Notes: 2, 4, 5, 7, 9, 10, 11, 12, 13, 14

SUTTER CREEK

The Foxes in Sutter Creek

77 Main Street, P.O. Box 159, 95685
(209) 267-5882; (800) 987-3344
FAX (209) 267-0712; e-mail: foxes@cdepot.net
www.foxesinn.com

Foxes Bed and Breakfast Inn is in the gold rush town of Sutter Creek, known as "the nicest town in Mother Lode." There are seven spacious guest rooms, all with private baths. Some with private entrances, wood-burning fireplaces and all with air conditioning. A full breakfast is served to each guest room, or in the garden, on silver service at the time guest chooses. Covered parking is available. "The Gold Country's most elegant inn"—*Motorland* magazine/CSAA-AAA. Skiing is an hour and fifteen minutes away. Closed Christmas Eve and Christmas day.

Hosts: Pete and Min Fox
Rooms: 7 (PB) $130-180
Full Breakfast
Credit Cards: A, B, D
Notes: 2, 7, 9, 10, 11, 12, 14

Sutter Creek Inn

75 Main Street, P.O. Box 385, 95685
(209) 267-5606; FAX (209) 267-9287
e-mail: info@suttercreekinn.com
www.suttercreekinn.com

The Sutter Creek Inn is full of surprises. Eighteen rooms with baths, 10 with fireplaces, some with hot tubs and TV. Some rooms have swinging beds that can be stabilized. A full hot breakfast is served each morning. Tree-shaded lawns with hammocks. Living room with library, piano, and game tables. Handwriting analysis and massages available. An hour's drive east of Sacramento on Highway 49.

Rooms: 18 (PB) $65-175
Full Breakfast
Credit Cards: A, B
Notes: 2, 5, 7, 9, 10, 11, 12, 13

Sutter Creek Inn

NOTES: Credit cards accepted: A MasterCard; B Visa; C American Express; D Discover; E Diner's Club; F Other; 2 Personal checks accepted; 3 Lunch available; 4 Dinner available; 5 Open all year; 6 Pets welcome;

Chaney House

TAHOE CITY

Chaney House

4725 West Lake Boulevard, P.O. Box 7852, 96145
(530) 525-7333; FAX (530) 525-4413
e-mail: www.chaneyhouse@thegrid.net

Built on the Lake Tahoe shore by Italian stonemasons, Chaney House has an almost medieval quality with its dramatic arched windows, 18-inch-thick stone walls, and enormous fireplace. The private beach and pier beckon guests. Bicycling, hiking, boating, fishing, and 19 ski areas are close at hand. Scrumptious breakfasts are served on the patio overlooking the lake on mild days. Children over 12 welcome.

Hosts: Gary and Lori Chaney
Rooms: 4 (PB) $110-195
Full Breakfast
Credit Cards: A, B
Notes: 2, 5, 7, 9, 10, 11, 12, 13, 14

Mayfield House

236 Grove Street, P.O. Box 5999, 96145
(530) 583-1001

Snug and cozy 1930s Tahoe home, one-half block from the beach. Premium skiing within five miles. Full breakfast. Home-made baked goods. Within walking distance of shops and restaurants in Tahoe City. Off-street parking.

Hosts: Cynthia and Bruce Knauss
Rooms: 6 (3 PB; 3 SB) $95-175
Full Breakfast
Credit Cards: A, B, C
Notes: 2, 5, 7, 9, 10, 11, 12, 13, 14

TAHOE VISTA

The Shore House at Lake Tahoe

7170 North Lake Boulevard, P.O. Box 343, 96148
(530) 546-7270; (800) 207-5160
FAX (530) 546-7130
e-mail: shorhse@inntahoe.com
www.inntahoe.com

On the north shore of Lake Tahoe, the Shore House is the ultimate romantic getaway, with a lakefront hot tub, private gardens and lawns, pier, and adjoining beach. Each floor is surrounded by balconies and decks offering views of the lake and snow-capped mountains. Each guest room has a private outdoor entrance, private bath, and mini-refrigerator. Decorated with gas log fireplaces, knotty pine walls and custom-built log beds, Scandia down comforters, and feather beds. There are 10 ski areas within 20 miles. Water sports, hiking, and biking are all within a few miles.

7 No smoking; 8 Children welcome; 9 Social drinking allowed; 10 Tennis nearby; 11 Swimming nearby; 12 Golf nearby; 13 Skiing nearby; 14 May be booked through a travel agent; 15 Handicapped accessible.

Hosts: Marty and Barb Cohen
Rooms: 9 (PB) $130-175
Full Breakfast
Credit Cards: A, B, D
Notes: 2, 5, 7, 8, 9, 10, 11, 12, 13, 14

Hosts: Betty and Dick Ryan
Rooms: 6 (PB) $100-150
Full Breakfast
Credit Cards: A, B, D
Notes: 2, 7, 9, 10, 11, 12, 14

TEMECULA

Bed and Breakfast International

P.O. Box 282910, San Francisco, 94128-2910
(650) 696-1690; (800) 872-4500
FAX (650) 696-1699; e-mail: info@bbintl.com
www.bbintl.com

TE-L61. In southern California's wine country, this lovely bed and breakfast has six uniquely decorated guest rooms with private baths. Full country breakfast is served. Sorry, smoking is not permitted. $95-125.

Loma Vista Bed and Breakfast

33350 La Serena Way, 92591
(909) 676-7047

Loma Vista, in the heart of Temecula's wine country, is convenient to any spot in southern California. This beautiful new Mission-style home is surrounded by citrus groves and premium vineyards. All six rooms have private baths; most have balconies. A full champagne breakfast is served. Closed Thanksgiving, Christmas, New Year's days.

TIBURON

Bed and Breakfast Exchange of Marin County— Referral Service

45 Entrata, San Anselmo, 94960
(415) 485-1971; FAX (415) 454-7179

High on a hilltop with wonderful view. Private cabin, private bath, garden setting, and very special ambiance. $125.

TRINIDAD

The Lost Whale Bed and Breakfast

3452 Patrick's Point Drive, 95570
(800) 677-7859; www.lost-whale-inn.com

Gorgeous oceanfront bed and breakfast on four wooded acres with a private beach and trail. Wake to barking sea lions and a spectacular ocean view. Chosen by *San Francisco Chronicle* as "one of the top ten dream vacation spots in California." Amenities include outdoor hot tub, afternoon tea, private baths, and queen-size beds. Fifteen minutes from the largest redwood forests in the world. Enjoy the gardens, decks, and gourmet breakfast. Families welcome.

Hosts: Lee Miller and Susanne Lakin
Rooms: 8 (PB) $95-170
Full Breakfast
Credit Cards: A, B, C, D
Notes: 2, 5, 7, 8, 10, 11, 12, 14

Trinidad Bay Bed and Breakfast

560 Edwards Street, P.O. Box 849, 95570
(707) 677-0840

A Cape Cod-style home overlooking beautiful Trinidad Bay. The inn offers spectacular views of the rugged coastline and fishing

NOTES: Credit cards accepted: A MasterCard; B Visa; C American Express; D Discover; E Diner's Club; F Other; 2 Personal checks accepted; 3 Lunch available; 4 Dinner available; 5 Open all year; 6 Pets welcome;

Trinidad Bay

harbor from two suites, one with a fireplace, and two upstairs bedrooms, all with private baths. Surrounded by beaches, trails, and redwood parks. Within walking distance of restaurants and shops. The suites enjoy breakfast delivered. The other two rooms enjoy breakfast at a family-style table.

Hosts: Paul and Carol Kirk
Rooms: (PB) $125-155
Full Breakfast
Credit Cards: A, B
Notes: 2, 7, 10, 12

TRUCKEE

Richardson House Bed and Breakfast Inn

10154 High Street, P.O. Box 2011, 96160
(916) 587-5388; (888) 229-0365
FAX (916) 587-0927

Fully restored Victorian, built by Warren Richardson, lumber baron, in the 1880s. Furnished with treasured antiques, fine linens. Victorian strolling garden, complete with gingerbread-adorned gazebo for weddings. On a hill overlooking the Sierras and Old Town Truckee. Train whistles and fresh mountain air to lull guests to sleep each night. Steeped in history and romance. Close to Lake Tahoe, Donner Lake, skiing, hiking, fishing, river rafting, and Amtrak. Twenty-four-hour snack bar, player piano. Children over 10 welcome.

Host: Jeannine Karnofsky
Rooms: 8 (6 PB; 2 SB) $100-150
Full Breakfast
Credit Cards: A, B, C, D
Notes: 2, 5, 7, 9, 11, 12, 13, 14, 15

UKIAH

Bed and Breakfast International

P.O. Box 282910, San Francisco, 94128-2910
(650) 696-1690; (800) 872-4500
FAX (650) 696-1699; e-mail: info@bbintl.com
www.bbintl.com

UK-V12I. This 1854 California historic landmark, once a favorite retreat of writers and U.S. presidents, still features warm, naturally carbonated mineral baths. The bed and breakfast is on 700 acres and features an Olympic-size pool, large Jacuzzi, indoor and outdoor mineral tubs, and massages. There are 12 guest rooms and two cottages with private baths and queen-size or twin beds. Hike or bike on the property. Many recreational opportunities are at nearby coast. Continental plus breakfast. No smoking. $125-170.

Vichy Hot Springs Resort and Inn

2605 Vichy Springs Road, 95482-3507
(707) 462-9515; FAX (707) 462-9516
e-mail: vichy@pacific.net
www.vichysprings.com

Vichy Hot Springs Resort, a delightful two-hour drive north of San Francisco, has 17 rooms and three self-contained cottages that have been renovated and individually decorated. All accommodations have their own heating and air-conditioning and either queen- or twin-size beds. Nearby are 10 mineral baths built in 1860 and used by the rich and famous in California's history. Vichy features naturally sparkling mineral baths, a communal hot pool, Olympic-size pool, 700 private acres with a waterfall, trails, and roads for hiking, jogging, picnicking, and mountain bicycling. Swedish massage, reflexology, and herbal facials.

7 No smoking; 8 Children welcome; 9 Social drinking allowed; 10 Tennis nearby; 11 Swimming nearby; 12 Golf nearby; 13 Skiing nearby; 14 May be booked through a travel agent; 15 Handicapped accessible.

Lunch and dinner available nearby. Smoking permitted outside only.

Hosts: Gilbert and Marjorie Ashoff
Rooms: 20 (PB) $99-195
Full Breakfast
Credit Cards: A, B, C, D, E, F
Notes: 2, 5, 7, 8, 9, 10, 11, 12, 14, 15

VALLEY FORD

Bed and Breakfast International
P.O. Box 282910, San Francisco, 94128-2910
(650) 696-1690; (800) 872-4500
FAX (650) 696-1699; e-mail: info@bbintl.com
www.bbintl.com

VF-141. This 1870 Victorian farmhouse, with library and wood-burning stove in the parlor, is set on lovely surroundings. Four guest rooms have private and shared baths and queen-size or double beds. Enjoy a Continental plus breakfast and afternoon refreshments. Excellent hiking, biking, and touring areas nearby. No smoking. $50-85.

VENICE

The Venice Beach House Bed and Breakfast
15 Thirtieth Avenue, 90291
(310) 823-1966; FAX (310) 823-1842

In 1911 Warren Wilson, the founder of the *Los Angeles Daily Journal*, and his family

Venice Beach House

built this home, just steps from the beach and all that makes Venice unlike anywhere else in the world. The house is decorated with dark oak antiques, hardwood floors, and a large living room with a wood-burning fireplace. Five suites have private baths and four rooms share two baths. There are also homemade cookies and hot and iced tea all afternoon.

Host: Karen Stern
Rooms: 9 (5 PB; 4 S2B) $85-165
Continental Breakfast
Credit Cards: A, B, C
Notes: 5, 7, 8, 9, 10, 11, 12, 14

VENTURA

Bella Maggiore Inn
67 South California Street, 93001
(805) 652-0277

This 1920s northern Italian-style inn was designed by A. C. Martin, architect of the Los Angeles City Hall. The inn is in the old business district near Mission San Buenaventura. Full breakfast served in the dining room or courtyard. Appetizers with beverages served in the afternoon. Telephone, TV in all rooms. Whirlpool, fireplace, and air conditioning in some rooms.

Host: Thomas Wood
Rooms: 24 (PB) $75-150
Full Breakfast
Cards: A, B, C, D, E
Notes: 3, 4, 5, 8, 9, 11, 12, 14, 15

Bed and Breakfast International
P.O. Box 282910, San Francisco, 94128-2910
(650) 696-1690; (800) 872-4500
FAX (650) 696-1699; e-mail: info@bbintl.com
www.bbintl.com

VE-B171. Three blocks from the beach, this inn with Mediterranean decor offers comfort and convenience. Seventeen rooms with private baths. Full breakfast and afternoon refreshments. $75-150.

VE-M5I. Bavarian-style hospitality is featured at this lovely bed and breakfast

NOTES: Credit cards accepted: A MasterCard; B Visa; C American Express; D Discover; E Diner's Club; F Other; 2 Personal checks accepted; 3 Lunch available; 4 Dinner available; 5 Open all year; 6 Pets welcome;

near the beach. Five guest rooms have queen- or king-size beds and private baths. Walking or biking distance from shops, restaurants, and attractions. Short commute to Santa Barbara, Ojai, and Santa Ynez Valley. Full breakfast. No smoking. $100-155.

La Mer Bed and Breakfast

411 Poli Street, 93001
(805) 643-3600; FAX (805) 653-7329

Nestled on a green hillside, this Cape Cod-style Victorian house overlooks the heart of historic Ventura and the spectacular California coastline. Originally built in 1890, La Mer has been faithfully decorated by host Gisela Baida to create an Old World atmosphere. Each guest room has been furnished to capture the feeling of a specific European country: France, Germany, Austria, Norway, and England. Wine or champagne and a Bavarian-buffet breakfast are included.

Hosts: Gisela and Mike Baida
Rooms: 5 (PB) $80-155
Full Breakfast
Credit Cards: A, B, C
Notes: 2, 5, 7, 9, 10, 11, 12, 14

WATSONVILLE

"Dunmovin" Bed and Breakfast

1006 Hecker Pass, 95076
(408) 728-4154

Seven miles from the ocean, nestled in redwood trees, this large English Tudor home, on 22 acres, overlooks Watsonville and Monterey Bay. The acreage is home to llamas, goats, peacocks, pot-bellied pigs, and one dog. Rooms are done in antiques. Full breakfast served with freshly ground coffee, French toast, homemade muffins, etc. Wine tasting a few miles away and factory outlets. All rooms have private baths.

Hosts: Ruth and Don Wakefield
Rooms: 3 (PB) $70-80
Full Breakfast

Credit cards: None
Notes: 2, 5, 7, 8, 9, 10, 11, 12

WESTPORT

DeHaven Valley Farm

39247 North Highway One, 95488
(707) 961-1660; FAX (707) 961-1677
e-mail: dehavenval@ad.com
www.dehaven-valley-farm.com

Eight comfortable rooms and cottages, private baths, hot tub, fireplaces. Twenty acres of hills, meadows, streams, and woods nestled next to the Pacific Ocean. Restaurants serving fresh, fabulous four-course dinners. Convenient to Mendocino, the Lost Coast, and the giant redwoods. A menagerie of animals provides endless entertainment. Full country-style breakfast included with fresh fruit, specialties like apple pancakes and kaiserschmaren.

Host: Christa Stapp
Rooms: 8 (6 PB; 2 SB) $85-140
Full Breakfast
Credit Cards: A, B
Notes: 2, 4, 5, 8, 9, 11, 12, 14, 15

Howard Creek Ranch

Box 121, 95488
(707) 964-6725; FAX (707) 964-1603
www.howardcreekranch.com

A historic 1867 farm on 40 acres, only 100 yards from the beach. A rural retreat adjoining wilderness. Suite and cabins; views of ocean, mountains, creek, or gardens; fireplace/wood stoves; period furnishings; hot

Howard Creek Ranch

tub, sauna, heated swimming pool, and horseback riding nearby. Gift certificates available. Pets welcome with prior arrangements. Inquire about accommodations for children. Limited smoking permitted.

Hosts: Charles (Sunny) and Sally Grigg
Rooms: 11 (9 PB; 2 SB) $75-160
Full Breakfast
Credit Cards: A, B
Notes: 2, 5, 6, 7

YOSEMITE

Bed and Breakfast California

P.O. Box 282910, San Francisco, 94128-2910
(650) 696-1690; (800) 872-4500
FAX (650) 696-1699; e-mail: info@bbintl.com
www.bbintl.com

Mariposa. On the old stagecoach route of historical Highway 49. The inn offers spacious, modern rooms with private baths and decks, TV/VCR, as well as in-room coffee maker and refrigerator. Hike or picnic among huge old oaks, pines, and ancient Indian grinding stones. Nearby attractions also include the Mariposa History Center and Museum, Badger Pass Ski area, and rafting. $85-110.

Restful Nest in Mariposa. A little corner of paradise on 11 acres of land has stunning surroundings. Three large suites and a guest house for four, all with private baths, private entrances, TV/VCR, refrigerator, and microwave. Full breakfast. Enjoy fishing in the pond or swimming in the pool. Barbecue area can accommodate 10 people at a time. Forty-five minutes from Yosemite, 10 minutes from beautiful Mariposa. $85-95.

Bed and Breakfast International

P.O. Box 282910, San Francisco, 94128-2910
(650) 696-1690; (800) 872-4500
FAX (650) 696-1699; e-mail: info@bbintl.com
www.bbintl.com

YO-K3I. Two miles from park entrance, this inn is five minutes from Mariposa Grove of giant sequoias and the narrow gauge railroad excursion. Full country breakfast. $85.

YO-P3I. Halfway between Yosemite Valley and Wawona is this beautiful new bed and breakfast with uniquely decorated rooms, each with fireplace and one with Jacuzzi for two. The three guest rooms have double, queen-, and king-size beds and private baths. Outdoor decks offer serenity, views, and a hot tub. Full breakfast. No smoking. $110-160.

YO-W2I. In Yosemite at 6,400 feet, 14 miles from Yosemite Valley, contemporary bed and breakfast offers a unique Yosemite holiday. The wooded area has excellent hiking trails. A suite and guest room with private baths are available. Full breakfast. Closed December through February. $68-88.

Château du Sureau

48688 Victoria Lane, P.O. Box 577,
Oakhurst, 93644
(209) 683-6860; FAX (209) 683-0800

On the rim of Yosemite National Park commanding extraordinary views of the Sierra Nevada sits this seven-and-one-half-acre French country estate. An enchanting, authentic European castle, the hotel offers exquisite guest rooms, all lovingly decorated with period antiques, canopied beds, wood-burning fireplaces, CD and stereo

Château du Sureau

systems, and gorgeous baths with deep Roman tubs. On the grounds, pathways meander through wildflower gardens, a European pool, and an outdoor chess and checkers court. Open year-round, except for three weeks in January.

Host: Mrs. Erna Kubin-Clanin
Rooms: 10 (PB) $285-485
Full Breakfast
Credit Cards: A, B, C
Notes: 3, 4, 7, 9, 11, 12, 13, 14, 15

Yosemite's River Resort

11399 Cherry Lake Road, 95321
(209) 962-7408; (800) 626-7408
FAX (209) 962-7400; e-mail: LMR@sonnet.com
www.sonnet.com/usr/yosemite/

Yosemite's River Resort, formerly Lee's Middle Fork Resort, on SR 120, just 150 miles from San Francisco and 11 miles from the Big Oak Flat entrance to Yosemite National Park, the most direct route into the park and the most scenic. For anglers, the Middle Fork of the Tuolumne River is well stocked with pan-size trout, and the river flows right through the resort. Other nearby activities include white-water rafting on the Tuolumne, hiking, swimming, and panning for gold, and in the winter downhill skiing. Nonsmoking rooms available.

Hosts: Roland and Robin Hilarides
Rooms: 20 (PB) $69-89
Full and Continental Breakfasts
Credit Cards: A, B, C, D, E, F
Notes: 3, 4, 5, 8, 9, 11, 12, 13, 14, 15

YOUNTVILLE

Vintage Inn

6541 Washington Street, 94599
(800) 351-1133

Vintage Inn in Napa Valley is a contemporary luxury country inn on a historic 23-acre winery estate in the walking town of Yountville. Centered amidst some of Napa Valley's finest vineyards, guests enjoy a unique resort atmosphere with pool, spa, tennis, cycling, and hot-air ballooning. A California champagne buffet breakfast is included with each guest stay. Superb accommodations for year-round comfort, featuring wood-burning fireplaces, whirlpool baths, compact refrigerators, and many other extras. Smoking permitted in designated areas only.

Host: Patti Larson
Rooms: 80 (PB) $160-325
Continental Breakfast
Credit Cards: A, B, C, D, E, F
Notes: 2, 3, 5, 6, 8, 9, 10, 11, 12, 14, 15

7 No smoking; 8 Children welcome; 9 Social drinking allowed; 10 Tennis nearby; 11 Swimming nearby; 12 Golf nearby; 13 Skiing nearby; 14 May be booked through a travel agent; 15 Handicapped accessible.

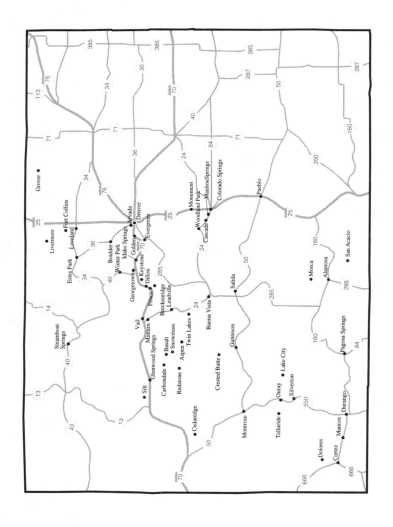

Colorado

Colorado

Cottonwood Inn and Gallery: A Bed and Breakfast Inn

123 San Juan Avenue, 81101
(719) 589-3882

Lovely turn-of-the-century Craftsman-style inn is decorated with antiques and local artwork. Packages available with the Cumbres Toltec Railway, golf courses, horseback riding outfitter, and four hot spring resort pools. Near the Great Sand Dunes, wildlife refuges, Adams State College, cross-country skiing, and the Rio Grande. Delicious full breakfasts featuring freshly ground coffee, homemade baked goods, and fresh fruit. Mobil-rated. Rated as one of Colorado's four best bed and breakfast by Frommer's.

Hosts: Julie Mordecai and George Sellman
Rooms: 9 (PB) $48-99
Full Breakfast
Credit Cards: A, B, C, D
Notes: 2, 5, 6, 7, 8, 9, 10, 11, 12, 13, 14

ARVADA

The TreeHouse

6650 Simms Street, 80004
(303) 431-6352; (888) 570-1105
e-mail: thetreehou@aol.com

This charming bed and breakfast takes its name from the 10-acre forest in which it lies. Guests may indulge themselves in the seclusion and beauty of the forest while sitting in the redwood Jacuzzi on the back deck. The rooms have fireplaces and private baths. Guests may enjoy the nightlife of Denver or the natural beauty of the Rocky Mountains before returning to the peaceful oak and maple forest for the night.

Hosts: Don and Sue Thomas
Rooms: 5 (PB) $69-109
Full Breakfast
Credit Cards: A, B, C
Notes: 2, 5, 7, 8, 10, 11, 12, 13, 14, 15

ARVADA (DENVER)

On Golden Pond Bed and Breakfast

7831 Eldridge, 80005
(303) 424-2296; FAX (303) 431-6580

A secluded retreat tucked in the Rocky Mountain foothills, this custom-built two-story brick house has dramatic views of the mountains, prairies, and downtown Denver. After a full breakfast swim laps in the pool, go horseback riding, or golf, play tennis, or ski. Less than 30 minutes away are downtown Denver, Boulder, Buffalo Bill Museum, Red Rocks Amphitheater, Central City, and many more Colorado escapes. Inquire about accommodations for pets and children. Smoking permitted outdoors only.

Host: Kathy Kula
Rooms: 5 (PB) $60-120
Full Breakfast
Credit Cards: A, B, C, D
Notes: 2, 5, 7, 9, 10, 11, 12, 14, 15

NOTES: Credit cards accepted: A MasterCard; B Visa; C American Express; D Discover; E Diner's Club; F Other; 2 Personal checks accepted; 3 Lunch available; 4 Dinner available; 5 Open all year; 6 Pets welcome; 7 No smoking; 8 Children welcome; 9 Social drinking allowed; 10 Tennis nearby; 11 Swimming nearby; 12 Golf nearby; 13 Skiing nearby; 14 May be booked through a travel agent; 15 Handicapped accessible.

ASPEN

Bed and Breakfast Reservation Agency of Colorado at Vail

2488 Garmisch Drive, Vail, 81657
(970) 476-0792; (800) 748-2666
FAX (970) 476-0711; e-mail: bbresser@vail.net

Aspen 100. Enjoy the Aspen ambiance in a variety of small inns and lodges. Some with hot tub/pool. Private baths. Walk or take free shuttle everywhere. Full or Continental breakfast. $95-250.

Boomerang Lodge

500 West Hopkins, 81611
(970) 925-3416; (800) 992-8852
www.boomeranglodge.com

This unique lodge in the quiet West End is within walking distance to downtown, Aspen Mountain ski gondola, or the music festival. All guest rooms and fireplace apartments have a sunny patio or balcony, thanks to the handsome design influenced by the owner-architect's teacher, Frank Lloyd Wright. Thoughtful touches include pool, whirlpool, and sauna. Additional winter amenities include afternoon tea and town courtesy van. Discover why devoted guests return to the Boomerang.

Hosts: Charles and Fonda Paterson
Rooms: 35 (PB) $105-280
Continental Breakfast
Credit Cards: A, B, C, D, E
Notes: 5, 7, 8, 10, 11, 12, 13, 14

Hotel Lenado

200 South Aspen Street, 81611
(970) 925-6246; (800) 321-3457
FAX (970) 925-3840; e-mail: hotlsard@rof.net

The Hotel Lenado welcomes guests with award-winning architecture and a warmth and style all its own. Nineteen guest rooms, each with a four-poster hickory or carved applewood bed, some with wood-burning stoves, wet bars, and whirlpool baths. A complimentary full breakfast is

served every day. Spend the afternoon relaxing in the rooftop hot tub with its magnificent view of Aspen Mountain or enjoying complimentary hors d'oeuvres in Marham's Bar.

Rooms: 19 (PB) $85-455
Full Breakfast
Credit Cards: A, B, C, E
Notes: 2, 8, 9, 10, 12, 13, 14

Independence Square Bed and Breakfast

404 Galena Street, 81611
(800) 633-0336; FAX (970) 920-2548

Aspen's bed and breakfast on the mall in the heart of town. This historic gem, built in 1889, features 28 rooms, each equipped with a queen-size bed and down comforter, private bath, mini-refrigerator, terry-cloth robes, and wet bar. Nightly rates include Continental breakfast, Aspen airport transfers, and, during the ski season, après-ski wine and cheese served in the library. The rooftop Jacuzzi and privileges at the Aspen Club health and racquet facility round out the amenity package provided by this cozy inn.

Rooms: 28 (PB) $89-345
Continental Breakfast
Credit Cards: A, B, C
Notes: 2, 7, 8, 9, 10, 11, 12, 13, 14

Sardy House

128 East Main Street, 81611
(970) 920-2525; (800) 321-3457
FAX (970) 920-4478; e-mail: hotlsard@rof.net

The Sardy House is a beautiful Victorian bed and breakfast hotel with 14 guest rooms and six suites. All rooms have four-poster cherrywood beds and armoires, terry-cloth robes, feather comforters, and whirlpool baths. The pool, Jacuzzi, and sauna area is perfect for relaxing in the afternoon. The garden area is a great spot for enjoying the complimentary breakfast. An elegant dinner or early evening cocktails are available in the bar and dining room. Inquire about accommodations for pets.

Rooms: 20 (PB) $90-750
Full Breakfast
Credit Cards: A, B, C, E
Notes: 2, 4, 8, 9, 10, 11, 12, 13, 14

BASALT

Altamira Ranch Bed and Breakfast

24384 Highway 82, 81621
(303) 927-3309

Beautiful ranch house 15 minutes from Aspen on the Roaring Fork River, a gold-medal trout stream. Enjoy quiet, peaceful country atmosphere adjacent to all the mountain activities, including skiing, hiking, river sports, and famous Glenwood Hot Springs. There is an antique shop on the premises of the inn. Guests can come enjoy a special home away from home. Children over six are welcome.

Host: Martha Waterman
Rooms: 2 (SB) $60-75
Full Breakfast
Credit Cards: A, B
Notes: 2, 5, 7, 9, 11, 12, 13, 14

Shenandoah Inn

600 Frying Pan Road, Box 560, 81621
(970) 927-4991; (800) 804-5520

Contemporary western Colorado bed and breakfast is on two riverfront acres on the Frying Pan River, one of North America's premier trout streams, in the heart of the White River National Forest. The inn is only 20 minutes from Aspen and Glenwood Hot Springs; year-round access to the best of Colorado's numerous outdoor activities. Enjoy the riverside hot tub, the warm, friendly atmosphere, and the exceptional cuisine.

Hosts: Bob and Terri Ziets
Rooms: 4 (2SB; 2 PB) $78-98
Cabin: $135-150
Full Breakfast
Credit Cards: A, B
Notes: 2, 5, 7, 9, 10, 11, 12, 13, 14

BOULDER

Bed and Breakfast at Sunset House

1740 Sunset Boulevard, 80304
(303) 444-0801

Two rooms offered with shared bath and a private entrance. Each room has its own telephone. The family room has a cozy fireplace, small library, and a TV. Outside patios overlook the city to the south and the Flatirons to the west. The Pearl Street Mall is a 10-minute walk away. Taikoo, a Shih Tzu mix, is the resident dog. Sunset House provides a nonsmoking environment.

Hosts: Phyllis and Roger Olson
Rooms: 2 (SB) $80
Full Breakfast
Credit Cards: None
Notes: 2, 5, 7

Bed and Breakfast Reservation Agency of Colorado at Vail

2488 Garmisch Drive, Vail, 81657
(970) 476-0792; (800) 748-2666
FAX (970) 476-0711; e-mail: bbresser@vail.net

Artist's Retreat. Tucked into a deep spruce forest 25 minutes from the bustle of Boulder one finds the serenity that only the mountains can provide. Explore the three and one-half acres of private, forested grounds with stunning views of the Continental Divide. Hot tub, TV, patios and decks to enjoy. $75-90.

Bldr 100. An exquisite boutique inn with downtown location, ambiance, fireplaces, jetted tubs, and gracious hosts to welcome guests. $144-167.

The Boulder Victoria Historic Inn

1305 Pine Street, 80302
(303) 938-1300

Downtown Boulder's exquisitely renovated Victorian inn offers seven unique guest

7 No smoking; 8 Children welcome; 9 Social drinking allowed; 10 Tennis nearby; 11 Swimming nearby; 12 Golf nearby; 13 Skiing nearby; 14 May be booked through a travel agent; 15 Handicapped accessible.

rooms that feature antique furniture, private baths, telephones, and TVs. Enjoy tea and scones in the elegant parlor, luxuriate in a private steam shower, or enjoy breakfast in the bay-windowed dining room. Soak in Boulder's sun on the spacious patio. Convenient to downtown, campus, and mountain activities.

Host: Meredith Lederer
Rooms: 7 (PB) $119-189
Continental Breakfast
Credit Cards: A, B, C
Notes: 2, 5, 7, 9, 10, 11, 12, 13, 14

Briar Rose Bed and Breakfast

2151 Arapahoe Avenue, 80302
(303) 442-3007; FAX (303) 786-8440
e-mail: brbbx@aol.com

Nine unique guest rooms in this English country cottage inn each have private baths, telephones, and most have queen-size beds. Two rooms have fireplaces. A delicious breakfast of fresh fruit, homemade granola, yogurt, croissants, and freshly baked muffins or nut bread with freshly squeezed orange juice, coffee, and tea is served. In the afternoon, tea and cookies are served to guests in the garden or in the privacy of their room. The inn is near the CU campus, about one mile from Pearl Street Mall, and within walking distance of many good restaurants.

Briar Rose

Hosts: Bob and Margaret Weisenbach
Rooms: 9 (PB) $99-160
Continental Breakfast
Credit Cards: A, B, C
Notes: 2, 5, 7, 9, 10, 11, 12, 13, 14

Earl House Historic Inn

Earl House Historic Inn

2429 Broadway, 80304
(303) 938-1400; FAX (303) 938-9710

Featured in *Country Inns* magazine and selected as one of the Year's Top Affordable Luxuries, this elegant 1880s Gothic Revival mansion has distinctive rooms with plush furnishings, telephones, TVs, and Jacuzzi tubs or steam showers. Relax by the fireplace during afternoon tea and enjoy homemade baked goods at breakfast in the sunny dining area. Pearl Street's shopping and restaurants, University of Colorado, and hiking are nearby. Two three-bedroom two-bath carriage houses are also available.

Host: Kathryn Ode
Rooms: 6 (PB) $119-189
Continental Breakfast
Credit Cards: A, B, C, E
Notes: 2, 5, 7, 9, 10, 11, 12, 13, 14

The House on 21st Street

2222-21st Street, 80302
(303) 443-4604; FAX (303) 545-0160

Designed by one of Boulder's most well-known contractors, Bill Coburn, the House on 21st Street is a new Victorian home in picturesque Boulder, convenient to the mountains, ski areas, lakes, golf courses,

NOTES: Credit cards accepted: A MasterCard; B Visa; C American Express; D Discover; E Diner's Club; F Other; 2 Personal checks accepted; 3 Lunch available; 4 Dinner available; 5 Open all year; 6 Pets welcome;

and Rocky Mountain National Park. Two beautiful bedrooms accommodate guests' special occasion, business trip, or romantic getaway. Upon request, professional massage, facials, local health club facilities, catered meals, and the use of host's bicycles are available.

Host: Donne Ruiz
Rooms: 2 (1 PB; 1 SB) $95-120
Continental Breakfast
Credit Cards: None
Notes: 2, 5, 7, 9, 10, 11, 12, 13

Pearl Street Inn

Pearl Street Inn

1820 Pearl Street, 80302
(303) 444-5584; (888) 810-1302
FAX (303) 444-6494; e-mail: ktbeeman@msn.com

This 1893 Queen Anne Victorian bed and breakfast is in the middle of downtown Boulder. Within walking distance of the historic Pearl Street Mall. Enjoy the serenity of a beautiful garden courtyard. All rooms have private baths, fireplaces, TVs, and telephones. Elegant organic homemade breakfasts made to order to accommodate all special dietary needs.

Host: Kate Beeman
Rooms: 7 (PB) $99-135
Full Breakfast
Credit Cards: A, B, C, E
Notes: 2, 3, 5, 7, 8, 9, 12, 13, 14

BRECKENRIDGE

Allaire Timbers Inn

9511 Highway 9, South Main Street, 80424
(970) 453-7530; (800) 624-4904
www.allairetimbers.com

An award-winning log bed and breakfast combining contemporary and rustic log furnishings in an intimate setting. Guest rooms have a private bath and deck with mountain views. Suites offer a private fireplace and hot tub. Great room has fireplace, sunroom, loft, and outdoor hot tub. All have spectacular views of the Colorado Rockies. Hearty breakfast and afternoon refreshments. Featured on the Travel channel's *Romantic Inns in America*.

Hosts: Jack and Kathy Gumph
Rooms: 10 (PB) $135-300
Full Breakfast
Credit Cards: A, B, C, D
Notes: 2, 5, 7, 9, 10, 11, 12, 13, 14, 15

Bed and Breakfasts on North Main Street

303 North Main Street, P.O. Box 2454, 80424
(970) 453-2975; (800) 795-2975 (outside Colorado)
FAX (970) 453-5258; e-mail: bnb@imageline.com
colorado-bnb.com/northmain

Unique river property in Breckenridge's historic district offering meticulously restored and antique-filled Williams House and separate Victorian cottage as featured on TV's *Romantic Inns of America*. Nestled on the willow-lined riverbank is the timber-framed Barn Above the River, established 1997, furnished country style with spectacular mountain views. Private baths. Some rooms

B & B on North Main Street (Williams House)

7 No smoking; 8 Children welcome; 9 Social drinking allowed; 10 Tennis nearby; 11 Swimming nearby; 12 Golf nearby; 13 Skiing nearby; 14 May be booked through a travel agent; 15 Handicapped accessible.

with fireplaces, whirlpool tubs for two, TV, views, balconies, telephones. Scrumptious breakfast, afternoon refreshments, complimentary beverages, outdoor spa, and in-town location.

Hosts: Fred Kinat and Diane Jaynes
Rooms: 11 (PB) $95-185
Cottage: 1 (PB) $175-235
Full Breakfast
Credit Cards: C
Notes: 2, 5, 7, 9, 10, 11, 12, 13, 14

Bed and Breakfast Reservation Agency of Colorado at Vail

2488 Garmisch Drive, Vail, 81657
(970) 476-0792; (800) 748-2666
FAX (970) 476-0711; e-mail: bbresser@vail.net

Elegance, location, breakfast, and private baths. Walk to everywhere or take the shuttle. $95-225.

Evans House

102 South French Street, P.O. Box 387, 80424
(970) 453-5509; e-mail: evans@imageline.com
colorado-bnb.com/evanshse

In the heart of beautiful, historic Breckenridge, the Evans House is a restored 1886 Victorian traditional bed and breakfast with a full view of the 10-mile range. A delicious seven-day-menu breakfast and afternoon refreshments are served. Winter activities are available at the front door via

Evans House

the free bus. Evening activities and restaurants are two blocks away. Spring, summer, and fall events, and sports make this area unforgettable. Supervised children welcome. Limited handicapped accessibility. AAA-approved. New! Hot tub!

Hosts: Pete and Georgette Contos
Rooms: 4 (2 PB; 2 SB) $65-109
Suite: 1 (PB) $86-127
Full Breakfast
Credit Cards: A, B, C, D, E
Notes: 2, 5, 7, 9, 10, 11, 12, 13, 14

Hunt Placer Inn

Hunt Placer Inn

275 Ski Hill Road, P.O. Box 4898, 80424
(970) 453-7573; (800) 472-1430
FAX (970) 453-2335; e-mail: hpi@colorado.net

Featured in *Newsday* (Long Island, New York) as one of 10 Favorite Rocky Mountain B&Bs and in the national television series *Romantic Inns of America*, the Bavarian chalet-style Hunt Placer Inn is in a lovely wooded area at the bottom of Peak 8, yet close to downtown. The inn features eight beautifully decorated guest rooms with balconies, including three suites with fireplaces and striking views. The three-course breakfasts, served on English china and silver, are truly memorable.

Hosts: Gwen and Carl Ray
Rooms: 8 (PB) $119-200
Full Breakfast
Credit Cards: A, B, C, D, E
Notes: 2, 5, 7, 9, 10, 11, 12, 13, 14, 15

NOTES: Credit cards accepted: A MasterCard; B Visa; C American Express; D Discover; E Diner's Club; F Other; 2 Personal checks accepted; 3 Lunch available; 4 Dinner available; 5 Open all year; 6 Pets welcome;

The Walker House

211 East Lincoln Avenue, P.O. Box 509, 80424
(970) 453-2426

An 1875 historic residence with original Victorian furnishings. Informal, quiet, and intimate. Two upstairs bedrooms with great views. Special foods on request. Dinners can be ordered "in." In the historic section of Breckenridge, one-half block from restaurants and shops, on free shuttle route. Catered dinner available.

Hosts: Sue Ellen and the Contos
Rooms: 2 (1 PB; 1 SB) $89-118
Full Breakfast
Credit Cards: None
Notes: 2, 7, 11, 13

The Wellington Inn

200 North Main Street, P.O. Box 5890, 80424
(970) 453-9464; (800) 655-7557
FAX (970) 453-0149

This Victorian inn is on historical Main Street within walking distance to many shops and restaurants and a short trolley ride to the ski area. Each guest room enjoys a balcony with breathtaking views of the mountain range and downtown Breckenridge. All rooms include whirlpool baths, goose-down comforters, complimentary sherry, coffee makers with complimentary beverages, and a hearty breakfast. The Wellington Inn's romantic restaurant specializes in fine dining nightly, featuring beef Wellington. Lunch is available during the summer months.

Rooms: 4 (PB) $129-249
Full Breakfast
Credit Cards: A, B, C, D
Notes: 2, 3, 4, 5, 7, 9, 10, 11, 12, 13, 14

BUENA VISTA

The Adobe Inn

303 North Highway 24, 81211
(719) 395-6340

Capture the flavor of an Old Southwest adobe hacienda. Three rooms and two suites provide a delightful range of styles and amenities. Each room has a private bath and color TV and guests can relax in the two-person Jacuzzi. In the upper Arkansas River Valley, home of the majestic Collegiate Peaks Range. Featured in AAA (three diamonds), Fodor's, and Mobil guides.

Hosts: Paul, Marjorie, and Michael Knox
Rooms: 5 (PB) $59-89
Full Breakfast
Credit Cards: A, B
Notes: 2, 3, 4, 5, 7, 8, 10, 11, 12, 13, 14

Meister House
Bed and Breakfast

414 East Main Street, P.O. Box 1133, 81211
(719) 395-9220; (888) 395-9220
FAX (719) 395-9128
e-mail: meisterhouse@vtinet.com
www.vtinet.com/meister

This two-story brick Western/Victorian structure began as a small first-class hotel, built in 1891 to accommodate railroad and mining executives traveling through central Colorado. Today it is the cherished home of Barbara and Frank Hofmeister, renovated with care to blend the Old West with the New West, offering seven uniquely different guest rooms, large reception/dining area, and bricked courtyard where Barbara's full gourmet breakfasts are served alfresco.

Meister House

Hosts: Barbara and Frank Hofmeister
Rooms: 7 (4 PB; 3 SB) $65-125
Full Breakfast
Credit Cards: A, B, C
Notes: 2, 5, 7, 8, 9, 10, 11, 12, 13, 14

Trout City Inn

P.O. Box 431, 81211
(719) 495-0348

Historic railway station on Trout Creek Pass in national forest has Victorian decor and antiques in depot rooms—plus elegant private Pullman car and Drover's caboose. Enjoy its own railroad, trout stream, beaver ponds, and gold mine, with grand view of canyon and Collegiate Peaks. White-water rafting, horseback riding, mountain hiking and climbing, mountain bike trails are just minutes away—plus great eating and shopping in historic Buena Vista. Trophy trout fishing in river and lakes, ghost towns, caves, Jeep tours, melodrama, antique shops all nearby.

Hosts: Juel and Irene Kjeldsen
Rooms: 4 (PB) $50-70
Full Breakfast
Credit Cards: A, B, C
Notes: 2, 7, 8, 9, 10, 11, 12, 14

CARBONDALE

The Ambiance Inn

66 North 2nd Street, 81623
(303) 963-3597

Enjoy Aspen, Glenwood Springs, and the beautiful Crystal Valley from this spacious chalet-style home featuring vaulted ceilings throughout. The 1950s ski lodge decor of the very large Aspen Suite or the Victorian elegance of the Sonoma Room featuring a romantic four-poster bed are ideal for getaways. The Santa Fe Room is alive with the warmth of the Southwest. The Kauai Room features special atmosphere and a two-person Jacuzzi. All rooms adjoin the library-sitting room.

Hosts: Norma and Robert Morris
Rooms: 4 (PB) $60-90

Full Breakfast
Credit Cards: A, B
Notes: 2, 5, 7, 9, 10, 11, 12, 13, 14

Mt. Sopris Inn

P.O. Box 126, 81623
(970) 963-2209; (800) 437-8675
FAX (970) 963-8975
e-mail: mt.soprisinn@juno.com
www.colorado.bnb.com/mtsopris

For a special relaxing treat stay at the Mt. Sopris Inn, central to Aspen, Redstone, and Glenwood Springs.

Rooms: 14 (PB) $85-175
Full Breakfast
Credit Cards: A, B
Notes: 5, 7, 11, 12, 13, 15

Van Horn House at Lions Ridge

0318 Lions Ridge Road, 81623
(970) 963-3605; (888) 453-0395
FAX (970) 963-1681; e-mail: jlaatsch@aol.com

Enjoy hiking, biking, trout fishing, skiing in the Roaring Fork Valley. Hosts offer the comfort of home away from home, featuring antiques, queen-size beds, and country charm; the lounge features satellite TV, VCR, books, movies, games, puzzles, and homemade cookies. Great views of Mount Sopris from the balconies, and a relaxing hot tub beckons. Full deluxe breakfast. Near Aspen, Snowmass, Redstone, and Glenwood Springs. Great restaurants nearby.

Hosts: Susan and John Laatsch
Rooms: 4 (2 PB; 2 SB) $65-80
Full Breakfast
Credit Cards: A, B
Notes: 2, 5, 7, 9, 13, 14

CASCADE

Black Bear Inn of Pikes Peak

5250 Pikes Peak Highway, 80809
(719) 684-0151

The Black Bear Inn of Pikes Peak is between the North Pole and the Pikes Peak tollgate. Guests enjoy breathtaking mountain views from each bedroom. At the end

---

NOTES: Credit cards accepted: A MasterCard; B Visa; C American Express; D Discover; E Diner's Club; F Other; 2 Personal checks accepted; 3 Lunch available; 4 Dinner available; 5 Open all year; 6 Pets welcome;

of a wooded trail guests are invited to enjoy the very private hot tub. Relax, read a book, or have special meetings or gatherings in the large common area. Hiking and nature trails are right outside the inn. "We will be happy to arrange banquets." Children 10 or older welcome.

Host: Christi Heidenreich
Room: 9 (PB) $75-85
Suites: $90
Full Breakfast
Credit Cards: A, B, D
Notes: 2, 5, 7, 14, 15

CEDAREDGE

Cedars' Edge Llamas Bed and Breakfast

2169 Highway 65, 81413
(970) 856-6836; www.llamaBandB.com

Beautiful cedar home is nestled high on the southern slope of Grand Mesa. This peaceful llama farm features a spectacular 100-mile view and a quiet, restful atmosphere. Rooms are filled with handmade country decor, quilts, and plants. Breakfast on the private deck or in the sunroom. Cottage features very private honeymoon suite with double tub. Close to hiking, fishing, skiing, and much more.

Hosts: Ray and Gail Record
Rooms: 4 (PB) $60-85
Full Breakfast
Credit Cards: A, B
Notes: 2, 5, 7, 8, 10, 11, 12, 13, 14

COLORADO SPRINGS

Cheyenne Cañon Inn

2030 West Cheyenne Boulevard, 80906
(800) 633-0625; FAX (719) 633-8826

Secluded in spectacular Cheyenne Cañon Park, this 13,000-square-foot Mission-style mansion with over 100 windows offers some of the best views in Colorado. The inn's seven spacious suites and honeymoon cottage are each deco-

rated for a different region of the world. Try a French chateau, a Spanish hacienda, an Italian villa, and more. Guests will also enjoy the amenities—antique soaking tubs, Jacuzzis, fireplaces, library, incredible hiking, rushing mountain streams—plus a hearty breakfast.

Hosts: Nancy, Steve, and Heather Stannard
Rooms: 10 (PB) $90-190
Full Breakfast
Credit Cards: A, B, C, D
Notes: 2, 5, 7, 8, 9, 10, 11, 12, 13, 14

Eastholme in the Rockies

Eastholme in the Rockies

4445 Haggerman Avenue, P.O. Box 98,
 Cascade, 80809
(719) 684-9901; (800) 672-9901

Charming 1885 Victorian nestled in the mountain village of Cascade. Close to all Colorado Springs attractions. Winner of Colorado's Historic Preservation award and a Ute Pass landmark, it offers a spectacular view of Pike National Forest. Graciously and comfortably decorated in antiques, with fine fabrics, lace, and oriental rugs. A bountiful breakfast is served each morning. There are also two romantic cottages that offer privacy and a whirlpool tub and fireplace.

Hostess: Terry Thompson
Rooms: 7 (5 PB; 2 SB) $69-135
Full Breakfast
Credit Cards: A, B, C, D, F
Notes: 2, 5, 7, 8, 9, 10, 11, 12, 13, 14

7 No smoking; 8 Children welcome; 9 Social drinking allowed; 10 Tennis nearby; 11 Swimming nearby; 12 Golf nearby; 13 Skiing nearby; 14 May be booked through a travel agent; 15 Handicapped accessible.

Holden House

Holden House—1902 Bed and Breakfast Inn

1102 West Pikes Peak Avenue, 80904
(719) 471-3980; FAX (719) 471-4740
e-mail: holdenhouse@worldnet.att.net
www.bbonline.com/co/holden/

A 1902 Victorian, a 1906 carriage house, and adjacent 1898 Victorian are filled with antiques and heirlooms. Immaculate accommodations in a residential area near historic district and central to the Pikes Peak region. Enjoy the parlor, living room with fireplace, or veranda with mountain views. Guest suites boast private sitting areas, fireplaces, and more. Complimentary refreshments and in-room telephones/modem add convenience. AAA- and Mobil-rated. Inquire about minimum-stay requirements. Friendly resident cats, Mingtoy and Muffin.

Hosts: Sallie and Welling Clark
Suites: 5 (PB) $120-135
Full Breakfast
Credit Cards: A, B, C, D, E, F
Notes: 2, 5, 7, 9, 10, 11, 12, 14, 15

Hughes Hacienda

12060 Calle Corvo, 80926
(719) 576-2060; e-mail: hacienda@kktv.com

Romantic, tranquil, secluded hacienda, high on a hill at the foot of Blue Mountain. Magnificent mountain setting minutes from Colorado Springs and the Broadmoor Hotel. A walk through the inn's soft sculpted adobe archway and into the courtyard leads to true serenity. Accommodations consist of one comfortable, very private suite with king-size bed, kiva fireplace, wet bar, stereo/CD player, TV, VCR, hot tub. Hiking trails. Gourmet dining.

Suite: 1 (PB) $85-130
Full Breakfast
Credit Cards: A, B, D
Notes: 2, 5, 7, 9, 10, 11, 12, 13, 14

Room at the Inn

618 North Nevada Avenue, 80903
(719) 442-1896; (800) 579-4621 (reservations)
FAX (719) 442-6802

Experience a peek at the past in this 1896 Victorian. Enjoy...the charm of a classic three-story turreted antique-filled Queen Anne featuring original wall murals, oak staircase, and pocket doors...the romance of fireplaces, plush robes, and whirlpool tubs for two...and gracious hospitality featuring full breakfasts, afternoon tea, and turndown service. Conveniently near downtown and Colorado College. A romantic retreat in the heart of the city. Three-star rating from Mobil.

Hosts: Jan and Chick McCormick
Rooms: 7 (PB) $85-135
Full Breakfast
Credit Cards: A, B, C, D, E
Notes: 2, 5, 7, 9, 10, 11, 12, 14, 15

Room at the Inn

NOTES: Credit cards accepted: A MasterCard; B Visa; C American Express; D Discover; E Diner's Club; F Other; 2 Personal checks accepted; 3 Lunch available; 4 Dinner available; 5 Open all year; 6 Pets welcome;

Serenity Pines Guest House

Serenity Pines Guest House

11910 Windmill Road, 80908
(719) 495-7141 (phone/FAX)
e-mail: serenpines@aol.com
www.colorado-bnb.com/serenpines

True Colorado getaway on acres of pines. This 1,200-square-foot guest house sleeps six. Rented by one party at a time. Full-size-stocked/equipped kitchen. New appliances (dishwasher), Continental breakfast supplies left for guests to prepare breakfast at their leisure. Like walking into country home. Bed-and-breakfast-style pampering. Private sun deck, picnic, barbecue area. Parklike setting. Cable, video library, telephone, answering machine, crib, fax, copier. Thirty minutes to area attractions.

Hosts: Kathy and Bob
Suite: 1 (PB) $99-129
Continental Breakfast
Credit Cards: A, B, C
Notes: 2, 4, 5, 7, 8, 11, 12, 13, 14, 15

COLORADO SPRINGS/PIKES PEAK AREA __

Silver Wood Bed and Breakfast at Divide

463 County Road 512, Divide, 80814
(719) 687-6784

Silver Wood is a tastefully decorated country home built in 1990 in a wooded area with abundant hiking trails and fantastic views of mountains and meadows. An ideal getaway from city life, yet near Colorado Springs and Cripple Creek. Two friendly resident cats, Lucy and Frisco. A country gourmet breakfast is served in the dining room. Enjoy country hospitality.

Hosts: Larry and Bess Oliver
Rooms: 2 (PB) $69-120
Full Breakfast
Credit Cards: A, B, C, D
Notes: 2, 5, 7, 8, 9, 14

CORTEZ

A Bed and Breakfast on Maple

P.O. Box 327, 81321
(970) 565-3906; (800) 665-3906
e-mail: maple@fone.net
www.subec.com/maple/home.htm/

"Where you get spoiled and pampered." Nine miles to Mesa Verde, 45 minutes to Durango. Antiques mixed with country charm. King- and queen-size beds, hot tub, water garden. Big appetite? Big breakfast! Downtown proximity—walk to restaurants, shopping, movies, and Indian dances. Packages available. Sack lunch available. Limited handicapped accessibility.

Hosts: Nonnie and Roy Fahsholtz
Rooms: 6 (PB) $59-119
Full Breakfast
Credit Cards: A, B, C, D
Notes: 2, 5, 7, 8, 9, 10, 11, 12, 13, 14

Grizzly Roadhouse Bed and Breakfast

3450 Highway 160 South, 81321
(970) 565-7738; (800) 330-7286
e-mail: grizbb@fone.net
www.subee.com/grizzly/home.html

On 30 acres of evergreen-studded hills and canyons, this newly remodeled country-style bed and breakfast and guest cottage provides a place to relax, expand, and be at peace. The "bear" necessities include walking trails, spa, uninterrupted views of the stars, native storytelling, and "hibernation" spiritual retreats. Dine on a full "gourbear"

7 No smoking; 8 Children welcome; 9 Social drinking allowed; 10 Tennis nearby; 11 Swimming nearby; 12 Golf nearby; 13 Skiing nearby; 14 May be booked through a travel agent; 15 Handicapped accessible.

breakfast featuring authentic native foods from family recipes. Each room has its own private bath and sitting area with TV/VCR and privacy.

Rooms: 4 (PB) $69-125
Full Breakfast
Credit Cards: A, B, C
Notes: 2, 3, 5, 7, 8, 9, 10, 11, 12, 13

CRESTED BUTTE

Bed and Breakfast Reservation Agency of Colorado at Vail

2488 Garmisch Drive, Vail, 81657
(970) 476-0792; (800) 748-2666
FAX (970) 476-0711; e-mail: bbresser@vail.net

CB 100. The best of both worlds: the history of the mining area with the comforts of the present. Close to shops and restaurants. Free shuttle to the ski mountain. Full breakfast and afternoon refreshments and a hot tub to relax in after a long day. $65-110.

Crystal Inn Bed and Breakfast

624 Gothic Avenue, P.O. Box 125, 81224-0125
(970) 349-1338; (800) 390-1338 (reservations only)
FAX (970) 349-1942
e-mail: reservations@crystalinn.com

Intimate five-bedroom inn features American antiques and 1800s iron beds. Each room offers queen-size bed, fluffy comforter, telephone, and private bath. Ameni-

Crystal Inn

ties include two parlors with fireplaces, large indoor hot tub, CATV, 24-hour coffee/tea bar, sunny balconies, unlimited views. Enjoy the full hearty family-style breakfast. Ample parking one and one-half blocks to free shuttle bus and a short walk to shops and restaurants.

Hosts: Dennis and Charlene Goree
Rooms: 5 (PB) $69-106
Full Breakfast
Credit Cards: A, B, C, D
Notes: 2, 5, 7, 9, 10, 11, 12, 13, 14

DENVER

Capitol Hill Mansion

Capitol Hill Mansion

1207 Pennsylvania Street, 80203
(303) 839-5221; (800) 839-9329 (reservations only)
FAX (303) 839-9046
www.capitolhillmansion.com

Award-winning 1891 mansion featuring antiques mixed with modern amenities, such as cable TV, refrigerators, complimentary beverages, hair dryers, telephones, desks, and off-street parking. Whirlpool tubs and fireplaces are available. A short walk to downtown, government offices, museums, galleries, shopping, and restaurants and a short drive to all major sports venues and the Rocky Mountains. Perfect for romance or business. Personal checks accepted with credit card numbers only. Inquire about accommodations for children. Partially handicapped accessible.

NOTES: Credit cards accepted: A MasterCard; B Visa; C American Express; D Discover; E Diner's Club; F Other; 2 Personal checks accepted; 3 Lunch available; 4 Dinner available; 5 Open all year; 6 Pets welcome;

Host: Kathy Robbins
Rooms: 8 (PB) $90-165
Full Breakfast
Credit Cards: A, B, C, D
Notes: 5, 7, 9, 10, 11, 12, 13, 14

Castle Marne

Castle Marne

1572 Race Street, 80206
(303) 331-0621; (800) 92 MARNE

Come, fall under the spell of one of Denver's grandest historic mansions. Built in 1889, the Marne is on both the local and national historic registers. Guests' stay is a unique experience in pampered luxury. Three rooms with private balconies and hot tubs for two. Two rooms with Jacuzzi tubs for two. Minutes from the finest cultural, shopping, sightseeing attractions, and the convention center. Lunch and dinner available by special arrangements. Ask about the candlelight dinners.

Hosts: The Peiker Family
Rooms: 9 (PB) $85-220
Full Breakfast
Credit Cards: A, B, C, D, E, F
Notes: 2, 5, 7, 9, 10, 11, 12, 13, 14

Haus Berlin

1651 Emerson Street, 80218
(303) 837-9527; (800) 659-0253
e-mail: haus.berlin@worldnet.att.net
www.hausberlinbandb.com

Century-old Victorian on a safe, quiet tree-lined street just minutes from downtown

Denver. European decor with original paintings and pieces of art. Off-street parking. Superior bed and bath linens. Telephones, TV, alarm radios, air dryers, fresh flowers add to guests' comfort and convenience. Hosts are urbane, friendly, and comfortable, just like their guests.

Hosts: Christiana and Dennis Brown
Rooms: 4 (PB) $95-130
Full Breakfast
Credit Cards: A, B, C, D, E
Notes: 2, 5, 7, 9, 10, 12, 13, 14

The Queen Anne Bed and Breakfast Inn

2147 Tremont Place, 80205
(303) 296-6666; (800) 432-INNS
FAX (303) 296-2151
www.bedandbreakfastinns.org/queenanne

Experience history, elegance, and warm hospitality in side-by-side Victorians facing a quiet park within walking distance of downtown Denver's pedestrian mall, state capitol, shops, museums, restaurants, convention center, businesses. Enjoy a hot breakfast, period furnishings, private baths, chamber music, fresh flowers, telephones, evening Colorado wine, free parking. Choose from 14 individually decorated rooms, including

The Queen Anne

four "gallery suites." Honors include 10 most romantic and 10 best nationally, Best of Denver. Inspected and rated by motor clubs and state associations.

Hosts: The King Family
Rooms: 14 (PB) $75-175
Full Breakfast
Credit Cards: A, B, C, D, E, F
Notes: 2, 5, 7, 9, 10, 12, 13, 14

DENVER AREA

Bed and Breakfast Reservation Agency of Colorado at Vail

2488 Garmisch Drive, Vail, 81657
(970) 476-0792; (800) 748-2666
FAX (970) 476-0711; e-mail: bbresser@vail.net

Urban settings downtown to suburban serenity. Decor depicting the history of Denver. The perfect setting for weddings, holidays, or that special occasion. King- or queen-size beds, private baths, some jetted tubs, hot tub. Full or Continental breakfast. $69-165.

DILLION

Bed and Breakfast Reservation Agency of Colorado at Vail

2488 Garmisch Drive, Vail, 81657
(970) 476-0792; (800) 748-2666
FAX (970) 476-0711; e-mail: bbresser@vail.net

Summit County provides the recreation in its four ski areas; the hosts provide the comforts of home with many extras. Private bath, full or Continental breakfast. Close to shuttle. $65-155.

DOLORES

Historic Rio Grande Southern

101 South Fifth Street, P.O. Box 516, 81323
(970) 882-7527; (800) 258-0434

The Rio Grande Southern hotel was built for the railroad in 1893 and has been in continu-

ous service as a hostelry ever since. The eight guest rooms are decorated in turn-of-the-century antiques with antique claw-foot high-backed tubs. The restaurant is still a popular stop for southwestern cuisine and setting. The hotel is in the national and state of Colorado lists of historic places. Inquire about accommodations for pets.

Hosts: Fred and Cathy Green
Rooms: 8 (3 PB: 4 SB) $50-130
Full Breakfast
Credit Cards: A, B, D
Notes: 2, 3, 4, 7, 8, 9, 10, 11, 12, 13, 14

Mountain View Bed and Breakfast

28050 County Road P, 81323
(970) 882-7861; (800) 228-4592
e-mail: bdunn@fone.net
www.subee.com/mtnview/home.html

Mountain View is in the Four Corners area one mile from the gateway to the San Juan Skyway, a nationally designated 238-mile scenic loop, 12 miles from the entrance to Mesa Verde National Park, and 4 miles from McPhee Lake, Colorado's second largest lake. On 22 acres, this ranch-style inn has porches, decks, and hot tub with marvelous mountain views. Eight guest rooms/suites, cabin, private baths, full breakfast, laundry. Singles, families, and groups welcome.

Hosts: Brenda and Cecil Dunn
Rooms: 8 (PB) $60-90
Full Breakfast
Credit Cards: A, B, D
Notes: 2, 5, 7, 8, 10, 11, 12, 13, 14, 15

NOTES: Credit cards accepted: A MasterCard; B Visa; C American Express; D Discover; E Diner's Club; F Other; 2 Personal checks accepted; 3 Lunch available; 4 Dinner available; 5 Open all year; 6 Pets welcome;

DURANGO

Apple Orchard Inn

7758 Country Road 203, 81301
(970) 247-0751; (800) 426-0751

The Apple Orchard Inn is a newly constructed farmhouse-style home with six country cottages on four and one-half acres of
orchards and gardens. From private covered
porch enjoy views of surrounding mountains.
Inside, be pampered with fresh flowers, fireplaces, quality furnishings and linens, feather
beds with down comforters, private baths,
and Jacuzzi tubs. A scrumptious full hot
breakfast is included and gourmet lunches
and dinners are available with advance reservations. Convenient to town and skiing.

Hosts: Celeste and John Gardiner
Rooms: 10 (PB) $85-150
Full Breakfast
Credit Cards: A, B, C, D
Notes: 2, 5, 7, 8, 9, 10, 11, 12, 13, 14, 15

Apple Orchard Inn

Bed and Breakfast Reservation Agency of Colorado at Vail

2488 Garmisch Drive, Vail, 81657
(970) 476-0792; (800) 748-2666
FAX (970) 476-0711; e-mail: bbresser@vail.net

Southern Colorado, Four Corners area,
Mesa Verde. Easy access to all area attractions. City or country. Cottage or in-home.
Queen-size beds, private baths, full breakfast, hot tub, and scenery second to none.
$85-225.

Country Sunshine

Country Sunshine Bed and Breakfast

35130 U.S. Highway 550 North, 81301
(970) 247-2853; (800) 383-2853
FAX (970) 247-1203

Enjoy southwest Colorado's splendor and
beauty while visiting this spacious six-
guest-room ranch-style home. Guests are
encouraged to indulge their senses and
spirit with mountain views, river songs,
abundant wildlife, and the aroma of ponderosa pines at this secluded location.
Relax under a star-filled sky in the large
outdoor hot tub. Wholesome country-style
breakfast offered. Seasonal rates.

Hosts: Beanie and Gary Archie
Rooms: 6 (PB) $70-85
Full Breakfast
Credit Cards: A, B, C, D, E
Notes: 2, 7, 8, 9, 10, 11, 12, 13, 14

Leland House Bed and Breakfast/Rochester Hotel

721 East Second Avenue, 81301
(970) 385-1920; (800) 664-1920
FAX (970) 385-1967
e-mail: leland@frontier.net
www.creativelinks.com/Rochester

Luxury accommodations in the Wild West!
Western movies, made in the Four Corners
area, were the inspiration for the decor in
this newly renovated 1890s hotel. Tall ceilings, wide hallways, and a beautifully landscaped courtyard add to the elegance.

7 No smoking; 8 Children welcome; 9 Social drinking allowed; 10 Tennis nearby; 11 Swimming nearby;
12 Golf nearby; 13 Skiing nearby; 14 May be booked through a travel agent; 15 Handicapped accessible.

Leland House

Designated "The Flagship Hotel of Colorado" by *Condé Nast's Traveler* magazine. Full gourmet breakfast provided. Children over 12 welcome.

Hosts: Diane and Kirk Komick
Rooms: 25 (PB) $112-185
Full Breakfast
Cards: A, B, C, D, E, G
Notes: 2, 5, 7, 9, 10, 11, 12, 13, 14, 15

Lightner Creek Inn

Lightner Creek Inn

999 CR 207, 81301
(970) 259-1226; (800) 268-9804
FAX (970) 259-9526; e-mail: lci@frontier.net

Convenient to town but with a country feeling on 20 pristine acres with pond and stream. Enjoy the privacy and comfort of a king-size feather bed in the carriage house or be spoiled with down comforters and king- or queen-size beds in the other seven rooms of the main house. This 1903 home has been lovingly renovated with country charm and attention to detail. Be pampered

with gourmet breakfasts served in the sunroom with a view. Ask to hear the player grand piano! Children over 10 welcome.

Hosts: Julie and Richard Houston
Rooms: 8 (PB) $105-150
Full Breakfast
Credit Cards: A, B, C, D
Notes: 2, 5, 7, 9, 12, 13, 14, 15

Logwood Bed and Breakfast

35060 US Highway 550 North, 81301
(970) 259-4396

Luxurious red cedar log home is a well-designed bed and breakfast lodge. View the beauty of the upper Animas River and mountains through the guest rooms' large windows. Every room has its own private bath. Suite with fireplace. Lounge on the 700-square-foot deck or the yard hammock, fish on the river while enjoying the views, or walk through the five acres of property while deer and bird watching. Full country breakfasts and evening award-winning desserts are served. Kitchen facilities available if entire lodge is rented. Children over eight are welcome.

Hosts: Debby and Greg Verheyden
Rooms: 8 (PB) $65-125
Suite: 1
Full Breakfast
Credit Cards: A, B
Notes: 2, 5, 7, 9, 11, 12, 13, 14

Logwood

River House Bed and Breakfast

495 Animas View Drive, 81301
(970) 247-4775; (800) 254-4775

River House is a large, sprawling southwestern home facing the Animas River.

River House

Guests eat in a large atrium filled with plants, a fountain, and eight skylights. Antiques, art, and artifacts from around the world decorate the seven bedrooms, snooker and music rooms. Enjoy a soak in the hot tub before a relaxing massage or retiring to the living room to watch a favorite video on the large screen TV, and enjoy the warmth of the fire in the beautiful stone and brass fireplace. Comfort, casualness, and fun are themes. New honeymoon cottage available.

Hosts: Crystal Carroll; Kate and Lars Enggren
Rooms: 7 (PB) $75-170
Full Breakfast
Credit Cards: A, B, C, D
Notes: 2, 5, 7, 8, 9, 10, 11, 12, 13, 14

Scrubby Oaks
Bed and Breakfast Inn
P.O. Box 1047, 81302
(970) 247-2176

On 10 acres overlooking the spectacular Animas Valley and surrounding mountains. Three miles from downtown Durango. Rooms are spacious and furnished with antiques, art works, and good books. Beautiful gardens and patios frame the inn outside, with large sitting areas inside for guest use. Closed November through April.

Host: Mary Ann Craig
Rooms: 7 (3 PB; 4 S2B) $70-80
Full Breakfast
Credit Cards: None
Notes: 2, 7, 8, 9, 10, 11, 12, 14

ESTES PARK

The Anniversary Inn
Bed and Breakfast
1060 Mary's Lake Road, 80517
(970) 586-6200

The Anniversary Inn is a turn-of-the-century two-story log home one mile from Rocky Mountain National Park. The living room with its beamed ceiling and moss rock fireplace provides a romantic and restful setting. Breakfast on the glass-enclosed porch starts the day with fruit, freshly baked breads, and a hearty entrée. Specially brewed coffee and a choice of juice complete the meal. The town of Estes Park is nearby and features quaint shops and many fine restaurants. Cross-country skiing, hiking, and fishing nearby.

Hosts: Norma and Harry Menke
Rooms: 4 (PB) $95-150
Full Breakfast
Credit Cards: A, B
Notes: 2, 5, 7, 9, 10, 12, 13

The Anniversary Inn

Black Dog Inn
650 South Saint Vrain Avenue,
P.O. Box 4659, 80517
(970) 586-0374

Snuggled in among towering pines overlooking the Estes Valley and the Mummy Range is the perfect romantic mountain retreat. The inn retains the warmth and charm of a bygone era. Hardwood floors

7 No smoking; 8 Children welcome; 9 Social drinking allowed; 10 Tennis nearby; 11 Swimming nearby; 12 Golf nearby; 13 Skiing nearby; 14 May be booked through a travel agent; 15 Handicapped accessible.

and pine-paneled walls are a perfect back-drop for Native American rugs and baskets, antique prints, and original art. Some of the guest rooms have whirlpool tubs and fire-places. Snacks, books, movies, and exten-sive trail information fill the library. Children over 12 welcome.

Hosts: Pete and Jane Princehorn
Rooms: 4 (PB) $80-150
Full Breakfast
Credit Cards: A, B
Notes: 2, 5, 7, 9, 10, 11, 12, 13, 14

Eagle Cliff House

2383 Highway 66, P.O. Box 4312, 80517
(970) 586-5425; (800) 414-0922

A warm and friendly facility is nestled in ponderosa pines at the base of Eagle Cliff Mountain. Relax in the comfort of soft colors native to southwestern decor, com-bined with the beautiful woods used in American antiques, to create warmth and hospitality. The abundant breakfast and never empty cookie jar keep guests ready for a full day of activities in the heart of Colorado's most spectacular landscapes.

Hosts: Nancy and Mike Conrin
Rooms: 3 (PB) $80-115
Full Breakfast
Credit Cards: D
Notes: 2, 5, 7, 8, 9, 10, 11, 12, 14

EVERGREEN

Bears Inn Bed and Breakfast

27425 Spruce Lane, 80439
(303) 670-1205; (800) 863-1205
FAX (303) 670-8542
e-mail: jenkins@bearsinn.com

Nestled in the pine trees, this 11-bedroom historic inn offers a true Colorado mountain experience. Each room offers a private bath, cable TV, and telephone. A full hearty breakfast is served in the great room which features a large stone fireplace. The outdoor hot tub, with great views of Mount Evans, helps to soothe away one's stress. Home-baked cookies and beverages are served in

the afternoons. Secluded setting, but next to an award-winning restaurant.

Hosts: Darrell and Chris Jenkins
Rooms: 11 (PB) $85-150
Full Breakfast
Credit Cards: A, B, C
Notes: 2, 5, 7, 9, 12, 13

FORT COLLINS

The Edwards House Bed and Breakfast

402 West Mountain Avenue, 80521
(970) 493-9191; (800) 281-9190
FAX (970) 484-0706
e-mail: edshouse@edwardshouse.com

The Edwards House bed and breakfast has been restored to capture the warmth of the Victorian era without sacrificing modern conveniences. All six rooms fea-ture a gas fireplace, private telephone, shower, and TV/VCR. The rooms with private baths in addition feature a Jacuzzi or claw-foot tub. Afternoon refreshments are provided. Near the historic Old Town shopping and restaurant district and Col-orado State University.

Host: Greg Belcher
Rooms: 6 (5 PB; 1 SB) $85-145
Full Breakfast
Credit Cards: A, B, C, D
Notes: 2, 5, 7, 10, 11, 12, 14

The Edwards House

FRISCO

Bed and Breakfast Reservation Agency of Colorado at Vail

2488 Garmisch Drive, Vail, 81657
(970) 476-0792; (800) 748-2666
FAX (970) 476-0711; e-mail: bbresser@vail.net

Whether one prefers an inn or a secluded private home, this reservation service has the perfect place for that getaway to the playgrounds of Summit County. Hike, bike, walk, ski, snowboard—it's all here. $79-160.

Galena Street Mountain Inn

First Avenue and Galena, Box 417, 80443
(800) 248-9138; FAX (970) 668-1569
www.colorado-bnb.com/galena

Fifteen beautifully furnished guest rooms with private baths, down comforters, cable TV, and in-room telephones. Large windows with window seats frame mountains so close guests can feel them. The inn provides easy access to Summit County's famous ski areas in winter and for cycling, hiking, or boating in the summer. The breakfasts include freshly baked breads, homemade granola, and an entrée served in

Galena Street Mountain Inn

the spacious dining room. Indoor hot tub and sauna also included.

Hosts: John and Sandy Gilfillan
Rooms: 15 (PB) $75-140
Full and Continental Breakfast
Credit Cards: A, B, C, D
Notes: 5, 7, 8, 12, 13, 14, 15

GEORGETOWN

Creekside Bed and Breakfast Inn

610 Seventh Street, Box 917, 80444
(303) 569-2664; (800) 484-9493 pin 5896

Creekside Bed and Breakfast is in the Victorian historic district of Georgetown. Antiques and a magnificent glass collection grace each room. Listen to the gentle symphony of the creek or lounge on the deck to capture the beauty that awaits. Near major ski and tourist areas. Fishing, seasonal hunting, snow shoeing, cross-country skiing, skating, snowmobiling, boating, hiking, biking, horseback riding, carriage rides, historical museums, Georgetown Loop Railroad, lovely restaurants, and shops nearby. Near Central City and Black Hawk. The inn is 42 miles from Denver and the international airport. A candlelight country breakfast served each morning. Children over eight welcome.

Host: Carol A. Curran
Rooms: 4 (PB) $69-95
Full Breakfast
Credit Cards: A, B, F
Notes: 2, 5, 7, 9, 10, 11, 12, 13, 14

Hardy House Bed and Breakfast

P.O. Box 156, 80444
(303) 569-3388; (800) 490-4802

This red and white Victorian home was built in 1880 and is in the historic district. There are four Victorian-decorated guest rooms, each with private bath, TV/VCR, and queen-size bed. There is a large outdoor hot tub in the back yard, and guests awake to a gourmet candlelight breakfast.

7 No smoking; 8 Children welcome; 9 Social drinking allowed; 10 Tennis nearby; 11 Swimming nearby; 12 Golf nearby; 13 Skiing nearby; 14 May be booked through a travel agent; 15 Handicapped accessible.

Hardy House

Georgetown is only 50 minutes from Denver, close to seven major ski areas in the heart of the Rocky Mountains. Romance and other packages available. Featured in *Country* magazine, December 1995 issue. Visa and MasterCard accepted for guarantee only. Children over 12 welcome.

Hosts: Carla and Mike Wagner
Rooms: 4 (PB) $73-82
Full Breakfast
Credit Cards: None
Notes: 2, 4, 5, 7, 9, 13, 14

GLENWOOD SPRINGS

Back in Time

927 Cooper, 81601
(303) 945-6183

A wonderful 1903 Victorian lovingly restored by owners. In the spacious home filled with antiques, family quilts, and clocks, three bedrooms are available. A full breakfast is served in the dining room. Enjoy skiing in the winter, swimming and rafting in the summer. Within walking distance to shopping, dining, and the world's largest hot springs. Forty miles from Aspen/Vail.

Hosts: June and Ron Robinson
Rooms: 3 (PB) $50-85
Full Breakfast
Cards: A, B, C, D
Notes: 2, 5, 7, 9, 10, 11, 12, 13, 14

The Bed and Breakfast on Mitchell Creek

1686 Mitchell Creek Road, 81601-2588
(970) 945-4002

This contemporary log home on Mitchell Creek in the mountains offers one spacious, romantic suite—private entrance, private bath, king-size bed, and living/dining area. Privacy, solitude, and romance await guests. Personal service is assured. Hiking trails and lower patio with fire pit. Horseback riding and hot mineral springs and spa minutes away. "Let us pamper you." Credit cards accepted only to hold reservation. In-state personal checks accepted.

Hosts: Stan and Carole Rachesky
Rooms: 1 (PB) $90
Full Breakfast
Credit Cards: None
Notes: 5, 7, 8, 9, 10, 11, 12, 13

The Kaiser House

932 Cooper Avenue, 81601
(970) 928-0101 (phone/FAX)

A blissful return to a Victorian fairy tale on the corner of 10th and Cooper, in the center of "the Spa of the Rockies." Eight bedrooms, each with a private bath and uniquely decorated in Victorian style. Enjoy a gourmet breakfast in a spacious dining room, breakfast area or outdoor patio during summer. An outside path provides an easy walk during summer to parks, shopping, fine restaurants, and the Hot Springs Pool and Vapor Caves.

Room: 8 (PB) $85-165
Full Breakfast
Credit Cards: A, B, C
Notes: 2, 3, 4, 5, 7, 8, 9, 10, 11, 12, 13, 14

GOLDEN

The Dove Inn

711 14th Street, 80401-1906
(303) 278-2209; FAX (303) 273-5272

Charming Victorian inn is in the west Denver vicinity in the small-town atmos-

The Dove Inn

phere of Golden. Close to Coors tours and Rocky Mountain National Park; one hour to ski areas. Children welcome. No pets.

Hosts: Tim and Connie Sheffield
Rooms: 6 (PB) $65-90
Full Breakfast
Credit Cards: A, B, C, D
Notes: 2, 5, 7, 8, 12, 13, 14

GROVER

West Pawnee Ranch Bed and Breakfast

29451 WCR 130, 80729
(970) 895-2482

In the heart of the Pawnee National Grasslands. Rest and relax with the hosts in the quiet of the vast prairie or take part on the

West Pawnee Ranch

working ranch. Horseback riding in the Chalk Bluffs. Spectacular sunsets. Enjoy newly opened two-room Prairie House with moss rock fireplace. Ranchers' breakfast served. Family friendly.

Hosts: Paul and Louanne Timm
Rooms: 3 (PB) $50-90
Full Breakfast
Credit Cards: F
Notes: 2, 3, 4, 5, 7, 8, 9, 12, 14

GUNNISON

The Eagle's Nest

206 North Colorado, 81230
(970) 641-4457

Originally built in 1923, this Early American former judge's home features stained glass and interior maple woodwork. Gunnison is an attractive place to visit in all four seasons. There is skiing at nearby Crested Butte, hunting in the fall, and fishing in either Blue Mesa Lake or the Gunnison River. During the gorgeous summer weather, there are numerous attractions: rafting, the Gunnison Rodeo, Crested Butte Wildflower Festival, etc. Credit cards accepted for reservations.

Hosts: Jane and Hugh McGee
Suite: 1 (PB) $45
Full and Continental Breakfast
Credit Cards: None
Notes: 2, 5, 7

Mary Lawrence Inn

601 North Taylor Street, 81230
(970) 641-3343; (800) 445-3861
www.gunnison.co.comm/main/lodging/maryl.htm

Make this Victorian home the center of excursions through Gunnison Country. The mountains, rivers, and lakes are extraordinary. Golf, swimming, rafting are accessible. The inn is furnished with antiques and collectibles. Breakfasts are bountiful and imaginative. Special fly-fishing weekends. Great ski package offered for Crested Butte skiing. Children welcome.

7 No smoking; 8 Children welcome; 9 Social drinking allowed; 10 Tennis nearby; 11 Swimming nearby; 12 Golf nearby; 13 Skiing nearby; 14 May be booked through a travel agent; 15 Handicapped accessible.

Hosts: Beth and Doug Parker
Rooms: 4 (PB) $69-85
Suites: 3 (PB) $99-129
Full Breakfast
Credit Cards: A, B
Notes: 2, 5, 7, 8, 9, 10, 11, 12, 13, 14

IDAHO SPRINGS

Riverside Bed and Breakfast

2130 Riverside Drive, P.O. Box 1535, 80452
(303) 567-9032; (303) 987-7450

The Riverside offers a friendly, comfortable stay. Guests can relax in the courtyard or the hot tub and view the nearby mountain scenery. Take a walk along Clear Creek River to Main Street and enjoy the many restaurants, museums, and galleries. If guests are adventurous, there is skiing, hiking, or rafting. Inquire about restrictions on social drinking.

Host: Theresa Gonzales
Rooms: 4 (1 PB: 3 S2B) $54-74
Full Breakfast
Credit Cards: A, B
Notes: 2, 5, 7, 13

Riverside

LAKE CITY

Old Carson Inn

P.O. Box 144, 81235
(970) 944-2511; (800) 294-0608

A secluded log inn filled with antiques and collectibles, 10 miles southwest of Lake City on the Alpine Loop. Seven guest rooms, private baths, common area with satellite TV, outdoor hot tub, large country breakfast with homemade bread. Baked goods and sack lunches available.

Hosts: Mary and Frank Wyant
Rooms: 7 (PB) $76-120
Full Breakfast
Credit Cards: A, B, C
Notes: 2, 7, 8

LEADVILLE

The Apple Blossom Inn

120 West 4th Street, 80461
(719) 486-2141; (800) 982-9279

This beautiful 1879 banker's home has been featured on two Victorian home tours. Recipient of 1998 Award of Excellence. Decorated with antiques, charm, and a flair for comfortable spaces. Breakfast is fully delicious. Free recreation center passes. Feather beds, fireplaces, home-baked goodies make guests' stay most memorable.

Host: Maggie Senn
Rooms: 8 (3 PB; 4 SB) $59-118
Full Breakfast
Credit Cards: A, B, C, D, E
Notes: 2, 3, 4, 5, 7, 8, 9, 10, 11, 12, 13, 14

Bed and Breakfast Reservation Agency of Colorado at Vail

2488 Garmisch Drive, Vail, 81657
(970) 476-0792; (800) 748-2666
FAX (970) 476-0711; e-mail: bbresser@vail.net

Restored Victorian hotels and homes offer the traveler a taste of Leadville's historic past. Close to shops, restaurants, and sur-

NOTES: Credit cards accepted: A MasterCard; B Visa; C American Express; D Discover; E Diner's Club; F Other; 2 Personal checks accepted; 3 Lunch available; 4 Dinner available; 5 Open all year; 6 Pets welcome;

rounded by spectacular scenery in this two-mile-high city. $70-125.

Historic Delaware Hotel

700 Harrison Avenue, 80461
(719) 486-1418; (800) 748-2004

Enjoy the ambiance of this historic hotel, circa 1886. Each of the 36 rooms features antique furnishings and heirloom-style bedspreads. Each room features a private bath and TV. A Jacuzzi, Victorian lobby and lounge are also available for guests to enjoy. No smoking in restaurant. First floor is handicapped accessible.

Rooms: 36 (PB) $70-120
Full Breakfast
Credit Cards: A, B, C, D, E
Notes: 5, 8, 9, 10, 11, 12, 13, 14

Historic Delaware Hotel

The Ice Palace Inn

813 Spruce Street, 80461
(719) 486-8272; (800) 754-2840
FAX (719) 486-0345; e-mail: ipalace@sni.net
www.colorado-bnb.com/icepalace

This gracious Victorian inn was built at the turn of the century, using the lumber from the famous Leadville Ice Palace. Romantic guest rooms, elegantly decorated with antiques, feather beds and quilts, each with an exquisite private bath, are named after the original rooms of the Ice Palace. Begin the day with a delicious gourmet breakfast served at individual tables in this historic

The Ice Palace Inn

inn. Afternoon teas and goodies are available every day. Turndown service in the evening. Hot tub.

Hosts: Giles and Kami Kolakowski
Rooms: 6 (PB) $79-119
Full Breakfast
Credit Cards: A, B, C, D
Notes: 2, 5, 7, 8, 9, 10, 11, 12, 13, 14

Wood Haven Manor Bed and Breakfast

809 Spruce, 80461
(800) 748-2570; FAX (719) 486-0210
e-mail: woodhavn@rmi.net
www.colorado-bnb.com/woodhavn

Casual elegance in Victorian fashion. Furnished with finest antiques. Romantic suites with sitting rooms, fireplaces, whirlpool, or

Wood Haven Manor

7 No smoking; 8 Children welcome; 9 Social drinking allowed; 10 Tennis nearby; 11 Swimming nearby;
12 Golf nearby; 13 Skiing nearby; 14 May be booked through a travel agent; 15 Handicapped accessible.

four-poster bed. Full gourmet breakfast. Hospitality, service, and wonderful atmosphere are just a few reasons pampered guests keep returning.

Hosts: Christy and Clint Burback
Rooms: 8 (PB) $59-129
Full Breakfast
Credit Cards: A, B, C, D
Notes: 2, 5, 7, 8, 9, 10, 11, 12, 13, 14

LIVERMORE

Cherokee Park Dude Ranch

436 Cherokee Hills Drive, 80536
(970) 493-6522; FAX (970) 493-5802
e-mail: thomas@pageplus.com

Nestled in the Colorado Rockies, Cherokee Park Ranch is only two hours from Denver. During the 1880s the ranch was a stagecoach stop, and much of the furnishings are from the ranch beginnings. Activities include horseback riding, river rafting, fishing, sightseeing trips, and more! Home-cooked meals are served family style. The ranch offers counseled programs for 3- to 12-year olds, creating a terrific place for kids to experience the West on a genuine dude ranch.

Hosts: Dickey and Christine Prince and family
Rooms: 12 (PB) $900-1100 weekly
Full Breakfast
Credit Cards: A, B
Notes: 2, 3, 4, 7, 8, 9, 14

LOVELAND

Apple Avenue Bed and Breakfast

3321 Apple Avenue, 80538
(970) 667-2665

Apple Avenue Bed and Breakfasts offers friendly service and pleasant accommodations in a quiet residential setting. Breakfasts range from pancakes and waffles served with pure Vermont maple syrup, to veggie-filled omelets and freshly baked muffins. Fruit and juice always are included, and special attention is paid to guests' dietary restrictions. Air conditioned, laundry facilities, gas barbecue grill. Benson Park Sculpture Garden is within an easy walk of Apple Avenue.

Hosts: Ann and Tom Harroun
Rooms: 2 (SB) $55-60
Full Breakfast
Credit Cards: A, B, C, D
Notes: 2, 5, 7, 8, 11, 12, 14

Derby Hill Inn Bed and Breakfast

2502 Courtney Drive, 80537
(970) 667-3193; (800) 498-8086
e-mail: DMcCue31@aol.com
www.guestinns.com/derbyhill

Rated in the top three for 1997 Inn of the Year in the small new inn category. In a quiet neighborhood close to retail and antique shops, art galleries, four-star golf course, Rocky Mountain National Park. Friendly hospitality welcomes the casual and business traveler to enjoy the well-decorated comfortable rooms with private baths, queen-size beds, in-room telephones, desk, TV, robes, and a delectable gourmet breakfast in the homelike atmosphere enhanced with art and antiques. Computer and fax are available.

Hosts: Dale and Bev McCue
Rooms: 2 (PB) $75-85
Full Breakfast
Credit Cards: A, B, C, E
Notes: 2, 5, 7, 10, 11, 12, 14

The Lovelander Bed and Breakfast Inn

217 West 4th Street, 80537
(970) 669-0798; (800) 459-6694 (reservations)
FAX (970) 669-0797

Nestled against the Rocky Mountain foothills, minutes from Rocky Mountain National Park, the Lovelander is a rambling Victorian-style inn. Its beauty and elegance are characteristic of the turn of the century, when the home was built. Near restaurants, shops, museums, and art galleries, the Lovelander is a haven for business and leisure travelers and a retreat for romantics. Meeting and reception facilities are available. Children over 10 are welcome. "We guarantee you will have a memorable stay, or your next stay is on us!"

Hosts: Lauren and Gary Smith
Rooms: 11 (PB) $100-150
Full Breakfast
Credit Cards: A, B, C, D
Notes: 2, 3, 5, 7, 9, 10, 11, 12, 14

MANCOS

Riversbend Bed and Breakfast

42505 Highway 160, 81328
(800) 699-8994; FAX (970) 533-1221
e-mail: riversbn@fone.net
www.riversbend.com

Riversbend Bed and Breakfast is on the San Juan Skyway—7 miles from Mesa Verde and 25 miles from Durango. This two-story log inn serves as a hub for the many area activities and is a haven for rest and relaxation when the day is over. Guests drift off to sleep between cool white sheets that smell of Colorado sunshine, and they awaken to the tantalizing scent of a scrumptious gourmet breakfast. Enjoy horseback riding, explore Mesa Verde National Park, or ride the narrow-gauge train.

Hosts: Gaye and Jack Curran
Rooms: 5 (PB) $75-125
Full Breakfast
Credit Cards: A, B, C, D
Notes: 2, 5, 7, 10, 11, 12, 13, 14

MANITOU SPRINGS

Gray's Avenue Hotel

711 Manitou Avenue, 80829
(719) 685-1277; (800) 294-1277
FAX (719) 685-1847
www. spectroweb.com/graysb&b.htm

This bed and breakfast is in the Manitou Springs Historic Preservation District. It was built in 1886 and opened as the Avenue Hotel, one of the original seven hotels in this resort town. Within minutes of most tourist attractions and easy walking distance of many shops and restaurants. Children over 10, please. Outdoor hot tub. Family suites. Small groups welcome. Fifteen dollars for extra person.

Hosts: Tom and Lee Gray
Rooms: 7 (3 suites) $60-80
Full Breakfast
Credit Cards: A, B, C
Notes: 2, 5, 7, 10, 11, 12, 13, 14

Red Crags Bed and Breakfast

302 El Paso Boulevard, 80829
(719) 685-1920; (800) 721-2248
e-mail: info@redcrags.com
www.redcrags.com

A magnificent four-story 1870s Victorian mansion. The 7,000-square-foot main house dominates the two-acre estate. High ceilings, hardwood floors, and beautiful antiques predominate. The large bedrooms, all with private baths, feature king-size beds with European feather mattresses and down comforters, fireplaces, and two suites with whirlpool tubs for two. Full gourmet breakfast. Beautiful views of Pikes Peak and the Manitou Valley. AAA three-diamond-rated, Mobil-, and BBIC-approved. Jackson, the friendly house dog, greets all guests. Children over 10 welcome.

Hosts: Howard and Lynda Lerner
Rooms: 8 (PB) $75-185
Full Breakfast
Credit Cards: A, B, C, D
Notes: 2, 5, 7, 9, 11, 12, 14

Red Crags

---

7 No smoking; 8 Children welcome; 9 Social drinking allowed; 10 Tennis nearby; 11 Swimming nearby; 12 Golf nearby; 13 Skiing nearby; 14 May be booked through a travel agent; 15 Handicapped accessible.

Rockledge Country Inn

328 El Paso Boulevard, 80829
(719) 685-4515; (888) 685-4515
FAX (719) 685-1031
e-mail: rockinn@webcom.com

Rockledge Country Inn, in the historic
Rockledge Manor House, is on three and
one-half fenced and gated acres of stone
terraces with panoramic views of Pikes
Peak and surrounding foothills. All suites
are spacious with king-size feather beds,
entertainment centers, some with fireplace
and spa—all have spectacular views. Guests
may enjoy large common areas which
include two fireplaces, an 1875 Steinway
grand piano, library, parlor games, solarium, patios and outdoor spa. A multi-course
gourmet breakfast is served each morning
and Colorado wines and hors d'oeuvres
each evening. Fresh cookies and chocolates
are always at hand.

Hosts: Hartman and Nancy Smith
Rooms: 3 (PB) $195-250
Full Breakfast
Credit Cards: A, B, C, D
Notes: 2, 4, 5, 7, 9, 10, 11, 12, 13, 14

MINTURN

Eagle River Inn

145 North Main; P.O. Box 100, 81645
(970) 827-5761; (800) 344-1750
FAX (970) 827-4020; e-mail: eri@vail.net

Directly between Vail and Beaver Creek
Resorts—a wonderful start-off point for
skiing, snowmobiling, snowshoeing, hiking,
rafting, or mountain biking. Breakfast, plus
evening wine and appetizers, are served by
the beehive fireplace in the cozy lobby. Hot
tub is out on the deck overlooking the Eagle
River. Twelve nonsmoking rooms with private baths. Unique shops, galleries, and eight
restaurants are within walking distance.

Host: Patty Bidez
Rooms: 12 (PB) $75-180
Full Breakfast
Credit Cards: A, B, C, D
Notes: 2, 7, 9, 10, 12, 13, 14

MONTROSE

Annie's Orchard Historic Bed and Breakfast

14963 63.00 Road, 81401
(970) 249-0298; e-mail: mneedham@montrose.net

Comfortably elegant country Tudor built in
1909. Quiet, romantic setting on two-acre
estate just outside Montrose in western Colorado. Three unique rooms, all with luxuriously appointed private baths and antique
furnishings. Romantic fireplace suite with
cozy feather bed. Hot tub under the stars.
Central to Black Canyon, San Juan Mountains, Telluride, Ouray Hot Springs, and
Grand Mesa. Hiking, skiing, fishing, jeeping nearby. Participant inn-to-inn bicycling.
Full gourmet breakfast and afternoon tea.

Host: Mary Needham
Rooms: 3 (PB) $45-75
Full Breakfast
Credit Cards: A, B, C, D
Notes: 2, 5, 7, 9, 10, 11, 12, 13, 14

MONUMENT

Cross Keys Inn Bed and Breakfast

20450 Beacon Lite Road, 80132
(719) 481-2772; (800) 250-KEYS
FAX (719) 481-8992
e-mail: innkeep@crosskeys.net
www.crosskeys.net

Cross Keys Inn is a comfortable log inn five
miles north of the U.S. Air Force Academy
between Colorado Springs and Castle Rock.
The first floor of the inn features an open
area for guests. It includes a hot tub in the
solarium, a living room with fireplace, a TV
room, and a private study for those needing
to finish up work in the evenings. On the
second floor, there are three comfortably furnished guest rooms. Children over 12 welcome. Small conference meetings welcome.

Hosts: Suzanne and Rick Laidlaw
Rooms: 5 (3 PB; 2 SB) $65-120

NOTES: Credit cards accepted: A MasterCard; B Visa; C American Express; D Discover; E Diner's Club;
F Other; 2 Personal checks accepted; 3 Lunch available; 4 Dinner available; 5 Open all year; 6 Pets welcome;

Full Breakfast
Credit Cards: A, B, C, D, E
Notes: 2, 5, 7, 14

MOSCA

Inn at Zapata Ranch

5303 Highway 150, 81146
(719) 378-2356; (800) 284-9213
FAX (719) 378-2428

Adjacent to the Great Sand Dunes National Monument, the inn is a secluded 15-room retreat at the heart of Colorado's legendary Zapata Ranch, high in the San Luis Valley. In the National Register of Historic Places, the inn is interesting in itself for its architecture and history. The world-class amenities include a championship 18-hole golf course, rustic hearty cuisine, heated outdoor pool, hot tub, sauna, and exercise room.

Innkeeper: Angela Moses
Owner: Nacho Martinez
Rooms: 15 (PB) $90-175
Full Breakfast
Credit Cards: A, B, C, D, E
Notes: 2, 3, 4, 7, 8, 9, 11, 12, 14, 15

OURAY

Bed and Breakfast Reservation Agency of Colorado at Vail

2488 Garmisch Drive, Vail, 81657
(970) 476-0792; (800) 748-2666
FAX (970) 476-0711; e-mail: bbresser@vail.net

Custom-designed with the guest in mind. Gorgeous views of the San Juan Mountains. Seven rooms, all with private baths and extraordinary decor. Hot tub, full breakfast. $65-125.

Main Street Bed and Breakfasts

322 Main Street, P.O. Box 641, 81427
(303) 325-4871

Two superbly renovated, turn-of-the-century residences offer three suites, three rooms, and a two-story cottage. All accommodations have private baths, queen-size beds, and cable TV. Five of the units have decks with spectacular views of the San Juan Mountains. Three units have fully equipped modern kitchens. Guests who stay in rooms without kitchens are served a full breakfast on antique china. Guests who stay in kitchen suites are provided with supplies for a hearty breakfast.

Hosts: Lee and Kathy Bates
Rooms: 7 (PB) $68-120
Full Breakfast
Credit Cards: A, B, C
Notes: 2, 7, 8, 9, 10, 11, 12, 14

St. Elmo Hotel

426 Main Street, P.O. Box 667, 81427
(303) 325-4951

Listed in the National Register of Historic Places and established in 1898 as a miners' hotel, St. Elmo's is now fully renovated with stained glass, antiques, polished wood, and brass trim throughout. An outdoor hot tub and aspen-lined sauna are available, as well as a cozy parlor and a breakfast room.

Hosts: Sandy and Dan Lingenfelter
Rooms: 9 (PB) $65-102
Full Breakfast
Credit Cards: A, B, C, D
Notes: 4, 5, 7, 8, 9, 10, 11, 12, 13, 14

PAGOSA SPRINGS

Davidson's Country Inn

P.O. Box 87, 81147
(970) 264-5863

On 30 acres, a log home converted to bed and breakfast with nine bedrooms and a two-bedroom suite. Furnished in all wood and antiques, and decorated in the style of country, frontier, and western. Game room, hay farm, great country breakfast. All kinds of things to do—hiking, fishing, hunting, rafting, train rides, and others. Hot tub. Not in a heavy tourist-oriented place, but a place to relax and have fun.

7 No smoking; 8 Children welcome; 9 Social drinking allowed; 10 Tennis nearby; 11 Swimming nearby; 12 Golf nearby; 13 Skiing nearby; 14 May be booked through a travel agent; 15 Handicapped accessible.

Hosts: Gilbert and Nancy Davidson
Rooms: 8 (3 PB: 5 SB)
Full Breakfast
Credit Cards: A, B, C, D
Notes: 2, 5, 7, 8, 10, 11, 12, 13, 14

Echo Manor Inn

3366 Highway 84, 81147
(970) 264-5646; e-mail: widmer@frontier.net

Beautiful country Dutch Tudor manor with towers, turrets, and gables, set in the majestic San Juan Mountains and described by many as a "fairy tale castle." This lovely bed and breakfast offers a honeymoon suite, gourmet-style breakfast, hot tub, horseback riding, rafting, snowmobiling, fishing, hunting, and boating. Airport shuttle. Across the street is beautiful Echo Lake. Guests are invited to enjoy cozy wood stoves and fireplaces. Children over 10 welcome.

Hosts: Maureen and John Widmer
Rooms:10 (PB) $65-160
Suite: 1
Full Breakfast
Credit Cards: A, B, C, D
Notes: 2, 5, 7, 9, 10, 11, 12, 13, 14

PUEBLO

Abriendo Inn

300 West Abriendo Avenue, 81004
(719) 544-2703; e-mail: abriendo@rmi.net

A classic bed and breakfast in the National Register of Historic Places, in the heart of

Abriendo Inn

Pueblo and one mile off I-25. Bask in the style and luxury of the past in rooms with all the comforts of today. All rooms have king- or queen-size beds, TVs, telephones, and air conditioning. Some with whirlpool tubs. Restaurants, shops, galleries, golf, tennis, and other attractions are all within five minutes of the inn. Children over seven welcome.

Host: Kerrelyn Trent
Rooms: 10 (PB) $59-115
Full Breakfast
Credit Cards: A, B, C, E
Notes: 2, 5, 7, 9, 10, 11, 12, 14

REDSTONE

Crystal Dreams Bed and Breakfast

0475 Redstone Boulevard, 81623
(970) 963-8240; e-mail: redstone@rof.net
www.net-unlimited.com/crystaldreams

Romantic country Victorian house on the Crystal River, in the historical town of Redstone. A perfect getaway in the Rockies. Guests receive special care and attention. Year-round sports activities for any enthusiast. Candlelight breakfast offered. Fly-fishing outside the back yard. Luxury at an affordable price.

Hosts: Lisa and Stephen Wagner
Rooms: 3 (PB) $90-100
Full Breakfast
Credit Cards: F
Notes: 2, 3, 5, 7, 9, 13

SALIDA

The Thomas House Bed and Breakfast

307 East First Street, 81201
(719) 539-7104; (888) 228-1410

The Thomas House reflects the comfortable, homey atmosphere that has earned the house a strong reputation among travelers for many years. The guest rooms

NOTES: Credit cards accepted: A MasterCard; B Visa; C American Express; D Discover; E Diner's Club; F Other; 2 Personal checks accepted; 3 Lunch available; 4 Dinner available; 5 Open all year; 6 Pets welcome;

The Thomas House

have private baths and the suite has its own kitchenette. The home is furnished with many family heirlooms, antiques, and collectibles, mixed with some modern pieces and hand-me-downs to provide a truly eclectic experience. An outdoor hot tub and spacious decks provide guests areas for relaxation.

Hosts: Tammy and Steve Office
Rooms: 5 (PB) $55-90
Continental Breakfast
Credit Cards: A, B
Notes: 2, 5, 7, 8, 9, 10, 11, 12, 13, 14

The Tudor Rose

6720 Paradise Road, P.O. Box 89, 81201
(719) 539-2002; (800) 379-0889

Stately country manor, high on a piñon hill overlooking the Arkansas River valley, is built on 37 acres of an 1890s homestead. Six distinctive rooms, including the Henry Tudor suite with its private Jacuzzi tub room, highlight the inn. A formal Queen Anne living room, relaxing Wolf's Den, deck with sunken spa, and a full hearty breakfast are complimentary. Facilities include a barn, fenced paddocks, access to thousands of federal acres, and outdoor dog accommodations.

Hosts: Jon and Terré Terrell
Rooms: 6 (4 PB; 2 SB) $50-120
Full Breakfast
Credit Cards: A, B, D
Notes: 2, 3, 5, 6, 7, 8, 9, 11, 12, 13, 14

SAN ACACIO

The Depot Historical Bed and Breakfast

Route 1, Box 186, 81150
(719) 672-3943; (719) 379-0349 (cell phone)
800) 949-3943

Casual, affordable getaway for families, couples, groups, and individuals in the last standing monument to the San Luis Southern Railroad. Built in 1910, the Depot today maintains much of its original character with its freight room, bank vault, ice house, and railroad memorabilia. The Depot is near Ski Rio, Cumbres-Toltec train, national forest lands, historic San Luis, Great Sand Dunes, and the southwestern culture of Taos, New Mexico. Excellent hiking, hunting, and fishing nearby.

Host: Neil Fletcher
Rooms: 4 (2-3 PB; 2 SB) $44-64
Full Breakfast
Credit Cards: B
Notes: 2, 5, 6, 7, 8, 9, 11, 12, 13

SILT

The Rieger Ranch

6536 County Road 331, 81652
(970) 876-2097

This 262-acre ranch sits among rolling hay fields, sweeping vistas of Grand

7 No smoking; 8 Children welcome; 9 Social drinking allowed; 10 Tennis nearby; 11 Swimming nearby; 12 Golf nearby; 13 Skiing nearby; 14 May be booked through a travel agent; 15 Handicapped accessible.

Mesa, Book Cliff mountains, and the flat tops. Part of the ranch house dates back to the 1800's. Charming guest rooms with shared bath. Participate in seasonal ranch activities, mountain bike, golf at Rifle Golf course, fish or raft the Colorado River, or swim at the Glenwood Hot Springs. Wake up to the sounds of Hans playing the zither and Sharon's country breakfasts with home-baked treats. The Riegers have been hosting guests for over 30 years. Lunch and dinner available by prior arrangement. Golf and swimming about 30 minutes away. Skiing about an hour and a half away.

Hosts: Hans and Sharon Rieger
Rooms: 3 (SB) $55-75
Full Breakfast
Credit Cards: None
Notes: 2, 7, 8, 9

SILVERTON

Wyman Hotel and Inn

1371 Greene Street, P.O. Box 780, 81433
(970) 387-5372; (800) 609-7845
FAX (970) 387-5745

Built in 1902; listed in the National Register of Historic Places. Recently featured as the historic hotel in Silverton on the Travel channel's *Historic Traveler*. Antiques throughout. All rooms have private bathrooms, telephones, TVs, VCRs, and comforters. Some rooms have canopied beds, and/or private whirlpool tubs. Gourmet breakfast and afternoon tea with homemade cookies included. Free videos from the 550 plus collection. AAA three-diamond rated. Step back in time by spending time at the Wyman Hotel and Inn.

Host: Lorraine Lewis
Rooms: 17 (PB) $90-165
Full Breakfast
Credit Cards: A, B, C, D
Notes: 2, 6, 7, 8, 9, 11, 13, 14, 15

SNOWMASS

Starry Pines Bed and Breakfast

2262 Snowmass Creek Road, 81654
(800) 527-4202

A contemporary luxurious bed and breakfast home on a 70-acre ranch 20 minutes from Aspen or Snowmass Village. Enjoy the trout stream, picnic area, spectacular mountain views, hot tub under the stars, cathedral ceiling, stone fireplace, and movie selection for VCR. Two guest rooms have private bath with shared shower and tub in between. Apartment sleeps three to four, private bath and entrance. Ski on four world-class mountains, hike, bike, or horseback trek into the wilderness. Boarding for horses available. Children over 10 welcome.

Host: Shelley Burke
Rooms: 3 (3 PB; 2 SB) $80-120
Continental Breakfast
Credit Cards: None
Notes: 2, 5, 7, 9, 10, 12, 13, 14

STEAMBOAT SPRINGS

Bed and Breakfast Reservation Agency of Colorado at Vail

2488 Garmisch Drive, Vail, 81657
(970) 476-0792; (800) 748-2666
FAX (970) 476-0711; e-mail: bbresser@vail.net

Mountainside ski lodges to Old Town private homes. Experience Steamboat at its best year-round. Single rooms and suites. Private bath, full or Continental breakfast, hot tub, pool, walk or take the free shuttle. $89-200.

Caroline's Bed and Breakfast

838 Merritt Street, P.O. Box 880013, 80488
(970) 870-1696; (800) 856-4029
e-mail: caroline@cmn.net
www.cmn.net/~caroline

This 1948 log house in one of Steamboat Springs's oldest neighborhoods has a spectacular view of Mount Werner. Large windows, arched ceilings and doorways, beautiful oak floors throughout, and an unusual handcrafted rock fireplace. Two guest rooms, furnished with family antiques, each with private bath and whirlpool tub. Three miles from Steamboat Ski Area, six blocks from downtown. Summer activities include mountain biking, hiking, kayaking, canoeing, fly-fishing, golf, horseback riding, Western Pro Rodeo Series, and balloon trips.

Hosts: Caroline and Oliver Fisher
Rooms: 2 (PB) $75-110
Full Breakfast
Credit Cards: A, B
Notes: 2, 5, 7, 9, 10, 11, 12, 13, 14

Iron Horse Inn

333 South Lincoln Avenue (Highway 40),
P.O. Box 771873, 80477
(970) 879-6505; (800) 856-6505
FAX (970) 879-6129

The accommodations at the Iron Horse Inn are clean, comfortable, and spacious. Whether guests' preference is a standard hotel room or a more spacious suite, complete with kitchenette, the hosts can make sure that guests feel right at home. Regardless of your choice of room at the inn, guests will enjoy a scenic view from the window while relaxing in comfort.

Rooms: 52 (PB) $49-122
Continental Breakfast
Credit Cards: A, B, C, E
Notes: 5, 7, 8, 11, 12, 13, 14, 15

Steamboat Valley Guest House

1245 Crawford Avenue, P.O. Box 773815, 80477
(970) 870-9017; (800) 530-3866
www.virtualcities.com

On spacious grounds, this western log house has spectacular views of skiing and Old Town. Family treasures and antiques accent log walls and lovely wallpapers. English and Scandinavian decor includes lace at every window. Great room features a fireplace, grand piano, and large sunny windows. Seasonal hot tub. Easy walk to restau-

rants, shops, bike path, river activities, and historic sites. Covered parking. Ski area is easily reached by town bus.

Hosts: George and Alice Lund
Rooms: 4 (PB) $80-132
Full Breakfast
Credit Cards: A, B, C, D, E
Notes: 2, 5, 7, 9, 11, 12, 13, 14

TELLURIDE

Alpine Inn Bed and Breakfast

440 West Colorado Avenue, P.O. Box 2398, 81435
(970) 728-6282; (800) 707-3344

Enjoy the charm and spectacular views at this restored Victorian inn in the historic district of Telluride. The inn is within walking distance of ski lifts, hiking trails, and festivals. Each room captures a Victorian serenity with antiques and soft colors. Enjoy breakfast with views from the sunroom or sun deck. Relax on the porch by the wildflower garden, read a good book by the fire, or enjoy sunsets from the hot tub.

Hosts: Denise and John Weaver
Rooms: 8 (6 PB; 2 SB) $80-220
Full Breakfast
Credit Cards: A, B, D
Notes: 2, 7, 9, 10, 11, 12, 13, 14

Bear Creek Bed and Breakfast

221 East Colorado Avenue, P.O. Box 2369, 81435
(970) 728-6681; (800) 338-7064
FAX (970) 728-3636; e-mail: colleenw@sni.net
www.telluridemm.com/bearcreek.html

European ambiance coupled with Old West hospitality. A steam room, cedar-lined dry sauna, and a rooftop terrace with a hot tub and panoramic views of the San Juan Mountains welcome guests after a day of outdoor activities. The inn has nine lovely guest chambers on the second and third floors of a red brick, Victorian-style structure on the sunny side of Telluride's historic Main Street opposite its namesake, Bear Creek Canyon. The location is ideal; close to summer festivals, dining, shopping, hiking,

7 No smoking; 8 Children welcome; 9 Social drinking allowed; 10 Tennis nearby; 11 Swimming nearby; 12 Golf nearby; 13 Skiing nearby; 14 May be booked through a travel agent; 15 Handicapped accessible.

biking, skiing, the river trail, and jeeping. Children 12 and older welcome.

Hosts: Tom and Colleen Whiteman
Rooms: 9 (PB) $75-185
Full Breakfast
Credit Cards: A, B, C, D
Notes: 5, 7, 9, 10, 11, 12, 13, 14

Johnstone Inn

403 West Colorado, Box 546, 81435
(970) 728-3316; (800) 752-1901
FAX (970) 728-0724; e-mail: bschiff@rmii.com
www.johnstoneinn.com

A true 100-year-old restored Victorian boarding house in the center of Telluride and the spectacular San Juan Mountains. Rooms are warm, romantic with Victorian marble and brass private baths. Full breakfast is served. Winter season includes après-ski refreshments. A sitting room with fireplace and outdoor hot tub complete guests' amenities. Nordic and alpine skiing, hiking, and jeep tours are within walking distance of the inn.

Johnstone Inn

Host: Bill Schiffbauer
Rooms: 8 (PB)
Full Breakfast
Credit Cards: A, B, C
Notes: 2, 7, 9, 12, 13, 14

TWIN LAKES

Mt. Elbert Lodge

Mt. Elbert Lodge and Cabins

10764 Highway 82, P.O. Box 40, 81251-0040
(719) 486-0594; (800) 381-4433
e-mail: mtelbert@amigo.net
www.colorado-bnb.com/mtelbert

Nestled in the Rockies, Mt. Elbert Lodge is a wonderful escape from the often hectic pace of everyday life. Beautiful mountain scenery and serenity will surround guests as they fish, hike, or just relax on the porch. In the center of a triangle created by Buena Vista, Leadville, and Aspen, guests are able to explore Colorado from its mining history to its glittery present. Please note, the access to Aspen is closed November through May.

Hosts: Scott and Laura
Room: 5 (3 PB; 2 SB) $59-84
Full Breakfast
Credit Cards: A, B, C, D
Notes: 2, 4, 5, 6, 7, 8, 9, 10, 11, 12, 13, 14

NOTES: Credit cards accepted: A MasterCard; B Visa; C American Express; D Discover; E Diner's Club; F Other; 2 Personal checks accepted; 3 Lunch available; 4 Dinner available; 5 Open all year; 6 Pets welcome;

VAIL

Intermountain Bed and Breakfast

2754 Basingdale Boulevard, 81657
(970) 476-4935; FAX (970) 476-7926
e-mail: vailbb@compuserve.com

This contemporary home is two miles from the ski lifts on a free shuttle bus route. Rooms have cable TV and refrigerators stocked with complimentary beverages. Breakfast includes home-baked pastries, fresh fruit, cereal, yogurt, and freshly squeezed orange juice. Enjoy an espresso or cappuccino on the garden patio. An award-winning fly-fishing creek and paved recreation path are just a short walk away, and a cozy hot tub is on the secluded patio.

Hosts: Kay and Sepp Cheney
Rooms: 2 (PB) $69-125
Continental Breakfast
Credit Cards: None
Notes: 2, 5, 7, 9, 10, 12, 13, 14

The Minturn Inn

442 Main Street, Minturn, 81645
(970) 827-9647; (800) MINTURN
FAX (970) 827-5590; www.minturninn.com

Discover the Minturn Inn, an authentic Rocky Mountain lodge nestled between Vail and Beaver Creek resorts in Minturn. Enjoy this mountain retreat in a completely refurbished 1915 hewn-log home. The distinctive accommodations feature custom-made log beds, antler chandeliers, river rock fireplaces, hardwood floors, and an elegant rustic atmosphere. Whether the ideal vacation consists of snuggling up by the fire with a good book, meandering through an alpine meadow in search of wildflowers, or skiing home on the famous Minturn Mile Backcountry Trail, the innkeepers look forward to sharing the secrets of the Vail Valley with guests, helping to make their stay at the Minturn Inn memorable. Recommended by *New York Times*, *Denver Post*, *Travel and Leisure*, and Fodor's.

Hosts: Tom and Cathy Sullivan; Mick Kelly
Rooms: 10 (8 PB; 2 SB) $65-219
Full Breakfast
Credit Cards: A, B, C, D, E
Notes: 2, 5, 7, 9, 10, 11, 12, 13, 14

VAIL (BEAVER CREEK)

Bed and Breakfast Reservation Agency of Colorado at Vail

2488 Garmisch Drive, 81657
(970) 476-0792; (800) 748-2666
FAX (970) 476-0711; e-mail: bbresser@vail.net

Alpenhaus. This Austrian-flavored home is one bus stop from Vail Village on the golf course. Great views from each bedroom, one overlooking the Gore Range and Vail Village; the other looks out on tall pines and aspens. Common gathering room available for après-ski with TV, VCR, and library. Kitchenette with microwave oven and refrigerator. No smoking. $105-115.

Alpine Creek. This beautiful house is on Alpine, just minutes from downtown. Two rooms with private baths are offered in this home. Elegantly decorated with European flair. Guests wake up to the rippling sound of the creek and the smell of freshly brewed coffee. A delicious breakfast starts off each day of winter skiing or summer recreation. $85-125.

At Home Suite. A lovely private apartment/suite. Charming handmade trim and decor with one bedroom, a sleeper sofa, efficiency kitchen, private bath. Close to bus route, four people maximum. Strictly nonsmoking. Prepare own light breakfast or afternoon snacks. Lots of privacy. $135-150.

Beaver Mountain. Newest bed and breakfast in the Vail area. Three rooms offer king-size beds, private baths, TV, and Continental plus breakfast. Five minutes from lifts at Beaver Creek. Free bus service to slopes

7 No smoking; 8 Children welcome; 9 Social drinking allowed; 10 Tennis nearby; 11 Swimming nearby; 12 Golf nearby; 13 Skiing nearby; 14 May be booked through a travel agent; 15 Handicapped accessible.

and shops. Soaring windows offer views of the surrounding mountains as guests enjoy the fireplace and the ambiance. Nonsmoking. No pets. $140-250.

The Eclectic Artist. Midway between Vail and Beaver Creek with bus service to both. Two bedrooms with private baths, full breakfast, and the serenity of the nearby Eagle River. Delightful long-time local hosts make guests' visit one to remember. $110-135.

Elk View. This gorgeous townhome nestled on the hillside of Beaver Creek boasts five levels with a breathtaking view of Beaver Creek Mountain. Beautifully decorated, each room has a charm of its own, and the house is impeccably furnished. In summer, breakfast can be enjoyed on one of the three outside decks, and in the winter, after a long day of skiing, relax in the outside hot tub. This property is perfect for honeymoon couples and guests wanting to relax with the locals. $85.

Intermountain Bed and Breakfast. This new home, nestled in a corner lot, offers a great view and serenity. Bedroom is spacious with TV, refrigerator, and a great view. Host is a ski instructor. Continental breakfast. $80-95.

Lodge in the Pines. This comfortable log duplex features one guest room with a large full bath including a jetted tub for guests' use. The outdoor hot tub is the perfect place to settle after a hard day of skiing or hiking. The large guest room is ideal for a family, as the hosts include two young children. Sleeps up to six. No smoking or pets, please. $135-200.

Matterhorn. TVs in rooms, telephone nearby, snow tires suggested for driveway. Enjoy a hearty breakfast with a magnificent view of the Gore valley. A European family (all speak German—daughter is bilingual) offers a comfortable, cozy home. Box lunch is provided for early rising convention attendants. Great for single travelers. $60-75.

Oberlohr Haus. Snuggle up in the living room next to the wood-burning stove after cooking dinner in the fully equipped kitchen. This two-bedroom, two-bath apartment is ready to let guests feel at home, with lots of privacy and space. Just three blocks from the free bus system, guests can feel fit and ready to hike or ski the day away. No smoking or pets, please. Ideal for a family or two couples. $150-200.

Snowed In. For affordable luxury, this home on an 18-hole golf course welcomes guests summer or winter. It is perfect for golfers, and in the winter, cross-country skiing is right out the back door. The guest rooms have a sitting room with TV, refrigerator, microwave, and dry bar right outside the door. Guests look forward to returning each season to sample the hospitality that reigns in this comfortably formal home. Breakfasts are unbeatable! Beaver Creek and Arrowhead Mountains are minutes away. $100-125.

Sportsman's Haven. Surrounded by pine trees and nestled on a creek, this home is a warm, spacious mountain home that beckons guests to snuggle in during the winter, or lounge on the sunny, private sun decks in summer. The hosts offer a ski home with two rooms. One is bright and cheery with pine trees outside every window, and the downstairs room has a private bath with a sauna and offers an adjoining family room with TV, pool table, shuffleboard, and fireplace. The home is within easy walking distance to the free bus. Discounted parking tickets available if guests should decide to drive. $79-95.

NOTES: Credit cards accepted: A MasterCard; B Visa; C American Express; D Discover; E Diner's Club; F Other; 2 Personal checks accepted; 3 Lunch available; 4 Dinner available; 5 Open all year; 6 Pets welcome;

Suite Retirement. In beautiful, quiet East Vail, just 5 minutes from the free town bus and only 15 minutes from the center of Vail Village, this private home-stay bed and breakfast will allow guests to relax with their hosts in the large, pine-ceilinged living room prior to retiring to the very private bedroom and bath. The unique furniture represents the host's international taste and lifestyle. The resident dog will happily greet guests at the door. No smoking. No pets. $115-150.

WINTER PARK

Alpen Rose Bed and Breakfast

244 Forest Trail, P.O. Box 769, 80482
(303) 726-5039

Fantastic mountain view surrounded by aspens and pine on three acres. Only 10 minutes' walking distance to town. Two miles from Winter Park Ski Area with Rocky Mountain National Park nearby. An outdoor lover's paradise. Handmade quilts, down puffs, and Austrian furnishings. Memorable, hearty breakfast with Austrian specialities. Crackling fire and hot tea and cookies in the afternoon. Owner is from Salzburg, Austria, and the inn reflects his love for his Austria.

Hosts: Robin and Rupert Sommerauer
Rooms: 6 (PB) $70-130
Full Breakfast
Credit Cards: A, B, C, D
Notes: 2, 5, 7, 9, 10, 11, 12, 13, 14

The Bear Paw Inn

871 Bear Paw Drive, P.O. Box 334, 80482
(970) 887-1351 (phone/FAX); (800) 474-0091

The Bear Paw Inn is a hand-hewn log lodge nestled among the pines and aspens high in the Colorado Rockies. Enjoy spectacular panoramic views from every window. Luxurious rooms feature feather beds and European down comforters, private decks, swings, Jacuzzis, and refrigerators. Easy access from Denver International Airport and Winter Park's world-class skiing. Summer activities include golf at Colorado's number one golf course, 600 miles of bike trails, boating, rodeos, music festivals, and spectacular Trail Ridge Road through Rocky Mountain National Park. "Our cool mountain air and crystal clear skies will have you convinced it is truly paradise."

Hosts: Rick and Susan Callahan
Rooms: 2 (PB) $125-160
Full Breakfast
Credit Cards: A, B, C
Notes: 2, 5, 7, 9, 10, 11, 12, 13, 14

Outpost Inn Bed and Breakfast

P.O. Box 41, 80482
(970) 726-5346; (800) 430-4538

The Outpost offers skiers a powder paradise at Winter Park. The inn, on a quiet 40-acre ranch, serves a full, elegant candlelight breakfast with hot homemade bread. Amenities include an atrium hot tub, a loft with TV, VCR, and CD player, games, books, and cards. Ten-minute drive to golf and just out the door for cross-country skiing, mountain biking, or hiking. The Outpost is just 40 minutes to Rocky Mountain National Park. Guests turn and return to the Outpost for the comfort, the food, but most of all the hospitality. Dinner available on winter weekdays.

Hosts: Ken and Barbara Parker
Rooms: 7 (PB) $70-110
Full Breakfast
Credit Cards: A, B, C, D
Notes: 2, 5, 7, 8, 9, 12, 13, 14

WOODLAND PARK

Woodland Inn
Bed and Breakfast

159 Trull Road, 80863-9027
(719) 687-8209; (800) 226-9565
FAX (719) 687-3112
e-mail: woodlandbb@aol.com
www.bbonline.com/co/woodland/

Come to a cozy country inn in the heart of
the Rocky Mountains where guests enjoy a
relaxing homelike atmosphere and fantastic
views. Peacefully secluded on 12 private
acres of woodlands, the inn is convenient to
a variety of attractions in the Pikes Peak
region. The hosts will prepare a picnic
lunch for a day of hiking, biking, or skiing,

or guests may join the hosts in a morning of
hot-air ballooning.

Hosts: Frank and Nancy O'Neil
Rooms: 7 (PB) $60-90
Full Breakfast
Credit Cards: A, B, C, D
Notes: 2, 5, 7, 8, 9, 10, 11, 12, 13, 14

NOTES: Credit cards accepted: A MasterCard; B Visa; C American Express; D Discover; E Diner's Club;
F Other; 2 Personal checks accepted; 3 Lunch available; 4 Dinner available; 5 Open all year; 6 Pets welcome;

Hawaii

The Rainbow Plantation

P.O. Box 122, 96704
(808) 323-2393; FAX (808) 323-9445
e-mail: konabnb@aloha.net
www.com/hawaii/rainbow.htm

Relax at Rainbow Plantation. Explore the peaceful surroundings. Stroll in the shade of the enchanting macadamia forest among coffee trees, tropical plants, and flowers. Listen to the birds and gentle breezes. Enjoy a tasty tropical breakfast on the ocean-view lanai overlooking koi ponds. Just seven miles south of Kona, near Kealakekua Bay, a marine sanctuary. Private entrances, private baths, TV, and refrigerators. Kayak rentals on premises. *On parle français; wir sprechen Deutsch.* No smoking in rooms.

Hosts: Marianna and Reiner Schrepfer
Rooms: 5 (PB) $65-95
Continental Breakfast
Credit Cards: A, B
Notes: 2, 5, 6, 9, 11, 12, 14

Bed and Breakfast Honolulu (Statewide)

3242 Kaohinani Drive, Honolulu, 96817
(808) 595-7533; (800) 288-4666
FAX (808) 595-2030; e-mail: bnbshl@aloha.net
www.planet-hawaii.com/bnb-honolulu

BBHS 22. A complete private downstairs unit on three and one-half acres of pastoral land. The lanai offers a view of the Waimea ranch lands, horses, cows, and the beautiful blue Pacific. Breakfast will be served on the lanai. There are a private bath and entrance, small refrigerator, coffee maker, color TV, and two single beds. A swimming beach is just a three-mile drive. Hike to the king's birthplace or a sacred heiau. Children over 12 are welcome. Smokers accepted. From $65.

Bed and Breakfast Hawaii

P.O. Box 449, Kapaa, 96746
(808) 822-7771; (800) 733-1632
FAX (808) 822-2723; e-mail: bandb@aloha.net

H1A. This home overlooking Hilo Bay was designed with bed and breakfast guests in mind. Hawaiian Continental breakfast served each morning. Each room features a private entrance, queen-size bed, and private bath. There is a guest sitting area with use of a refrigerator and microwave. Outside smoking only, please. Three-night minimum. $65-75.

Bed and Breakfast Honolulu (Statewide)

3242 Kaohinani Drive, Honolulu, 96817
(808) 595-7533; (800) 288-4666
FAX (808) 595-2030; e-mail: bnbshl@aloha.net
www.planet-hawaii.com/bnb-honolulu

BBHS 1. Experience authentic rural Hawaii from this four-acre floral nursery set halfway between Hilo and Volcanoes National Park. Enjoy the rich cultural surroundings of the spacious home of a well-known island artist couple. These hosts offer four guest rooms; two rooms share a bath and two rooms have private baths. A gourmet breakfast of fresh island fruits, breads, and Kona coffee. Must have own crib. From $65.

7 No smoking; 8 Children welcome; 9 Social drinking allowed; 10 Tennis nearby; 11 Swimming nearby; 12 Golf nearby; 13 Skiing nearby; 14 May be booked through a travel agent; 15 Handicapped accessible.

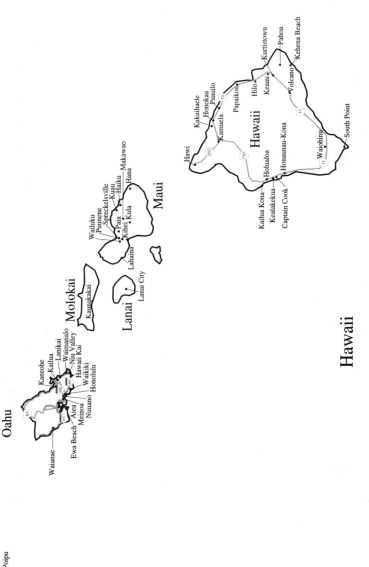

Hawaii

Kauai

Anini Beach
Princeville
Hanalei
North Shore
Kilauea
Anahola
Kapaa
Wailua
Koloa
Poipu
Kalaheo
Lawai

Oahu

Waianae
Kaneohe
Kailua
Lanikai
Waimanalo
Niu Valley
Hawaii Kai
Waikiki
Honolulu
Nuuano
Meinoa
Aiea
Ewa Beach

Molokai

Kaunakakai

Lanai

Lanai City

Maui

Wailuku
Puunene
Spreckelsville
Kuau
Paia
Haiku
Kihei Kula
Makawao
Hana
Lahaina

Hawaii

Hawi
Kukuihaele
Honokaa
Paauilo
Papaikou
Kamuela
Hilo
Keaau
Kurtistown
Pahoa
Kehena Beach
Volcano
South Point
Kailua Kona
Holualoa
Kealakekua
Captain Cook
Honaunau-Kona
Waiohinu

BBHS 2. Two miles outside of Hilo on a cliff overlooking Hilo Bay, this Hawaiian-type home has a private yard with lovely pool. Charming long-time resident offers two bedrooms. A full bath and a half-bath are reserved for bed and breakfast guests. These bathrooms are shared by the guest rooms when both rooms are booked. The yard is beautifully landscaped, and a charming tea house is by the pool. Children over 12 welcome. Smoking outside. From $60.

BBHS 8. Just five minutes into Hilo in lush tropical surroundings and comfortably furnished. Host offers a spacious and private guest studio. Separate from the main home over the garage, the studio contains a queen-size bed, two twin beds, a queen-size sleeper-sofa, private bath with shower, color cable TV and VCR, stereo, and kitchenette sink, refrigerator, microwave, and hot plate for light cooking. Guests are provided a Continental breakfast each morning. Only minutes away from the Rainbow Falls, Lyman house museum, and Hilo's farmer's market. Children and nonsmokers welcome. From $65.

BBHS 28. In cool upper Hilo on a quiet cul-de-sac overlooking Hilo Bay and the city lights. Fifteen minutes to airport and five minutes to downtown, restaurants, supermarkets and stores, and Hilo Bay. Host offers two rooms, each with private entrance and bath, and guest living room. Queen-size bed, refrigerator, and microwave in both rooms. Both are wheelchair accessible. Continental breakfast of tropical fruits and juices, Hawaiian breads and coffee, tea and herbal teas provided in the morning. Five-dollar surcharge for less than three night's stay. From $65.

BBHS 185. Two luxury oceanfront units only 25 feet from the ocean. Both units have king-size beds, private baths with tub/shower, refrigerator, microwave, toaster, coffee maker. A telephone is available in the common area. Private lanais and TV. Continental breakfast served daily. Children welcome. No smoking on the property. One nighter accepted. From $95.

HAWAII—HOLUALOA

Bed and Breakfast Honolulu (Statewide)

3242 Kaohinani Drive, Honolulu, 96817
(808) 595-7533; (800) 288-4666
FAX (808) 595-2030; e-mail: bnbshl@aloha.net
www.planet-hawaii.com/bnb-honolulu

BBHS 10. Just 15 minutes south of Kailua-Kona, this host offers three guest rooms in her newly constructed home. All rooms have private baths and entrances. From the wraparound lanai, enjoy the ocean views. After a day of shopping, swimming, or exploring the Big Island, spend the evening relaxing in the hot tub. Continental breakfast served. From $75.

Holualoa Inn

P.O. Box 222, 96725
(808) 324-1121; (800) 392-1812
FAX (808) 322-2472; e-mail: inn@aloha.net
www.konaweb.com

The Holualoa Inn is characterized as the "crown jewel" of bed and breakfasts in the state of Hawaii. Set upon a 40-acre working coffee farm and pasture land. At the elevation of 1,250 feet, the inn is cool, quiet, and comfortable. Guests may enjoy the custom-tiled swimming pool, billiard table, garden hot tub, and rooftop gazebo. Also provided to guests is a kitchenette to prepare light meals. Most outstanding features are the eucalyptus floors and the view—16 miles of the beautiful Kona coast.

NOTES: Credit cards accepted: A MasterCard; B Visa; C American Express; D Discover; E Diner's Club; F Other; 2 Personal checks accepted; 3 Lunch available; 4 Dinner available; 5 Open all year; 6 Pets welcome; 7 No smoking; 8 Children welcome; 9 Social drinking allowed; 10 Tennis nearby; 11 Swimming nearby; 12 Golf nearby; 13 Skiing nearby; 14 May be booked through a travel agent; 15 Handicapped accessible.

Hosts: Michael and Lei'a Twigg-Smith;
   Thea Brown
Rooms: 6 (PB) $135-175
Full Breakfast
Credit Cards: A, B, C, E
Notes: 2, 5, 7, 9, 10, 11, 12, 14

The Kona Escape Bed and Breakfast

78-7025 Mamalahoa Hwy, P.O. Box 197, 96725
(808) 322-3295 (phone/FAX)
www.settingsun.com/kona-escape

A newly built house on seven and one-half acres is designed with the guests' needs in mind. A large lanai encircles the main house where guests can have breakfast while enjoying the expansive view of the ocean. A grass courtyard separates the main house from the guest buildings. Each room has a private entrance, TV, queen-size or twin beds, full bath, and angled high windows that act as skylights. Relax in the hot tub under an umbrella of stars.

Host: Patricia Barlow
Rooms: $65
Continental Breakfast
Credit Cards: None
Notes: 2, 5, 8, 9, 10, 11, 12, 14, 15

HAWAII—HONAUNAU

Bed and Breakfast Honolulu (Statewide)

3242 Kaohinani Drive, Honolulu, 96817
(808) 595-7533; (800) 288-4666
FAX (808) 595-2030; e-mail: bnbshl@aloha.net
www.planet-hawaii.com/bnb-honolulu

BBHS 3. Above the city of refuge, this host offers a downstairs studio apartment with private entrance, private bath, and color cable TV. In addition to a Continental breakfast, there is also a small refrigerator, microwave, and coffeepot for light cooking. The unit opens out onto a cool, quiet private half-acre of gardens. Only three miles to the closest beach for snorkeling, 25 miles from airport, 15 minutes to Kona village. From $65.

HAWAII—HONOKAA

Bed and Breakfast Honolulu (Statewide)

3242 Kaohinani Drive, Honolulu, 96817
(808) 595-7533; (800) 288-4666
FAX (808) 595-2030; e-mail: bnbshl@aloha.net
www.planet-hawaii.com/bnb-honolulu

BBHS 181. At the 1200-foot level on a five-acre plantation estate with ocean views on three sides, this home offers three luxury accommodations. The master suite has a king-size bed with fireplace, color TV, large lanai, and adjoining double bedroom via the private full baths, color TV, and views of the gardens. The home itself has 12-foot ceilings, a den with color TV, wet bar, adjoining billiard room, and library overlooking the formal garden. After the Continental breakfast, guests may wish to enjoy the basketball or tennis courts. Laundry service and crib available as well. From $105.

HAWAII—KAILUA-KONA

Bed and Breakfast Hawaii

P.O. Box 449, Kapaa, 96746
(808) 822-7771; (800) 733-1632
FAX (808) 822-2723; e-mail: bandb@aloha.net

H10. A spacious home surrounded by tropical foliage. A five-minute drive from the ocean. The downstairs accommodation includes a private lanai with an ocean view and a separate entrance through glass doors to the bedroom. Mini-refrigerator, microwave, TV, and telephone. Continental breakfast. No smoking. Two-night minimum stay. $70.

Bed and Breakfast Honolulu (Statewide)

3242 Kaohinani Drive, Honolulu, 96817
(808) 595-7533; (800) 288-4666
FAX (808) 595-2030; e-mail: bnbshl@aloha.net
www.planet-hawaii.com/bnb-honolulu

NOTES: Credit cards accepted: A MasterCard; B Visa; C American Express; D Discover; E Diner's Club; F Other; 2 Personal checks accepted; 3 Lunch available; 4 Dinner available; 5 Open all year; 6 Pets welcome;

BBHS 184. One bedroom with queen-size bed, private entrance, and bath. Kitchenette (microwave, refrigerator, coffeepot, etc.), large sitting room with color cable TV. Pool access, use of washer/dryer, all antiques, very deluxe. Sleeps two to four people. Tennis court, hot tub, pool access. Continental breakfast. Futons available. From $100.

Hale Maluhia Country Inn Bed and Breakfast

76-770 Hualalai Road, 96740
(808) 329-5773; (800) 559-6627
FAX (808) 326-5487
e-mail:hawaii-inns@aloha.net
www.hawaii-bnb.com/halemal.html

Gracious upcountry Swiss Family Robinson living in the heart of the Kona recreational paradise. In beautiful Holualoa coffee land. Breakfast lovers' buffet. Large rooms, private baths, good beds, and Japanese stone spa, deep with massage jets. Old Hawaii living with native woods, open-beam ceilings, koa cabinets, big lanais, four common areas, and a stream with waterfalls and lily ponds. Two and one-half miles from the Kailua-Kona village; easy (KOA) airport access. Cable TV/VCR with movie library. No smoking inside buildings.

Hosts: Ken and Ann Smith
Rooms: 5 (PB) From $65
Cottages: 2 (PB) From $125
Full Breakfast
Credit Cards: A, B, C, D
Notes: 2, 5, 7, 8, 9, 10, 11, 12, 13, 14, 15

HAWAII—KAMUELA

Bed and Breakfast Honolulu (Statewide)

3242 Kaohinani Drive, Honolulu, 96817
(808) 595-7533; (800) 288-4666
FAX (808) 595-2030; e-mail: bnbshl@aloha.net
www.planet-hawaii.com/bnb-honolulu

BBHS 4. This quaint bed and breakfast getaway is to be found at the end of a three-mile drive thru the pasturelands of upcountry Hawaii. Three guest rooms with one private and two shared baths. A hearty healthy Continental breakfast is served. Adults only. Smoking permitted outside. From $75.

BBHS 9. On Kalaki Road, this beautiful two-bedroom suite borders the ranch lands of Mauna Kea. The two-bedroom guest unit is on the first floor with its own private entrance, fireplace, full bath, and full kitchen. Two-night minimum. Smoking outside only. The home was built in 1988, and is three miles from Kamuela town center and 14 miles from the island's best white-sand beaches and Waipio Valley. From $65.

Kamuela Inn

P.O. Box 1994, 96743
(808) 885-4243; FAX (808) 885-8857

Comfortable, cozy rooms and suites with private baths, with or without kitchenettes, all with cable TV. Continental breakfast served on a sunny lanai each morning. In a quiet, peaceful setting near shops, parks, museums, and restaurants. Hawaii's white sand beaches, golf, and valley and mountain tours are only minutes away.

Host: Carolyn Cascavilla
Rooms: 31 (PB) $59-185
Continental Breakfast
Credit Cards: A, B, C, D, E
Notes: 2, 5, 8, 9, 10, 11, 12, 13, 14

HAWAII—KEAAU

Rainforest Retreat

HCR 1, Box 5655, 96749
(808) 982-9601 (location); (888) 244-8074
FAX (808) 966-6898; (808) 966-7712 (nursery)
e-mail: orchids@ilhawaii.net

Relax and enjoy country paradise. Experience an alternative retreat. Lori practices acupuncture and Chinese herbal medicine.

7 No smoking; 8 Children welcome; 9 Social drinking allowed; 10 Tennis nearby; 11 Swimming nearby; 12 Golf nearby; 13 Skiing nearby; 14 May be booked through a travel agent; 15 Handicapped accessible.

Rejuvenate oneself this trip. The peaceful relaxing atmosphere on the slopes of Kileua Volcano eases one's body and spirit. Soak away pain and tension in the hot tub. Revel in comfort and privacy. The guest unit is amidst native forests and wild orchids. Most units offer private bath, king-size bed, and kitchenettes. Near Hilo, thermal springs, and Volcanoes National Park.

Hosts: Lori and Mark Campbell
Rooms: 6 (PB) $55-165
Full Breakfast
Credit Cards: A, B, C, D
Notes: 5, 8, 9, 10, 11, 12, 13, 14

HAWAII—KEALAKEKUA-KONA

Merryman's Bed and Breakfast

P.O. Box 474, 96750
(808) 323-2276; (800) 545-4390
FAX (808) 323-3749

Beautiful and quiet ocean-view upcountry estate in Kealakekua/Captain Cook. Minutes from the best snorkeling, historical sites, activities. Enjoy spacious, charming rooms, pretty linens, fresh flowers, cable TV. Complimentary Hawaiian breakfast, Jacuzzi. AAA-rated three diamonds.

Hosts: Don and Penny Merryman
Rooms: 4 (2 PB; 2 SB) $75-125
Full Breakfast
Credit Cards: A, B, D
Notes: 2, 5, 9, 10, 11, 12, 14

HAWAII—KEHENA BEACH

Kalani Oceanside Retreat

Rural Route 2, Box 4500, 96778
(808) 965-7828; (800) 800-6886
e-mail: kalani@kalani.com
www.kalani.com

Experience the only coastal lodging within Hawaii's largest conservation area. Kalani Honua, meaning "Harmony of Heaven and Earth," is the ideal location for culture and relaxation. Private cot-

tages with ocean views. Three delicious, healthful meals served each day. Take an ongoing class. Enjoy a massage or relax at the spa. Many natural wonders nearby, including a black-sand beach, warm springs, and Volcanoes National Park. Limited smoking.

Hosts: Richard Koob and Dottie Kaiser
Rooms: 30 (11 PB; 19 SB) $75-130
Camping: $20-25
Full Breakfast
Credit Cards: A, B, C, E, F
Notes: 3, 4, 5, 8, 9 10, 11, 14, 15

HAWAII—KONA

Bed and Breakfast Honolulu (Statewide)

3242 Kaohinani Drive, Honolulu, 96817
(808) 595-7533; (800) 288-4666
FAX (808) 595-2030; e-mail: bnbshl@aloha.net
www.planet-hawaii.com/bnb-honolulu

BBHS 13. Kona Sundown is conveniently three miles from Kailua-Kona, off All'l Drive. The hosts offers three units. One studio has light cooking, twin beds, TV, and an ocean view. The second studio has a double bed, light cooking. There is also a two-bedroom apartment, one room with queen-size bed, the other with twin beds. Full kitchen, large living/dining area. All units have access to a washer/dryer. Beautiful sunsets. Less than two miles to a swimming beach, but only one-half mile to the ocean. Host speaks German. From $55.

BBHS 182. The detached 480-square-foot cottage is one-half mile from the quaint village of Kailua-Kona. Equipped with full-size refrigerator, microwave, toaster oven, coffee maker, blender, queen-size bed, queen-size Hide-a-Bed, TV, and stereo. The cottage will sleep four comfortably as well as provide a lovely garden setting to enjoy the Continental breakfast that is provided as well. Tennis courts available in subdivision. Children welcome.

NOTES: Credit cards accepted: A MasterCard; B Visa; C American Express; D Discover; E Diner's Club; F Other; 2 Personal checks accepted; 3 Lunch available; 4 Dinner available; 5 Open all year; 6 Pets welcome;

HAWAII—KUKUIHAELA

Bed and Breakfast Honolulu (Statewide)

3242 Kaohinani Drive, Honolulu, 96817
(808) 595-7533; (800) 288-4666
FAX (808) 595-2030; e-mail: bnbshl@aloha.net
www.planet-hawaii.com/bnb-honolulu

BBHS 11. On more than four acres overlooking majestic Waipio Bay and the Hamakua Cliffs, waterfalls, and tropical valleys. Host offers two new units. Both units have a private bath with tub, private entrance, wraparound lanai, kitchenette with two-burner range, refrigerator, sink, microwave, and coffee supplies. Continental breakfast fixings are stocked in kitchen area. Both have living/dining areas with ceiling fan. There are many nearby trails, or go for a swim at the nearby black-sand beach. From $85.

HAWAII—PAAUILO

Suds' Acres Bed and Breakfast

43-1973 Paauilo Mauka Road, P.O. Box 277, 96776
(808) 776-1611 (phone/FAX); (800) 735-3262
e-mail: aphesis@interpac.net
www.hawaii-bnb.com/sudsac.html

Suds' Acres Bed and Breakfast is on a six-acre macadamia nut farm on the Hamakua coast of the Big Island of Hawaii. There is a cozy two-bedroom rustic cottage that sleeps five. In the main house the privacy of the ground floor is available for up to seven people, with a private entrance, kitchenette, bath, fireplace, and wheelchair accessibility. The upstairs includes a separate bedroom with double bed and private bath. Continental breakfast. Color TVs. Smoking permitted outside only.

Rooms: 3 (PB) $65
Continental Breakfast
Credit Cards: A, B, C, D, E, F
Notes: 5, 7, 8, 10, 11, 12, 14, 15

HAWAII—PAHOA

Bed and Breakfast Honolulu (Statewide)

3242 Kaohinani Drive, Honolulu, 96817
(808) 595-7533; (800) 288-4666
FAX (808) 595-2030; e-mail: bnbshl@aloha.net
www.planet-hawaii.com/bnb-honolulu

BBHS 7. A beautiful new home in the Puna rain forest, 23 miles from Hilo. Four miles to Pahoa, a historic mill town. Many fruit farms in the area. Host is very friendly and invites guests to enjoy a cup of Kona coffee or a tropical fruit drink in the comfort of her living room or enjoy the spa. Spacious bedrooms with either two double beds or a double bed and a twin bed. Both with private bath. Breakfast includes locally grown fruit as well as a wide selection of breakfast foods. From $60.

BBHS 186. The budget traveler has a choice of two bed and breakfast rooms. One room has an attached full bathroom. The second room shares a bath with the hosts. There is a microwave on the guest lanai. Guests may use hosts' refrigerator (limited space). Twenty-five miles from Hilo. Smoking outside only. TV shared with hosts. Hosts are Unitarians. Full breakfast. From $40.

HAWAII—PAPAIKOU

Bed and Breakfast Honolulu (Statewide)

3242 Kaohinani Drive, Honolulu, 96817
(808) 595-7533; (800) 288-4666
FAX (808) 595-2030; e-mail: bnbshl@aloha.net
www.planet-hawaii.com/bnb-honolulu

BBHS 15. This host has a large cedar home with four guest rooms with private and shared baths. Enjoy the tropical view, and the singing stream from each of the guest rooms. All have private lanais. The

7 No smoking; 8 Children welcome; 9 Social drinking allowed; 10 Tennis nearby; 11 Swimming nearby; 12 Golf nearby; 13 Skiing nearby; 14 May be booked through a travel agent; 15 Handicapped accessible.

home is on a one-half acre lot with tropical surroundings, but it's only a short walk into the small town of Papaikou for restaurants and shopping. There is a common room for the bed and breakfast travelers to enjoy TV, fireplace, or the grand piano. Children 12 and up, as well as smokers, are welcome. Hearty breakfast served. There is also an outside dog. From $65.

Our Place Papaikou's Bed and Breakfast

P.O. Box 469, 96781-0469
(808) 964-5250; (800) 245-5250
e-mail: rplace@aloha.net
www.best.com/~ourplace

A private, lush, tropical retreat. Four miles north of Hilo, Our Place Papaikou's Bed and Breakfast is a cedar home set amid a lush tropical garden overlooking Kapua stream. The great room, splendid with its cathedral ceiling, has a library, fireplace, grand piano, and cable TV for guests to enjoy. Four rooms share a Hawaiian-style lanai that looks out over Kapua stream. Nearby attractions include surfing and snorkeling at beaches and ocean parks, the Hawaii Tropical Botanical Garden, Akaka Falls, and Hawaii Volcanoes National Park. Continental plus breakfast. Children over 12 welcome. Smoking permitted on lanai only.

Hosts: Ouida Trahan and Sharon Miller
Rooms: 4 (1 PB; 3 SB) $55-90
Continental Breakfast
Credit Cards: A, B
Notes: 5, 7, 9, 10, 11, 12, 13, 14

Bed and Breakfast Honolulu (Statewide)

3242 Kaohinani Drive, Honolulu, 96817
(808) 595-7533; (800) 288-4666
FAX (808) 595-2030; e-mail: bnbshl@aloha.net
www.planet-hawaii.com/bnb-honolulu

BBHS 180. Midway between Kona and volcano on the Big Island of Hawaii, this bed and breakfast offers guests comfortable, attractive, quiet rooms. The host offers one room with a private bath and entrance with a private porch, and a second room with a private bath. Enjoy a full breakfast on the wraparound lanai and take in the flowers and view of South Point and the ocean. Explore Kalae (South Point) site of the first Polynesian landings in the islands. Enjoy spectacular views of the cliffs and shoreland. Hike to famous green-sand beaches from South Point road. About one and one-half hours south of the Kona airport. From $55.

Bed and Breakfast Hawaii

P.O. Box 449, Kapaa, 96746
(808) 822-7771; (800) 733-1632
FAX (808) 822-2723; e-mail: bandb@aloha.net

H51. Just two miles from Volcanoes National Park. Helpful hosts offer a king-size bedroom with its own entrance and private bath and a futon for a third person. Great breakfasts are served every morning. $70-95.

Bed and Breakfast Honolulu (Statewide)

3242 Kaohinani Drive, Honolulu, 96817
(808) 595-7533; (800) 288-4666
FAX (808) 595-2030; e-mail: bnbshl@aloha.net
www.planet-hawaii.com/bnb-honolulu

BBHS 19. Positively charming, restored turn-of-the-century two-bedroom guest

NOTES: Credit cards accepted: A MasterCard; B Visa; C American Express; D Discover; E Diner's Club; F Other; 2 Personal checks accepted; 3 Lunch available; 4 Dinner available; 5 Open all year; 6 Pets welcome;

cottage with wood-burning fireplace. Nestled on two and one-half acres of beautifully landscaped property. One bedroom has a four-poster bed and the other has two twin beds. Some breakfast fixings provided. TV/VCR, beautifully furnished and maintained. Smoking permitted outside only. Two-night minimum stay. From $85.

BBHS 121. At the 3,800-foot elevation, this historic missionary home, built about 1886, has a large botanical garden that blooms year-round. The main house has a room on each of the floors. All guests share the two and one-half baths, Hawaiian library, and living room with TV. The host can provide picnic coolers, flashlights, and specially prepared maps and hiking guides for day or night trips. Their specialty is a full "all you can eat" breakfast and all the macadamia nuts guests can eat (in season). Children, smokers, and one-night stays welcome. Cat in residence. From $55.

BBHS 183. Nestled in the cool higher elevation at about the 3,500 foot level. Hostess offers two guest rooms in her home. One room has a queen-size bed plus a double futon. The other has a king-size bed. Both rooms have electric heat, private entrance, bath, and TV. Telephone is available for local calls. Continental plus breakfast served each morning. Guests may socialize in the common area. Just two miles to the national park. Restaurants and shops just minutes away. Families and one-night stays welcome. Seven-person hot tub is available.

Chalet Kilauea— The Inn at Volcano

P.O. Box 998, Volcano Village, 96785
(808) 967-7786; (800) 937-7786
FAX (808) 967-8660 or (800) 577-1849
e-mail: innkeeper@volcano-hawaii.com
www.volcano-hawaii.com

This inn at 3,500 feet amid the lush splendor of a tropical rain forest is near Volcanoes National Park. Choose from superior theme rooms and suites including the Treehouse Suite and separate spacious vacation homes. Awaken to a candlelit, three-course full gourmet breakfast featuring international and local cuisine. Enjoy afternoon tea in the living room filled with stunning and fascinating art from around the world or outside on the huge covered veranda. All units have private entrances and private baths, featuring marble Jacuzzi tubs. Other features include fireplaces, outside Jacuzzi, TV, VCR, and a video, music, and book library, tropical flower arrangements, and plush robes.

Hosts: Lisha and Brian Crawford
Rooms: 12 (PB) $125-395
Full Breakfast
Credit Cards: A, B, C, D, E, F
Notes: 2, 5, 7, 8, 9, 10, 11, 12, 14

Kilauea Lodge

Kilauea Lodge

P.O. Box 116, 96785
(808) 967-7366; FAX (808) 967-7367

Charming mountain lodge one mile from Volcanoes National Park. Full-service dining room with excellent wine list. Full breakfast readies guests for an active day of hiking and viewing the wonders of Pele, the volcano goddess. Private baths. Some rooms and cottages have fireplaces. Common area.

Rooms: 14 (PB) $95-145
Full Breakfast
Credit Cards: A, B, C
Notes: 2, 4, 5, 7, 8, 9, 12, 14, 15

---

7 No smoking; 8 Children welcome; 9 Social drinking allowed; 10 Tennis nearby; 11 Swimming nearby; 12 Golf nearby; 13 Skiing nearby; 14 May be booked through a travel agent; 15 Handicapped accessible.

The Lodge at Volcano

The Lodge at Volcano

P.O. Box 998, 96785
(808) 967-7244; (800) 736-7140
FAX (808) 967-8660 or (800) 577-1849
e-mail: innkeeper@volcano-hawaii.com
www.volcano-hawaii.com

The Lodge at Volcano is a seven-bedroom, six-bathroom, ranch-style lodge on 30 beautiful acres in upcountry Volcano. On the premises guests can enjoy an extensive trail throughout the native fern forest, wrap-around covered deck with eight-person Jacuzzi, spacious living rooms with fire-places, and game room with TV/VCR and video library. Mornings start with a delight-ful, hearty breakfast featuring local tropical fruit, assorted cereals, breads, waffles, juice, and Kona coffee.

Host: Lisha and Brian Crawford
Rooms: 7 (PB) $85-125
Continental Breakfast
Credit Cards: A, B, C, D, E, F
Notes: 2, 5, 7, 8, 9, 10, 11, 12, 14

Volcano Bed and Breakfast

P.O. Box 998, 96785
(808) 967-7779; (800) 736-7140; (800) 577-1849
FAX (808) 967-8660
e-mail: innkeeper@volcano-hawaii.com
www.volcano-hawaii.com

This renovated 1912 three-story home, on landscaped grounds, is an excellent choice for travelers looking for low-priced com-fortable accommodations. Guests are invited to relax and enjoy a reading room, cable TV, VCR, and sunroom. Just five minutes away is Volcanoes National Park offering year-round opportunities for hiking, bird watch-ing, and spectacular lava viewing.

Host: Henry Haan
Rooms: 5 (SB) $45-65
Continental Breakfast
Credit Cards: A, B, C, D, E, F
Notes: 2, 5, 7, 8, 9, 10, 11, 12, 14

HAWAII—WAIOHINU

Hawaii South Point Banyan Tree House

Mamalahoa Highway
(888) 451-0880

The newly constructed guest house is nes-tled up inside a huge Chinese banyan tree in the picturesque and historic village of Waiohinu. The South Point Banyan Tree House is next to a classic Missionary-era Kauaha'ao Congregational Church (c. 1841) on the corner of Pinao Street and the Mamalahoa Highway. This luxury designer studio features a unique Lexan see-through roof, giving an airy, open feeling as guests look up into the dense canopy of the mas-sive banyan tree by day or enjoy the subtle lighting of its splendor at night. The tree house is conveniently near Hawaii Volca-noes National Park, the massive cliffs, and the green-sand beach of South Point, as well as Punalu'u's black-sand beach where snorkelers enjoy swimming among the giant sea turtles.

Hosts: Ululani and Kamaka Kelekolio
Rooms: 1 (PB) $110
Continental Breakfast
Credit Cards: None
Notes: 2, 5, 8, 9, 11, 12

KAUAI—ANAHOLA

Bed and Breakfast Honolulu (Statewide)

3242 Kaohinani Drive, Honolulu, 96817
(808) 595-7533; (800) 288-4666
FAX (808) 595-2030; e-mail: bnbshl@aloha.net
www.planet-hawaii.com/bnb-honolulu

NOTES: Credit cards accepted: A MasterCard; B Visa; C American Express; D Discover; E Diner's Club; F Other; 2 Personal checks accepted; 3 Lunch available; 4 Dinner available; 5 Open all year; 6 Pets welcome;

BBHS 60. This host has a two-bedroom, one-bath cottage. There is a fully equipped kitchen. Living room has a garden view. There is a large deck. This property is a two-minute walk to a long sandy beach. Also on this property are two 500-square-foot one-bedroom apartments with kitchenette, living room, private bath. Ocean view from one of these, mountain view from the other. Both of the apartments have use of a large gazebo and an indoor/outdoor kitchen, wet bar, and barbecue. Ocean view from the gazebo. From $85.

BBHS 63. Enjoy a peaceful vacation or a romantic honeymoon in this completely private studio. Color cable TV. Laundry facilities, mini-refrigerator, wet bar, complete kitchenette. Continental breakfast fixings provided for guests to have at their leisure. The bath has a tub/shower combo. Central on the island for easy access to all sightseeing and touring. The beach is directly across the road. Reef protected for beautiful swimming or sunning on the white sands. Sit in own private yard and enjoy the tropical birds, flowers, trees, and the beautiful mountain view, or take a walk in the hills and valleys just behind the home. Adults preferred. Smoking outside only. The host has no pets. From $75.

BBHS 176. Luxury bed and breakfast on a seven-acre estate with tropical fruit and flower garden with breathtaking ocean views and elegantly furnished suites with Indonesian art and furniture. Aloha Mana is just steps away from the Allomanu Bay beach and a short drive away from recreational activities. Accommodates one to five people in the guest house with ocean view, and the farm house suite with lovely garden/waterfall view is for one to two people only. Units each have a private balcony, telephone, TV/VCR, kitchenette. Homegrown Continental breakfast. Use of outdoor Jacuzzi. From $100.

KAUAI—HANALEI

Bed and Breakfast Honolulu (Statewide)

3242 Kaohinani Drive, Honolulu, 96817
(808) 595-7533; (800) 288-4666
FAX (808) 595-2030; e-mail: bnbshl@aloha.net
www.planet-hawaii.com/bnb-honolulu

BBHS 73. Breathtaking views of lush mountains, tropical jungles, cascading waterfalls, and Hanalei Bay just 100 yards away. This host offers three guest rooms in her elegantly decorated home. On the second floor are two rooms, one with a private bath off the hall and the other with a private bath and TV. On the third floor is the honeymoon suite with extra-large private bath. All are welcome to enjoy the views from the 1,000-square-foot wraparound, second-floor lanai. Continental breakfast. Two-night minimum stay. From $65.

KAUAI—KALAHEO

Bed and Breakfast Honolulu (Statewide)

3242 Kaohinani Drive, Honolulu, 96817
(808) 595-7533; (800) 288-4666
FAX (808) 595-2030; e-mail: bnbshl@aloha.net
www.planet-hawaii.com/bnb-honolulu

BBHS 61. Three delightful, self-contained, cottages adjacent to a custom-built home on landscaped half acre. These unique cottages feature antique stained and leaded windows from New Zealand, plus all the comforts of home. Fully furnished, carpeted, full kitchens, TV. The host also offers a 440-square-foot attached studio with full kitchen. Ten minutes by car to the golden beaches and playground of the sunny south shores of Poipu. Five minutes to Kukuiolono golf course. Hot tub. Tennis nearby. From $65.

BBHS 70. Minutes from the quaint town of Kalaheo, surrounded by open meadows with bananas and palm trees that frame the ocean views. This host offers two private units in her lovely home. The Seaview Suite is a spacious one bedroom with a complete kitchen. There is a queen-size and a single bed in the extra-large, tiled bedroom. Also, cable TV/VCR, stereo, and telephone. Can be combined with the Ti room for larger parties. Extra futons are available. From $60.

KAUAI—KAPAA

Bed and Breakfast Hawaii

P.O. Box 449, Kapaa, 96746
(808) 822-7771; (800) 733-1632
FAX (808) 822-2723; e-mail: bandb@aloha.net

K6. These three fresh and comfortable accommodations overlook a horse pasture skirted by Opaekaa stream. Waterfalls are often visible in the distance from the lanai. Private entrances to all suites decorated in wicker and rattan. All rooms feature king- or queen-size beds, kitchen areas, and private baths. Smoking outside only. $60-100.

Bed and Breakfast Honolulu (Statewide)

3242 Kaohinani Drive, Honolulu, 96817
(808) 595-7533; (800) 288-4666
FAX (808) 595-2030; e-mail: bnbshl@aloha.net
www.planet-hawaii.com/bnb-honolulu

BBHS 23. Nestled behind the Sleeping Giant mountain on a lovely landscaped one-half acre, this host offers six guest rooms in her bed and breakfast home, all with private baths. Three of the rooms are off the common area with cable TV, VCR, and kitchenette for light cooking. In the other wing of the home are three other rooms with private entrances. One room has cable TV, and all three have refrigerators, microwaves, dishes, etc. Continental breakfast. From $55.

BBHS 71. In a friendly neighborhood, atop a country mountainside plateau, this host

offers two units. The first unit has private bath and entrance, shower/tub, living room with sofa bed. Both units have lanais, mini wet bars, refrigerators, microwave ovens, and color TV. A gazebo with a Jacuzzi and sauna is available for guests' relaxation. No smoking. From $75.

BBHS 171. Adjacent to Opaeka'a Falls is one of the most beautiful bed and breakfast homes on the island. It has three wonderfully appointed rooms and a studio. Two guest rooms share a bath. The third room has a private bath. All units have ceiling fans, full carpeting, and are tastefully decorated with original artwork. Continental breakfast. The studio has a kitchenette, TV, and ceiling fan. No breakfast is provided for the studio. Hot tub. Children over 16 welcome. From $70.

KAUAI—KILAUEA

Bed and Breakfast Hawaii

P.O. Box 449, Kapaa, 96746
(808) 822-7771; (800) 733-1632
FAX (808) 822-2723; e-mail: bandb@aloha.net

K15. Hale Li'i is mauka (mountainside) of the rural area of Kilauea town, just minutes from the beach. A detached private cottage nestled in the gardens of a three-acre citrus orchard offers a king-size bed with an additional futon available for a third guest or child. The cottage has a well-equipped efficiency kitchenette stocked daily with breakfast basics. Other amenities include TV/VCR, telephone, fans, and washer with private clothesline area. Hosts also offer guests use of beach gear. Outside smoking only. Ten dollars for each additional guest. $85.

K48. Hosts offer a separate Hawaiian country cottage with two bedrooms, full kitchen, dining room, and living room. From the two decks, guests have views of the mountain, valley, and the ocean in the

NOTES: Credit cards accepted: A MasterCard; B Visa; C American Express; D Discover; E Diner's Club; F Other; 2 Personal checks accepted; 3 Lunch available; 4 Dinner available; 5 Open all year; 6 Pets welcome;

distance. The bedrooms offer queen- and full-size beds and hosts can provide a Port-a-crib. A small library area offers books of local interest and novels and the living room is equipped with TV/VCR. Enjoy the backyard with mango, lychee, coconut, jabong, and other local fruit trees and flowers. A welcome basket of fruit, coffees, and breads is provided. Children are welcome. No smoking. Three-night minimum stay. Ten dollars for each additional guest. $75.

Bed and Breakfast Honolulu (Statewide)

3242 Kaohinani Drive, Honolulu, 96817
(808) 595-7533; (800) 288-4666
FAX (808) 595-2030; e-mail: bnbshl@aloha.net
www.planet-hawaii.com/bnb-honolulu

BBHS 64. This magnificent split-level home is overlooking a fresh-water stream and pond on five acres. The Pineapple Room features a seven-foot round bed and a private full bath; the Guava Room has a canopied bed, sitting area with table/chairs, private bath and entrance; the Mango Room has two beds and a shared bath; and the Papaya Room has a shared full bath. Each room has TV and telephone. Continental breakfast. Kitchen privileges. Washer/dryer, surf and boogie boards, snorkle gear, and gas barbecue. Fifteen-minute walk to secret beach. From $55.

BBHS 174. Spacious, cozy one-bedroom apartment hideaway on the edge of the Kilauea River valley. Telephone, washer/dryer, TV/VCR. Kitchenette is fully equipped with the exception of a cook top/oven. Beautiful valley views. Continental breakfast served daily. Two miles to beaches. Smoking outside only. One-nighters accepted at $90. From $80.

BBHS 175. Truly a gorgeous, peaceful setting. On two jungle-like acres including the running river that will lull guests to sleep.

Studio one sleeps three and has a full kitchen, full bath, living room, bedroom, TV/VCR, telephone, lanai overlooking the river. Studio two sleeps three in a spacious one room with a bed, double futon sofa, kitchenette with small refrigerator, microwave, coffee maker, TV/VCR, private lanai overlooking the river, telephone. Continental breakfast. Two-night minimum stay. Smoking permitted outside only. Fifteen dollars for extra guests. $80-100.

Kai Mana Bed and Breakfast

P.O. Box 612, 96754
(808) 828-1280; (800) 837-1782
FAX (808) 828-6670; e-mail: datine@aloha.net
www.nataraj.com/npweb/km.html

Shakti Gawain's home on Kauai. Magnificent suites and cottages with kitchen and bath on five luscious acres overlooking secluded beach. Completely remodeled and comfortable. Massage, acupuncture, etc., on-site. Trail to Secret Beach!

Hosts: Sara Cash and Chris Mildwater
Rooms: 4 (PB) $95-150
Continental Breakfast
Credit Cards: None
Notes: 2, 5, 7, 9, 10, 11, 12, 14

KAUAI—KOLOA

Bed and Breakfast Hawaii

P.O. Box 449, Kapaa, 96746
(808) 822-7771; (800) 733-1632
FAX (808) 822-2723; e-mail: bandb@aloha.net

K51-KOLOA. This private guest cottage is in the hills of Omao on the south shore just minutes away from sunny Poipu and some of the most magnificent beaches in the world. The secluded lanai enjoys views of the majestic mountains and ocean. The cottage offers a large bedroom with queen-size bed, private bath (shower only), sitting room that includes TV/VCR, and a full kitchen. Guests have a choice of breakfasts or no breakfast at a reduced rate. Smoking outside only. An additional $15 for extra guest. $80.

---

7 No smoking; 8 Children welcome; 9 Social drinking allowed; 10 Tennis nearby; 11 Swimming nearby; 12 Golf nearby; 13 Skiing nearby; 14 May be booked through a travel agent; 15 Handicapped accessible.

Bed and Breakfast Honolulu (Statewide)

3242 Kaohinani Drive, Honolulu, 96817
(808) 595-7533; (800) 288-4666
FAX (808) 595-2030; e-mail: bnbshl@aloha.net
www.planet-hawaii.com/bnb-honolulu

BBHS 67. Only four miles from sunny Poipu, this 500-square-foot one-bedroom garage apartment tropically decorated with rattan furniture has beamed ceilings, a wraparound lanai with panoramic views of Poipu and Black Mountain. The bedroom has a bed and the living room has a sofa bed. A full kitchen is stocked with breakfast fixings, TV/VCR, cassette stereo, telephone, snorkel gear, beach chairs, cooler, boogie boards, and golf clubs. Outdoor shower. From $65.

BBHS 131. This host is between the two ends of the island for easy sightseeing. The host offers a guest room with twin beds, private bath and entrance. Continental breakfast is provided. Small refrigerator, color TV, private patio. The sandy beaches of Poipu are an easy 15-20 minute walk away. Two-night minimum stay. Outside cat. Smokers welcome. From $55.

KAUAI—LAWAI

Bed and Breakfast Honolulu (Statewide)

3242 Kaohinani Drive, Honolulu, 96817
(808) 595-7533; (800) 288-4666
FAX (808) 595-2030; e-mail: bnbshl@aloha.net
www.planet-hawaii.com/bnb-honolulu

BBHS 62. Victoria Place overlooks thick jungle, whispering cane fields, and the beckoning Pacific. It's an oasis of pampered comfort and privacy for travelers. Three guest rooms in one wing of the spacious skylit home open directly through glass doors onto a pool surrounded by flowering walls. The Calla Lily Room has a full bath off the hallway and makes an ideal romantic getaway. The Raindrop Room is for one person with a private half-bath. The Shell Room has a private bath and a portable ramp for wheelchair use. Non-smoking house. From $65.

BBHS 170. Just 10 minutes from beautiful Poipu Beach. Terrific one-bedroom cottage with full kitchen, living room, dining area, and telephone. Mountain view from dining area. Covered lanai. Continental breakfast provided in unit. Smoking permitted. From $65.

BBHS 172. Secluded high up in the Lawai Valley, these hosts offer three suites in their home. All three suites have private entrances, queen-size beds, private baths, small refrigerators, ceiling fans. A telephone and a fax are available for guests' use. There is a reading room with TV/VCR with plenty of videos. Island delights are served each morning, fresh from local suppliers. Prepared as available or to suit guests' own dietetic or nutritional needs. There is no cooking. One nighters accepted. Smoking outside only. Only 20 minutes to Poipu Beach, and 25 minutes to the airport. From $75.

KAUAI—POIPU

Bed and Breakfast Hawaii

P.O. Box 449, Kapaa, 96746
(808) 822-7771; (800) 733-1632
FAX (808) 822-2723; e-mail: bandb@aloha.net

K22. This plantation house offers two lovely rooms with private baths. Relax in the screened-in lanai or in the common living room. Continental breakfast. Two-night minimum stay is preferred. Smoking outside. $70-75.

K24. Poipu Plantation is not really a bed and breakfast accommodation because as many as 20 people can be accommodated in

---

NOTES: Credit cards accepted: A MasterCard; B Visa; C American Express; D Discover; E Diner's Club; F Other; 2 Personal checks accepted; 3 Lunch available; 4 Dinner available; 5 Open all year; 6 Pets welcome;

the small inn. Nine rooms feature a variety of bed sizes, face the garden or ocean, and have their own telephone lines. Two units are two-bedroom, two-bath suites. A barbecue, sunning area, and laundry facilities are available. $85-125.

Bed and Breakfast Honolulu (Statewide)

3242 Kaohinani Drive, Honolulu, 96817
(808) 595-7533; (800) 288-4666
FAX (808) 595-2030; e-mail: bnbshl@aloha.net
www.planet-hawaii.com/bnb-honolulu

BBHS 173. The beautiful Harbor Room has a ceiling fan, stereo, TV/VCR, refrigerator, and private bath. Sitting right on the water's edge with panoramic views of the ocean, boat harbor, Spouting Horn, Mt. Kahill, Black Mountain, and lush cane fields, all from guests' own private balcony. A wonderful breakfast served daily. No smoking on premises. Rates slightly lower for stay of three nights. From $115.

KAUAI—WAILUA

Bed and Breakfast Honolulu (Statewide)

3242 Kaohinani Drive, Honolulu, 96817
(808) 595-7533; (800) 288-4666
FAX (808) 595-2030; e-mail: bnbshl@aloha.net
www.planet-hawaii.com/bnb-honolulu

BBHS 66. Wailua country bed and breakfast offers guests a personal touch of Hawaiian country hospitality. On two acres tucked behind the famous Sleeping Giant mountain. This host offers several guest rooms, studio apartment, and a two-bedroom cottage. Both private units have been newly redecorated. Breakfast is served daily. Fifteen minutes from the airport, five minutes to swimming beaches, restaurants, golf courses, shopping. From $65.

BBHS 74. Mohala Ke Ola is high above the lush Wailua River. It offers three spacious

guest rooms with Continental breakfast. Private and shared baths. The magnificent mountain and waterfall views wait to greet guests. Relax around the pool and Jacuzzi. Enjoy the gardens and valley views. Host speaks Japanese and does professional massage. One-quarter mile to Opaeka'a Falls. Three-minute drive to the beach. Nonsmoking home. From $65.

LANAI—LANAI CITY

Bed and Breakfast Honolulu (Statewide)

3242 Kaohinani Drive, Honolulu, 96817
(808) 595-7533; (800) 288-4666
FAX (808) 595-2030; e-mail: bnbshl@aloha.net
www.planet-hawaii.com/bnb-honolulu

BBHS 141. This host offers two bed and breakfast rooms with private baths. Continental breakfast. The guests are welcome to use the TV in the living room and the kitchen. Ten minutes from the airport, 15 minutes from the beach, and within walking distance of the community recreation center with pool. There is a shuttle to this home from airport. From $65.

MAUI—HAIKU

Bed and Breakfast Honolulu (Statewide)

3242 Kaohinani Drive, Honolulu, 96817
(808) 595-7533; (800) 288-4666
FAX (808) 595-2030; e-mail: bnbshl@aloha.net
www.planet-hawaii.com/bnb-honolulu

BBHS 48. Designed along the line of the old gracious Hawaiian-style plantation homes, this is a lovely cottage that can sleep three. There is a glass sitting room and an adjacent screened in veranda. King-size bed and double bed in the glass room. Kitchenette. Continental breakfast included first morning. Beautiful, peaceful, open and airy. From $85.

---

7 No smoking; 8 Children welcome; 9 Social drinking allowed; 10 Tennis nearby; 11 Swimming nearby; 12 Golf nearby; 13 Skiing nearby; 14 May be booked through a travel agent; 15 Handicapped accessible.

BBHS 164. On a peaceful two-acre farm with macadamia, coconut, avocado, citrus, and banana trees. Off the beaten path, it is a tropical setting with a gazebo which overlooks the ocean. The bedrooms each have queen-size beds and refrigerators. Gourmet teas and coffee served with European charm for breakfast. German is spoken by the West German host. Only international squash court in Hawaii on premises. Minutes to international wind surfing beach and Haleakala crater district. From $60.

Haikuleana Bed and Breakfast Plantation

555 Haiku Road, 96708-5884
(808) 575-2890 (reservations); (808) 575-7459
(guests' use); FAX (808) 575-9177
e-mail: blumblum@maui.net

Fully licensed, Haikuleana is the gateway to upcountry. Built in the 1870s amid Cook Island pines and lush foliage. Renovated in 1992. Elegant and relaxing. Hawaiian and New England antiques, beautiful fabrics, and fresh orchids enhance traditional fretwork of Colonial architecture. Convenient to Hana and Haleakala Crater. Ceiling fans. Private guest telephones. Cable TV and VCR. Gourmet breakfast. True aloha atmosphere. Children over seven are welcome. Additional charge for third person. Smoking outside only. Ten-person whirlpool hot spa.

Hosts: Ralph H. and Jeanne Elizabeth Blum
Rooms: 4 (PB) $95-125
Full Breakfast
Credit Cards: None
Notes: 2, 5, 9, 11, 12, 14

Halfway to Hana House

P.O. Box 675, 96708
(808) 572-1176; FAX (808) 572-3609
e-mail: gailp@maui.net; www.maui.net/~gailp

This cozy private studio, with its spectacular location, is nestled in lush seclusion 20 minutes from Paia town on the Hana road. Sparkling clean, airy, with a minikitchen

and private bath and entrance, it features a breakfast patio overlooking a tropical valley with panoramic ocean views. Freshwater pools and waterfalls are nearby. The hostess, a long-time Maui resident and avid outdoor enthusiast, delights in graceful touches like chocolate-covered macadamia nuts by the pillow and dazzling floral arrangements. She's helpful with restaurant and adventure tips and might invite guests to go snorkeling or kayaking on a Sunday morning.

Host: Gail Pickholz
Room: 1 (PB) $70
Continental Breakfast
Credit Cards: None
Notes: 2, 5, 7, 8, 9, 11, 14

MAUI—HANA

Affordable Accommodations Maui

2825 Kauhale Street, Kihei, 96753
(808) 879-7865; FAX (808) 874-0831
e-mail: llittle@maui.net
www.maui.net/~llittle/affordable.html

1. Bed and breakfast in Hana town. Fifteen-minute walk to Hana Bay. Three comfortable, spacious rooms with queen-size and twin beds in each. Private baths. Two rooms have decks looking out to the garden area with fruit trees and tropical plants. In-room refrigerator. Outdoor kitchenette and barbecue available to guests. Additional guests $10 each. $55-65.

Hana Plantation Houses

P.O. Box 249, 96713
(808) 923-0772; (800) 228-HANA
FAX (808) 922-6068; e-mail: hana@kestrok.com
www.kestrok.com/~hana

Discover Hana, the other Maui, with waterfalls, secluded beaches, and hiking in bamboo jungles just steps from the tropical and beachfront cottages. Exotic black-sand beaches, and natural sparkling pools once known only to Hawaiian royalty. Many of the homes have spas, TVs, and kitchens. A café is in the botanical gardens. Hana Plantation also has accommodations on Molokai, a private island.

Hosts: Blair Shurtleff and Tom Nunn
Rooms: 18 (PB) $60-185
Full and Continental Breakfast
Credit Cards: A, B, C
Notes: 2, 3, 5, 7,. 8, 9, 10, 11, 14

MAUI—KIHEI

Affordable Accommodations Maui

2825 Kauhale Street, Kihei, 96753
(808) 879-7865; FAX (808) 874-0831
e-mail: llittle@maui.net
www.maui.net/~llittle/affordable.html

Listing bed and breakfast accommodations throughout Maui and the outer islands. Some bed and breakfasts may include pools and/or Jacuzzis. There are more than 50 available listings, which include guest rooms, studios, and cottages. Continental breakfast. Open year-round. $50-150.

1. Lovely Hawaiian pole-style home in garden setting with barbecue and picnic table available for guests. Tiki torches give that wonderful Hawaiian feeling. Two spacious one-bedroom one-bath suites, one studio suite, and a master bedroom. One with ocean view. Nicely furnished. Warm hosts offer breakfast on their lanai with sweeping ocean views. $75-95.

2. Enchanting bed and breakfast right above Wailea. Immaculately clean. Garden Room with private bath, queen-size bed. Huge master bedroom with king-size bed, private bath, and entrance. Property has many fruit trees, a courtyard to relax and read a book, and a lovely gazebo with a koi pond and waterfall to sit and reflect on the wonders of Maui. Charming hostess to help guests with all their needs. $75-95.

3. Large, light airy room with king-size bed, private bath in south Kihei home.

Three blocks from the beach. TV, refrigerator. Breakfast served on ocean-view lanai, weather permitting. $50-60.

4. Private, set apart one-bedroom one-bath deluxe cottage bordering Wailea. Small ocean view. Full kitchen equipped with everything guests need. TV, VCR, tape deck, radio/CD player. Washer and dryer, air conditioned for those warm summer days. Skylight in the bedroom for viewing the stars at night. $80-90.

5. A tropical haven in North Kihei. Lush, tropical gardens with waterfall. Three units each with private entrance and bath. Large oversize rooms. Two of the rooms are wheelchair accessible. Kitchenettes. A short stroll to long sandy beach. $95-110.

Aloha Bed and Breakfast

811 South Kihei Road, #1F, 96753
(808) 875-4517; (800) 484-6748 ext. 5582

Enjoy magical Maui at this beautiful condominum resort. For guests' pleasure there is a near-Olympic-size swimming pool, hot tub, 18-hole putting green, and two tennis courts. Across the street there is a five-mile-long beach where guests can enjoy walks, swimming, or watching beautiful sunsets. Enjoy the luscious breakfast in the elegant dining area or on the airy lanai that is surrounded by lovely tropical flowers.

Hosts: Eric and Karen Miller
Rooms: 1 (PB) $65
Full Breakfast
Credit Cards: F
Notes: 5, 7, 9, 10, 11, 12, 14

Aloha Pualani

15 Wailana Place, 96753
(808) 874-9265; (800) PUALANI
FAX (808) 874-9127

"Our heavenly flowers welcome you." Experience the best of both worlds—a bed and breakfast and a condominium. Five private

7 No smoking; 8 Children welcome; 9 Social drinking allowed; 10 Tennis nearby; 11 Swimming nearby; 12 Golf nearby; 13 Skiing nearby; 14 May be booked through a travel agent; 15 Handicapped accessible.

suites surround a tropically landscaped courtyard and heated swimming pool. Best of all, Aloha Pualani is just across the street from beautiful Maalaea Bay and the longest sandy beach on Maui. Enjoy spectacular sunsets from either guests' private ocean-view lanai or from the beach only 100 feet away. Centrally placed on the island for convenient sightseeing.

Hosts: Marina and Keith Dinsmoor
Rooms: 5 (PB) $89-119
Continental Breakfast
Credit Cards: A, B, C, D, E
Notes: 2, 5, 7, 8, 9, 10, 11, 12, 14

Bed and Breakfast Hawaii

P.O. Box 449, Kapaa, 96746
(808) 822-7771; (800) 733-1632
FAX (808) 822-2723; e-mail: bandb@aloha.net

M22. This hideaway sits at the top of a hill overlooking the beautiful south beaches of Maui. Two accommodations are available. The Pink Shell Room is spacious with a king-size bed and private bath across the hall. Air conditioning, ceiling fans, telephone, and TV. The Blue Ocean Room offers a private entrance, queen-size bed, private bath, private lanai, telephone, TV, and ceiling fans. Continental breakfast is served on the lanai. Guests are welcome to use the large ohana room including kitchen area, dining, and living room. Two-night minimum. No smoking allowed. $55.

Bed and Breakfast Honolulu (Statewide)

3242 Kaohinani Drive, Honolulu, 96817
(808) 595-7533; (800) 288-4666
FAX (808) 595-2030; e-mail: bnbshl@aloha.net
www.planet-hawaii.com/bnb-honolulu

BBHS 46. Ocean view and only three blocks to beautiful Mai Poina 'Oe la'U Beach Park. This host offers two bed and breakfast guest rooms with private baths and Continental breakfast. Guests are also welcome to use the cheerful living/dining room and the kitchen. From $55.

BBHS 49. Less than 1,000 feet from Mai Poina 'Oe la'U Beach that stretches for three miles. Beautiful three-story plantation-style home in north Kihei. Offers three guest rooms on the second floor. One unit has a private bath and the other two units share a bath. Ocean and mountain views from every room. Climb the open stairway to a third-story sitting area with lanai, perfect for whale watching or spectacular sunset views. Continental breakfast. Smoking permitted outside only. $50-65.

BBHS 52. At the top of Maui meadows, just above Wailea, overlooking the islands of Lanai, Molokini, and Kahoolawe. The home is divided into four living sections, one which is occupied by the owner. The studio has one bedroom, a full kitchen, and private bath. The apartment has two bedrooms, private bath, and kitchenette. The cottage is separate and has one bedroom, living room with sofa bed, full kitchen, and wraparound lanai. Kitchens are stocked with breakfast foods. Minutes from beaches, golf courses, shopping. From $90.

BBHS 54. Only one-half mile stroll to Kamaole II beach. Guests may select from four exceptional units in this beautiful pole home with lovely grounds. Beach gear is provided. Four units with private baths. One unit has a full kitchen and two units have kitchenettes. All units include a full breakfast served family style. Air conditioning, hot tub, barbecue, telephone, TV/VCR. $65-95.

BBHS 163. Walled and gated for privacy, three bed and breakfast rooms. Large outdoor entertainment area with large Jacuzzi and gas barbecue. Continental breakfast. Smoking outside only. One room has a private bath and the other two rooms share a bath. Short walk to beach. From $50-65.

BBHS 165. The bed and breakfast room is in the lovely five and one-half acre condo

---

NOTES: Credit cards accepted: A MasterCard; B Visa; C American Express; D Discover; E Diner's Club; F Other; 2 Personal checks accepted; 3 Lunch available; 4 Dinner available; 5 Open all year; 6 Pets welcome;

development known as Koa Resort. Queen-size bed, TV, private bath with shower. Continental breakfast. Smoking outside only. Heated pool, Jacuzzi, tennis courts. Approximately two blocks to the beach. One nighter welcome. From $65.

BBHS 166. Only one-half mile up the street from Kamaole III beach and adjoining the beautiful Wailea resort area. Host offers a bed and breakfast suite with private bath with shower and private entrance. A coffee maker and small refrigerator are in the suite. Continental breakfast. Smoking outside only. Ten dollars for additional person over five. From $85.

BBHS 168. Gorgeous setting at the ocean's edge (no beach, one-half mile to swimming beach). Very large master suite bed and breakfast with king-size bed and a full-size sleeper-sofa. Private entrance. Small refrigerator, microwave, and coffee maker. Fabulous for whale watching, Maui sunsets. Continental breakfast. Inquire about one-night stays. Children under five free. Additional guests $15. From $95.

MAUAI—KUAU

Affordable Accommodations Maui

2825 Kauhale Street, Kihei, 96753
(808) 879-7865; FAX (808) 874-0831
e-mail: llittle@maui.net
www.maui.net/~llittle/affordable.html

1. Just past Paia guests will find a charming bed and breakfast with the feel of old Hawaii. Beautifully decorated with Hawaiian fabrics of the 40s and touches of Hawaiiana everywhere guests look. The property has a large grass area for lounging around and listening to the birds sing. Walk a few steps and guests will be in a private cove with the waves lapping at the shore. A five-minute walk will take guests to several

sandy beaches. Two bed and breakfast rooms are offered with private baths and a dining/relaxing area. World-famous wind-surfing beach, Hookipa, is just minutes away. $85.

MAUI—KULA

Bed and Breakfast Honolulu (Statewide)

3242 Kaohinani Drive, Honolulu, 96817
(808) 595-7533; (800) 288-4666
FAX (808) 595-2030; e-mail: bnbshl@aloha.net
www.planet-hawaii.com/bnb-honolulu

BBHS 81. Host offers several accommodations in a recently renovated ranch home. This home has six bedrooms with private baths. Guests are invited to use the kitchen. The bunkhouse is a U-shaped building with five small apartments. These units all have kitchens and one has a fireplace for cooler evenings. The Lahaina cottage is the honeymoon suite. It has an old wood-burning stove, complete kitchen, king-size bed, a big red bathtub with ocean views. Families and one-nighters welcome. Smoking outside only. From $85.

BBHS 167. On the slopes of Haleakala with beautiful views of the west Maui mountains and the Kihei coastline sits a lovely home that offers two bed and breakfast rooms. The master bedroom has a private bath with views of pasture lands, ferns, orchids, and anthurium flowers. The second bedroom shares a bath with the host only. There is a very large lanai to relax and just enjoy the gorgeous surroundings. Breakfast is served in the dining room.

Kula View Bed and Breakfast

140 Holopuni Road, P.O. Box 322, 96790
(808) 878-6736

Glorious sunrise and sunsets, sweeping ocean, mountain, and garden views from

---

7 No smoking; 8 Children welcome; 9 Social drinking allowed; 10 Tennis nearby; 11 Swimming nearby; 12 Golf nearby; 13 Skiing nearby; 14 May be booked through a travel agent; 15 Handicapped accessible.

Kula View

All tile floors. Guests share exclusive kitchen. Delicious full breakfast served each morning. Air conditioned for those warm Lahaina days. Hosts with worldly interests. Rooms and suites include queen-size bed, mini-refrigerator, and private baths. $85-125.

2. Just a short walk to Lahaina town, Lahaina Harbor, and the beach from this bed and breakfast on a quiet street in Lahaina. Friendly hostess happy to share her knowledge about this historic town. Rooms with queen-size or twin beds share a bath in this quaint home. $55-70.

every guest room. Raised 2,000 feet above sea level on the slopes of the dormant volcano Haleakala, Kula View is surrounded by two acres of lush greenery, fruits, flowers, banana and coffee trees, and yet is close to the Kahului airport, shopping centers, hiking parks, and beaches. The upper-level suite has a private entrance, deck, and private bath luxuriously appointed with a queen-size bed, reading area, wicker breakfast nook, and mini-refrigerator. Kula View offers personal old-fashioned Maui upcountry-style hospitality. Two-night minimum stay required.

Host: Susan Kauai
Room: 1 (PB) $85
Continental Breakfast
Credit Cards: None
Notes: 2, 5, 9, 11, 12, 14

MAUI—LAHAINA _____

Affordable Accommodations Maui

2825 Kauhale Street, Kihei, 96753
(808) 879-7865; FAX (808) 874-0831
e-mail: llittle@maui.net
www.maui.net/~llittle/affordable.html

1. Large home with six accommodations. Amenities include pool, barbecue area, large lanai with tables to watch the sunset.

Bed and Breakfast Hawaii

P.O. Box 449, Kapaa, 96746
(808) 822-7771; (800) 733-1632
FAX (808) 822-2723; e-mail: bandb@aloha.net

M5. This guest house is a private home where every guest room offers optimum privacy, with TV, refrigerator, ceiling fan, and air conditioning. All rooms have private baths, and one includes a Jacuzzi tub. The shared family room has a VCR, and the living room has a 350-gallon marine aquarium. A short walk to shops and restaurants as well as the beach, or relax beside the pool. $75-95.

Bed and Breakfast Honolulu (Statewide)

3242 Kaohinani Drive, Honolulu, 96817
(808) 595-7533; (800) 288-4666
FAX (808) 595-2030; e-mail: bnbshl@aloha.net
www.planet-hawaii.com/bnb-honolulu

BBHS 39. Hosts offer two units in their luxurious waterfront home. The oceanfront room has a private bath and entrance with lanai. The ocean-view room has a private bath and entrance. Both have TV and refrigerator. Continental breakfast. The beach is ideal for snorkeling, kayaking, or wind surfing. A great swimming beach is just

NOTES: Credit cards accepted: A MasterCard; B Visa; C American Express; D Discover; E Diner's Club; F Other; 2 Personal checks accepted; 3 Lunch available; 4 Dinner available; 5 Open all year; 6 Pets welcome;

moments away. Nonsmokers welcome. From $75.

BBHS 53. This recently remodeled 7,000-square-foot residence offers six spacious guest rooms five with outside access. Guest lounges, pool with slide and separate Jacuzzi. A full complimentary breakfast served in the main dining room or on the terrace. Guests also have the convenience of a separate kitchen. Four rooms accommodate up to four persons. Private baths. Smoking outside only. From $85.

BBHS 130. Each unit has a queen-size bed, plus a pull-out single or twin, a private Jacuzzi or hot tub, air conditioning, color TV, ceiling fan, small refrigerator, private bath, and private lanai. Relax around the large pool, join other guests in the family room for the latest videos or just relax in the quiet comfort of the living room. Continental breakfast provided and use of the kitchen is permitted. Outstanding accommodations at a modest price. From $90.

Old Lahaina House

P.O. Box 10355, 96761
(808) 667-4663; (800) 847-0761
FAX (808) 667-5615
www.mauiweb.com/maui/olhouse/

This convenient, relaxing place from which to visit Maui allows guests to enjoy the romantic, secluded ambiance of a private pool in a tropical courtyard. Only steps from a serene beach and convenient walking distance to dining and shopping in historic Lahaina town, a culturally rich and diverse old whaling town. Old Lahaina House is a home away from home, a special retreat, an intimate piece of paradise! Special tropical breakfast by the pool. Personal checks accepted for deposit. Smoking permitted outside.

Hosts: John and Sherry Barbier and Family
Rooms: 4 (PB) $69-95
Continental Breakfast
Credit Cards: A, B, C, D
Notes: 5, 7, 8, 9, 10, 11, 12, 14

MAUI—MAKAWAO

Affordable Accommodations Maui

2825 Kauhale Street, Kihei, 96753
(808) 879-7865; FAX (808) 874-0831
e-mail: llittle@maui.net
www.maui.net/~llittle/affordable.html

1. Charming plantation-style home in upcountry Makawao. Two lovely rooms and one suite decorated with antiques. The suite has a TV, refrigerator, and private bath which includes a shower and the original claw-foot tub. Room one is decorated in collectible Hawaiana and has an antique brass bed with a private bath. The second room is spacious and comfortable and feature a queen-size bed and private bath. The newest addition is a two-bedroom suite complete with a sleeper-sofa and private bath. Rambling country kitchen perfect for families. Walk to Makawao, the paniolo (Hawaiian cowboy) town of the past. The gracious hostess serves breakfast on the sideboard. $60-130.

2. Cozy one-bedroom, 700-square-foot cottage, walking distance to Makawao. Queen-size bed in bedroom and sofa bed in living area. Covered patio, nice garden. Amenities include TV, VCR. Decorated with a romantic flair. Ten dollars for each additional person. $75-85.

MAUI—MAUI MEADOWS

Bed and Breakfast Honolulu (Statewide)

3242 Kaohinani Drive, Honolulu, 96817
(808) 595-7533; (800) 288-4666
FAX (808) 595-2030; e-mail: bnbshl@aloha.net
www.planet-hawaii.com/bnb-honolulu

BBHS 30. Above Wailea, this redwood pole house sits on an acre and is surrounded by 75 fruit trees and large tropical garden. It has a lanai that wraps around the

7 No smoking; 8 Children welcome; 9 Social drinking allowed; 10 Tennis nearby; 11 Swimming nearby; 12 Golf nearby; 13 Skiing nearby; 14 May be booked through a travel agent; 15 Handicapped accessible.

home for beautiful ocean views. There are two accommodations offered. The guest rooms have private entrances and baths. On the garden level is the two-bedroom apartment with a full bath, kitchen, and private lanai. Less than a mile to the beach and shopping. Continental breakfst. Twelve miles from the airport. The Swedish-born hostess is a great help with coolers, snorkeling gear, beach mats, and lounge chairs. From $55.

BBHS 40. In a quiet residential area above Wailea. This host has two studios with private baths and entrances. These large studios have light cooking facilities with refrigerator, coffee maker, and microwave. The host stocks breakfast fixings for guests to use when they want. There is an ocean view from the lanai above the units. Just a short drive to the beaches, shopping, and restaurants. Three-night minimum stay. From $65.

MAUI—PAIA

Bed and Breakfast Hawaii

P.O. Box 449, Kapaa, 96746
(808) 822-7771; (800) 733-1632
FAX (808) 822-2723; e-mail: bandb@aloha.net

M12. Right on the beach and convenient for sightseeing, this large plantation-style home is in an exclusive neighborhood adjacent to the Maui Country Club. It offers a large guest room with a private bath. A short walk leads to a stretch of white sandy beach. No smoking inside. $80.

MAUI—SPRECKELSVILLE

Affordable Accommodations Maui

2825 Kauhale Street, Kihei, 96753
(808) 879-7865; FAX (808) 874-0831
e-mail: llittle@maui.net
www.maui.net/~llittle/affordable.html

1. Charming studio attached to a beautiful old plantation-style home with kitchenette/full refrigerator, lovely lanai to sit in and view the garden. Private bath, TV, VCR, and telephone. Just a few steps to baby beach and the Maui Country Club. Gracious hostess. $65-75.

MAUI—UPCOUNTRY

Bed and Breakfast Honolulu (Statewide)

3242 Kaohinani Drive, Honolulu, 96817
(808) 595-7533; (800) 288-4666
FAX (808) 595-2030; e-mail: bnbshl@aloha.net
www.planet-hawaii.com/bnb-honolulu

BBHS 161. Walking distance to charming Makawao. Gracious old plantation home built in 1924. Host offers three bed and breakfast rooms, all with private baths. Each room is furnished with Old World charm. TV in the main common area and the Rose Room. Continental breakfast. Refrigerator, microwave, and coffee maker available for guests. Smoking permitted outside only. Children welcome. One-nighters welcomed. From $60-70.

MAUI—WAILUKU

Bed and Breakfast Honolulu (Statewide)

3242 Kaohinani Drive, Honolulu, 96817
(808) 595-7533; (800) 288-4666
FAX (808) 595-2030; e-mail: bnbshl@aloha.net
www.planet-hawaii.com/bnb-honolulu

BBHS 162. Built in 1924 by a wealthy island banker. Down to the smallest detail it represents 1920s Hawaii at its best intertwined with the conveniences and luxuries modern travelers expect. Seven gracious rooms each named for an island flower. Each room has a private bath, telephone, and an heirloom Hawaiian quilt. A few of the rooms have a whirlpool bath. Full gourmet breakfast is served. Smoking per-

NOTES: Credit cards accepted: A MasterCard; B Visa; C American Express; D Discover; E Diner's Club; F Other; 2 Personal checks accepted; 3 Lunch available; 4 Dinner available; 5 Open all year; 6 Pets welcome;

mitted outside only. Twenty dollars for each additional guest. From $120-180.

MOLOKAI—KAUNAKAKAI

Bed and Breakfast Hawaii

P.O. Box 449, Kapaa, 96746
(808) 822-7771; (800) 733-1632
FAX (808) 822-2723; e-mail: bandb@aloha.net

MO2. Across the road from Father Damien's historic St. Joseph Church stands Kamalo Plantation, a five-acre tropical garden and lime orchard at the foot of Mount Kamakou. Ancient stone ruins beside the plantation offer a unique sense of peace and tranquility. Stay at the country cottage with a fully equipped kitchen or in the main house with two rooms and a shared bath. No smoking allowed. $65-75.

OAHU—AIEA

Rainbow Inn

98-1049 Mahola Place, 96701
(808) 488-7525 (phone/FAX)
e-mail: gsmith3777@aol.com

This beautiful bed and breakfast has easy access to sights and airport, yet is in a secluded tropical setting with marvelous views of Pearl Harbor, mountains, and the entire south coast of Oahu. Private garden apartment, separate entrance, private pool, beautiful private bath. In one of Oahu's nicest executive neighborhoods on valley filled with rainbows. Fully furnished, plenty of extras: refrigerator, microwave, air conditioning, color cable TV, many interesting books on Hawaii. Use of washer/dryer. Stores, ethnic restaurants, theaters nearby.

Hosts: Cdr. (Ret) USN Gene and Betty Smith
Rooms: 1 (PB) $65
Full Breakfast
Credit Cards: None
Notes: 2, 5, 7, 9, 10, 11, 12

OAHU—EWA BEACH

Bed and Breakfast Honolulu (Statewide)

3242 Kaohinani Drive, Honolulu, 96817
(808) 595-7533; (800) 288-4666
FAX (808) 595-2030; e-mail: bnbshl@aloha.net
www.planet-hawaii.com/bnb-honolulu

BBHS 158. If one yearns to get away from the crowds and find an uncrowded white-sand beach, then come to Oahu's southern shore. This home offers four bedrooms and two baths. Full kitchen. Common area. TV. More than one family could share this home. Full breakfast. Views of the shoreline and Diamond Head. Nonsmoking property. From $60.

OAHU—HAWAII KAI

Bed and Breakfast Hawaii

P.O. Box 449, Kapaa, 96746
(808) 822-7771; (800) 733-1632
FAX (808) 822-2723; e-mail: bandb@aloha.net

O-19. The hosts, mother and daughter, are from England and make sure that their guests have a great time in Hawaii. In this beautiful home in east Honolulu close to a bus route, hosts offer two rooms for guests. A downstairs bedroom is furnished with a queen-size bed, has private bath with shower, TV/VCR, and microwave. The upstairs bedroom is furnished with a king-size bed, private full bath. Everyone is welcome for breakfast each morning. No smoking. Two-night minimum. $65-75.

Bed and Breakfast Honolulu (Statewide)

3242 Kaohinani Drive, Honolulu, 96817
(808) 595-7533; (800) 288-4666
FAX (808) 595-2030; e-mail: bnbshl@aloha.net
www.planet-hawaii.com/bnb-honolulu

BBHS 79. The hosts, mother and daughter, are originally from England where bed and

---

7 No smoking; 8 Children welcome; 9 Social drinking allowed; 10 Tennis nearby; 11 Swimming nearby; 12 Golf nearby; 13 Skiing nearby; 14 May be booked through a travel agent; 15 Handicapped accessible.

breakfast started. The upstairs guest room has a private bath, TV, refrigerator. The downstairs room has a private bath, TV, VCR, microwave. A hearty Continental breakfast served. Ten-minute drive to swimming beaches and Hanauma Bay (famous for snorkeling). No smoking. Adults only. Two-night minimum. Hosts have a dog. From $65.

BBHS 150. This host offers two newly renovated guest rooms with shared bath. Each room has a private entrance through a private patio/garden area. Both have TV, radio-alarm clock, ceiling fan, and small refrigerator. Guests may also eat and sunbathe on the marina side of the house where there is a gas grill. Convenient to Hanauma Bay, Sandy Beach, shopping centers, and many restaurants. It is 9 miles to Waikiki, 11 miles to Ala Moana shopping center. Continental breakfast. Smoking permitted outside. From $55.

BBHS 151. Luxurious marina waterfront property. Foyer has moss rock waterfall with fish pool. Enjoy a beautiful lagoon-shaped pool with waterfalls. A four-poster brass bed. Private full bath, small refrigerator, TV, air conditioning, Continental breakfast. Smoking permitted outside only. From $80.

BBHS 152. Gorgeous home right on a waterway (not a beach). There is also a pool for guests' enjoyment. The room has a queen-size bed. The bathroom is shared with one resident only. Continental breakfast. Smoking permitted outside only. Two-night minimum. Host has a small cat and two love birds. Only minutes from Haunama Bay. Private bath would require higher rate. From $55.

BBHS 160. This home on Mariners Ridge, in an executive community, has many pluses. The large deck offers marvelous ocean views, and has a patio table which is a perfect place to have breakfast or just relax in the early evening. Swimming pool available for guests' use. These hosts offer two rooms in their home with a shared bathroom. The king-size room has an ocean view, while the room with twin beds has its own TV, looks out on a small tropical garden. This bed and breakfast is minutes from Hanauma Bay and other beaches, shopping centers, and restaurants. Also, there is absolutely no smoking.

OAHU—HONOLULU

Bed and Breakfast Honolulu (Statewide)

3242 Kaohinani Drive, Honolulu, 96817
(808) 595-7533; (800) 288-4666
FAX (808) 595-2030; e-mail: bnbshl@aloha.net
www.planet-hawaii.com/bnb-honolulu

BBHS 101. In Foster Village, about two miles from Pearl Harbor and the Arizona Memorial. This home has two bed and breakfast rooms. Kitchen privileges with microwave and regular ovens, freezer, refrigerator, range, laundry facilities, and color TV. Not directly on the bus line, so a car is probably necessary. Children and smokers welcome. Two blocks from Tripler Hospital busline. From $50.

Bed and Breakfast Manoa

2651 Terrace Drive, 96822
(808) 988-6333; FAX (808) 988-2515
e-mail: mcdevitt@hawaii.edu

Bed and Breakfast Manoa is a comfortable, casual bed and breakfast home in Manoa Valley, one of Honolulu's best-loved neighborhoods. Guests are invited to relax on the lanai (deck) and enjoy the cool mountain breezes, colorful rainbows, and spectacular view of Diamond Head and Waikiki. Near some of Oahu's best tropical hiking trails, Bed and Breakfast Manoa is conveniently just a short drive or bus ride from Waikiki

NOTES: Credit cards accepted: A MasterCard; B Visa; C American Express; D Discover; E Diner's Club; F Other; 2 Personal checks accepted; 3 Lunch available; 4 Dinner available; 5 Open all year; 6 Pets welcome;

and downtown Honolulu. Smoking permitted on the deck only.

Host: Colleen Boyle
Rooms: 2 (1 PB; 1 SB) $70-75
Continental Breakfast
Credit Cards: None
Notes: 2, 5, 8, 9, 10, 11, 12, 14

OAHU—KAILUA

Akamai Bed and Breakfast

172 Kuumele Place, 96734
(808) 261-2227; (800) 642-5366
FAX (808) 259-8238; e-mail: joe@makai.com

In a quiet and separate wing of the house are two large, comfortably furnished, nonsmoking studios. Each has its own private entrance, bathroom, cable TV, and radio. Breakfast foods are stocked in rooms for three mornings. The kitchen area has a full-size refrigerator, light cooking appliances, dishes, and flatware. Guests can enjoy the lovely tropical setting of the lanai and pool. The rooms are also ideal for couples traveling together. "As your hosts, we will help you in every way we can to enjoy our beautiful island."

Host: Diane VanRyzin
Rooms: 2 (PB) $75
Full Breakfast
Credit Cards: None
Notes: 2, 5, 7, 9, 10, 11, 12, 14

All Islands Bed and Breakfast

463 Iliwahi Loop, 96734-1837
(808) 263-2342; (800) 542-0344 (U.S. & Canada)
FAX (808) 263-0308; e-mail: cac@aloha.net
www.planet-hawaii.com/all-island

Experience the real Hawaii! More than 700 private accommodations on all Hawaiian islands. Rooms in private homes average $55-75. Studios in private homes average $65-85. Ohana cottages average $75-95. Excellent rental car and interisland air rates. Free brochure.

Rooms: 1,500 (900 PB; 100 SB) $45-260
Continental Breakfast
Cards: A, B, C
Notes: 2, 5, 7, 8, 9, 10, 11, 12, 14

Bed and Breakfast Hawaii

P.O. Box 449, Kapaa, 96746
(808) 822-7771; (800) 733-1632
FAX (808) 822-2723; e-mail: bandb@aloha.net

O25. Ka Hale La'i means "House of Peacefulness" in Hawaiian and this delightful home is just that. Two rooms, each with a queen-size bed, private bath, and air conditioning. The main bedroom has sliding glass doors opening onto a covered lanai area by the pool, cable TV, and a bathroom with a sunken shower. The second bedroom is only used when two couples are traveling together. Two miles from Kailua Beach, a very pretty, safe beach for swimming and a popular spot for windsurfing. Snorkel to Flat Island to turtle watch. Golf courses are nearby. A very loving golden Labrador retriever lives here. No smoking. Adults only. Three-night minimum. $75-140.

Bed and Breakfast Honolulu (Statewide)

3242 Kaohinani Drive, Honolulu, 96817
(808) 595-7533; (800) 288-4666
FAX (808) 595-2030; e-mail: bnbshl@aloha.net
www.planet-hawaii.com/bnb-honolulu

BBHS 89. Walk to Kailua town and only one-half mile to gorgeous Kailua Beach. Beautiful tropical yard with pool. The bed and breakfast unit has private entrance and bath, TV, coffee maker, refrigerator, microwave, toaster, and ceiling fan. The large private studio is also equipped for light cooking. Futons can be used for additional guests. Both units are given Continental breakfast fixings for the first day only. Children welcome. Smoking permitted outside only. From $75.

BBHS 91. Only 200 yards from the ocean. Host offers two units with private entrances and baths. Each unit has built-in microwave, coffee maker, and refrigerator for light cooking. The host provides breakfast fixings in the unit for the first morning only. Air conditioning. Swimming pool for

---

7 No smoking; 8 Children welcome; 9 Social drinking allowed; 10 Tennis nearby; 11 Swimming nearby; 12 Golf nearby; 13 Skiing nearby; 14 May be booked through a travel agent; 15 Handicapped accessible.

guests' use. The property is enclosed and very private. Children over 16 welcome. Smokers welcome. Host has an Irish setter. Three-night minimum. From $70.

BBHS 96. Welcome to this beautiful open Hawaiian-style home enhanced by gorgeous flower arrangements in all rooms. Back yard is picture perfect with a large pool and gentle stream that empties into the ocean two blocks away. Lovely golf course rimmed by mountains completes the view. Room offers a private bath, TV, chair, ceiling fan, and refrigerator. Inquire about nonbreakfast option. Two aloof cats on premises. From $65.

BBHS 153. This host offers two guest rooms, with private baths, in her newly decorated home furnished with oriental art gathered from around the world. It's a three and one-half-minute walk to Kailua Beach. Both have TVs and share the guest refrigerator off the hall between the rooms. The common rooms are large and spacious with a lovely garden in the back of the house. Continental breakfast. Entrance is through an oriental arch. Husband fluent in Chinese and some Japanese. Nonsmokers welcome. From $60.

BBHS 154. Enjoy this oceanfront unit sitting right on the breakers of Kailua Beach—not for swimming due to lava rock. Five-minute walk to a swimming area. Attached to single-family home. Hosts offer studio with king-size or twin beds. Futon available for extra guest. TV in room along with light cooking facilities. Breakfast fixings stocked for guests' convenience. Private entrance and full bath. Golden retriever on property. From $85-90.

BBHS 155. Just four houses from Kailua Beach, is a small studio with private entrance. It has a private bath, microwave, refrigerator, and small eating area. The host serves a bountiful Continental breakfast. Relax at the pool or in the small private sit-ting area adjacent to the studio. There is a convenient right of away to the beach available. From $65.

BBHS 159. Away from the clamor of Waikiki on a quiet dead end street, Kailua Beach park is one-half mile walk. This host offers two guest rooms. Both share the guest bath with shower/tub combo. Continental breakfast. Guests are welcome to use the coolers, beach mats, and beach chairs. On bus line. Dog on premises. Smoking permitted on lanai only. Adults only. Two-night minimum. From $45.

Papaya Paradise

395 Auwinala Road, 96734
(808) 261-0316 (phone/FAX)

Private, quiet, tropical, and near all attractions. Enjoy the pool. Relax in the Jacuzzi. Stroll Kailua Beach. Savor breakfast on the lanai surrounded by Hawaiian plants, trees, and flowers with Mount Olomana in the background. Rooms with private bath, private entry, refrigerator, air conditioning, telephone, and TV. Tennis, golf, and all kinds of water sports nearby. Just 20 miles from Waikiki and the Honolulu airport. Minimum three-night stay. Personal checks accepted for deposit only. AAA-approved.

Hosts: Bob and Jeanette Martz
Rooms: 2 (PB) $75-80
Continental Breakfast
Credit Cards: None
Notes: 5, 8, 9, 10, 11, 12

OAHU—KANEOHE

Bed and Breakfast Honolulu (Statewide)

3242 Kaohinani Drive, Honolulu, 96817
(808) 595-7533; (800) 288-4666
FAX (808) 595-2030; e-mail: bnbshl@aloha.net
www.planet-hawaii.com/bnb-honolulu

BBHS 95. On the bay. This host has two guest rooms with private baths and entrance. The King room has an adjacent sitting room with a twin daybed (fine for third person), microwave, coffee maker, refrigerator, and TV. The Queen room has a small dinette, coffee maker, toaster oven (refrigerator also available). Guests can enjoy sitting poolside. Picture postcard views available from the lanai or the boat-dock. Near village shopping center, super-market, cinema, and nice restaurants. Two miles to one of the loveliest beaches on the island. Fifteen miles from airport. Smoking outside only. From $65.

OAHU—LANIKAI

Bed and Breakfast Honolulu (Statewide)

3242 Kaohinani Drive, Honolulu, 96817
(808) 595-7533; (800) 288-4666
FAX (808) 595-2030; e-mail: bnbshl@aloha.net
www.planet-hawaii.com/bnb-honolulu

BBHS 94. A lovely 350-square-foot studio two blocks from gorgeous Lanikai Beach. Queen-size and twin beds. Bath with tub/shower, TV, coffee maker, toaster oven, refrigerator, bath towels, and beach chairs. Recessed on the lower part of hosts property. Very secluded and private. No smoking on property. There are 16 steps down to the property. Breakfast fixings in the unit for guests to prepare at their leisure. No use of telephone except for emergency calls. No children. No laundry facilities. Two-night minimum. From $95.

OAHU—MANOA

Bed and Breakfast Honolulu (Statewide)

3242 Kaohinani Drive, Honolulu, 96817
(808) 595-7533; (800) 288-4666
FAX (808) 595-2030; e-mail: bnbshl@aloha.net
www.planet-hawaii.com/bnb-honolulu

BBHS 82. In Manoa Valley (known for its rainbows and waterfalls), this host offers two comfortably decorated units to the bed

and breakfast traveler. One bedroom has a private bath with shower only. The second room has a private half bath and shared shower/tub. Entry is connected to the room. Continental breakfast. A 5- to 10-minute drive to beaches of Waikiki, hike to Manoa Falls, or visit Lyon Arboretum. Children welcome. Smoking permitted outside only. From $70.

OAHU—NIU VALLEY

Bed and Breakfast Honolulu (Statewide)

3242 Kaohinani Drive, Honolulu, 96817
(808) 595-7533; (800) 288-4666
FAX (808) 595-2030; e-mail: bnbshl@aloha.net
www.planet-hawaii.com/bnb-honolulu

BBHS 157. In the lower middle portion of quiet Niu Valley this host offers two bed and breakfast rooms at very modest prices making this an exceptional value. Room one has twin beds and room for a futon, TV, and small refrigerator. Room two has a ceiling fan and a double bed. The rooms share a bath. Continental breakfast. Three blocks to bus. Thirty minutes to airport. Nonsmokers only. No pets. From $50.

OAHU—NUUANU

Bed and Breakfast Honolulu (Statewide)

3242 Kaohinani Drive, Honolulu, 96817
(808) 595-7533; (800) 288-4666
FAX (808) 595-2030; e-mail: bnbshl@aloha.net
www.planet-hawaii.com/bnb-honolulu

BBHS 78. These units are in the home/office of the owners of this service. It's 10 minutes to downtown Honolulu, 20 minutes to Waikiki, or the airport. Each unit has color TV, private telephone, coffee maker, toaster, refrigerator, table, chairs, dishes, and private shower bath. The second-floor unit has a small bedroom. The first floor unit also has a small dining area and a daybed. Microwave

7 No smoking; 8 Children welcome; 9 Social drinking allowed; 10 Tennis nearby; 11 Swimming nearby; 12 Golf nearby; 13 Skiing nearby; 14 May be booked through a travel agent; 15 Handicapped accessible.

and hot plate available nearby, so only an aloha welcome basket is provided for the first day. Three blocks to bus stop. One-nighters welcome, but surcharge, if fewer than three. Smokers and children welcome. Hosts have dogs in the main house and outdoor cats. Fax, e-mail, and copying available for a modest fee. From $55.

OAHU—WAIANAE

Bed and Breakfast Honolulu (Statewide)

3242 Kaohinani Drive, Honolulu, 96817
(808) 595-7533; (800) 288-4666
FAX (808) 595-2030; e-mail: bnbshl@aloha.net
www.planet-hawaii.com/bnb-honolulu

BBHS 156. Nine-tenths of a mile from Pokai Beach and Waianae Army beach. Twenty-two miles from airport. Continental breakfast. Smoking permitted outside only. Two-night minimum. Two rooms with either shared or private bath. From $60-65.

OAHU—WAIKIKI

Aston Waikiki Beachside Hotel

2452 Kalakaua Avenue, Honolulu, 96815
(808) 931-2100; (800) 922-7866 (reservations)
FAX (808) 931-2129

An elegant boutique hotel with a prestigious address overlooking famous Waikiki Beach features 18th-century European and Asian artwork and antiques. Imported French-milled toiletries, English goose down pillows, and a seashell in a silk purse left with a welcome note on the eve of arrival are special touches that complement the friendly and enthusiastic Hawaiian hospitality. On the weekends, afternoon tea is offered in the hotel's outdoor courtyard. Ask for the special bed and breakfast rate for 30 percent discount.

Hosts: Donna Wheeler, general manager
  Bobbie Quitan, director of sales

Rooms: 79 (PB) $180-375
Continental Breakfast
Credit Cards: A, B, C, D, E, F
Notes: 2, 5, 9, 10, 11, 12, 14

Bed and Breakfast Honolulu (Statewide)

3242 Kaohinani Drive, Honolulu, 96817
(808) 595-7533; (800) 288-4666
FAX (808) 595-2030; e-mail: bnbshl@aloha.net
www.planet-hawaii.com/bnb-honolulu

BBHS 109. Only two blocks to Waikiki Beach, this host offers one guest room in his two-bedroom, air-conditioned condo. This room has a queen-size bed with private bath. Enjoy the view of downtown, Waikiki, the beach in the daytime, and the beautiful stars and sunsets in the evening. Continental breakfast. Easy walking distance to shopping and restaurants. Guests may use the kitchen. Smoking permitted outside on the lanai only. Parking on street. From $50.

OAHU—WAIMANALO

Bed and Breakfast Honolulu (Statewide)

3242 Kaohinani Drive, Honolulu, 96817
(808) 595-7533; (800) 288-4666
FAX (808) 595-2030; e-mail: bnbshl@aloha.net
www.planet-hawaii.com/bnb-honolulu

BBHS 92. This host offers a separate cottage with light cooking. Refrigerator, microwave, and coffee maker available. Host provides some breakfast materials. The cottage has a queen-size bed. There is a tub/shower combination and air conditioning is available. The main house fronts the ocean and the cottage is a distance behind the house. There is no ocean view from the cottage, although there is direct access to the beach which is about 100 feet away. Bus service is two blocks away. Telephone in unit shares host's line. Three-night minimum. Two people maximum. From $70.

Idaho

Marsh Creek Inn

386 South Main, 83311
(208) 673-6259

On Highway 77 in Albion, Marsh Creek Inn is named after the beautiful stream that flows through the property accenting the parklike atmosphere with horseshoe pits and a fire pit for evening enjoyment. All rooms have cable TV, telephones, and refrigerators. An outdoor covered spa is also available. The rustic lobby is in a restored log house that was originally built in 1879. Sightseeing, fishing, and rock climbing are just minutes away.

Host: Gary Erickson
Rooms: 12 (PB) $38.50-59.00
Continental Breakfast
Credit Cards: A, B, D
Notes: 2, 5, 8, 9, 12, 13, 14, 15

ATHOL

The Ponderosa

2555 Brunner Road, 83801
(208) 683-2251; (888) 683-2251
FAX (208) 683-5112; e-mail: pondrosa@ior.com
www.onlinenow.com/theponderosa/

A breathtaking log home nestled on a 10-acre wooded estate with beautiful mountain views. Three rooms have queen-size log beds; one room has twin beds. Country atmosphere. Complimentary wine tasting in hosts' 2,000-bottle wine cellar. Each room has "His and Her" robes for the walk to the enclosed whirlpool spa. Area attractions include Silverwood Theme Park (May thru October), Farragut

State Park, shopping malls, antique shops, and numerous outdoor activities.

Hosts: Jack and Betty Bonzey
Rooms: 4 (PB) $85-125
Full Breakfast
Credit Cards: A, B
Notes: 2, 5, 7, 9, 10, 11, 12, 13

BEAR LAKE

Bear Lake Bed and Breakfast

500 Loveland Lane, Fish Lake, 83287
(208) 945-2688

Guests are encouraged to make themselves at home in this spacious secluded log home. Sitting on the deck guests can absorb the peace and beauty of the turquoise blue lake below. The national forest is half a mile behind the bed and breakfast. Each guest room is decorated in a different style. Guests will find total hospitality here and yummy aromas coming from the kitchen each morning.

Host: Esther Harrison
Rooms: 4 (1 PB; 3 SB) $79-89
Full Breakfast
Credit Cards: A, B
Notes: 2, 5, 7, 9, 10, 11, 12, 13

BOISE

Idaho Heritage Inn

109 West Idaho, 83702
(208) 342-8066

This inn was a former governor's mansion and home to the late Sen. Frank Church. In the historic Warm Springs district, the inn enjoys the convenience of natural geothermal water. The inn is surrounded by other distinguished turn-of-the-century

7 No smoking; 8 Children welcome; 9 Social drinking allowed; 10 Tennis nearby; 11 Swimming nearby; 12 Golf nearby; 13 Skiing nearby; 14 May be booked through a travel agent; 15 Handicapped accessible.

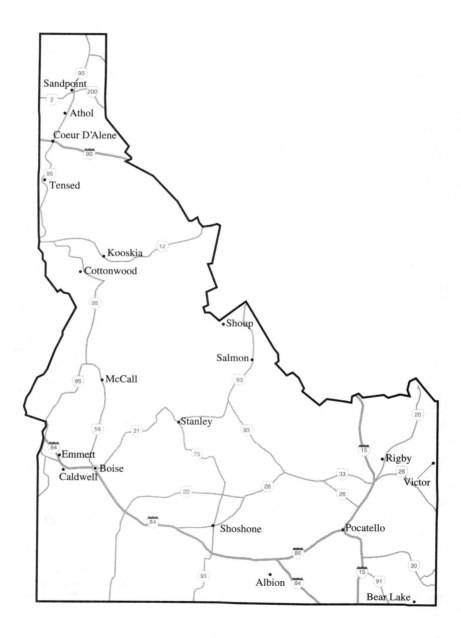

Idaho

Idaho Heritage Inn

homes and is also within walking distance of downtown, beautiful parks, museums, and Boise's famous Greenbelt river walkway. All rooms have been comfortably and charmingly appointed with private baths, period furniture, and crisp linens.

Hosts: Phyllis and Tom Lupher
Rooms: 6 (PB) $60-95
Full Breakfast
Credit Cards: A, B, C, D
Notes: 2, 5, 7, 9, 10, 11, 12, 13, 14

CALDWELL

Harvey House Bed and Breakfast

13466 Highway 44, 83605
(208) 454-9874

Big Sky Country hospitality at its best! Circa 1910 home furnished in comfortable—with a capital *C*. Fresh flowers, complimentary local wines, as well as fruit and cheese plate upon arrival. Spacious rooms furnished in antiques adjoin a main receiving area that includes TV, VCR, stereo, and sitting area. In addition, rooftop decking which overlooks Emmett Butte or the Owyhee Mountains. Hot tub under the stars. Near golf courses, ski area, antiques. White-water rafting and vineyards.

Hosts: Bill and Angela Cyr
Rooms: 3 (1 PB; 2 SB) $85-110
Full Breakfast
Credit Cards: A, B, C
Notes: 2, 3, 4, 5, 7, 8, 9, 11, 12, 13

COEUR D'ALENE

Baragar House Bed and Breakfast

316 Military Drive, 83814
(208) 664-9125; (800) 615-8422
FAX (208) 765-2427; e-mail: baragar@dmi.net
www.baragarhouse.com

Craftsman-style bungalow in historic Fort Sherman near downtown, park, and beach of Lake Coeur d'Alene. All rooms have queen-size beds, cable TV/VCRs, air conditioning, robes, and private use of indoor spa and sauna. Exquisite honeymoon suite has a romantic bathroom with an antique tub and a unique glass shower. Morning coffee tray. Complimentary snacks. Delicious breakfasts. Honeymooners are served breakfast in bed. Laundry privileges.

Hosts: Bernie and Carolyn Baragar
Rooms: 3 (1 PB; 2 SB) $95-125
Full Breakfast
Credit Cards: A, B, C, D
Notes: 2, 5, 7, 9, 10, 11, 12, 13, 14

Berry Patch Inn Bed and Breakfast

North 1150 Four Winds Road, 83814
(208) 765-4994; FAX (208) 667-7336
www.bbhost.com/berrypatchinn

Nationally acclaimed by *National Geographic Traveler* as "One of the 20 Best Inns in the Rockies," and featured by Nordstrom stores. Private, elegant mountaintop chalet, backed to pristine forest. Only three and one-half miles to dining and shopping. Lakes, golf, and skiing. Heart-healthy delicious full breakfast with berries from the garden. Down comforters for sweet sleep.

NOTES: Credit cards accepted: A MasterCard; B Visa; C American Express; D Discover; E Diner's Club; F Other; 2 Personal checks accepted; 3 Lunch available; 4 Dinner available; 5 Open all year; 6 Pets welcome; 7 No smoking; 8 Children welcome; 9 Social drinking allowed; 10 Tennis nearby; 11 Swimming nearby; 12 Golf nearby; 13 Skiing nearby; 14 May be booked through a travel agent; 15 Handicapped accessible.

Tea and wine complimentary. Gift certificates. Adults only. Honeymoons. Air conditioned. Parking for boat trailers and RVs.

Host: Ann M. Caggiano
Rooms: 3 (PB) $125-150
Full Breakfast
Credit Cards: A, B
Notes: 2, 5, 7, 9, 11, 12, 13

Gregory's McFarland House Bed and Breakfast

601 Foster Avenue, 83814
(208) 667-1232; (800) 335-1232
www.bbhost.com/mcfarlandhouse

Surrender to the elegance of this award-winning historical home, circa 1905. Breakfast is gourmet, the cookie jar always full. Guests will find an ideal blending of beauty, comfort, and clean surroundings. Jerry Hulse of the *Los Angeles Times* says, "Entering Gregory's McFarland House is like stepping back 100 years to an unhurried time when four-posters were in fashion, and lace curtains fluttered at the windows." Air conditioning. Small, intimate and/or church weddings available.

Hosts: Winifred, Carol, and Stephen
Rooms: 5 (PB) $85-135
Full Breakfast
Credit Cards: A, B, D
Notes: 2, 5, 7, 10, 11, 12, 13, 14

Katie's Wild Rose Inn

East 5150 Coeur d' Alene Lake Drive, 83814
(208) 765-WISH (9474)
www.dmi.net/idaho-bandb/

Katie's welcomes all who enjoy a cozy, warm atmosphere. The house is decorated country cottage style, offering four guest rooms. The suite includes a view of the lake from its deck, large spa bathtub, and queen-size bed. Three and one-half miles east of Coeur d'Alene, it is on the Centennial Trail for hikers and bicyclists. Relax and enjoy the library, TV, or a game of pool. Weddings are a specialty.

Hosts: Lee and Joisse Knowles
Rooms: 4 (2 PB; 2 SB) $55-117

Katie's Wild Rose Inn

Full Breakfast
Credit Cards: A, B
Notes: 2, 5, 7, 9, 10, 11, 12, 13, 14, 15

Kingston 5 Ranch Bed and Breakfast

42297 Silver Valley Road, P.O. Box 130, Kingston, 83839
(208) 682-4862; (800) 254-1852
FAX (208) 682-9445; e-mail: k5ranch@nidlink.com
www.nidlink.com/~k5ranch

This picturesque 1930s farmhouse offers a quiet, relaxing retreat or a wonderful romantic getaway. Private suites have in-room fireplaces, private baths with jetted tubs, and private outdoor spas. Lazy mornings begin with the wonderful tastes and smells of homemade specialities. Ten minutes west of Silver Mountain Ski Area and 25 minutes east of Coeur d'Alene. Easy access, just south of I-90. Special weekday package available year-round except February, July, August, and all holidays.

Hosts: Walt and Pat Gentry
Rooms: 2 (PB) $85-125
Full Breakfast
Credit Cards: A, B
Notes: 2, 5, 7, 9, 10, 11, 12, 13, 14

COTTONWOOD

Mariel's Bed and Breakfast

Route 1, Box 207, 83522
(208) 962-5161

Experience the peace and quiet of rural Idaho in this big, comfortable home on a

NOTES: Credit cards accepted: A MasterCard; B Visa; C American Express; D Discover; E Diner's Club; F Other; 2 Personal checks accepted; 3 Lunch available; 4 Dinner available; 5 Open all year; 6 Pets welcome;

dryland wheat farm. From the windows of the seven spacious bedrooms view the Camad Prairie, with its rolling hills, surrounded by canyons and framed by mountains. Enjoy walking along quiet country roads, then relax in the indoor hot tub. Five of the bedrooms have private baths, queen-size or twin beds. Guests are served a full country breakfast in the family dining room.

Rooms: 7 (5 PB; 2 SB) $46
Full Breakfast
Credit Cards: D
Notes: 2, 5, 7, 9, 10, 11, 12, 13

EMMETT

Frozen Dog Digs

4325 Frozen Dog Road, 83617
(208) 365-7372

Frozen Dog Digs is as unique as its name. Nestled in the foothills and surrounded by fruit orchards, the Digs offers a panoramic view of the Emmett Valley. Sunsets viewed from the romantic gazebo are an artist's dream. Amenities the owner designed and built include a racquetball court, chip-and-putt golf greens, landscaped gardens with secluded spa, and sports bar. For the adventuresome, world-famous recreational areas and white-water rapids are within an echo and beckon.

Host: Jon Elsberry
Rooms: 4 (2 PB; 2 SB) $59-99
Full Breakfast
Credit Cards: A, B, D
Notes: 2, 5, 7, 9, 10, 11, 12, 13

KOOSKIA

Dream's Bed and Breakfast

Milepost 86 US Hwy. 12, P.O. Box 733, 83539
(208) 926-7540; e-mail: dreams@camasnet.com

On the Lewis-Clark Highway (US 12) which parallels the route of the famous explorers Captains Lewis and Clark. Panoramic river view—total privacy—country breakfast.

Dream's 18 acres are part of the Wild and Scenic corridor along the middle fork of the Clearwater River. With the assistance of local guides, explore some of the endless wilderness mountains—or just relax in the hot tub under the sky.

Hosts: Gene and Helga Tennies
Rooms: 2 (PB) $65
Full Breakfast
Credit Cards: A, B
Notes: 2, 5, 7, 9, 11, 15

Three Rivers Bed and Breakfast

Highway 12, HC 75, Box 61, 83539
(208) 926-4430

In the heart of the Idaho wilderness these bed and breakfast cabins sit high on the hill in privacy. A log cabin with grand open-beam A-frame. The view is spectacular. Each cabin has a fireplace, a Jacuzzi, and an antique brass bed in a mountain paradise.

Hosts: Mike and Marie Smith
Rooms: 15 (PB) $45-97.50
Full Breakfast
Credit Cards: A, B, C, D, E
Note: 2, 3, 4, 5, 6, 8, 9, 11, 14

MCCALL

Northwest Passage Bed and Breakfast

201 Rio Vista, P.O. Box 4208, 83638
(208) 634-5349; (800) 597-6658
FAX (208) 634-4977

The Northwest Passage Bed and Breakfast is in the Rocky Mountain town of McCall on the shores of Payette Lake. The Northwest Passage was originally built to house the cast of the 1938 MGM movie *Northwest Passage*. The hostess serves a full breakfast, the menu changing daily. Complimentary wines and sherry in the afternoon also available. The McCall area is a full service four-season resort destination but still maintains its small town ambiance and affordability. Winter activities include alpine and cross-country skiing, ice skating, and snowmobiling.

7 No smoking; 8 Children welcome; 9 Social drinking allowed; 10 Tennis nearby; 11 Swimming nearby; 12 Golf nearby; 13 Skiing nearby; 14 May be booked through a travel agent; 15 Handicapped accessible.

Summer activities include all water sports, fishing, golf, and hiking.

Hosts: Steve and Barbara Schott
Rooms: 6 (PB) $65-85
Full Breakfast
Credit Cards: A, B, C
Notes: 2, 5, 9, 11, 12, 13, 14

POCATELLO

Back O' Beyond

Back O' Beyond
Bed and Breakfast Inn

404 South Garfield Avenue, 83204
(208) 232-3825; (888) 232-3820
FAX (208) 232-2771
e-mail: backbeyond@gemstate.net

Back O' Beyond Bed and Breakfast is an 1893 Victorian home, restored with lovely antiques. "Your home along the Oregon Trail" features three comfortable rooms with private baths and a pioneer patio where guests may hear the author discuss his books about the trail. The old-fashioned front porch beckons guests to linger awhile with cookies, tea, or lemonade. A full country breakfast is served in the old dining room for rested and nostalgic guests. The inn is near downtown Old Pocatello and the Fort Hall Replica.

Hosts: Jay and Sherrie Mennenga
Rooms: 3 (PB) $60
Full Breakfast
Credit Cards: A, B, C, D
Notes: 2, 3, 4, 5, 7, 8, 9, 10, 12, 13, 14

Hales Half Acre

Route 2, Box 26, 83202
(208) 237-7130

"We are small but we're great!" The rooms are at the end of a ranch-style home on a little acreage. Electric heat, comfortable beds, jet tub, and a full farm breakfast of homemade bread, home-canned jam, honey butter, and more. A tree house and large play area are available for children to enjoy. The big window looks out on a well-kept vegetable garden with mountains in the distance.

Hosts: Delos and Betty Hale
Rooms: 2 (S1B) $40-45
Full Breakfast
Credit Cards: None
Notes: 2, 5, 7, 8, 12, 13

Z Bed and Breakfast

620 South 8th Avenue, 83201
(208) 235-1095; (888) 235-1095

This beautifully renovated 1915 home is just one-half block from Idaho State University campus. A warm welcome awaits guests. The guest rooms feature queen-size brass beds, colorful comforters, and private baths. The cozy fireplace, screened sun room, shady patio, and spacious front porch all invite guests to relax. Guests will enjoy the friendly hospitality, fine food, and quiet, comfortable atmosphere of Z Bed and Breakfast. "We are looking forward to meeting you!" Children 12 and older welcome.

Hosts: Greg and Naoni Zervas
Rooms: 3 (PB) $75
Full Breakfast
Credit Cards: None
Notes: 2, 5, 7, 12, 13

Z Bed and Breakfast

NOTES: Credit cards accepted: A MasterCard; B Visa; C American Express; D Discover; E Diner's Club; F Other; 2 Personal checks accepted; 3 Lunch available; 4 Dinner available; 5 Open all year; 6 Pets welcome;

RIGBY

Blacksmith Inn

227 North 3900 East, 83442
(208) 745-6280; (888) 745-6280
FAX (208) 745-0602

The Blacksmith Inn is a contemporary, round "eagles nest" home, cedar sided to give a western flavor. Each room features a mural depicting the western heritage or landscape. Locally made quilts adorn every bed. Guests will decide what to have for breakfast or sample it all, including the freshly ground estate coffees. Each room has a private bath, cable TV/VCR, and clock radio. The inn is only a short drive to museums, golf course, galleries, and shops, on the way to West Yellowstone. There is plenty of summer and winter fun nearby from fly-fishing to skiing. Inspected and rated three crowns by ABBA.

Hosts: Mike and Karla Black
Rooms: Rooms: 4 (PB) $60-75
Full Breakfast
Credit Cards: A, B, D
Notes: 2, 5, 7, 8, 9, 10, 11, 12, 13, 15

Blacksmith Inn

SALMON

Greyhouse Inn Bed and Breakfast

HC 61, Box 16, 83467
(800) 348-8097

Built in 1894, this fully restored Victorian farmhouse is near the Frank Church-River of No Return Wilderness. Surrounded by the Bitteroot, Beaverhead, and Salmon

Greyhouse Inn

Mountains. Fishing, hiking, hot springs, white-water rafting, and skiing are just a few of the things to do while staying at the Greyhouse Inn. The rooms are furnished with antiques and wonderfully comfortable beds in every room. A full breakfast will be ready for guests each morning with homemade muffins and scones.

Hosts: Dave and Sharon Osgood
Rooms: 4 (2 PB: 2 SB) $65-80
Full Breakfast
Credit Cards: A, B
Notes: 2, 3, 4, 5, 7, 8, 9, 11, 12, 13

SANDPOINT

The Coit House Bed and Breakfast

502 North 4th Avenue, 83804
(208) 265-4035

Walk through the doors and experience the magnificent beauty of a restored 1907 Victorian manor. All rooms feature private baths, air conditioning, and are uniquely decorated with antiques. Enjoy mountain hospitality with the full homemade breakfast. Conveniently one block from downtown shopping, dining, and City Beach. An easy drive to Schweitzer Mountain Ski area. Open year-round. AAA-approved, three diamonds.

Hosts: Julie and Seth Coit
Rooms: 4 (PB) $65-85
Full Breakfast
Credit Cards: A, B
Notes: 2, 5, 7, 10, 11, 12, 13, 14

7 No smoking; 8 Children welcome; 9 Social drinking allowed; 10 Tennis nearby; 11 Swimming nearby; 12 Golf nearby; 13 Skiing nearby; 14 May be booked through a travel agent; 15 Handicapped accessible.

SHOSHONE

Governor's Mansion Bed and Breakfast Inn

315 South Greenwood, P.O. Box 326, 83352
(208) 886-2858

First occupied in 1906, the Governor's Mansion was built by the Gooding family. It was owned by Thomas Gooding, older brother of Frank Gooding, once governor of Idaho. Come to a small-town atmosphere 55 miles from Sun Valley and near many Idaho attractions, including Shoshone Falls and the Craters of the Moon. Host offers a friendly, homelike atmosphere and breakfast to guest's order. Air conditioned.

Host: Edith Collins
Rooms: 7 (2 PB; 5 SB) $45-65
Full Breakfast
Credit Cards: None
Notes: 2, 5, 6, 8, 9

SHOUP

Smith House Bed and Breakfast

49 Salmon River Road, 83469
(208) 394-2121; (800) 238-5915

The perfect place to relax and let the stress of city life slide by. Caters to small groups—birthdays, reunions, anniversaries, weddings. Guest house sleeps 10 and has separate living and dining rooms from the log home. Hiking, fishing, rafting, photography, and more both off and on the property. Delightful Continental plus breakfast served. One small house pet allowed for additional charge. Smoking outside only and children are always welcome. The outdoor hot tub and front lawn are natural gathering spots.

Hosts: Aubrey and Marsha Smith
Rooms: 5 (1 PB; 4 SB) $35-55
Continental Breakfast
Credit Cards: A, B
Notes: 2, 7, 8, 9, 11, 14

STANLEY

Idaho Rocky Mountain Ranch

HC 64, Box 9934, 83278
(208) 774-3544

One of Idaho's oldest and finest guest ranches, offering comfortably decorated lodge and cabin accommodations. Beautiful mountain vistas from the front porch. Delightful meals served by a friendly staff. Hiking, fishing, horseback riding, mountain biking, rafting, cross-country skiing, wildlife viewing, and much more, both on and off the ranch. Fifty miles north of Sun Valley in the Sawtooth National Recreation Area and on Highway 75. Brochure available; weekly rates available. Closed April 1 through May 31 and September 30 through November 20.

Hosts: Bill Leavell and Sandra Bakwith
Rooms: 21 (PB) $130-220
Credit Cards: A, B, D
Notes: 2, 3, 4, 7, 8, 9, 11, 13

Idaho Rocky Mountain Ranch

NOTES: Credit cards accepted: A MasterCard; B Visa; C American Express; D Discover; E Diner's Club; F Other; 2 Personal checks accepted; 3 Lunch available; 4 Dinner available; 5 Open all year; 6 Pets welcome;

TENSED

Seven Springs Farm— A Country Inn

HCR 1, Box 310, 83870
(208) 274-2470

Experience the Northwest: the valley of Sanders, in the Idaho panhandle, is nestled between rolling Palouse farmland and majestic timbered mountains, five miles from McCroskey State Park. The round two-story home which overlooks a working 160-acre farm is dedicated to the principles of earth and sky, the four seasons, peace and personal well-being. The inn grows most of its own vegetables and much fruit following organic principles. Every country breakfst is home cooked and northwestern fresh.

Host: Christina Crawford
Rooms: 5 (4 PB; 1 SB) $65-75
Full Breakfast
Credit Cards: A, B
Notes: 2, 3, 4, 5, 7, 9, 12, 13, 14

VICTOR

Moose Creek Ranch

219 East Moose Creek Road, P.O. Box 350, 83455
(208) 787-2784; (800) 676-0075
FAX (208) 787-2284
e-mail: moosecreekranch@pdt.net

Moose Creek Ranch is just an hour from Wyoming's famous western town Jackson. It's a beautiful drive over the mountain pass into Idaho from Wyoming. Moose Creek offers a traditional dude ranch experience with an emphasis on families and children. Surrounded by the Targhee National Forest with Moose Creek running through the ranch. Guests are taught to groom and saddle their own horses and how to ride properly in the high-mountain terrain. Horses from the Adopt a Wild Mustang Program are trained and intergrated into the remuda. Moose Creek Ranch offers sincere and wholesome western hospitality for the entire family.

Hosts: Kelly and Roxann Van Orden
Rooms: 9 (PB) $65-350
Full Breakfast
Credit Cards: A, B, C, D
Notes: 2, 3, 4, 7, 8, 9, 10, 12, 13, 14, 15

7 No smoking; 8 Children welcome; 9 Social drinking allowed; 10 Tennis nearby; 11 Swimming nearby; 12 Golf nearby; 13 Skiing nearby; 14 May be booked through a travel agent; 15 Handicapped accessible.

Montana

Montana

Burggraf's Countrylane

BIGFORK

Burggraf's Countrylane Bed 'n' Breakfast on Swan Lake

Rainbow Drive, 59911
(406) 837-4608; (800) 525-3344
FAX (406) 837-2468
e-mail: burggrafs@digisys.net

Custom-made log home on seven acres beside Swan Lake with panoramic view. Forty-five miles south of Glacier National Park. "All you can eat" breakfast. Complimentary wine, fruit and cheese upon arrival. All rooms with private bath and walk-in showers. King-, queen-, or single-size beds. Lawn croquet; free use of canoes, paddle and fishing boats available. Cabin by the lake. Honeymoon suite with Jacuzzi/whirlpool tubs. Children over 12 welcome.

Hosts: Natalie and R. J. Burggraf
Rooms: 5 (PB) $90-125
Full Breakfast
Credit Cards: A, B
Notes: 2, 3, 6, 7, 9, 10, 11, 12, 13, 14, 15

O'Duachain Country Inn

675 Ferndale Drive, 59911
(406) 837-6851; (800) 837-7460
FAX (406) 837-0778

Enjoy the beauty and solitude of Flathead Valley's original bed and breakfast inn. Make vacation or business travel comfortable and memorable. Luxurious log lodging with full breakfast. Five acres of naturally landscaped beauty including wildflowers, pond, wild game, water fowl, and enchanting peacocks. Enjoy nearby Glacier National Park; Flathead Lake; National Bison Range; historic Jesuit mission; Bob Marshall Wilderness; Swan Lake; Big Mountain Ski Resort; Bigfork Summer Theater; Jewel Basin Hiking; Bigfork's numerous world-class restaurants. Two-bedroom suite also available. Inquire about accommodations for pets.

Hosts: Bill Knoll and Mary Corcoran Knoll
Rooms: 4 (PB) $110
Suite: $180
Full Breakfast
Credit Cards: A, B, C, D
Notes: 2, 5, 7, 8, 9, 10, 11, 12, 13, 14, 15

O'Duachain Country Inn

NOTES: Credit cards accepted: A MasterCard; B Visa; C American Express; D Discover; E Diner's Club; F Other; 2 Personal checks accepted; 3 Lunch available; 4 Dinner available; 5 Open all year; 6 Pets welcome; 7 No smoking; 8 Children welcome; 9 Social drinking allowed; 10 Tennis nearby; 11 Swimming nearby; 12 Golf nearby; 13 Skiing nearby; 14 May be booked through a travel agent; 15 Handicapped accessible.

BIG TIMBER

The Grand Hotel

139 McLeod Street, P.O. Box 1242, 59011
(406) 932-4459; FAX (406) 932-4248

Built in 1890 and listed today in the
National Register of Historic Places, the
Grand Hotel had been lovingly restored to
her original dignity and is now operated as
a bed and breakfast. The Grand Hotel Bed
and Breakfast offers original hotel rooms
dressed and appointed in their Victorian
best: high-ceilinged, sunlit rooms with
period furnishings. The Grand also features
one of Montana's premier restaurants which
serves locally raised lamb and beef and
fresh seafood that has been flown in. Proud
winners of the Wine Spectator Award of
Excellence. The bed and breakfast offers
fishing on two classic rivers, the Yellowstone River and the Boulder River, two
blue-ribbon trout streams.

Host: Larry Edwards
Rooms: 11 (4 PB; 7 SB) $59-145
Full Breakfast
Credit Cards: A, B, D
Notes: 3, 4, 5, 7, 12

BOULDER

Boulder Hot Springs Hotel and Spa

3 Miles South of Boulder on Highway 69 (location)
P.O. Box 930, 59632-0930 (mailing)
(406) 225-4339; FAX (406) 225-4345

An 1888 historic inn, newly renovated, bed
and breakfast rooms decorated with antique
furniture and lace curtains. Hot springs available for use in indoor pool (105°) and an outdoor swimming pool (98°). Substantial
breakfast served. Massage services available
at additional cost. On 274 acres adjacent to
Deerlodge National Forest. Hiking, fishing,
cross-country skiing, and many surrounding
activities. Reservations recommended.
Sunday buffet available 12:00 to 3:00 P.M.
Golf and skiing one hour away.

Host: Barb Reher (manager)
Rooms: 33 (18 PB; 15 SB) $70-90
Full Breakfast
Credit Cards: A, B
Notes: 2, 5, 7, 8, 11, 15

BOZEMAN

Fox Hollow Bed and Breakfast at Baxter Creek

545 Mary Road, 59718
(406) 582-8440; (800) 431-5010

A country setting in the heart of the Gallatin
River Valley. Enjoy panoramic views of
majestic mountain ranges from the wraparound deck or hot tub spa. This 1993
country-style home offers spacious guest
rooms with plush queen-size beds and private
baths. Wake to full gourmet breakfasts every
morning. Montana is a traveler's paradise.
Choose from world-famous fly-fishing,
hiking, mountain biking, or alpine and cross-
country skiing. Yellowstone National Park is
only 90 minutes away.

Hosts: Michael and Nancy Dawson
Rooms: 5 (PB) $78-108
Full Breakfast
Credit Cards: A, B, C, D
Notes: 2, 5, 7, 9, 10, 11, 12, 13, 14

The Lehrkind Mansion Bed and Breakfast

719 North Wallace Avenue, 59715
(406) 585-6932; (800) 992-6932
e-mail: lehrkindmansion@imt.net
www.imt.net/~lehrkindmansion/index.html

Listed in the national register and built in 1897,
the Lehrkind Man-
sion offers one of
Montana's finest
examples of Vic-
torian Queen
Anne architec-
ture. Spacious
yard and gar-
dens, porches,
and the large corner tower are among the

NOTES: Credit cards accepted: A MasterCard; B Visa; C American Express; D Discover; E Diner's Club;
F Other; 2 Personal checks accepted; 3 Lunch available; 4 Dinner available; 5 Open all year; 6 Pets welcome;

mansion's spectacular features. Period Victorian antiques throughout; the music parlor features Victrolas and a very rare 1897 Regina music box—seven feet tall! Queen-size beds, comforters, overstuffed chairs; a large hot tub will soak away an active day. A stay at the Lehrkind Mansion is not just a room for the night—it's an experience!

Hosts: Jon Gerster and Christopher Nixon
Rooms: 5 (3 PB; 2 SB) $75-155
Full Breakfast
Credit Cards: A, B, C
Notes: 2, 5, 7, 8, 9, 10, 11, 12, 13, 14

The Silver Forest Inn Bed and Breakfast

15325 Bridger Canyon Road, 59715
(406) 586-1882; (888) 835-5970
FAX (406) 582-0492; e-mail: silverforest@aol.com

A 1934 log-hewn home in the Rocky Mountains of southwest Montana. Surrounded by National Forest service land, 15 miles from Bozeman and one-fourth mile from Bridger Bowl Ski area. Centered among three blue-ribbon trout streams. Hot tub, Jacuzzi, and wonderful gourmet breakfast.

Hosts: Finn and Tara Nelson
Rooms: 6 (4 PB; 2 SB) $75-115
Full Breakfast
Credit Cards: A, B, C, D
Notes: 2, 5, 6, 7, 8, 9, 13, 14

Torch and Toes Bed and Breakfast

309 South Third Avenue, 59715
(406) 586-7285; (800) 446-2138

Set back from the street, it looks much as it did when it was built in 1906. A tall, trim brick-and-frame house in the Colonial Revival style. Just enough lace curtains and turn-of-the-century furniture to remind guests that this is a house with a past. Smells of blueberry muffins, coddled eggs, and fresh fruit will entice guests to breakfast in the oak-paneled dining room with the wood-burning fireplace.

Hosts: Ronald and Judy Hess
Rooms: 4 (PB) $70-100

Torch and Toes

Full Breakfast
Credit Cards: A, B
Notes: 2, 5, 7, 8, 9, 10, 11, 12, 13, 14

Voss Inn Bed and Breakfast

319 South Wilson, 59715
(406) 587-0982

Magnificently restored Victorian inn in the historic district with elegant guest rooms and private baths. A delightful gourmet breakfast is served in the privacy of guests' rooms or family style in guest parlor. Bozeman is 90 miles north of Yellowstone Park, near skiing, fishing, hiking, and snowmobiling. Full afternoon tea. Airport transportation available. Children over five welcome.

Hosts: Bruce and Frankee Muller
Rooms: 6 (PB) $85-95
Full Breakfast
Credit Cards: A, B, C
Notes: 2, 5, 7, 9, 10, 11, 12, 13, 14

Voss Inn

7 No smoking; 8 Children welcome; 9 Social drinking allowed; 10 Tennis nearby; 11 Swimming nearby; 12 Golf nearby; 13 Skiing nearby; 14 May be booked through a travel agent; 15 Handicapped accessible.

COLSTRIP

Lakeview Bed and Breakfast and Specialty Dining

7437 Castle Rock Lake Drive, P.O. Box 483, 59323
(406) 748-3653; (888) LAKE BNB (525-3262)

In the heart of southeastern Montana, weary travelers can enjoy the peaceful beauty of Castle Rock Lake. Boating, fishing, swimming, bird watching, lovely walking path. Nearby golf course. Thirty minutes from Lewis and Clark Trail. An hour's drive to Custer Battlefield. Garden, woodland, castle rooms have gorgeous queen-size beds, telephones, TVs. Delicious, full breakfast. Evening refreshments. Other meals offered. "Relax in beautiful, comfortable surroundings while we take care of the little details that make you feel right at home..."

Host: Debby Vetsch
Rooms: 3 (1 PB: 2 SB) $57.20-69.68
Full Breakfast
Credit Cards: A, B, C
Notes: 2, 3, 4, 5, 7, 8, 9, 10, 11, 12, 14

Lakeview

COLUMBIA FALLS

Bad Rock Country Bed and Breakfast

480 Bad Rock Drive, 59912
(800) 422-3666

For the visitor to Glacier National Park. On 30 rolling country acres. Spectacular views of nearby Rocky Mountains. Three rooms in the house; Old West antiques; four rooms in

two new square-hewn log buildings with handmade lodgepole pine furniture. Selected one of 1995's 12 top inns in U.S. and Mexico by *Country Inns* magazine. Inspected and approved by AAA and Mobil, and the Montana Bed and Breakfast Association.

Hosts: Jon and Susie Alper
Rooms: 7 (PB) $110-155
Full Breakfast
Credit Cards: A, B, C, D, E
Notes: 2, 5, 7, 9, 12, 13, 14

Meadow Lake View Bed and Breakfast

180 Meadow Lake Drive, 59912
(406) 892-0900; (800) 897-3182

Just a mile from a Meadow Lake golf course, 10 miles from Big Mountain ski resort, and 17 miles from Glacier National Park. Rooms have queen-size beds, TV, VCR, telephone, and private bath. Lots of activities available all around. Antique shops, golfing, white-water rafting, hiking, mountain biking, horseback riding. After a long day, the hot tub may be inviting.

Hosts: Nando and Fran Marolt
Rooms: 4 (PB) $75-95
Full Breakfast
Credit Cards: A, B
Notes: 2, 5, 7, 8, 12, 13

EMIGRANT

Paradise Gateway Bed and Breakfast and Guest Log Cabin

P.O. Box 84, 59027
(403) 333-4063; (800) 541-4113
e-mail: paradise@gomontana.com

Paradise Gateway Bed and Breakfast, nestled in the majestic Absaroka Mountains, is just minutes away from scenic Yellowstone National Park. The bed and breakfast offers quiet, comfortable guest rooms. Each room has a private bath and a large, relaxing parlor in between for reading, music, and conversation. The surrounding area boasts many activities including hiking, horseback riding,

NOTES: Credit cards accepted: A MasterCard; B Visa; C American Express; D Discover; E Diner's Club; F Other; 2 Personal checks accepted; 3 Lunch available; 4 Dinner available; 5 Open all year; 6 Pets welcome;

fishing, rafting, sightseeing, and much more. Also available: two-bedroom log cabin on 26 acres next to the Yellowstone River. Very private with mountain views. Homemade Continental breakfast served at the cabin. The bed and breakfast receives a full breakfast. Inquire about accommodations for pets. Children welcome in cabin only.

Hosts: Pete and Carol Reed
Rooms: 4 (PB) $85-110
Cabin: $150
Full and Continental Breakfast
Credit Cards: A, B
Notes: 2, 5, 7, 9, 10, 11, 12, 13, 14, 15

Yellowstone Riverview Lodge

186 East River Road, 59027
(406) 848-2156; (888) 848-2550
e-mail: riverview@imt.net
www.wtp.net/go/riverview

The Yellowstone Riverview Lodge is a beautiful hand-hewn log home overlooking the Yellowstone River, minutes from Yellowstone National Park. Nestled between the Absaroka and Gallatin Mountains in the spectacular Paradise Valley, it offers breathtaking views, blue-ribbon fly fishing and endless outdoor activities. The home, which sits on 20 wild acres, provides guests with an entire floor to themselves: four bedrooms, private entrance, lounge, kitchenette/dining area, and patio. Open year-round.

Hosts: Steve Koester and Bill Wagner
Rooms: 4 (2 PB; 2 SB) $65-105
Full Breakfast
Credit Cards: A, B
Notes: 2, 3, 4, 5, 6, 7, 8, 9, 11, 13

EUREKA

Huckleberry Hannah's Montana Bed and Breakfast

3100 Sophie Lake Road, 59917
(888) 889-3381 (for reservations and free brochure)
e-mail: huckhana@libby.org
www.libby.org/HuckleberryHannah

Nearly 5,000 square feet of old-fashioned charm. Fifty wooded acres, fabulous trout-

filled lake, glorious views of the Rockies. This bed and breakfast depicts a quieter time in history—a walk in the woods or a moonlight swim, not to mention comfortable, sunny rooms and wonderful food. Owned and operated by the author of one of the Northwest's best-selling cookbooks, *Huckleberry Hannah's Country Cooking Sampler*. Questions cheerfully answered. Inquire about accommodations for pets. Smoking permitted outside only. Senior discounts.

Hosts: Jack and Deanna Doying
Rooms: 5 (PB) $55-90
Cottage: 1 (PB)
Full Breakfast
Credit Cards: A, B
Notes: 2, 3, 5, 7, 8, 9, 11, 12, 13, 14

GALLATIN GATEWAY

Wild Rose Bed and Breakfast

1285 Upper Tom Burke Road, 59730
(406) 763-4692; FAX (406) 763-5424
e-mail: gallatin@avicom.net

A peaceful country setting 15 miles southwest of Bozeman, midway between Big Sky and Bridger Bowl Ski areas. Cross-country skiing, fishing, rafting, hiking, and horseback riding in nearby Gallatin National Forest and Yellowstone National Park. Breakfast includes banana-blueberry muffins baked fresh daily, fresh fruit, a main entrée, juice, and coffee or tea.

Hosts: Dennis and Diana Bauer
Rooms: 3 (1 PB; 2 SB) $55-65
Full Breakfast
Credit Cards: A, B
Notes: 2, 5, 7, 8, 9, 10, 11, 12, 13

GLENDIVE

The Hostetler House Bed and Breakfast

113 North Douglas Street, 59330
(406) 365-4505; (800) 965-8456
FAX (406) 365-8456

Two blocks from downtown shopping and restaurants, the Hostetler House is a

7 No smoking; 8 Children welcome; 9 Social drinking allowed; 10 Tennis nearby; 11 Swimming nearby; 12 Golf nearby; 13 Skiing nearby; 14 May be booked through a travel agent; 15 Handicapped accessible.

The Hostetler House

charming 1912 historic Frank Lloyd Wright Prairie School home with two comfortable guest rooms, sitting room filled with books, enclosed sun porch, gazebo, and hot tub. Casual country decor mix with handmade and heirloom furnishings and many special touches. Full gourmet breakfast is served on Grandma's china. On I-94 and the Yellowstone River, close to parks, antique shops, churches, and Makoshika State Park.

Hosts: Craig and Dea Hostetler
Rooms: 2 (SB) $50
Full Breakfast
Credit Cards: A, B, D
Notes: 2, 5, 7, 9, 10, 11, 12, 13, 14

HAMILTON

Deer Crossing
Bed and Breakfast

396 Hayes Creek Road, 59840
(406) 363-2232; (800) 763-2232
e-mail: deercros@bitterroot.net
www.wtp.net/go/deercrossing

Old West charm and hospitality at its best. Deer Crossing is on 25 acres of pines and

Deer Crossing

pasture overlooking the beautiful Bitterroot Valley. After watching the sun rise over the Sapphire Mountains, enjoy a hearty ranch breakfast and plan the day. Visit historic sites, explore on horseback, hike, or fly-fish in one of the numerous sparkling creeks. Inspected and approved by Montana Bed and Breakfast Association and Mobil Travel Guide. "Kick off your boots, hang your hat, and make yourself at home!" Guests' horses are welcome.

Host: Mary Lynch
Rooms: 5 (4 PB; 1 SB) $70-100
Full Breakfast
Credit Cards: A, B, C,
Notes: 2, 3, 4, 5, 7, 8, 9, 10, 11, 12, 13, 14, 15

Trout Springs
Bed and Breakfast

721 Desta Street, 59840
(406) 375-0911; (888) 67-TROUT
FAX (406) 375-0988
e-mail: tsprings@bitterroot.net
www.wtp.net/go/troutsprings

Nestled against the backwaters of the Bitterroot River lies an elegant western, spacious bed and breakfast. Breakfast is five courses with fresh trout caught from the private ponds where hosts encourage their guests to catch their own. Enjoy an evening social time and campfire. Walking distance to downtown.

Hosts: Maynard and Brenda Gueldenhaer
Rooms: 5 (PB) $70-90
Full Breakfast
Credit Cards: A, B, C
Notes: 2, 5, 7, 9, 10, 11, 12, 13

HARDIN

Kendrick House Inn
Bed and Breakfast

206 North Custer Avenue, 59034
(406) 665-3035

The Kendrick House Inn was built in 1914 as a boarding house. In 1988 the boarding house was restored as a bed and breakfast and now is in the historic register. The inn's five guest

NOTES: Credit cards accepted: A MasterCard; B Visa; C American Express; D Discover; E Diner's Club; F Other; 2 Personal checks accepted; 3 Lunch available; 4 Dinner available; 5 Open all year; 6 Pets welcome;

Kendrick House

rooms feature comfy antique beds, dressers, and a sink, true to the boarding houses of yesteryear. Shared bathrooms are unique with antique tubs, showers, and pull-chain toilets. The common areas include two glassed-in verandas, a library, and a parlor. A full Montana breakfast is served in the formal dining room. Within 15 miles of the Little Bighorn Battlefield National Monument.

Hosts: Steve and Marcie Smith
Rooms: 5 (S2B) $65
Full Breakfast
Credit Cards: A, B, F
Notes: 2, 7, 9, 10, 11, 12, 14

HAVRE

West Prairie Inn Bed and Breakfast and Antiques

9855 US Highway 2 Northwest, 59501
(406) 265-7281; (800) 268-3545
e-mail: wpi@hi-line.net

The West Prairie Inn is a 1927 Sears, Roebuck home that has been completely restored and decorated with antique furnishings. It is in north-central Montana five miles west of Havre on Highway 2. The guest rooms, each with a decorative theme, are on the second floor. All rooms offer a spacious view of the surrounding landscape. Antiques are for sale in the three restored one-room-school buildings on the grounds.

Hosts: Margaret and Ed Hencz
Rooms: 3 (1 PB: 2 SB) $50-65

Full Breakfast
Credit Cards: A, B

HELENA

Appleton Inn Bed and Breakfast

1999 Euclid Avenue, 59601
(406) 449-7492; (800) 956-1999
FAX (406) 449-1261; e-mail: appleton@ixi.net
www.appletoninn.com

Relax in splendor at this beautiful Victorian built in 1890 and listed in the national historic register. Individually decorated rooms with antique and hand-crafted furnishings, private in-room baths, telephones, data ports. Enjoy afternoon refreshments in the parlors or perennial gardens. Awake to a delicious full breakfast served on antique Franciscan appleware. Close to hiking trails, golf course, and a lake. Mountain bikes are available. Minutes from all of the city's historic attractions. Pets welcome with prior approval.

Hosts: Tom Woodall and Cheryl Boid
Rooms: 5 (PB) $65-95
Full Breakfast
Credit Cards: A, B, C, D, E
Notes: 5, 7, 8, 9, 11, 12, 13, 14

Barrister Bed and Breakfast

406 North Ewing, 59601
(406) 443-7330; (800) 823-1148
FAX (406) 442-7964

Relax in an 1874 Victorian mansion in the heart of Montana's capital city. Enjoy more than 2,000 square feet of common area, including parlor, formal dining room, den and TV room, library, office, and enclosed sun porch. The five guest bedrooms are spacious and carefully decorated to provide an intimate atmosphere, along with warmth and comfort. All rooms have private baths, TV, and queen-size beds. Hors d'oeuvres and full gourmet breakfast included. Not suitable for children under 10.

Rooms: 5 (PB) $85-115
Full Breakfast
Credit Cards: A, B, C, E
Notes: 2, 5, 6, 7, 9, 10, 11, 12, 13, 14

7 No smoking; 8 Children welcome; 9 Social drinking allowed; 10 Tennis nearby; 11 Swimming nearby; 12 Golf nearby; 13 Skiing nearby; 14 May be booked through a travel agent; 15 Handicapped accessible.

HUSON

The Schoolhouse and the Teacherage

18815 Remount Road, 59846
(406) 626-5879

The Schoolhouse and the Teacherage is 27 miles northwest of Missoula. The bed and breakfast, built by the Anaconda Company in early 1900 for the loggers' children, has four guest rooms with featherbeds, down comforters, and handmade quilts plus a separate guest house. Each room has a different theme: Amish, Swedish, Dutch, and Montana. Reasonable rates, full breakfast. Owners are craftsmen, designers, and Hanneke is a published author.

Hosts: Les and Hanneke Ippisch
Rooms: 5 (5 SB) $65
Full Breakfast
Credit Cards: A, B, C, D, E
Notes: 2, 5, 7, 8, 9, 12, 13, 15

KALISPELL

Bonnie's Bed and Breakfast

265 Lake Blaine Road, 59901
(406) 755-3776; (800) 755-3778
www.wtp.net/go/montana/sites/bonnie.html

An English Tudor with Montana hospitality. Minutes to Glacier Park and Flathead Lake. Hiking, white-water rafting, antiquing, fine dining, and skiing nearby. Member of the Montana Bed and Breakfast Association.

Hosts: Leonard and Bonnie Boles
Rooms: 3 (2 PB; 2 SB) $75-115
Full Breakfast
Credit Cards: A, B
Notes: 2, 5, 7, 8, 9, 12, 13, 14

Creston Country Inn

70 Creston Road, 59901
(406) 755-7517; (800) 257-7517

Quiet charm and rural serenity are waiting at this delightful two-story farmhouse with mountain and valley views. The inn's rooms

Creston Country Inn

are furnished in old-country style and offer the finest in overnight accommodations. A hearty Montana breakfast is served. Minutes away from Glacier National Park, Flathead Lake, golf, skiing, white-water rafting, antiquing, and theater.

Hosts: Rick and Ginger Lockner-Malloch
Rooms: 4 (PB) $80-95
Full Breakfast
Credit Cards: A, B
Notes: 2, 7, 8, 9, 10, 11, 12, 13, 14

LIVINGSTON

The River Inn on the Yellowstone

4950 Highway 89 South, 59047
(406) 222-2429; FAX (406) 222-2625
e-mail: riverinn@alipnet.net
www.wtp.net/go/riverinn

Bed and breakfast, rustic cabin, and sheepherder's wagon. A beautifully restored historic farmhouse, 30 feet from the Yellowstone

The River Inn on the Yellowstone

NOTES: Credit cards accepted: A MasterCard; B Visa; C American Express; D Discover; E Diner's Club; F Other; 2 Personal checks accepted; 3 Lunch available; 4 Dinner available; 5 Open all year; 6 Pets welcome;

River. Secluded old cottonwoods on five acres with plenty of riverfront to meander or fish. Three fine bedrooms offer private baths. Spectacular river and mountain views. Guided canoe, hiking, and biking trips. Exceptional dining. Twenty-six miles east of Bozeman and just minutes from Livingston, a lively Old West town. Children nine and older are welcome. Cats on premises.

Hosts: DeeDee VanZyl and Ursula Neese
Rooms: 3 (PB) $70-90
Full Breakfast
Credit Cards: A, B
Notes: 2, 3, 4, 7, 9, 11, 12, 13, 14

MISSOULA

Foxglove Cottage Bed and Breakfast

2331 Gilbert Avenue, 59802
(406) 543-2927

Foxglove Cottage is a cozy 100-year-old house surrounded by a lovely garden just seven minutes from downtown Missoula, the University of Montana, and the Rattlesnake Wilderness National Recreation Area. Swimming pool, sun room, TVs, VCRs, 500-tape video library, croquet, and horseshoes available.

Hosts: John Keegan and Anthony Cesare
Rooms: 3 (1 PB; 2 SB) $65-95
Continental Breakfast
Credit Cards: F
Notes: 2, 7, 9, 10, 11, 12, 13

RED LODGE

Willows Inn

224 South Platt Avenue, P.O. Box 886, 59068
(406) 446-3913

Spectacular mountain scenery surrounds this delightful turn-of-the-century inn. Flanked by giant evergreens and colorful flower beds, it is reminiscent of a bygone era, complete with white picket fence, gingerbread trim, and a porch swing. Guest rooms have brass-and-iron four-poster beds. Delicious home-

baked pastries and afternoon refreshments are served. Close to hiking, fishing, and Yellowstone Park. Video movies, books, games, and a large sun deck are available. Two storybook cottages are ideal for families.

Hosts: Kerry, Carolyn, and Elven Boggio
Rooms: 5 (3 PB: 2 SB) $50-75
Cottages: 2; $80-110
Continental Breakfast
Credit Cards: A, B, D
Notes: 2, 5, 6, 7, 8, 9, 10, 11, 12, 13, 14

ST. IGNATIUS

Stoneheart Inn

P.O. Box 236, 59865
(406) 745-4999; (888) 291-4970, pin #7038
e-mail: sti4999@montana.com

Fortunate is the traveler who finds the Stoneheart Inn. The journey to Montana will be enhanced by a unique bed and breakfast experience. The inn is a historic hotel nestled at the base of the magnificent Mission Mountains in St. Ignatius. It has been beautifully recreated as a reflection of Montana, a place where guests will be treated to western pampering, gourmet food, and scenery as awe-inspiring as Glacier Park without the crowds. Inquire about accommodations for pets. Seven golf courses and three downhill ski areas within 60 miles.

Hosts: Judith-Ellis Tholt and Mike Tholt
Rooms: 4 (PB) $30-60
Full Breakfast
Credit Cards: A, B
Notes: 2, 5, 7, 8, 9

SEELEY LAKE

The Emily A. Bed and Breakfast

P.O. Box 350, 59868
(406) 677-3474 (phone/FAX)
e-mail: SLK3340@montana.com
www.theemilya.com

Grand 11,000-square-foot log home overlooking the headwaters of the Clearwater River. Private lake and fishing dam. Fourth-generation Montana family will share stories

7 No smoking; 8 Children welcome; 9 Social drinking allowed; 10 Tennis nearby; 11 Swimming nearby; 12 Golf nearby; 13 Skiing nearby; 14 May be booked through a travel agent; 15 Handicapped accessible.

and adventures. Hiking, fishing, wildlife viewing on the 160 acres. Family antiques and a remarkable western art collection.

Hosts: Marilyn and Keith Peterson
Rooms: 5 (2 PB: 3 SB) $95-150
Full Breakfast
Credit Cards: A, B
Notes: 2, 5, 6, 7, 8, 9, 11, 12, 13, 14, 15

SOMERS

Osprey Inn Bed and Breakfast

5557 Highway 93 South, 59932
(406) 857-2042; (800) 258-2042
FAX (406) 857-2019
e-mail: ospreyin@cyberport.net
www.sierranet.net/montana/osprey

The Osprey Inn is on the shore of Flathead Lake. There is a private pebble beach, boat dock, and hot tub. Use hosts' canoe or bring own boat, or just sunbathe on the beach. A guest lounge has a fireplace, player piano, library, and cable TV. Enjoy boating, canoeing, swimming, fishing, bird watching, the evening campfire, and fresh mountain air. Only one hour from Glacier National Park.

Hosts: Wayne and Sharon Finney
Rooms: 5 (4 PB: 2 SB) $100-110
Full Breakfast
Credit Cards: A, B
Notes: 2, 5, 7, 9, 11, 12, 13

STEVENSVILLE

The Country Caboose

852 Willoughby Lane, 59870
(406) 777-3145

This authentic 1923 wooden caboose is set on rails in the quiet countryside. The red caboose sleeps two (plus) and offers a spectacular view of the Bitterroot Mountains, right from one's pillow. The Country Caboose is off the beaten path, but not hard to find. It is the essence of a hidden treasure with unexpected pleasures.

Host: Lisa Thompson
Rooms: 1 (PB) $59
Full Breakfast

Credit Cards: None
Notes: 2

SULA

Camp Creek Inn Bed and Breakfast Guest Ranch

7674 Highway 93 South, 58971
(406) 821-3508; FAX (406) 821-3808

Old-fashioned western comfort awaits guests at this 160-acre ranch. Accommodations include three guest rooms in the original 1920 ranch house and two cabins with kitchens. A hearty ranch breakfast is included with all stays. Guided horseback rides are nearby and stalls for guest horses are available in the summer. Miles of gorgeous Bitterroot Forest trails surround the ranch. Excellent trout fishing is nearby. Ski packages are available, with Lost Trail Powder Mountain only nine miles away.

Host: Sandy Skorupa
Rooms: 5 (4 PB; 1 SB) $55-65
Full Breakfast
Credit Cards: None
Notes: 2, 5, 7, 8, 9, 11, 13, 14

THREE FORKS

Sacajawea Inn

Box 648, 59752
(406) 285-6515

Since William Howard Taft was president, guests have enjoyed the gracious hospitality of the Sacajawea Inn. Come savor the casual elegance of this landmark which is listed in the National Register of Historic Places. Graced by rocking chairs, a large front porch welcomes guests to a spacious lobby and newly renovated nostalgic guest rooms. One hundred miles from Yellowstone, the inn is a perfect spot from which to explore the Gallatin Valley. The Missouri headwaters are filled with Lewis and Clark history and are less than five miles from the inn.

Hosts: Smith and Jane Roedel
Rooms: 32 (PB) $59-99
Continental Breakfast
Credit Cards: A, B, C, D
Notes: 7, 8, 9, 12, 14, 15

VIRGINIA CITY

Just An Experience

1570 Mount Highway 287, P.O. Box 98, 59755
(406) 843-5402

A perfect getaway any time of year, Just An Experience offers comfortable lodging, excellent meals, wonderful atmosphere, and gracious hosts. In the historic gold towns of Virginia City/Nevada City, the inn is close to live entertainment and excellent outdoor activities. Relax in a rustic log cabin furnished with full bathroom, kitchen, living area, and private master bedroom. In the main house, the decor of the three guest rooms is eclectic antique. Relax in the main living area of wood and native stone with a coffee or cappuccino. Excellent breakfasts of fresh fruit, gourmet French toast, or special egg dishes and homemade syrups and jams. Smoking permitted outside.

Hosts: John and Carma Sinerius
Rooms: 5 (3 PB; 2 SB) $48-75
Full Breakfast
Credit Cards: A, B, C, D
Notes: 2, 3, 4, 5, 7, 8, 9, 10, 11, 12, 13, 14

WEST YELLOWSTONE

Sportsman's High Bed and Breakfast

750 Deer Street, 59758
(406) 646-7865; FAX (406) 646-9288
e-mail: sportsmanshigh@wyellowstone.com

Since its opening in 1989, this bed and breakfast has accommodated guests from

Sportsman's High

every state in the United States and all over the world. It offers five exquisitely decorated guest rooms, all with private baths, and antique furnishings. It is renowned for its fabulous breakfasts, its decidedly informal and peaceful atmosphere, along with its bird- and wildlife-viewing opportunities. If one is looking for a low-key and comfortable getaway close to Yellowstone Park—then they have just found it!

Hosts: Diana and Gary Baxter
Rooms: 5 (PB) $65-115
Full Breakfast
Credit Cards: A, B, C, D, E, F
Notes: 2, 5, 7, 12, 13

WHITEFISH

Edgewood

12 Dakota Avenue, 59937
(406) 862-9663 (phone/FAX)
e-mail: bnbdoll@cyberport.net

The Edgewood is a friendly nonsmoking country-style bed and breakfast on the road to Whitefish Lake City Beach. Open year-round. Moderate rates. Full breakfast served. Children welcome. Guests have use of family area with cable TV, a VCR, games, and reading material.

Rooms: 3 (3 SB) $65
Full Breakfast
Credit Cards: None
Notes: 2, 5, 7, 8, 11, 12, 13, 14

7 No smoking; 8 Children welcome; 9 Social drinking allowed; 10 Tennis nearby; 11 Swimming nearby; 12 Golf nearby; 13 Skiing nearby; 14 May be booked through a travel agent; 15 Handicapped accessible.

Gasthaus Wendlingen

700 Monegan Road, 59937
(406) 862-4886 (phone/FAX); (800) 811-8002
www.wtp.net/go/montana/sites/gasthaus.html

A place for all seasons and sports! Barbara and Bill welcome guests with German-western hospitality. Enjoy a full breakfast with homemade specialties. The off-highway location, two miles from Whitefish center, has a real Montana setting on eight acres. Spectacular views of Big Mountain to the gateway of Glacier National Park. The spacious bedrooms with private baths view Haskell Creek and Whitefish River. Sit by the fire or relax on the porch or patio.

Hosts: Barbara and Bill Klein
Rooms: 3 (2 PB; 1 SB) $70-125
Full Breakfast
Credit Cards: A, B, F
Notes: 5, 7, 9, 10, 11, 12, 13

Good Medicine Lodge

537 Wisconsin Avenue, 59937
(800) 860-5488; FAX (406) 862-5489
www.wtp.net/go/goodrx

This classic Montana getaway hewn from solid cedar timbers has nine guest rooms with private baths, direct-dial telephones, balconies, mountain views, custom-made lodgepole beds, hearty breakfasts, laundry, and ski room. Only minutes from guests' favorite outdoor activity, shopping, dining, the airport, and Amtrak. Relax in front of a fireplace or unwind in the outdoor spa. AAA-rated three diamonds. Handicapped accessible.

Hosts: Christopher and Susan Ridder
Rooms: 9 (PB) $85-125
Full Breakfast
Credit Cards: A, B, C, D
Notes: 2, 5, 7, 8, 9, 10, 11, 12, 13,14, 15

WHITE SULPHUR SPRINGS

The Columns

19 East Wright Street, P.O. Box 611, 59645
(406) 547-3666

The Columns

Recently renovated red brick 1882 private home with an eclectic blend of yesterday's charm and today's comfort in the middle of cow country. Big Sky hospitality at its best. Delicious ranch-style breakfasts. Children welcome with previous arrangement.

Host: Dale N. McAfee
Rooms: 3 (1 PB; 2 SB) $45-65
Full Breakfast
Credit Cards: A, B
Notes: 2, 5, 7, 9, 10, 11, 12, 13, 14

Sky Lodge Bed and Breakfast

4260 Highway 12 East, P.O. Box 428, 59645
(406) 547-3999; (800) 965-4305

Sky Lodge is a spacious log lodge that provides affordable luxury and homelike accommodations in large, comfortable guest rooms with private baths. There are large common areas—a game room with pool table and Ping-Pong, two living rooms for reading, TV and VCR movies, and a deck with awesome views of the surrounding mountains. In the beautiful Smith River valley of central Montana. Outdoor recreation: hiking, bicycling, skiing, fishing, and hunting. Deluxe hot tub outdoors with great view of mountains.

Hosts: Marc and Debbie Steinberg
Rooms: 4 (PB) $62-72
Full Breakfast
Credit Cards: A, B
Notes: 4, 5, 7, 8, 9, 11, 13

NOTES: Credit cards accepted: A MasterCard; B Visa; C American Express; D Discover; E Diner's Club; F Other; 2 Personal checks accepted; 3 Lunch available; 4 Dinner available; 5 Open all year; 6 Pets welcome;

Nevada

CARSON CITY (WASHOE VALLEY)

Deer Run Ranch
Bed and Breakfast

5440 Eastlake Boulevard, 89704
(702) 882-3643

Western ambiance in a unique timber-framed ranch house on this family-owned and -operated alfalfa ranch. Private guest wing with two comfortable rooms, private baths, a sitting room and library, all with its own private entry. Twenty minutes south of Reno, 10 minutes north of Carson City, and a half-hour to Lake Tahoe or Virginia City. The ranch is adjacent to Washoe Lake State Park and affords lots of privacy and wildlife viewing.

Hosts: David and Muffy Vhay
Rooms: 2 (PB) $80-105
Full Breakfast
Credit Cards: A, B, C, D
Notes: 2, 5, 7, 9, 11, 12, 13

EAST ELY

Steptoe Valley Inn

P.O. Box 151110, 220 East 11th Street, 89315-1110
(702) 289-8687 (June-September)
www.nevadaweb.com/steptoe

Elegantly reconstructed in 1990 from the Ely City Grocery of 1907, this inn is one-half block from the Nevada Northern Railway Museum with its weekend train excursions, and 70 miles from the Great Basin National Park. Its individually decorated guest rooms are on the second floor and have private balconies with views of

Steptoe Valley Inn

the mountains and valley or the gazebo and rose garden. Guests have use of the veranda, Victorian living/dining room, and library. Open June through September.

Hosts: Jane and Norman Lindley
Rooms: 5 (PB) $84-90
Full Breakfast
Credit Cards: A, B, C
Notes: 2, 7, 10, 12, 14

GENOA

The Genoa House Inn
Bed and Breakfast

180 Nixon Street, P.O. Box 141, 89411
(702) 782-7075

The Genoa House Inn is an authentic Victorian home listed in the National Register of Historic Places. The house has been restored to the charm and tranquility of an earlier time. Take a romantic step into the past, and enjoy the gracious accommodations accented by antiques and collectibles. Wine in the afternoon; a coffee tray delivered to room, followed by a full breakfast.

NOTES: Credit cards accepted: A MasterCard; B Visa; C American Express; D Discover; E Diner's Club; F Other; 2 Personal checks accepted; 3 Lunch available; 4 Dinner available; 5 Open all year; 6 Pets welcome; 7 No smoking; 8 Children welcome; 9 Social drinking allowed; 10 Tennis nearby; 11 Swimming nearby; 12 Golf nearby; 13 Skiing nearby; 14 May be booked through a travel agent; 15 Handicapped accessible.

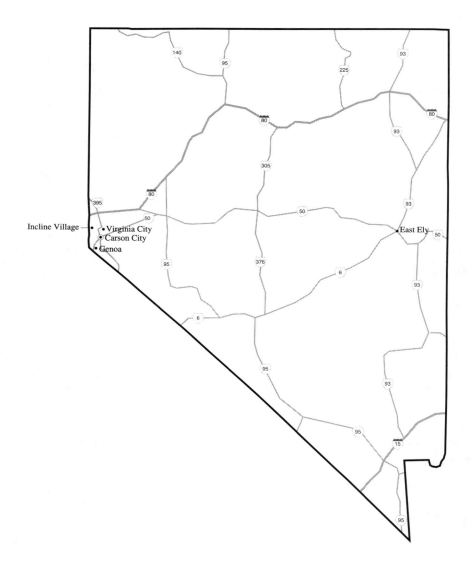

Nevada

Guests have use of Walley's Hot Springs spa nearby. Inquire about accommodations for pets and children.

Hosts: Bob and Linda Sanfilippo
Rooms: 3 (PB) $104-150
Full Breakfast
Credit Cards: A, B, D
Notes: 2, 5, 7, 9, 10, 11, 12, 13, 14

INCLINE VILLAGE

Haus Bavaria

P.O. Box 9079, 89452
(702) 831-6122; (800) 731-6222
FAX (702) 831-1238

Haus Bavaria is a European-style guest house, built in 1980. Each of the five upstairs guest rooms opens onto a balcony, offering a view of the surrounding mountains, while the living room, with its rustic wood paneling and collection of German bric-a-brac, retains an alpine charm. Breakfast is served in the cozy dining room downstairs and includes freshly baked goods, seasonal fruits and juices, freshly ground coffee, and a selection of teas. Children over 12 welcome.

Host: Bick Hewitt
Rooms: 5 (PB) $85-145
Full Breakfast
Credit Cards: A, B, C, D
Notes: 2, 5, 7, 9, 10, 11, 12, 13, 14

VIRGINIA CITY

Gold Hill Hotel

Highway 342, P.O. Box 710, 89440
(702) 847-0111

The Gold Hill Hotel is Nevada's oldest hotel, circa 1859. This country inn is a wonderful combination of luxury and rustic charm, placed in a setting that is fascinating for its history, beauty, and personalities. Guests enjoy a range of accommodations: 12 of the 14 rooms have private baths and four very spacious rooms have fireplaces and balconies. All rooms are decorated with period antiques. Fabulous dinners accented with a choice of over 160 wines create a memorable escape. The cozy bar with its stone and dark wood decor and forge-like fireplace is reminiscent of Old World country inns.

Hosts: Carol and Bill Fain
Rooms: 14 (12 PB; 2 SB) $40-135
Continental Breakfast
Credit Cards: A, B
Notes: 2, 4, 5, 8, 9, 10, 11, 12, 13, 14, 15

Gold Hill Hotel

7 No smoking; 8 Children welcome; 9 Social drinking allowed; 10 Tennis nearby; 11 Swimming nearby; 12 Golf nearby; 13 Skiing nearby; 14 May be booked through a travel agent; 15 Handicapped accessible.

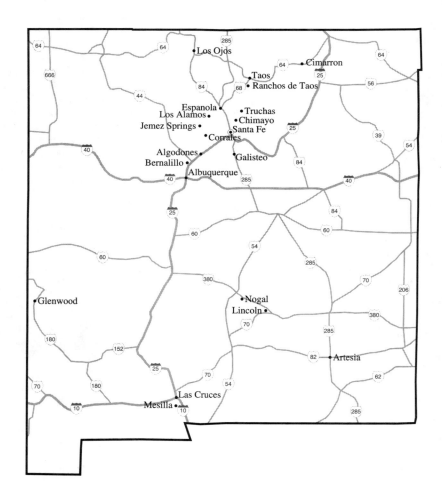

New Mexico

New Mexico

Brittania and W.E. Mauger Estate Bed and Breakfast

701 Roma Avenue Northwest, 87102
(505) 242-8755; (800) 719-9189
FAX (505) 842-8835
www.thuntek.net/tc_arts/mauger

This wonderful 1897 Queen Anne Victorian in the National Register of Historic Places has eight unique rooms with private baths, robes, TV/VCR, and down comforters. The property features a wonderful front porch for enjoying New Mexico summer evenings. Within walking distance of Old Town, downtown, convention center, and many restaurants. Elegant and gracious, this is the place to stay for leisure or business travel. Earn InnPoints for every stay.

Hosts: Mark Brown and Keith Lewis
Rooms: 8 (PB) $89-179
Full Breakfast
Credit Cards: A, B, C, D, E
Notes: 2, 5, 6, 7, 8, 9, 10, 11, 12, 13, 14

Hacienda Antigua Bed and Breakfast

6708 Tierra Drive Northwest, 87107
(800) 201-2986; FAX (505) 345-3855
e-mail: antigua@swcp.com

A 200-year-old adobe hacienda welcomes guests to the rich history of Spanish colonial times. Relax in the peaceful, sun-splashed courtyard, flower gardens, pool, or hot tub. In winter, enjoy a crackling piñon fire. Spacious rooms, antique furnishings, private baths, warm hospitality, and hearty breakfasts. Quiet splendor on El Camino Real. Featured on TLC's *Great Country Inns.* Frommer's: one of the four best bed and breakfasts in New Mexico.

Hosts: Ann Dunlap and Melinda Moffitt
Rooms: 5 (PB) $85-150
Full Breakfast
Credit Cards: A, B, C, D
Notes: 2, 5, 7, 9, 10, 11, 12, 13, 14

Mi Casa Su Casa/Old Pueblo Homestays Bed and Breakfast Reservation Service

P.O. Box 950, Tempe, AZ 85280-0950
(602) 990-0682; (800) 456-0682
FAX (602) 990-3390
e-mail: micasa@primenet.com
www.azres.com

6011. Just 20 minutes from downtown Albuquerque, this southwestern-style home is in a quiet, residential neighborhood, decorated in a delightful mix of antiques, handmade collectibles, and family memorabilia. Surrounded by fruit trees with a large vegetable garden in the corner side yard, this bed and breakfast brings a taste of the country to a convenient city location. Four rooms with private or shared baths available. Dogs in residence. Smoking restricted. Full breakfast is served. $50-60.

6151. The only bed and breakfast accommodation in Old Town proper, this spacious mansion with shaded grass and garden courtyard is visible from the plaza. In the National Register of Historic Places, the

1912 Victorian mansion was built in four-square style and is unusual when compared to most of Old Town's architecture. The decor, food, and hospitality reflect the Indian, Spanish, and Anglo cultures of the area. Seven sets of accommodations are available. Full breakfast. No pets. Smoking restricted. Minimum two-night stay on weekends. Credit cards accepted. $79-139.

6152. In one of Albuquerque's most beautiful areas, this bed and breakfast is within walking distance of the Rio Grande Nature Conservancy and eight miles to the airport. Walking and riding paths crisscross this North Valley area along the bosque. In one wing of this adobe home is a southwestern guest suite with a private entrance and bath by the flower-filled courtyard. The Quilt Room is in the same wing with a private hall bath. There is a large greenhouse with comfortable lounging which is available for guests. Continental plus breakfast. $75-85.

6153. An elegant 1897 three-story Queen Anne historic landmark with a Victorian sitting room and a living room with an organ and a fireplace. Seven guest rooms and a two-room suite have private baths, air conditioning, coffee maker, TVs, and all the comforts of a luxury inn. Refrigerators in the second- and third-floor rooms. Laser disc player available with 200 movies. Walk to the convention center, downtown business center, shops, restaurants, Old Town, and the Indian Cultural Center. Six miles from the airport. Three-course gourmet breakfast, evening treats. Additional guests, $15. Inquire about rates for children. Small pet with special arrangement permitted in one room only, $15. Health club privileges. Indoor/outdoor dining room. German and Spanish spoken. $79-179.

6154. Territorial adobe home with southwestern decor. There is an outdoor kiva fireplace. Seven guest rooms or suites in the main house and the guest house, each with a private bath, fireplace, and many amenities. The largest suite is perfect for families. Afternoon refreshments. Sumptuous full breakfast includes local specialties. Full air conditioning, TV, hot tub. Smoking outdoors only. No pets. Children five and older welcome. Three-night minimum stay during the Balloon Fiesta. For business travelers, there are a fully equipped office, meeting room, and catered meals. Additional person $20. $79-149.

1836. This southwestern/Mediterranean home is on one acre in a quiet neighborhood. Private parking for the two guest suites. Jogging/biking trail nearby. Guests are welcome to use the barbecue. The two very private, spacious suites each can accommodate one to four persons. Each suite has a small refrigerator, microwave, breakfast bar, TV, and telephone. One suite has a whirlpool bath and private veranda. Continental plus breakfast. Smoking outside. One small dog or a horse possible. Spanish spoken. Children under 12 free. Additional person $10. Senior discount. $64-72.

6155. This 200-year-old hacienda and the rich history of Spanish colonial times. There are four rooms and one suite for guests. They can enjoy the warm hospitality, spacious rooms with antique furnishings, kiva fireplaces, and private baths. Amenities include a courtyard with pool, hot tub, and peaceful gardens. The full breakfast often includes southwestern specialities. Two small dogs live here. No smoking or pets. Children over six welcome. $85-150.

Old Town Bed and Breakfast

707 Seventeenth Street Northwest, 87104
(505) 764-9144; (888) 900-9144

Beautiful adobe home, quiet residential area a few blocks from historic Old Town.

NOTES: Credit cards accepted: A MasterCard; B Visa; C American Express; D Discover; E Diner's Club; F Other; 2 Personal checks accepted; 3 Lunch available; 4 Dinner available; 5 Open all year; 6 Pets welcome;

Charming upstairs guest room, queen-size bed, private bath, provides views of Sandia Mountains and tree-lined neighborhood streets. Spacious first-floor suite has king-size bed, kiva fireplace, adjacent Jacuzzi bath shared with owner only. Single beds, additional sleeping accommodations available. Enjoy a short walk to museums, shops, restaurants, or relax on the premises in secluded garden setting. Generous breakfast. Gracious hospitality.

Host: Nancy Hoffman
Rooms: 2 (1 PB; 1 SB) $65-80
Continental Breakfast
Credit Cards: None
Notes: 2, 5, 7, 8, 9, 10, 12, 13, 14

ALGODONES/SANTA FE

Hacienda Vargas

P.O. Box 307, 87001
(505) 867-9115; (800) 261-0006

Romantic, secluded, and historic. Elegantly renovated. Amid the majestic New Mexico mesas, beside the Rio Grande, and lined by cottonwood trees. Seven rooms with fireplaces, private baths, and private entrances. Four suites with two-person Jacuzzi. Barbecue. Thirty minutes south of Santa Fe and north of Albuquerque. Romance packages available. A place of enchantment in the land of enchantment. Children over 12 welcome.

Hosts: Pablo and Julia De Vargas
Rooms: 7 (PB) $79-149
Full Breakfast
Credit Cards: A, B
Notes: 2, 5, 7, 9, 12, 13, 14

ALGODONES

Mi Casa Su Casa/Old Pueblo Homestays Bed and Breakfast Reservation Service

P.O. Box 950, Tempe, AZ 85280-0950
(602) 990-0682; (800) 456-0682
FAX (602) 990-3390
e-mail: micasa@primenet.com
www.azres.com

6201. Gracious hosts welcome guests to a delightful 200-year-old spacious hacienda halfway between Albuquerque and Santa Fe. The Hacienda Vargas is full of light, has polished tile floors, southwestern art, Indian arts and crafts, and a nice mix of antiques. Guests are welcome in the living room or library. The chef presents special full breakfasts. Six guest rooms each have kiva fireplace, private bath, and private entrance to courtyard or hot tub. The large Wagner Room has a whirlpool tub. No resident pets. Smoking outside. Rollaway bed available. $69-139.

ARTESIA

Heritage Inn

1211 West Main Street, 88210 (mailing)
209 West Main Street, 88210 (location)
(505) 748-2552

The Heritage Inn hosts strive to pamper guests with a delightful and unique home-away-from-home inn experience. There are queen-size beds, private baths, and a remote-control color TV. Local calls are free. Newly decorated in country Victorian. Continental breakfast. Deck. Fax service available. No smoking. No pets. AAA-rated three diamonds.

Hosts: James and Wanda Maupin
Rooms: 9 (PB) $50-65
Continental Breakfast
Credit Cards: A, B, C, D
Notes: 2, 5, 7, 11, 12

---

7 No smoking; 8 Children welcome; 9 Social drinking allowed; 10 Tennis nearby; 11 Swimming nearby; 12 Golf nearby; 13 Skiing nearby; 14 May be booked through a travel agent; 15 Handicapped accessible.

BERNALILLO

La Hacienda Grande

21 Baros Lane, 87004
(505) 867-1887; (800) 353-1887
FAX (505) 771-1436; e-mail: lhg@swcp
www.lahaciendagrande.com

On the way to Santa Fe, this superbly restored 250-year-old Spanish hacienda has been a storehouse for Spanish gold as well as a former stagecoach stop. Today the inn reflects historic southwestern architecture with two-inch-thick adobe walls, wood ceilings, stone/tile floors, and fireplaces in almost every room. Six spacious suites are built around a central courtyard with private entrances, private baths, and comfortable sitting areas with fireplaces. Mobil-rated three stars and AAA-rated three diamonds.

Host: Shoshana Zimmerman
Rooms: 6 (PB) $99-129
Full Breakfast
Credit Cards: A, B, C, D, E
Notes: 3, 4, 5, 8, 12, 13, 14

Mi Casa Su Casa/Old Pueblo Homestays Bed and Breakfast Reservation Service

P.O. Box 950, Tempe, AZ 85280-0950
(602) 990-0682; (800) 456-0682
FAX (602) 990-3390
e-mail: micasa@primenet.com
www.azres.com

6231. Magnificent 250-year-old Spanish hacienda built around a central courtyard. Full gourmet breakfast with a southwestern flair. Six guest rooms with private baths; one has a double whirlpool tub. Five rooms have beehive-shaped kiva fireplaces and ceilings with vigas. Coffee served to guests in their room in the morning. Afternoon refreshments available. Romance packages with intimate dinners for two can be arranged. The hacienda is available for special events or business meetings. Air conditioning. Telephones, TVs, and a VCR are available. Downhill and cross-country

skiing less than a half-hour away. Golfing, fishing, boating, and swimming are just minutes from the inn. Rated three diamonds by AAA. No smoking inside. Pets possible, $20. Meals other than breakfast by special arrangement. $89-109.

CHIMAYO

Mi Casa Su Casa/Old Pueblo Homestays Bed and Breakfast Reservation Service

P.O. Box 950, Tempe, AZ 85280-0950
(602) 990-0682; (800) 456-0682
FAX (602) 990-3390
e-mail: micasa@primenet.com
www.azres.com

6251. The inn is 30 miles north of Santa Fe, within a half-hour's drive of several Indian pueblos, national forests, and archaeological sites. On six acres, surrounded by mountains, Casa Escondida ("the hidden house") is a serene home in a Spanish Colonial adobe style, typical of northern New Mexico. Five rooms all have private full baths and are decorated with American arts and crafts. Living area includes a full kitchenette with microwave oven. Hot tub available. Full breakfast. Smoking outside. No pets. Visa and MasterCard accepted. Weekly rates. $65-150.

CIMARRON

Casa del Gavilan

Highway 21 South, P.O. Box 518, 87714
(505) 376-2246; (800) GAVILAN
FAX (505) 376-2247

Nestled in the majestic foothills of the Sangre de Cristo Mountains, the Casa del Gavilan is a place of spirit where hawk and eagle soar. Secluded turn-of-the-century adobe villa. Enjoy elegant hospitality and breathtaking views in a historic setting. Four guest rooms with private baths, plus a two-room suite. "Come join us—and expe-

NOTES: Credit cards accepted: A MasterCard; B Visa; C American Express; D Discover; E Diner's Club; F Other; 2 Personal checks accepted; 3 Lunch available; 4 Dinner available; 5 Open all year; 6 Pets welcome;

Casa de Gavilan

rience the uncommon tranquility of Casa del Gavilan."

Hosts: Bob and Helen Hittle
Rooms: 6 (4 PB; 2 SB) $70-100
Full Breakfast
Credit Cards: A, B, C, D
Notes: 2, 5, 7, 8, 9, 14, 15

CORRALES

Mi Casa Su Casa/Old Pueblo Homestays Bed and Breakfast Reservation Service

P.O. Box 950, Tempe, AZ 85280-0950
(602) 990-0682; (800) 456-0682
FAX (602) 990-3390
e-mail: micasa@primenet.com
www.azres.com

6271. This traditional adobe-style inn was built in 1986 around an inner courtyard with flowers and hummingbirds. Navajo rugs, kachina dolls, carved santos, and pueblo pottery reflect the richness of New Mexico's cultural and artistic background. Within a short walk the visitor will encounter the bosque (cottonwood forest) of the Rio Grande, several fine restaurants, and art galleries. All six guest rooms have private entrances, full baths, and individual heating and cooling. A hot tub and meeting rooms/facilities are available. Rates include a full breakfast, afternoon snacks, complimentary wine or sherry. No smoking or pets. Children possible. $75-95.

6272. This bed and breakfast is a secluded adobe hacienda hidden behind traditional New Mexico walls. An old wooden turquoise gate leads visitors to the shaded patio, intimate gardens, and a hot tub. The suite has a bedroom, sitting room, sofa bed, and kitchenette. Three guest rooms have private baths and a TV is available. Enjoy memorable breakfasts on the patio. Fourteen miles from the Albuquerque airport, 45 miles to Santa Fe. Ten dollars for additional person in the suite. Rates for extended stays and business travelers. Fax available. $85-135.

6273. A private, lush 30-acre estate which has one of the most unusual private collections of animals in the Southwest. There are more than 50 llamas, two potbellied pigs, two water buffalo, two Watusi cows, six peacocks, eight draft horses, a Scottish Highland cow, miniature horses and donkeys, pheasants, a kangaroo, a spider monkey, and a camel. The llama farm stays open to visitors year-round and is free to visit. A conference center with seating is available for groups up to 75. There are mountain bike trails, hiking, basketball, and beach volleyball. All bed and breakfast units are private apartments throughout the barn areas of the farm. They are all completely separate from each other. They feature two bedrooms, living room, kitchen, and bathroom. Families and livestock welcome. Self-catered Continental breakfast placed in kitchen. $65-95.

6274. This contemporary adobe overlooks twinkling city lights and mountain views. The four guest rooms have private full baths with showers and tubs. A morning coffee tray is placed outside the door, and a warm delectable breakfast is on the buffet. There are comfy robes for relaxing and hot tubbing. Loaner mountain bikes. For business guests, conference areas available. Short pleasant distance from Intel and other area businesses. Telephones, fax available. Memorable balloon rides are $200 for two people. $75-99.

7 No smoking; 8 Children welcome; 9 Social drinking allowed; 10 Tennis nearby; 11 Swimming nearby; 12 Golf nearby; 13 Skiing nearby; 14 May be booked through a travel agent; 15 Handicapped accessible.

ESPAÑOLA

Mi Casa Su Casa/Old Pueblo Homestays Bed and Breakfast Reservation Service

P.O. Box 950, Tempe, AZ 85280-0950
(602) 990-0682; (800) 456-0682
FAX (602) 990-3390
e-mail: micasa@primenet.com
www.azres.com

6291. Hostess welcomes guests to handsome, new New Mexico-style home, an easy drive to many places of interest, such as Santa Fe, Taos, Los Alamos, and Bandelier National Monument. Two guest rooms, each with private bath and TV, are available. Guests are welcome in the large living room with a fireplace, ceramic tile floors, and log-beamed ceilings. Afternoon refreshments. Seasonal lap pool. Hot tub. Full breakfast offers New Mexican specialities. Smoking outside. No children, please. Two-night minimum stay. $80.

ESPAÑOLA/ABIQUIU

Casa del Rio

P.O. Box 92, 87532
(505) 753-2035; e-mail: casadelr@roadrunner.com

Casa del Rio, a small ranch on the Chama River, amidst Georgia O'Keeffe's red cliffs. Horses, sheep, hand-carved furniture, local crafts—gracious, genuine, and

Casa del Rio

understated. For an enchanted getaway or a romantic rendezvous, with Casa del Rio as the hub guests can enjoy a wide variety of attractions—hiking, bird watching, biking, skiing, white-water rafting, gambling, fishing, hot springs, horseback riding. This bed and breakfast is in the heart of it all midway between Santa Fe and Taos. Extravagant breakfasts, spectacular view.

Hosts: Eileen Sopanen and Mel Vigil
Rooms: 2 (PB) $85-125
Full Breakfast
Credit Cards: A, B
Notes: 2, 5, 7, 9, 11, 13, 14

GALISTEO

The Galisteo Inn

The Galisteo Inn

HC 75, Box 4, 87540
(505) 466-4000

Visit this 240-year-old adobe hacienda in the beautiful countryside of northern New Mexico, 23 miles southeast of Santa Fe. Enjoy the hot tub, sauna, pool, bicycles, horseback riding, and massage. The dinners feature creative southwestern cuisine nightly, except Monday and Tuesday. Reservations required for accommodations and dining. A buffet breakfast is offered. Smoking in designated areas only.

Hosts: Joanna Kaufman and Wayne Aarniokoski
Rooms: 12 (9 PB; 3 SB) $100-175
Full Breakfast

Credit Cards: A, B, D
Notes: 2, 3, 4, 9, 10, 11, 13, 14, 15

GLENWOOD

Los Olmos Guest Ranch

P.O. Box 127, 88039
(505) 539-2311

A quiet country inn in a narrow valley amidst a bulky mountain range. Situated in a popular outdoor recreation area; hiking, bird watching, and fishing abound. Guest recreation room is in the main building, and guest accommodations are in individual stone cottages with private baths. A swimming pool, spa, bicycles, and horseback riding are all available. Please inquire about pets.

Hosts: Jerry and Tiffany Hagemeier
Rooms: 13 (PB) $65-80
Full Breakfast
Credit Cards: A, B, C, D
Notes: 2, 4, 7, 8, 9, 11

JEMEZ SPRINGS

Bed and Breakfast Southwest Reservation Service

P.O. Box 51198, Phoenix, AZ 85076-1198
(602) 947-9704; (800) 762-9704
FAX (602) 874-1316

Jemez Springs 201. Nestled on three and one-half acres beneath the towering Jemez Mountain Virgin Mesa, on the Jemez River, this adobe-style bed and breakfast inn has six guest rooms each named and decorated after a southwestern Indian tribe. A certified hummingbird sanctuary, the open air plaza in the center of this beautiful inn is filled with birds, hummingbirds, and other wildlife with an underground spring supplying an oversize, continuous-flowing bird bath. Hot tub, barbecue facilities, gym, and complimentary snack bar. No smoking. Children over 12 welcome. $89-109.

LAS CRUCES

Hilltop Hacienda Bed and Breakfast

2600 Westmoreland, 88012
(505) 382-3556; FAX (505) 382-0308

Just minutes from downtown, Hilltop Hacienda is an unusual two-story adobe dwelling of Spanish Moorish architecture offering spectacular views of the city, river valley, and mountains. Guests stay comfortable in the summer and winter and enjoy spectacular sunrises, sunsets, and skies full of stars. Guest quarters are filled with family heirlooms, paintings, and southwestern craft collectibles. Bob and Teddi are full of tips on how to spend time most productively. Smoking outside only. Inquire about accommodations for pets. Children 12 and older welcome.

Hosts: Bob and Teddi Peters
Rooms: 3 (PB) $75-85
Full Breakfast
Credit Cards: A, B
Notes: 2, 5, 7, 9, 10, 11, 12, 13, 14, 15

Lundeen Inn of the Arts

618 South Alameda Boulevard, 88005
(505) 526-3326; FAX (505) 647-1334

Built in 1893, the Lundeen Inn is a historic Mexican/Territorial restored adobe home. Known for the Merienda Room (gathering room), with soaring 18-foot ceilings and Palladian windows that allow the guests to enjoy the sun rising over the majestic Organ Mountains. Guest rooms are named after southwestern artists and decorated accordingly. The Linda Lundeen Art Gallery is nestled in the bed and breakfast.

Hosts: Linda and Gerald Lundeen
Rooms: 20 (PB) $64-105
Full Breakfast
Credit Cards: A, B, C, D, E
Notes: 2, 5, 6, 7, 8, 10, 11, 12, 13, 14

---

7 No smoking; 8 Children welcome; 9 Social drinking allowed; 10 Tennis nearby; 11 Swimming nearby; 12 Golf nearby; 13 Skiing nearby; 14 May be booked through a travel agent; 15 Handicapped accessible.

Mi Casa Su Casa/Old Pueblo Homestays Bed and Breakfast Reservation Service

P.O. Box 950, Tempe, AZ 85280-0950
(602) 990-0682; (800) 456-0682
FAX (602) 990-3390
e-mail: micasa@primenet.com
www.azres.com

6341. This inn is a 100-year-old restored Mexican Territorial inn. It is two double-story guest houses joined by a vast great room with 18-foot ceilings and tall arched windows. All guest accommodations have private baths. Seven suites have kitchenettes, cable TV, telephones. Library, patio, gazebo, media room, exercise room, Ping-Pong room. Full breakfast. Smoking outside. Children and pets welcome with prior arrangement. AAA three-diamond-rated. Weekly and long-term accommodations available. $75-105.

T. R. H. Smith Mansion Bed and Breakfast

909 North Alameda Boulevard, 88005
(505) 525-2525; (800) 526-1914
FAX (505) 524-8227

This stately 1914 mansion was built by bank president T. R. H. Smith and designed by Henry Trost, a Frank Lloyd Wright contemporary, in the heart of the fertile Mesilla Valley. Four distinctive bedrooms are named for the owners' favorite vacation areas: Europe, Southwest, Polynesia, and Latin America. Formal dining and living rooms, sun porch, and basement game/TV room offer relaxing respites alone or to enjoy with other guests. Full breakfast features fresh fruits or fruit drinks.

Hosts: Marlene and Jay Tebo
Rooms: 4 (2 PB; 2 SB) $60
Full Breakfast
Credit Cards: A, B, C, D
Notes: 2, 5, 7, 9, 10, 11, 12, 14

LINCOLN

Mi Casa Su Casa/Old Pueblo Homestays Bed and Breakfast Reservation Service

P.O. Box 950, Tempe, AZ 85280-0950
(602) 990-0682; (800) 456-0682
FAX (602) 990-3390
e-mail: micasa@primenet.com
www.azres.com

6371. The prominent vigas, high ceilings, and new Mexican tiled baths add to the charm of this (circa 1860) historic home. The one-story Old Trail House (circa 1995) with two new rooms offers spaciousness, privacy, gardens, and vistas of the gentle hillsides. The Eastburn (country garden) Room has a bath with double Jacuzzi and shower, fireplace, wet bar, porch, and private entrance. The Vaquero (cowboy) Room has a private bath with roomy shower and built-in seat, fireplace, wet bar, porch, and private entrance. It is handicapped accessible. A hearty country breakfast is served in the main house. Guests in the Old Trail House and the casitas are furnished with Continental plus breakfasts. Evening meals are available with prior arrangement for registered guests. Smoking outdoors. No pets. Additional persons are $6-15 each. $79-107.

LOS ALAMOS

Casa del Rey

305 Rover Street, 87544
(505) 672-9401

Quiet residential area, friendly atmosphere. In White Rock, minutes from Los Alamos and 40 minutes from Santa Fe. Excellent recreational facilities and restaurants nearby. The area is rich in Indian and Spanish history. Breakfast features homemade granola and breads served on the sun porch overlooking flower gardens, with views of the mountains. Children over eight welcome.

Host: Virginia King
Rooms: 2 (SB) $45
Continental Breakfast
Credit Cards: None
Notes: 2, 5, 7, 9, 10, 11, 12, 13

LOS OJOS

Mi Casa Su Casa/Old Pueblo Homestays Bed and Breakfast Reservation Service

P.O. Box 950, Tempe, AZ 85280-0950
(602) 990-0682; (800) 456-0682
FAX (602) 990-3390
e-mail: micasa@primenet.com
www.azres.com

6391. Nine miles south of Chama, this historic, beautifully converted adobe residence was built in 1859 and has been in the same family for several generations. Choose from four guest rooms and two suites, four of which have a private bath. One large first-floor guest suite has a private bath and fireplace. There is a small conference room and gift shop. There are no telephones or TVs. Attractions in the area include train rides over the Rocky Mountains, fishing, hunting, and cross-country skiing. Full breakfast. No smoking or pets. Age restrictions may apply for children. Weekly and monthly rates available. Open February through October. Possible handicapped accessibility. AAA three-diamond-rated. $55-95.

MESILLA

Mesón de Mesilla

1803 Avenida de Mesilla, 88046
(505) 525-9212; (505) 525-2380; (800) 732-6025
FAX (505) 527-4196

A bed and breakfast country inn, in the European tradition, gourmet dining in a southwestern atmosphere. Inquire about accommodations for pets.

Hosts: Gina and Stanley Grudzinski
Rooms: 15 (PB) $55-87
Full Breakfast
Credit Cards: A, B, C, D, E, F
Notes: 2, 4, 5, 7, 8, 9, 11, 14

NOGAL

Monjeau Shadows

HC 67, Box 87, 88341
(505) 336-4191

Four-level Victorian farmhouse on 10 acres of beautiful, landscaped grounds, picnic area, nature trails. King- and queen-size beds, honeymoon suite, antiques. Just minutes from Lincoln National Park and White Mountain Wilderness. Fishing, cross-country skiing, and horseback riding available in area. For fun and relaxation, enjoy Monjeau Shadows' year-round comfort.

Hosts: Billie and Gil Reidland
Rooms: 4 (PB) $75-100
Full Breakfast
Credit Cards: A, B, D
Notes: 2, 5, 7, 10, 11, 12, 13

RANCHOS DE TAOS

Mi Casa Su Casa/Old Pueblo Homestays Bed and Breakfast Reservation Service

P.O. Box 950, Tempe, AZ 85280-0950
(602) 990-0682; (800) 456-0682
FAX (602) 990-3390
e-mail: micasa@primenet.com
www.azres.com

6411. This 160-year-old adobe home is on four acres of pines, fruit trees, and pasture on the tranquil outskirts of Taos. Fifteen minutes to the Rio Grande Gorge and 25 minutes to Taos Ski Valley. All four luxurious, romantic guest rooms in the main house and one guest cottage have private

---

7 No smoking; 8 Children welcome; 9 Social drinking allowed; 10 Tennis nearby; 11 Swimming nearby; 12 Golf nearby; 13 Skiing nearby; 14 May be booked through a travel agent; 15 Handicapped accessible.

entrances, baths, fireplaces. Two-night minimum stay on weekends. Smoking restricted. No pets. Children over 12 welcome. Major credit cards accepted. Full gourmet breakfast. An additional $20 for third person in room. $85-145.

6412. This handcrafted southwestern guest house is the perfect country-town adobe. It sleeps four. There are Saltillo tile flooring, coved-plaster ceilings, living room, dining area, fully-equipped kitchen, kiva fireplace, and hand-carved decorative doors. There are a large supply of piñon firewood, TV, complete linens, and laundry room. A starter breakfast is furnished. No smoking or pets. Children welcome. Minimum stay of two to five nights. Rates vary according to season. Ten dollars for each additional person. $75-175.

SANTA FE

Adobe Abode

202 Chapelle, 87501
(505) 983-3133; FAX (505) 986-0972

Just three blocks from the plaza, this is a historic adobe home restored into an inviting and intimate inn. Decorated with flair and authentic southwestern charm, the inn has private baths, telephones, and TVs in all guest rooms. There are two guest rooms and a two-room suite in the main house, plus three detached casitas with fireplaces, pri-

Adobe Abode

vate entrances, and landscaped patios, all in pure Santa Fe style. Complimentary sherry, cookies, and morning newspaper are offered in the stylish guest living room with fireplace. A full gourmet breakfast is served.

Host: Pat Harbour
Rooms: 6 (PB) $115-155
Full Breakfast
Credit Cards: A, B, D
Notes: 2, 5, 7, 8, 9, 10, 11, 12, 13, 14

Alexander's Inn

Alexander's Inn

529 East Palace, 87501
(505) 986-1431

Enjoy the luxury of this award-winning historic inn near the plaza, surrounded by beautiful gardens of roses and lilacs. The sun-filled rooms are lovingly decorated with antiques, lace, and stenciling. Guests are pampered by hosts with home-baked goodies, a hot tub under the stars, and incredible personal service. Pets welcome. Cottages for families.

Host: Carolyn Lee
Rooms: 16 (14 PB; 2 SB) $75-160
Continental Breakfast
Credit Cards: A, B
Notes: 2, 5, 6, 7, 8, 9, 10, 11, 12, 13, 14

Bed and Breakfast Southwest Reservation Service

P.O. Box 51198, Phoenix, 85076-1198
(602) 947-9704; (800) 762-9704
FAX (602) 874-1316

Santa Fe 203. The finest retreat in historic downtown Santa Fe. Nineteen fully restored casitas surrounded by gardens. Guests may choose from a studio or one-bedroom casita, each with living room, bath, kitchen (stocked with drinks and snacks), cable TV, VCR, and Kiva fireplaces. Relaxing southwestern ambiance. Full health club, pool, and hot tub. Close to fine dining and entertainment, two blocks from the plaza. No smoking. Children welcome. $129 and up.

Casa de la Cuma Bed and Breakfast

105 Paseo de la Cuma, 87501
(505) 983-1717; (888) 366-1717
www.casacuma.com/bb

Casa de la Cuma is a beautiful bed and breakfast inn just four blocks from the Santa Fe Plaza, the historic and artistic center of the city. The living room and each of the three bedrooms are richly decorated with Navajo textiles, Mexican antiques, and original art. Friendly, southwestern hospitality offers afternoon snacks in front of the fireplace or on the guest patio. Vacation rentals (with kitchens) are also available near the Plaza.

Hosts: Art and Donna Bailey
Rooms: 3 (PB) $75-135
Continental Breakfast
Credit Cards: A, B
Notes: 2, 5, 7, 9, 10, 11, 12, 13, 14

Dunshee's

986 Acequia Madre, 87501
(505) 982-0988

A romantic adobe getaway in the historic east side, about a mile from the Plaza. Guests can choose either a two-room suite or a two-bedroom guest house with kitchen. Both units have kiva fireplaces, antiques, folk art, fresh flowers, homemade cookies, phone, TV, pretty linens, private bath, patio, and great breakfasts. Two-night minimum stay weekends and holidays.

Host: Susan Dunshee
Rooms: 2 (PB) $125
Full or Continental Breakfast
Credit Cards: A, B
Notes: 2, 5, 7, 8, 9, 13

El Paradero

El Paradero

220 West Manhattan, 87501
(505) 988-1177; e-mail: elparadero@nets.com

Just a short walk from the busy Plaza, this 200-year-old Spanish farmhouse was restored as a charming southwestern inn. Enjoy a full gourmet breakfast, caring service, and a relaxed, friendly atmosphere. The inn offers lots of common space and a patio for afternoon tea and snacks. Pets welcome by prior arrangements. AAA- and Mobil-rated.

Hosts: Thom Allen and Ouida MacGregor
Rooms: 14 (10 PB; 4 SB) $65-135
Full Breakfast
Credit Cards: A, B
Notes: 2, 5, 6, 7, 8, 9, 10, 11, 12, 13, 14

Four Kachinas Inn

512 Webber Street, 87501
(505) 982-2550; (800) 397-2564
FAX (505) 989-1323
e-mail: 4kachina@swcp.com
www.southwesterninns.com/fourkach.htm

Four Kachinas Inn, a short walk from Santa Fe's historic Plaza, offers six rooms with private baths. The rooms are furnished with Navajo rugs, Hopi kachina dolls, and handcrafted wooden furniture. Three rooms

7 No smoking; 8 Children welcome; 9 Social drinking allowed; 10 Tennis nearby; 11 Swimming nearby; 12 Golf nearby; 13 Skiing nearby; 14 May be booked through a travel agent; 15 Handicapped accessible.

have individual garden patios, while an upstairs room offers a view of the Sangre de Cristo Mountains. Two rooms are in the 1910 landmark cottage. A Continental plus breakfast, including award-winning baked goods, is served in the room. The old adobe guest lounge features afternoon tea and cookies. One room and the guest lounge are handicapped accessible. Children 10 and older welcome.

Hosts: John Daw and Andrew Beckerman
Rooms: 6 (PB) $70-127
Continental Breakfast
Credit Cards: A, B, D
Notes: 7, 9, 10, 11, 12, 13

Grant Corner Inn

122 Grant Avenue, 87501
(505) 983-6678

An exquisite Colonial manor home in downtown Santa Fe. Just two blocks from the historic plaza, the inn is nestled among intriguing shops, restaurants, and galleries.

Grant Corner Inn

Each room is individually appointed with antiques and treasures from around the world: quilts, brass and four-poster beds, armoires, and art. Private telephones, cable TV, and ceiling fans. Complimentary wine is served in the evening.

Host: Louise Stewart
Rooms: 12 (10 PB; 2 SB) $70-155
Full Breakfast
Credit Cards: A, B
Notes: 2, 3, 5, 7, 9, 10, 11, 12, 13, 14, 15

Inn of the Animal Tracks

707 Paseo de Peralta, 87501
(505) 988-1546; FAX (505) 982-8098
e-mail: animal@trail.com
www.santafe.org/animaltracks

Three blocks from the Plaza, this highly acclaimed (by *Frommers*, *Fodor's*, and many other travel directories) cozy and whimsical inn has a distinctive personality. Each of its five rooms has a private bath, queen-size feather bed, and is named and decorated after an animal or a bird. A central living room is filled with big pillows, soft chairs, and a fireplace. A full breakfast is prepared daily. A large shaded patio is available. All rooms are air conditioned and have TVs and telephones.

Innkeeper: Myrna Wheeler
Rooms: 5 (PB) $90-130
Full Breakfast
Credit Cards: A, B, C
Notes: 2, 5, 6, 7, 8, 9, 10, 11, 12, 13, 14, 15

La Tienda Inn

445-447 West San Francisco Street, 87501
(505) 989-8259; (800) 889-7611
FAX (505) 820-6931
www.latiendabb.com/inn/

Just four blocks from the Santa Fe Plaza, the compound includes a turn-of-the-century Territorial-style house and a meandering adobe building which began as a small neighborhood market—La Tienda. Individually decorated guest rooms, some with fireplaces and all overlooking a courtyard or garden area. Private entrances, private bath-

NOTES: Credit cards accepted: A MasterCard; B Visa; C American Express; D Discover; E Diner's Club; F Other; 2 Personal checks accepted; 3 Lunch available; 4 Dinner available; 5 Open all year; 6 Pets welcome;

La Tienda Inn

rooms, cable color TV, and telephones are provided in each room. Enjoy the refreshing afternoon tea in the Old Store Common Room and a generous Continental plus breakfast delivered to guests' room in the morning—or in the garden in summer.

Hosts: Leighton and Barbara Watson
Rooms: 7 (PB) $90-160
Continental Breakfast
Credit Cards: A, B
Notes: 2, 5, 7, 10, 11, 12, 13, 14, 15

Mi Casa Su Casa/Old Pueblo Homestays Bed and Breakfast Reservation Service

P.O. Box 950, Tempe, AZ 85280-0950
(602) 990-0682; (800) 456-0682
FAX (602) 990-3390
e-mail: micasa@primenet.com
www.azres.com

6431. Santa Fe Territorial-style unhosted accommodation in the Canyon Road Historic District, a mixed zoning area of shops, restaurants, and residences. Guests can choose from two separate accommodations sharing a courtyard behind a shop. The suite consists of a bedroom, a sitting room with futon and fireplace, full bath, and kitchenette. The compact casita has a bedroom, kitchenette, and bath. Santa Fe furnishings, quality linens and toiletries, original art, and Mexican tile floors. Self-catered Continental breakfast. Two-week minimum stay. Call for rates.

6432. This two-story, 1903 Craftsman inn and cottage has a friendly atmosphere. In keeping with the turn-of-the-century style, inside are found hardwood floors, fireplaces, antiques, quilts, and stenciling. In the main house, three guest rooms have private baths and two share one bath, and three separate suites have private baths. Continental plus breakfast served. Garden hot tub, mountain bikes, health club guest privileges, concierge services. French spoken. Two-night minimum stay on weekends. No smoking inside. Children six and older welcome in main house; children all ages welcome in suites. Well-behaved pets welcome. $75-200.

1817. This historic inn, which was built in 1906, is a large two-story adobe house within easy walking distance of the Plaza. The four guest rooms' decor reflects different Santa Fe cultures. Each guest room has a private bath, private entrance, and outside patio, garden, or balcony. Visa and MasterCard accepted. Smoking restricted. No pets. Children over 12 welcome. Full breakfast. Seasonal rates available. $85-148.

6433. Constructed in 1948, this small, two-bedroom New Mexico Territorial-style house is in a residential historic neighborhood in a excellent location. There is one guest room available with a private bath in the hall. Near public transportation. Two-night minimum stay weekends. Handicapped accessible. Full breakfast. Smoking outside. An infant or small child welcome. Upon request, hostess will arrange for a crib. Pets welcome with prior arrangement. Weekly rates available. Less in off-season except during holidays. $65-75.

6434. This bed and breakfast is in a hilly area and has beautiful city and mountain views. Walk to the Plaza from the bed and breakfast in 15 minutes. Guests are welcome in the living room where there are a TV, fireplace, VCR, radio, and many books. The large guest room has a full bath en

7 No smoking; 8 Children welcome; 9 Social drinking allowed; 10 Tennis nearby; 11 Swimming nearby; 12 Golf nearby; 13 Skiing nearby; 14 May be booked through a travel agent; 15 Handicapped accessible.

suite, door to outside patio. The extra-large room has a semiprivate full hall bath. Rollaway beds are available. Six guests maximum. Continental plus breakfast. Cats in residence. Two-night minimum preferred. Smoking outside. No pets. No children. German, a little Spanish, and French spoken. For a stay of over two weeks, 10 percent less. $70-85.

Preston House

106 Faithway Street, 87501
(505) 982-3465; (888) 877-7622
FAX (505) 988-2397
e-mail: prestonhouse@aol.com

Santa Fe's first bed and breakfast is a historically plaqued Queen Anne-style house built in 1886 offering eight guest rooms, furnished with antiques and sumptuous, individually chosen linens and lace. The inn is comfortably on a quiet street near the Plaza and Canyon Road. Gardens, fireplaces, stained-glass windows, fresh breads and pastries, personalized service, and an English afternoon tea make Preston House the premier inn of Santa Fe. Continental plus breakfast served. Children 12 and older welcome.

Host: Signe Bergman
Rooms: 8 (6 PB; 2 SB) $65-165
Continental Breakfast
Credit Cards: A, B
Notes: 2, 5, 6, 7, 9, 13, 14

Pueblo Bonito
Bed and Breakfast Inn

138 West Manhattan Avenue, 87501
(505) 984-8001; (800) 461-4599
FAX (505) 984-3155

Historic adobe estate in downtown Santa Fe, three blocks south of the Plaza. Eighteen guest rooms, each with private bath, kiva fireplace, telephone, TV, and 12-inch-thick adobe walls. While the rooms vary in size, the decor is enchantingly Santa Fe—boasting hand-carved wooden furniture and southwestern attire. A bountiful Continental

"create your own" breakfast buffet and afternoon tea (including margaritas) are the perfect complement to any visit. Hot tub facility on premises.

Rooms: 18 (PB) $65-140
Continental Breakfast
Credit Cards: A, B, C, D
Notes: 2, 5, 7, 8, 9, 10, 11, 12, 13, 14, 15

Spencer House Inn

Spencer House Inn

222 McKenzie Street, 87501
(800) 647-0530; www.spencerhse-santafe.com

Spencer House Inn is a four-bedroom cozy and charming traditional bed and breakfast inn. Recipient of the 1994 Historical Preservation award by the Santa Fe Historical Board for restoring the property. Just three blocks from the downtown plaza near the finest restaurants, galleries, and retail stores. Fine bed linens, private baths, and a full breakfast served by the innkeeper. A cozy retreat in downtown Santa Fe. Fully air-conditioned.

Rooms: 5 (PB) $95-167
Full Breakfast
Credit Cards: A, B, C
Notes: 2, 5, 7, 9, 12, 13, 14

Territorial Inn

215 Washington Avenue, 87505
(800) 745-9910

The Territorial Inn is a historic 1890s mansion one and one-half blocks north of the Plaza. Each room is uniquely decorated in a beautiful Victorian style. Eight rooms have private baths and two rooms feature a private fireplace. Breakfast can be enjoyed either outside in the rose garden during the summer or it can be brought to guests in the privacy of their own room each morning.

Hosts: Mary Beath Hokum and Jeanette Arellano
Rooms: 10 (8 PB; 2 SB) $80-165
Continental Breakfast
Credit Cards: A, B, C, E
Notes: 2, 3, 5, 7, 9, 12, 13, 14, 15

TAOS

Adobe and Stars Bed and Breakfast

P.O. Box 2285, 87571
(800) 211-7076

A brand new luxury inn, southwestern style, is at the edge of a national forest and the entrance to famous Taos Ski Valley—perfect for outdoor enthusiasts. Nearby are hiking, biking, horseback riding, Rio Grande rafting, fishing, world-class skiing, and golfing. Visit historic Taos, a pueblo town loaded with museums and art galleries. Unparalleled views from every room, kiva fireplaces, and Jacuzzi tubs. AAA-rated three diamonds and Mobil Travel Guide.

Owner: Judy Salathiel
Rooms: 8 (PB) $75-175
Full Breakfast
Credit Cards: A, B, C, D
Notes: 2, 5, 6, 7, 8, 9, 10, 11, 12, 13, 14, 15

American Artists Gallery House

132 Frontier Road, P.O. Box 584, 87571
(505) 758-4446; (800) 532-2041
e-mail: aagh@taos.newmex.com
www.americanartistsbandb.com

Charming southwestern hacienda filled with artwork by American artists of the Southwest. "Like sleeping in a gallery"—*Bon Appétit*. Tucked away on a secluded dead end road with magnificent views of Taos Mountain. Enjoy gourmet breakfast specially created by the host, kiva fireplaces, Jacuzzi suites, private entrances,

American Artists Gallery House

private baths, outdoor hot tub, and gardens. Minutes from galleries, restaurants, museums, and shops. Let hosts arrange a gallery or historical walking tour to round out a Taos visit.

Hosts: LeAn and Charles Clamurro
Rooms: 10 (PB) $85-185
Full Breakfast
Credit Cards: A, B
Notes: 2, 5, 7, 9, 10, 11, 12, 13, 14

The Brooks Street Inn

119 Brooks Street, P.O. Box 4954, 87571
(505) 758-1489; (800) 758-1489
e-mail: brooks@taos.newmex.com
www.aoswebb.com/hotel/brooks-street/

"One of the Ten Best Inns of North America!"—*Country Inns* magazine. A short walk from Taos Plaza, discover this adobe home, the perfect mix of comfort and elegance, a place of southwestern history, style, and warmth. Enjoy local art, fireplaces, cozy reading nooks, spacious gardens. Indulge in gourmet breakfasts and specialty coffees from the espresso bar. Like Taos itself, the host offers a tradition of gracious hospitality. Children over 10 welcome.

7 No smoking; 8 Children welcome; 9 Social drinking allowed; 10 Tennis nearby; 11 Swimming nearby; 12 Golf nearby; 13 Skiing nearby; 14 May be booked through a travel agent; 15 Handicapped accessible.

Host: Carol Frank
Rooms: 6 (PB) $80-105
Full Breakfast
Credit Cards: A, B, C
Notes: 2, 5, 7, 9, 10, 11, 12, 13, 14

Casa Encantada

416 Liebert Street, 6460 NDCBU, 87571
(505) 758-7477; (800) 223-TAOS

A few short blocks from Taos Plaza—in a world of its own—experience Casa Encantada. Peace, beauty, and warm hospitality abound. The 10 rooms have private entrances and baths. Each room and suite is designed for charm and comfort, portraying the diversity of the area. Healthy breakfasts include fruit, cereals, home-baked goodies, and southwestern delights and are served in a sunny, plant-filled atrium. Information to enhance the Taos experience is generously provided.

Hosts: The Ruffino Family
Rooms: 10 (PB) $95-165
Full Breakfast
Credit Cards: A, B, C
Notes: 2, 5, 7, 10, 11, 12, 13, 14

Casa Europa Inn and Gallery

840 Upper Ranchito Road, HC 68 Box 3F, 87571
(505) 758-9798; (888) 758-9798

Spacious 17th-century pueblo-style inn rests under giant cottonwoods a little over one mile from Taos Plaza. Surrounded with open pastures, grazing horses, and majestic mountain views. Seven elegant guest rooms offer fireplaces, private baths (two with hot tubs), and comfortable furnishings of European antiques and southwestern style. Full gourmet breakfasts and European pastries or evening hors d'oeuvres included. Walled courtyards with flowers, fountains, hot tub, and Swedish sauna. Enjoy the best of the Southwest! America's Favorite Inn Award 1997, Mobil-rated three stars.

Hosts: Rudi and Marcia Zwicker
Rooms: 7 (PB) $75-135
Full Breakfast
Credit Cards: A, B
Notes: 2, 5, 7, 8, 9, 10, 11, 12, 13, 14

Cottonwood Inn Bed and Breakfast

HCR 74, Box 24609, 87529
(800) 324-7120; FAX (505) 776-1141
e-mail: cottonbb@taos.newmex.com
www.taosnet.com/cottonbb/

Relax in adobe elegance at the Cottonwood Inn, surrounded by original art and artifacts of the Southwest. This country inn is serenely set at the foot of the Sangre de Cristo Mountains amidst a grove of cottonwoods. Each of the inn's seven rooms is distinctive, offering spectacular views and a range of amenities from private spa and whirlpool bath to private deck and kiva fireplace. The inn provides a savory full breakfast and evening appetizers. AAA-rated three diamonds.

Hosts: Bill and Kit Owen
Rooms: 7 (PB) $85-155
Full Breakfast
Credit Cards: A, B
Notes: 2, 5, 7, 8, 9, 10, 11, 12, 13, 14, 15

Hacienda del Sol

P.O. Box 177, 87571
(505) 758-0287
www.taoswebb.com/hotel/haciendasol

A 190-year-old historic, charming, quiet adobe with fireplaces, viga ceilings, surrounded by century-old trees. Guest rooms have down comforters, carefully selected furnishings, and fine art. Enjoy an unobstructed view of the mountains from the deck of the outdoor hot tub. Generous breakfasts are served by a crackling fire in the winter, or on the patio in the summer. Chosen by USA Weekend as one of America's 10 most romantic inns. One mile north of Taos Plaza. Mobil-rated three stars.

Hacienda del Sol

Host: Dennis Sheehan
Rooms: 10 (PB) $78-145
Full Breakfast
Credit Cards: A, B
Notes: 2, 5, 7, 8, 9, 10, 11, 12, 13, 14, 15

Hosts: Bill Swan and Nancy Brooks-Swan
Rooms: 6 (PB) $85-135
Full Breakfast
Credit Cards: None
Notes: 2, 5, 7, 8, 9, 12, 13, 14, 15

La Doña Luz Inn formerly El Rincón Inn: An Historic Bed and Breakfast

114 Kit Carson, 87571
(505) 758-4874; FAX (505) 758-4541

In the heart of Taos, this charming adobe inn offers authentic decor, resplendent with fine artwork, Indian, Anglo, and Spanish colonial artifacts representing the three cultures of Taos. Original structure dates to 1802. All rooms feature private baths and all modern amenities; most have fireplaces, Jacuzzi baths, or private hot tubs. A lovely blend of old and new. Recommended by the *New York Times*, *USA Today Weekend*, the *Denver Post*, *Honeymoon* magazine, and featured on the Travel channel series *Romantic Inns of America*. Five rooms are nonsmoking rooms. One room is handicapped accessible.

Hosts: Nina C. Meyers and Paul C. Castillo
Rooms: 16 (PB) $59-125
Continental Breakfast
Credit Cards: A, B, C, D
Notes: 2, 5, 6, 8, 9, 10, 11, 12, 13, 14

La Posada de Taos

309 Juanita Lane, P.O. Box 1118, 87571
(800) 645-4803; FAX (505) 751-3294
e-mail: laposada@taos.newmex.com
www.taosnet.com/laposada/

Escape to a romantic, secluded adobe inn, two and one-half blocks from Plaza in the historic district. First bed and breakfast in Taos. Walk to galleries, museums, restaurants, shops. Return to casual elegance of country pine antiques, handmade quilts, private baths, courtyards, fireplaces. Savor a delicious full breakfast. Two rooms with whirlpool tubs. Separate honeymoon house. Local knowledge of shops and nearby mountains. *New York Times* on Taos "Where to Stay." AAA three-diamond-rated.

Mi Casa Su Casa/Old Pueblo Homestays Bed and Breakfast Reservation Service

P.O. Box 950, Tempe, AZ 85280-0950
(602) 990-0682; (800) 456-0682
FAX (602) 990-3390
e-mail: micasa@primenet.com
www.azres.com

1824. This 50-year-old updated and enlarged adobe home has three spacious guest rooms. Two of the rooms share a private living room with kiva fireplace, refrigerator, and private entrance. The third room has a private bath, kiva fireplace, sitting area, and private entrance. Full breakfast. Dogs, cats, llamas on property. Rates are higher during holidays. Crib available. Fifteen dollars for each additional person. $75-85.

6461. This inn is on a secluded acre surrounded by an adobe wall in the heart of Taos. Each of the inn's five guest rooms has a private entrance and private bath plus a welcoming kiva fireplace and a lot of privacy. Listed in the national and state historic registries. TV, stereo, and library of more than 500 classical and jazz CDs. Guided fishing trips are available upon request. Full breakfast. Afternoon refreshments. Fifteen dollars for each additional guest. $95-130.

6463. This two-story bed and breakfast has three guest rooms with private baths. There are a wraparound "coyote fence," flower beds, a fountain, fish pond, deck, and portal. The living room has a fireplace and baby grand piano. Continental breakfast. No smoking or pets. Children welcome. Handicapped possible. $75-95.

7 No smoking; 8 Children welcome; 9 Social drinking allowed; 10 Tennis nearby; 11 Swimming nearby; 12 Golf nearby; 13 Skiing nearby; 14 May be booked through a travel agent; 15 Handicapped accessible.

Old Taos Guest House

1028 Witt Road, Box 6552, 87571
(800) 758-5548; FAX (505) 758-5448 (call first)
www.taoswebb.com/hotel/oldtaoshouse/

Discover the magic of Taos from this historic adobe hacienda with spectacular views. On seven and one-half acres yet only five minutes to the Plaza, this bed and breakfast offers cozy rooms and exquisite suites in a rural setting. Don't miss the wonderful hot tub, romantic fireplaces, healthy breakfasts and an intimate knowledge of rivers, trails, and mountains.

Hosts: Tim and Leslie Reeves
Rooms: 9 PB) 70-125
Continental Breakfast
Credit Cards: B
Notes: 2, 5, 7, 8, 9, 10, 11, 12, 13

Orinda Bed and Breakfast

461 Valverde, 87571
(800) 847-1837

A beautiful 50-year-old adobe estate that combines spectacular views with country privacy and is still within walking distance of Taos Plaza. Four bedrooms are available with private baths and entrances. A delicious and hearty breakfast is served each morning.

Hosts: Cary and George Pratt
Rooms: 4 (PB) $70-90
Full Breakfast
Credit Cards: A, B, C, D
Notes: 2, 5, 7, 8, 9, 10, 11, 12, 13, 14

Orinda

The Ruby Slipper Bed and Breakfast

P.O. Box 2069, 87571
(505) 758-0613

This restored adobe farmhouse with classic gabled roof is just a 10-minute walk from the historic Taos Plaza. The rooms, each with fireplace or woodstove and tea and coffe service, are romantic and private. The scrumptious breakfasts include apple-cheddar omelets, breakfast burritos with homemade green chile, pumpkin spice pancakes, and more. A memorable stay will include great conversation in a warm atmosphere. Private hot tub available.

Rooms: 7 (PB) $79-119
Full Breakfast
Credit Cards: A, B, C, D
Notes: 2, 5, 7, 8, 9, 10, 11,1 2, 13, 14, 15

Salsa del Salto Bed and Breakfast

P.O. Box 1468, El Prado, 87529
(505) 776-2422; (800) 530-3097
e-mail: salsa@taos/newmex.com
www.taoswebb.com/salsa

Taos's most beautiful blend of southwestern style and ambiance. Soaring mountain views, stunning sunsets, a million stars, and a hot tub. Turquoise pool, tennis court, and beautiful gardens. Ten rooms with king- or queen-size beds, some with jetted tubs, and fireplaces. Close to Taos Ski Valley and Taos Plaza. French chef, gourmet breakfast, and afternoon snacks.

Hosts: Dadou Mayer and Mary Hockett
Rooms: 8 (PB) $85-160
Full Breakfast
Credit Cards: A, B
Notes: 2, 5, 7, 9, 10, 11, 12, 13, 14

Sagebrush Inn

Box 557, 87571
(800) 428-3626

A charming southwestern inn with warm hospitality. Request a room with an adobe

NOTES: Credit cards accepted: A MasterCard; B Visa; C American Express; D Discover; E Diner's Club; F Other; 2 Personal checks accepted; 3 Lunch available; 4 Dinner available; 5 Open all year; 6 Pets welcome;

fireplace and hand-carved furniture. Authentic Taos artwork throughout the inn. Full-service bar and dining room. Live country-western music nightly in the cantina. Golf, ski, and river rafting packages available. Close to health club.

Rooms: 100 (PB) $55-140
Full Breakfast
Credit Cards: A, B, C, D, E
Notes: 2, 4, 5, 6, 7, 8, 9, 10, 11, 12, 13, 14, 15

Taos Bed and Breakfast Association

P.O. Box 2772, 87571
(505) 758-4747; (800) 876-7857
FAX (505) 758-7875
e-mail: tbba@taos.newmex.com
www.taoswebb.com/bedandbreakfast

Casa de las Chimeneas. (505) 758-4777. "Just two and one-half blocks from the plaza, secluded behind thick adobe walls, the House of Chimneys with its formal gardens...could serve as the approach to a castle."—*Fodor's*. "...a perfect romantic hideaway"—*Ski*. Featured in *Bon Appétit* and *Gourmet*. A luxury bed and breakfast with spectacular amenities since 1988. AAA three-diamond-rated and Mobil three-star-rated. Eight rooms. $125-190.

Old Taos Guesthouse. (505) 758-5448. Nestled amid a grove of stately old trees, this historic adobe hacienda sits peacefully on seven and one-half rural acres above Taos, just five minutes from the plaza. Quiet spots and spectacular views are easy to find on these spacious grounds. Cozy rooms, exquisite suites, skylights, fireplaces, private baths, star-lit hot tub, perfect for outdoor enthusiasts. Nine rooms. $70-125.

The Willows Inn. (505) 758-2558. Discover romance in an artist's historic walled adobe estate. This bed and breakfast is on a secluded parklike acre where massive willows and expansive gardens create an oasis

just a short walk to the plaza. Experience southwestern cultures in the deluxe themed rooms: Cowboy, Anasazi, Conquistador, Santa Fe, or Hennings' Studio. Enjoy lavish, full breakfasts and afternoon hors d'oeuvres. $95-130.

Inn on La Loma. (505) 758-1717. An elegant and luxurious walled adobe estate on the national historic register, two and one-half blocks from the plaza. Quiet park setting with towering trees and commanding mountain views. Beautifully appointed, spacious guest areas with fountains. Romantic rooms with private baths, hand-crafted furniture, fireplaces, and a healthy gourmet breakfast. Seven rooms. $95-195.

Salsa del Salto. (505) 776-2422. Exquisite southwestern inn with soaring mountain views and stunning sunsets. Enjoy the private tennis court, heated pool, and hot tub. Tastefully decorated rooms with down comforters, full baths, some with fireplaces and whirlpool tubs. "In short, you will want for nothing here."—*Frommer's*. Gourmet breakfast, snacks. Ten rooms. $85-160.

Casa Europa. (505) 758-9798. Be immersed in the magical Southwest when staying at this classic 17th-century inn. On six lush acres with mountain vistas, horses, fountains, garden hot tub and sauna. Be pampered in one of the seven luxury rooms offered with marble baths, fireplaces, hot tubs, fine antiques, all with southwestern flair. Full gourmet breakfast, European pastries and hors d'oeuvres included. Mobil three-star-rated and ABBA plus. $85-135.

Alma del Monte. (505) 776-8888. Quality-built for romance and luxury, this exquisite five-guest-room hacienda exudes an ambiance of casual elegance and southwestern charm with magnificent panoramic vistas of the mountains and the mesas. Each spacious guest room has a fireplace, whirlpool, skylight, antiques, down comforter, etc. Sumptuous gourmet breakfasts and afternoon refreshments. $125-200.

The Willows Inn

412 Kit Carson Road at Dolan Street
Box 6560 NDCBU, 87571-6223
(505) 758-2558; (800) 525-TAOS (8267)
(505) 758-5445 (guestline/FAX)
e-mail: willows@taos.newmex.com
www.taoswebb.com/hotel/willows

Nestled under two of America's largest willow trees is this national historic register estate. The walled adobe estate was the home and studio of E. M. Hennings, member of the elite 1920s Taos Society of Artists. The innkeeper/owners share their hospitality beginning with a gourmet, family-style breakfast and visiting over lavish afternoon refreshments. Each of the

The Willows Inn

inn's guest rooms has an outside entrance, private bath, queen-size bed, and year-round kiva fireplace. The individual room decors reflect cultures special to Taos. Guided fly-fishing trips available. Walk to the plaza. Limited handicapped accessibility.

Hosts: Janet and Doug Camp
Rooms: 5 (PB) $95-130
Full Breakfast
Credit Cards: A, B, C
Notes: 2, 5, 7, 8, 9, 10, 11, 12, 13, 14

TRUCHAS

Rancho Arriba

P.O. Box 338, 87578
(505) 689-2374
www.redbay.com/web/rancho

A European-style bed and breakfast with an informal and tranquil atmosphere, this traditional adobe hacienda is on a historic Spanish land grant. Spectacular mountain view in every direction, amid colonial villages featuring traditional arts and architecture. Adobe churches, hand weaving, wood carving, and quilting. Smoking in designated areas only.

Host: Curtiss Frank
Rooms: 4 (SB) $70
Full Breakfast
Credit Cards: A, B
Notes: 2, 4, 5, 8, 9, 13

NOTES: Credit cards accepted: A MasterCard; B Visa; C American Express; D Discover; E Diner's Club; F Other; 2 Personal checks accepted; 3 Lunch available; 4 Dinner available; 5 Open all year; 6 Pets welcome;

Oregon

Adams Cottage
Bed and Breakfast

737 Siskiyou Boulevard, 97520
(541) 488-5405; (800) 345-2570

Adams Cottage, built in 1900, offers picket-fence country charm with beautiful grounds surrounding the two-story house and secluded carriage house. Private bath, air conditioning, antiques, in-room fireplace, and gourmet breakfast. Short walk to shops, theater, University of Southern Oregon. An ABBN member. Full breakfast available May through October.

Host: Jeff von Hauf
Rooms: 4 (PB) $55-115
Full Breakfast
Credit Cards: A, B, F
Notes: 2, 5, 7, 8, 9, 10, 11, 12, 13, 14

Country Willows
Bed and Breakfast Inn

1313 Clay Street, 97520
(541) 488-1590; (800) WILLOWS
FAX (541) 488-1611; www.willowsinn.com

Combine Ashland's theatrical attractions with a peaceful rural setting at Country Willows. Guest rooms have views of the Siskiyou and Cascade Mountains. Guests may relax in the Jacuzzi, on the inn's porches, or in the Willows's swing. Hiking trails are also available. The five-acre, 1896 farmhouse was remodeled in 1985 for maximum comfort. Rooms are in the main house, a separate guest cottage, and in an 1899 barn. The swimming pool is heated spring through fall. Rates include a full breakfast served at individual tables on the porch or in the sunroom. Guests looking for a special romantic getaway will love the two barn suites with king-size beds, fireplaces, and Jacuzzis for two.

Host: Dan Durant
Suite: 9 (PB) $90-185
Full Breakfast
Credit Cards: A, B, C, D
Notes: 2, 5, 7, 9, 10, 11, 12, 13, 14, 15

Cowslip's Belle
Bed and Breakfast

159 North Main Street, 97520
(541) 488-2901; (800) 888-6819
FAX (541) 482-6138; e-mail: stay@cowslip.com
www.cowslip.com/cowslip

Teddy bears, chocolate truffles, sweet dreams, and scrumptious breakfasts can be enjoyed here. Just three blocks to the heart of town. Beautiful 1913 Craftsman bungalow and carriage house. Four queen/twin rooms with private baths and entrances. Featured in *McCall's* "Most Charming Inns in America," *Weekends for Two in the Pacific Northwest—50 Romantic Getaways*, *Best Places to Kiss in the Northwest*, and *Northwest Best Places*. Country accents. "A garden of many splendored delights." Member of the Oregon Bed and Breakfast Guild. Children over nine welcome.

Cowslip's Belle

---

7 No smoking; 8 Children welcome; 9 Social drinking allowed; 10 Tennis nearby; 11 Swimming nearby; 12 Golf nearby; 13 Skiing nearby; 14 May be booked through a travel agent; 15 Handicapped accessible.

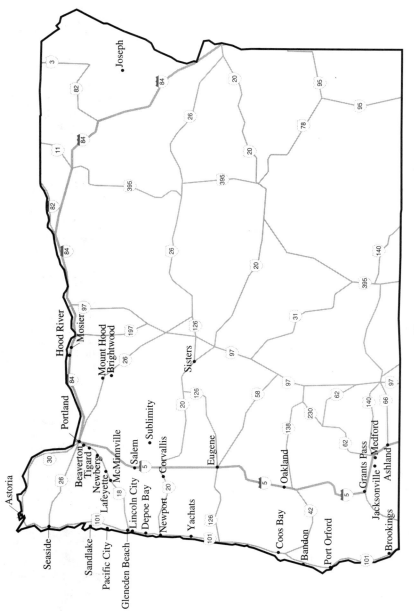

Oregon

Hosts: Jon and Carmen Reinhardt
Rooms: 5 (PB) $95-175
Full Breakfast
Credit Cards: A, B
Notes: 2, 5, 7, 9, 10, 11, 12, 13, 14

Hersey House

Hersey House

451 North Main Street, 97520
(541) 482-4563; (800) 482-4563
FAX (541) 488-9317; e-mail: herseybb@mind.net
www.mind.net/hersey

Relaxed living in restored Victorian with a colorful English country garden. Also a separate bungalow for families or groups that sleeps two to six. Sumptuous breakfasts. Air conditioning. Walk to plaza and three Shakespeare theaters. Nearby, guests will find white-water rafting on the Rogue and Klamath Rivers, Crater Lake National Park, Britt Music Festival, Jacksonville national historic district, and Oregon wineries.

Hosts: Paul and Terri Mensch
Rooms: 4 (PB) $75-119
Bungalow: 1 (PB) $99-149
Full and Continental Breakfast
Credit Cards: A, B, D
Notes: 2, 5, 7, 8, 10, 11, 12, 13, 14

The Iris Inn

59 Manzanita Street, 97520
(541) 488-2286; (800) 460-7650
FAX (541) 488-3709; e-mail: irisinnbb@aol.com

A favorite since 1982. A 1905 Victorian furnished with antiques. Elegant breakfasts fea-

ture eggs Benedict and cheese-baked eggs. Mountain views, quiet neighborhood. Near the Oregon Shakespeare Festival and the Rogue River for rafting. Cross-country and downhill skiing also nearby. The Oregon Cabaret Theater operates year-round, and the Britt Music Festival is enjoyed during the summer. Children over seven welcome.

Host: Vicki Lamb
Rooms: 5 (PB) $110
Full Breakfast
Credit Cards: A, B
Notes: 2, 5, 7, 10, 11, 12, 13

Morical House Garden Inn

668 North Main Street, 97520
(541) 482-2254; (800) 208-0960
FAX (541) 482-1775; e-mail: moricalhse@aol.com
www.garden-inn.com

Eastlake Victorian farmhouse on two acres of gardens with mountain views, ponds, and stately trees provides rural setting only seven blocks from Oregon Shakespeare Festival. Some guest rooms feature fireplaces, wet bars, and double whirlpool tubs. All have private baths. Superb breakfasts served at individual tables in dining room or on sun porch. AAA-rated three diamonds, ABBA-rated three crowns.

Hosts: Gary and Sandye Moore
Rooms: 7 (PB) $88-160
Full Breakfast
Credit Cards: A, B, C, D
Notes: 2, 5, 7, 9, 10, 11, 12, 13, 14, 15

Morical House Garden Inn

Mount Ashland Inn

Mount Ashland Inn

550 Mount Ashland Ski Road, 97520
(541) 482-8707; (800) 830-8707

Enjoy mountain serenity and spectacular views from this beautifully handcrafted log inn 16 miles from Ashland. Relax in comfortable, welcoming surroundings accented by the sunny deck, rock fireplace, stained glass, hand carvings, oriental rugs, and antiques. The new Finnish sauna and outdoor jetted spa have fabulous mountain views. Hike and cross-country ski from the door; closest lodging to downhill ski area. AAA- and Mobil-recommended. Member of the Oregon Bed and Breakfast Guild and the Professional Association of Innkeepers International. Included in room rates is a large gourmet breakfast and use of snowshoes, cross-country skis and boots, sleds, and mountain bikes. Children over 10 welcome.

Hosts: Chuck and Laurel Biegert
Rooms: 5 (PB) $79-190
Full Breakfast
Credit Cards: A, B, C, D
Notes: 5, 7, 9, 10, 12, 13, 14

The Mousetrap Inn

312 Helman Street, 97520
(541) 482-9228; (800) 460-5453
e-mail: mousetrapinn@stealthcom.com
www.stealthcom.com/mousetrap

A comfortable, colorful 1890s restored home in Ashland's historic railroad district. Only four blocks from the theater area, it has six rooms with private baths, queen-size beds, air conditioning, an English garden, and deck. Breakfast includes freshly squeezed orange juice, smoothies, delicious baked goods, local fruits, and good coffee, with an emphasis on low-fat, organic ingredients. The decor is eclectic and whimsical, combining antiques with contemporary art, as well as pottery made by the hosts.

Hosts: Rob and Linda Joseph
Rooms: 6 (PB) $73-98
Full Breakfast
Credit Cards: A, B
Notes: 2, 7, 8, 9, 12, 13, 14

Neil Creek House
Bed and Breakfast

341 Mowetza Drive, 97520
(541) 482-6443; (800) 460-7860
FAX (541) 482-1074; e-mail: neilcrk@mindnet.
www.mind.net/neilcrk

Nestled in the foothills of the Siskiyou Mountains with magnificent views of the Cascades is this country retreat. The tranquil parklike setting offers a wildlife pond and creek that wanders lazily through the property. Stroll through the woods, bird watch, or relax in the gazebo with a cool afternoon refreshment. Merely six picturesque miles from the Shakespearean experience and many other exciting activities. Call for additional information or a brochure. Service dogs welcome. Children 12 and older welcome.

Hosts: Paul and Gayle Negro
Rooms: 2 (PB) $85-175
Full Breakfast
Credit Cards: None
Notes: 2, 4, 5, 7, 9, 10, 11, 12, 13, 14

Neil Creek House

Oak Hill Country

Oak Hill Country Bed and Breakfast

2190 Siskiyou Boulevard, 97520
(541) 482-1554; (800) 888-7434
FAX (541) 482-1378; e-mail: oakhill@mind.net
www.bbonline.com/or/oakhill

This charming 1910 farmhouse, minutes from the Oregon Shakespeare Festival, offers the convenience of the city with the ambiance and tranquillity of the country. An old-fashioned veranda, spacious living room, gardens, deck, and bicycles provide variety for guests' relaxation. Each of the inn's six air-conditioned bedrooms has a queen-size bed and a private bath. The delicious family-style breakfast served in the sunny dining room is truly the main event at Oak Hill. AAA two-diamonds- and Mobil two-stars-rated. Children 12 and older welcome. "What a terrific find—charming, immaculate, warm, and inviting, absolutely wonderful food, and a loving and generous innkeeper."

Rooms: 6 (PB) $65-105
Full Breakfast
Credit Cards: A, B
Notes: 2, 5, 7, 9, 11, 12, 13, 14

Pinehurst Inn at Jenny Creek

17250 Highway 66, 97520
(541) 488-1002

Constructed in 1923 with logs harvested from the property, the lodge accommodated travelers on the new State Highway 66 built to replace the old southern Oregon wagon road. The inn is on the west bank of Jenny Creek, where the Cascade and Siskiyou

Mountains meet, 23 miles east of Ashland and 39 miles west of Klamath Falls. The restaurant serves breakfast, lunch, and dinner to the inn's guests and the public.

Hosts: Mike and Mary Jo Moloney
Rooms: 4 (PB) $75-105
Suites: 2 (PB)
Full Breakfast
Credit Cards: A, B, D
Notes: 2, 3, 4, 7, 9, 11, 12, 13

The Redwing Bed and Breakfast

115 North Main Street, 97520
(541) 482-1807; (800) 461-6743

The Redwing, nestled in Ashland's charming historic district, is a 1911 Craftsman-style home with its original lighting fixtures, beautiful wood, and comfortable decor. Each of the inviting guest rooms enjoys its own distinctive intimacy, queen-size bed, and private bath. One city block from the Oregon Shakespeare Festival, Lithia Park, restaurants, and gift shops. Downhill and cross-country skiing, river rafting, and fishing are nearby. *Bon Appétit*, July 1994, and *Breakfast For Chocolate*, May 1997.

Hosts: Judi and Mike Cook
Rooms: 3 (PB) $70-125
Full Breakfast
Credit Cards: A, B, D
Notes: 2, 5, 7, 9, 10, 11, 12, 13

The Redwing

Romeo Inn

295 Idaho Street, 97520
(541) 488-0884; (800) 915-8899
FAX (541) 488-0817

An elegant Cape Cod amid pines and beautiful gardens in a quiet residential

7 No smoking; 8 Children welcome; 9 Social drinking allowed; 10 Tennis nearby; 11 Swimming nearby; 12 Golf nearby; 13 Skiing nearby; 14 May be booked through a travel agent; 15 Handicapped accessible.

neighborhood near downtown. Hand-stitched Amish quilts, swimming pool, hot tubs, fireplaces, library, air conditioning, gourmet breakfasts. Mobil-rated three stars, AAA-rated three diamonds. Featured in *Country Inns* magazine, August 1995. Selected as one of the few Special Places. "Professional innkeeping with a personal touch."

Hosts: Deana and Don Politis
Rooms: 6 (PB) $95-180
Full Breakfast
Credit Cards: A, B, D
Notes: 2, 5, 7, 9, 10, 11, 12, 13, 14

The Wood's House

The Wood's House Bed and Breakfast Inn

333 North Main Street, 97520
(541) 488-1598; (800) 435-8260
FAX (541) 482-8027
e-mail: woodshse@mind.net
www.mind.net/woodshouse/

In the historic district, four blocks from the Shakespeare theaters, Lithia Park, restaurants, and shops, this 1908 Craftsman-style home offers six sunny and spacious guest rooms. Simple furnishings of warm woods, antique furniture, fine linens, watercolors, oriental carpets, leather books, and private-label amenities create a sophisticated comfortable ambiance. The one-half-acre terraced English gardens provide many areas for guests to relax, read, and socialize. Golf, swimming, hiking, biking, and river rafting are nearby.

Hosts: Françoise and Lester Roddy
Rooms: 6 (PB) $65-118
Full Breakfast
Credit Cards: A, B, D
Notes: 2, 5, 7, 9, 10, 11, 12, 13, 14

ASTORIA

Astoria Inn Bed and Breakfast

3391 Irving Avenue, 97103
(503) 325-8153; (800) 718-8153

Relax and be pampered in the comfort of an 1890s Victorian. Magnificent views of the Columbia River. Hiking trails in the forest behind the inn. Beautifully decorated guest rooms with private baths. Full breakfast and daily snacks. Beautiful, quiet residential neighborhood just three minutes from shopping and restaurants.

Host: Mickey Cox
Rooms: 4 (PB) $60-85
Full Breakfast
Credit Cards: A, B, D
Notes: 2, 5, 7, 9, 10, 11, 12, 14

Columbia River Inn Bed and Breakfast

1681 Franklin Avenue, 97103
(503) 325-5044; (800) 953-5044

A five-star Victorian charmer. Elegant "painted lady" when guests enter. Built in

Columbia River Inn

NOTES: Credit cards accepted: A MasterCard; B Visa; C American Express; D Discover; E Diner's Club; F Other; 2 Personal checks accepted; 3 Lunch available; 4 Dinner available; 5 Open all year; 6 Pets welcome;

the late 1870s. Nearby, Columbia River Maritime Museum and Captain George Flavel House. Ocean is five miles away. Full breakfast, river view, off-street parking available. Enjoy Stairway to the Stars, a unique terraced garden. Gazebo available for outdoor weddings and parties; write and ask for details and prices. During the summer and holidays a two-night minimum stay is required. New seafood lab.

Host: Karen N. Nelson
Rooms: 4 (PB) $75-125
Full Breakfast
Credit Cards: A, B
Notes: 2, 5, 11, 12

Franklin Street Station Bed and Breakfast

1140 Franklin Street, 97103
(503) 325-4314; (800) 448-1098

This Victorian home is rated one of the finest bed and breakfast establishments by many publications. Five rooms, all with private baths (two suites), and three rooms with views of the Columbia River. Try the Captain's Quarters, with a fabulous view, wet bar, fireplace, TV, VCR, stereo, and luxurious bath. Full breakfast. Close to downtown and within walking distance of museums. Make reservations in advance, if possible.

Host: Renee Caldwell
Rooms: 5 (PB) $68-120
Full Breakfast
Credit Cards: A, B, C, D
Notes: 2, 5, 7, 8, 9, 10, 11, 12

BANDON

Lighthouse Bed and Breakfast

650 Jetty Road, P.O. Box 24, 97411
(541) 347-9316

The gateway of the Pacific Ocean meets the mouth of the Coquille River with the Bandon historical lighthouse illuminating the scene. Walking distance to historical old downtown Bandon or the beach and surf.

Unsurpassed views. Five guest rooms, two king-size with whirlpool and fireplace. Full breakfast. Children over 12 welcome by prior arrangement. Complimentary wine.

Host: Shirley Chalupa
Rooms: 5 (PB) $90-145
Full Breakfast
Credit Cards: A, B
Notes: 2, 5, 7, 9, 11, 12

Sea Star Guesthouse

370 First Street, 97411
(503) 347-9632

This guest house is a comfortable, romantic coastal getaway with European ambiance. It is on the harbor and provides harbor, river, and ocean views. The shops, galleries, theater, and other sights of the Oldtown Harbor District are just a step away. The newly decorated rooms offer a warm, private retreat. Some rooms have skylights, open-beam ceilings, and fireplaces; all have decks. All rooms have refrigerators, toaster ovens, and in-room coffee and tea service.

Host: Eileen Sexton
Rooms: 4 (PB) $40-85
Credit Cards: A, B, D
Notes: 5, 7, 8, 9, 10, 11, 12

BEAVERTON

The Yankee Tinker Bed and Breakfast

5480 Southwest 183rd Avenue, 97007
(503) 649-0932; (800) 846-5372
e-mail: yankeetb7b@aol.com
www.yankeetinker.com

Easy access to Beaverton, Hillsboro businesses, 10 miles west of Portland, in Washington County wine country. Comfortable home operating as bed and breakfast since 1988, filled with family heirlooms, antiques, quilts, and flowers. Private yard and gardens. Spacious deck. Quiet retreat, perfect for a day or a week. Fireplace in guest sitting room. Fully air conditioned. Acclaimed breakfasts, timed and scaled to

7 No smoking; 8 Children welcome; 9 Social drinking allowed; 10 Tennis nearby; 11 Swimming nearby; 12 Golf nearby; 13 Skiing nearby; 14 May be booked through a travel agent; 15 Handicapped accessible.

meet guests' needs, utilize the abundant variety of locally grown fruits and berries. Featured in *Hidden Oregon*.

Hosts: Jan and Ralph Wadleigh
Rooms: 3 (2 PB; 1 SB) $65-75
Full Breakfast
Credit Cards: A, B, C, D, E
Notes: 2, 5, 7, 9, 10, 11, 12, 14

BRIGHTWOOD

Pacific Bed and Breakfast Agency

P.O. Box 46894, Seattle, WA 98146
(206) 439-7677; FAX (206) 431-0932
e-mail: pacificb@nwlink.com
www.seattlebedandbreakfast.com

149. East of Portland, on two acres on historic Barlow Trail and surrounded by a clear mountain stream and tall firs is guests' very own guest house with its own Japanese water garden for that special getaway. A complimentary gourmet breakfast can accommodate special diets if there is advanced notice. A variety of bikes, books, videos, games, and puzzles are provided. Make sure to make reservations for lodging early for this lovely spot.

BROOKINGS

Brookings South Coast Inn

516 Redwood Street, 97415
(541) 469-5557; (800) 525-9273
FAX (541) 469-6615; e-mail: scoastin@wave.net
www.virtualcities.com

A 1917 vintage home designed in the Craftsman style by Bernard Maybeck. Restored and furnished with antiques and treasures, this home has a happy, warm feeling. Large parlor, indoor hot tub/sauna, in-room TV/VCRs, spacious bedrooms upstairs. Ocean view. Just a few blocks from the river and harbor. Gourmet breakfast includes Norwegian waffles. A private garden cottage is also available. Fully

licensed. AAA-approved and *Northwest Best Places*. Children over 12 are welcome.

Hosts: Ken and Keith
Rooms: 4 (PB) $84-94
Full Breakfast
Credit Cards: A, B, C, D
Notes: 2, 5, 7, 9, 10, 11, 12, 14

Chetco River Inn

21202 High Prairie Road, 97415
(541) 670-1645
(800) 327-2688 (Pelican Bay Travel)
FAX (503) 469-4341

Relax in the peaceful seclusion of 35 forested acres. Near the seacoast town of Brookings. The inn is small, so guest numbers are limited. Surrounded on three sides by the lovely Chetco River, the inn uses alternative energy, but it will offer guests all modern amenities. Delicious big meals. River fishing, swimming, hiking, bird watching, mushrooming, and just plain relaxing. Smoking in designated areas. Inquire about accommodations for children. Social drinking permitted if self-provided. Swimming is available in the river. May book through a travel agent if called direct.

Host: Sandra Brugger
Rooms: 4 (3 PB; 1 SB) $115-135
Full Breakfast
Credit Cards: A, B, C, D
Notes: 2, 3, 4, 5, 11

Chetco River Inn

COOS BAY

Blackberry Inn
Bed and Breakfast

843 Central, 97420
(541) 267-6951; (800) 500-4657

On the southern Oregon coast, this charming bed and breakfast offers the elegant atmosphere of an old Victorian home. Since the inn is separate from the hosts' residence, guests can enjoy the hospitality and have privacy, too. A quick walk to several restaurants, stores, a theater, an art museum, and the city park, with its lovely Japanese gardens, tennis courts, and picnic areas.

Hosts: John and Louise Duncan
Rooms: 4 (3 PB; 1 SB) $35-50
Continental Breakfast
Credit Cards: A, B
Notes: 2, 5, 7, 9, 10

Blackberry Inn

This Olde House
Bed and Breakfast

202 Alder Avenue, 97420
(541) 267-5224

Elegant home built in 1893 by the Lord Bennett family. Convenient location to watch ships and tugboats working in the port and to stroll along the waterfront. This Olde House is close to shops, galleries, cultural centers, casino, antique shops, and fine dining. There are four beautifully furnished bedrooms, private baths, complimentary wine, and full breakfasts.

Owner: Sally White
Rooms: 4 (PB) $75-115
Full Breakfast
Credit Cards: A, B
Notes: 2, 5, 7, 9, 10, 11, 12

Pacific Bed and
Breakfast Agency

P.O. Box 46894, Seattle, WA 98146
(206) 439-7677; FAX (206) 431-0932
e-mail: pacificb@nwlink.com
www.seattlebedandbreakfast.com

148. Built in 1912, this Colonial-style house has an open-air banister that surrounds the second floor and the detailed woodworking throughout the entire home makes for a warm and inviting atmosphere. Choose from five rooms with private or shared baths. A Continental plus breakfast is included in the room rate.

CORVALLIS

Bed and Breakfast on the Green

2515 Southwest 45th Street, 97333
(541) 757-7321; (888) 757-7321
FAX (541) 753-4332
e-mail: neoma@bandbonthegreen.com
www.bandbonthegreen.com

Critique passing golfers from the back deck, or be spoiled in the outdoor spa. Visit in Victorian splendor in the living room, or relax in comfort in the TV/reading room. Sleep in country quiet on a king- or queen-size bed. Then awake to juice and coffee, fresh fruit compote, hot entrée, and homemade pie served on china and crystal in the dining room. Life is good! Three miles to downtown and Oregon State University.

Hosts: Neoma and Herb Sparks
Rooms: 4 (PB) $80-87
Full Breakfast
Credit Cards: A, B, C, D, E
Notes: 2, 5, 7, 9, 10, 11, 12, 14

---

7 No smoking; 8 Children welcome; 9 Social drinking allowed; 10 Tennis nearby; 11 Swimming nearby; 12 Golf nearby; 13 Skiing nearby; 14 May be booked through a travel agent; 15 Handicapped accessible.

DEPOE BAY

The Channel House Inn, Inc.

35 Ellingson, P.O. Box 56, 97341
(541) 765-2140; (800) 477-2140
FAX (541) 765-2191; www.channelhouse.com

The Channel House Inn is perched on a cliff high above the rugged coastline of Oregon's Depoe Bay. Enjoy spectacular views of the Pacific Ocean, with abundant whale watching and captivating winter storms. Charter fishing and whale watching cruises are available. Whirlpool tubs for two on private oceanfront decks and cozy gas log fireplaces make Channel House the perfect romantic getaway. Two and one-half hours southwest of Portland, just off Highway 101. Buffet breakfast served.

Host: Vicki Mix and Carl Finseth
Rooms: 14 (PB) $75-225
Continental Breakfast
Credit Cards: A, B, C, D
Notes: 2, 5, 7, 12, 14

The Channel House Inn, Inc.

Gracie's Landing Bed and Breakfast Inn

235 SE Bayview Avenue, P.O. Box 29, 97341
(541) 765-2322; (800) 228-0448

This Cape Cod-style Oregon coast inn is charming and relaxing. Parlor with baby grand piano; dining room with teas and coffees and homemade cookies available; and library/game room with fireplace. Fireplaces and whirlpool bathtubs lend romance to the rooms. Ocean fishing and whale watching tours add adventure. All rooms have TV/VCRs, telephones, and "fishing village"

views of the harbor. Receptions, retreats, and reunions welcome. Hors d'oeuvres, luncheons, or culinary extravaganzas can be arranged. Smoking permitted on porch only.

Rooms: 13 (PB) $85-115
Full Breakfast
Credit Cards: A, B, C, D, E
Notes: 2, 5, 9, 10, 12, 15

EUGENE

The Campbell House, "A City Inn"

252 Pearl, 97401
(541) 343-1119; (800) 264-2519
FAX (541) 343-2258
e-mail: campbellhouse@campbellhouse.com

Built in 1892 and restored in the tradition of a fine European hotel. All of the 18 elegant guest rooms feature private baths, telephones with data ports, TV with VCR, and luxury amenities. Some rooms feature Jacuzzi tub for two and fireplace. Just two blocks to boutique shops and restaurants. Nearby hiking, rock climbing, bicycling on riverside bike paths, golfing, jogging, fishing, and white-water rafting. "Rated top 25 in nation." Weddings, receptions, and meeting rooms.

Host: Myra Plant
Rooms: 18 (PB) $80-350
Full Breakfast
Credit Cards: A, B, C, D
Notes: 5, 7, 8, 9, 10, 11, 12, 14, 15

Kjaer's House in the Woods

814 Lorane Highway, 97405
(541) 343-3234

A 1910 Craftsman-style bungalow designated as a city historic landmark, the Young-Pallett House, in a peaceful wooded setting with abundant wildlife. Near jogging, biking, and hiking trails. Furnished with comfortable antiques, oriental carpets, square grand piano, music and reading libraries. This home offers urban convenience with suburban tranquility. Full breakfasts with careful

NOTES: Credit cards accepted: A MasterCard; B Visa; C American Express; D Discover; E Diner's Club; F Other; 2 Personal checks accepted; 3 Lunch available; 4 Dinner available; 5 Open all year; 6 Pets welcome;

Kjaer's House in the Woods

attention to dietary needs served at guests' convenience. No smoking or pets. Inquire about accommodations for children.

Rooms: 2 (PB) $65-80
Full Breakfast
Credit Cards: None
Notes: 2, 5, 7, 10, 11, 12, 14

Maryellen's Guest House

1583 Fircrest, 97403
(541) 342-7375

Maryellen's Guest House is on a wooded hillside near Hendricks Park and the University of Oregon. A contemporary home with casual elegance. Guests enjoy private and spacious rooms opening onto cedar decks that lead to a swimming pool and hot tub. Breakfasts are catered to guests' preference. Guest refrigerator and microwave are available as well as a variety of books, games, and videos.

Hosts: Maryellen and Bob Larson
Rooms: 2 (PB) $82-96
Full Breakfast
Credit Cards: A, B
Notes: 2, 5, 7, 9, 10, 11, 12, 13, 14

McKenzie View, A Riverside Bed and Breakfast

34922 McKenzie View Drive, 97478
(541) 726-3887; (888) MCKVIEW
e-mail: mckenzieview@worldnet.att.net

Spacious country getaway on a quiet bend of the McKenzie River, but only 15 minutes from downtown Eugene. Towering Douglas firs and perennial gardens dot the six acres of grounds. Picture window views of the river can be enjoyed throughout the house. All the guest rooms are elegantly decorated and have antique furnishings and comfortable seating areas. Let the river lull one to sleep, rest in a hammock, or relax in front of a fire. McKenzie View is a great place to refresh body and spirit.

Hosts: Roberta and Scott Bolling
Rooms: 4 (PB) $70-225
Full Breakfast
Credit Cards: A, B
Notes: 2, 5, 7, 10, 11, 12, 13, 14

The Oval Door

988 Lawrence at Tenth, 97401
(541) 683-3160; FAX (541) 485-5339
www.ovaldoor.com

Recently built as a bed and breakfast inn, this 1920s farmhouse-style home in the heart of Eugene has a wraparound porch and an inviting front door with an oval glass. Guest rooms are spacious and comfortable, each with large private bathroom. The Tub Room with Jacuzzi for two is a relaxing haven with bubbles, candles, and music. Hearty breakfast with homemade specialities. Guests love the porch swing and cozy library.

Hosts: Judith McLane and Dianne Feist
Rooms: 4 (PB) $75-100
Full Breakfast
Credit Cards: A, B, C, D
Notes: 2, 5, 8, 9, 12

Pookie's Bed 'n' Breakfast on College Hill

2013 Charnelton Street, 97405
(503) 343-0383; (800) 558-0383
FAX (503) 343-0383
www.travelassist.com

This restored Craftsman home built in 1918 offers distinctive rooms with many antiques. The three rooms with queen-size bed and twin beds are upstairs and share a cozy sitting room. In a quiet, older neighborhood close to the University of Oregon, downtown, shopping, and fine restaurants. The hosts pamper their guests with a full breakfast served in the formal dining room at guests' convenience. Beautiful grounds with rose garden and wonderful yard where guests can relax. This is a nonsmoking facility, but smoking is permitted outside. Children six and older are welcome.

Hosts: Pookie and Doug Walling
Rooms: 3 (2 PB; 1 SB) $70-95
Full Breakfast
Credit Cards: None
Notes: 2, 5, 7, 9, 10, 11, 12, 13, 14

The Ivy House

GLENEDEN BEACH

Pacific Bed and Breakfast Agency

P.O. Box 46894, Seattle, WA 98146
(206) 439-7677; FAX (206) 431-0932
e-mail: pacificb@nwlink.com
www.seattlebedandbreakfast.com

151. If one is looking for a peaceful hideaway on the Oregon coast, this is the right place to stay. Guest rooms are native wood structures built in harmony with the naturally landscaped surroundings with sheltered, covered walkways, and bridges leading to the main lodge. The ambiance is heightened by the variety and caliber of the Pacific Northwest dining. Play golf, indoor/outdoor tennis, take a swim in the indoor pool or just relax before own fireplace. Large conference and social events rooms available. Seasonal rates.

GRANTS PASS

The Ivy House

139 Southwest "I" Street, 97526
(541) 474-7363 (phone/FAX)

Enjoy fine English tradition in downtown Grants Pass. Easy walking distance to historic district, shops, and restaurants. This 1908 brick historic home offers beautifully

appointed rooms. Tea and biscuits in bed. Full English breakfast follows. Jacuzzi bathtub for guests' pleasure. Air conditioning. Homey, friendly, and comfortable. Fishing and trips down Rogue River available.

Host: Doreen Pontius
Rooms: 5 (1 PB; 4 SB) $60-80
Full Breakfast
Credit Cards: None
Notes: 2, 5, 6, 7, 8, 10, 11, 12, 13

Lawnridge House Bed and Breakfast

1304 Northwest Lawnridge, 97526
(541) 476-8518

Since 1984, guests have enjoyed the privacy and peace of this 1907 restored Craftsman two-story. Large rooms, guest friendly antiques, beamed ceilings, and a large wooded lot framed by 200-year-old oak trees are features of this inn. Bedrooms

Lawnridge House

NOTES: Credit cards accepted: A MasterCard; B Visa; C American Express; D Discover; E Diner's Club; F Other; 2 Personal checks accepted; 3 Lunch available; 4 Dinner available; 5 Open all year; 6 Pets welcome;

have king- or queen-size canopied beds, TV, VCR, mini-refrigerators, and air conditioning. Northwest regional focus is a specialty, and dietary requests are catered to when possible. The family suite sleeps from two to six people, while the king-size suite is used frequently for honeymoons and anniversary celebrations.

Host: Barbara Head
Rooms: 3 (2 PB; 1 SB) $65-85
Full Breakfast
Credit Cards: None
Notes: 2, 5, 7, 8, 9, 10, 11, 12, 13, 14

Morrison's Rogue River Lodge

8500 Galice Road, Merlin, 97532
(541) 476-3825; (800) 826-1963
FAX (541) 476-4953

Morrison's Rogue River Lodge is in southern Oregon on the famous Rogue River. It was built in the 1940s and has grown from a fishing lodge to a full-service destination resort catering to romantics as well as families, outdoorsmen, rafting enthusiasts, and fishermen. First-class accommodations in cozy river-view cottages with fireplaces or lodge rooms. Well known for its fabulous cuisine. Overnight accommodations include a four-course gourmet dinner and a bountiful country breakfast. Full service conference facilities are available.

Host: Michelle Hanten
Rooms: 13 (PB) $160-260
Full Breakfast
Credit Cards: A, B, D
Notes: 2, 3, 4, 7, 8, 9, 10, 11, 12, 14

Pine Meadow Inn Bed and Breakfast

1000 Crow Road, Merlin, 97532
(541) 471-6277 (phone/FAX); (800) 554-0806
e-mail: pmi@pinemeadowinn.com
www.pinemeadowinn.com

A distinctive country retreat on nine acres of meadow and woods near the Wild and Scenic area of the Rogue River. Enjoy nearby white-water rafting, Shakespeare

Pine Meadow Inn

Festival, historic Jacksonville, and California redwoods. Wraparound porch with wicker furniture, English cutting and herb gardens, a hot tub under the pines, koi pond. Guest rooms are sunny and well lit for reading, with queen-size, pillow-top mattresses, and private baths. Delicious, healthy breakfasts. Central air. Children over 10 welcome. AAA-rated three diamonds and Mobil-rated three stars.

Hosts: Maloy and Nancy Murdock
Rooms: 4 (PB) $80-110
Full Breakfast
Credit Cards: A, B, D
Notes: 2, 5, 7, 9, 12, 14

HOOD RIVER

Brown's Bed and Breakfast

3000 Reed Road, 97031
(541) 386-1545

This house is a functioning farmhouse built in the early 1930s and remodeled in 1985. It has a modern kitchen where the large farm-style breakfasts are prepared and a new bathroom that is shared by the two bedrooms. One bedroom has twin beds and overlooks beautiful Mount Hood, the other bedroom has a king-size bed and overlooks the orchard. Nestled in the forest and at the end of the road; the only noise to be heard

---

7 No smoking; 8 Children welcome; 9 Social drinking allowed; 10 Tennis nearby; 11 Swimming nearby; 12 Golf nearby; 13 Skiing nearby; 14 May be booked through a travel agent; 15 Handicapped accessible.

is that of birds chirping. There are nature trails for hiking or jogging.

Hosts: Al and Marian Brown
Rooms: 2 (SB) $65
Full Breakfast
Credit Cards: A, B
Notes: 2, 5, 7, 8, 10, 11, 12, 13, 14

Columbia Gorge Hotel

4000 Westcliff Drive, 97031
(541) 386-5566; (800) 345-1921
FAX (541) 387-5414; e-mail: cghotel@gorge.net

The Columbia Gorge Hotel, 60 miles east of Portland, was built in 1921 as a gracious oasis for travelers along the Columbia River Scenic Highway. At the top of a 210-foot waterfall above the majestic Columbia River, the hotel has a national reputation for fine cuisine and elegant surroundings. The hotel boasts 40 unique guest rooms, an award-winning dining room, and exquisite wedding facilities on six beautifully landscaped acres. Complimentary "world-famous farm breakfast."

Hosts: Boyd and Halla Graoes
Rooms: 40 (PB) $150-250
Full Breakfast
Credit Cards: A, B, C, D, E
Notes: 2, 3, 4, 5, 6, 7, 9, 10, 11, 12, 13, 14

JACKSONVILLE

Jacksonville Inn

175 East California Street, P.O. Box 359, 97530
(541) 899-1900; (800) 321-9344
e-mail: jvinn@mind.net
www.jacksonvilleinn.com

In the national historic landmark town of Jacksonville, the Jacksonville Inn, built in 1861, offers eight elegantly decorated hotel rooms, modernized for comfort and opulence with whirlpool tubs, steam showers, and air conditioning, as well as three luxurious honeymoon cottages that cater to romance and privacy. An award-winning dinner house features gourment dining with more thatn 1,500 wines and a full service lounge.

Jacksonville Inn

Hosts: Jerry and Linda Evans
Rooms: 11 (PB) $100-245
Full Breakfast
Credit Cards: A, B, C, D, E
Notes: 2, 3, 4, 5, 7, 9, 10, 11, 12, 13, 14

JOSEPH

Chandlers' Bed, Bread and Trail Inn

700 Main Street, P.O. Box 639, 97846
(541) 432-9765; (800) 452-3781
FAX (541) 432-4303; www.eoni.com/~chanbbti

The Chandlers' post-and-beam inn offers warm hospitality. At the base of the Wallowa Mounatins, it provides a snug home base as guests explore the Eagle Cap Wilderness, visit bronze-casting foundries, galleries, or swim and fish at nearby Wallowa Lake. In the winter, Nordic skiing and snowmobiling are popular activities.

Chandlers' Bed, Bread and Trail Inn

NOTES: Credit cards accepted: A MasterCard; B Visa; C American Express; D Discover; E Diner's Club; F Other; 2 Personal checks accepted; 3 Lunch available; 4 Dinner available; 5 Open all year; 6 Pets welcome;

Innkeepers: Ethel and Jim Chandler
Manager: Crystal Sanchez
Rooms: 5 (3 PB: 2 SB) $70-80
Full Breakfast
Credit Cards: A, B
Notes: 2, 5, 7, 9, 10, 11, 12, 13, 14

LAFAYETTE

Kelty Estate
Bed and Breakfast

675 Third Street, P.O. Box 817, 97127
(503) 864-3740; (800) 867-3740

Built in 1872 in historic Lafayette, this Early Colonial-style home is listed in the National Register of Historic Places. In the heart of Oregon wine country, perfect for visiting the entire Willamette Valley. Browse at the antique mall, visit the county museum, or one of the many nearby wineries. Less than an hour's drive to Salem or Portland. Within two hours' drive of scenic Mount Hood, the Columbia River Gorge, or the colorful Oregon coast. Convenient for both Linfield College and George Fox University.

Hosts: Ron and JoAnn Ross
Rooms: 2 (PB) $65-75
Full Breakfast
Credit Cards: None
Notes: 2, 5, 7, 9, 12

LINCOLN CITY

Brey House Ocean View
Bed and Breakfast Inn

3725 Northwest Keel Avenue, 97367
(541) 994-7123
www.moriah.com/breyhouse

This three-story Cape Cod-style house has a nautical theme that shows throughout the home. Across the street from the ocean, it is a short walk to shops and restaurants. Queen-size beds are in all the rooms, and all rooms have private entrances. Close to sea lion caves and the world's smallest harbor. Lincoln City is also the kite capital of the world. Keiko, the *Free Willy* orca, is 20 miles away in the Oregon Coast Aquarium. Enjoy watching the ocean while eating a fantastic breakfast served by the hosts.

Hosts: Milt and Shirley Brey
Rooms: 4 (PB) $70-135
Full Breakfast
Credit Cards: A, B, D
Notes: 5, 7, 9, 10, 11, 12, 14

MCMINNVILLE

Youngberg Hill Vineyard
Bed and Breakfast

10660 Southwest Youngberg Hill Road, 97128
(503) 472-2727; FAX (503) 472-1313
e-mail: martin@youngberghill.com
www.youngberghill.com

This magnificent hilltop farmhouse commands breathtaking views across the property's 12 acres of pinot noir vineyards, over the Willamette Valley towards the Cascades and Coast Range. Every room has a romantic view (two have fireplaces), a private bath, lovely oak furnishings, fresh flowers, and bedtime chocolates. Breakfasts are a treat. Among the inn's special attractions are a well-stocked wine cellar with an emphasis on Oregon wines.

Hosts: Kevin and Tasha Byrd
Rooms: 5 (PB) $130-150
Full Breakfast
Credit Cards: A, B
Notes: 2, 5, 7, 9, 10, 11, 12, 14, 15

Youngberg Hill Vineyard

7 No smoking; 8 Children welcome; 9 Social drinking allowed; 10 Tennis nearby; 11 Swimming nearby; 12 Golf nearby; 13 Skiing nearby; 14 May be booked through a travel agent; 15 Handicapped accessible.

MEDFORD

Waverly Cottages

305 North Grape, 97501
(541) 779-4716; FAX (541) 732-1718
www.aaaabbcom.

In a historic area just north of downtown Medford, Waverly Cottage offers complete privacy with authentic Victorian charm. Built in 1898, the cottage has been restored to accurately maintain its ornate Queen Anne style. Central heating and air conditioning. Fully furnished suites offer complete privacy, cable TV, private telephones, and ample living areas. This central location is within walking distance of the Craterian Theater, government offices, dozens of restaurants, nightclubs, a microwbrewery, and a historic walking tour. Inquire about accommodations for children and pets. One unit is handicapped accessible. All units have kitchens. On request, the host will do fruit baskets with muffins, coffee, and juice for an additional $10.

Host: David K. Fisse
Rooms: 2 (PB) $40-90
Credit Cards: None
Notes: 2, 7, 9, 10, 11, 12, 13, 14

MOSIER

The Mosier House

704 Third Avenue, 97040
(541) 478-3640

The Mosier House bed and breakfast is an elegantly restored Queen Anne Victorian in the town of Mosier where cherry orchards weave through the volcanic bluffs of the Columbia River Gorge and a landscape of Oregon oak, ponderosa pine, and wildflowers. Just five miles east of Hood River and 65 miles from Portland, the Mosier House is the perfect base for exploration of the gorge.

Hosts: The Koerners
Rooms: 5 (1 PB; 4 SB) $75-100

The Mosier House

Full Breakfast
Credit Cards: A, B
Notes: 2, 5, 7, 8, 9, 10, 11, 12, 13, 14

MOUNT HOOD AREA

Falcon's Crest Inn

87287 Government Camp Loop Highway
P.O. Box 185, 97028
(503) 272-3403; (800) 624-7384
FAX (503) 272-3454

Elegance Mount Hood-style features three rooms and two suites with private baths. Individually decorated with family heirlooms, in-room telephones, bed turndown service, morning refreshment tray. A full breakfast is served in the morning. In the heart of a year-round recreation area. Skiing, hiking, fishing, and golf are all nearby. Corporate, private, and mystery parties. Ski packages, holiday, and special events. Fine evening dining and spirits available.

Hosts: Melody and Bob Johnson
Rooms: 5 (PB) $95-179
Full Breakfast
Credit Cards: A, B, C, D
Notes: 2, 4, 5, 7, 8, 9, 10, 11, 12, 13, 14

NOTES: Credit cards accepted: A MasterCard; B Visa; C American Express; D Discover; E Diner's Club; F Other; 2 Personal checks accepted; 3 Lunch available; 4 Dinner available; 5 Open all year; 6 Pets welcome;

NEWBERG

Avellan Inn: A Bed and Breakfast

16900 Northeast Highway 240, 97132
(503) 537-9161

Discover the magic that is Avellan Inn. Twelve acres of grounds invite guests to wander through the gardens, forest, and hazelnut orchard. Gourmet breakfast features Oregon products and homemade breads. Each room offers panoramic view, down featherbed on queen-size mattress, and private bath with bidet. Enjoy the hosts' lavish attention to detail, from the homemade hazelnut truffle on the pillow upon arrival to the "brown bag cookie" on departure. Explore Portland (30 miles northeast), the ocean (60 miles west), the wineries (more than a 10-mile radius), or simply relax and enjoy the private, country peacefulness and outdoor spa. Close to George Fox University and Linfield College. Optional suite available.

Hosts: Ken and Carol Bond Williams
Rooms: 2 (PB) $85-115
Full Breakfast
Credit Cards: A, B
Notes: 2, 5, 6, 7, 8, 9, 14

NEWPORT

Oar House

520 Southwest Second Street, 97365
(541) 265-9571; (800) 252-2358
e-mail: oarhouse@newportnet.com
www.newportnet.com/oarhouse

Oar House, a Lincoln County historic landmark in the picturesque Nye Beach area of Newport, has offered comfort and conviviality to guests since the early 1900s. Originally a boarding house, later a bordello, and now a bed and breakfast, Oar House continues to attract visitors because of its history, mystery, ghost, and hospitality. Each guest room has a queen-size bed; four rooms have ocean views. The lighthouse tower provides 360-degree views from Yaquina Head to Yaquina Bay.

Host: Jan LeBrun
Rooms: 5 (PB) $90-120
Full Breakfast
Credit Cards: A, B, D
Notes: 5, 7, 9, 10, 11, 12

Ocean House Bed and Breakfast

4920 Northwest Woody Way, 97365
(503) 265-6158; (800) 56 B AND B
e-mail: garrard@oceanhouse.com
www.oceanhouse.com

Ocean House at beautiful Agate Beach has guest rooms that overlook gardens and the surf. A private trail leads to beach and tidal pools. Nearby attractions include the lighthouse, aquarium, marine science center, and bay front, with restaurants and galleries. Storm and whale watching lure winter guests, and the spacious great room is just the place to gather. Morning coffee for early birds is followed by breakfast in the sunroom. All rooms with private baths, some with Jacuzzis. Special winter rates and gift certificates are available.

Host: Bob Garrard
Rooms: 5 (PB) $90-150
Full Breakfast
Credit Cards: A, B, D
Notes: 2, 5, 7, 9, 10, 11, 12

OAKLAND

Beckley House Bed and Breakfast

338 Southeast Second Street, P.O. Box 198, 97462
(541) 459-9320 (phone/FAX)

The Beckley House is a historic two-story Classical Revival Victorian home listed in

---

7 No smoking; 8 Children welcome; 9 Social drinking allowed; 10 Tennis nearby; 11 Swimming nearby; 12 Golf nearby; 13 Skiing nearby; 14 May be booked through a travel agent; 15 Handicapped accessible.

the historic register. Reflecting a nostalgic era, the home is comfortably furnished in period-style antiques. Enjoy wine tours, Rochester covered bridge, or the Umpqua River. Two rooms with private baths. Fresh bread, muffins, and a great breakfast are served.

Hosts: Karene and Rich Neuharth
Rooms: 2 (PB) $60-85
Full Breakfast
Credit Cards: A, B, C
Notes: 2, 5, 7, 8, 9, 10, 12, 14

PACIFIC CITY

Eagle's View Bed and Breakfast

37975 Brooten Road, P.O. Box 901, 97135
(503) 965-7600; (888) TIME AWAY (846-3292)
www.moriah.com/eaglesview/

The inn is decorated country comfortable including pine vaulted ceiling fans, and lots of quilts. This custom-built inn was carved high on a mountain overlooking beautiful Nestucca Bay and River. All rooms have private baths, queen-size beds, a TV, a VCR, a CD player, and direct-dial telephones. Three guest rooms have Jacuzzi tubs. Enjoy a hearty country breakfast in the privacy of own room or dine in the great room.

Hosts: Mike and Kathy Lewis
Rooms: 5 (PB) $95-115
Full Breakfast
Credit Cards: A, B, D
Notes: 2, 5, 7, 9, 11, 12, 14, 15

PORTLAND

General Hooker's Bed and Breakfast

125 Southwest Hooker, 97201
(503) 222-4435; (800) 745-4135
FAX (503) 295-6410
e-mail: ghbandb@teleport.com
www.teleport.com/~ghbandb

In a quiet district and within walking distance of downtown, General Hooker's is a casually classic Victorian townhouse that

General Hooker's

combines the mellow warmth of the 19th century with the comfort and convenience of the 20th. Knowledgeable host, a fourth-generation Portlander and a charter member of the Oregon Bed and Breakfast Guild, can be a veritable gold mine of information for newcomers to her city. Two-night minimum stay is often required. Sociable Abyssinian cat in residence. AAA- and Mobil-listed.

Host: Lori Hall
Rooms: 4 (2 PB; 2 SB) $70-120
Continental Breakfast
Credit Cards: A, B, C
Notes: 5, 7, 9, 10, 11, 12

Georgian House Bed and Breakfast

1828 Northeast Siskiyou, 97212
(503) 281-2250; (888) 282-2250 (toll-free)
FAX (503) 281-3301

Step back in time to charming Olde England at this restored, handsome brick Georgian Colonial featured in *Better Homes and Gardens* magazine. Relax on the sun deck or in the gazebo. Stroll through the colorful rose garden or the quiet, historic Irvington neighborhood. Close to shopping, restaurants, theaters; easy freeway access to I-5, I-205, and I-84. Close to convention center, coliseum,

NOTES: Credit cards accepted: A MasterCard; B Visa; C American Express; D Discover; E Diner's Club; F Other; 2 Personal checks accepted; 3 Lunch available; 4 Dinner available; 5 Open all year; 6 Pets welcome;

Georgian House

Lloyd Center Mall, downtown, and MAX Light Rail. Winding staircase to second floor, hardwood floors, and antiques. Rooms are air conditioned.

Host: Willie Ackley
Rooms: 4 (2 PB: 2 SB) $65-85
Full Breakfast
Credit Cards: A, B
Notes: 2, 5, 7, 10, 11, 12, 13

Pacific Bed and Breakfast Agency

P.O. Box 46894, Seattle, WA 98146
(206) 439-7677; FAX (206) 431-0932
e-mail: pacificb@nwlink.com
www.seattlebedandbreakfast.com

142. Villa on the Butte. On a volcanic cone above the city this host home has wonderful views of Mount St. Helens, Mount Hood, and the Columbia River Gorge. One suite is offered to guests and there is a king-size bed and private bath, TV, and VCR for guests' enjoyment. A special exercise room is available for guests' morning workout followed by a full breakfast. Seasonal rates.

143. Georgian Colonial. This is one of only three true Georgian Colonial homes in Portland. There are several gold coins placed in the house foundation for good luck. Leaded windows, a winding staircase, and oak floors have been lovingly restored. Three

bedrooms give guests the choice of shared or private bath and king- or queen-size bed. Full breakfast served. $70-100.

144. Elegant historic landmark. Six rooms all with private baths featuring claw-foot tubs make this historic home a special place for a romantic weekend or business trip. Guests will enjoy the friendly atmosphere in a quiet residential area. Continental buffet breakfast is served in the formal dining room. Room rates vary.

145. City and mountain views. A garden-level suite with a private entrance can be guests' home-away-from-home just 10 minutes by car from the city center. This two-room suite has a choice of king-size or twin beds and has a Hide-a-Bed to accommodate a total of four persons. A fireplace, TV, and VCR are provided and a full breakfast is served in the dining room. Call for prices and availability.

Pittock Acres Bed and Breakfast

103 Northwest Pittock Avenue, 97210
(503) 226-1163

This delightful 24-year-old contemporary with traditional, Victorian, and country furnishings is on a quiet country lane just five minutes from downtown Portland and within easy walking distance to the historic Pittock Mansion. From the mansion grounds, stroll/jog beautiful forested trails to the zoo, Hoyt Arboretum, Washington Park, and the beautiful Japanese and Rose Test Gardens. Enjoy Nob Hill offering exciting fine restaurants, art galleries, quality specialty shops, all minutes away from this peaceful atmosphere of

7 No smoking; 8 Children welcome; 9 Social drinking allowed; 10 Tennis nearby; 11 Swimming nearby; 12 Golf nearby; 13 Skiing nearby; 14 May be booked through a travel agent; 15 Handicapped accessible.

nature. Children 14 and older welcome. ABBA-rated Excellent.

Hosts: Linda and Richard Matson
Rooms: 3 (2 PB; 1 SB) $95
Full Breakfast
Credit Cards: A, B, C, D
Notes: 2, 5, 7, 10, 12

Portland Guest House

1720 Northeast Fifteenth Street, 97212
(503) 282-1402; e-mail: pgh@teleport.com
www.teleport.com/~pgh/

This 1890 Victorian is in the historic Irvington neighborhood. All rooms have telephones, antiques, heirloom linens, and great beds. Luscious breakfasts. Family suite with three beds, two rooms with two beds, and five rooms with private baths. Herb, vegetable, and flower gardens. Closest bed and breakfast to convention center. Convenient transit to downtown. Walk to restaurants, delis, coffee shops, and boutiques. Central air conditioning. Mount Hood is 50 miles away.

Host: Susan Gisvold
Rooms: 7 (5 PB; 2 SB) $65-95
Full Breakfast
Credit Cards: A, B
Notes: 2, 5, 7, 8, 9, 10, 11, 12

Portland Guest House

Portland White House

Portland White House Bed and Breakfast Inn

1914 Northeast Twenty-second Avenue, 97212
(503) 287-7131; (800) 272-7131
FAX (503) 249-1641; e-mail: pdxwhi@aol.com

Listed in the National Register of Historic Places, this stately home and Carriage House have been restored to its original splendor with circular drive and classic Greek columns. Romantic elegance with bronze and crystal chandeliers, fountains, grand dining room, and period furnishings. The inn is in the historic Irvington district, convenient to Broadway shops, downtown Portland, convention center, fine dining, and local sights. Eight elegantly furnished rooms, all with private baths, private telephone, data ports, and air conditioning. Full gourmet breakfast.

Rooms: 8 (PB) $98-149
Full Breakfast
Credit Cards: A, B, D
Notes: 5, 7, 10

PORT ORFORD

Home by the Sea Bed and Breakfast

444 Jackson Street, P.O. Box 606, 97465-0606
(541) 332-2855; www.homebythesea.com

The hosts built their contemporary wood home on a spit of land overlooking a dramatic stretch of Oregon coast. Queen-size Oregon myrtlewood beds and cable TV are featured in both accommodations, which make ideal quarters for two couples traveling together.

NOTES: Credit cards accepted: A MasterCard; B Visa; C American Express; D Discover; E Diner's Club; F Other; 2 Personal checks accepted; 3 Lunch available; 4 Dinner available; 5 Open all year; 6 Pets welcome;

Home by the Sea

It's a short walk to restaurants, public beaches, and the town's harbor. Amenities include a beautiful ocean view, direct beach access, smoke-free environment, laundry privileges, and telephone jacks in rooms. America On-line access. Macintosh spoken.

Hosts: Alan and Brenda Mitchell
Rooms: 2 (PB) $95-105
Full Breakfast
Credit Cards: A, B
Notes: 2, 5, 7, 9, 10, 12

SALEM

State House Bed and Breakfast

2146 State Street, 97301
(800) 800-6712; FAX (503) 363-2774
e-mail: mikwin@teleport.com

Delightfully refurbished 1920s home on Mill Creek. Close to Willamette University, Mission Mill Museum, and downtown shopping. In addition, it is only one hour or less to the Oregon beaches, the mountains, or to Portland. It's charming inside, with warm, homey furnishings and pleasant color schemes. All rooms include a telephone. Behind the bed and breakfast guests will discover a handsomely landscaped garden area along the creek and a large deck with a view of ducks, geese, and other aspects of wildlife. Includes a full breakfast of guests' choice served between 8:30 and 10:00 A.M.

Hosts: Mike and Judy Winsett
Rooms: 4 (2 PB; 2 SB) $50-70
Full Breakfast
Credit Cards: A, B, D, E
Notes: 2, 5, 7, 9, 12, 14

SANDLAKE (PACIFIC CITY)

Sandlake Country Inn

8505 Galloway Road, Cloverdale, 97112
(503) 965-6745

It's a secret hideaway on the awesome Oregon coast—a private, peaceful place for making memories. This 1894 shipwreck-timbered farmhouse on the Oregon historic register is tucked into a bower of old roses. Hummingbirds, Mozart, cookies at midnight, fireplaces, whirlpools for two, honeymoon cottage, breakfast en suite, vintage movies, no smoking, wheelchair accessible. Togetherness baskets available.

Hosts: Femke and David Durham
Rooms: 4 (PB) $90-135
Full Breakfast
Credit Cards: A, B, C, D
Notes: 2, 7, 12, 14, 15

SEASIDE

Pacific Bed and Breakfast Agency

P.O. Box 46894, Seattle, WA 98146
(206) 439-7677; FAX (206) 431-0932
e-mail: pacificb@nwlink.com
www.seattlebedandbreakfast.com

146. Oceanfront bed and breakfast hotel. With breathtaking ocean views, this small inn has 14 rooms. Room sizes range from cozy hideaway to large penthouse suites and family units with kitchens. Chef-prepared meals, jetted tubs, individual heating and air conditioning, private baths, and maybe a fireplace become a special retreat for guests. There is a wide range of prices.

147. Share the charm. This turn-of-the-century bed and breakfast has two rooms, each with a private bath, and one room is spacious enough to accommodate two children. Wake up each morning to hot beverages delivered to guests' room followed by a full breakfast featuring homemade breads and delicious fruits. Affordable rates.

7 No smoking; 8 Children welcome; 9 Social drinking allowed; 10 Tennis nearby; 11 Swimming nearby; 12 Golf nearby; 13 Skiing nearby; 14 May be booked through a travel agent; 15 Handicapped accessible.

SISTERS

Conklin's Guest House

69013 Camp Polk Road, 97759
(541) 549-0123; (800) 559-4262
FAX (541) 549-4481

The house offers guests a truly peaceful environment within walking distance of the bustling shops and restaurants of Sisters. All guests are served evening refreshments and a full country breakfast in the morning. Trout ponds are stocked for catch and release fishing, the swimming pool is heated, and there are plenty of places around the grounds to relax in privacy. Groups, reunions, parties, and weddings are welcome. Children over 12 welcome.

Rooms: 5 (PB) $90-120
Full Breakfast
Credit Cards: None
Notes: 2, 5, 7, 10, 11, 12, 13, 14, 15

SUBLIMITY

Silver Mountain Bed and Breakfast

4672 Drift Creek Road Southeast, 97385
(503) 769-7127; (800) 952-3905
FAX (503) 769-3549

Visit a working farm in the foothills of the Cascade Mountains 20 miles east of Salem. Stay in a modernized "barn" with Jacuzzi, sauna, pool table, fireplace, kitchen, swimming pool. Five minutes to Silver Falls State Park. Fishing, rafting, float trips, golf, tennis available nearby. Join in farm chores or enjoy solitude. Open May through October.

Hosts: Jim and Shirley Heater
Rooms: 2 (PB) $65-75
Full or Continental Breakfast
Credit Cards: None
Notes: 2, 6, 7, 8, 10, 11, 12

TIGARD

Woven Glass Inn

14645 Beef Bend Road, 97224
(503) 590-6040

A large rambling historic country home in the heart of the wine country just 12 miles south of Portland. The house abounds with stained-glass windows of unique design and purpose in every room. The Garden Suite (queen-size bed) and the French Room (four-poster bed) both have private baths and are tastefully decorated, complete with down comforters, luxurious linens, and seasonal flowers. Two fireplaces entice peaceful relaxation, or stroll through the sunken garden and rose gardens.

Hosts: Renée and Paul Giroux
Rooms: 2 (PB) $65-75
Full Breakfast
Credit Cards: A, B, C
Notes: 2, 5, 7, 11

Woven Glass Inn

YACHATS

The Kittiwake

95368 Highway 101 South, 97498
(541) 547-4470
e-mail: jszewc@orednet.org
compuserve:70413,3636

A calm ambiance of personal relaxation and restoration permeates this romantic two-

NOTES: Credit cards accepted: A MasterCard; B Visa; C American Express; D Discover; E Diner's Club; F Other; 2 Personal checks accepted; 3 Lunch available; 4 Dinner available; 5 Open all year; 6 Pets welcome;

story, 4,000-square-foot contemporary home on the ocean. This grown-ups' place for grown-up people was completed in 1993. Amenities include two guest rooms with breathtaking ocean views, queen-size beds, afghans, down comforters, window seats, decks, and private baths with double whirlpool tubs. Guest reading/whale watching room; coffee bar. Fantastic European breakfasts. The Germans have a word for the Kittiwake's warmth: *gemütlichkeit*.

Hosts: Brigitte and Joseph Szewc
Rooms: 2 (PB) $125-140
Full and Continental Breakfast
Credit Cards: A, B, C, D
Notes: 2, 5, 7, 9, 10, 11, 12, 14

The Sanderling Bed and Breakfast

7304 Southwest Highway 101, Milepost #160, 97498
(541) 563-4752

The Sanderling Bed and Breakfast is 100 percent oceanfront. All rooms are large with an extra-large private bath with two-person Jacuzzis and showers; three rooms have king-size beds and one room has two full-size beds. All rooms have feather mattresses. Wake-up beverage outside the door. Full breakfast. Nonsmoking. No children or pets. Private entrance to and from eight miles of easy-walking sandy beach.

Hosts: Ernie and Pat
Rooms: 4 (PB) $100-130
Full Breakfast
Credit Cards: A, B, D
Notes: 2, 5, 7, 9, 12, 14

Sea Quest Bed and Breakfast

95354 Highway 101, 97498
(541) 547-3782; (800) 341-4878
FAX (541) 547-3719
e-mail: seaquest@newportnet.com
www.seaq.com

A spectacular two-story cedar and glass house. Built on two and one-half acres just 100 feet from the Pacific Ocean. All rooms have unobstructed views of the ocean. Private baths with Jacuzzi tubs. Floor to ceiling used-brick fireplace to sit by. Eclectic and antique furnishing. Comfortable places to sit and read.

Hosts: Elaine and George
Rooms: 5 (PB) From $140
Full Breakfast
Credit Cards: A, B, D
Notes: 5, 7, 9, 10, 11, 12

7 No smoking; 8 Children welcome; 9 Social drinking allowed; 10 Tennis nearby; 11 Swimming nearby; 12 Golf nearby; 13 Skiing nearby; 14 May be booked through a travel agent; 15 Handicapped accessible.

Texas

Texas

Bolin's Prairie House
Bed and Breakfast
508 Mulberry, 79601
(915) 675-5855

Nestled in the heart of Abilene is a 1902 home furnished with antiques and modern luxuries combined to create a warm, home-like atmosphere. Downstairs, there are high ceilings, hardwood floors, and a wood-burning stove. Upstairs are four unique bedrooms (Love, Joy, Peace, and Patience), each beautifully decorated. Breakfast of special baked-egg dishes, fruit, and home-made bread is served in the dining room that is decorated with a collection of cobalt glass and blue-and-white china.

Hosts: Sam and Ginny Bolin
Rooms: 4 (2 PB; 2 SB) $50-65
Full Breakfast
Credit Cards: A, B, C, D
Notes: 2, 5, 7

Parkview House
Bed and Breakfast
1311 South Jefferson, 79101
(806) 373-9464; FAX (806) 373-3166
e-mail: parkviewbb@aol.com
www.members.aol.com/parkviewbb

This 1908 Prairie Victorian in the heart of the Texas panhandle has been lovingly restored by the present owners to capture its original charm. It is furnished with antiques and comfortably updated. Guests may relax,

Parkview House

read, or engage in friendly conversation on the wicker-filled front porch; browse through the garden; or soak leisurely in the romantic hot tub under stars. Convenient to biking, jogging, tennis, hiking, and the award-winning musical drama *Texas* in Palo Duro State Park. Old Route 66, antique shops, restaurants, various museums, and West Texas A&M University are nearby. Continental plus breakfast. Smoking outside only. Inquire about accommodations for children.

Hosts: Nabil and Carol Dia
Rooms: 5 (3 PB; 2 SB) $65-85
Cottage: $105
Continental Breakfast
Credit Cards: A, B, C
Notes: 2, 5, 7, 9, 10, 12, 14

Austin-Lake Travis
Bed and Breakfast
4446 Eck Lane, 78734
(512) 266-3386; (800) 484-9095 (#5348)
   (reservations only)
www.laketravisbb.com

This unique waterfront retreat is a 20-minute drive from downtown Austin.

NOTES: Credit cards accepted: A MasterCard; B Visa; C American Express; D Discover; E Diner's Club; F Other; 2 Personal checks accepted; 3 Lunch available; 4 Dinner available; 5 Open all year; 6 Pets welcome; 7 No smoking; 8 Children welcome; 9 Social drinking allowed; 10 Tennis nearby; 11 Swimming nearby; 12 Golf nearby; 13 Skiing nearby; 14 May be booked through a travel agent; 15 Handicapped accessible.

Cliffside location, crystal water, hills, and expansive view provide the setting for a luxurious getaway. The natural beauty of the surroundings is reflected in the hill country home with each of the four guest suites having a deck with view of the lake. "Intimate resort" describes the amenities available: private boat dock, pool, hot tub, fitness center, massage and spa services, and sailing/boat charters. Inside is a stone fireplace, game room, pool table, and library/theater. Nearby are a boat and Jet Ski rentals, horseback riding, bicycling, hiking, steam train, and wineries to tour. Breakfast is served in bed.

Hosts: Judy and Vic Dwyer
Rooms: 4 (PB) $145-195
Full Breakfast
Credit Cards: A, B, C
Notes: 5, 7, 9, 10, 11, 12, 14

Austin's Wildflower Inn

1200 West 221/2 Street, 78705
(512) 477-9639; FAX (512) 474-4188
e-mail: kjackson@io.com

Austin's Wildflower Inn, built in the early 1930s, is a lovely Colonial-style two-story home tucked away in a very quiet neighborhood of tree-lined streets in the center of

Austin's Wildflower Inn

Austin. Convenient to the University of Texas, the state capitol, and the downtown shopping and entertainment district. Every room has been carefully restored to create an atmosphere of warmth and comfort. "I invite you to come and relax here and enjoy our beautiful grounds and have one of our special breakfasts in our lovely back garden. I wish you happiness and prosperity, and may your road lead to mine."

Host: Kay Jackson
Rooms: 4 (2 PB; 2 SB) $74-89
Full Breakfast
Credit Cards: A, B, C
Notes: 2, 5, 7, 9, 10, 11, 12

Bed and Breakfast Texas Style

4224 West Red Bird Lane, Dallas, 75237
(972) 298-8586; (800) 899-4538
FAX (972) 298-7118; e-mail: bdtxstyle1@aol.com
www.bnbtexasstyle.com

Carter Lane Bed and Breakfast. This large sprawling residence in a quiet area of bustling Austin has two guest areas, a well-stocked fish pond, pool, picnic area, and a weight and exercise room. The home is newly decorated with upscale furnishings; each guest room has a private bath. Guests are encouraged to relax in the hammock by the lake, or workout while watching a video in the exercise room. Weekday breakfasts are Continental. On weekends guests are served a full breakfast with all the trimmings. The lucky guest who lands a bass from the lake may enjoy having it for breakfast. The host will also prepare vegetarian and healthy recipes. $75-85.

The Brook House Bed and Breakfast

609 West 33rd Street, 78705
(512) 459-0534

The Brook House was built in 1922 and restored to its present country charm. It is seven blocks from the University of Texas with easy access to local restaurants and live music. Enjoy one of six guest rooms, each of which has a private bath, TV, and

The Brook House

telephone. A full breakfast is served daily in the dining room which has a fireplace or, weather permitting, outside on the veranda. No smoking in rooms. Partial handicapped accessibility.

Host: Barbara Love
Rooms: 6 (PB) $72-99
Full Breakfast
Credit Cards: A, B, C, D, E, F
Notes: 2, 5, 6, 8, 9, 10, 11, 12

Fairview—A Bed and Breakfast Establishment

1304 Newning Avenue, 78704
(512) 444-4746; (800) 310-4746
FAX (512) 444-3494; e-mail: fairview@io.com
www.fairview~bnb.com

Surrounded by huge live oak trees on an acre of landscaped grounds, this turn-of-

Fairview

the-century Colonial Revival historic landmark offers gracious accommodations. Carefully selected antique furnishings give each room its own unique style and romance. Fairview's six rooms range from luxury suites to elegant retreats. The gardens are a wonderful place to relax after a busy day. "Fairview is probably the grandest bed and breakfast in Austin (and one of the top two or three in the state)"—*Texas Monthly*, August 1993.

Hosts: Duke and Nancy Waggoner
Rooms: 6 (PB) $99-149
Full Breakfast
Credit Cards: A, B, C, D, E
Notes: 2, 5, 7, 9, 10, 11, 12, 14

Gregg House and Gardens

4201 Gregg Lane, 78744
(512) 928-9777; FAX (512) 928-9776
e-mail: jim6611@aol.com

This in-town country retreat with hardwood floors and a stone fireplace is set on two acres with huge trees and a fish pond. Downtown and state capitol are 10 minutes; LBJ presidential library and shopping 15 minutes. Full kitchen, TV room, living/dining and laundry available for guests' use. Large patio and deck; bus stop. Airport 20 minutes. Hosts will help guests with their special interests and provide directions and maps. A large organic garden and nature trails are being developed. Fifteen dollars per each additional person.

Hosts: Nelda and Jim Haynes
Rooms: 2 (PB) $35-45
Full or Continental Breakfast
Credit Cards: None
Notes: 3, 4, 5, 7, 9, 10, 11, 12

Southard House

908 Blanco, 78703
(512) 474-4731

Centrally downtown off West Sixth Street are three beautifully restored homes. A two-block stroll will take guests to the wonderful West End area, full of restaurants and shopping. All of the antique-decorated

7 No smoking; 8 Children welcome; 9 Social drinking allowed; 10 Tennis nearby; 11 Swimming nearby; 12 Golf nearby; 13 Skiing nearby; 14 May be booked through a travel agent; 15 Handicapped accessible.

rooms and suites have private baths and telephones. Some of the rooms have features such as claw-foot tubs, fireplaces, coffee makers, TVs, and small refrigerators. Continental buffet is served on weekdays; full breakfast is served on weekends. Enjoy the new swimming pool.

Hosts: Jerry and Rejina Southard
Rooms: 16 (PB) $69-169
Full and Continental Breakfast
Credit Cards: A, B, C, D, E
Notes: 2, 5, 7, 8, 11, 15

BELTON

Bed and Breakfast Texas Style

4224 West Red Bird Lane, Dallas, 75237
(972) 298-8586; (800) 899-4538
FAX (972) 298-7118; e-mail: bdtxstyle1@aol.com
www.bnbtexasstyle.com

The Belle of Belton. A beautiful antebellum home right in town with four bedrooms to charm and pamper guests. The rooms are named after the four seasons: Spring, with twin four-poster beds and claw-foot tub across the hall; Summer, with king-size bed, white wicker furniture, and shared bath; Fall, with brass bed, rocking chairs in the triple window, and private bath with shower; Winter, with a corner cupola where poinsettias are displayed, queen-size bed, and private bath. Continental breakfast includes quiche or croissants, fresh fruit, and specially blended coffees or teas. $75.

BEN WHEELER

Bed and Breakfast Texas Style

4224 West Red Bird Lane, Dallas, 75237
(972) 298-8586; (800) 899-4538
FAX (972) 298-7118; e-mail: bdtxstyle1@aol.com
www.bnbtexasstyle.com

The Arc Ridge Guest Ranch. This 600-acre ranch in East Texas near Canton and Tyler has its own lake. Three guest houses have two bedrooms, living room, complete kitchen, and shower. Fishing and paddle-boats are available. No hunters allowed in this environmentally protected area. Breakfast will be left in the refrigerator for guests to prepare themselves. Family rates will be considered. Two-night minimum stay. $95.

BOERNE

Boerne Sunday House Bed and Breakfast Inn

911 South Main, 78006
(210) 249-9563; (800) 633-7339

In a quaint and appealing setting in the beautiful Texas Hill Country. Each room is unique and most are furnished with antiques. All guest rooms are delightfully decorated, cozy, and immaculate. A bountiful breakfast is served in the restored German Sunday House. Close to antique and craft shops. Twenty-five miles from San Antonio and Sea World. Fifteen miles from Fiesta Texas theme park. Smoking restricted. Inquire about accommodations for children. Minimal accessibility for handicapped.

Hostess: Faye Wilson
Owners: Lou and Mary Lou Borgman
Rooms: 13 (PB) $48-70
Full Breakfast
Credit Cards: A, B, C, D, E
Notes: 2, 5, 8, 10, 11, 12

Boerne Sunday House

Guadalupe River Ranch

605 F.M. 474, 78006
(830) 537-4837; (800) 460-2005
FAX (830) 537-5249; e-mail: grranch@gvtc.com
www.guadalupe-river-ranch.com

The main lodge was built in 1929 (formerly owned by actress Olivia de Havilland) and restored to its original elegance. With 360 acres, the ranch provides one of the most spectacular views in the Texas Hill Country. The Guadalupe River Ranch is renowned for its gourmet cuisine, fine wines, Vintner Events, and also offers a variety of activities; river tubing, canoeing, horseback riding, and hiking trails. If one is seeking rest and relaxation, find a hammock, or the overlook swing. Enjoy the peace and serenity.

Host: Elisa McClure
Rooms: 46 (PB) $209-229
Full Breakfast
Credit Cards: A, B, C, D
Notes: 2, 3, 4, 7, 8, 9, 10, 11, 12, 14, 15

BRADY

Brady House

704 South Bridge, 76825
(915) 597-5265; (888) 272-3901
e-mail: bradyhs@centex.net

Brady is at the geographic center of Texas: the northern gateway to the Hill Country, the southern door to the Texas plains, and the portal to West Texas. Six blocks south

Brady House

of the square, Brady House amid its acre of landscaped grounds has three spacious guest rooms, each with private bath. The Craftsman-style home built in 1908 is furnished to reflect not only the period but also family collections.

Hosts: Bobbie and Kelly Hancock
Rooms: 3 (PB) $85-95
Full Breakfast
Credit Cards: A, B, C, D
Notes: 3, 4, 5, 7, 10, 11, 12

BRECKENRIDGE

Bed and Breakfast Texas Style

4224 West Red Bird Lane, Dallas, 75237
(972) 298-8586; (800) 899-4538
FAX (972) 298-7118; e-mail: bdtxstyle1@aol.com
www.bnbtexasstyle.com

The Blue Rose Bed and Breakfast. This Victorian cottage is charmingly decorated with lovely antiques. The cottage has been completely remodeled and has the comforts of today, including central heat and air, washer and dryer, and a microwave oven in the kitchen. There are two bedrooms, each with one bed; one bathroom. There is also a rollaway. Breakfast fixings are left in the well-stocked kitchen and will include the Blue Rose breakfast cake. Breckenridge is a historic town south of Possum Kingdom Lake. The owners live across the street and will meet and welcome guests. Ten dollars for each additional person. $79.

The Keeping Room Bed and Breakfast. This large two-story brick inn is a place for comfort and refuge from the busy world. It was built in 1929 and has been faithfully restored to "better than original" condition. There are two large suites, Bluebonnet and Walker, that each have a sitting room, a bedroom with queen-size beds and matching day bed, and a private bath. The other two rooms, Goodwin and Rustic, also have queen-size beds and share a hall bath. All rooms have TVs.

7 No smoking; 8 Children welcome; 9 Social drinking allowed; 10 Tennis nearby; 11 Swimming nearby; 12 Golf nearby; 13 Skiing nearby; 14 May be booked through a travel agent; 15 Handicapped accessible.

Guests will be pampered with a hearty breakfast of biscuits, sausage, eggs, muffins, juice, and coffee. $65-75.

BRYAN

Bed and Breakfast Texas Style

4224 West Red Bird Lane, Dallas, 75237
(972) 298-8586; (800) 899-4538
FAX (972) 298-7118; e-mail: bdtxstyle1@aol.com
www.bnbtexasstyle.com

Wilderness Bed and Breakfast. This charming home is at the end of a cul-de-sac just three miles from Texas A&M University. There are three bedrooms, two with queen-size beds, one with two twin beds, and a private sitting room with a sleeper-sofa. The master suite downstairs has a private bath; the two rooms upstairs share a hall bath. Breakfast may be Continental with homemade breads or muffins, lots of fruit and cereals, or it may be a traditional Canadian/Texan-style breakfast. This is a nonsmoking facility. Children over 15 years welcome. $75-85.

CANTON

Heavenly Acres Bed and Breakfast

Route 3, Box 470, Mabank, 75147
(800) 283-0341; www.heavenlyacres.com

A 100-acre ranch, with two lakes and two ponds, all spring fed and fully stocked for fishing. Twelve miles southwest of Canton. Each private cabin provides unique decor, with kitchen, TV/VCR, porches with rockers to overlook water. Perfect for romantic getaways. Enjoy video library, mountain bikes, fishing, paddle boats, barnyard petting zoo, and walking paths. Conference center available for church retreats, corporate seminars, etc. No smoking indoors.

Hosts: Vickie J. and Marshall E. Ragle
Cabins: 6 (PB) $85.50-95

Full Breakfast
Credit Cards: A, B, C, D
Notes: 2, 3, 4, 5, 7, 9, 10, 11, 12, 14, 15

Texas Star Bed and Breakfast

Route 1, Box 187, Edgewood, 75117
(903) 896-4277; FAX (903) 896-7061
e-mail: ohohm@integrityonline2.com

Enjoy a peaceful day in the country nestled among large oaks, cedar trees, and green pasturelands in the gently rolling hills of East Texas. Each of the six rooms reflects a different theme of Texas history—Spanish, Native American, Old West, German, Texas country. Private baths, private entrances, and private patios are available. Full course country breakfasts. Five minutes from the world-famous First Monday Trade Days in Canton. Dinner is available by advance request.

Hosts: David and Marie Stoltzfus
Rooms: 6 (4 PB; 2 SB) $65-85
Full Breakfast
Credit Cards: A, B, C, D
Notes: 2, 5, 7, 8, 12

CANYON

Hudspeth House

1905 Fourth Avenue, 79015
(806) 655-9800; (800) 655-9809
FAX (806) 655-7457
www.Hudspethinn.com

This historic bed and breakfast is on the road to and only 20 minutes from Palo Duro Canyon, home of the famous *Texas* musical drama. The facilities offer beautiful accommodations, good ol' American breakfasts. Take a stroll to the Panhandle-Plains Historic Museum or just relax and enjoy the warm hospitality. Special candlelight dinner served in privacy of guests' room is available with reservations.

Hosts: Mark and Mary Clark
Rooms: 8 (PB) $55-110
Full Breakfast
Credit Cards: A, B, C, D, E, F
Notes: 5, 7, 8, 9, 10, 11, 12, 14

NOTES: Credit cards accepted: A MasterCard; B Visa; C American Express; D Discover; E Diner's Club; F Other; 2 Personal checks accepted; 3 Lunch available; 4 Dinner available; 5 Open all year; 6 Pets welcome;

CHAPPELL HILL

Stagecoach Inn

Main at Chestnut, P.O. Box 339, 77426
(409) 836-9515

The inn, built in 1850 by Jacob and Mary Haller, the founders of Chappell Hill, was a favorite stopping place for many notable Texans traveling from Houston to Austin or Waco over the first stagecoach line organized in Texas in 1841 by Smith and Jones. The inn, listed in the National Register of Historic Places, is a 14-room Greek Revival structure with six fireplaces, on three beautifully landscaped acres. A country breakfast is served. Two guest houses also available.

Host: Elizabeth Moore
Rooms: 5 (3 PB; 2 SB) $90
Full Breakfast
Credit Cards: None
Notes: 2, 5, 7, 9, 15

Stagecoach Inn

CLEBURNE

Bed and Breakfast Texas Style

4224 West Red Bird Lane, Dallas, 75237
(972) 298-8586; (800) 899-4538
FAX (972) 298-7118; e-mail: bdtxstyle1@aol.com
www.bnbtexasstyle.com

Cleburne Guest House. This lovely historical Queen Anne Victorian house was built near the turn of the century and is near downtown Cleburne. There are four guest rooms, two with private baths and two sharing a hall bath. All rooms have color TVs and fresh flowers. Coffee bar and refrigerator upstairs for guests' needs. A Continental breakfast will be served in the main dining room or out on the New Orleans-style patio. Area attractions include antiquing, candlewalk, Springfest, and Hot Air Balloon Festival. Walk to antique malls, tearoom, and shopping. $95-115.

CLIFTON

Bed and Breakfast Texas Style

4224 West Red Bird Lane, Dallas, 75237
(972) 298-8586; (800) 899-4538
FAX (972) 298-7118; e-mail: bdtxstyle1@aol.com
www.bnbtexasstyle.com

The Sweetheart Cottage. A historical home, once damaged in a tornado, now restored for a perfect weekend getaway. A loft room has a queen-size bed, and a pull-out sofa is available downstairs. Country breakfast fare is left in the complete kitchen for the guests to prepare. No smoking. Two-night minimum stay required. $65-75.

COLLEGE STATION

Bed and Breakfast Texas Style

4224 West Red Bird Lane, Dallas, 75237
(972) 298-8586; (800) 899-4538
FAX (972) 298-7118; e-mail: bdtxstyle1@aol.com
www.bnbtexasstyle.com

Country Gardens. A sense of peace and tranquility will descend on guests as they enter this little country hideaway on four acres. Stroll through the wooded glen, fruit orchard, grapevines, and berry patches and enjoy the birds and wildflowers. The hosts will prepare a delicious breakfast of wheat pancakes or homemade bread; coffee, tea, or milk; and fruit in season. $65-75.

7 No smoking; 8 Children welcome; 9 Social drinking allowed; 10 Tennis nearby; 11 Swimming nearby; 12 Golf nearby; 13 Skiing nearby; 14 May be booked through a travel agent; 15 Handicapped accessible.

COMFORT

The Comfort Common

717 High Street, P.O. Box 539, 78013
(830) 995-3030
e-mail: comfortcommon@hctc.net
www.bbhost.com/comfortcommon

Historic limestone hotel, circa 1880, listed in the National Register of Historic Places. Rooms and suites are furnished with antiques. The downstairs of the hotel features numerous shops filled with American antiques. A stay at the Comfort Common will put guests in the heart of the Texas Hill Country with Fredericksburg, Kerrville, Boerne, Bandera, and San Antonio all a brief 15-30 minutes away. Fiesta Texas theme park is only 20 minutes away. Featured in *Southern Living* and *Travel & Leisure* magazines.

Hosts: Jim Lord and Bobby Dent
Rooms: 9 (PB) $65-110
Full Breakfast
Credit Cards: A, B, C, D
Notes: 2, 5, 7, 9, 12

The Comfort Common

CORPUS CHRISTI

Bay Breeze Bed and Breakfast

201 Louisiana, 78404
(512) 882-4123
www.go-native.com/inns/0121.html

Within view of the sparkling bay waters, this fine older home features bedroom suites with private baths that radiate the

Bay Breeze

charm and ambiance of days gone by. Less than a five-minute drive from the business district and city marinas, where sea vessels of every description are berthed. One can enjoy fine dining, recreation, or purchase shrimp direct from the net. Travel only a short distance to the Bayfront Convention Center, art and science museums, the Columbus ships, the preservation homes of Heritage Park, and the Harbor Playhouse Community Theater. Beach nearby.

Hosts: Frank and Perry Tompkins
Rooms: 4 (PB)
Full Breakfast
Credit Cards: A, B
Notes: 2, 5, 7, 9, 10, 11, 12

Sand Dollar Hospitality

3605 Mendenhall Drive, 78415
(512) 853-1222; (800) 528-7782
FAX (512) 814-1285
www.ccinternet.net/sand-dollar

Bay Breeze. Within view of the sparkling bay waters, this fine older home offers four accommodations, all with private baths. Guests are invited to enjoy the large sunroom, the 1930s billard table, watch TV, or just relax. A five-minute drive to the business district and city marinas, where guests can enjoy fine dining and recreation or purchase shrimp direct from the net. It is only a short stroll to the city's finest bayfront park and fishing pier. Resident cat. Full breakfast. Smoking permitted outside only. $65-90.

NOTES: Credit cards accepted: A MasterCard; B Visa; C American Express; D Discover; E Diner's Club; F Other; 2 Personal checks accepted; 3 Lunch available; 4 Dinner available; 5 Open all year; 6 Pets welcome;

Camden at Villa Del Sol. A one-bedroom tastefully furnished condominium overlooking Corpus Christi Bay and the USS *Lexington* aircraft carrier/naval history musuem. The compact kitchen is stocked with basic cooking and serving ware. Sleeping accommodations include a queen-size bed, queen-size sofa bed, and two built-in bunks in the hallway. Laundry facilities are close by and elevator is down the hall. The complex includes two swimming pools, three hot tubs, and four barbecue pits. Weekly and monthly rates available. $96.

Camden House. Just five-minute's walking time from beautiful Corpus Christi Bay, this rambling white brick ranch-style home offers a spacious guest suite with a king-size bed and private bath. The adjoining sitting room is furnished with a small couch, easy chair, and has full cable TV. Step out from the suite to own private Jacuzzi or join the hosts at the pool. Have breakfast in the privacy of own suite, or in the dining room, or out by the pool. $96.

Colley House (formerly the Seagull). New England antiques collected by the hosts, a retired navy couple, add to the charm and ambiance of this lovely home. Only one block from Corpus Christi Bay, this 50-year-old home is in a quiet up-scale neighborhood just a five-minute walk from the city's largest bayside park. Guests are invited to relax in the enclosed patio/den with TV, wet bar, and cozy surroundings. Two bedrooms with private baths are available. Older children are welcome. Full breakfast. Smoking permitted outside only. $65.

Inn on the Bay. With an unencumbered view of Corpus Christi Bay and the downtown skyline, this host home offers the discriminating guest a luxurious retreat. An attractively furnished one-bedroom apartment is in the guest wing of the home with own private entrance. Within three miles of Corpus Christi Naval Air Station and Texas A&M University, this home is conveniently on Ocean Drive, a scenic expressway to downtown Corpus Christi. It is also only about 15 minutes' driving time to the gulf beaches on nearby Padre Island. $125.

La Maison du Soleil. Within a quiet gated community, reminiscent of the medieval cities of Provence, this scenic home offers a guest room with private bath, a heated pool, and access to nearby tennis courts. This charming French Provincial-style home is midway between downtown and the gulf beaches—driving time being 25 minutes in either direction. A full gourmet breakfast served. Smoking permitted outside only. $90.

Manitou Cottage. Nestled among the trees behind a charming New England-style farm house, this guest cottage is three blocks from Corpus Christi Bay and less than 10 minutes from downtown. An antique brass bed, wood floors, skylights, and ceiling fans combine to offer a relaxed and cozy atmosphere. Rockers on the porch facing the swimming pool add to the relaxed ambiance. Bicycles are available for riding through the neighborhood. Other amenities include cable TV, telephone, and fax service. A full hot breakfast is delivered to the cottage door. $96.

Smith Place. A colorfully landscaped back yard with pool and hot tub is the setting for two charming guest houses—the Garden Room and the Lodge. The sleeping accommodations for the Garden Room include a queen-size bed in the bedroom and a queen-size sofa bed in the adjoining sitting room. The Lodge has just a queen-size bed and easy chair. Other amenities include private entrances, off-street parking, refrigerator, microwave, coffee center, and cable TV. Breakfast provisions are brought in daily. Small pets permitted. $90.

7 No smoking; 8 Children welcome; 9 Social drinking allowed; 10 Tennis nearby; 11 Swimming nearby; 12 Golf nearby; 13 Skiing nearby; 14 May be booked through a travel agent; 15 Handicapped accessible.

DALLAS

Bed and Breakfast Texas Style

4224 West Red Bird Lane, Dallas, 75237
(972) 298-8586; (800) 899-4538
FAX (972) 298-7118; e-mail: bdtxstyle1@aol.com
www.bnbtexasstyle.com

Artist's Haven. This private home offers two upstairs guest rooms with lovely amenities and shared bath. One room has twin beds, and the other room has a king-size bed. Breakfast is Continental plus, with fruit, pastries, and beverages. Cat in residence. No smoking. Children are welcome. $75.

The Cloisters. This lovely home is one block from White Rock Lake in a secluded area of Dallas. There are two guest rooms, each with a private bath. Both rooms have double beds, one with an antique Mexican headboard that is a conversation piece. Breakfast will be lots of protein, eggs, and/or blueberry pancakes. A bicycle is available for riding around the lake. No smoking. $75.

Fan Room. The antique fan displayed in this lovely twin bedroom is the focal point and was the start of a large collection of fans. The home is near Prestonwood, Marshall Fields, and the Galleria Mall. Southfork Ranch is a 15-minute drive north. A full country breakfast includes jalapeño muffins for first-time Texas visitors. Second bedroom near the kitchen with a double bed and private bath. $70.

The Rose. This historical home was built in 1901 and has four guest bedrooms, each with a private bath. Guests are treated to special breakfasts on the weekends, Continental during the week. Children over 12 are welcome. Smoking is permitted. $60-85.

Tudor Mansion. Built in 1933 in an exclusive neighborhood in the shadow of down-town, this Tudor-style mansion offers queen-size bed and private bath. A full gourmet breakfast of cheddar on toast, Texas-style creamed eggs with jalapeño, or fresh vegetable omelet is served. The bus line is three blocks away. Spanish and French are spoken. Three miles from down-town. Close to a public golf course. $80.

DEL RIO

The 1890 House

609 Griner Street, 78840
(210) 775-8061; (800) 282-1360
FAX (210) 775-4667

Nestled in the heart of Del Rio guests will find this magnificent turn-of-the-century home. It boasts five charming guest rooms, private soaking tubs, and Jacuzzi. It possesses the relaxing Victorian elegance of years gone by. Awaken every morning to the aromas of homemade breads, muffins, and freshly ground coffee. Make this visit an international event by traveling three miles south of the border to Acuna, Mexico.

Hosts: Alberto and Laura Galvan
Rooms: 5 (PB)
Full Breakfast
Credit Cards: A, B, D
Notes: 5, 7, 8, 9, 10, 11, 12, 14

EL PASO

Cowboys and Indians Board and Bunk

P.O. Box 13752, 79913
(505) 589-2653; www.softaid.net/cowboys

Lie back and enjoy the wonderful panoramic view of Franklin Mountains and desert sunsets of southern New Mexico. Bunk down in one of the four theme rooms that are comfortable and decorated to make guests feel like they are a part of the Old West. Relax in the large gathering room. The grub is the best in southwestern- and chuckwagon-style cooking. Special packages for year-round

NOTES: Credit cards accepted: A MasterCard; B Visa; C American Express; D Discover; E Diner's Club; F Other; 2 Personal checks accepted; 3 Lunch available; 4 Dinner available; 5 Open all year; 6 Pets welcome;

golf, horseback riding, sightseeing, seminars, and workshops. Lunch and dinner available but catered only. Smoking permitted outside only. Children over 12 welcome. One room is handicapped accessible.

Hosts: Irene and Don Newlon
Rooms: 4 (PB) $64-87 per night
Full and Continental Breakfast
Credit Cards: A, B, C
Notes: 2, 5, 7, 9, 10, 11, 12, 14

FORT DAVIS

The Veranda Country Inn

The Veranda Country Inn

210 Court Avenue, P.O. Box 1238, 79734
(888) 383-2847; e-mail: veranda@overland.net
www.theveranda.com

The Veranda is a spacious historic inn built in 1883. This unique adobe building, with 2-foot-thick walls and 12-foot ceilings, has eight large rooms and suites furnished with antiques and collectibles. Its walled gardens and quiet courtyards provide travelers with a change of pace and lifestyle in mile-high Fort Davis. A large, separate Carriage House is next to the gardens in the shade of a large pecan tree. The Veranda is within minutes of sites renowned for astronomy, historical forts and buildings, and scenic hiking, biking, and bird watching.

Hosts: Paul and Kathie Woods
Rooms: 8 (PB) $67.50-99
Carriage House: $95-135
Full Breakfast
Credit Cards: A, B, D
Notes: 2, 5, 7, 9,

FORT WORTH

Bed and Breakfast at the Ranch

8275 Wagley Robertson Road, 76131
(817) 232-5522; (888) 593-0352
e-mail: bbranch@flash.net
www.fortworthians.com/bbranch

A true taste of Texas on 15 acres. Bed and Breakfast at the Ranch offers four spacious rooms with their own private baths. Two rooms have special tubs—a Jacuzzi and antique claw-foot tub. Three rooms have their own private patio. The spacious living room offers a stone fireplace, TV with video library, board games, upright grand piano, and library of books. Enclosed patio room is complete with hot tub, patio furniture, wet bar, guest refrigerator, and free pinball. Gourmet breakfast served by resident innkeeper—full on weekends and Continental on weekdays. Grounds offer tennis, putting green, gazebo, swing, and smokehouse. Unique!

Hosts: Scott and Cheryl Stewart
Rooms: 4 (PB) $85-159
Full or Continental Breakfast
Credit Cards: A, B, C
Notes: 2, 4, 5, 7, 9, 10, 11, 12

Bed and Breakfast at the Ranch

Bed and Breakfast Texas Style

4224 West Red Bird Lane, Dallas, 75237
(972) 298-8586; (800) 899-4538
FAX (972) 298-7118; e-mail: bdtxstyle1@aol.com
www.bnbtexasstyle.com

Bloomsbury House. Escape to this beautifully restored 1908 two-story Queen Anne home in one of Texas's largest historic neighborhoods, just south of downtown. Guests will be pampered in one of the four guest bedrooms; each room has its own private bath. Enjoy desserts upon arrival and full home-cooked breakfast in the morning. Attractions in Fort Worth include the Sundance Square, Kimbell Art Museum, and Billy Bob's (famous "kicker dance" club). $99-110.

Miss Molly's Hotel

109 1/2 West Exchange Avenue, 76106
(817) 626-1522; (800) 99-MOLLY (996-6559)
FAX (817) 625-2723
e-mail: missmollys@travelbase.com

An authentic turn-of-the-century boarding house in the Fort Worth stockyards national historic district, the heart of the North Texas cattle industry. Reminiscent of the Old West, seven rooms share three antique-appointed full baths (custom robes are provided during guests' stay), and Miss Josie's, the premier suite, boasts an elegant Victorian decor with draped-fabric ceiling and private bath. A Continental plus breakfast is served in the central parlor beneath a stained-glass skylight. Lunch and dinner are available within walking distance.

Host: Alice Hancock
Rooms: 8 (1 PB; 7 SB) $75-170
Full Breakfast
Credit Cards: A, B, C, D, E, F
Notes: 2, 5, 7, 8, 9, 14

The Texas White House

1417 Eighth Avenue, 76104
(817) 923-3597; (800) 279-6791
FAX (817) 923-0410

This historically designated, award-winning country-style home has been restored to its original 1910 grandeur of simple, yet elegant decor. Within five mintues of downtown, medical center, Fort Worth zoo, the cultural district, botanic gardens, water gardens, and Texas Christian University. Three guest rooms with sitting areas and private baths with claw-foot tubs. Breakfast served in either the dining room or sent to guests'

room. Amenities include telephone, TV, early morning coffee service, afternoon snacks and beverages, secretarial services, laundry service for extended stays, and off-street parking.

Hosts: Jamie and Grover McMains
Rooms: 3 (PB) $85-105
Full Breakfast
Credit Cards: A, B, C, D
Notes: 2, 5, 7, 9, 10, 11, 12, 14

FREDERICKSBURG

Das College Haus

106 West College, 78624
(830) 997-9047; (800) 654-2802

Visit historic Fredericksburg and stay at Das College Haus, just three blocks from downtown. Spacious rooms with private baths; all have access to the porches, balcony with porch swing, and wicker rockers, where guests can relax and visit. Das College Haus is beautifully appointed with comfortable period furniture and original art for a wonderful "at home" atmosphere. Enjoy a full breakfast served in the old-fashioned dining room. Central heat and air, cable TV, VCR, and a collection of movies. Coffee makers and refrigerators in rooms.

Host: Myrna Dennis
Rooms: 4 (PB) $80-100
Full Breakfast
Credit Cards: A, B
Notes: 2, 5, 7, 9, 10, 11, 12, 15

Schildknecht-Weidenfeller House

Gästehaus Schmidt Reservation Service
231 West Main, 78624
(830) 997-5612; FAX (830) 997-8282

Guests can relive history in the Schildknecht-Weidenfeller House in the heart of Fredericksburg's historic district. Decorated with antiques and handmade quilts, this guest house accommodates up to 10 people. A German-style Continental plus breakfast is left for guests to enjoy at their leisure around the antique farm table in the kitchen. This 1870s German limestone house

NOTES: Credit cards accepted: A MasterCard; B Visa; C American Express; D Discover; E Diner's Club; F Other; 2 Personal checks accepted; 3 Lunch available; 4 Dinner available; 5 Open all year; 6 Pets welcome;

Schildknecht-Weidenfeller House

has been featured on tours of historic homes and in *Country Decorating Ideas*. Member of Historic Accommodations of Texas. Children 12 and older welcome. Rates increase with number of people in party.

Owners: Ellis and Carter Schildknecht
House: $125
Continental Breakfast
Credit Cards: A, B, D
Notes: 2, 5, 7, 9, 10, 11, 12, 14

Schmidt Barn Bed and Breakfast

Gästehaus Schmidt Reservation Service
231 West Main, 78624
(210) 997-5612; FAX (210) 997-8282

The remnants of an 1860s limestone barn were lovingly saved to turn it into a guest house. Stone walls, brick floors, timber beams maintain century-old charm. Bathroom invites guests to a long soak in a sunken tub. Quilts, antique linens, samplers, and a collection of toys enliven the wooden-beamed loft bedrooms. Hosts live next door. Featured in *Country Living* and *Travel and Leisure*. German Continental plus breakfast is left for guests to enjoy at their leisure.

Hosts: Charles and Loretta Schmidt
Rooms: 1 (PB) $85
Continental Breakfast
Credit Cards: A, B
Notes: 2, 5, 6, 8, 9, 10, 11, 14

Watkins Hill

608 East Creek Street, 78624
(800) 899-1672; FAX (830) 997-6057

The hosts' goal for guests is relaxation and privacy. Two acres with seven buildings, seven antique-filled guest rooms, private entrances, private baths, telephone line, TV/VCR, breakfast brought to guests' door. Meeting, retreat, reunion, wedding facility for 50 persons with 1840 frontier log barn, including stage, ballroom, dining room, library, parlor, conservatory, and kitchen. Catering available. The hosts can accommodate or create guests' own special occasion or event.

Hosts: Betty O'Connor and Susan Martin
Rooms: 7 (PB) $110-165
Full Breakfast
Credit Cards: A, B
Notes: 5, 6, 7, 8, 9, 10, 11, 12, 14

GAINESVILLE

Alexander Bed and Breakfast Acres, Inc.

Route 7, Box 788, 76240
(903) 564-7440; (800) 887-8794
www.bbhost.com/alexanderbbacres

Three-story Queen Anne Victorian home on 65 peaceful acres of woods and meadows. Large wraparound porch for lounging; walking trails; near two large lakes, antiques, country farms, and zoo. Each bedroom decorated with different theme: western, antique, canopied, or Amish. Full breakfast included. Separate conference room and extra lodging on third floor. Two-story guest cottage offers three bedrooms sharing one and one-half baths, kitchen, laundry, living area, and large screened porch. Children and pets welcome in cottage only. Dinner available by arrangement.

Hosts: Jim and Pamela Alexander
Rooms: 8 (5 PB; 3 SB) $60-125
Full Breakfast
Credit Cards: A, B, D
Notes: 2, 5, 7, 9, 11, 12, 13, 14

7 No smoking; 8 Children welcome; 9 Social drinking allowed; 10 Tennis nearby; 11 Swimming nearby; 12 Golf nearby; 13 Skiing nearby; 14 May be booked through a travel agent; 15 Handicapped accessible.

GALVESTON

Madame Dyer's Bed and Breakfast

1720 Postoffice Street, 77550
(409) 765-5692

From the moment guests enter this carefully restored turn-of-the-century Victorian home built in 1889, they will be entranced by such period details as wraparound porches, high airy ceilings, wooden floors, and lace curtains. Each room is furnished with delightful antiques that bring back memories of days gone by. In the morning, on an antique buffet sideboard on the second floor, guests will find teas and freshly brewed coffee provided for the early riser. Breakfast is a special treat, served abundantly in the dining room. Smoking permitted on outside porches only. Children over 12 are welcome.

Hosts: Linda and Larry Bonnin
Rooms: 3 (PB) $100-125
Full Breakfast
Credit Cards: A, B
Notes: 2, 5, 7, 9, 10, 11, 12, 14

Madame Dryer's

The Queen Anne Bed and Breakfast

1915 Sealy Avenue, 77550-2312
(409) 763-7088; (800) 472-0930

This home is a four-story Queen Anne Victorian built in 1905. Stained-glass windows, beautiful floors, large rooms, pocket doors, and 12-foot ceilings with transom doors; beautifully redecorated in 1991. Walk to the historic shopping district, restaurants, 1886 opera house, museums, and the historic homes district. A short drive to the beach. A visit to Queen Anne is to be anticipated, relished, and long-remembered.

Hosts: John McWilliams and Earl French
Rooms: 5 (3 PB; 2 SB) $85-145
Full Breakfast
Credit Cards: A, B, C
Notes: 2, 5, 7, 9, 10, 11, 12, 13, 14

GALVESTON ISLAND

Bayview Inn with Hot Tub and Boatpier

P.O. Box 1326, 77553
(409) 741-0705

Waterfront casual luxury and elegance in a romantic setting complete with huge swaying palms, exotic waterfowl, and hot tub. Water views from all rooms with private baths; furnished with fabulous rare antiques from world travels. Boat dock. Golf course and beach two minutes away. Ms. Pat is an island character well worth meeting. Her specialty is adult getaways. Nearby are flight and car museums, historical homes, IMAX, rainforest-pyramid, trolley, fishing, beach, boating; 45 minutes to Houston.

Host: Ms. Pat Hazlewood
Rooms: 3 (PB) $65-145
Continental Breakfast
Credit Cards: F
Notes: 2, 5, 7, 9, 10, 11, 12, 13

GARLAND

Bed and Breakfast Texas Style

4224 West Red Bird Lane, Dallas, 75237
(972) 298-8586; (800) 899-4538
FAX (972) 298-7118; e-mail: bdtxstyle1@aol.com
www.bnbtexasstyle.com

Catnip Creek. Right on Spring Creek, the hot tub on the deck overlooks a wooded

---

NOTES: Credit cards accepted: A MasterCard; B Visa; C American Express; D Discover; E Diner's Club; F Other; 2 Personal checks accepted; 3 Lunch available; 4 Dinner available; 5 Open all year; 6 Pets welcome;

creek. The guest room has a queen-size bed, private bath, and private entrance. Breakfast has granola and cinnamon-raisin biscuits or other homemade muffins and breads. Weekend guests are treated to a healthy quiche or pancakes. Herbal teas and specially blended coffees are offered. Bicycles are provided. Just 30 minutes from downtown Dallas and very near Hypermart, the newest tourist attraction of the metroplex. Also near Southfork Ranch. $60-75.

Heron Hill Farm

GEORGETOWN

Claibourne House

912 Forest, 78626
(512) 930-3934; (512) 913-2272 (voice mail)

Claibourne House is three blocks west of the historic courthouse square in the heart of old Georgetown. Built in 1896, this spacious Victorian residence was restored during 1987-88 and adapted as a bed and breakfast inn. Guests are graciously accommodated in four bedrooms, each with private bath. An intimate upstairs sitting room and downstairs grand hall and parlor and wraparound porch are available for guests. The guest rooms are handsomely furnished with treasured family furniture, antiques, and distinctive fine art.

Host: Clare Easley
Rooms: 4 (PB) $85-120
Continental Breakfast
Credit Cards: A, B
Notes: 2, 5, 7, 9

Heron Hill Farm Bed and Breakfast

1350 County Road 143, 78626
(512) 863-0461; (800) 439-3828 (reservations)

New, old-fashioned Texas farmhouse built in 1997 especially for bed and breakfast. House sits high on a hill overlooking 13 acres of wildlife habitat and a large vegetable garden. Pick own veggies in season. The four guest rooms, each with private bath, are on the second floor. Rooms feature country decor which mixes new and antique furniture. Three rooms have queen-size beds, one room has two twin antique white iron beds. Full breakfast served daily. Enjoy antiquing, hiking, biking, and swimming and boating at local lake; golf also available nearby. Inner Space Caverns and Lady Bird Johnson Wildflower Center make good day trips.

Hosts: Ed and Linda Devine
Rooms: 4 (PB) $75
Full Breakfast
Credit Cards: A, B
Notes: 2, 5, 7, 8, 9, 11, 12

GLADEWATER

Honeycomb Suites

111 North Main Street, 75647
(800) 594-2253; FAX (903) 845-2448
www.pageboyz.com/honeycomb

Specializing in romantic getaways, offering seven suites, each in a different motif. Five suites are above scratch-recipe bakery in the antique district of Gladewater. Two suites (including the honeymoon suite) are in an adjacent building. Four suites have whirlpool tubs for two. Saturday evenings, candlelight dinners with horse-drawn carriage rides are available by reservation. Romance packages and gift certificates are available. Gladewater is 120 miles east of Dallas or 60 miles west of Shreveport.

Hosts: Bill and Susan Morgan
Rooms: 7 (PB) $85-150
Full Breakfast
Credit Cards: A, B, C, D
Notes: 2, 3, 4, 5, 7, 9, 10, 11, 12

GLEN ROSE

Bed and Breakfast Texas Style
4224 West Red Bird Lane, Dallas, 75237
(972) 298-8586; (800) 899-4538
FAX (972) 298-7118; e-mail: bdtxstyle1@aol.com
www.bnbtexasstyle.com

Hummingbird Lodge. The motto of the owners for this extraordinary bed and breakfast is "Come find the trees and streams, the deer and the birds, the peace. Come find yourself." Just about two miles south of Glen Rose off the beaten path, surrounded by cedar trees and small hills, a weary city dweller will find complete serenity. There are large porches and decks with rocking chairs; the "hummers" are most entertaining; or just curl up with a book down by the hot tub in the swinging hammock. There are well marked walking trails, a waterfall, and a pond for the energetic fisherman. There are six guest rooms, all with private baths. A full gourmet breakfast is provided. $85-115.

Bussey's Something Special
202 Hereford Street, P.O. Box 1425, 76043
(817) 897-4843; (800) 700-4843 (#13)

Relax in a private country cottage in downtown Glen Rose historic district. Family-friendly with crib upstairs. Enjoy hand-crafted lounges, artwork, books, games, and toys. Seashell and oak bathroom with shower (no tub). Experience the Early American decor in a private cozy cottage with tropical bath, whirlpool jet tub/shower, and small kitchen. Both cottages have a king-size bed. Continental plus breakfast, private front porches, and attractive decor.

Sweetheart packages for special occasions are available upon request.

Hosts: Susan and Morris Bussey
Cottage: 2 (PB) $80-100
Continental Breakfast
Credit Cards: A, B, C
Notes: 2, 5, 7, 8, 10, 11, 12, 14

GOLIAD

The Linburg House
736 North Jefferson Street (Highway 183 North), 77963
(512) 645-1997; e-mail: mheskett@viptx.net

An 1888 Victorian Craftsman-style residence that has been made comfortable with country antique furnishings, central air and heat. After a busy day, be prepared to relax in the exquisite charm and comfort of one of the three gracious bedrooms. Each suite has its own cable color TV. There is a front porch to relax on or guests can choose the enclosed screened back porch and enjoy a country view. Just a short drive to the historic fully restored Spanish fort Presidio La Bahia, Goliad State Historical Park, wildlife observation areas, and Coleto Creek Reservoir, which has year-round fishing.

Hosts: Mike and Terry Heskett
Rooms: 3 (PB) $65-85
Full Breakfast
Credit Cards: None
Notes: 2, 5, 7

GONZALES

St. James Inn
723 St. James, 78629
(830) 672-7066

A former cattle baron's mansion. This elegant bed and breakfast is a welcome respite from the busy life. Furnished with antiques, colorful collections, and warm hospitality. The rural area offers a fun opportunity for hiking, biking, antiquing, and roaming. Relax in the lovely setting of one of the grand historic homes of Gonzales, "the

Lexington of Texas"—once alive with cotton and cattle ranches. This area of Texas is rich in history and great scenic adventures. Experience historic and hospitable Gonzales Country. Member of Professional Innkeepers, Inc., and Texas Historic Accommodations Association.

Hosts: Ann and J. R. Covert
Rooms: 5 (4 PB) 85-100
Full Breakfast
Credit Cards: A, B, C
Notes: 2, 3, 4, 9, 10, 11, 12, 14

Pearl Street Inn

GRAHAM

Bed and Breakfast Texas Style

4224 West Red Bird Lane, Dallas, 75237
(972) 298-8586; (800) 899-4538
FAX (972) 298-7118; e-mail: bdtxstyle1@aol.com
www.bnbtexasstyle.com

Victorian Memories. Victorian ambiance adorns this 1900s Folk Victorian-style bed and breakfast guest house, built by one of Graham's pioneer families. Established in 1885, it has been lovingly preserved with unique stained glass, wood floors, and high ceilings. There are two guest rooms, each complimented by English ivy, floral wreaths, quilts, and charming antiques. There are two baths, one with a claw-foot tub. There is a fully equipped kitchen, where a Continental breakfast is left for guests' leisure. Relax in the sunroom while enjoying the pleasures of fresh flowers and plants. Visit historic Graham with America's largest downtown square only two blocks away. Inquire about rates for the entire house. $79.

GRANBURY

Pearl Street Inn Bed and Breakfast

319 West Pearl Street, 76048
(817) 579-7465; (888) PEARL ST

Relax and reminisce in the stately, stylish comfort of a 1912 Prairie-style home. Three blocks from Granbury's historic square, this tastefully restored historical home features antique furnishings, two porches, cast-iron tubs, pocket doors, outdoor hot tub, and scrumptious breakfasts. Enjoy live theater, state parks, drive-in movies, antique shopping, or festivals in a charming country setting, 30 miles south of the Dallas/Fort Worth metroplex. Enjoy overnight accommodations in a delightful home "where days move gently in all seasons."

Host: Danette D. Hebda
Rooms: 5 (PB) $59-109
Full Breakfast
Credit Cards: None
Notes: 2, 5, 7, 9, 10, 11, 12, 14

HOUSTON

The Lovett Inn

501 Lovett Boulevard, 77006
(713) 522-5224; (800) 779-5224
FAX (713) 528-6708; www.lovettinn.com

Once the home of Houston mayor and federal court judge Joseph C. Hutcheson, the Lovett Inn has all of the amenities of a first-class hotel. Within walking distance to some of the city's finest restaurants, clubs, and shopping. The George R. Brown Convention Center, downtown, Greenway Plaza, Texas Medical Center, Hobby Airport, and the Galleria are also nearby. Each room has been comfortably decorated to evoke the inn's historic past, while adding such modern amenities as in-room telephones, remote color TV, and

7 No smoking; 8 Children welcome; 9 Social drinking allowed; 10 Tennis nearby; 11 Swimming nearby; 12 Golf nearby; 13 Skiing nearby; 14 May be booked through a travel agent; 15 Handicapped accessible.

private bathrooms. To accommodate the most discriminating traveler, suite accommodations, meeting rooms, fax service, and in-room whirlpool are available.

Host: Tom Fricke
Rooms: 9 (8 PB; 1 SB) $85-150
Continental Breakfast
Credit Cards: A, B, C, D
Notes: 5, 6, 7, 8, 9, 10, 11, 12, 14, 15

Robin's Nest

4104 Greeley, 77006
(713) 528-5821; (800) 622-8343
FAX (713) 521-2154; www.houstonbnb.com

Historic, circa 1897, two-story wooden Queen Anne. Feather beds atop fine mattresses, convenience of central location, and taste (buds) make the stay worthwhile. The rooms are spacious, furnished in eclectic Victorian with custom-made drapes, bed covers, etc. Robin's Nest is decoratively painted in concert with her sister "painted ladies." In the Museum and Arts district, surrounded by museums, art galleries, downtown, excellent restaurants, and the theater district. Inquire about accommodations for pets and children.

Host: Robin Smith
Rooms: 4 (PB) $85-120
Full Breakfast
Credit Cards: A, B, C, D
Notes: 2, 5, 7, 9, 10, 11, 12, 13

Sara's Bed and Breakfast Inn

941 Heights Boulevard, 77008
(713) 868-1130; (800) 593-1130

This Queen Anne Victorian is in the historic Heights district of Houston, a neighborhood of historic homes, many of which are in the National Register of Historic Places. Each bedroom is uniquely furnished, having either single, double, queen, or king-size beds. The balcony suite consists of two bedrooms, two baths, kitchen, living area, and balcony. The sights and sounds of downtown are only four miles away.

Sara's

Hosts: Donna and Tillman Arledge
Rooms: 14 (12 PB; 2 SB) $55-150
Continental Breakfast
Credit Cards: A, B, C, D, E, F
Notes: 2, 5, 7, 8, 9, 10, 11, 12, 14

JEFFERSON

Captain's Castle Bed and Breakfast

403 East Walker Street, 75657
(800) 650-2330
www.jeffersontx.com/captainscastle

The Captain's Castle was so named by Captain Thomas J. Rogers, a Confederate officer and local pioneer banker. In the early 1870s, he combined two older houses—the two-story front portion he moved across town on log rollers, with oxen, from down on the riverfront. This colorful old home, furnished with antiques, has a Texas Historical Medallion and is listed in the national register of homes.

Hosts: Buck and Barbara Hooker
Rooms: 7 (PB) $95-110
Full Breakfast
Credit Cards: A, B, C
Notes: 2, 5, 7, 9, 11, 12, 14

NOTES: Credit cards accepted: A MasterCard; B Visa; C American Express; D Discover; E Diner's Club; F Other; 2 Personal checks accepted; 3 Lunch available; 4 Dinner available; 5 Open all year; 6 Pets welcome;

Excelsior House Hotel

211 West Austin, 75657
(903) 665-2513

The historic Excelsior House was built in the 1850s by riverboat captain William. Perry. Currently owned and operated by the Jessie Allen Wise Garden Club, the brick and timber structure has 15 guest rooms, each furnished in exquisite period furniture. The ballroom, once the location of gala balls, and the dining room are the perfect setting to enjoy the Excelsior's famous plantation breakfast, or to host receptions, weddings, luncheons, or dinners by reservation.

Rooms: 15 (PB) $65-100
Full Breakfast
Credit Cards: A, B
Notes: 2, 5, 7, 9, 11, 12

Hale House
Bed and Breakfast

702 South Line Street, 75657
(903) 665-8877

Hale House Bed and Breakfast is spacious, comfortable, and furnished with gorgeous period antiques. Completely restored to include modern conveniences, the home glows with hardwood floors, antique mirrors, and chandeliers. Owners James and Nancy Rice offer a warm southern welcome to guests, along with a gourmet breakfast served with china and crystal in the formal dining room. Six beautifully appointed guest rooms, an enclosed sun porch, a

Hale House

broadside porch, and spacious gazebo make Hale House a delightful, romantic setting.

Hosts: James and Nancy Rice
Rooms: 6 (PB) $75-100
Full Breakfast
Credit Cards: A, B, D
Notes: 2, 5, 7, 12

McKay House

McKay House
Bed and Breakfast Inn

306 East Delta Street, 75657
(903) 665-7322
(800) 468-2627 (reservations 9 A.M.-5 P.M.)

Jefferson is a riverport town from the frontier days of the Republic of Texas. It has historical mule-drawn tours, 30 antique shops, boat rides on the Big Cypress Bayou, and a mysterious lake made famous by Walt Disney. The McKay House, an 1851 Greek Revival cottage, offers period furnishings, cool lemonade, porch swings, and fireplaces. Seven rooms that vary from the keeping room to the garden suite (with his and her antique footed tubs). A full gentleman's breakfast is served in the garden conservatory. Victorian nightclothes are laid out for guests. VIP guests have included Lady Bird Johnson, Alex Haley, and Fabio. Mobil Travel Guide.

Owner: Peggy Taylor
Innkeepers: Lisa and Roger Cantrell
Rooms: 4 (PB) $99
Suites: 3 (PB) $125-155
Full Breakfast
Credit Cards: A, B, C
Notes: 2, 5, 7, 8, 11, 12, 14

7 No smoking; 8 Children welcome; 9 Social drinking allowed; 10 Tennis nearby; 11 Swimming nearby; 12 Golf nearby; 13 Skiing nearby; 14 May be booked through a travel agent; 15 Handicapped accessible.

Urquhart House of Eleven Gables

301 East Walker Street, 75657
(903) 665-8442

The Urquhart House of Eleven Gables is an experience of luxuries and historical elegance. Turn-of-the-century quality of life comes alive with period decor and antiques. Further creating the yesteryear ambiance are equestrian carriages and wagons clip-clopping the street that fronts the wraparound porch of this expansive 1890 Queen Anne house. Antique wicker swing and furniture occupy the abundantly pleasant wraparound porch inviting guests to come and "sit a spell." Gourmet breakfast served with antique linens, crystal, and china.

Host: Joyce Jackson
Rooms: 4 (PB) $125
Full Breakfast
Credit Cards: A, B, C, D, E
Notes: 2, 5, 7, 8, 9, 12, 14

Urquhart House of Eleven Gables

Shady Rest at the Junction

massive refurbishing inside and out. Relax on the beautiful wraparound front porch, or leisurely lounge at the umbrella table, as guests enjoy this picturesque setting nestled between the North and South Llano Rivers. Guests will be treated to a sumptuous breakfast by candlelight to Victorian love songs.

Hosts: Bill and Debbie Bayer
Rooms: 1 (PB) $65
Full Breakfast
Credit Cards: None
Notes: 2, 3, 4, 7, 12

KEMALT

The Ark on the Bay

705 Sixth Street, 77565 (location)
1302 First Street, Seabrook, 77586 (mailing)
(281) 474-5295; FAX (281) 474-7840

The Ark has a nautical theme with incredible views. The house has been carefully decorated and will make guests feel as if they were the captain of the ship. Rent a room or the whole house for a fun-packed memorable vacation. Bring one's watercraft, fishing poles, crab traps, swimsuits, beach towels, and lots of suntan lotion for a great time. Outside, under the house is a 10-person hot tub, stereo speakers, a patio area, and access to the water via a small pier. It is only three blocks from the marina and some of the best seafood restaurants on the Texas

JUNCTION

Shady Rest at the Junction Bed and Breakfast Inn

101 North 11th Street, 76849
(915) 446-4067 (phone/FAX); (888) 892-8292

Junctions's one-of-a-kind Victorian-style bed and breakfast offers guests a unique stay in downtown. This beautiful turn-of-the-century home has recently undergone a

NOTES: Credit cards accepted: A MasterCard; B Visa; C American Express; D Discover; E Diner's Club; F Other; 2 Personal checks accepted; 3 Lunch available; 4 Dinner available; 5 Open all year; 6 Pets welcome;

Coast. There are also many speciality and gift shops within a half block to browse through. Unhosted.

Managed by: Suzanne Silver
Rooms: 3 (2 PB; 1 SB) $85-120
Continental Breakfast
Credit Cards: A, B, C, D
Notes: 2, 5, 7, 9, 12, 14

KINGSVILLE

B Bar B Ranch Inn

325 East County Road 2215, 78363
(512) 296-3331; FAX (512) 296-3337
e-mail: bbarb@rivnet.com

Quietly nestled beneath the rippling leaves of a south Texas mesquite grove, this 80-acre working ranch is host to a wide variety of native plants and wildlife. Originally part of the historic King Ranch, the B Bar B is a bird watching hot spot. The hosts also offer fishing and hunting trips. Their gourmet restaurant is sure to tempt guests' taste buds.

Hosts: Luther and Patti Young
Rooms: 16 (PB) $85-125
Full Breakfast
Credit Cards: A, B, D
Notes: 2, 4, 5, 11, 12, 14

LA COSTE

Bed and Breakfast Texas Style

4224 West Red Bird Lane, Dallas, 75237
(972) 298-8586; (800) 899-4538
FAX (972) 298-7118; e-mail: bdtxstyle1@aol.com
www.bnbtexasstyle.com

Swan and Railway Inn. At one time this inn was known as the City Hotel and it had only three guest bedrooms. It has now increased to five rooms, three with private baths. There is a new pool for guests to enjoy. Breakfast may be yogurt and granola or bran muffins, fruit, and herb teas. About 18 to 20 minutes from San Antonio and 10 minutes from Sea World. La Coste was a French settlement, and nearby Castroville has German roots. $75-85.

LEDBETTER

Ledbetter Bed and Breakfast

208 FM 1291, P.O. Box 212, 78946-0212
(409) 249-3066; (800) 240-3066
FAX (409) 249-3330; e-mail: jjervis@fais.net
www.ledbetter-tx.com

Ledbetter Bed and Breakfast, established in 1988, is a collection of multigenerational, family, 1800-1900s homes within walking distance of the remaining 1870s downtown businesses. A full country breakfast buffet can serve up to 70 guests daily. Hay rides, walks, fishing, horse and buggy rides, games, Christmas lights, chuck wagon or romantic dinners, indoor heated swimming pool, VCR, TV. A telephone can be made available on advance request. Each unit accommodates approximately four people. Only nonalcoholic beverages are allowed outside private quarters. Only outdoor smoking is permitted. Water skiing nearby. Establishment is semi-handicapped accessible.

Hosts: Chris and Jay Jervis
Rooms: 20 (18 PB; 2 SB) $70-150
Full or Continental Breakfast
Credit Cards: A, B, C
Notes: 2, 3, 4, 5, 7, 8, 10, 11, 12, 13, 14

MASON

Hasse House Ranch

1221 Ischar, P.O. Box 58, 76856
(888) 41-HASSE (414-2773)

The Hasse House, circa 1883, is where country quality lives in historical architecture laced with modern conveniences. Complete with period furniture, microwave, dishwasher, washer-dryer, central air, two bedrooms, two baths, living room, and complete kitchen. Guests may explore the 320-acre ranch with two-mile nature trail and abundant wildlife. Owner lives in town so party will be only one in the house. "Let us invite you to the complete peace of rural living."

7 No smoking; 8 Children welcome; 9 Social drinking allowed; 10 Tennis nearby; 11 Swimming nearby; 12 Golf nearby; 13 Skiing nearby; 14 May be booked through a travel agent; 15 Handicapped accessible.

Host: Laverne Lee
Rooms: 2 (PB) $95
Continental Breakfast
Credit Cards: A, B
Notes: 2, 5, 8, 9, 12

MINEOLA

The Lott Home Bed and Breakfast Cottages

311 East Kilpatrick Street, 75773
(888) 232-LOTT (5688); e-mail:
  lotthomecottages@tyler.net

The Lott Home Cottages, circa 1918, offers old-fashioned southern hospitality at its best. The charming, romantic cottages include queen-size beds, private baths, cable TV, antique furnishings, and a kitchen, with microwave, refrigerator, and coffee maker, fully stocked with refreshments and snacks. Each cottage has its own private porch with wooden rockers for guests to relax and view a beautiful East Texas sunset. Treat oneself to an unforgettable night, relive a moment in time and take home wonderful memories at the Lott Home Bed and Breakfast Cottages.

Hosts: Mark and Sharon Chamblee
Rooms: 2 (PB) $95
Full Breakfast
Credit Cards: A, B, D
Notes: 2, 5, 7, 9, 12, 14, 15

MONTGOMERY

Honeysuckle Rose Bed and Breakfast

820 Caroline Street, P.O. Box 1447, 77356
(409) 597-7707; (800) 341-9151
FAX (409) 582-4404; e-mail: rosebb@mcia.com

A Victorian-style home two blocks from antique shopping in downtown Montgomery. Three rooms with private baths, parlor, and library. A European-style Continental plus breakfast provided—no set time for breakfast. Hosts live off premises. The English Rose Room (queen-size bed) and Tea Room (double bed) have Victorian

decor. The Rambling Rose Room is country style with twin beds. Front and back porches have rockers and a swing for guests to enjoy.

Hosts: Charlotte and Dix Cottingham
Rooms: 3 (PB) $75-85
Continental Breakfast
Credit Cards: A, B, D
Notes: 2, 5, 7, 12, 14, 15

NACOGDOCHES

PineCreek Lodge Bed and Breakfast Country Inn

Route 3, Box 1238, 75964
(409) 560-6282; (888) 714-1414
e-mail: pitts@lcc.net
www.pinecreeklodge.com

On a peaceful 140-acre wooded property near a flowing creek. Acres of beautiful grounds and flowers. Miles of surrounding country roads for driving and hiking enjoyment. Special features include large decks with swings and rocking chairs, hammock, pool, spa, fishing pond, and hiking trail. Each room has a private bath and deck with swing, air conditioning, ceiling fans, TV and VCR, refrigerator, telephone, monogrammed robes, and fresh flowers. Refreshments at check-in. Smoking outdoors only.

Hosts: The Pitts Family
Rooms: 11 (PB) $55-95
Full Breakfast
Credit Cards: A, B, C, D
Notes: 2, 3, 4, 5, 8, 12

PineCreek Lodge

NOTES: Credit cards accepted: A MasterCard; B Visa; C American Express; D Discover; E Diner's Club; F Other; 2 Personal checks accepted; 3 Lunch available; 4 Dinner available; 5 Open all year; 6 Pets welcome;

NEW BRAUNFELS

Historic Kuebler-Waldrip Haus

1620 Heuco Springs Loop, 78132
(830) 625-8372; (800) 299-8372
www.cruisingamerica.com/kuebler-waldrip

Come relax on a 43-acre ranch near San Antonio. Enjoy a delightful stay in either the Historic Kuebler-Waldrip Haus (circa 1847), a German Roch house, or the historic Danville School House (circa 1863), an original one-room schoolhouse. Rooms have air conditioning and central heat, private baths, some with whirlpool tubs, TVs, telephones, kitchen access, and porch. Create great memories when planning reunions, a wedding, honeymoon, anniversaries, receptions, or vacation. Meeting and party facility is now available. Free brochure. Quiet, well-behaved pets welcome. Airport nearby.

Hosts: Margaret and son, Darrell Waldrip
Rooms: 10 (PB) $95-145
Full Breakfast
Credit Cards: A, B, C, D
Notes: 2, 5, 7, 8, 9, 10, 11, 12, 13, 14, 15

Karbach Haus Bed and Breakfast

487 West San Antonio Street, 78130
(830) 625-2131; (800) 972-5941
FAX (830) 629-1126

Lovingly restored turn-of-the-century mansion on an acre estate in downtown New Braunfels. Walk to fine restaurants, museums, antique stores, local attractions. Experience *Gemütlichkeit* of a German *Gasthaus* with amenities of a small resort. Spacious guest rooms have private tile baths, queen- or king-size beds, cable TVs, VCRs, robes, ceiling fans, down quilts, and many antiques. Central heat and air, heated pool and spa, video library, butler's pantry with guest refrigerator, ice machine. World-class German-style breakfasts. Long-term rental available. Owner/hosts on premises.

Hosts: Captain Ben Jack Kinney, USN (Retired)
  and Kathleen Karbach Kinney, Ph.D.

Rooms: 6 (PB) $105-175
Full Breakfast
Credit Cards: A, B, D
Notes: 2, 5, 7, 9, 10, 11, 12

The Old Hunter Road Stagecoach Inn Bed and Breakfast

5441 FM 1102, 78132
(830) 620-9453 (phone/FAX)
e-mail: stagecoach@sat.net

Step back in time to a bygone era of Texas history and hospitality. The inn—with its hand-hewn log cabins and *fachwerk* house redolent of early Texas—was used as a stagecoach stop between 1850 and 1865. Each guest room is impeccably appointed with the rustic elegance of Texas antiques, laces, linens, quilts, and fresh flowers. All have private baths, entrances, and porches with rockers surrounded by gardens of fragrant herbs and antique roses. A gourmet breakfast with guests in mind is served in the candlelit dining room.

Rooms: 3 (PB) $85
Full Breakfast
Credit Cards: A, B, C
Notes: 2, 5, 7, 8, 9, 10, 11, 12

Prince Solms Inn

295 East San Antonio Street, 78130
(800) 625-9169; FAX (830) 625-9169

Historic landmark in historic Hill Country, circa 1898. Oldest continuous business in the state. City location in historic downtown. Two blocks from museums, water sports, and so forth. Ideal for family  gatherings, small weddings, and corporate retreats. Mystery weekends (spring and fall), romance packages which include dinner in renowned Wolfgang's Keller Restaurant,

7 No smoking; 8 Children welcome; 9 Social drinking allowed; 10 Tennis nearby; 11 Swimming nearby; 12 Golf nearby; 13 Skiing nearby; 14 May be booked through a travel agent; 15 Handicapped accessible.

rated one of the 10 most romantic restaurants by *Ultra* magazine. Continental plus breakfast served. Restaurant on premises. Smoking permitted in courtyard only.

Hosts: Larry Patton and
   Beverly Talbot (general manager)
Rooms: 10 (PB) $90-150
Continental Breakfast
Credit Cards: A, B, C, D
Notes: 2, 3, 4, 5, 7, 8, 9, 10, 11, 12, 13, 14

Carson House

PADRE ISLES

Sand Dollar Hospitality

35 Mendenhall Drive, Corpus Christi, 78415
(512) 853-1222; (800) 528-7782
FAX (512) 814-1285
www.ccinternet.net/sand-dollar

Fortuna Bay. This enchanting hideaway on Texas's North Padre Island is cradled between the Laguna Madre and the Gulf of Mexico. A unique bed and breakfast inn, Fortune Bay presently consists of three one-bedroom fully furnished condominums in a 10-unit complex. Each unit has a living room with cable TV, a bedroom with a queen-size bed, a fully equipped kitchen with microwave, and a washer and dryer. There is also an outside grill near the pool. The three-story, red-tile-roof structure is at the intersection of five canals. Provisions for a Continental plus breakfast are supplied. A complimentary boat ride through the canal system is offered. Weekly and monthly rates are available. $96.

PITTSBURG

Carson House Inn and Grille

302 Mount Pleasant Street, 75686
(903) 856-2468; (888) 302-1878
FAX (903) 856-0709
e-mail: carsonig@1starnet.com

Built in 1878, the inn is a study in charm and elegance. Turn-of-the-century antiques fill the beautifully appointed rooms. The unique wood trim and wainscotting is from the now extinct curly pine tree. The serene, cozy atmosphere of the Carson House beckons guests for a relaxing long weekend or a romantic getaway. The Grille brings inviting atmosphere and exceptional food to the table. The staff is ready to make guests feel right at home.

Rooms: 5 (3 PB; 2 SB) $55-85
Full Breakfast
Credit Cards: A, B, C, D
Notes: 2, 3, 4, 5, 7, 8, 11, 12

PORT ARANSAS

Sand Dollar Hospitality

35 Mendenhall Drive, Corpus Christi, 78415
(512) 853-1222; (800) 528-7782
FAX (512) 814-1285
www.ccinternet.net/sand-dollar

Harbor View. Three-story Mediterranean-style home on the Port Aransas Municipal Harbor, offers three large bedrooms, one with private bath. The inn is within easy walking distance of the restaurants, shops, charter boats, and fishing operations. On-site mooring facilities are available for crafts up to 50 feet in length. Bikes are available at no additional charge. Full breakfast. Cots for children are available at $15 per child. $75-90.

ROCKPORT

Sand Dollar Hospitality

35 Mendenhall Drive, Corpus Christi, 78415
(512) 853-1222; (800) 528-7782
FAX (512) 814-1285
www.ccinternet.net/sand-dollar

Anthony's by the Sea. The innkeepers at Anthony's offer four guest bedrooms in the guest wing of the residence plus two guest cottages. All units throughout the inn include a refrigerator, cable TV and VCR. A spacious plant-filled patio with lounge chair and tables connects the main house and the two guest cottages. There guests will also find a barbecue grill for guests' use. Off to the side is a swimming pool and hot tub. A full breakfast is served. The renowned Aransas Wildlife Refuge is less than an hour's drive away. Group, weekly, and monthly rates available. $66-95.

Chandler House. The upper-level veranda of this 123-year-old house offers a view of the gulf and the town's shopping area with its many specialty shops and galleries. Each of the two large upstairs bedrooms has two queen-size beds and its own private bath. The downstairs bedroom has a king-size bed, a private attached bath, fireplace, and TV. The common area includes a great room with fireplace and parlor games and a spacious breakfast room. Lunch is also available and open to the public at the unique Chandler House Tea Room. Children over 12 welcome at $25 per each child. $100.

Cygnet. A cozy, secluded country cottage on 16 acres with a double bed, top of the line queen-size sleeper sofa, kitchenette, TV/VCR, and country Jacuzzi outside. This delightful country retreat is about five miles south of Rockport and was designed to provide guests with privacy and comfort. Guests will be provided with farm-fresh eggs, homemade bread, cereals, milk, and fresh fruit. Five dollars for each additional person. $67.

The Habitat. A unique haven of seven plus acres, in the heart of the Lamar Peninsula and near the Aransas Wildlife Refuge, this bed and breakfast consists of three log cabins. Each cabin has a fully stocked kitchen, screened front porch, and outdoor grill. Bird watchers will have a chance to identify and photograph a myrid of bird life in and around the two-acre lake that fronts each cabin. Self-serve Continental breakfast. No pets.

ROCKWALL

Bed and Breakfast Texas Style
4224 West Red Bird Lane, Dallas, 75237
(972) 298-8586; (800) 899-4538
FAX (972) 298-7118; e-mail: bdtxstyle1@aol.com
www.bnbtexasstyle.com

Barton on Boydstun. Individual cottage suites are on this large property right near downtown Rockwall. Other buildings are an art gallery, working studio, and the Bois d'Arc Chapel. The cottages are new and built specifically for guests. Each one has its own screened porch and small kitchen. Perfect place for a small wedding or honeymoon retreat. Breakfast is a prepared treat that is left in the cottage for guests to zap in the microwave. $110-140.

ROUND TOP

Broomfields
801 North Nassau Road, 78954
(409) 249-3706; FAX (409) 249-3852
e-mail: brmflds@fais.net

Country retreat five miles from Round Top on 40 acres of meadowland with wooded tracts, stocked pond with boats and gazebo. Historic restorations, classical music, and semiannual antique shows nearby. Spectacular displays of wildflowers in spring and foliage in fall. An 1800s Texas-vernacular modern home built with 100-year-old barn

Broomfields

beams and furnished with selected European and American antiques. Comfortable, well-appointed rooms and baths. Antiques and decorative arts gallery on the premises. Miniature donkeys raised.

Hosts: Julia and Bill Bishop
Rooms: 3 (PB) $90-140
Full Breakfast
Credit Cards: None
Notes: 2, 5, 9, 10, 11, 12

SAN ANTONIO

Academy House of Monte Vista

Academy House of Monte Vista

2317 North Main Avenue, 78212
(888) 731-8393; e-mail: academyh@netxpress.com
www.ahbnb.com

A gracious, unpretentious 1897 Victorian in San Antonio's century-old Monte Vista historic neighborhood, only minutes from the Riverwalk and Alamo. Each guest bedroom has its own unique character; elegantly decorated in rich shades of wine and burgundy, furnished with period antiques, private baths, cable TV, king-size beds. Full country breakfast. Private garden cottage with Jacuzzi. Excellent restaurants nearby. Member of Texas Historical Accommodations.

Hosts: Kenneth and Johnnie Walker Staggs
Rooms: 4 (PB) $85-145
Full Breakfast
Credit Cards: A, B
Notes: 2, 5, 7, 10, 12, 14, 15

Adams House Bed and Breakfast

231 Adams Street, 78210
(210) 224-4791; (800) 666-4810
FAX (210) 223-5125
www.san-antonio-texas.com

Enjoy gracious, southern hospitality at the Adams House Bed and Breakfast, in the King William Street Historic District of downtown San Antonio. The Riverwalk is a short two-block stroll, and the Alamo is a 15-minute walk. The two-story Adams House has been lovingly restored to its original 1902 splendor. Full-width verandas grace both floors, front and back. All rooms are furnished with period antiques, oriental rugs, and handmade reproductions. AAA three-diamond and Mobil Travel Guide.

Hosts: Nora Peterson and Richard Green
Rooms: 4 (PB) $89-125
Full Breakfast
Credit Cards: A, B, C, D
Notes: 2, 5, 8, 9, 10, 11, 12, 14

Beckmann Inn and Carriage House

222 East Guenther Street, 78204
(210) 229-1449; (800) 945-1449
FAX (210) 229-1061
www.beckmanninn.com

This elegant Victorian inn is in the heart of San Antonio in the King William Street

Beckmann Inn and Carriage House

NOTES: Credit cards accepted: A MasterCard; B Visa; C American Express; D Discover; E Diner's Club; F Other; 2 Personal checks accepted; 3 Lunch available; 4 Dinner available; 5 Open all year; 6 Pets welcome;

Historic District. The wraparound porch welcomes guests to this beautiful home. All rooms are colorfully decorated, featuring ornately carved Victorian queen-size beds, antiques, private baths, TVs, telephones, refrigerators, desks, and robes. Ride the trolley or take the Riverwalk to the Alamo, restaurants, shops, Mexican market, and much more. Guests receive gracious and warm hospitality during their stay. Gourmet breakfast with a breakfast dessert. AAA-, Mobil-, and IIA-rated excellent.

Hosts: Betty Jo and Don Schwartz
Rooms: 5 (PB) $90-140
Full Breakfast
Credit Cards: A, B, C, D, E
Notes: 2, 5, 7, 8, 9, 11, 12, 14

Bonner Garden Bed and Breakfast

145 East Agartia, 78212
(800) 396-4222; FAX (210) 733-6129
e-mail: noels@onr.com
www.travelbase.com

An award-winning replica of an Italian Renaissance villa built in 1910 for internationally known artist Mary Bonner. The original villa was built in Italy in the early 1600s. Fireplaces, tile, fixtures, etc., were imported from Italy. A large swimming pool and a rooftop patio provide enjoyable respites for guests. Guest rooms have private baths, some with Jacuzzi tubs, TVs, VCRs, and telephones. A film

Bonner Garden

library and Texarkana library are available for guests' enjoyment. A full gourmet breakfast is served.

Hosts: Jan and Noel Stenoien
Rooms: 5 (PB) $85-115
Full Breakfast
Credit Cards: A, B, C, D, E
Notes: 2, 5, 7, 9, 10, 11, 12, 14

Brackenridge House

Brackenridge House: A Bed and Breakfast Inn

230 Madison, 78204
(210) 271-3442; (800) 221-1412
FAX (210) 226-3139; e-mail: benniesueb@aol.com
www.brackenridgehouse.com

Native Texan owners and innkeepers will guide guests through their visit to this beautiful Greek Revival home in historic King William. Gourmet breakfast served in formal dining room or veranda, hot tub, private baths, and country Victorian decor add to guests' comfort and pleasure. Pets and children are welcome in the carriage house.

Owners and Innkeepers: Bennie and Sue Blansett
Rooms: 5 (PB) $89-175
Guest house: 2 (PB)
Full Breakfast
Credit Cards: A, B, C, D, E
Notes: 2, 5, 6, 7, 8, 9, 10, 11, 12, 14

7 No smoking; 8 Children welcome; 9 Social drinking allowed; 10 Tennis nearby; 11 Swimming nearby; 12 Golf nearby; 13 Skiing nearby; 14 May be booked through a travel agent; 15 Handicapped accessible.

Chabot Reed House

403 Madison, 78204
(210) 223-8697; (800) 776-2424
FAX (210) 734-2342; e-mail: sister@txdirect.net
www.ivylane.com/chabot

George Stooks Chabot built this Victorian home in 1876 in the heart of what is known today as the King William Street Historic District. The property, masterfully and authentically restored, is listed in the National Register of Historic Places and is a Texas historic landmark. This magnificent home offers beautiful, private, and romantic accommodations within walking distance to downtown San Antonio, Riverwalk, and the convention center. Smoking permitted outside only. Partially handicapped accessible.

Hosts: Sister and Peter Reed
Rooms: 5 (PB) $125-175
Full Breakfast
Credit Cards: None
Notes: 2, 5, 7, 8, 9, 10, 11, 12, 14

The Columns on Alamo

1037 South Alamo, 78210
(800) 233-3364
www.bbonline.com/tx/columns

Resident innkeepers welcome guests to their gracious 1892 Greek Revival home and guest house in the historic King William area. Blocks from Riverwalk,

The Columns on Alamo

restaurants, shopping, convention center, and Alamo; short drive to Sea World and Fiesta Texas. Marvelous antiques and period reproductions, queen- and king-size beds, Jacuzzis, fireplace, telephones, TVs, large common areas, verandas, gardens, off-street parking. Full gourmet breakfast is served in the main house. Smoke free except for verandas, outdoors. Two-night minimum Saturday.

Hosts: Ellenor and Art Link
Rooms: 11 (PB) $89-148
Full Breakfast
Credit Cards: A, B, C, D, E, F
Notes: 5, 7, 9, 12, 14

Noble Inns

Noble Inns

107 Madison Street, 78204
(210) 225-4045; (800) 221-4045
FAX (210) 227-0877; e-mail: nobleinns@aol.com
www.nobleinns.com

Noble Inns operates two luxury Victorian properties in downtown San Antonio's King William historic district. Meticulously restored, the 1890-era bed and breakfasts are decorated with period antiques and offer full modern amenities. All accommodations feature private, marble bath with two-person Jacuzzi or claw-foot tub; antique mantel gas fireplace; sumptuous fabrics, wallpapers; color cable TV with HBO; telephone with data port and voicemail. Full

NOTES: Credit cards accepted: A MasterCard; B Visa; C American Express; D Discover; E Diner's Club; F Other; 2 Personal checks accepted; 3 Lunch available; 4 Dinner available; 5 Open all year; 6 Pets welcome;

and Continental breakfasts. Beautiful patios, outdoor pool and heated spa or indoor swim spa. Transportation in classic 1960 Rolls Royce available.

Hosts: Don and Liesl Noble
Rooms: 9 (PB) $120-175
Full and Continental Breakfast
Credit Cards: A, B, C, D
Notes: 2, 5, 7, 9, 10, 11, 12, 14

The Ogé House on the Riverwalk

209 Washington Street, 78204
(800) 242-2770; FAX (210) 226-5812
e-mail: ogeinn@swbell.net
www.ogeinn.com

Elegant historic antebellum mansion shaded by massive pecans and oaks, on one and one-half landscaped acres along the banks of the famous San Antonio Riverwalk in the King William Street Historic District. The inn, beautifully decorated with antiques, has large verandas and a grand foyer. All rooms have air conditioning, telephones, and TVs, many with fireplaces. Dining, entertainment, convention centers, trolley, and the Alamo are steps away. Featured in the *New York Times*, *Glamour*, *Victoria*, *Southern Living*, Travel channel. IIA-rated excellent, Mobil three-star-rated. Complimentary *Wall Street Journal*, *New York Times*, and *San Antonio Express News*. Smoking restricted. Gourmet breakfast.

Hosts: Patrick and Sharrie Magatagan
Rooms: 10 (PB) $145-205
Continental Breakfast
Credit Cards: A, B, C, D, E
Notes: 2, 5, 9, 10, 12, 14

Riverwalk Inn

329 Old Gailbeau Road, 78204
(210) 212-8300; (800) 254-4440
FAX (210) 229-9422

The Riverwalk Inn is comprised of five two-story log homes, circa 1840, that have been restored on the San Antonio Riverwalk and are tastefully decorated in period

antiques. Amenities include fireplaces, refrigerators, private baths, telephones, balconies, 80-foot porch, and conference area. Continental plus breakfasts and desserts served. Swimming nearby. Smoking permitted outside only. No children.

Hosts: Johnny Halpenny; Jan and Tracy Hammer
Rooms: 11 (PB) $99-155
Continental Breakfast
Credit Cards: A, B, C, D
Notes: 2, 5, 7, 10, 11, 12, 14, 15

The Victorian Lady Inn

The Victorian Lady Inn

421 Howard Street, 78212
(210) 224-2524; (800) 879-7116
www.viclady.com

This 1898 historic mansion offers spacious guest rooms furnished with period antiques. High-back beds, claw-foot tubs, fireplaces, and verandas complete guests' pampered retreat. Savor a fabulous full breakfast each morning. Relax in the outdoor hot tub surrounded by tropical palms and banana trees. The Alamo, Riverwalk, convention center, and trolley are just blocks away. Package plans, corporate rates, and meeting space available.

Hosts: Joe and Kathleen Bowski
Rooms: 8 (PB) $69-135
Full Breakfast
Credit Cards: A, B, C, D
Notes: 2, 5, 7, 9, 10, 11, 12, 14

7 No smoking; 8 Children welcome; 9 Social drinking allowed; 10 Tennis nearby; 11 Swimming nearby; 12 Golf nearby; 13 Skiing nearby; 14 May be booked through a travel agent; 15 Handicapped accessible.

A Yellow Rose

229 Madison, 78204
(210) 229-9903; (800) 950-9903
www.bbonline.com/tx/yellowrose/

A Yellow Rose bed and breakfast is an 1878 Victorian home in the King William Street Historic District. It has five wonderful guest rooms appointed with antiques, and each has private bath, cable TV, and queen-size bed. Off-street, covered parking is also provided. Breakfast is served daily in the elegant 18th-century dining room, and afterwards or in the afternoon or evening guests will enjoy relaxing on the veranda. Two blocks from the Riverwalk, one block from the 50¢ trolley, five blocks from the Alamo and convention center, and within three blocks from three of the finest restaurants in San Antonio.

Hosts: Deb Field-Walker and Kit Walker
Rooms: 5 (PB) $95-140
Full Breakfast
Credit Cards: A, B, C, D
Notes: 2, 5, 7, 9, 12, 14

SANDIA

Knolle Farm and Ranch Bed, Barn, and Breakfast

Route 1, Box 81, Farm Road 70, 78383
(512) 547-2546; FAX (512) 547-3934

Bed, Barn, and Breakfast in renovated, historic dairy barn. Once boasting "World's Largest Jersey Herd," the Knolles are now pampering guests. Nestled in the Nueces River valley among towing oaks and rolling fields, upscale guest cottages contain antiques, full kitchens, patios, laundry facilities. Guests may bring private horses or ride bed and breakfast's horses. Fully equipped barn, arenas, acres of trail riding. Guided dove/duck/goose hunting, fishing, canoeing, game room all on premises. Superb bird watching, catered gourmet meals and picnics. Fun for entire family.

Host: Beth Knolle
Rooms: 4 (2 PB; 2 SB) $65-125

Full Breakfast
Credit Cards: A, B
Notes: 2, 3, 4, 5, 6, 8, 9, 11, 15

Sand Dollar Hospitality

35 Mendenhall Drive, Corpus Christi, 78415
(512) 853-1222; (800) 528-7782
FAX (512) 814-1285
www.ccinternet.net/sand-dollar

Knolle Farm and Ranch Bed and Breakfast. A true Texas ranch experience with sufficient "citified" amenities to make for a comfortable and enjoyable stay. There are four guest rooms. There are eight stalls as well as outside paddock and arena. Additional attractions and/or activities include canoeing, fishing, skeet shooting, and bird watching. Ten dollars for each additional person. $125.

SAN MARCOS

Crystal River Inn

326 West Hopkins, 78666
(512) 396-3739

Romantic, luxurious Victorian mansion that captures all the fun and flavor of the Texas Hill Country. Close to headwaters of crystal-clear San Marcos River. Antiques, fireplaces, and fresh flowers adorn the rooms. Wicker-strewn veranda, gardens, and fountains offer hours of peaceful rest

Crystal River Inn

and relaxation. Enjoy sumptuous brunches including gourmet items such as stuffed French toast and bananas Foster crêpes. Mystery weekends, river trips, and romantic getaways are the hosts' specialities.

Hosts: Mike and Cathy Dillon
Rooms: 12 (10 PB; 2 SB) $75-135
Full Breakfast
Credit Cards: A, B, C, D, E, F
Notes: 2, 5, 7, 9, 10, 11, 12, 14

SEABROOK

Bed and Breakfast Texas Style

4224 West Red Bird Lane, Dallas, 75237
(972) 298-8586; (800) 899-4538
FAX (972) 298-7118; e-mail: bdtxstyle1@aol.com
www.bnbtexasstyle.com

Crew's Quarters. Right on Galveston Bay at the channel where shrimp boats and ocean liners go in and out, this Cape Cod-style cottage is available for families or romantic getaways. It will sleep seven to nine people with two bedrooms downstairs, each with a private bath. A loft room upstairs with two double beds and a twin bed has a half-bath. A large deck with chairs is perfect for sunning and watching birds and boats. Continental breakfast. $75-95.

The Pelican House Bed and Breakfast Inn

1302 First Street, 77586
(713) 474-5295; FAX (713) 474-7840

This 90-year-old home can be found on the Back Bay just down the street from Galveston Bay and is in the Old Seabrook Art and Antique Colony. The Pelican House is the closest bed and breakfast to Space Center Houston and is less than five minutes to the 19 Clear Lake area marinas. The Pelican House is decorated whimsically with pelicans and fish. Relax in rocking chairs on the front porch or on the back deck where water bird viewing is at its best. Children over 10 welcome.

The Pelican House

Host: Suzanne Silver
Rooms: 4 (PB) $65-75
Full Breakfast
Credit Cards: A, B, C, D
Notes: 2, 5, 7, 9, 12, 14

SEADRIFT

Hotel Lafitte

302 Bay Avenue, 77983
(512) 785-2319

A unique bed and breakfast on San Antonio Bay. Built in 1909 and fully restored in 1988. Furnished in antique Victorian style. In Seadrift, Texas, 30 miles south of Victoria on Highway 185.

Hosts: Frances and Weyman Harding
Rooms: 10 (4 PB; 6 SB) $60-115
Full Breakfast
Credit Cards: A, B, C
Notes: 2, 9, 10, 11, 12, 14

SMITHVILLE

Bed and Breakfast Texas Style

4224 West Red Bird Lane, Dallas, 75237
(972) 298-8586; (800) 899-4538
FAX (972) 298-7118; e-mail: bdtxstyle1@aol.com
www.bnbtexasstyle.com

The Doll House. A private guest area on the second level of this residence in the Lost Pines area near Bastrop is available for visitors. The large sitting-bedroom is

7 No smoking; 8 Children welcome; 9 Social drinking allowed; 10 Tennis nearby; 11 Swimming nearby; 12 Golf nearby; 13 Skiing nearby; 14 May be booked through a travel agent; 15 Handicapped accessible.

furnished with lovely antiques and collectibles and has its own private bath. There is a small kitchen area with refrigerator and microwave. If guests prefer to eat in, Continental fixings will be left in the room. A hearty breakfast downstairs in the dining area will be served by the gracious hosts. Two decks are available for bird watching or sunning. A lovely patio is a few steps down the trail. The state park is a few miles away. Two public golf courses are within a 10-minute drive. $110-125.

SOUTH PADRE ISLAND

Brown Pelican Inn

207 West Aries, P.O. Box 2667, 78597
(956) 761-2722

The Brown Pelican Inn is a place to relax, make oneself at home, and enjoy personalized service. The porches are a great spot to sit and watch the sun set over the bay. The inn is comfortably furnished with European and American antiques; all guest rooms have private baths, and most rooms have spectacular bay views. Breakfast in the parlor includes freshly baked bread or muffins, fresh fruit, cereal, juice, and gourmet coffee or tea. Children over 12 welcome.

Hosts: Vicky and Ken Conway
Rooms: 8 (PB) $70-150
Continental Breakfast
Credit Cards: A, B
Notes: 2, 5, 7, 9, 10, 11, 12, 14, 15

STEPHENVILLE

The Oxford House

563 North Graham Street, 76401
(817) 965-6885

Stephenville is in the northern tip of the beautiful Texas Hill Country on Highway 377 west of Lake Granbury and east of Proctor Lake. Tarleton State University is in town. Only 30 minutes from Fossil Rim Wildlife Center and Dinosaur Valley State

The Oxford House

Park. The Oxford House was built in 1898 by Judge W. J. Oxford Sr., and the completely restored, two-story Victorian, presently owned by the grandson of the judge, has antique furnishings. Enjoy a quiet atmosphere and country breakfast. Shopping within walking distance. Smoking permitted in designated areas only. Children over 10 are welcome.

Hosts: Bill and Paula Oxford
Rooms: 5 (4 PB; 1 SB) $65-85
Full Breakfast
Credit Cards: A, B, C, D
Notes: 2, 4, 5, 9, 10, 11, 12, 14

TERRELL

The Bluebonnet Inn

310 West College, 75160
(972) 524-2534

The turn of the century brought the railroad to Terrell, and with it, prosperity. This fine old home was a part of Terrell's grand old days, and despite many changes through the years, the Victorian beauty remains. Relax in the large rooms, all with private baths. Enjoy this house full of antiques with its two parlors, sunroom dining, country kitchen, and service area, where guests can help themselves to snacks and fountain

NOTES: Credit cards accepted: A MasterCard; B Visa; C American Express; D Discover; E Diner's Club; F Other; 2 Personal checks accepted; 3 Lunch available; 4 Dinner available; 5 Open all year; 6 Pets welcome;

sodas. A full breakfast is served each morning at nine, or choose a private Continental breakfast at one's leisure. Innkeepers and owners Bryan and Jan Jobe look forward to guests' visit and will answer any questions when they call.

Rooms: 4 (PB) $75-105
Full and Continental
Credit Cards: A, B, C, D
Notes: 4, 5, 7, 10, 11, 12

TURKEY

Hotel Turkey Bed and Breakfast

Third and Alexander Streets, 79261
(806) 423-1151; (800) 657-7110
www.llano.net/turkey/hotel

Built in 1927 for the early railroad traveler and rancher, it was converted to a bed and breakfast eight years ago, maintaining the 1927 decor. Listed in the National Register of Historic Places in 1991 and the Texas historic registry in 1985. Three blocks from the Rails-to-Trails park system for hiking, biking, and horseback riding. With a lovely outside patio and enclosed glass porch with 12 rocking chairs, the hotel can accommodate up to 35 guests. Group rates available.

Hosts: Gary and Suzie Johnson
Rooms: 15 (6 PB: 9 SB) $69
Full Breakfast
Credit Cards: A, B, C
Notes: 2, 5, 7, 10

TYLER

Bed and Breakfast Texas Style

4224 West Red Bird Lane, Dallas, 75237
(972) 298-8586; (800) 899-4538
FAX (972) 298-7118; e-mail: bdtxstyle1@aol.com
www.bnbtexasstyle.com

Vintage Farm Home. This newly renovated, circa 1836-1864, home, once an original dogtrot plantation home, sits in the piney woods of East Texas. Catch the morning sun or evening breeze on the large veranda where rocking chairs and a swing invite relaxation. Take a stroll through the trails during dogwood or fall foliage season. The guest room has a king-size bed and private bath. Breakfast is served downstairs in the cozy nook. $85.

Rosevine Inn Bed and Breakfast

415 South Vine, 75702
(903) 592-2221; e-mail: rosevine@iamerica.net

Rosevine Inn is in the historic Brick Street district. Come rest and relax at Rosevine Inn. Amenities include a lovely courtyard with fountain and fireplace. There are also an outdoor hot tub and game room complete with billiards for guests' enjoyment. There are now two suites available. A full gourmet breakfast is served. The hosts look forward to meeting guests and welcoming them to the Rose Capital of the World. A picnic lunch is available.

Hosts: Bert and Rebecca Powell
Rooms: 7 (PB) $85-150
Full Breakfast
Credit Cards: A, B, C, D, E
Notes: 2, 3, 5, 7, 8, 9, 10, 11, 12, 14

VAN

Tumble on Inn

P.O. Box 1249, 75790
(903) 963-7669; (888) 707-3992
e-mail: tumbleoninn@aol.com

Country casual comfort in the pine woods of East Texas. One hour from Dallas, one and one-half hours from Shreveport. Five minutes to Canton First Monday Trade Days. Community room with movies, books, music for all tastes. Hot tub under the stars. Balcony for stargazing. Deck for relaxing. Children 12 and older welcome. No pets. Discounts for two-night stay, AARP, Texas Passport.

Hosts: Gordon and Jean Jensen
Rooms: 5 (5 SB) $75
Full Breakfast
Credit Cards: A, B
Notes: 2, 3, 4, 5, 9, 15

---

7 No smoking; 8 Children welcome; 9 Social drinking allowed; 10 Tennis nearby; 11 Swimming nearby; 12 Golf nearby; 13 Skiing nearby; 14 May be booked through a travel agent; 15 Handicapped accessible.

VANDERPOOL

Texas Stagecoach Inn

HC02, Box 166, Highway 187, 78885
(830) 966-6272; (888) 965-6272
FAX (830) 966-6273 (call first)
e-mail: stageinn@swtexas

Year-round nature tourism awaits guests at
Lost Maples State Natural Area and Texas
Stagecoah Inn within this undiscovered area
of the Texas Hill Country. The spacious
riverside inn, on three acres, is designed to
ensure a peaceful respite. Guest rooms and
common rooms are generously appointed
with Hill Country elegance and original
landscapes. Breakfast buffet feasts greet
each morning. If one's desire is to relax in
the tranquility of the Sabinal Canyon, or
enjoy nature and all its activites, guests will
find it here. Smoking permitted outside only.

Hosts: Karen and David Camp
Rooms: 2 (PB) $85-115
Suites: 2 (PB)
Full Breakfast
Credit Cards: None
Notes: 2, 5, 7, 8, 9, 10, 11, 12, 14

VICTORIA

Friendly Oaks Bed and Breakfast

210 East Juan Linn Street, 77901
(512) 575-0000; e-mail: innkprbill@aol.com
www.bbhost.com/friendlyoaks

In the shelter of ancient live oaks, history
comes alive at the Friendly Oaks bed and
breakfast in a preservation area of 80
restored Victorian homes. Each of four
guest rooms has a private bath, its own
individual decor reflecting the preservation
efforts of Victoria. A conference room provides a quiet setting for retreats, meetings,
seminars, parties, showers, and small weddings. Here "Bed means Comfortable,
Breakfast means Scrumptious."

Hosts: Bill and Cee Bee McLeod
Rooms: 4 (PB) $55-75

Full Breakfast
Credit Cards: A, B, C, D
Notes: 2, 5, 7, 9, 10, 11, 12, 14, 15

WACO

The Judge Baylor House

908 Speight, 76706
(888) JBAYLOR; FAX (817) 756-0711
e-mail: jbaylor@iamerica.net
www.eyeweb.com/jbaylor

Two blocks from Baylor University and its
Armstrong Browning Library, five minutes
from Waco Convention Center. A two-story
red brick home with five spacious and beautifully appointed guest rooms. All have private baths and either king-, queen-size, or
twin beds. Sitting in the swing hanging from
a large ash tree in the front lawn, playing the
grand piano, or enjoying a new book, guests
are sure to relax and feel at home.

Hosts: Bruce and Dorothy Dyer
Rooms: 5 (PB) $69-89
Full Breakfast
Credit Cards: A, B, C
Notes: 2, 4, 5, 6, 7, 8, 9, 10, 11, 12, 14, 15

WIMBERLEY

Bed and Breakfast Texas Style

4224 West Red Bird Lane, Dallas, 75237
(972) 298-8586; (800) 899-4538
FAX (972) 298-7118; e-mail: bdtxstyle1@aol.com
www.bnbtexasstyle.com

Casa de Angelitas. In the heart of the Hill
Country, close to what makes Wimberley so
special, and yet it has a peaceful, being in
the country feeling. This lovely cottage has
a fireplace, three bedrooms with adjoining
bath for each room, and is available for private getaways, families, or retreats. A Continental breakfast is left in the fully
equipped kitchen. A special gourmet breakfast may be served upon request. A massage therapist lives nearby and private
appointments can be arranged for additional
fee. Lots of quaint shops and artists' galleries are nearby. $75-95.

NOTES: Credit cards accepted: A MasterCard; B Visa; C American Express; D Discover; E Diner's Club;
F Other; 2 Personal checks accepted; 3 Lunch available; 4 Dinner available; 5 Open all year; 6 Pets welcome;

Southwind Bed and Breakfast

2701 FM 3237, 78676
(512) 847-5277; (800) 508-5277

Southwind is five minutes from the quaint village of Wimberley and one hour from Austin or San Antonio. Rocking chairs on the porches are good places to view hills and valleys, wildlife, and sunsets, and the hot tub is grand for star gazing. Fireplaces, queen- and king-size beds, and antique and reproduction furniture. In addition to the inn, two cabins, each with king-size bed, fireplace, and whirlpool tub, are nestled in the woods and hills. No smoking. Children are welcome in cabins. Inquire about accommodations for pets. Cabins are handicapped accessible.

Host: Carrie Watson
Rooms: 3 (PB) $80-90
Full Breakfast
Credit Cards: A, B, C, D
Notes: 2, 5, 7, 9, 10, 11, 12, 14

WINNSBORO

Thee Hubbell House

307 West Elm, 75494
(800) 227-0639; FAX (903) 342-6627
e-mail: hubhouse@bluebonnet.netcom
www.bluebonnet.net/hubhouse

Ninety miles east of Dallas in beautiful northeast Texas. Two-acre landscaped plantation estate with four designated Texas historical houses. Twelve bedrooms and suites. Romantic candlelight dining, hot tub house, massage. One hundred antique shops, ten lakes, and seven golf courses. Pets are welcome at the pet motel. Children are welcome in the family cottage.

Hosts: Dan and Laurel Hubbell
Rooms: 12 (PB) $75-175
Full or Continental Breakfast
Credit Cards: A, B, C, D, E, F
Notes: 2, 4, 5, 7, 9, 10, 11, 12, 14, 15

7 No smoking; 8 Children welcome; 9 Social drinking allowed; 10 Tennis nearby; 11 Swimming nearby; 12 Golf nearby; 13 Skiing nearby; 14 May be booked through a travel agent; 15 Handicapped accessible.

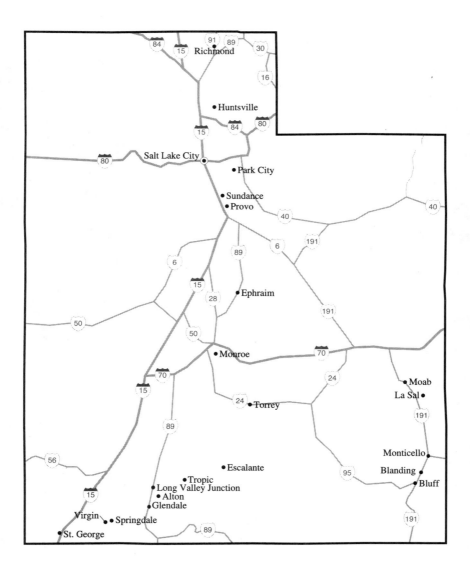

Utah

Utah

ALTON

Mi Casa Su Casa/Old Pueblo Homestays Bed and Breakfast Reservation Service

P.O. Box 950, Tempe, AZ 85280-0950
(602) 990-0682; (800) 456-0682
FAX (602) 990-3390
e-mail: micasa@primenet.com
www.azres.com

7011. On five acres, there are two large A-frame houses on this heavily wooded lot. There are four guest rooms. The room on the main floor has a private bath. On the first floor are three rooms that share one bath in the hall. Weather permitting, the host couple has a campfire each night overlooking the meadow. Smoking outside. With advance notice, pets are possible. Children welcome. Unique RV garage that will house up to a 32-foot RV with complete hookups. Kitchen privileges. Barbecue and fireplace. Satellite TV and VCR. Business center with computer and fax. Exercise equipment. Full breakfast. $40-65.

BLANDING

Grayson Country Inn Bed and Breakfast

118 East 300 South (86-6), 84511
(801) 678-2388; (800) 365-0868

Grayson Country Inn sits in the heart of San Juan County, known for Lake Powell, Monument Valley, Canyonlands, Arches, Rainbow Bridge, and Natural Bridges. The inn is off Main Street near a pottery factory and gift shops. Great hiking in the back country. Grayson has 11 guest rooms, each with private bath and TV. Welcome singles, couples, families. Three-bedroom cottage available for groups. The hosts specialize in home cooking and home atmosphere.

Hosts: Dennis and Lurlene Gutke
Rooms: 11 (PB) $42-59
Full Breakfast
Credit Cards: A, B, C
Notes: 5, 7, 8, 11, 14

BLUFF

Pioneer House Inn

189 North 3rd East, P.O. Box 219, 84512
(435) 672-2446 (phone/FAX)
e-mail: rmcbluff@att.net

Built in 1898 and in Bluff's historic district, the Pioneer House Inn is a much welcomed home away from home for travelers of all ages. The home features private entrances, private baths, and a relaxing atmosphere in

Pioneer House Inn

the desert Southwest. The hosts serve healthy, hearty breakfasts and arrange sunset cookouts. The most popular as well as unexplored attractions surrounding the Four Corners area are all nearby and guided trips are available.

Hosts: Thomas Rice and Kelly McAndrews
Rooms: 5 (PB) $49-175
Full Breakfast
Credit Cards: A, B
Notes: 2, 5, 7, 8, 9, 15

EPHRAIM

Ephraim Homestead Bed and Breakfast

135 West 100 North (43-2), 84627
(801) 283-6367

Ephraim Homestead offers lodging in a pioneer log cabin or a rustic barn. Both are furnished with antiques and surrounded by old-fashioned gardens under a canopy of trees. Breakfast is cooked on a century-old Monarch stove and served privately to guests in the cabin; others are served in the hosts' dining room. A delicious nighttime treat is also provided. Truly a unique and memorable experience. Smoking permitted outside only. Cross-country skiing nearby.

Hosts: Sherron and McKay Andreasen
Log Cabin: 1 (PB) $85
Barn: 2 (SB) $55-65
Full Breakfast
Credit Cards: None
Notes: 2, 5, 7, 8, 10, 11, 12, 13

Ephraim Homestead

ESCALANTE

Rainbow Country Tours and Bed and Breakfast

586 East 300 South, P.O. Box 333, 87426-0333
(800) 252-UTAH (8824)
e-mail: rainbow @color-country.net
www.color-country.net/~rainbow/

In the heart of the new Grand Staircase—Escalante National Monument. Visit Escalante and experience the stunning beauty of its narrow canyons, slick rock hills, and towering sandstone formations. Explore ancient petrified forests and marvel at prehistoric Indian rock art. Visit nearby serene lakes in Dixie National Forest. Rainbow Country Bed and Breakfast offers guests an idyllic place to unwind after a day of traveling adventures. Comfortable and peaceful, it provides all the amenities of a traditional bed and breakfast, rooms with private baths, hearty food, plus hot tub and wraparound sun deck with sweeping vistas of the surrounding mountains and desert.

Host: Gene Windle
Rooms: 4 (PB) $55-65
Full Breakfast
Credit Cards: A, B
Notes: 2, 5, 6, 7, 8, 9, 11, 14

Rainbow Country Tours

GLENDALE

Arizona Trails Bed and Breakfast Reservation Service

P.O. Box 18998, Fountain Hills, 85269-8998
(602) 837-4284; (888) 799-4284
FAX (602) 816-4224
e-mail: aztrails@arizonatrails.com
www.arizonatrails.com

NOTES: Credit cards accepted: A MasterCard; B Visa; C American Express; D Discover; E Diner's Club; F Other; 2 Personal checks accepted; 3 Lunch available; 4 Dinner available; 5 Open all year; 6 Pets welcome;

AZ 142. This four-room bed and breakfast sits amidst 13 acres and is the perfect tranquil, romantic getaway and great for those touring the canyon areas. Halfway between Bryce and Zion Canyons and only two hours to the North Rim of the Grand Canyon. All rooms have private baths, two come with fireplaces. Each is decorated with a unique collection of artifacts and art collected from around the world. A full breakfast served in the dining room will get the day started. $60-107.

Eagle's Nest Bed and Breakfast

500 Lydia's Canyon Road, P.O. Box 160, 84729
(435) 648-2200; (800) 293-6378
FAX (435) 648-2221
e-mail: innkeeps@eaglesnestbb.com
www.eaglesnestbb.com

Enjoy the tranquility of Lydia's Canyon in the heart of southwest Utah off US Highway 89. Zion, Bryce, and Grand Canyon National Parks and Cedar Breaks National Monument are easily accessible. Every room is detailed to provide a relaxed and romantic setting with unique furnishings from around the world. Enjoy a full gourmet breakfast in the sunlit, antique-filled dining room. Soak carelessly in the spa. All rooms have private baths, two with fireplaces. Extra amenities.

Hosts: Shanoan and Dearborn Clark
Rooms: 4 (PB) $69-117
Full Breakfast
Credit Cards: A, B, D
Notes: 2, 4, 5, 7, 9, 12, 14

Mi Casa Su Casa/Old Pueblo Homestays Bed and Breakfast Reservation Service

P.O. Box 950, Tempe, AZ 85280-0950
(602) 990-0682; (800) 456-0682
FAX (602) 990-3390
e-mail: micasa@primenet.com
www.azres.com

7031. On 13 acres, this romantic bed and breakfast is nestled in a side canyon of Lydia's Canyon, in what is known as the Grand Circle of the Southwest within America's highest concentration of scenic national parks and monuments, including the Grand Canyon, Zion, Bryce Canyon, and the Lake Powell recreation area. Choose from four rooms all with private baths, two with fireplaces. A full gourmet breakfast is served and special dietary needs are accommodated with prior notice. Smoking permitted outside. No pets. Inquire about children. Twenty dollars per extra guest. $68-107.

Smith Hotel

P.O. Box 106, 84729
(435) 648-2156

This historic hotel-boarding house was built in 1927 by Mormon settlers. Enjoy western charm. Screened porch overlooking the hills of southern Utah's beautiful Long Valley. Close to the scenic wonders of Zion, Bryce, and Grand Canyon National Parks and the recreational facilities of Lake Powell. All rooms have private baths. Late 1800s private family cemetery on property. Continental plus breakfast served in family dining room. Meet other guests from all over the world. Easy to find, right on Highway 89.

Host: Shirley Phelan
Rooms: 7 (PB) $42-65

Smith Hotel

---

7 No smoking; 8 Children welcome; 9 Social drinking allowed; 10 Tennis nearby; 11 Swimming nearby; 12 Golf nearby; 13 Skiing nearby; 14 May be booked through a travel agent; 15 Handicapped accessible.

Continental Breakfast
Credit Cards: A, B
Notes: 7, 9, 12

HUNTSVILLE

Jackson Fork Inn
7345 East 900 South, 84317
(801) 745-0051; (800) 255-0672

The Jackson Fork Inn was originally a dairy barn built in the 1930s. It was converted in 1980 to an inn and restaurant. All rooms have private bathrooms and some rooms have Jacuzzi tubs. Restaurant serves steaks, chicken, and fish dinners. Close to ski resorts and golf courses.

Host: Vicki Petersen
Rooms: 8 (PB) $50-115
Continental Breakfast
Credit Cards: A, B, C, D
Notes: 2, 4, 5, 7, 8, 9, 11, 12, 13, 14

LONG VALLEY JUNCTION

Color Country Bed and Breakfast
P.O. Box 100771, Alton, 84710
(800) 575-9486; FAX (801) 648-2618
e-mail: jimp@color-country.net
www.xpressweb.com/colorcountry/

Nestled high in the pines of southern Utah at the corner of Highways 89 and 14 (Long Valley Junction), this unique facility is in the heart of Utah's Color Country. Zion and Bryce National Parks are within 30 minutes. This new A-frame was completed in the spring of 1997. The bed and breakfast is just off the main highways overlooking a meadow with pink cliffs in the background. Beautiful view from the large spa available to all guests. Smoking permitted on decks and patio only. Main floor is handicapped accessible.

Hosts: Jim and Bonnie Pollock
Rooms: 3 (2 PB; 1 SB) $55-85
Full Breakfast
Credit Cards: A, B
Notes: 3, 4, 5, 6, 8, 13, 14

MOAB

Mi Casa Su Casa/Old Pueblo Homestays Bed and Breakfast Reservation Service
P.O. Box 950, Tempe, AZ 85280-0950
(602) 990-0682; (800) 456-0682
FAX (602) 990-3390
e-mail: micasa@primenet.com
www.azres.com

7041. The casual atmosphere of a ranch-style home nestled between the snow-capped La Sal Mountains and the red rock canyons of the Colorado River. Mountain biking, white-water challenging, and downhill or cross-country skiing are nearby. This home is a perfect place to relax at the end of the day. Three guest rooms with private baths. Two rooms share a bath. Cable TV, hot tub. Maximum 14 guests. Full breakfast. Bicycles to rent. Resident cats. No smoking. Children six and older are welcome. Rollaway beds are available. Weekly and seasonal rates. $70-105.

7042. The host couple has renovated the original adobe farmhouse built about 100 years ago, added extra rooms, and a cozy cottage. There are six rooms including two two-bedroom units. Some rooms have air conditioning, telephones. All rooms have private baths and video cassette players. Adventure library, outdoor hot tub, lush gardens, patios, barbecue. Three blocks from downtown. Outstanding breakfast buffet. No smoking or pets. Children welcome by prior arrangement. Fifteen dollars per each additional person. Seasonal rates. $65-140.

Pack Creek Ranch
P.O. Box 1270, 84532
(801) 259-5505; FAX (801) 259-8879

Fifteen miles southeast of Moab. The 300-acre spread is in the foothills of the La Sal Mountains, a locale favored by moderate summertime temperatures, while offering superb views of mountains and desert alike.

NOTES: Credit cards accepted: A MasterCard; B Visa; C American Express; D Discover; E Diner's Club; F Other; 2 Personal checks accepted; 3 Lunch available; 4 Dinner available; 5 Open all year; 6 Pets welcome;

Pack Creek has a history as a working ranch, retaining the whipsawed look of the Old West. Lodge and cabins are rustic, though fully renovated. Most have rock fireplaces. All have modern furnishings as well as fully equipped kitchens. No telephones or TVs in the rooms, however. Guests' peace of mind is hosts' first concern. Winter rates are lower and there are no meals included. Pets on leash welcome. Handicapped accessible with help.

Hosts: Ken and Jane Sleight
Rooms: 12 (PB) $270
Full Breakfast
Credit Cards: A, B, C, D
Notes: 2, 3, 4, 5, 7, 8, 9, 11, 12, 13, 14

Westwood Guest House

81 East 100 South, 84532
(801) 259-7283; (800) 526-5690

Seven uniquely decorated condos. Reasonable; clean. Living room, bathroom, bedroom, kitchen with do-it-yourself breakfast food (eggs, bagels, pancakes, coffee, tea, milk, and juice). Sleeps two to eight comfortably. Telephones, TV, hot tub in private back yard, decks, patios. Visitor center, museum, tennis courts, ball park, shopping, bars, restaurants in immediate area. Golf course within four miles, the river within two miles, city park with pool within five blocks. Mild winters. Biking, hiking, hunting, and cross-country skiing are 40 minutes away.

Host: Betty Beck
Rooms: 7 (PB) $59
Continental Breakfast
Credit Cards: A, B, C, D
Notes: 2, 5, 7, 8, 9, 10, 11, 12, 14

MONROE

Mi Casa Su Casa/Old Pueblo Homestays Bed and Breakfast Reservation Service

P.O. Box 950, Tempe, AZ 85280-0950
(602) 990-0682; (800) 456-0682
FAX (602) 990-3390
e-mail: micasa@primenet.com
www.azres.com

7051. Halfway between Denver and Los Angeles a considerate hostess, who is known for her cookbooks and cooking skills, offers three guest rooms. Room one has a private entrance, private bath with shower, small refrigerator, and electric coffee maker. Room two, which adjoins room one, has a small TV and children's games. The third room has a full bath across the hall, TV, and refrigerator. Outdoor furniture in private, fully fenced yard. A 100-year-old apple tree provides ample shade. Easy driving distance to five national parks and four national forests. Full breakfast. Fifteen dollars for each additional person. $65.

Peterson's

Peterson's Bed and Breakfast

95 North 300 West, P.O. Box 142, 84754-0142
(435) 527-4830

Halfway between Los Angeles and Denver, this modern rural community offers mountain ranges, peaceful community near fishing, rivers, and scenic beauty. Comfortable L-shaped home has private quarters for guests. Private yard fully fenced with carport, motion lights, country atmosphere. Main room has refrigerator stocked with cold drinks (honor system), in-room coffee, tea, cocoa furnished. Adjoining room (suite) has cable TV, double recliner. Double bed room has private full bath, refrigerator, TV. Gourmet breakfast with Gevalia coffee, homemade bakery items. No one goes away hungry. In business for more than 22 years with people from around the globe. Open April through November.

7 No smoking; 8 Children welcome; 9 Social drinking allowed; 10 Tennis nearby; 11 Swimming nearby; 12 Golf nearby; 13 Skiing nearby; 14 May be booked through a travel agent; 15 Handicapped accessible.

Host: Mary Ann Peterson
Rooms: 3 (2 PB; 1 SB) $55-115
Full Breakfast
Credit Cards: F
Notes: 2, 7, 8, 10, 11, 12, 13

MONTICELLO

Mi Casa Su Casa/Old Pueblo Homestays Bed and Breakfast Reservation Service

P.O. Box 950, Tempe, AZ 85280-0950
(602) 990-0682; (800) 456-0682
FAX (602) 990-3390
e-mail: micasa@primenet.com
www.azres.com

7161. This salt-box structure was built in 1933 at the foot of the Blue Mountains. The three-story building was originally known as the Old Monticello Flour Mill. Six beautiful suites, all with private baths. Several attractions are within driving distance, including the Four Corners area, Lake Powell, Natural Bridges National Monument, Canyonlands and Arches National Parks, and Monument Valley. Guests are welcome to enjoy the sitting room with fireplace, the library with a view of the Blue Mountains, the TV room, the deck, and the whirlpool. There is a local golf course. No smoking. No pets. Inquire about bringing children. $52.

OLD LA SAL

Mt. Peale Bed and Breakfast

1415 East Highway 46, P.O. Box 366, 84530
(888) MT PEALE

This bed and breakfast is a log home nestled at the base of Mount Peale. The inn has three guest rooms, an informal dining area, fireplace comfort room, and outdoor deck and hot tub. The inn has a premier location for guests who choose to experience Canyonlands, Arches National Park, Moab, and La Sal Mountains. The guests can experience unexplored mountain biking,

hiking, cross-country ski trails, and pure country dining. Inquire about accommodations for pets. Smoking permitted outside only. Inquire about accommodations for children. Golf nearby in Moab. Skiing nearby in Telluride.

Hosts: Teague and Lisa
Rooms: 3 (PB) $70-85
Full Breakfast
Credit Cards: A, B
Notes: 2, 3, 4, 5, 7, 9, 11, 14, 15

PARK CITY

The Blue Church Lodge

424 Park Avenue, P.O. Box 1720, 84060
(435) 649-8009; (800) 626-5467
FAX (435) 649-0686; e-mail: bcl@ditell.com

Listed in the Utah and the national historic registers, the church was originally built in 1897. A Victorian-era church on the outside. Inside, the lodge houses seven charmingly quaint and cozy, distinctively different condominiums, ranging from a room with a private bath up to a four-bedroom suite. Amenities include indoor spa, game room, laundry, private telephones, cable TV, VCR, CD player, private parking, ski lockers, maid service, and gas-burning fireplaces.

Host: Nancy Schmidt
Rooms: 7 (PB) $105-330
Continental Breakfast
Credit Cards: A, B
Notes: 2, 7, 8, 9, 13, 14

1904 Imperial Hotel, A Bed and Breakfast Inn

221 Main Street, P.O. Box 1628, 84060-1628
(435) 649-1904; (800) 669-8824
FAX (435) 645-7421

On historic Main Street in Park City, the 1904 Imperial Hotel warmly captures the spirited charm and hospitality of Park City's illustrious past. Although it once boarded weary miners, served as a hospital, and was known to be a house of ill-repute,

NOTES: Credit cards accepted: A MasterCard; B Visa; C American Express; D Discover; E Diner's Club; F Other; 2 Personal checks accepted; 3 Lunch available; 4 Dinner available; 5 Open all year; 6 Pets welcome;

1904 Imperial Hotel

the 1904 Imperial Hotel's 10 guest rooms have since been restored with period decor and furnishings, many featuring oversized tubs. Breakfast greets guests in the morning and a revitalizing hot tub welcomes them back in the afternoon.

Host: Nancy McLaughlin
Rooms: 10 (PB) $65-245
Full Breakfast
Credit Cards: A, B, C, D
Notes: 2, 5, 7, 8, 9, 10, 11, 12, 13, 14

The Old Miners' Lodge

615 Woodside Avenue, Box 2639, 84060
(435) 645-8068; (800) 648-8068
FAX (435) 645-7420

A restored 1889 miners' boarding house in the national historic district of Park City, with 12 individually decorated rooms

filled with antiques and older pieces. Close to historic Main Street, with the Park City ski area in its back yard, the lodge is "more like staying with friends than at a hotel!" A nonsmoking inn. Minimum-stay requirements Christmas and some special events.

Hosts: Susan Wynne and Liza Simpson
Rooms: 12 (PB) $65-250
Full Breakfast
Credit Cards: A, B, C, D, E
Notes: 2, 5, 7, 8, 9, 10, 11, 12, 13, 14

Old Town Guest House

1011 Empire Avenue, Box 162, 84060
(435) 649-2642; (800) 290-6423 ext. 3710
FAX (435) 649-3320
e-mail: dlovci@compuserve.com
ww.utahusa.com/otgh

This beautiful, historically registered home is the perfect place for active skiers, hikers, and bikers. Guests may walk to the ski area as well as the historic Main Street. All the rooms are furnished with lodgepole pine furniture. Afternoon snacks are available for when guests return from their active day and there is a hot tub to soothe any aching muscles.

Host: Deb Lovci
Rooms: 4 (2 PB; 2 SB) $60-175
Full Breakfast
Credit Cards: A, B, C
Notes: 2, 5, 7, 8, 9, 10, 11, 12, 13

Washington School Inn

P.O. Box 536, 84060
(801) 649-3800; (800) 824-1672

Historic restoration of an old schoolhouse, decorated with modified Victorian furnishings. Hot tub and sauna on the property. Full breakfast and afternoon tea service included in rates. In downtown historic Park City, close to Salt Lake area airport (45 minutes) and some of the best skiing in the world.

Hosts: Nancy Beaufait and Delphine Covington
Rooms: 15 (PB) $100-300
Full Breakfast
Credit Cards: A, B, C, D, E
Notes: 5, 7, 8, 9, 10, 11, 12, 13, 14

---

7 No smoking; 8 Children welcome; 9 Social drinking allowed; 10 Tennis nearby; 11 Swimming nearby; 12 Golf nearby; 13 Skiing nearby; 14 May be booked through a travel agent; 15 Handicapped accessible.

PROVO

R. Spencer Hines Mansion

383 West 100 South, 84601
(801) 374-8400; (800) 428-5636
FAX (801) 374-0823

R. Spencer Hines Bed and Breakfast is
housed in a 100-year-old Victorian mansion.
Much of the original decor such as wood
moldings, brick walls, and stained glass has
been left in place. The nine bedrooms are
decorated with antique and reproduction
furniture from the period, using a variety of
themes. King- and queen-size beds, with a
two-person whirlpool tub and private baths
in each room. Full gourmet breakfast, complimentary cookies and fruit and Martinelli
apple cider.

Hosts: Sandi and Gene Henderson
Rooms: 9 (PB) $99-199
Full Breakfast
Credit Cards: A, B, C
Notes: 2, 5, 7, 11, 12, 13, 14

R. Spencer Hines Mansion

RICHMOND

Clint's Bed and Breakfast

165 North State Street, 84333
(435) 258-3768 (Bed and Breakfast)
(435) 753-0951 (ask for Bonnie during daytime)
FAX (435) 753-1101

Enjoy the beautiful countryside of Cache
Valley in northern Utah on US Highway 91.

Clint's

Guests will appreciate the peaceful quiet in
the small rural communtiy of Richmond.
Guests are within two blocks of a small
grocery store, video store, post office,
church, and park. Enjoy beautiful sunsets
and a mountain view from the deck and
wake to a full breakfast by Clint, a retired
ranger, who can share stories and great
home-cooked food.

Hosts: Clint and Bonnie Groll
Rooms: 2 (2 SB) $35-45
Full Breakfast
Credit Cards: None
Notes: 5, 7, 8, 10, 13

ST. GEORGE

Mi Casa Su Casa/Old Pueblo Homestays Bed and Breakfast Reservation Service

P.O. Box 950, Tempe, AZ 85280-0950
(602) 990-0682; (800) 456-0682
FAX (602) 990-3390
e-mail: micasa@primenet.com
www.azres.com

7261. In the historic district of St. George,
across from the Brigham Young home,
guests will find traditional western hospitality in this inn, which has two buildings.
One is an 1873 Colonial with three stories.
The other is an 1883 Victorian Colonial
with two stories. Decorated with antiques
collected in America and Europe, some of
the bedrooms are named after the seven
wives of an ancestor of the innkeepers, who
really did have seven wives. All 12 guest
rooms have private baths, two with
whirlpool tubs. Some have wood-burning
stoves and most have outside doors to

NOTES: Credit cards accepted: A MasterCard; B Visa; C American Express; D Discover; E Diner's Club;
F Other; 2 Personal checks accepted; 3 Lunch available; 4 Dinner available; 5 Open all year; 6 Pets welcome;

downstairs porches or upstairs balconies. Pool. No smoking. No pets. Credit cards accepted. $50-100.

Quicksand and Cacti's Bed and Breakfast

346 North Main Street, 84770
(435) 674-1739; (800) 381-1654
e-mail: quicksand@infowest.com
www.infowest.com/quicksand/

This historic pioneer home is where the renowned author and historian, Juanita Brooks, lived and wrote. On the North Main Street hill, there is a great view of the city with the entire downtown historic district within walking distance. The original two rooms of this house were built by George Brooks, with chips and irregular stones from the cleanup of the temple and tabernacle construction sites. Rooms have private baths and TV/VCRs. Covered porches abound.

Host: Carla Fox
Rooms: 3 (PB) $55-85
Full Breakfast
Credit Cards: A, B, D
Notes: 5, 7, 9, 10, 11, 12, 14

Seven Wives Inn

217 North 100 West, 84770
(435) 628-3737; (800) 600-3737

The inn consists of two adjacent pioneer adobe homes with massive hand-grained moldings, framing windows, and doors. Bedrooms are furnished with period antiques and handmade quilts. Some rooms

Seven Wives Inn

have fireplaces; three have whirlpool tubs. Swimming pool on premises.

Hosts: Donna and Jay Curtis
Rooms: 13 (PB) $55-125
Full Breakfast
Credit Cards: A, B, C, D, E
Notes: 2, 3, 5, 7, 8, 9, 10, 11, 12, 14, 15

SALT LAKE CITY

The Anton Boxrud Inn

The Anton Boxrud Bed and Breakfast Inn

57 South 600 East, 84102
(801) 363-8035; (800) 524-5511
FAX (801) 596-1316

This "Grand Old Home" is a half-block from the governor's mansion and six blocks from Temple Square and city center. The Anton Boxrud Bed and Breakfast Inn is within walking distance to many restaurants and the ski bus. Whether enjoying a cozy fire, a soothing soak in the hot tub after a great day of skiing, or simply relaxing on a cool summer evening on the front porch after a day of sightseeing, guests find life at the Anton Boxrud truly uncomplicated—an invitation to relax and unwind.

Host: Jane E. Johnson
Rooms: 7 (5 PB; 2 SB)
Full Breakfast
Credit Cards: A, B, C, D, E
Notes: 2, 3, 4, 5, 7, 8, 9, 10, 11, 12, 13, 14

---

7 No smoking; 8 Children welcome; 9 Social drinking allowed; 10 Tennis nearby; 11 Swimming nearby; 12 Golf nearby; 13 Skiing nearby; 14 May be booked through a travel agent; 15 Handicapped accessible.

Mi Casa Su Casa/Old Pueblo Homestays Bed and Breakfast Reservation Service

P.O. Box 950, Tempe, AZ 85280-0950
(602) 990-0682; (800) 456-0682
FAX (602) 990-3390
e-mail: micasa@primenet.com
www.azres.com

7201. Well known for its superior luxury and hospitality, this inn, a beautifully preserved 1915 home, takes great pride in providing its guests with one of the most beautiful settings in the Southwest. Secluded canyon close to hiking trails, ski resorts. Six accommodations, each with a theme, with a maximum of 16 guests. One two-bedroom unit. Some rooms have air conditioning, kitchens, telephones, cable TVs. Additional person $20. Outstanding full breakfasts. No smoking. No pets. Children 10 and older welcome. Credit cards accepted. AAA-rated four diamonds. $70-175.

7202. The Salt Lake City Historical Society has recognized this two-and-one-half-story brick house as one of Salt Lake's "Grand Old Homes." The beveled-glass windows and beautiful woodwork have been carefully restored according to the original 1901 plans. Rooms are furnished with antiques, including a hand-carved German dining table where a full breakfast is served. Close to the governor's mansion, downtown, University of Utah, and Temple Square. Five guest rooms on the second floor have queen-size or double beds, private and shared baths. Hot tub. Smoking allowed outside. Full breakfast. $69-129.

7203. Welcoming guests with homegrown hospitality has become a tradition at this oldest continuously operating bed and breakfast in Utah. The owners have collected antiques from the 19th and early 20th century and have enjoyed placing them so

the decor is simple and comfortable. In a residential area of Salt Lake City within minutes of the Utah state capitol, Temple Square, the genealogy library, and Symphony Hall. Seven Wasatch Front ski resorts are all within a 40-minute drive. There are five rooms and three baths in the main house. There are two cottages with full facilities. Refreshments. Full breakfast. $65-134.

Saltair Bed and Breakfast

164 South 900 East, 84102
(801) 533-8184; (800) 733-8184
e-mail: saltair@travelbase.com
www.travelbase.com/destinations/
   salt-lake-city/saltair

Antiques and charm complement queen-size brass beds, Amish quilts, and period lamps. A full breakfast featuring house juice and wake-up favorites such as pumpkin-walnut waffles and Saltair mc(muffins) greet each guest. Hospitality offered by innkeepers includes snacks and use of parlor, dining room, TV, and telephone. Close to the University of Utah, historic downtown, skiing, canyons, and seasonal recreation.

Hosts: Jan Bartlett and Nancy Saxton
Rooms: 5 (2 PB; 3 SB) $55-105
Full Breakfast
Credit Cards: A, B, C, D, E
Notes: 2, 5, 7, 9, 11, 12, 13, 14

Wildflowers, A Bed and Breakfast

936 East 1700 South, 84105
(801) 466-0600; e-mail: ls2939@aol.com

Wildflowers is an 1891 Victorian home surrounded by blue spruce and an abundance of wildflowers. Listed in the National Register of Historic Places, it is five minutes from downtown and 30 minutes from skiing. In their careful restoration, the owners have kept the delights of the past and added the comforts of the present, including air conditioning. Hand-

Wildflowers

carved staircases, stained-glass windows, claw-foot bathtubs, original chandeliers, oriental rugs, antiques, private baths, and deck make up the present Wildflowers. Guests will be warmly welcomed by owners and hosts who serve a gourmet breakfast. Suite available with balcony and view of mountains.

Hosts: Cill Sparks and Jeri Parker
Rooms: 5 (PB) $80-170
Full Breakfast
Credit Cards: A, B, C, D
Notes: 2, 5, 7, 8, 9, 10, 11, 12, 13, 14

SPRINGDALE

Mi Casa Su Casa/Old Pueblo Homestays Bed and Breakfast Reservation Service

P.O. Box 950, Tempe, AZ 85280-0950
(602) 990-0682; (800) 456-0682
FAX (602) 990-3390
e-mail: micasa@primenet.com
www.azres.com

7251. Built in 1988 in a contemporary pioneer ranch style, this two-story inn is on a quiet dead-end street less than one mile from the south entrance to Zion National Park. Comfortable, clean, and bright with a contemporary interior, original artwork, and collectibles. One room is on the first floor with a private bath. Three rooms on the second floor all have private baths. Children are welcome by prior arrangement. No smoking. Complimentary beverages. Breakfast is a culinary event! Hot tub. Credit cards are accepted. AAA-rated three diamonds. Fifteen dollars for each additional person. $75-90.

7252. At this two-story bed and breakfast, guests can choose one of 10 rooms, each with a private bath. In the center of a panoramic arc of spectacular red rock mountains, this inn is within walking distance of shops and restaurants. The entrance to Zion National Park is about a mile away, and the Utah Shakespearean Festival or the shops of St. George are about an hour away. There are three smaller rooms without TVs, and seven extra-large rooms with TVs. English-style afternoon tea. Gourmet breakfast. Handicapped accessible. AAA-rated three diamonds. Seasonal rates. $75-95.

SUNDANCE

Sundance

Rural Route 3, Box A-1, 84604
(801) 225-4107; FAX (801) 226-1937

Sundance is a year-round mountain community set among spruce groves and meandering streams on 6,000 pristine acres at the base of 12,000-foot Mount Timpanogos. In 1969, Robert Redford envisioned the careful growth of a community that would foster the alliance of arts and recreation while preserving the integrity of the land. Today, Sundance offers a full range of activities for day and night guests in the Sundance Village and on the Sundance mountain.

Rooms: 100 (PB) $150-425
Full Breakfast
Credit Cards: A, B, C, D, E, F
Notes: 2, 3, 4, 5, 7, 8, 9, 10, 11, 12, 13, 14, 15

7 No smoking; 8 Children welcome; 9 Social drinking allowed; 10 Tennis nearby; 11 Swimming nearby; 12 Golf nearby; 13 Skiing nearby; 14 May be booked through a travel agent; 15 Handicapped accessible.

TORREY

Mi Casa Su Casa/Old Pueblo Homestays Bed and Breakfast Reservation Service

P.O. Box 950, Tempe, AZ 85280-0950
(602) 990-0682; (800) 456-0682
FAX (602) 990-3390
e-mail: micasa@primenet.com
www.azres.com

7271. This two-story Territorial-style house is on 75 acres seven miles west of Capitol Reef National Park. The five guest rooms have private baths, video cassette players, antiques, art furniture, and folk sculpture. Some have telephones, a private deck or patio. One unit has a private hot tub on an enclosed open air deck. There are interior and exterior corridors. No smoking. Near bicycling and hiking trails. Full breakfast. Credit cards accepted. AAA-rated four diamonds. Fifteen dollars per each additional person. $72-102.

TROPIC

Mi Casa Su Casa/Old Pueblo Homestays Bed and Breakfast Reservation Service

P.O. Box 950, Tempe, AZ 85280-0950
(602) 990-0682; (800) 456-0682
FAX (602) 990-3390
e-mail: micasa@primenet.com
www.azres.com

7281. In tiny picturesque Tropic, this bed and breakfast is within walking distance of Bryce Canyon National Park's western boundary. The house was built in the early 1930s and a two-story addition was built in 1990. There are wraparound decks with spectacular views. Five spacious guest rooms, each with queen-size bed, private bath, and picture windows. The new guest cottage has a living room, bedroom, kitchen. Children are welcome. Full break-

fast served. No smoking. Ten dollars for each additional person in room. $77-99.

7282. This bed and breakfast is a modern two-story log home with flower gardens. It is a working farm of 10 acres that produces grain and hay. Farm animals. Nine miles from Bryce Canyon Park entrance and a few miles from Kodachrome Basin. The three rooms all have private baths. Enclosed spa. Children are welcome. Full breakfast served. No smoking or pets. Possible handicapped accessibility. Ten dollars for each additional person in room. $55-70.

VIRGIN

Snow Family Guest Ranch Bed and Breakfast

Zion Canyon, 633 East Highway 9,
    P.O. Box 790190, 84779
(801) 635-2500; (800) 308-7669
FAX (801) 635-2758
www.snowfamilyranch.com

The Snow Family Guest Ranch is just east of the town of Virgin, on the north side of Highway 9. This beautiful horse ranch lies in a picturesque setting just 15 minutes from entrance to Zion National Park, on 12 acres of lush green pastures, surrounded by white-rail fencing. Area attractions include Zion National Park, Bryce Canyon, the North Rim of the Grand Canyon, and Lake Powell. The ranch has very mild winters, and year-round activities are plentiful. The western hospitality of the ranch provides a quiet, private atmosphere. It is perfect for a relaxing peaceful getaway. Pool, spa, trail rides on site.

Hosts: Steve and Shelley Penrose
Rooms: 9 (PB) $85-150
Full Breakfast
Credit Cards: A, B, C, D
Notes: 5, 7, 11, 12, 14

NOTES: Credit cards accepted: A MasterCard; B Visa; C American Express; D Discover; E Diner's Club; F Other; 2 Personal checks accepted; 3 Lunch available; 4 Dinner available; 5 Open all year; 6 Pets welcome;

Washington

Cooney Mansion

ABERDEEN (COSMOPOLIS)

Cooney Mansion

1705 Fifth Street, Cosmopolis, 98537
(360) 533-0602; (800) 9-spruce
www.techline.com/~cooney/

This historically registered Craftsman-style lumber baron's retreat features original furniture and private baths. Relax in the Jacuzzi, exercise room, or sauna. Play golf, tennis, or curl up with a book from the extensive library. Sit in the rose garden or amble through Mill Creek Park with its bridges and waterfalls. The Cooney Mansion exudes an old-fashioned warmth and relaxed atmosphere. The Cooney Suite features fireplace, sitting areas, and original rainfall shower. Two minutes' drive from Aberdeen and Hoquiam. Close to beaches, antique shops, and historic seaport. Serving national award-winning breakfast.

Hosts: Judi and Jim Lohr
Rooms: 8 (5 PB; 3 SB) $75-165
Full Breakfast
Credit Cards: A, B, C, D, E, F
Notes: 5, 7, 10, 12

ALGONA

Pacific Bed and Breakfast Agency

P.O. Box 46894, Seattle, 98146
(206) 439-7677; FAX (206) 431-0932
e-mail: pacificb@nwlink.com
www.seattlebedandbreakfast.com

065. Homestyle Bed and Breakfast. Guests are on the right track at the host home that features carousel horses in its decor. Private bath, TV, and telephones. A game and exercise room for guests' comfort and enjoyment. Full breakfast. $55-65.

ANACORTES

Albatross Bed and Breakfast

5708 Kingsway West, 98221
(360) 293-0677; (800) 622-8864

Across from the Skyline Marina, this 1927 Cape Cod-style home features delicious full breakfasts, king- and queen-size beds, private baths, fine art, antiques, and island views. The marina offers charter boats, a deli, and fine dining. Nearby are Washington Park and ferries to the San Juan Islands and Victoria, British Columbia. AAA-approved.

7 No smoking; 8 Children welcome; 9 Social drinking allowed; 10 Tennis nearby; 11 Swimming nearby; 12 Golf nearby; 13 Skiing nearby; 14 May be booked through a travel agent; 15 Handicapped accessible.

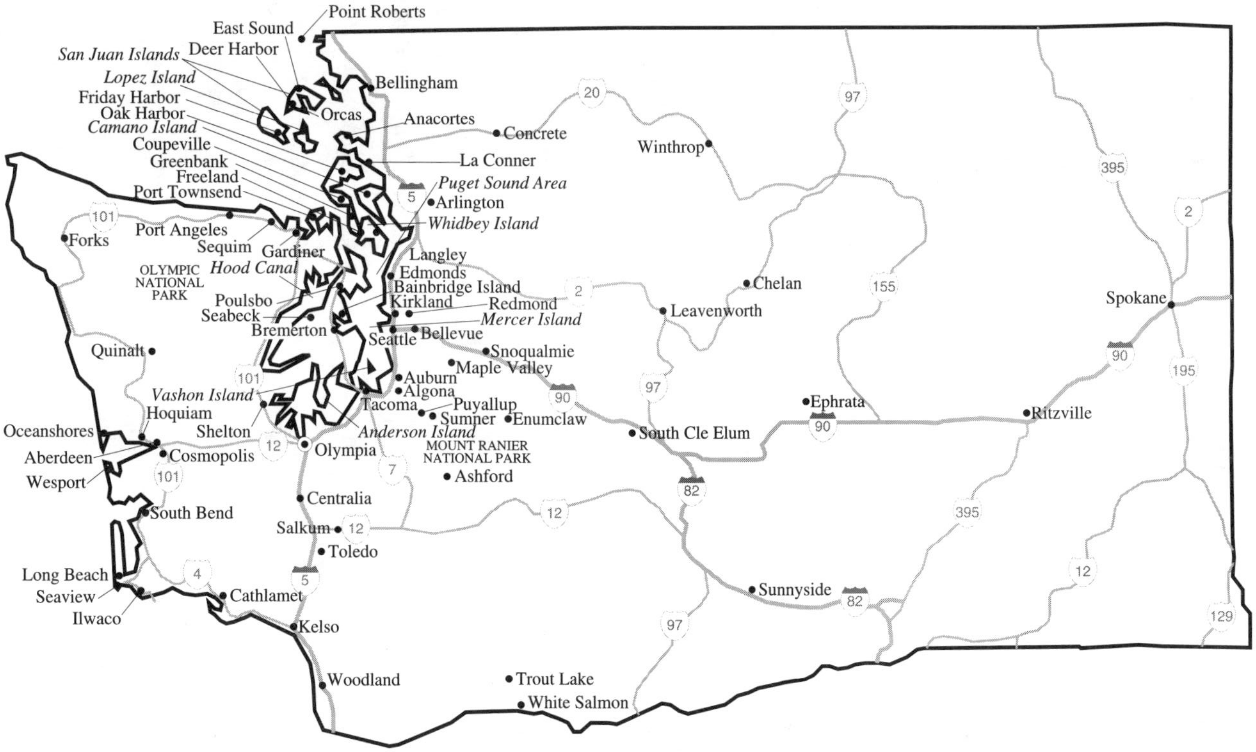

Washington

Point Roberts

Spokane
Ritzville
Ephrata
Sunnyside
Chelan
Leavenworth
Winthrop
South Cle Elum
Trout Lake
White Salmon
Anacortes
Concrete
La Conner
Puget Sound Area
Arlington
Whidbey Island
Langley
Edmonds
Redmond
Mercer Island
Snoqualmie
Maple Valley
Bainbridge Island
Kirkland
Bellevue
Seattle
Tacoma
Auburn
Algona
Puyallup
Sumner
Enumclaw
Anderson Island
MOUNT RANIER
NATIONAL PARK
Ashford
Bellingham
Orcas
East Sound
San Juan Islands
Lopez Island
Friday Harbor
Oak Harbor
Camano Island
Coupeville
Greenbank
Freeland
Port Townsend
Port Angeles
OLYMPIC
NATIONAL
PARK
Sequim
Gardiner
Hood Canal
Poulsbo
Seabeck
Bremerton
Olympia
Centralia
Toledo
Woodland
Kelso
Cathlamet
Salkum
Shelton
Vashon Island
Cosmopolis
Hoquiam
Oceanshores
Aberdeen
Wesport
South Bend
Long Beach
Seaview
Ilwaco
Quinalt
Forks
Deer Harbor

2
195
129
395
90
12
395
155
82
97
90
82
97
20
5
2
90
7
12
12
101
4
5
101
101

Hosts: Linda and Lorrie Flowers
Rooms: 4 (PB) $75-95
Full Breakfast
Credit Cards: A, B, C
Notes: 2, 5, 6, 7, 8, 9, 10, 11, 12, 13, 14, 15

Hasty Pudding House Bed and Breakfast

1312 8th Street, 98221
(360) 293-5773; (800) 368-5588

Celebrate romance in this delightful 1913 heritage home. A wonderful example of Craftsman-style architecture, this home is filled with Victorian antiques, fresh flowers, window seats, and wonderful private rooms, all with turn-of-the-century charm and comfort guests will enjoy. Snuggle in king- and queen-size top-of-the-line beds that Grandmother would envy. Melinda's luscious breakfasts and table setting will begin this Anacortes adventure each day of guests' stay.

Hosts: Mike and Melinda Hasty
Rooms: 4 (PB) $75-109
Full Breakfast
Credit Cards: A, B, C, D
Notes: 2, 5, 7, 9, 10, 11, 12, 14

Old Brook Inn

530 Old Brook Lane, 98221
(360) 293-4768; (800) 503-4768

Old Brook Inn is a four-bedroom Cape Cod home nestled into a quiet little valley four miles outside of Anacortes. A rambling brook finds its way to a dammed-up pond full of rainbow trout. Ten acres give the bird watchers their exercise. There is plenty of room for the golfers to practice their approach shots. The upstairs room is big; one queen-size plus two twin beds. There is even room for a rollaway.

Host: Dick Ash
Rooms: 2 (PB) $80-90
Continental Breakfast
Credit Cards: A, B
Notes: 2, 5, 6, 7, 8, 9, 12, 14

Pacific Bed and Breakfast Agency

P.O. Box 46894, Seattle, 98146
(206) 439-7677; FAX (206) 431-0932
e-mail: pacificb@nwlink.com
www.seattlebedandbreakfast.com

118. 1902 Host Home. This Victorian home, designed and built for an Italian count in 1902, is a lovely bed and breakfast furnished with antiques in each room. Just a few minutes from the San Juan Islands ferry dock, guests have views of Puget Sound and Guemes Channel. Each room has its own special decor and private bath. In the Rose Cottage guests will find two rooms with fireplaces and jetted tubs for that special occasion. The outdoor hot tub is nearby and is for all the guests to enjoy. A wonderful homemade gourmet breakfast is served in the dining room and will start guests' day perfectly. $69-105.

119. Anacortes Marina. With 52 rooms, a guest spa and Jacuzzi rooms, this modern inn will accommodate any guest or group of guests. Queen- or king-size beds, cable TV/VCRs, and a Continental breakfast that will satisfy even the most seasoned traveler for a night or a longer stay. $55-85.

158. Restored Farmhouse. Originally built in 1915, this two-story farmhouse was moved and completely restored in 1990. The atmosphere is relaxed and quiet with warm hospitality. The acreage is small but wooded affording the ambiance of a peaceful spot for a getaway bed and breakfast. The master bedroom has a private bath with claw-foot tub and the other two rooms share a very large bath. Full breakfast.

173. Hotel, bistro, and pub. Dating from 1889, this small, grand hotel will welcome guests with friendly and personalized

NOTES: Credit cards accepted: A MasterCard; B Visa; C American Express; D Discover; E Diner's Club; F Other; 2 Personal checks accepted; 3 Lunch available; 4 Dinner available; 5 Open all year; 6 Pets welcome; 7 No smoking; 8 Children welcome; 9 Social drinking allowed; 10 Tennis nearby; 11 Swimming nearby; 12 Golf nearby; 13 Skiing nearby; 14 May be booked through a travel agent; 15 Handicapped accessible.

service. The 23 unique rooms are furnished with antiques and down comforters, soaking tubs, wet bars, and have view decks. A Continental breakfast is complimentary. A Victorian Pub and banquet and meeting rooms are available.

Sunset Beach Bed and Breakfast

100 Sunset Beach, 98221
(360) 293-5428; (800) 359-3448

On the exciting Rosario Strait overlooking seven of the San Juan Islands, this bed and breakfast invites guests to enjoy the water scenery that includes water birds, deer, fishing boats, and more. Take a stroll and enjoy the scenic view of the Olympic Mountains, or amble down the beach. Close to the ferry, marina, and excellent restaurants, and adjacent to Washington Park. Full breakfasts, queen-size beds, and private baths. Hot tub on request.

Hosts: Joann and Hal Harker
Rooms: 3 (PB) $82-95
Full Breakfast
Credit Cards: A, B
Notes: 2, 5, 7, 9, 11, 12, 14

ANDERSON ISLAND

The Inn at Burg's Landing

8808 Villa Beach Road, 98303
(206) 884-9185; (206) 488-8682

Catch the ferry from Steilacoom to stay at this contemporary log homestead built in 1987. It offers spectacular views of Mount Rainier, Puget Sound, and Cascade Mountains. The inn has a private beach. Collect seashells and agates, swim in one of the two freshwater lakes nearby, or enjoy a game of tennis or golf. Tour the scenic island by bicycle or on foot. Relax in the hot tub. Families are welcome.

Hosts: Ken and Annie Burg
Rooms: 3 (2 PB; 1 SB) $77-110
Full Breakfast

Credit Cards: A, B
Notes: 2, 5, 7, 8, 9, 10, 11, 12, 13

ARLINGTON

Mt. Higgins House

29805 State Route 530 Northeast, 98223
(360) 435-8703; (888) 296-3700
FAX (360) 435-9757

A secluded retreat on a 70-acre farm in the Stillaguamish River Valley 17 miles east of Arlington. All rooms with mountain views. A large deck overlooks a stocked trout pond. The common areas include the living room with a river rock fireplace, piano, satellite TV and CD player; a large dining area and a cozy library. Enjoy bird watching, fishing, and hiking. River access; private baths. Adults only. Smoke-free. A generous buffet breakfast is included.

Host: Renee Ottersen
Rooms: 2 (PB) $85-105
Full Breakfast
Credit Cards: A, B
Notes: 2, 5, 7, 12, 14

ASHFORD

Growly Bear Bed and Breakfast

37311 State Road 706, 98304
(360) 569-2339; (800) 700-2339

Experience a bit of history and enjoy a mountain stay at a rustic homestead house built in 1890. Hike in nearby Mount Rainier National Park. Dine at unique restaurants

Growly Bear

NOTES: Credit cards accepted: A MasterCard; B Visa; C American Express; D Discover; E Diner's Club; F Other; 2 Personal checks accepted; 3 Lunch available; 4 Dinner available; 5 Open all year; 6 Pets welcome;

within walking distance of guests' room. Be lulled to sleep by the whispering sounds of Goat Creek just outside the window. Awake in the morning to the sight of tall evergreen trees and the early morning melodies of the mountain birds. Indulge in a basket of warm scrumptious pastries.

Host: Susan Jenny Johnson
Rooms: 2 (1 PB; 1 SB) $70-110
Full Breakfast
Credit Cards: A, B, C
Notes: 2, 5, 7, 9, 13, 14

Mountain Meadows Inn Bed and Breakfast

28912 State Route 706 East, P.O. Box 291, 98304-0291
(360) 569-2788

Built in 1910 as the home of a lumber mill superintendent, Mountain Meadows Inn is on 11 acres of serene cedar groves amidst the grandeur of the northwestern landscape. Guests enjoy forested trails, garden, wildlife pond, evening campfires, and an impressive Northwest Coast Native American artifact collection. The nature library of more than 1,000 books includes a John Muir archive. The large comfortable rooms are highlighted with a hearty country breakfast. Smoking permitted outside only.

Hosts: Harry and Michelle Latimer
Rooms: 6 (PB) $65-110
Full Breakfast
Credit Cards: A, B
Notes: 2, 5, 7, 8, 9, 11, 12, 13, 14

Pacific Bed and Breakfast Agency

P.O. Box 46894, Seattle, 98146
(206) 439-7677; FAX (206) 431-0932
e-mail: pacificb@nwlink.com
www.seattlebedandbreakfast.com

067. Country Inn near Mount Rainier. The original register of this inn includes such famous names as Presidents Theodore Roosevelt and William Howard Taft. Built in 1912 and restored in 1984, it features 11 newly renovated rooms, 6 with private baths. Guests will enjoy the handmade quilts, the antiques, Tiffany lamps, and stained-glass windows. Also at this inn is a critically acclaimed restaurant that serves delicious food in a relaxed, genteel fashion by a big stone fireplace. Join in for a fun country experience. Seasonal rates. $104.31-148.23.

AUBURN

Pacific Bed and Breakfast Agency

P.O. Box 46894, Seattle, 98146
(206) 439-7677; FAX (206) 431-0932
e-mail: pacificb@nwlink.com
www.seattlebedandbreakfast.com

062. Contemporary Bed and Breakfast. Choose from three different accommodations in this peaceful setting. One is a suite with fireplace and private entrance. The second has a bathroom with jetted tub and the third has a private bath. Full breakfast and afternoon refreshments are included. $65-110.

063. Ranch-style Experience. This authentic 21-acre family ranch is home to the hostess and her family and their pets, two horses, a pony, and two dogs. The bed and breakfast accommodation offered is a two-bedroom suite with two baths (one with a one-person jetted tub). There is a scenic bicycle route and a wide array of activities are offered for guests' enjoyment while visiting this unique host home. Continental plus breakfast served. $65-85.

064. A Step Back In Time. Choose either a king-size bedroom with private bath or a double bedroom with shared bath. The ample vegetarian breakfasts include homemade breads and granola, waffles with fruit topping or real maple syrup. A special feature is

7 No smoking; 8 Children welcome; 9 Social drinking allowed; 10 Tennis nearby; 11 Swimming nearby; 12 Golf nearby; 13 Skiing nearby; 14 May be booked through a travel agent; 15 Handicapped accessible.

an hour-long Swedish massage at an additional charge. $70-90.

Rose Arbor Inn Bed and Breakfast and Massage

514 A Street Northeast, 98002
(253) 931-8564; www.moriah.com/inns

Come to this cozy, old-fashioned home for a reprieve from a busy life and enjoy renewal of body, mind, and soul. Enjoy homemade chocolate chip cookies and ample vegetarian breakfasts. Four guest rooms with one shared bath and one private. Swedish massage and hot tub available. Near SuperMall, Emerald Downs Race Track, and Seattle International Raceway. Twenty minutes from airport. No smoking or pets.

Host: Rae Boggs
Rooms: 4 (1 PB; 3 SB) $60-90
Full Breakfast
Credit Cards: A, B
Notes: 2, 5, 7, 11, 12, 13

BAINBRIDGE ISLAND

Bombay House

8490 Beck Road, 98110
(206) 842-3926; (800) 598-3926

The Bombay House is a spectacular 35-minute ferry ride from downtown Seattle. The house was built in 1907 and sits high on a hillside in the country overlooking Rich Passage. Widow's walk; rustic, rough-cedar gazebo; masses of gardens exploding with seasonal color. Watch the ferry pass and see the lights of Bremerton in the distance. Just a few blocks from the beach, a country theater, and fine dining. A great spot for the Seattle business traveler or vacationer.

Hosts: Bunny Cameron and Roger Kanchuk
Rooms: 5 (3 PB; 2 SB) $59-149
Continental Breakfast
Credit Cards: B, C, D
Notes: 2, 5, 7, 9, 10, 11, 12, 14

BELLEVUE

Pacific Bed and Breakfast Agency

P.O. Box 46894, Seattle, 98146
(206) 439-7677; FAX (206) 431-0932
e-mail: pacificb@nwlink.com
www.seattlebedandbreakfast.com

044. Host Home. Hospitable retired hosts offer guests a suite with two bedrooms, each with private bath, living room, kitchenette, and private entrance. A tasty breakfast is served. Super handy location. $85.

045. Bellevue Square. Secluded, yet near downtown Bellevue, this modern home offers either king/twin- or queen-size bedroom sharing one bath. Enjoy the hot tub on the deck during the summer. Full breakfast. $65.

046. Two Acres of Grounds. Near Bridal Trail State Park, this Spanish Colonial bed and breakfast offers two rooms and a suite with kitchen, each with a private bath. This bed and breakfast is unique with exotic animals such as llamas, emus, rheas, and peacocks for guests' enjoyment. Children welcome. Full breakfast. $85.

047. British-Style Bed and Breakfast. The British hostess welcomes guests to her lovely contemporary home. Two rooms with a shared bath are available. Guests are welcome to use the sitting room with TV and VCR. Full breakfast. $60-65.

Petersen Bed and Breakfast

10228 Southeast Eighth, 98004
(206) 454-9334

Petersen Bed and Breakfast is in a well-established neighborhood five minutes from shopping in the Bellevue Square and 20 minutes from Seattle. It offers two rooms,

---

NOTES: Credit cards accepted: A MasterCard; B Visa; C American Express; D Discover; E Diner's Club; F Other; 2 Personal checks accepted; 3 Lunch available; 4 Dinner available; 5 Open all year; 6 Pets welcome;

with a queen-size bed or two twin beds, and a spa on the deck off the atrium kitchen. Home-style breakfast.

Hosts: Eunice and Carl Petersen
Rooms: 2 (SB) $60-75
Full Breakfast
Credit Cards: None
Notes: 2, 5, 7, 8

BELLINGHAM

Pacific Bed and Breakfast Agency

P.O. Box 46894, Seattle, 98146
(206) 439-7677; FAX (206) 431-0932
e-mail: pacificb@nwlink.com
www.seattlebedandbreakfast.com

134. Victorian. A restored Victorian that overlooks the bay is proudly shared with guests by the innkeepers. Two rooms only, each with a private bath. The house is decorated with stained glass and etchings crafted by the hostess. Lots of advice and friendly help are given by the hosts who have lived in the area a long time. Guests are assured of a warm welcome. Full breakfast served. No smoking in house. No small children. $59-69.

135. Historic Queen Anne Mansion. In the national register, the inn is a unique and very special bed and breakfast that offers guests splendid views over Bellingham Bay and 10 rooms from which to choose. A Steinway grand piano adorns the entry, and music suggests names for each room. A variety of bed sizes and private or shared bath accommodations will meet the needs of any traveler. Full breakfast. $45-84.

Schnauzer Crossing

4421 Lakeway Drive, 98226
(360) 733-0055; (800) 562-2808;
FAX (360) 734-2808; e-mail: schnauzerx@aol.com

Schnauzer Crossing is a luxury bed and breakfast between Seattle and Vancouver,

British Columbia. Enjoy this destination bed and breakfast, with its lakeside ambiance, outdoor hot tub, and its master suite with fireplace and Jacuzzi. There is also a new cottage available for guests to stay in. Sail in the beautiful San Juan Islands or climb 10,000-foot Mount Baker. Experience the many wonders of Washington State!

Hosts: Vermont and Donna McAllister
Rooms: 3 (PB) $115-190
Full Breakfast
Credit Cards: A, B, D
Notes: 2, 5, 7, 8, 9, 10, 11, 12, 13, 15

Stratford Manor

1416 Van Wyck Road, 98226
(360) 715-8441; FAX (360) 671-0840
e-mail: llohse@aol.com
www.site-works.com/stratford

Quiet, peaceful Tudor-style country home on 30 acres with views of the Pacific Northwest countryside. Golfing, hiking, skiing, shopping, and fine dining are nearby. A comfortably luxurious home with three guest rooms with gas fireplaces, suite amenities, and wonderful baths. A full delectable country breakfast is served in the formal dining room. Conveniently between Seattle and Vancouver, British Columbia.

Hosts: Leslie and Jim Lohse
Rooms: 3 (PB) $125-165
Full Breakfast
Credit Cards: A, B
Notes: 2, 5, 7, 9, 11, 12, 13

BELLINGHAM (FAIRHAVEN DISTRICT)

The Castle Bed and Breakfast

1103 15th and Knox Streets, 98225
(360) 676-0974

High on a hill above historic Fairhaven looms the castle. Excellent views of Bellingham Bay and the San Juan Islands can be viewed from any guest room of this majestic 1889 mauve mansion. The owners, Gloria and Larry Harriman, have restored the castle for 20 years. A bed and breakfast

7 No smoking; 8 Children welcome; 9 Social drinking allowed; 10 Tennis nearby; 11 Swimming nearby; 12 Golf nearby; 13 Skiing nearby; 14 May be booked through a travel agent; 15 Handicapped accessible.

since 1986. It is only a few blocks to the Alaska and Victoria ferries, Amtrak train and Greyhound bus depots. Extensive lamp and clock collections and castle furnishings dominate the castle and can be purchased. Ask about Seagoat Cottage, a beachfront getaway. Children over 12 welcome. Skiing is 60 miles away.

Hosts: Gloria and Larry Harriman
Rooms: 3 (PB) $75-95
Continental Breakfast
Credit Cards: None
Notes: 2, 5, 7, 9, 10, 11, 12

BREMERTON

Pacific Bed and Breakfast Agency

P.O. Box 46894, Seattle, 98146
(206) 439-7677; FAX (206) 431-0932
e-mail: pacificb@nwlink.com
www.seattlebedandbreakfast.com

115. High Society. "An opulent retreat to yesteryear" is the description of this stately mansion built in 1936 and it became the hub of high society on the Canal in 1937. The Gable Room is named for Clark Gable who was a frequent visitor. Six rooms, all with private baths, offer wonderful choices for guests' stay. Breakfast is a special treat. The mansion has an interesting history and special spaces to explore. $115-175.

CAMANO ISLAND

Peifferhaus

1462 East Larkspur Lane, 98292
(360) 629-4746; FAX (360) 629-4785

This country-style home on Camano Island is designed for relaxing. Enjoy the panoramic view from the room or on the wraparound covered porch. There are four and one-half acres of beautiful grounds and flower gardens. A short drive from Seattle, this island retreat has the charisma of the San Juan Islands, without the ferry lines and expenses. Gourmet breakfasts are served in a peaceful country setting. Enjoy lawn games and mini-golf course on-site.

Hosts: Tom and Mary Ann Peiffer
Rooms: 4 (PB) $85-95
Full Breakfast
Credit Cards: A, B, D
Notes: 2, 3, 4, 5, 6, 7, 8, 9, 10, 11, 12, 13

CATHLAMET

Rodfern Farm Bed and Breakfast

277 Crossdike Road, 98612
(360) 849-4108

In the lower Columbia River estuary and on rural Puget Island, Redfern Farm is about two hours from Portland, Oregon, and Olympia. There is easy access by bridge from Cathlamet or by the historic ferry from Westport, Oregon. The 1940s farmhouse has two second-story guest rooms, each with queen-size beds and private bath. Furnishings are an eclectic mix of old and new. Enjoy the quiet of the country garden and outdoor spa; walk, hike, bicycle, and bird watch on this portion of Columbia White-tailed Deer Refuge.

Host: Winnie
Rooms: 2 (PB) $55
Full Breakfast
Credit Cards: None
Notes: 2, 5, 7, 12

CENTRALIA

Candalite Mansion

402 North Rock, 98531
(360) 736-4749; (800) 849-4749
e-mail: candal@localaccess.com

Candalite Mansion, one of Centralia's oldest homes. Built in 1903 as the Gurrier Mansion. Very beautiful with large rooms; king-, queen-size, double or twin beds, furnishings to match the era of the home, and a candle in every window. Three blocks from downtown Centralia. Quiet residential street; smoke-free Christian atmosphere.

NOTES: Credit cards accepted: A MasterCard; B Visa; C American Express; D Discover; E Diner's Club; F Other; 2 Personal checks accepted; 3 Lunch available; 4 Dinner available; 5 Open all year; 6 Pets welcome;

Candalite Mansion

Full breakfast served weekends; Continental breakfast weekdays.

Rooms: 5 (2 PB; 3 SB) $50-65
Full or Continental Breakfast
Credit Cards: None
Notes: 2, 5, 7

CHELAN

Highland Guest House

121 East Highland Avenue, P.O. Box 2089, 98816
(509) 682-2892; (800) 681-2892
www.lakechelan.com/highland.htm

This 1902 Queen Anne Victorian sits high above town on the north hill. The view of Lake Chelan and surrounding mountains is breathtaking. Relax on the wraparound veranda on either the porch swing or wicker furniture. In summer, enjoy your full gourmet breakfast on the veranda. Unwind in the parlor complete with hand-stenciled ceilings and period antiques. All

Highland Guest House

rooms are theme decorated and stenciled including private baths. The Rose Room also has a private porch overlooking lake. All rooms have air conditioning, fresh flowers, and fruit.

Hosts: Brad and Marilee Stolzenburg
Rooms: 3 (PB) $55-104
Full Breakfast
Credit Cards: A, B
Notes: 2, 5, 7, 8, 9, 10, 11, 12, 13, 14

CONCRETE-BIRDSVIEW

Cascade Mountain Inn

3840 Pioneer Lane, 98237
(360) 826-4333

The inn has five guest rooms, each with its own theme and, of course, each room has its own bathroom. A full breakfast is included in the room rate and is served in the breakfast room or, weather permitting, on the patio. Here are a few suggestions of activities guests may want to do while staying at the inn: hiking, fishing, river rafting, bald eagle watching (winter only), hang-gliding, hunting, snowmobiling, cross-country skiing.

Hosts: John and Sally Brummett
Rooms: 5 (PB) $120
Full Breakfast
Credit Cards: A, B
Notes: 2, 5, 7, 9, 12

COSMOPOLIS

Pacific Bed and Breakfast Agency

P.O. Box 46894, Seattle, 98146
(206) 439-7677; FAX (206) 431-0932
e-mail: pacificb@nwlink.com
www.seattlebedandbreakfast.com

110. Lumber Baron's Mansion. A circular driveway leads guests to the portico of this lumber baron's mansion built in

7 No smoking; 8 Children welcome; 9 Social drinking allowed; 10 Tennis nearby; 11 Swimming nearby; 12 Golf nearby; 13 Skiing nearby; 14 May be booked through a travel agent; 15 Handicapped accessible.

1908. In the state and national registers. Guests will find that old-fashioned charm and warmth are tangible qualities here. Five rooms have private baths and four additional rooms with shared baths are offered. The first-floor living room, dining room, and two parlors are all available for ceremonies and receptions and on the lower level, the ballroom is ideal for banquets for large groups. Jacuzzi, sauna, and exercise rooms are an added bonus. $65-115.

Palmer's Chart House

COUPEVILLE

Pacific Bed and Breakfast Agency

P.O. Box 46894, Seattle, 98146
(206) 439-7677; FAX (206) 431-0932
e-mail: pacificb@nwlink.com
www.seattlebedandbreakfast.com

130. Two Victorian Host Homes. Two lovely Victorian host homes sit side-by-side and offer a truly unique stay in a bygone era. Dating from 1887 and 1891 and restored in a loving manner, the rooms will give guests the feeling of days long gone. All six rooms have private baths with clawfoot tubs and either king- or queen-size beds. The master rooms have a gas fireplace and Jacuzzi tub. $65-125.

DEER HARBOR (ORCAS ISLAND)

Palmer's Chart House

Box 51, 98243
(360) 376-4231

The first bed and breakfast on Orcas Island (since 1975) with a magnificent water view. The 33-foot private yacht *Amante* is available for a minimal fee with Skipper Don. Low-key, private, personal attention makes this bed and breakfast unique and attractive. Well-traveled hosts speak Spanish. Children over 10 welcome.

Hosts: Majean and Donald Palmer
Rooms: 2 (PB) $50-70
Full Breakfast
Credit Cards: None
Notes: 2, 5, 9, 10, 11, 12, 14

EASTSOUND (ORCAS ISLAND)

Kangaroo House Bed and Breakfast

Box 334, 98245-0334
(360) 376-2175; (888) 371-2175
FAX (360) 376-3604
e-mail: kangaroo@thesanjuans.com
www.pacificws.com/kangaroo

A centrally positioned base for enjoying all that Orcas Island has to offer, Kangaroo House provides comfortable accommoda-

Kangaroo House

NOTES: Credit cards accepted: A MasterCard; B Visa; C American Express; D Discover; E Diner's Club; F Other; 2 Personal checks accepted; 3 Lunch available; 4 Dinner available; 5 Open all year; 6 Pets welcome;

tions, relaxed, and unpretentious atmosphere, and fine breakfasts. Large guest living room, stone fireplace, garden hot tub. Families welcome. Walk to village shops, restaurants, and beach. Panoramic view from nearby Moran State Park.

Hosts: Peter and Helen Allen
Rooms: 5 (2 PB; 3 SB) $75-125
Full Breakfast
Credit Cards: A, B, C, D
Notes: 2, 5, 7, 8, 9, 10, 11, 12, 14

Turtleback Farm Inn and the Orchard House at Turtleback Farm

Route 1, Box 650 (Crow Valley Road), 98243
(360) 376-4914; (800) 376-4914
www.turtlebackinn.com

This meticulously restored farmhouse has been described as a "marvel of bed and breakfastmanship decorated with country finesse and a sophisticated sense of the right antiques." Seven bedrooms with private baths. Award-winning breakfasts. Lunch and dinner available by special arrangements. Children eight and older welcome. Inquire about handicapped accessibility.

Hosts: William and Susan Fletcher
Rooms: 11 (PB) $80-210
Full Breakfast
Credit Cards: A, B, D
Notes: 2, 5, 7, 9, 10, 11, 12, 14

EDMONDS

Harrison House

210 Sunset Avenue, 98020
(206) 776-4748

New waterfront home with sweeping view of Puget Sound and the Olympic Mountains. Many fine restaurants within walking distance. Each spacious room has private bath, private deck, TV, wet bar, telephone, and king-size bed. University of Washington is nearby.

Hosts: Jody and Harve Harrison
Rooms: 2 (PB) $45-65
Continental Breakfast
Credit Cards: None
Notes: 2, 5, 7, 9, 10, 11, 12

ENUMCLAW

Pacific Bed and Breakfast Agency

P.O. Box 46894, Seattle, 98146
(206) 439-7677; FAX (206) 431-0932
e-mail: pacificb@nwlink.com
www.seattlebedandbreakfast.com

138. Magnificent Mansion. This 1922 Colonial mansion has 22 rooms and took two years to build. Master craftsmen decorated the interior with beautiful millwork using old-growth Honduran mahogany and oak. Four guest rooms are offered, all with private bath. Awaken to the aroma of freshly brewed coffee and a gourmet breakfast. $85-95.

EPHRATA

Ivy Chapel Inn Bed and Breakfast

164 D Street Southwest, 98823
(509) 754-0629

The inn is in the former Presbyterian church. The original brick building was built in the 1940s and refurbished in 1994. The inn features six unique theme rooms including the Blue Suite, the Outdoorsman's Room, the Safari Room, the Southwest Room, the Ivy Room, and the Bridal Room. Each room has a private bath. A large parlor, breakfast room, deck with hot tub, and the 1,800-square-foot chapel complete the inn.

Hosts: Kirk and Cheryl McClelland
Rooms: 6 (PB) $75-100
Full Breakfast
Credit Cards: A, B, C
Notes: 2, 5, 7, 9, 11, 12

---

7 No smoking; 8 Children welcome; 9 Social drinking allowed; 10 Tennis nearby; 11 Swimming nearby; 12 Golf nearby; 13 Skiing nearby; 14 May be booked through a travel agent; 15 Handicapped accessible.

Miller Tree Inn

654 East Division Street, P.O. Box 1565, 98331
(360) 374-6806; FAX (360) 374-6807
e-mail: milltree@ptinet.net
www.northolympic.com/millertree

Wonderful 1917 country homestead.
Twelve miles from Pacific beaches, Hoh
Rain Forest, and five fish-filled rivers.
Breakfast is served 7:30-9:00 A.M., consisting of fresh fruit, cereal, and pastry bar followed by mouth-watering entrée. Two
living rooms, hot tub, and reasonable rates.
For the fisherman: guide referrals, trailer
shuttles, pre-dawn breakfasts (October
through April), secure off-road parking,
and river reports. AAA two-diamond, 12
years *Best Places*.

Hosts: Bill and Susan Brager
Rooms: 7 (3 PB; 4 SB) $60-100
Full Breakfast
Credit Cards: A, B
Notes: 2, 5, 7, 8, 9, 14

Cliff House and Seacliff Cottage

727 Windmill Drive, 98249
(360) 331-1566
www.whidbey.com/cliffhouse

On Whidbey Island, a setting so unique
there is nothing anywhere quite like Cliff
House. In a private world of luxury, this
stunning home and/or cottage is the guests'
alone. Secluded in a forest on the edge of
Puget Sound. Views are breathtaking. Stone
fireplace, spa, and miles of driftwood
beach. Gourmet kitchen. Two-night minimum stay required. Children 14 and older
or tiny babies.

Hosts: Peggy Moore and Walter O'Toole
House: $385
Cottage: $165
Continental Breakfast
Credit Cards: None
Notes: 2, 5, 7, 9, 12, 14

Argyle House

685 Argyle Avenue, P.O. Box 2569, 98250
(360) 378-4084; (800) 624-3459

Argyle House is a 1910 vintage Craftsman
design. Two blocks from downtown, it is a
short walk from the ferry. The house is surrounded by beautiful landscaping with lots
of flowers. Guests may choose from three
cozy rooms with private baths, a two-room
suite for four people, or a private charming
honeymoon cottage. A fabulous full breakfast is served. There is also an inviting hot
tub on the deck. Recommended by *Best
Places to Kiss in the Northwest*.

Hosts: Bill and Chris Carli
Rooms: 5 (4 PB; 1 SB) $75-135
Full Breakfast
Credit Cards: A, B
Notes: 2, 5, 10, 11, 12

Mariella Inn and Cottages

630 Turn Point Road, 98250
(360) 378-3622; (800) 700-7668
FAX (360) 378-6822

Classic 1902 waterfront estate and country
inn. Gorgeous water views and grand parlors. Hot tubs. Cozy waterfront cottages
with kitchenettes and wood stoves or fireplaces. Kayak and bicycle rental/tours.
Moorage dock. Volleyball and croquet.
Lovely trout-filled pond and perennial gardens. Less than a half-mile from ferry. Perfect for family reunions, weddings, or quiet
getaways. Sixty-foot classic 1927 wooden
motor launch for charter. Continental breakfast buffet is offered to inn guests; Continental breakfast basket is delivered to
cottage guests. A la carte country breakfast
available at supplemental prices. Children
welcome in cottages.

Hosts: Arthur and Alison Lohrey
Rooms: 11 (PB) $115-275
Cottages: 12 (PB) $195-375
Full and Continental Breakfast
Credit Cards: A, B, C
Notes: 4, 5, 7, 8, 9, 12, 14

NOTES: Credit cards accepted: A MasterCard; B Visa; C American Express; D Discover; E Diner's Club;
F Other; 2 Personal checks accepted; 3 Lunch available; 4 Dinner available; 5 Open all year; 6 Pets welcome;

States Inn

States Inn

2039 West Valley Road, 98250
(360) 378-6240; FAX (360) 378-6241
e-mail: paschal@rockisland.com
www.karuna.com/statesinn

In a scenic valley seven miles from town, States Inn is on a 60-acre horse ranch on the west side of San Juan Island. It is a fully updated 10-room inn (including a three-room suite) originally built circa 1910. Each guest room is decorated with a theme from a different state. AAA has rated the inn three diamonds since it opened in 1991, the top rating for San Juan Islands bed and breakfast inns.

Hosts: Alan and Julia Paschal
Rooms: 10 (8 PB; 2 SB) $85-125
Full Breakfast
Credit Cards: A, B
Notes: 2, 5, 14, 15

Tower House Bed and Breakfast

1230 Little Road, 98250
(360) 378-5464; (800) 858-4276
e-mail: towerhouse@san-juan-island.com
www.san-juan-island.com

This Queen Anne-style home on 10 acres overlooks the San Juan Valley. Two suites offer a blend of Victorian spirit and contemporary comfort. Retreat to the library and the sunroom or watch sunsets through stained glass from the window seat of the Tower Room. Cherished old linens, china, and crystal recall the ceremony of the past as guests enjoy breakfast. Play the piano or view a movie by the fire in the paneled

parlor. Vegan breakfast (no animal products) available with advance notice.

Hosts: Chris and Joe Luma
Rooms: 2 (PB) $95-120
Full Breakfast
Credit Cards: A, B, C, D
Notes: 2, 5, 7, 12, 14

Trumpeter Inn Bed and Breakfast

420 Trumpeter Way, 98250
(360) 378-3884; (800) 826-7926
FAX (360) 378-8235

The inn enjoys views of the San Juan Valley's meadows and ponds with a distant view of the strait and Olympic Mountains. There are five beautifully decorated rooms, all with private baths—one is handicapped accessible. Hot tub in the garden. A scrumptious, hearty breakfast awaits guests in the morning. Children over 12 welcome.

Hosts: Don and Bobbie Wiesner
Rooms: 5 (PB) $90-135
Full Breakfast
Credit Cards: A, B, C, D
Notes: 2, 5, 7, 9, 10, 11, 12, 14, 15

Trumpeter Inn

Tucker House Bed and Breakfast with Cottages

260 B Street, 98250
(800) 965-0123; FAX (306) 378-6437
e-mail: tucker@rockisland.com
www.rockisland.com/~tucker

This 1898 Victorian home has two upstairs bedrooms with queen-size beds, TV/VCRs, accent furniture plus three self-contained cottages with private baths, queen-size beds, wood stoves/electric heat, kitch-

7 No smoking; 8 Children welcome; 9 Social drinking allowed; 10 Tennis nearby; 11 Swimming nearby; 12 Golf nearby; 13 Skiing nearby; 14 May be booked through a travel agent; 15 Handicapped accessible.

enettes, TV/VCR. An outdoor hot tub. A full gourmet breakfast in the solarium. One block from ferry landing. Families welcome in the cottage or children 10 and older upstairs. Small dogs permitted in cottages with prior arrangement and extra charge. Gift certificates available.

Hosts: Skip and Annette Metzger
Rooms: 5 (3 PB; 2 SB) $85-210
Full Breakfast
Credit Cards: A, B, C, D
Notes: 2, 5, 7, 9, 10, 11, 12, 14

FRIDAY HARBOR (SAN JUAN ISLAND)

Pacific Bed and Breakfast Agency

P.O. Box 46894, Seattle, 98146
(206) 439-7677; FAX (206) 431-0932
e-mail: pacificb@nwlink.com
www.seattlebedandbreakfast.com

124. On the Water. If guests would like the experience of staying on a 60-foot sailboat, there is just the perfect one for them at the harbor on San Juan Island. Two cabins are available, one with double bed and bunk beds, shared bath; the other with queen-size bed and private bath. Breakfasts are special here. Two-night minimum required. $90-95.

126. Victorian Inn. Enjoy the hospitality and the relaxed days of yesteryear where quaintness, comfort, and charm await guests at this Victorian inn at Friday Harbor. Each guest room reflects the nostalgic atmosphere of days gone by and the old-fashioned garden provides fresh flowers each day. Shared and private bath accommodations have reasonable rates.

GARDINER

Diamond Point Inn

241 Sunshine Road, 98334
(360) 797-7720; (888) 797-0393
FAX (360) 797-7723

A refuge away from the stress of work and city living. Nestled in the center of 10

Diamond Point Inn

acres, the inn offers tranquility in a country retreat setting. Comfortable furnishings and cozy wood stoves beckon guests to rest and rejuvenate. The main house offers two rooms with private baths and two rooms that share a bath. Also two cottage units with private baths, coffee makers, and refrigerators. Enjoy a full breakfast in the dining room, sunroom, or outside on the large deck. Children over five welcome.

Hosts: Doug and Barbara Billings
Rooms: 6 (4 PB; 2 SB) $75-125
Full Breakfast
Credit Cards: A, B
Notes: 2, 7, 9, 12, 15

GREENBANK

Guest House Log Cottages

24371 State Route 525, 98253
(360) 678-3115; e-mail: guesthse@whidbey.net
www.whidbey.net/logcottages

A couple's romantic retreat, this AAA four-diamond-rated bed and breakfast hideaway

Guest House Log Cottages

NOTES: Credit cards accepted: A MasterCard; B Visa; C American Express; D Discover; E Diner's Club; F Other; 2 Personal checks accepted; 3 Lunch available; 4 Dinner available; 5 Open all year; 6 Pets welcome;

offers five storybook cottages and one log mansion in cozy settings on 25 acres. Fireplaces, VCRs, more than 400 complimentary movies, in-room Jacuzzis, kitchens, country antiques, and wildlife pond. Continental plus breakfast. Pool and spa. Privacy, peace, and pampering. Near winery. Special midweek rates October 31 through March 15. Minimum-stay requirements for weekends and holidays.

Hosts: Don and Mary Jane Creger
Rooms: 6 (PB) $125-285
Full and Continental Breakfast
Credit Cards: A, B, C, D
Notes: 2, 5, 7, 9, 10, 11, 12, 14

HOQUIAM

Pacific Bed and Breakfast Agency

P.O. Box 46894, Seattle, 98146
(206) 439-7677; FAX (206) 431-0932
e-mail: pacificb@nwlink.com
www.seattlebedandbreakfast.com

109. Elegant Inn. Much more than an elegant inn, it is a gallery, museum, and workshop where furniture, collectibles, and antiques can be purchased. Each room at the inn is uniquely furnished with queen-size beds and a choice of shared or private bath accommodations. Freshly brewed coffee starts the day and a full buffet breakfast awaits guests in the dining room. $75-140.

ILWACO

Kola House Bed and Breakfast

211 Pearl, P.O. Box 646, 98624
(360) 642-2819; e-mail: ljl@willapa.org

Walk to fishing, plenty of parking for boat trailers. View of Columbia River and Astoria. Suite has fireplace and sauna. Pool table in basement. Cabin with kitchen available. Quaint 1919 home. Quiet neighborhood. Rates available for groups and winter. Kitty on premises.

Host: Linda Luokkala
Rooms: 5 (PB) $65-75
Full Breakfast
Credit Cards: A, B
Notes: 2, 5, 7, 9, 10, 11, 12

KELSO

Longfellow House Bed and Breakfast Cottage

203 Williams Finney Road, 98626
(360) 423-4545; e-mail: lngfelhs@pacifier.com
www.pacifier.com/~lngfelhs

Longfellow House is the ideal private destination for that special occasion or business trip. A secluded cottage for two in a rural setting one mile east of I-5. The main floor is guests' alone. Enjoy the 1913 player piano and collection of works by and about Henry Wadsworth Longfellow. Sleep as long as you like. Wake to the smell of gourmet coffee and the breakfast guests selected being prepared. Off-street parking, telephone, modem jack, and business services. Visit Mount St. Helens, Pacific beaches, and Columbia Gorge.

Hosts: Richard and Sally Longfellow
Rooms: 1 (PB) $89
Full Breakfast
Credit Cards: None
Notes: 2, 5, 7, 10, 12

KIRKLAND

Pacific Bed and Breakfast Agency

P.O. Box 46894, Seattle, 98146
(206) 439-7677; FAX (206) 431-0932
e-mail: pacificb@nwlink.com
www.seattlebedandbreakfast.com

054. Historic Mansion. The mansion has eight wonderfully appointed bed and breakfast rooms, each with a queen-size bed and private bath. An inviting buffet breakfast is served in the dining room, complemented with candles and flowers. Each evening there are homemade goodies with beverages as the season suggests. Children over 12 welcome. $70-105

7 No smoking; 8 Children welcome; 9 Social drinking allowed; 10 Tennis nearby; 11 Swimming nearby; 12 Golf nearby; 13 Skiing nearby; 14 May be booked through a travel agent; 15 Handicapped accessible.

Shumway Mansion

Shumway Mansion

11410 99th Place Northeast, 98033
(425) 823-2303

Overlook Lake Washington from this award-winning 23-room mansion dating from 1909. Eight individually decorated guest rooms with private baths. Variety-filled breakfast. Complimentary use of athletic club. Short distance to all forms of shopping; 20 minutes to downtown Seattle. Water and snow recreation close at hand. Children over 12 welcome.

Hosts: Richard and Salli Harris
Rooms: 8 (PB) $70-105
Full Breakfast
Credit Cards: A, B, C
Notes: 2, 5, 7, 9, 10, 11, 12, 13, 14

LA CONNER

Benson Farmstead

1009 Avon-Allen Road, Bow, 98232
(206) 757-0578
www.bbhost.com/bensonbnb

The Benson Farmstead is a 1914 restored 17-room farmhouse with antiques, quilts, and a cozy decor. It is surrounded by flower gardens and farmland and is just off I-5 near La Conner, Burlington, Chuckanut Drive, and the tulip fields. Third-generation Skagit Valley farmers Jerry and Sharon are friendly hosts who

serve a full country breakfast every morning and dessert and coffee in the evening.

Hosts: Jerry and Sharon Benson
Rooms: 4 (PB) $75-85
Full Breakfast
Credit Cards: A, B
Notes: 2, 5, 7, 8, 9, 10, 11, 12, 13

Pacific Bed and Breakfast Agency

P.O. Box 46894, Seattle, 98146
(206) 439-7677; FAX (206) 431-0932
e-mail: pacificb@nwlink.com
www.seattlebedandbreakfast.com

128. Country Inn. A beautiful Victorian-style country inn at the entrance to La Conner with views over fields, meadows, and mountains offers guests 10 rooms, each with a private bath. Some rooms feature fireplace and view. Telephone and TV in each room. The honeymoon suite has a Jacuzzi. An outdoor hot tub invites guests to relax their cares away. Continental breakfast included. $69-155.

157. Samish Bay Guest Houses. On a bluff above Samish Bay are these two Cape Cod-style guest houses. Views of Samish Bay and the Canadian mountains. Individual rooms can be rented as well as an entire house. Decks, outdoor spa, breakfast in the morning. From $100.

185. Historic Bed and Breakfast. Relax in the serenity of country living at this turn-of-the-century farmhouse with sweeping views of the farmlands and Mount Baker. Relax in the hot tub on the back deck or gather in the parlor around the wood-burning ceramic fireplace. There are eight rooms to choose from with a variety of personal touches and either shared or private bath accommodations. Breakfasts are satisfying and wholesome served on the windowed front porch or in the dining room.

NOTES: Credit cards accepted: A MasterCard; B Visa; C American Express; D Discover; E Diner's Club; F Other; 2 Personal checks accepted; 3 Lunch available; 4 Dinner available; 5 Open all year; 6 Pets welcome;

The White Swan Guest House

The White Swan Guest House

15872 Moore Road, Mount Vernon, 98273
(360) 445-6805; www.cnw.com/~wswan

The White Swan is a "storybook" farm-house only six miles from the historic waterfront town of La Conner. Fine restaurants, great antiquing, and interesting shops are all available in Washington's favorite artist's community. Just an hour north of Seattle and 90 miles south of Vancouver. Separate honeymoon cottage available. Gardens seen in *Country Home* magazine. Two stars in *Northwest Best Places*. Children welcome in cottage.

Host: Peter Goldfarb
Rooms: 4 (1 PB; 3 SB) $65-85
Cottage: $125-150
Continental Breakfast
Credit Cards: A, B
Notes: 2, 5, 7, 12

LANGLEY

Dove House and Chauntecleer House

3557 & 5081 Saratoga Road, P.O. Box 659, 98260
(360) 221-5494; (800) 637-4436
FAX (360) 221-0397
e-mail: bunny@dovehouse.com
www.dovehouse.com

A short ferry ride from Seattle takes guests to Whidbey Island and these two fully furnished private cottages with fireplaces. The cottages are surrounded by six acres of ponds, meadows, and gardens. Chaunte-cleer House sits on a high bluff with panoramic views of Puget Sound and the Cascade Mountains. Handcrafted furniture and stained-glass windows adorn the little lodge, Dove House. Walk to the seaside village of Langley from both cottages.

Hosts: Bunny and Bob Meals
Rooms: 3 (PB) $175
Continental Breakfast
Credit Cards: A, B
Notes: 2, 5, 7, 9, 12, 14

Eagles Nest Inn

4680 Saratoga Road, 98260
(360) 221-5331; www.eaglesnestinn.com

The inn's rural setting on Whidbey Island offers a sweeping view of Saratoga Passage and Mount Baker. Casual elegance and natural splendor abound. Superbly appointed guest suites with private bath, TV/VCR, water-view decks. Beautiful common rooms, outdoor spa, library, bird watching, and acres of adjacent trails. Children over 12 welcome. Also private honeymoon waterfront cottage. Fireplace, Jacuzzi, fluffy feather bed. A romantic getaway for a very private affair. Couples only. Two-night minimum stay.

Hosts: Joanne and Jerry Lechner
Rooms: 4 (PB) $95-125
Cottage: $235
Full Breakfast
Credit Cards: A, B, D
Notes: 5, 7, 10, 11, 12, 14

Eagles Nest Inn

7 No smoking; 8 Children welcome; 9 Social drinking allowed; 10 Tennis nearby; 11 Swimming nearby; 12 Golf nearby; 13 Skiing nearby; 14 May be booked through a travel agent; 15 Handicapped accessible.

Island Tyme

Island Tyme Bed and Breakfast Inn

4940 South Bayview Road, 98260
(360) 221-5078; (800) 898-8963
e-mail: islandty@whidbey.com

Peaceful, elegant country Victorian on secluded estate. Five rooms, all with private baths, Jacuzzis, fireplaces, decks, gourmet breakfasts, beverage bars, homemade cookies. Friendly pygmy goats. Near Langley, a quaint village by the sea, a popular tourist attraction. Local art, antiques, fine dining, golf, beaches, parks, wineries, and microbrewery tours. AAA-rated three diamonds. Pets welcome in one room. Children five and older welcome. One room is handicapped accessible.

Hosts: Phil and Lyn Fauth
Rooms: 5 (PB) $95-140
Full Breakfast
Credit Cards: A, B, C, D
Notes: 2, 5, 7, 9, 11, 12, 14

Log Castle

4693 Saratoga Road, 98260
(360) 221-5483

On Whidbey Island, 30 miles north of Seattle. Log lodge on secluded beach. Big stone fireplace, turret bedrooms, panoramic views of Puget Sound and the Cascade Mountains. The lodge's breakfast is a legend. Watch for bald eagles and seals, herons

from the widow's walk. Two-night minimum stay required for holidays.

Owners: Representative Jack and Norma Metcalf
Innkeepers: Karen and Phil Holdsworth
Rooms: 4 (PB) $95-120
Full Breakfast
Credit Cards: A, B, D
Notes: 2, 5, 7, 10, 11, 12, 13, 14

LANGLEY (WHIDBEY ISLAND)

Heron Haven Bed and Breakfast

513 Anthes Avenue, 98260
(360) 221-9121; FAX (360) 221-7506
e-mail: sybil@whidbey.com

A 1930s Cape Cod cottage on beautiful Whidbey Island, 30 minutes north of Seattle, plus a short ferry ride. View of water and mountains. Enjoy beautiful antiques and luscious gardens. Full breakfast is served in dining room, on the deck, or under wisteria-covered arbor. Walk to everything in town—antique shops, restaurants, and performing arts center. Queen-size beds, private half-baths in rooms and shared shower, common area, TV, fireplace, spectacular views.

Host: Sybil Yates
Rooms: 2 (2 P1/2B; 2 SB) $90
Full Breakfast
Credit Cards: A, B
Notes: 2, 5, 7, 9, 12

Pacific Bed and Breakfast Agency

P.O. Box 46894, Seattle, 98146
(206) 439-7677; FAX (206) 431-0932
e-mail: pacificb@nwlink.com
www.seattlebedandbreakfast.com

129. New Victorian Style. The inn is newly built in the Victorian style and is wheelchair accessible. Five guest rooms are offered with either king- or queen-size beds and all have private baths; two have fireplaces and one has a Jacuzzi tub. Full breakfast. Children welcome. $85-140.

133. Modern Inn. Built into a bluff overlooking the sound, each of the 24 rooms has a 180-degree waterfront view. Each room features a wood-burning fireplace, refrigerator, coffee maker, and Jacuzzi tub facing both the fireplace and the water view. Continental breakfast is served. Rates start at $170.

161. Saratoga Modern View Inn. New inn in Langley, features 15 guest rooms each with a fireplace and views of Saratoga Passage or the Cascade Mountains. All private baths, oversize showers, breakfast, and afternoon tea with appetizers. Also available is a cabin suite with private deck, fireplace, kitchen, and antique tub. From $110.

LEAVENWORTH

Pacific Bed and Breakfast Agency

P.O. Box 46894, Seattle, 98146
(206) 439-7677; FAX (206) 431-0932
e-mail: pacificb@nwlink.com
www.seattlebedandbreakfast.com

140. Bavarian Inn. A perfect place for business or pleasure. Ample space, courteous staff, and restaurant on premises are features guests will enjoy as they come home from exploring the many recreational activities of this unique town. Exercise room, spa, and pool available. Continental breakfast. Seasonal rates.

141. European-style Country Inn. The brochure for this unique inn tells guests that they will find a bit of the Alps in the foothills of the Cascades, two minutes from the center of Leavenworth and a world away from daily cares. Settle into one of 10 comfortable, cozy rooms in the main house or stay in a snug chalet with kitchen. This location is perfect any time of the year with a special festival during the holidays. Full country breakfast. $65-160.

Run of the River Bed and Breakfast

9308 East Leavenworth Road, P.O. Box 285, 98826
(509) 548-7171; (800) 288-6491

Imagine the quintessential northwestern log bed and breakfast inn. Spacious rooms feature private baths and hand-hewn log beds. The suite has its own wood stove, jetted Jacuzzi surrounded by river rock, and a bird's-eye loft. View Icicle River, surrounding bird refuge, and the Cascade peaks, appropriately named the Enchantments. Take a spin on complimentary mountain bikes. A delicious hearty northwestern breakfast sets the day in motion! The inn is an ideal base for side trips to Winthrop, Lake Chelan, and Grand Coulee.

Hosts: Monty and Karen Turner
Rooms: 5 (PB) $100-155
Full Breakfast
Credit Cards: A, B, D
Notes: 2, 5, 7, 9, 10, 11, 12, 13, 14

LONG BEACH

Boreas Bed and Breakfast Inn

607 North Boulevard, P.O. Box 1344, 98631
(360) 642-8069; (888) 642-8069
e-mail: boreas@boreasinn.com
www.boreasinn.com

This 1920s beach house, remodeled in eclectic style, skillfully combines art and

Boreas

7 No smoking; 8 Children welcome; 9 Social drinking allowed; 10 Tennis nearby; 11 Swimming nearby; 12 Golf nearby; 13 Skiing nearby; 14 May be booked through a travel agent; 15 Handicapped accessible.

antiques with comfort and casualness. Romantic ocean-view bedrooms and spacious living rooms with stereo, musical instruments, and marble fireplace. A custom-designed cedar-and-glass gazebo houses a state-of-the-art spa facing the dunes. Delicious full breakfast is served. Walk or bike to the boardwalk, shopping, and restaurants. Ten minutes to lighthouses and beautiful state parks for hiking, kayaking, and the many other outdoor activities Washington has to offer.

Hosts: Susie Goldsmith and Bill Verner
Rooms: 5 (PB) $115-135
Full Breakfast
Credit Cards: A, B, C, D, E
Notes: 2, 5, 7, 9, 10, 11, 12, 14

LOPEZ ISLAND

Inn at Swifts Bay

Route 2, Box 3402, 98261
(360) 468-3636; FAX (360) 468-3637
e-mail: inn@swiftsbay.com
www.swiftsbay.com

Recognized nationally as one of the finest bed and breakfasts in the San Juan Islands, the Inn at Swifts Bay offers guests a choice of five rooms, three with private baths and fireplaces, all with white-goose down comforters to dive under, fresh flowers, books everywhere guests look, and an ambiance that is best described as "a weekend in the country!" Dine on gourmet breakfasts unparalleled among the islands, immerse in the hot tub, or perhaps enjoy the quiet reverence of a stroll along the many Lopez beaches. Above all, indulge in the romantic ambiance and quiet retreat that is the Inn at Swifts Bay.

Hosts: Rob Aney, Carol Ortner, and Margie Zener
Rooms: 5 (3 PB; 2 SB) $95-175
Full Breakfast
Credit Cards: A, B, C, D
Notes: 2, 5, 7, 9, 12, 14

MAPLE VALLEY

Maple Valley Bed and Breakfast

20020 Southeast 228th Street, 98038
(425) 432-1409; FAX (425) 413-1459

Welcome to this warm cedar home in the wooded Northwest. Spacious grounds, wildlife pond, and fine feathered friends. Experience the "Good Morning" rooster, hootenanny pancakes, "hot babies," and gracious family hospitality. Crest Airpark is just minutes away. Be special. Be a guest at Maple Valley. Extra person in room is an additional $15-25.

Hosts: Jayne and Clarke Hurlbut
Rooms: 2 (SB) $75
Full Breakfast
Credit Cards: None
Notes: 2, 3, 5, 7, 8, 9, 10, 11, 12, 13, 14

Maple Valley

MERCER ISLAND

Pacific Bed and Breakfast Agency

P.O. Box 46894, Seattle, 98146
(206) 439-7677; FAX (206) 431-0932
e-mail: pacificb@nwlink.com
www.seattlebedandbreakfast.com

048. Lakefront Cottage. This lovely two-bedroom cottage is just steps from Lake

Washington. The large private yard gives guests a relaxed and peaceful setting. The hostess provides a Continental breakfast each day and guests will have a full kitchen, bath, living room, and study, and TV and VCR. No smoking. No pets. Children welcome. $115-125.

049. View Home. This contemporary home has three different bed and breakfast spaces for the folks with different needs. The first is a garden-level two-room suite with private bath; the second has a private bath and is on the main floor. On the top floor guests can choose a one-bedroom apartment with private deck. Breakfast is a special occasion and is served in the dining room by the German hostess. No pets. No smoking. Inquire about accommodations for children. $65-80.

050. Tudor with a View. On Mercer Island with easy access to the I-90 bridge, guests can be in Seattle in about 10 minutes. Two rooms that share a bath are offered. Breakfast is served by the hostess. No smoking. No pets. Inquire about accommodations for children. $80-90.

051. Ivy Lane Bed and Breakfast. Totally furnished private suite with private parking and private entrance is at garden level for those folks who need to avoid steps. Very private with TV and telephone just one minute from I-90 and into Seattle in 10 minutes. Self-serve breakfast. No pets. No smoking. Inquire about accommodations for children. $75-95.

052. Lakeview Bed and Breakfast. This bed and breakfast, in a lovely neighborhood just minutes away from downtown Seattle, has four bedrooms with private or shared baths. Continental breakfast. No smoking. No pets. Inquire about accommodations for children. $60-90.

053. Modern View Home. This English hostess welcomes guests to her lovely home. There is one room with a private bath. This room has its own sitting area for guests' comfort. Full breakfast. No smoking, pets, or children. $60-90.

MOUNT RAINIER

Jasmers Bed and Breakfast and Cabins

30005 State Road 706 East, Ashford, 98304
(360) 569-2682
www.mashell.com/mrba/jasmers.html

A perfect balance of pampering and privacy! A love nest! Two rooms apart from the main house, private baths with showers for two, queen-size beds, refrigerator and microwave, TV/VCR, and one room with a fireplace. All of this on a gorgeous three-acre farm with a hot tub. The "cabin on Big Creek" has a complete kitchen, bath, two bedrooms, wood stove, deck with hot tub, and a picture perfect wooded setting on the creek. Come! See! Smell! Relax amid the splendors of nature! Children over 10 are welcome.

Hosts: Luke and Tanna Osterhaus
Rooms: 8 (PB) $75-125
Continental Breakfast
Credit Cards: A, B
Notes: 2, 5, 7, 13

OAK HARBOR (WHIDBEY ISLAND)

Pacific Bed and Breakfast Agency

P.O. Box 46894, Seattle, 98146
(206) 439-7677; FAX (206) 431-0932
e-mail: pacificb@nwlink.com
www.seattlebedandbreakfast.com

131. Oak Harbor. On the beach just steps away from the sand, this modern bed and breakfast will give guests a panoramic view

---

7 No smoking; 8 Children welcome; 9 Social drinking allowed; 10 Tennis nearby; 11 Swimming nearby; 12 Golf nearby; 13 Skiing nearby; 14 May be booked through a travel agent; 15 Handicapped accessible.

of Puget Sound and guests can sit in the hot tub on the deck on a warm summer's evening. Three rooms with private and shared baths. Full breakfast. $65-85.

OCEAN SHORES

Pacific Bed and Breakfast Agency

P.O. Box 46894, Seattle, 98146
(206) 439-7677; FAX (206) 431-0932
e-mail: pacificb@nwlink.com
www.seattlebedandbreakfast.com

107. On the Beach. The ocean is just outside the door and the view is spectacular. There are fireplaces in each room and Jacuzzi suites are available. Many amenities are offered to make guests' stay very personal and special with exercise room, indoor pool and spa, and color TV and VCR. Continental breakfast. $85-175.

108. Ocean View Elegance. In the national register. Much more than an elegant inn, it is a gallery, museum, and workshop where furniture, collectibles, and antiques can be purchased. Each room at the inn is uniquely furnished with a choice of shared or private bath accommodations. Freshly brewed coffee starts the day and a full buffet breakfast awaits guests in the dining room. $75-140.

OLYMPIA

Pacific Bed and Breakfast Agency

P.O. Box 46894, Seattle, 98146
(206) 439-7677; FAX (206) 431-0932
e-mail: pacificb@nwlink.com
www.seattlebedandbreakfast.com

061. Historic Mansion. Built in 1893, this stately Queen Anne/Eastlake mansion is an Olympia landmark, listed in both the city and state historical registers. Guests are

invited to relax with a hot or cold beverage in the drawing room or stroll among the inn's half-acre of gardens and orchard. Four rooms with private baths and a honeymoon suite with jetted tub. Full breakfast. $85-115.

Puget View Guesthouse

7924 61st Avenue Northeast, 98516
(360) 413-9474

Classic Puget Sound. This quaint waterfront guest cottage suite sleeps four and is on the shore of Puget Sound next to the hosts' log home. Gorgeous and expansive marine-mountain view is breathtaking. Breakfast is served privately in the cottage. Great for a special honeymoon or romantic retreat. Near Tolmie State Park, only five minutes off of I-5, just north of downtown Olympia.

Hosts: The Yunkers
Cottage: 1 (PB) $89
Continental Breakfast
Credit Cards: A, B
Notes: 2, 5, 6, 7, 8, 9, 11, 12, 14

Swantown Inn

1431 11th Avenue Southeast, 98501
(360) 753-9123

Built in 1893, this stately Queen Anne/Eastlake mansion in an Olympia landmark, listed in both the city and state historical registers. Guests are invited to relax with a hot or cold beverage in the drawing room, or stroll among the inn's half-acre of gardens and orchard. The inn is close to the state capital campus, farmers' market, downtown restaurants, and waterfront boardwalk. Further afield, the Olympic Peninsula, Mount St. Helens, Mount Rainier, and the cities of Seattle and Portland are all an easy day's trip. Children over 11 welcome.

Hosts: Ed and Lillian Peeples
Rooms: 4 (PB) $75-125
Full Breakfast

NOTES: Credit cards accepted: A MasterCard; B Visa; C American Express; D Discover; E Diner's Club; F Other; 2 Personal checks accepted; 3 Lunch available; 4 Dinner available; 5 Open all year; 6 Pets welcome;

Credit Cards: A, B
Notes: 2, 3, 4, 5, 7, 9, 14

ORCAS ISLAND

Pacific Bed and Breakfast Agency

P.O. Box 46894, Seattle, 98146
(206) 439-7677; FAX (206) 431-0932
e-mail: pacificb@nwlink.com
www.seattlebedandbreakfast.com

121. Log Inn. This modern log inn is on a hill with a view over Puget Sound looking to the west to give guests the bonus of lovely sunsets. Eight rooms all have private baths. A full restaurant is on the main floor for guests' convenience and a self-serve breakfast will be delivered to guests' room. Three cottages also available. $100.

122. Historic Waterfront Inn. On the water on Orcas Island, the inn looks as if it had been transplanted from the coast of Maine. A private beach, small pond, and flower gardens welcome guests to relax and forget the busy city. Ask about its colorful history beginning in 1888. Choose from 30 different rooms with private or shared baths or select a suite for a stay. Seasonal rates.

POINT ROBERTS

Maple Meadow Bed and Breakfast

101 Goodman Road, 98281
(360) 945-5536; FAX (360) 945-2855
e-mail: mplmedbb@whidbey.com
www.travel-wise.com/maple/index.html

Discover a geographical quirk: Point Roberts, five square miles of peninsula which guests can reach by land only through Canada or via water through Juan de Fuca. The 1910 farmhouse and Old Pump House cottage offer a romantic getaway one block from the tidal beaches of Boundary Bay.

Great crabbing, hiking, bike trails, and restaurants await guests. Enjoy the hearty breakfast with a view of the horses grazing under the landmark maple tree.

Rooms: 4 (2 PB; 2 SB) $65-140
Full Breakfast
Credit Cards: A, B
Notes: 2, 5, 9, 12

PORT ANGELES

Bavarian Inn Bed and Breakfast

1126 East 7th, 98362
(360) 457-4098

The Bavarian Inn is a delightful Bavarian chalet nestled in the foothills of the Olympic Peninsula Alps, with a panoramic view of the harbor and Victoria, British Columbia. Guests rooms have private baths, marvelously comfortable beds with down comforters. The hosts serve bountiful, delicious breakfasts and are cheerfully hospitable and sensitive to guests' needs and expectations. To assure guests' comfort and quietude, the hosts regretfully exclude children and pets. The inn is a nonsmoking facility.

Hosts: Gene and Joy Robinson
Rooms: 4 (PB) $85-145
Full Breakfast
Credit Cards: F
Notes: 2, 5, 7, 9, 10, 11, 12, 13

Domaine Madeleine

146 Wildflower Lane, 98362
(360) 457-4174; FAX (360) 457-3037
www.northolympic.com/dm

Four-star rating from Mobil Travel Guide. Secluded, elegant, five-acre waterfront estate with water and mountain views. Four rooms with Jacuzzis for two. All rooms have fireplaces. Monet garden replica. Lawn games; whale, eagle, and deer watching; golf and skiing nearby. Breakfast so good that the inn pays if guests have lunch before 2:00 P.M. Practice languages with the hostess. Take a nature walk with the botanist host.

7 No smoking; 8 Children welcome; 9 Social drinking allowed; 10 Tennis nearby; 11 Swimming nearby; 12 Golf nearby; 13 Skiing nearby; 14 May be booked through a travel agent; 15 Handicapped accessible.

Hosts: Madeleine and John Chambers
Rooms: 4 (PB) $135-175
Full Breakfast
Credit Cards: A, B, C, D
Notes: 2, 5, 7, 9, 10, 11, 12, 13, 14

Klahhane Inn

1203 East 7th Street, 98362-0012
(360) 417-0260; (888) 552-4263
FAX (360) 457-4269; e-mail: james@olypen.com
www.northolympic.com/klahhane

Better Homes and Gardens-featured, award-winning, contemporary dwelling. On a quiet dead-end street with ground-level rooms. King-size beds, private and shared baths. Full breakfast. Smoke free. Children five and over are welcome.

Hosts: Al and June James
Rooms: 4 (2 PB; 2 SB) $65-95
Full Breakfast
Credit Cards: A, B
Notes: 2, 5, 7, 10, 11, 12, 13, 14

Pacific Bed and Breakfast Agency

P.O. Box 46894, Seattle, 98146
(206) 439-7677; FAX (206) 431-0932
e-mail: pacificb@nwlink.com
www.seattlebedandbreakfast.com

104. Country Elegance. In the foothills two miles from Port Angeles overlooking the Strait of Juan de Fuca, this contemporary bed and breakfast has four rooms with private or shared baths, or if guests prefer, a cottage may be theirs for their stay on the peninsula. The largest suite has a water view, a private bath with double Jacuzzi tub, cable TV, exercise bike, and a telescope to watch the ships go by. $69-120.

105. Chalet-style Lodging. The inn is a delightful chalet nestled in the foothills of the Olympic Alps with a view of the harbor. The rooms will have a private bath and comfortable beds with down comforters. A bountiful breakfast is served or guests may ask for an early breakfast to be on the ferry the early sailing to Victoria. Cheerful hospitality. $80-95.

The SeaSuns Bed and Breakfast Inn

1006 South Lincoln Street, 98362
(360) 452-8248
www.northolympic.com/seasuns

Peaceful gardens with towering evergreens surround this elegant 1926 Dutch Colonial home with antique period furnishings, water and mountain views. Five minutes to Olympic National Park and a short walk to downtown and ferry dock. Pacific Northwest breakfast and pleasant memories are the specialty. AAA-approved. Mobil Travel Guide.

Hosts: Bob and Jan Harbick
Rooms: 5 (3 PB; 2 SB) $60-115
Full Breakfast
Credit Cards: A, B
Notes: 2, 3, 5, 7, 9, 10, 11, 12, 13, 14

Tudor Inn

1108 South Oak, 98362
(360) 452-3138

Between the mountains and the sea, this half-timbered Tudor home was built by an Englishman in 1910 and has been tastefully restored and furnished with European antiques and an English garden. Five rooms, all with private baths, one with fireplace and balcony. Two-night minimum stay required for weekends July through September and for holidays. Children over 12 welcome.

Host: Jane Glass
Rooms: 5 (PB) $75-125
Full Breakfast
Credit Cards: A, B, C, D
Notes: 2, 5, 7, 9, 10, 11, 12, 13

PORT TOWNSEND

Ann Starrett Mansion Bed and Breakfast Inn

744 Clay Street, 98368
(360) 385-3205; (888) 385-3205

Victorian mansion, circa 1889, epitomizes the heart and soul of this Victorian seaport community. Internationally renowned for its classical architecture, antiques, and excellent service and food. In a quiet residential area within walking distance to town, theater, restaurants, beach, and ferry. Tennis, swimming, golf, and skiing nearby. Jacuzzi and fireplace. Panoramic water and mountain views from most rooms. Won the National Trust for Historic Preservation American Home Award for bed and breakfast restoration in 1996. Full breakfast served. Fourteen-day cancellation policy.

The English Inn

Hosts: Edel and Bob Sokol
Rooms: 11 (PB) $80-225
Full Breakfast
Credit Cards: A, B, C, D
Notes: 2, 5, 7, 8, 9, 10, 11, 12, 13, 14, 15

Bishop Victorian Guest Suites

714 Washington, 98368
(360) 385-6122; (800) 824-4738

This Victorian hotel built in 1890 has been restored and is in the heart of downtown Port Townsend. The lower floor of the building is used as a storefront and a flight of steps leads to the main lobby. Thirteen suites are furnished with period pieces and offer private baths, sitting areas, full kitchens, and one or two bedrooms. Eight suites have fireplaces and two have soaking tubs. Off-street parking and athletic club facilities are available.

Rooms: 13 (PB) $79-150
Continental Breakfast
Credit Cards: A, B, C, D
Notes: 2, 5, 7, 8, 9, 10, 12, 14

The English Inn

718 F Street, 98368
(360) 385-5302; (800) 254-5302
FAX (360) 385-6562
e-mail: nancy@english-inn.com
www.english-inn.com

Built on a hill overlooking a valley with the Olympic range in the distance, the English Inn is an Italianate Victorian home built in 1885. Full, delectable four-course breakfast served in the formal dining room or in

guests' room. The large garden offers a gazebo to enjoy the sunsets and a hot tub where guests can relax. Fifty miles from Seattle, Port Townsend is a Victorian seaport providing visitors with quaint shops, fine restaurants, and cultural events. Weddings and corporate advances welcomed. Children over 14 welcome. Internet access in all rooms.

Host: Nancy Borino
Rooms: 5 (PB) $75-105
Full Breakfast
Credit Cards: A, B, C, D, E
Notes: 2, 5, 7, 9, 10, 11, 12, 14

The James House

1238 Washington Street, 98368
(360) 385-1238; (800) 385-1238
www.jameshouse.com

The first bed and breakfast in the Northwest, the James House is on the bluff overlooking this charming Victorian seaport town. With unobstructed views of Puget Sound, Mount Rainier, the Olympic and Cascade mountain ranges, the James House offers 12 rooms, including a cottage, master/bridal suite, and lovely two-bedroom suites. A full breakfast, afternoon sherry, homemade cookies, and lovely gardens are just a few of the amenities at this beautiful inn.

Host: Carol McGough
Rooms: 12 (10 PB; 2 SB) $75-175
Full Breakfast
Credit Cards: A, B, C
Notes: 2, 5, 7, 10, 12

7 No smoking; 8 Children welcome; 9 Social drinking allowed; 10 Tennis nearby; 11 Swimming nearby; 12 Golf nearby; 13 Skiing nearby; 14 May be booked through a travel agent; 15 Handicapped accessible.

Lizzie's Victorian

Lizzie's Victorian Bed and Breakfast

731 Pierce Street, 98368
(360) 385-4168; (800) 700-4168
e-mail: wickline@olympus.net

An 1888 Victorian mansion within walking distance of shops and restaurants. The inn is decorated in antiques and some original wallpaper. Parlors are comfortable retreats for reading or conversation. Gateway to the Olympic Mountains, San Juan Islands, and Victoria. Wonderful breakfasts! Children over 10 welcome.

Hosts: Bill and Patti Wickline
Rooms: 7 (PB) $70-135
Full Breakfast
Credit Cards: A, B, D
Notes: 2, 5, 7, 9

Manresa Castle

Seventh and Sheridan, P.O. Box 564, 98368
(360) 385-5750; (800) 732-1281

This historic landmark, listed in the National Register of Historic Places, now houses 40 Victorian-style guest rooms, an elegant dining room, and an Edwardian-style lounge set atop Castle Hill. Almost all rooms, including the dining room and lounge, have spectacular views of the town, harbor, marina, and/or Olympic Mountains. The guest rooms offer private baths, direct dial telephones, TVs, and Continental breakfast.

Hosts: Lena and Vernon Humber
Rooms: 40 (PB) $68-175
Continental Breakfast
Credit Cards: A, B, D
Notes: 2, 4, 5, 8, 9, 10, 11, 12, 14

Pacific Bed and Breakfast Agency

P.O. Box 46894, Seattle, 98146
(206) 439-7677; FAX (206) 431-0932
e-mail: pacificb@nwlink.com
www.seattlebedandbreakfast.com

096. 1876 Victorian. Experience elegant hospitality with an eclectic flair, sumptuous cuisine garnished by the live magic melodies of the classical concert harp. Five superbly appointed guest accommodations with private baths, down comforters, and feather beds. Enjoy luxurious ambiance accented by art and antiques. Full breakfast. $88-133.

097. Romantic Cabin. The perfect spot for a honeymoon, this 800-square-foot cabin with arched ceilings has two murals in the peaks depicting pristine views of Mount Rainier and the early days of Port Townsend. Lots of northwestern woods and tiles accent the floor-to-ceiling fireplace facing the king-size bed, jetted tub, full kitchen, TV/VCR, and washer/dryer. Breakfast is self-serve Continental with some food provided by the hostess. Inquire about special honeymoon package and weekly rates. $125.

098. Classic Seaport Inn. Experience the joy of awakening to a golden sunrise over the water as boats of all descriptions glide by on the bay. A gourmet breakfast plus a morning concert on the Steinway grand will give guests' day the best possible start. Eight rooms with private baths. $67-175.

099. 1892 Castle. This castle sits on a hill with commanding marine views. It features rooms with private baths and Victorian decor; lovely gardens. The landmark mansion is in the national register and was totally restored to former glory in 1973, yet the historic character was retained. Enjoy this splendid luxury while in Port Townsend. The honeymoon suite in the tower is a favorite for all romantics. Continental breakfast is served in the restaurant. $75-175.

100. Grand Dame. On the bluff overlooking mountains and Puget Sound, the lovingly restored grand mansion epitomizes the soul of historic Port Townsend. It is known for its classic Victorian architecture with a spiral staircase leading to a unique domed ceiling. Nine delightful rooms are individually decorated and offer private or shared baths. Rates are seasonal and a full breakfast is included.

101. Victorian Grandeur. Today, historic preservation has allowed visitors in this town a chance to relive a time when lumber tycoons and ship captains built their futures. This Italianate-Victorian inn was built in 1883 on a hill overlooking a broad farming valley and the Olympic Mountains. The five guest rooms have private baths. A cozy gazebo in the garden offers guests a quiet spot or they may prefer a few relaxed minutes in the hot tub. $85-115.

The Palace Hotel
1004 Water Street, 98368
(360) 385-0773; (800) 962-0741 (US only)

Awarded again this year as a Northwest Best Place to Stay, the Palace Hotel on Water Street is a beautifully restored Victorian hotel in the heart of Port Townsend's historic district. Close to galleries and shops, it offers convenient off-street parking and is within blocks of ferry and bus services. Accommodations range from superior rooms with fabulous views and beautiful baths, to family-style suites with equipped kitchens to the most economical Continental-style bedrooms. Any stay at the Palace includes a complimentary Continental breakfast. All rooms have cable TVs,

coffee, and tea. Two nonsmoking rooms are available, and children are welcome. Off-season discounts offered during the winter.

Rooms: 15 (12 PB; 3 SB) $65-129
Continental Breakfast
Credit Cards: A, B, C, D
Notes: 2, 4, 5, 6, 8, 9, 10, 11, 12, 14

Quimper Inn

Quimper Inn, Ltd.
1306 Franklin Street, 98368
(360) 385-1060; (800) 557-1060

This 1886 mansion in the historic uptown district offers lovely water and mountain views. Four comfortable bedrooms, plus a two-room suite with a sitting room and bath. Antique period furniture, lots of books, and two porches for relaxation. A short walk to historic downtown with its many shops and restaurants. A wonderful breakfast is served. Off-season rates October through May.

Hosts: Ron and Sue Ramage
Rooms: 5 (3 PB; 2 SB) $70-140
Full Breakfast
Credit Cards: A, B
Notes: 2, 5, 7, 9, 10, 11, 12

Ravenscroft Inn
533 Quincy Street, 98360
(800) 782-2691; FAX (360) 385-6724
e-mail: ravenscroft@olympus.net
www.ravenscroftinn.com

Imagine a delightful blend of old and new while offering the most modern amenities. Relax and enjoy a beautifully appointed, spacious guest room or suite with private

7 No smoking; 8 Children welcome; 9 Social drinking allowed; 10 Tennis nearby; 11 Swimming nearby; 12 Golf nearby; 13 Skiing nearby; 14 May be booked through a travel agent; 15 Handicapped accessible.

Ravenscroft Inn

bath. Choose from eight rooms, some with fireplaces, soaking tubs, and private access to the veranda where guests can enjoy views of the quaint Victorian seaport of Port Townsend, Admiralty Inlet, and the snow-clad Cascade Mountains. The inn is ideally positioned for exploring Olympic National Park and surrounding ocean beaches. Port Townsend offers many fine galleries, boutiques, restaurants, and cultural events.

Host: Leah Hammer
Rooms: 8 (PB) $67-175
Full Breakfast
Credit Cards: A, B, C, D
Notes: 2, 5, 7, 9, 10, 11, 12, 13

Swan Hotel

Water and Monroe Street, 98368
(360) 385-1718; (800) 776-1718
e-mail: swan@waypt.com
www.waypt.com/bishop

Enjoy views of the Olympic and Cascade Mountains and the sea from a one-bedroom suite with kitchen and TV. Charming garden cottages offer queen-size beds, minikitchenettes, and TVs. The penthouse has an expansive reception and dining area with four bedrooms, fully equipped kitchen, and a large Jacuzzi bath. Guests are welcome to a complimentary Continental breakfast at the Bishop Victorian.

Hosts: Joe and Cindy Finnie
Rooms: 9 (PB) $65-200
Continental Breakfast
Credit Cards: A, B, C
Notes: 2, 5, 7, 8, 9, 10, 11, 12, 14, 15

Water Street Hotel

635 Water Street, 98368
(360) 385-5467; (800) 735-9810
www.virtualwebdesign.com/hotel/home.htm

Built in 1889 and completely renovated in 1990, the Water Street Hotel is in a secluded waterfront community. It combines the Old World charm of historic downtown Port Townsend with a panoramic view of Puget Sound and the majestic Olympic Mountains. It's within walking distance of downtown shops, restaurants, and the Keystone ferry. A Continental breakfast is served across the street at the bakery. Only in-state personal checks accepted. Pets welcome at an additional charge. No smoking available.

Hosts: Mary Hewitt and Dawn Pfeiffer
Rooms: 16 (11 PB; 5 SB) $45-125
Continental Breakfast
Credit Cards: A, B, C, D
Notes: 5, 8, 10, 11, 12

POULSBO

Pacific Bed and Breakfast Agency

P.O. Box 46894, Seattle, 98146
(206) 439-7677; FAX (206) 431-0932
e-mail: pacificb@nwlink.com
www.seattlebedandbreakfast.com

114. Hospitality. This elegant bed and breakfast overlooks the picturesque Scandinavian town, the bay, and the marina. A variety of rooms are available with shared or private baths, and a combination of rooms can be arranged for a group of adults for a special occasion. Full breakfast. $59-140.

PUYALLUP

Tayberry Victorian Cottage

7406 80th Street East, 98371
(206) 848-4594

A charming Victorian with beautiful valley views. Guests are pampered with warm hospitality, delicious country breakfasts, queen-size beds, TV and VCR, private baths, and a hot tub from which to take in the enchanting view. Convenient to the Tacoma Dome, Emerald Downs, and three large shopping malls, and just minutes from Puyallup's antique shops and fair grounds. Beautifully decorated. Bed and Breakfast Association of Tacoma and Mount Rainier and Washington State Association of Bed and Breakfasts.

Hosts: Terry and Vicki Chissus
Rooms: 4 (3 PB) $65-85
Full Breakfast
Credit Cards: A, B, C
Notes: 2, 5, 7, 8, 9, 10, 12, 13, 14

REDMOND

Pacific Bed and Breakfast Agency

P.O. Box 46894, Seattle, 98146
(206) 439-7677; FAX (206) 431-0932
e-mail: pacificb@nwlink.com
www.seattlebedandbreakfast.com

055. Host Home. Welcome to a private woodland cottage. It is large, self-contained, and furnished with antiques and includes a private entrance, queen-size bed, private bath, TV, and telephone. The large deck and wooded picnic area will give guests privacy and breakfast will be brought to guests' suite. This is a smoke- and alcohol-free environment. No pets or children. $85.

RITZVILLE

The Portico Bed and Breakfast

502 South Adams, 99169
(509) 659-0800

The Portico Bed and Breakfast is in a lovely 1902 house in the National Register of Historic Places. Gleaming oak woodwork and turn-of-the-century wallpaper and lighting are part of the rich detail. The rooms are comfortable and well appointed—a discreet TV to catch guests up on the news. Rest on the porch, relax in the hot tub, enjoy the

The Portico

gardens. Easy access to I-90 and Highway 395. "Come refresh yourself—We're on your way!"

Rooms: 2 (PB) $59-74
Full Breakfast
Credit Cards: A, B, C, D
Notes: 2, 5, 7, 9, 10, 11, 12

SALKUM

The Shepherd's Inn

168 Autumn Heights Drive, 98582
(800) 985-2434

Experience warm hospitality in a quiet country setting between Mount St. Helens and Mount Rainier. The inn is nestled among the trees on 40 wooded acres. The 5,000-square-foot home features a wrap-around deck for star gazing and enjoying the sunsets over the Cowlitz Valley and the rolling hills beyond. Enjoy bird watching and deer grazing in the morning and evening. Relax with music in the private double Jacuzzi. Individual tables to dine privately or for large groups in the main dining room. Feast on a full breakfast featuring the inn speciality of wild huckleberry crêpes, and more. Take exit 68 from I-5, go 13 miles east on highway 12, turn right on Fischer Road and follow signs. WBBG. AAA three-diamond-rated. Children welcome by prior arrangement.

Hosts: Richard and Ellen Berdan
Rooms: 5 (3 PB; 2 SB) $65-80
Full Breakfast
Credit Cards: A, B, C, D
Notes: 2, 5, 7, 11, 13, 14

7 No smoking; 8 Children welcome; 9 Social drinking allowed; 10 Tennis nearby; 11 Swimming nearby; 12 Golf nearby; 13 Skiing nearby; 14 May be booked through a travel agent; 15 Handicapped accessible.

SEABECK

Willcox House

2390 Tekiu Road, Northwest, 98380
(360) 830-4492; (800) 725-9477
FAX (360) 820-0506; www.willcoxhouse.com

With spectacular views of Hood Canal and the Olympic Mountains, this waterfront country house inn is in a forest setting between Seattle and the Olympic peninsula. The 1930s mansion estate offers parklike grounds, private pier, rowboat, and an oyster-laden saltwater beach. Comfortable period pieces and antiques are featured in guest rooms, the great room, billiard room, pub, library, theater, and dining room. Included is afternoon wine and cheese social hour, and a full breakfast served at private tables in the view dining room. The inn is under two hours west of Seattle, and one and one-half hours from Seattle/Tacoma airport. Accolades given by *Country Inns* magazine. *Best Places to Stay in the Pacific Northwest, Best Places to Kiss in the Pacific Northwest.*

Hosts: Cecilia and Phillip Hughes
Rooms: 5 (PB) $115-175
Full Breakfast
Credit Cards: A, B, D
Notes: 2, 3, 4, 5, 7, 9, 11, 12, 14

SEATTLE

Bacon Mansion

959 Broadway East, 98102
(206) 329-1864; (800) 240-1864
FAX (206) 860-9025

This is one of Seattle's most gracious mansions, within two blocks of the Broadway shopping district. The Bacon Mansion is in the Harvard-Belmont historic district. Most of the rooms have their own private baths. There are a beautiful grand staircase and a turn-of-the-century library in the house; breakfast is served in the formal dining room.

Host: Daryl King
Rooms: 10 (8 PB; 2 SB) $74-144

Bacon Mansion

Continental Breakfast
Credit Cards: A, B, C, D
Notes: 2, 5, 7, 8, 9, 10, 15

Capitol Hill House

2215 East Prospect Street, 98112
(206) 322-1752; (888) 323-1752
FAX (206) 323-6252

Old World charm is the hallmark of this classic brick house built in 1923 on a tree-lined street in an exclusive residential neighborhood. Three guest rooms provide elegance unmatched by modern accommodations and are equipped with telephones and color TVs. Accommodations include daily maid service. Near Broadway, one of the more exciting and diverse shopping areas in the city. Within walking distance to the Seattle Asian Art Museum and University of Washington and 10 to 15 minutes from downtown Seattle, theaters, shopping, and the Washington State Convention and Trade Center.

Host: Mary A. Wolf
Rooms: 3 (1 PB; 2 SB) $55-75
Full Breakfast
Credit Cards: A, B, C
Notes: 2, 5, 7, 8, 9, 10, 11, 12, 13, 14

NOTES: Credit cards accepted: A MasterCard; B Visa; C American Express; D Discover; E Diner's Club; F Other; 2 Personal checks accepted; 3 Lunch available; 4 Dinner available; 5 Open all year; 6 Pets welcome;

Chambered Nautilus

Chambered Nautilus

5005 22nd Avenue Northeast, 98105
(206) 522-2536; (800) 545-8459
FAX (206) 528-0898
e-mail: chamberednautilus@msn.com

Enjoy the gracious ambiance of the classic
Chambered Nautilus inn, an elegant 1915
Georgian Colonial perched on a peaceful
hill in the university district overlooking the
Cascade Mountains. Ten minutes from
downtown attractions and a short walk to
University of Washington. Relax by the
living room fireplace or in the large guest
rooms. Sip afternoon tea on the sun porches.
Sumptuous full breakfast features house
specialties, such as stuffed French toast or
northwestern breakfast pie.

Hosts: Joyce Schulte and Steven Poole
Rooms: 6 (PB) $89-119
Full Breakfast
Credit Cards: A, B, C
Notes: 2, 5, 7, 9, 10, 11, 12

Chelsea Station on the Park Bed and Breakfast Inn

4915 Linden Avenue North, 98103
(206) 547-6077; (800) 400-6077
FAX (206) 632-5107; e-mail: jsg@nwlink.com
www.bandbseattle.com

Refresh your spirit! Feel the welcome of
the warm and comfortable mood in one of
Seattle's finest neighborhood inns. Built in
1929, Chelsea Station offers unique rooms
including large suites with mountain views.

Relax in Mission-style furniture and enjoy
antiques throughout. Stroll to Woodland
Park, the zoo, the rose garden, and wonderful restaurants. Ten minutes to the heart of
downtown and city activities. Sumptuous
breakfasts, a bottomless cookie jar, and
smoke-free comfort. Guests will want to
return. Children over 12 welcome.

Hosts: John Griffin and Karen Carbonneau
Rooms: 9 (PB) $75-135
Full Breakfast
Credit Cards: A, B, D, E
Notes: 2, 5, 7, 9, 10, 11, 12

Chelsea Station on the Park

Gaslight Inn

1727 15th Avenue, 98122
(206) 325-3654; FAX (206) 328-4803

This beautifully restored turn-of-the-century
home is on Capitol Hill in downtown Seattle.
Oak paneling, fireplaces, decks, and a heated
in-ground pool make the Gaslight a very
special place for the guests, whether they are
visiting for pleasure or business. Guests may
choose among nine rooms and seven suites.

Gaslight Inn

7 No smoking; 8 Children welcome; 9 Social drinking allowed; 10 Tennis nearby; 11 Swimming nearby;
12 Golf nearby; 13 Skiing nearby; 14 May be booked through a travel agent; 15 Handicapped accessible.

Hosts: Steve Bennett and Trevor Logan
Rooms: 16 (11 PB; 3 SB) $68-148
Continental Breakfast
Credit Cards: A, B, C
Notes: 2, 5, 7

Green Gables Guesthouse

Green Gables Guesthouse

1503 Second Avenue West, 98119
(206) 282-6863; FAX (206) 286-8525

A tranquil, in-city retreat on historic Queen
Anne Hill. Walk to many restaurants, shops,
the Space Needle, and performing arts. Built
in 1904, this home is filled with antiques,
costumes, and family heirlooms. Spectacular
box-beam ceilings and leaded-glass windows make for a truly vintage setting. A private garden leads to a 1906 Sears, Roebuck
kit house, offering longer stays. Guests are
served generous family-style breakfasts. Private telephones, fax, and TVs.

Hosts: David and Lila Chapman; Reonn Rabon
Rooms: 8 (3 PB; 2 SB) $79-139
Houses: 2 @ 8 (4 PB; 4 SB)
Full Breakfast
Credit Cards: A, B, C, D
Notes: 2, 5, 7, 8, 9, 11

Hill House Bed and Breakfast

1113 East John Street, 98102
(206) 720-7161; (800) 720-7161
FAX (206) 323-0772
e-mail: hillhouse@foxinternet.net

This 1903 Victorian is just minutes from
downtown Seattle. Featuring superb gourmet
breakfasts served on china and crystal and
seven rooms, tastefully appointed with

antiques. All rooms have queen-size beds
with down comforters, crisp cotton sheets,
and plenty of pillows. Walk to numerous
shops and restaurants just blocks away.
Three-fourths mile from downtown attractions, the convention center, and Pike Place
Market. Close to transportation, off-street
parking. AAA-rated three diamonds, *Best
Places to Kiss in the Northwest*, Seattle Bed
and Breakfast Association.

Hosts: Herman and Alea Foster
Rooms: 7 (5 PB; 2 SB) $75-135
Full Breakfast
Credit Cards: A, B, C, D, E
Notes: 4, 5, 7, 10, 12

Mildred's Bed and Breakfast

1202 15th Avenue East, 98112
(206) 325-6072

A traditional 1890 Victorian gem in an elegant style. Old-fashioned hospitality awaits.
Red carpets, lace curtains, fireplace, grand
piano, and wraparound porch. Across the
street is the Seattle Asian Art Museum,
flower conservatory, and historic 44-acre
Volunteer Park. Electric trolley at the front
door. Minutes to city center, freeways, and
all points of interest.

Hosts: Mildred Sarver and Melodee Sarver
Rooms: 3 (PB) $85-120
Full Breakfast
Credit Cards: A, B, C
Notes: 2, 5, 7, 8, 9, 10, 11, 12, 14

Mildred's

NOTES: Credit cards accepted: A MasterCard; B Visa; C American Express; D Discover; E Diner's Club;
F Other; 2 Personal checks accepted; 3 Lunch available; 4 Dinner available; 5 Open all year; 6 Pets welcome;

Pacific Bed and Breakfast Agency

P.O. Box 46894, 98146
(206) 439-7677; FAX (206) 431-0932
e-mail: pacificb@nwlink.com
www.seattlebedandbreakfast.com

001. New Elegant Bed and Breakfast. Recently opened, Seattle's newest downtown luxury bed and breakfast featuring rooms with fireplaces, Jacuzzi tubs, turndown service, afternoon tea and hors d'oeuvres, and full country breakfasts. It also offers exercise facilities, lap pool, 24-hour front desk, and morning newspapers. One block to the waterfront shops and restaurants and three blocks to Pike Place Market. $150-200.

002. New View Bed and Breakfast. Just opened! Five blocks north of the Pike Place Market and three blocks east of the Victoria Clipper Terminal. This location features 20 rooms, some with views of Elliott Bay or the Space Needle, all with private baths, some kitchen units, TV, telephones. Continental plus breakfast served. $100.

005. 1920s Hotel. Conveniently close to everything downtown, this hotel was completely renovated a few years ago but retains the original tiled bathrooms of the 1920s. Double, twin, or queen-size beds, private baths, TVs, telephones, and Continental breakfast. Smoking permitted in designated areas only. No pets. Children welcome. $64-94.

007. Cruising. Enjoy the life of the rich and famous aboard a 56-foot Chris Craft motor yacht. Guests will leave Seattle on Friday night, spend the night in Port Orchard. Saturday, cruise to the Scandinavian village of Poulsbo. Return to Seattle on Sunday afternoon. Breakfast and lunch aboard the boat are included in the price. Two private staterooms, huge salon with queen-size sleeper-sofa. The yacht is fully equipped. Well-behaved children are welcome. Some holiday weekends not available; moorage and docking fees are extra (approximately $18 per night). No smoking or pets. $600.

008. Room with a View. Enjoy the view of Puget Sound from private deck while having a Continental breakfast. The large guest room has a private bath, TV, and telephone. Small refrigerator for guests' convenience. $65.

009. Romantic Apartment with a View. Small unit in a triplex that has a great view looking over Elliott Bay to the southwest, ferry traffic, Vashon Island, Blake Island, Duwamish Head, and the tip of Bainbridge Island. Beautifully decorated studio apartment, full kitchen, private entrance, TV, telephone, and balcony. Hostess provides food for self-serve breakfast. Bus is at the front door and two and one-half miles to downtown. $90.

011. Historic 1904 Mansion. Laura Ashley prints and original artwork greet guests at this stunning bed and breakfast on Queen Anne Hill about five minutes' drive from downtown Seattle. Four bedrooms and one suite have either a private or shared bath. This home has been featured in many publications around the U.S. and is one that is unique. Full breakfast. Smoking permitted outside only. Inquire about accommodations for pets. Children welcome. $59-105.

017. Heritage Home. Directly across from Volunteer Park and the Seattle Asian Art Museum is this delightful Seattle heritage home that has been lovingly restored; leaded windows, French doors, a blend of antiques and contemporary furnishings. Main guest room has a private bath, TV, and telephone. Another bedroom is available that would share the bath with the

---

7 No smoking; 8 Children welcome; 9 Social drinking allowed; 10 Tennis nearby; 11 Swimming nearby; 12 Golf nearby; 13 Skiing nearby; 14 May be booked through a travel agent; 15 Handicapped accessible.

Pacific Bed and Breakfast Agency (continued)

main room. Afternoon tea, freshly baked cookies, cakes, or finger sandwiches. Full gourmet breakfast delivered to guests' door, in the dining room, or on the garden patio. No smoking; there are a resident cat and dog. $60-115.

019. Turn of the Century Home. Built in 1903 and in the Capitol Hill area of the city, this host home has three rooms with double beds which share one bath. The front room spans the entire front of the house and is very sunny and light. The two smaller rooms overlook the garden and one has its own sink for guests' convenience. Continental breakfast served. Two-night minimum stay. Smoking permitted outside. No pets or children. $55-68.

020. Mary's Retreat. Furnished with elegant antiques and copies of Old Master paintings, this host home offers three rooms with private or shared baths, TVs, telephones. About two miles from downtown. Continental plus breakfast. Smoking permitted outside. No pets. Children welcome. From $55.

021. Victorian Charm. A true Victorian, built in 1890, with stained-glass windows, fine period furniture, original woodwork, and an ambiance that is unequaled. All the little touches that make that special bed and breakfast experience for guests happen here. The breakfasts are legendary. Come and experience this personally. Three rooms with private baths. No smoking, pets, or children. $115.

023. Beacon Hill-View. Two miles south of downtown on Beacon Hill with Spanish decor and serving either American or Spanish-style breakfasts. Five rooms with private baths. Views out over the Kingdome, Elliott Bay, and the Olympic Mountains from the two west rooms and from the dining room. Inquire about accommodations for children. No pets. Smoking permitted outside only. $60-95.

024. Seward Park. With a view of Lake Washington, this suite has two bedrooms and can accommodate a family. The kitchenette is small but convenient for making snacks and lunches. The hostess offers a self-serve breakfast in the refrigerator. No smoking, pets, or children. $50-55.

025. Lake Washington View Home. A contemporary host home with a spectacular view from the exclusive guest room is one's accommodation in this south Seattle location. A large room with a king-size bed and four-piece private bath will wrap guests in luxury and give guests the privacy they want for that special day in Seattle. Full breakfast is served. No smoking, pets, or children. $90.

026. Park View. Up on a hill, this room with a view shows guests the Seattle skyline and sunsets over the Olympic Mountains. The suite has private bath, TV, private entrance, and private parking. Pick-up from the train or plane for an additional $7. Full breakfast. No pets. Children welcome. $49.

027. Betty's Place. This 1930s brick home is on a quiet cul-de-sac in the Magnolia area of the city. The upstairs room has an in-room TV and a private bath with a large shower. Breakfast is served in the dining room. Two-night minimum stay. No smoking or pets. Children welcome. $65.

028. Discovery Park Bed and Breakfast. Northwest of downtown Seattle, in a woodsy setting by a stream frequently visited by local wildlife, is this Tudor-style bed and breakfast featuring the master suite with king-size bed, fireplace, French doors opening to the balcony with a view of the forest and Puget Sound, private bath, dressing room, TV, telephone, and full gourmet breakfast. Also four other rooms with private or shared bath. Smoking permitted outside. No pets or children. $60-100.

029. Bed and Breakfast. On a quiet neighborhood street, this lovely Tudor host home offers six rooms, four with shared baths and two with full private bath. This home is perfect for a visiting family and does welcome children. Smoking permitted outside only. No pets. Full breakfast. $55-65.

030. Private Guest Suite. In the Ballard neighborhood, this garden-level suite features a living room, full kitchen, separate bedroom with queen-size bed and three-quarter bath, TV, and telephone. Some staple foods are provided for guests' convenience. Two-night minimum stay required. $65.

031. Crown Hill Suite. This host home offers guests a private suite with private entrance, queen-size bed, private bath, TV, telephone, and a self-serve breakfast. Two-night minimum stay. No smoking, pets, or children. $75.

033. Cottage. West of the university and north of Lake Union is this stand-alone cottage beside the main house. On a quiet residential street within two blocks of the bus line. Features private bath, full kitchen, TV, telephone, and even a piano. Hostess provides food so that guests can make their own breakfast. Smoking permitted outside only. No pets. Children welcome. Two-night minimum stay. $65.

034. Mr. Monroe's 85th Street Guest House. For family or business groups nothing compares to the comfort and convenience of a fully equipped house with separate bedrooms, full kitchen, full bath, and staple foods for breakfast. This house has the capability of expanding to accommodate up to 16 persons with extra bedrooms and other half-bath. Children welcome and there is a crib available. Two color TVs, two VCRs, movies for everyone, toys for the children, and other pleasant surprises to make a stay here enjoyable. Fifteen dollars for each additional person. $95.

036. Luxury Suite. The four-room guest suite has a vaulted ceiling bedroom with a four-poster queen-size bed, private bath, kitchenette, and sitting room. Relax in the private sauna and enjoy the partially enclosed sunrise deck with outdoor shower. TV/VCR and library with books-on-tape are there for guests to enjoy. Continental breakfast. Smoking permitted outside only. No pets or children. $85-125.

037. Country Comfort with City Convenience. This contemporary home has three rooms. One room has a private bath and the other two share a bath. Breakfast is served homestyle or Continental with emphasis on dietary preferences. Extra meals, business center, or pet accommodations need to be arranged in advance. $60-75.

038. Bed and Breakfast. Contemporary northwestern home on a wooded greenbelt area north of the university campus. Gracious hostess who will make guests' stay a delight. Two-night minimum. Full breakfast. No smoking, pets, or children. $75-85.

039. Country Cottage. Charming English country cottage bed and breakfast near the Vashon Island ferry terminal. One of the nicest rooms in Seattle is the Victorian Suite. The suite includes the library/sitting room with a day bed and a trundle bed,

7 No smoking; 8 Children welcome; 9 Social drinking allowed; 10 Tennis nearby; 11 Swimming nearby; 12 Golf nearby; 13 Skiing nearby; 14 May be booked through a travel agent; 15 Handicapped accessible.

coffee service for early morning, master bedroom with king-size bed, cable TV, telephone, and the private bath with claw-foot tub. A full gourmet breakfast served. No smoking or pets. Children over 13 welcome. $55-95.

040. Alki Beach. If guests like to walk, jog, play at the beach, enjoy sunrises or sunsets, and spectacular views of the sound and downtown the Alki Beach area will fit their needs. This apartment is one-half block from the beach. Fully equipped and furnished two bedroom unit, full kitchen, TV, telephone, and food provided for self-serve breakfast. Three-day minimum. Ten dollars for each additional person. Weekly rates available. $100.

041. Beach Drive. On Beach Drive in west Seattle, one-half mile from Lincoln Park, is a small bed and breakfast with views of the sound, mountains, and ship traffic. One room features a queen-size bed, a ship's bunk bed/window seat, four-head European shower, TV, telephone. Two-night minimum stay. Full breakfast. No smoking or pets. Inquire about accommodations for children. $85.

043. Ultimate Luxury Suite. Beautiful suite featuring open-canopied bed, fireplace, large marbled Jacuzzi, double shower, bidet, terry-cloth robes, TV/VCR, sitting room with hand-painted ceiling, separate office, French doors opening to the balcony, views of the Olympic Mountains and Puget Sound, waterfront on a bluff with wooded trail leading to the beach. Full gourmet breakfast served. Smoking permitted outside only. Please, no pets or children. $180-195.

137. Rooms with a View. Sitting on the west side of Queen Anne Hill are two condominium units where the owners have converted the first floors into guest rooms, one with a kitchen. Food is provided at both so that guests can make their own breakfast. About two and one-half miles north of the Pike Place Market. No pets or children. $75.

Pioneer Square Hotel

77 Yesler Way, 98104
(206) 340-1234; FAX (206) 467-0707
e-mail: info@pioneersquare.com
www.pioneersquare.com

Seventy-five beautifully appointed rooms and suites with private tiled bathrooms with brass fixtures, individual room climate controls, and color cable remote control TVs. Computer data port, guest room telephones. Board room meeting facility. Tratoria Michelli and al Bocalino restaurants adjacent to hotel. The Pioneer Square Saloon and Juice and Java coffee bar within the hotel building. Walk to the ferry terminal, Pike Place Market, the Kingdome, Amtrak station, and historic Pioneer Square's shopping, restaurants, nightlife, and tourist attractions.

Rooms: 75 (PB) $99-209
Continental Breakfast
Credit Cards: A, B, C, D, E, F
Notes: 3, 4, 5, 7, 8, 9, 10, 11, 12, 13, 14, 15

Prince of Wales Bed and Breakfast

133 13th Avenue East, 98102
(206) 325-9692; (800) 327-9692
FAX (206) 322-6402
e-mail: addicott2@earthlink.net

Convenient to the business and convention traveler. Within walking distance of or a short bus ride to downtown Seattle and the Washington State Convention and Trade Center. A charming turn-of-the-century bed and breakfast on scenic Capitol Hill. Rooms include a romantic attic hideaway with private deck and panoramic view of the city skyline, Puget Sound, and Olympic Mountains. Restaurants and shops are

NOTES: Credit cards accepted: A MasterCard; B Visa; C American Express; D Discover; E Diner's Club; F Other; 2 Personal checks accepted; 3 Lunch available; 4 Dinner available; 5 Open all year; 6 Pets welcome;

Prince of Wales

nearby. Healthful breakfasts! Rates vary with seasons.

Host: Faith Addicott
Rooms: 4 (PB) $90-125
Full Breakfast
Credit Cards: A, B, D
Notes: 2, 5, 7, 8, 9, 10, 11, 12

Salisbury House

750 16th Avenue East, 98112
(206) 328-8682; www.salisburyhouse.com

An elegant turn-of-the-century home on Capitol Hill, just minutes from Seattle's cultural and business activities. Gracious guest rooms with private baths. A well-stocked library and wraparound porch

Salisbury House

invite relaxation. In a historic neighborhood with parks, shops, and restaurants. Two friendly cats in residence. Recommended by Frommer's and Fodor's. Mobil-rated three stars. A suite is also available.

Hosts: Mary and Cathryn Wiese
Rooms: 4 (PB) $75-140
Full Breakfast
Credit Cards: A, B, C
Notes: 2, 5, 7, 10, 11, 12, 13

Three Tree Point Bed and Breakfast

17026 33rd Avenue Southwest, 98166
(206) 669-7646; (888) 369-7696
e-mail: whisler@publiconline.com
www.3treepointbnb.com

A private suite with spectacular views of Puget Sound and Mount Rainier. Enjoy beach walks, ship watching, quiet neighborhood, and membership at local health club. Breakfast in guests' room. Private patio. Minutes from Sea-Tac. Come and enjoy a unique Seattle experience with hosts, Penny, Doug, Braly, and Brita Whisler.

Hosts: Penny and Doug Whisler
Rooms: 1 (PB) $110-125
Full Breakfast
Credit Cards: A, B, C
Notes: 2, 5, 7, 8, 9, 10, 11

SEAVIEW

The Shelburne Inn

P.O. Box 250, 98644-0250
(360) 642-2442; FAX (360) 642-8904

The Shelburne Inn, established in 1896, is a true American classic. It has offered travelers warm hospitality, wonderful food, and comfortable shelter for more than a century. A relaxing retreat for city dwellers, a sublime sanctuary for nature lovers, this country inn houses 15 thoughtfully appointed, antique-filled guest rooms, all with private bath, and most with a private deck.

Hosts: David Campiche and Laurie Anderson
Rooms: 15 (PB) $105-200

7 No smoking; 8 Children welcome; 9 Social drinking allowed; 10 Tennis nearby; 11 Swimming nearby; 12 Golf nearby; 13 Skiing nearby; 14 May be booked through a travel agent; 15 Handicapped accessible.

The Shelburne Inn

Full Breakfast
Credit Cards: A, B, C
Notes: 2, 3, 4, 5, 7, 8, 10, 12, 14, 15

SEQUIM

Glenna's Cuthrie Cottage Bed and Breakfast— Antique and Gift Shop

10083 Old Olympic Highway, 98382
(360) 681-4349; (800) 930-4349

Historic farm house viewing the snow-capped Olympic Mountains and the Olympic National Park. Hosts invite guests to come and visit them while exploring the area. Suites with private baths and private outside entrance, cable TV, and RV and boat parking. Enjoy the friendly service, hot tub under the stars, gourmet breakfast. Cooking classes, fax, and bikes available. With the mild winters, golf and other sports are enjoyed year-round. Great shopping and colorful attractions nearby.

Rooms: 4 (PB) $60-95
Full Breakfast
Credit Cards: A, B, C, D
Notes: 5, 7, 8, 9, 10, 11, 12, 13, 14, 15

Greywolf Inn

395 Keeler Road, 98382
(360) 683-5889; (800) 914-WOLF
FAX (360) 683-1487; e-mail: grywolf@olypen.com
www.northolympic.com/greywolf

Greywolf Inn, a five-acre country estate, is the ideal starting point for light adventure on the Olympic Peninsula. Enjoy nearby bird watching, boating, or golfing, or head for the woods. Choices include Olympic National Park, Hurricane Ridge, Hoh Rain Forest, and Sequim's own Dungeness Spit and Wildlife Refuge. A steaming hot tub, a good night's sleep, and plenty of pampering are waiting for guests at Greywolf Inn. Join the hosts for fine food and good cheer at their splendid little inn. Picnic lunch available. Children over 12 welcome.

Hosts: Peggy and Bill Melang
Rooms: 5 (PB) $65-125
Full Breakfast
Credit Cards: A, B, C, D
Notes: 2, 5, 7, 9, 10, 11, 12, 13, 14

Greywolf Inn

Pacific Bed and Breakfast Agency

P.O. Box 46894, Seattle, 98146
(206) 439-7677; FAX (206) 431-0932
e-mail: pacificb@nwlink.com
www.seattlebedandbreakfast.com

102. A 100-Year-Old Victorian. Sequim is called "the Banana Belt" of the Northwest, known for its good weather, protected by the Olympic Mountains. The inn was built at the turn of the century and the original decor remains. The five guest rooms have queen- or king-size beds and offer private or shared bath accommodations. Most rooms have TV/VCRs. Breakfast is served in the dining room. $85-110.

NOTES: Credit cards accepted: A MasterCard; B Visa; C American Express; D Discover; E Diner's Club; F Other; 2 Personal checks accepted; 3 Lunch available; 4 Dinner available; 5 Open all year; 6 Pets welcome;

103. Craftsman-style. Set in the rural quiet north of Sequim, this bed and breakfast is tastefully decorated with English antiques in comfortable elegance. Three rooms have queen-size beds, lace curtains, and a peek-a-boo view of the Strait of Juan de Fuca. Breakfast is served at 8:30 A.M. and the menu is varied, with egg and sausage main dishes, fruit, breads, coffee, tea, and dessert. Hot beverages and snacks are offered in the evening. $85-95.

SHELTON

Twin River Ranch Bed and Breakfast

5730 Highway 3, 98584
(360) 426-1023

Rural 1918 manor house is on the Olympic Peninsula. Stone fireplace, antiques, and granny rooms tucked under the eaves overlooking the garden and stream. One hundred forty acres of pasture surrounded by old-growth trees. Puget Sound laps the marsh, and gulls, blue heron, and eagles circle overhead in season. By reservation only. No smoking upstairs.

Hosts: Phlorence and Ted Rhode
Rooms: 2 (SB) $59
Full Breakfast
Credit Cards: A, B
Notes: 2, 12

SOUTH BEND

The Russell House

902 East Water Street, P.O. Box F, 98586
(360) 875-6487; (888) 484-6907
e-mail: srown@willapabay.org

A Queen Anne Victorian bed and breakfast, built in 1891. Furnished and decorated elegantly with antiques. Enjoy a lavish breakfast served in the dining room. Birds and deer are plentiful. Lots of history in the town. John Russell is the architect of this beautiful building and several others in town. One hour from beach, one hour from shopping mall. No smoking inside.

Hosts: Sylvia and Steve Rowan
Rooms: 3 (PB) $60-75
Full Breakfast
Credit Cards: None
Notes: 2, 3, 4, 5, 6, 7, 8, 9, 12, 14

SOUTH CLE ELUM

The Moore House Bed and Breakfast Country Inn

526 Marie Avenue, P.O. Box 629, 98943
(509) 674-5939

Former 1909 Milwaukee Railroad crew hotel, now offering 12 bright and airy rooms ranging from economical to exquisite, including two genuine cabooses and a bridal suite with jetted tub. Now in the national historic register, the inn has a museum-like atmosphere with an extensive collection of railroad memorabilia and artifacts. Nestled in the Cascade Mountain foothills, the Moore House is close to cross-country skiing, hiking, biking, rafting, fishing, horseback riding, and also fine dining.

Hosts: Eric and Cindy Sherwood
Rooms: 12 (6 PB; 6 SB) $50-125
Full Breakfast
Credit Cards: A, B, C, D
Notes: 2, 5, 7, 8, 9, 12, 13, 14

SPOKANE

Angelica's Bed and Breakfast

West 1321 Ninth Avenue, 99204
(509) 624-5598; (800) 987-0053

Romantic 1907 Craftsman mansion. Listed in the local register of historical places. Elegant atmosphere. Peaceful setting. Queen-size beds. Down comforters. Luxurious linens. Private baths. Savor freshly ground gourmet coffee and assorted teas in

Angelica's

staircase. The recent award-winning restoration of the exterior and grounds returns this inn to its rightful place as one of the finest homes in historic Browne's Addition. Period furniture, wraparound porch, player piano, evening tea, and nearby antique shops will delight all guests. Museum and excellent restaurants are within walking distance.

Hosts: Jackie and Graham Johnson
Rooms: 4 (1 PB; 3 SB) $75-90
Full Breakfast
Credit Cards: A, B, C, D
Notes: 2, 5, 7, 9, 10, 12, 13, 14

the sunroom. Full breakfast served in the dining room or outside on the veranda. Continental breakfast served in privacy of room. Close to dining, shopping, museum, Spokane arena, Spokane Falls, Riverfront Park, golf, and biking trails.

Hosts: Lynette and Arielle White
Rooms: 4 (2 PB; 2 SB) $85-100
Full Breakfast
Credit Cards: A, B
Notes: 2, 5, 7, 12, 13, 14

The Fotheringham House

2128 West Second Avenue, 99204
(509) 838-1891; FAX (509) 838-1807
e-mail: fotheringham.bnb@ior.com
www.ior.com/fotheringham

This 1891 Victorian home of the city's first mayor features beautiful hand-carved woodwork, tin ceilings, and an open, curved

The Fotheringham House

Marianna Stoltz House

Marianna Stoltz House

East 427 Indiana, 99207
(509) 483-4316; (800) 978-6587
FAX (509) 483-6773

Established in 1987, the Marianna Stoltz House has earned a reputation for pampering its guests. This 1908 historic landmark is beautifully decorated. Private baths with a tub for two, air conditioning, cable TV, secure on-site parking, and a hearty breakfast each morning are just a few of the amenities that await guests. Minutes from I-90, downtown, Spokane Arena, Opera House, Convention Center, Centennial Trail, and Gonzaga University.

NOTES: Credit cards accepted: A MasterCard; B Visa; C American Express; D Discover; E Diner's Club; F Other; 2 Personal checks accepted; 3 Lunch available; 4 Dinner available; 5 Open all year; 6 Pets welcome;

Host: Phyllis Maguire
Rooms: 4 (2 PB; 2 SB) $65-85
Full Breakfast
Credit Cards: A, B, C, D
Notes: 2, 5, 7, 9, 10, 11, 12, 13, 14

SUMNER

Pacific Bed and Breakfast Agency

P.O. Box 46894, Seattle, 98146
(206) 439-7677; FAX (206) 431-0932
e-mail: pacificb@nwlink.com
www.seattlebedandbreakfast.com

066. Lake Tapps. The hostess suggests a variety of activities from water skis to swimming or fishing, all at the doorstep. There are four rooms to choose from with king- or queen-size beds and private baths with oversized double tubs, TVs, and private entrances. The view of Mount Rainier is an added bonus and the natural setting is special. Breakfast is served by the hostess. $99-250.

SUNNYSIDE

Sunnyside Inn Bed and Breakfast

800 East Edison Avenue, 98944
(509) 839-5557; (800) 221-4195

In the heart of Washington wine country with more than 20 wineries and 300 days of sunshine. Seven of the rooms have in-room double Jacuzzi tubs. All rooms have cable TVs, telephones, and private baths. A full country breakfast is served as well as popcorn, cookies, and ice cream for snacks. Come enjoy a stay that is a cut above the common experience.

Hosts: Karen and Donavon Vlieger
Rooms: 10 (PB) $50-90
Full Breakfast
Credit Cards: A, B, C, D
Notes: 2, 5, 7, 8, 9, 10, 11, 12, 14

TACOMA

Commencement Bay Bed and Breakfast

3312 North Union Avenue, 98407
(253) 752-8175; FAX (253) 759-4025
e-mail: greatviews@aol.com
www.bestinns.net/sa/wa/cb.html

From its elevated perch above the scenic waterfront, this stately Colonial home affords breathtaking views of  Mount Rainier, Puget Sound, and the Cascades. Three elegantly appointed guest rooms, all with private baths, TVs, VCRs, and telephones with data ports. A variety of common areas offer a fireplace, hot tub, game room, and office area for business travelers. Full breakfasts and gourmet coffees daily. Exercise room and bikes available. Ten minutes to state historical museum. Special rates for winter. AAA three-diamond-rated and Mobil-approved. Featured in *Northwest Best Places*, 11th edition. Children over 12 welcome.

Hosts: Bill and Sharon Kaufmann
Rooms: 3 (PB) $85-125
Full Breakfast
Credit Cards: A, B, C, D
Notes: 2, 5, 7, 9, 10, 11, 12, 14

A Greater Tacoma Bed and Breakfast Reservation Service

3312 North Union Avenue, 98407
(253) 759-4088; (800) 406-4088
FAX (253) 759-4025
e-mail: reservations@tacoma-inns.org
www.tacoma-inns.org

A. Olalla Orchard Bed and Breakfast. Savor quiet rural country charm in a modern home with mountain views. An orchard and pond beautify the grounds.

7 No smoking; 8 Children welcome; 9 Social drinking allowed; 10 Tennis nearby; 11 Swimming nearby; 12 Golf nearby; 13 Skiing nearby; 14 May be booked through a travel agent; 15 Handicapped accessible.

Suite with private bath and Jacuzzi tub. Full breakfast. $75-95.

B. Inn at Burley Lagoon. A spacious contemporary home on a scenic quiet bay in a rural setting with lots of privacy. Two rooms with private baths and living room. Kitchen, hot tub, sauna, and horse pasture available. Full breakfast. $100-120.

C. Harbor's Edge Bed and Breakfast. Watch the seagulls passing boats from the deck of this private cottage on Gig Harbor Bay. Full bath, kitchen, and living room with fireplace, TV/VCR. Boat moorage and kayak are available. Self-serve breakfast included. From $125.

D. Sunny Bay Cottage. Private and relaxing, this one-bedroom cottage overlooks Puget Sound and the Olympics. Bath with shower, sitting room with wood stove, TV/VCR, kitchen, outdoor hot tub. Self-serve breakfast included. $100-120.

E. Rosedale Bed and Breakfast. Guests are encouraged to make themselves at home in this large contemporary home. Enormous waterfront suite with fireplace, TV, VCR, and private bath. Second-floor room has private bath. Full breakfast. $75-95.

F. Beachside Bed and Breakfast. Relax on the beach of this waterfront English Tudor-style home with private entrance. A large suite with private full bath, fireplace, TV/VCR, kitchen, and hot tub. Self-serve breakfast included. $75-95.

G. Hideaway House. Nestled in the trees, this is a lovely contemporary home with comfortable country decor. Two guest rooms with private baths, Jacuzzi tub, TV/VCR. Golf, tennis, and marina nearby. Full breakfast. $50-70.

H. Burg's Landing. A real northwestern treat. This majestic waterfront log home overlooks Mount Rainier with lots of modern comforts, a hot tub, skylight, and deck. Four rooms with private or shared baths. Full breakfast. $100-120.

I. Foxglove Bed and Breakfast. Exquisite panoramic views of old town Stellacoom, Puget Sound, and the Olympics from every room. A suite with private bath, Jacuzzi tub, and private deck. Elevator available. A relaxing retreat. Full breakfast. From $100.

J. Sally's Bear Tree Cottage. A brass bed and crackling fireplace make this secluded private cottage in the woods warm and inviting. Private bath, small kitchen area with refrigerator and microwave. Golf nearby. Continental breakfast. $75-95

K. Oakes Street Barn Bed and Breakfast. This Dutch Colonial home offers country decor and great hospitality. Two bedrooms with private or shared baths, a large sitting area with TV/VCR, and an outdoor hot tub. Close to shopping. Full breakfast. $50-70.

L. Dove Cottage Bed and Breakfast. Walk to the beach from this one-bedroom cottage getaway. Private bath, full kitchen, living room with TV/VCR, fireplace, laundry room, and a white picket fence. Short walk to private beach. Self-serve breakfast included. $75-95.

M. Blue Willow Cottage. Enjoy country charm minutes from the university area or downtown. Main floor suite with private bath and private garden deck, or upstairs room with shared bath. Full breakfast. $75-95.

N. Plum Duff House Bed and Breakfast. A warm and charming 1901 house near down-

NOTES: Credit cards accepted: A MasterCard; B Visa; C American Express; D Discover; E Diner's Club; F Other; 2 Personal checks accepted; 3 Lunch available; 4 Dinner available; 5 Open all year; 6 Pets welcome;

town in the historic Stadium District. Three large rooms with private baths, TVs, and telephones. Afternoon tea, evening desserts, fax/modem available. Full breakfast. $75-120.

O. Commencement Bay Bed and Breakfast. This award-winning Colonial home features elegant decor, dramatic bay and mountain views, hot tub, fireplace, game and exercise rooms, three rooms, all with bay views, private baths, telephones, TVs, and VCRs. Business guest service. Full breakfast. $75-120.

P. Palisades Bed and Breakfast. An elegant European-style home with beautiful surroundings and a sumptuous breakfast. A very private view suite with canopied bed, fireplace, TV/VCR, and marbled Jacuzzi spa tub. Full breakfast. From $125.

Q. Angels of the Sea Bed and Breakfast. Guests will think they are in heaven in this historic 1917 country church bed and breakfast. Three rooms with private or shared baths, one with Jacuzzi tub. Live harp music during breakfast by the hostess. TV/VCR, golf, and pool available. Children welcome. Full breakfast. From $75.

R. Emerald Inn Bed and Breakfast. A large home on two lovely landscaped acres. Three rooms, one with fireplace and private entrance. Private baths, TV/VCR, and video library. Golf and racing nearby. Airport pickup available. Full breakfast. $50-120.

S. Rose Arbor Inn. Just minutes from downtown, this 1940s home offers warm hospitality and relaxation. Three rooms have private and shared baths and are decorated with antiques and lots of charm. On-site Swedish massage available by appointment. Full breakfast. $50-95.

T. Carousel Bed and Breakfast. A charming home offering two rooms with private baths, TV, telephone, and game/exercise rooms. Full breakfast. $75-95.

U. Tayberry Victorian Cottage Bed and Breakfast. Just minutes from both Puyallup and Tacoma, this graceful Victorian-style home overlooks a quiet farming valley. Three very charming rooms are decorated with antiques, TV/VCR, and lots of atmosphere. Private baths. Full breakfast. $50-95.

Keenan House

2610 North Warner, 98407
(206) 752-0702

Clean, comfortable, attractive rooms. Complimentary full breakfast. Seven blocks from University of Puget Sound. Ten minutes from Point Defiance Park. Five minutes from Commencement Bay with a fine selection of restaurants. Just off I-5 and near Highway 16.

Host: Lenore Keenan
Room: 4 (2 PB; 2 SB) $60-70
Full Breakfast
Credit Cards: A, B
Notes: 2, 5, 7, 8, 9, 10, 12, 14

Pacific Bed and Breakfast Agency

P.O. Box 46894, Seattle, 98146
(206) 439-7677; FAX (206) 431-0932
e-mail: pacificb@nwlink.com
www.seattlebedandbreakfast.com

057. Victorian Guest Houses. Ten minutes from Point Defiance Park and near the University of Puget Sound, on a tree-lined street, these two Victorian host homes offer a variety of rooms with shared or private baths. Decorated with comfortable country-style furnishings. Guests will find a relaxed atmosphere. Full breakfast. $45-65.

058. On the national registry. With echoes of the drama of the historical Pantages Theatre, the master suite of this true Victorian home

---

7 No smoking; 8 Children welcome; 9 Social drinking allowed; 10 Tennis nearby; 11 Swimming nearby; 12 Golf nearby; 13 Skiing nearby; 14 May be booked through a travel agent; 15 Handicapped accessible.

has views of the harbor from the bay window, queen-size bed, and private bath with Jacuzzi. The second suite also features a fireplace. The Garden Room has a queen-size bed and private bath with claw-foot tub. A two-story cottage is also available with two suites, each with private bath, queen-size bed, and a small kitchenette. $85-200.

059. Secluded Cottage. For that cozy, comfortable place of one's own for a getaway, consider this small cottage in a wooded setting. The cottage has a queen-size bed, private bath with sunken tub, kitchenette, and Swedish fireplace. Breakfast is self-serve. $75.

TOLEDO

Pacific Bed and Breakfast Agency

P.O. Box 46894, Seattle, 98146
(206) 439-7677; FAX (206) 431-0932
e-mail: pacificb@nwlink.com
www.seattlebedandbreakfast.com

112. The Farm. Nestled in the foothills of Mount St. Helens, this 80-acre farm is home to a herd of cashmere goats, livestock, guard dogs, horses, geese, ducks, and chickens. The farm borders Salmon Creek where guests can find arrowheads, agates, and copperlight. The host and hostess maintain this working farm and the chef prepares a memorable farm breakfast to start the day off right. Five guest rooms, all with private baths with showers. $85.

TROUT LAKE

The Farm: A Bed and Breakfast

490 Sunnyside Road, 98650
(509) 395-2488; FAX (509) 395-2127
e-mail: farmbnb@gorge.net
www.gorge.net/business/farmbnb

Circa 1890. The Farm is a charming three-story farmhouse filled with antiques and art on six acres in beautiful Trout Lake Valley at the base of Mount Adams. Twenty-five miles north of Hood River, Oregon, and the Columbia River Gorge—home of world-class wind surfing. Quiet and comfortably decorated two rooms are available. Mountain bikes provided for guests. Hike, raft the White Salmon River, bird watch, cross-country ski, pick wild huckleberries, or just relax.

Hosts: Dean and Rosie Hostetter
Rooms: 2 (SB) $70-80
Full Breakfast
Credit Cards: F
Notes: 2, 5, 7, 8, 12, 13

VASHON ISLAND

Betty MacDonald Farm

12000-99th Avenue Southwest, 98070
(206) 567-4227

Spectacular view of Mount Rainier, the sunrise, and eagles over Puget Sound. Private cedar loft and an all-cedar cottage. Cozy, secluded, intimate retreat. Rustic elegance sleeps two to four, full kitchen, private baths with claw-foot tubs. Lovely gardens, beach access, six wooded acres. Ideal for writers, bird watchers, honeymooners, nature lovers. A unique one-of-a-kind place. Miles/worlds away from the city. Cable TV/VCR. Great decks. Betty MacDonald wrote *Egg and I*, *Onions in the Stew*, and *Mrs. Piggle Wiggle's Farm Magic*. Twenty-five minutes to airport and Sea-Tac. Smoking permitted outside only. One and one-half hours to Mount Rainier.

Host: Judith Manerud Lawrence
Rooms: 2 (PB) $100-120
Continental Breakfast
Credit Cards: None
Notes: 2, 5, 7, 8, 9, 10, 11, 12

WHITE SALMON

Llama Ranch Bed and Breakfast

1980 Highway 141, 98672
(509) 395-2786; (800) 800-LAMA

This inn stands between two snow-capped mountains. The hosts offer hands-on expe-

---

NOTES: Credit cards accepted: A MasterCard; B Visa; C American Express; D Discover; E Diner's Club; F Other; 2 Personal checks accepted; 3 Lunch available; 4 Dinner available; 5 Open all year; 6 Pets welcome;

rience with llamas, including guided llama walks through the woods. Get better acquainted with these beautiful, intelligent animals. The bedrooms have queen-size beds and spectacular views. Nearby are refreshing waterfalls and natural lava bridges. Other activities in the area include white-water rafting, golf, plane trips over Mount St. Helens, fishing, hunting, hiking, cave exploration, and huckleberry picking. Cross-country skiing and snowmobiling in the winter. Close to nice restaurants.

Hosts: Jerry Stone and Dee Kern
Rooms: 7 (2 PB; 5 SB) $55-75
Full Breakfast
Credit Cards: A, B, D
Notes: 2, 5, 7, 8, 9, 12, 13, 14

WINTHROP

Dammann's Bed and Breakfast
716 Highway 20, 98862
(509) 996-2484

These antique-filled guest rooms are on the banks of the Methow River. Winthrop has been westernized and all buildings look old. Also board sidewalks. It is a real tourist attraction. The valley is a recreation paradise for photography, seasonal hunting, fishing, hiking, camping, and skiing. Eight lakes within six to eight miles; right at the foot of the Cascade Mountains.

Hosts: Hank and Jean Dammann
Rooms: 2 (PB) $55
Continental Breakfast
Credit Cards: None
Notes: 2, 7, 9, 10, 11, 12, 13

WOODLAND

Grandma's House
4551 Lewis River Road, 98674
(360) 225-7002; e-mail: gmasbb@pacifier.com

Quaint 1917 farmhouse on 35 secluded acres overlooking the North Fork of the Lewis River. Gateway to Mount St. Helens. Eight miles east of Woodland and 20 miles west of Couger on State Route 503.

Hosts: Warren and Louise Moir
Rooms: 3 (SB) $55
Full Breakfast
Credit Cards: A, B
Notes: 2, 5, 7, 8, 9, 11, 12

7 No smoking; 8 Children welcome; 9 Social drinking allowed; 10 Tennis nearby; 11 Swimming nearby; 12 Golf nearby; 13 Skiing nearby; 14 May be booked through a travel agent; 15 Handicapped accessible.

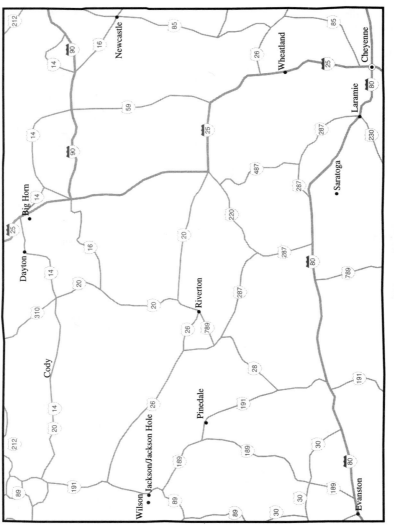

Wyoming

Wyoming

BIG HORN

Spahn's Bighorn Mountain Bed and Breakfast

Box 579, 82833
(307) 674-8150

Towering log home and secluded guest cabins on the mountainside in whispering pines. Borders one million acres of public forest with deer and moose. Gracious mountain breakfast served on the deck with binoculars to enjoy the 100-mile view. Owner was a Yellowstone ranger. Just 15 minutes from Sheridan and I-90. Wildlife trips. Mobil- and AAA-approved: three-diamond rating.

Hosts: Ron and Bobbie Spahn
Rooms: 4 (PB) $65-120
Full Breakfast
Credit Cards: A, B
Notes: 4, 5, 7, 8, 9

CHEYENNE

Adventurers' Country Bed and Breakfast

3803 I-80 S. Service Road, 82009
(307) 632-4087 (phone/FAX)
e-mail: fwhite1@juno.com
www.cruising-america.com/country.html

Modern, southwestern ranch home on 120 acres. Has four large bedrooms, all with private baths, a three-room suite with jet tub, king-size bed, and private bath. Guest living room, TV, videos, games, books, and fireplace. A 150-foot rambling porch out into a garden courtyard. Ranch animals to pet. Short and long horse-riding adventures. Full homemade breakfasts. Porch and dining room dinners available. On the way to Yellowstone, Jackson Hole, and Black Hills.

Hosts: Chuck and Fern White
Rooms: 4 (PB) $55-75
Suite: $135
Full Breakfast
Credit Cards: F
Notes: 2, 3, 4, 5, 6, 7, 8, 9, 10, 11, 12, 14

The Howdy Pardner

1920 Tranquility Road, 82009
(307) 634-6493; FAX (307) 634-2822
e-mail: janp9999@aol.com
www.cruising-america.com/howdy.html

Western atmosphere with a Big Wyoming Welcome. A ranch-style home on 10 acres in a serene country setting perched high on a hill with spectacular views all around that invite walkabouts. Only 10 minutes from Frontier Park, Interstates 25 and 80, and the airport. All rooms have queen-size beds, private baths, telephones, and TV/VCR. Afternoon refreshments await guests' arrival, and a full gourmet country breakfast will start guests off the next morning in the true western tradition. Gather in the evening to gaze at the ever-changing sunset. Join other guests at a game of pool or Ping Pong.

NOTES: Credit cards accepted: A MasterCard; B Visa; C American Express; D Discover; E Diner's Club; F Other; 2 Personal checks accepted; 3 Lunch available; 4 Dinner available; 5 Open all year; 6 Pets welcome; 7 No smoking; 8 Children welcome; 9 Social drinking allowed; 10 Tennis nearby; 11 Swimming nearby; 12 Golf nearby; 13 Skiing nearby; 14 May be booked through a travel agent; 15 Handicapped accessible.

Belly-up to the bar on tractor-seat stools. Tour the sheepherder's wagon, sit by the Lucky Horseshoe Pond. Children and pets welcome. Resident cat and dog provide companionship at no additional charge.

Rooms: 3 (PB) $65-105
Full Breakfast
Credit Cards: A, B
Notes: 2, 5, 6, 7, 8, 9, 10, 11, 12, 14

Nagle Warren Mansion

Nagle Warren Mansion Bed and Breakfast

222 East 17th Street, 82001
(307) 637-3333; (800) 811-2610
FAX (307) 638-6835

This 1888 national historic register mansion has been newly restored to its original glory with all of today's necessities. On the quiet edge of downtown, it is convenient to all of Cheyenne, especially for business people. Public areas include parlor, sitting room, library, conference rooms, workout room, and the tower. All rooms are spacious and individually appointed. Luxuriate in the Victorian elegance while exploring the public spaces and private places.

Hosts: Jim and Jacquie Osterfoss
Rooms: 12 (PB) $85-125
Full Breakfast
Credit Cards: A, B, C
Notes: 2, 5, 7, 9, 10, 12, 14, 15

CHEYENNE (LARAMIE)

A. Drummond's Ranch Bed and Breakfast

399 Happy Jack Road, State Highway 210, 82007
(307) 634-6042 (phone/FAX)
e-mail: adrummond@juno.com

Quiet, gracious retreat on 120 acres; 20 minutes to Cheyenne or Laramie, by national forest. Mountain bike, hike, rock climb, llama trek, cross-country ski, or relax. Bring own horse and train at 7,500 feet. Boarding for horses and pets in transit. "Adventure at your pace" packages. Private outdoor Jacuzzi. Suite with fireplace, sauna, private deck with Jacuzzi, and pantry closet kitchen. Privacy with personalized attention. Featured in *Country Inns* and *Country Extra* magazines. Superb breakfast, fine dining. Beverages, fresh fruit, and homemade snacks always available. AAA- and Mobil-approved. Reservations required. Partially handicapped accessible.

Host: Taydie Drummond
Rooms: 4 (2 PB; 2 SB) $65-175
Full Breakfast
Credit Cards: A, B, D
Notes: 2, 3, 4, 5, 6, 7, 8, 9, 12, 13, 14

CODY

Hunter Peak Ranch

Box 1731, Painter Route, 82414
(307) 587-3711

During 1999, the Cary family celebrates 50 years of welcoming guests to their mountain ranch. At 6,700 feet elevation, year-round recreational activities abound: photography, wildlife viewing, scenic drives, hiking, trout fishing, horseback riding, pack trips, biking, fall hunting, cross-country skiing, snowshoeing, snowmobiling. Accommodations are cozy cabins and spacious lodge rooms, each with private bath and kitchen. Western decor is throughout. Delicious ranch-style

NOTES: Credit cards accepted: A MasterCard; B Visa; C American Express; D Discover; E Diner's Club; F Other; 2 Personal checks accepted; 3 Lunch available; 4 Dinner available; 5 Open all year; 6 Pets welcome;

meals available in dining room. Call for 1999 specials.

Hosts: Louis and Shelley Cary
Rooms: 8 (PB) $94
Full Breakfast
Credit Cards: A, B
Notes: 2, 3, 4, 5, 6, 8, 9, 11, 13, 15

DAYTON

Cabin Creek

Box 431, 82836
(307) 655-2455; FAX (307) 655-2455
e-mail: lofgren@wave.com

Nature at its finest! The Little Tongue River and the Big Horn Mountains are at the doorstep. In addition to skiing and golfing, there is some of the best snowmobiling, hunting, fishing, hiking, and mountain biking in the country. Use the whole cabin or cuddle up in the loft or one on the two bedrooms. Make yourself at home with a fully furnished kitchen and laundry room. Twenty miles from Sheridan on the way to Yellowstone Park.

Hosts: Joyce and Doug Lofgren
Rooms: 3 (1 PB; 2 SB) $60-150
Full Breakfast
Credit Cards: None
Notes: 2, 5, 7, 9, 12, 13

EVANSTON

Pine Gables Inn Bed and Breakfast

1049 Center Street, 82930
(307) 789-2069; (307) 789-2787; (800) 789-2069

Framed by majestic pine trees, historic Pine Gables was built in 1883 and is an ideal location for a romantic getaway, celebration, or travel. This Eastlake Victorian-style mansion offers four lovely guest rooms, dining room, and formal parlor with hand-painted murals and walls. Relax in newly redecorated antique-filled rooms. Cross-country skiing in winter; hiking and fishing

Pine Gables Inn

in the summer. Private baths, color TVs, and telephones in all rooms. A full home-made breakfast is served. Visit soon.

Hosts: Nephi and Ruby Jensen
Rooms: 4 (PB) $50-60
Full Breakfast
Credit Cards: A, B, C, D
Notes: 2, 5, 7, 10, 11, 12, 13, 14

JACKSON

The Alpine House

Box 20245, 83001
(307) 739-1570; (800) 753-1421
FAX (307) 734-2850
e-mail: alpinhouse@compuserve.com

The Alpine House is a little bit of Scandinavia in the heart of Jackson Hole. It is a new timber-frame lodge that is bright and airy. Light and spotless guest rooms, each with its own private bath, await guests' arrival. Each of the seven rooms has a private balcony with French doors leading to it, heated tile floors, down comforters, plush towels, and simple country antique furniture. A full healthy homemade breakfast served each morning. Brand new hot tub in 1999.

Hosts: Hans and Nancy Johnstone
Rooms: 7 (PB) $80-120
Full Breakfast
Credit Cards: A, B
Notes: 2, 5, 7, 8, 9, 10, 11, 12, 13, 14, 15

7 No smoking; 8 Children welcome; 9 Social drinking allowed; 10 Tennis nearby; 11 Swimming nearby; 12 Golf nearby; 13 Skiing nearby; 14 May be booked through a travel agent; 15 Handicapped accessible.

The Huff House Inn Bed and Breakfast

240 East Deloney, P.O. Box 1189, 83001
(307) 733-4164; FAX (307) 739-9091
e-mail: huffhousebnb@blissnet.com

Innkeepers Jackie and Weldon Richardson have dedicated themselves to retaining the characteristics that make this lovely home special. Old-fashioned kitchen cupboards with pull-out flour bins, beveled-glass doors, original light fixtures, fine antiques, and pedestal sinks. At the same time, they have added the amenities that bed and breakfast guests appreciate, such as whirlpool tubs, in-room telephones, TVs, and outdoor hot tub.

Hosts: Jackie and Weldon Richardson
Rooms: 9 (PB) $105-195
Full Breakfast
Credit Cards: A, B, D
Notes: 2, 5, 7, 8, 9, 10, 11, 12, 13, 14

The Wildflower Inn

P.O. Box 11000, 83002
(307) 733-4710

A lovely log home with five sunny guest rooms, this bed and breakfast is on three acres of land only 5 minutes from the Jackson Hole ski area, 10 minutes from the town of Jackson, and 30 minutes from Grand Teton.

Hosts: Ken and Sherrie Jern
Rooms: 5 (PB) $140-225
Full Breakfast
Credit Cards: A, B
Notes: 2, 5, 7, 8, 9, 10, 11, 12, 13, 14

The Wildflower Inn

LARAMIE

Annie Moore's Guest House

Annie Moore's Guest House

819 University Avenue, 82070
(307) 721-4177; (800) 552-8992

Restored Princess Anne home with six individually decorated guest rooms, four with sinks. Large, sunny common living rooms, second-story sun deck. Across the street from the University of Wyoming; two blocks from the Laramie Plains Museum; six blocks from downtown shops, galleries, and restaurants. Just 15 minutes from skiing, camping, biking, and fishing in uncrowded wilderness areas.

Hosts: Ann Acuff and Joe Bundy
Rooms: 6 (SB) $55-65
Continental Breakfast
Credit Cards: A, B, C, D
Notes: 2, 5, 7, 9, 12, 13

Vee Bar Guest Ranch

2091 State Highway 130, 82070
(307) 745-7036; (800) 483-3227
FAX (307) 745-7433

The historic Vee Bar Guest Ranch is nestled in the shadows of the beautiful Snowy Range mountains where the Little Laramie River winds its way through the Centennial

NOTES: Credit cards accepted: A MasterCard; B Visa; C American Express; D Discover; E Diner's Club; F Other; 2 Personal checks accepted; 3 Lunch available; 4 Dinner available; 5 Open all year; 6 Pets welcome;

Valley. The riverside cabins have decks, gas fireplaces, access to the hot tub, and are decorated in country-western comfort. Guests at the Vee Bar enjoy a wonderful blend of western tradition, contemporary comfort, and personal, old-fashioned service. Activities are varied and there is something for everyone on this year-round ranch.

Host: Jim "Lefty" and Carla Cole (owners)
Rooms: 9 (PB) $100-150
Full Breakfast
Credit Cards: A, B
Notes: 2, 4, 5, 7, 8, 9, 13, 14, 15

NEWCASTLE

EVA—Great Spirit Ranch Bed and Breakfast

1262 Beaver Creek Road, 82701
(307) 746-2537; e-mail: rspilln@trib.com

Secluded log home on historic Cheyenne/ Deadwood stagecoach route. On 525 acres of scenic grounds in the beautiful Black Hills. Roomy bedrooms, private baths, full country breakfast. Great room with fireplace, movie and reading libraries, board games and puzzles. An outdoor gas grill and kitchen are available to guests. Hiking, exploring, cross-country skiing, wildlife, serenity. Adjoins national forest. Hunting packages are available. Fishing, horseback riding, rock climbing, snowmobile trails are all within minutes. Mount Rushmore, Devil's Tower, Crazy Horse Mountain, Deadwood gaming, and more are within 90 minutes' drive. Dog in residence.

Host: Irene Spillane
Rooms: 4 (2 PB; 2 SB) $50-80
Full Breakfast
Credit Cards: A, B
Notes: 2, 5, 7, 9, 11, 12, 13, 15

4W Ranch Recreation

1162 Lynch Road, 82701
(307) 746-2815

Looking for the unbeaten path? Spend a few days on this working cattle ranch with 20,000 acres of diversified rangeland to explore at leisure. Rates include three meals a day.

Hosts: Bob and Jean Harshbarger
Rooms: 2 (SB) $100-125 (American plan)
Full Breakfast
Credit Cards: None
Notes: 2, 3, 4, 7, 8, 9, 11

PINEDALE

Pole Creek Ranch Bed and Breakfast

P.O. Box 278, 82941
(307) 367-4433

Rustic log home has breathtaking view of the Wind River Mountains. It features barn, corrals, horse rides, wagon and sleigh rides, and an outdoor hot tub. Horse boarding is also available. One bedroom with private bath; two bedrooms share a bath. Try the Indian teepee, too. The peace and beauty of Pole Creek Ranch is unsurpassed.

Hosts: Dexter and Carole Smith
Rooms: 3 (SB) $55
Full Breakfast
Credit Cards: None
Notes: 2, 3, 4, 5, 6, 7, 8, 10, 11, 12, 13, 15

Window on the Winds

10151 Highway 191, Box 996, 82941
(307) 367-2600; (888) 367-1345

The McClains invite guests to this rustic log home. The hosts offer lodgepole pine queen-size beds, a large common room, all decorated in western and Plains Indian decor. Enjoy the breathtaking view of the Winds or relax in the hot tub. Only minutes from year-round mountain adventures such as hiking, fishing, skiing, and snowmobiling, and less than two hours from Jackson and Yellowstone. The perfect base for a western Wyoming vacation.

Host: Leanne McClain
Rooms: 4 (SB) $60-95
Full Breakfast
Credit Cards: A, B
Notes: 2, 3, 4, 5, 6, 7, 8, 9, 11, 12, 13, 14

7 No smoking; 8 Children welcome; 9 Social drinking allowed; 10 Tennis nearby; 11 Swimming nearby; 12 Golf nearby; 13 Skiing nearby; 14 May be booked through a travel agent; 15 Handicapped accessible.

RIVERTON

Cottonwood Ranch Bed and Breakfast
951 Missouri Valley Road, 82501
(307) 856-3064

This 250-acre working farm/ranch was founded in 1937, raising cattle, barley, hay, corn, and oats. Thirteen rooms, two-story farm house with three bed and breakfast rooms upstairs that share a bath and family room. Full farm breakfast served by former cateress and cooking columnist. Three hours to Yellowstone or Jackson Hole, one hour to Sinks Canyon and Hot Springs State Parks. Good hunting, fishing, hiking, and boating nearby. Lunch and dinner available by reservation. Outdoor pets welcome. Supervised children welcome. Moderate social drinking permitted.

Hosts: Earl and Judie Anglen
Rooms: 3 (3 SB) $50-55
Full Breakfast
Credit Cards: None
Notes: 2, 5, 7, 10, 11, 12

Cottonwood Ranch

SARATOGA

Hotel Wolf
P.O. Box 1298, 82331
(307) 326-5525

The historic Hotel Wolf, built in 1893, served as a stagecoach stop. During its early years, the hotel was the hub of the community and noted for its fine food and convivial atmosphere. The same holds true today. The dining room is acclaimed as one of the finest in the region. AAA-rated restaurant. Nearby is a mineral hot spring and excellent fishing. On the North Platte River.

Hosts: Doug and Kathleen Campbell
Rooms: 6 (PB) $30-47
Suites: 3 (PB) $58-105
Credit Cards: A, B, C, E
Notes: 2, 3, 4, 5, 7, 8, 9, 10, 11, 12, 13, 14

WHEATLAND

The Blackbird Inn
1101 Eleventh, 82201
(307) 322-4540

This elegant three-story brick home has four bedrooms and one suite sharing three baths. Each bedroom has a different decorating theme. The Blackbird Inn is noted for its wonderful front porch, complete with swing, wicker furniture, and lemonade in the summer. On chilly days, sit by the fireplace and sip a cup of herbal tea or hot chocolate. Great biking, fishing, and bird watching nearby. Thirty minutes from the mountains and the Oregon Trail. Outdoor hot tub. Lunch and dinner available by reservation.

Hosts: Scotty and Alice Anderson
Rooms: 5 (SB) $50-60
Full Breakfast
Credit Cards: None
Notes: 2, 5, 6, 7, 8, 9, 10, 11, 12, 14

WILSON (JACKSON HOLE)

Teton View Bed and Breakfast
2136 Coyote Loop, Box 652, 83014
(307) 733-7954

Rooms all have mountain views, cozy country decor, orthopedic mattresses, private entrance, private deck overlooking Teton Mountain range, and comfortable lounge area with books and refrigerator. Convenient location to Yellowstone and Grand Teton National Parks. Closed November, April.

Hosts: John and Jo Engelhart
Rooms: 3 (1 PB; 2 SB) $70-95
Full Breakfast
Credit Cards: None
Notes: 2, 7, 8, 9, 10, 11, 12, 13, 14

NOTES: Credit cards accepted: A MasterCard; B Visa; C American Express; D Discover; E Diner's Club; F Other; 2 Personal checks accepted; 3 Lunch available; 4 Dinner available; 5 Open all year; 6 Pets welcome;

Canada

Alberta

Alberta

Big Springs Bed and Breakfast

Rural Route 1, T4B 2A3
(403) 948-5264; FAX (403) 948-5851
e-mail: bigsprings@bigsprings-bb.com
www.bigsprings-bb.com

DeWitt's

Peaceful country setting. Excellent access to Calgary (15 minutes), airport (22 minutes), Kananaskis Country, Banff, Lake Louise, and famous Calgary Stampede. This 5,500-square-foot home is on 35 acres overlooking valley. Elegantly appointed rooms: Manor, Victorian, Arbour, Bridal Suite (Thermo-masseur tub). Secluded English Garden sitting room. Gourmet breakfast experience— china, silver, linen. Patios, hot tub, sauna, fireplace, piano, and nature path. Evening snacks. Romantic package, self-guided day trips available. Extra personal touches. Canada Select three-stars-rated.

Hosts: Earle and Carol Whittaker
Rooms: 4 (PB) $90-125
Full Breakfast
Credit Cards: A, B
Notes: 5, 7, 8, 10, 11, 12, 13, 14

DeWitt's Bed and Breakfast

Rural Route 1, T4B 2A3
(403) 948-5356; FAX (403) 912-0788
e-mail: dewitbnb@cadvision.com

"Welcome to our home." Warmly decorated clean rooms and flower-filled patio beckon guests' to relax with hosts. The home is guests to enjoy during their stay. Only 10.8 kilometers west of Airdrie/Highway 2 on the south junction of Highways 567 and 772. Twenty minutes to Calgary and the international airport. The closeness to the city and airport, yet the quietness of the country make this a great place to begin or end a tour of western Canada.

Hosts: Irene DeWitt and Wendy Kelly
Rooms: 3 (1 PB; 2 SB) $75-85
Full Breakfast
Credit Cards: B
Notes: 5, 7, 8, 10, 11, 12, 13

Eleanor's House

125 Kootenay Avenue, P.O. Box 1553, T0L 0C0
(403) 760-2457; FAX (403) 762-3852
e-mail: info@bbeleanor.com; www.bbeleanor.com

Banff's finest guest home reflects mid-century elegance for the discerning traveler. Spacious superior bedrooms have private full bathrooms. Mountain views from all windows. In a quiet, prestigious neighborhood, walking distance from the town center or the famous Banff Springs Hotel. The hosts provide guests with an individual daily itinerary to make the best of their days in the area. Together they have more than 50 years' experience in mountain hospitality and national park management. Closed November, December, and January.

Hosts: Eleanor House and Rick Kunelius
Rooms: 2 (PB) $125 Canadian
Continental Breakfast
Credit Cards: A, B
Notes: 2, 7, 9, 10, 11, 12, 13, 14

NOTES: Credit cards accepted: A MasterCard; B Visa; C American Express; D Discover; E Diner's Club; F Other; 2 Personal checks accepted; 3 Lunch available; 4 Dinner available; 5 Open all year; 6 Pets welcome; 7 No smoking; 8 Children welcome; 9 Social drinking allowed; 10 Tennis nearby; 11 Swimming nearby; 12 Golf nearby; 13 Skiing nearby; 14 May be booked through a travel agent; 15 Handicapped accessible.

CALGARY

Barb's Bed and Breakfast
1308 Carlyle Road SW, T2V 2T8
(403) 255-6596; FAX (403) 543-3354
www.bbcanada.com/274.html

A quiet, spacious home in a well-treed residential area, close to Heritage Park, and minutes from downtown and transit. Small kitchen, spacious lounge area with TV. Private entrance from garden area. Full Continental breakfast at the guests' leisure. Only two rooms, queen-size and double. Shared shower room. Smoking restricted. Canada Select Recommended Accommodation.

Host: Barbara I. Cook
Rooms: 2 (SB) $65 Canadian
Continental Breakfast
Credit Cards: None
Notes: 5, 9, 10, 12, 13

Bed and Breakfast at Harrison's
6016 Thornburn Drive NW, T2K 3P7
(403) 274-7281; FAX (403) 531-0069

Harrison's is a cozy bungalow in a quiet residential area of Calgary. Fifteen minutes to Calgary International Airport and city center. Good access to public transit. Guests share comfortable living room and sheltered patio with host. Two main-floor rooms: queen-size bedroom and twin-size bedroom, each with private bath. Children over 10 welcome. Smoking outside only.

Host: Susan Harrison
Rooms: 2 (PB) $60-70 Canadian
Full Breakfast
Credit Cards: None
Notes: 2, 5, 7, 9, 12, 13, 14

Hilltop Ranch Bed and Breakfast
Box 54, Priddis, T0L 1W0
(800) 801-0451; e-mail: hilltopr@cybersurf.net

A hobby ranch in the foothills. Mountain view. All rooms with private bathrooms. Guest lounge with TV, VCR, fireplace, and private deck. Fifteen minutes southwest of Calgary. A beautiful spot. "If you are coming to Calgary, you should have a western bed and breakfast experience."

Hosts: Gary and Barb Zorn
Rooms: 3 (PB) $60-105
Full Breakfast
Credit Cards: A, B, C
Notes: 5, 6, 7, 8, 9, 10, 11, 12, 13, 14

Paradise Acres Bed and Breakfast
243105 Paradise Road, Box 20, Site 2,
   Rural Route 6, T2M 4L5
(403) 248-4748; FAX (403) 235-3916

On Paradise Road just minutes away from the Calgary International Airport. Guests can enjoy a beautiful lake, golf course, shopping, and recreation nearby. Hosts have four rooms fitted with queen-size beds. Two baths en suite and two private baths. Relax next to a luxurious marble fireplace or enjoy the city or mountain view. Inquire about accommodations for children. CAA- and AAA-approved. Skiing 80 miles away.

Hosts: Brian and Char Bates
Rooms: 4 (PB) $67.50-82.50 Canadian
Full and Continental Breakfast
Credit Cards: A, B, C
Notes: 5, 7, 10, 11, 12, 14

CANMORE

Alpenglow Inn Bed and Breakfast
230 Lady Macdonald Drive, T1W 1H3
(403) 678-3389; FAX (403) 609-2879
e-mail: info@AlpenglowInn.com
www.AlpenglowInn.com
www.canadianrockies.net/alpenglow

In the scenic Canadian Rockies, on the sunny side of Bow Valley in a quiet residential neighborhood. Modern cedar home only five minutes from Banff National Park, less than an hour from six major ski resorts, and 1.5 hours from the Calgary International Airport. Near hiking and

---

NOTES: Credit cards accepted: A MasterCard; B Visa; C American Express; D Discover; E Diner's Club; F Other; 2 Personal checks accepted; 3 Lunch available; 4 Dinner available; 5 Open all year; 6 Pets welcome;

biking trails; climbing routes; and other adventure possibilities like white-water rafting, dogsledding, horseback riding. Private guest entrance. Guest rooms are furnished with TV, VCR, and en suite bath. Shared sitting area/common room, a kitchenette with refrigerator, sink, microwave oven. Inquire about accommodations for pets. Limited handicapped accessibility.

Hosts: Mike and Tina Howard
Rooms: 2 (PB) $40-90 Canadian
Continental Breakfast
Credit Cards: A, B
Notes: 5, 7, 8, 9, 10, 11, 12, 13, 14

Ambleside Lodge

123 A Rundle Drive, T1W 2L6
(403) 678-3976; FAX (403) 678-3919
e-mail: amblside@telusplanet.net
www.comcept.ab.ca/cantravel/amble.html

This home offers the beauty of a pine interior, along with the largest fireplace in all of Canmore, reported to have 18 tons of local stone. The mountain view from the decks is simply spectacular. Each room has its own individual ambiance. Take in the mountain view by day and the stars at night, through the skylights in all the bedrooms. Just a short walk to downtown, the Bow River, and the Nordic Centre. There are pets in the house and smoking is restricted to the deck only.

Hosts: Maureen and John Whitlock
Rooms: 2 (PB) $75-105
Full Breakfast
Credit Cards: A, B
Notes: 5, 7, 9, 10, 11, 12, 13

Cougar Creek Inn Bed and Breakfast

240 Grizzly Crescent, T1W 1B5
(403) 678-4751

Quiet, rustic cedar chalet with mountain views in every direction. Grounds border on Cougar Creek. Hiking trail borders property. Hostess is an outdoor enthusiast with a strong love for mountains and can assist guests' plans for local hiking, skiing, canoeing, mountain biking, and backpack-

ing. Bonfire pit, private entrance, fireplace, sitting room with TV, games, private dining, serving area, and sauna. Personal checks accepted for deposit. Open May through September. Large room available for families—sleeps five.

Host: Patricia Doucette
Rooms: 2 (PB) $65-85 Canadian
Full Breakfast
Credit Cards: None
Notes: 2, 3, 7, 8, 9, 10, 11, 12, 13

The Georgetown Inn

1101 Bow Valley Trail T1W 1N4
(403) 678-3439; FAX (403) 678-6909

At the eastern gateway to Banff National Park, a Tudor-style 24-bedroom inn with private dining room and a licensed guest lounge. All bedrooms are nonsmoking and have private baths, antique furnishings, TVs, telephones, and majestic mountain views. Each room is individually decorated, several with gas fireplaces, and some with jetted tubs. Easy to find and close to all conveniences. Smoking is permitted in the snug and the outdoor patios. Doreen and Barry built the inn in 1993 from scratch, patterning it after those in their native England.

Hosts: Barry and Doreen Jones and Family
Rooms: 24 (PB) $79-149 Canadian
Full Breakfast
Credit Cards: A, B, C, D
Notes: 2, 5, 8, 9, 10, 11, 12, 13, 14, 15

Monarch Bed and Breakfast

317 Canyon Close, T1W 1H4
(403) 678-2566; FAX (403) 609-2122
e-mail: ogawa@telusplanet.net
www.canadianrockies.net/monarch

A brand new modern home in the Canadian Rockies, only 15 minutes from the famous site of Banff. A private 1,600-square-foot area featuring kitchen/dining area, two private entrances, living room with cable TV, VCR and movie selection, two bedrooms with brass beds, bathroom, and recreation room with billiard table.

---

7 No smoking; 8 Children welcome; 9 Social drinking allowed; 10 Tennis nearby; 11 Swimming nearby; 12 Golf nearby; 13 Skiing nearby; 14 May be booked through a travel agent; 15 Handicapped accessible.

Central to hiking and climbing trails, world-famous ski-resorts, 1988 Olympic site of Winter Olympics, and much more. Perfect for families, couples, and groups. Suite rentals available.

Hosts: Charlie and Joscelyne Ogawa
Rooms: 2 (2 SB) $40-95 Canadian
Continental Breakfast
Credit Cards: A, B, F
Notes: 5, 7, 8, 9, 10, 11, 12, 13, 14

Paintbox Lodge

629 10th Street, T1W 2A2
(403) 678-3956; FAX (403) 678-4134

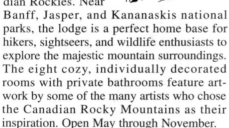

The Paintbox Lodge is a small lodge in the heart of Canmore, a scenic former coal mining town nestled in the heart of the Canadian Rockies. Near Banff, Jasper, and Kananaskis national parks, the lodge is a perfect home base for hikers, sightseers, and wildlife enthusiasts to explore the majestic mountain surroundings. The eight cozy, individually decorated rooms with private bathrooms feature artwork by some of the many artists who chose the Canadian Rocky Mountains as their inspiration. Open May through November.

Hosts: Tristan and Damian Jones
Rooms: 8 (PB) $89
Full Breakfast
Credit Cards: A, B
Notes: 7, 8, 9, 11, 12, 14

COCHRANE

Dickens Inn Bed and Breakfast

Rural Route 1, T0L 0W0
(403) 932-3945; e-mail: dickens@nucleus.com
www.bbcanada.com/275.html

Beautifully decorated Victorian-style home designed as a bed and breakfast. Close proximity to Cochrane, Calgary, Kananaskis Country, Banff, and Lake Louise. All guest rooms have a queen-size four-poster bed and private (en suite) bathroom. Each room has a view of the majestic Rocky Mountains. Excellent base location for day trips to the Rockies. Only 10 minutes to the Western Heritage Centre. Evening refreshments by the fireplace.

Hosts: Elsa Peterson and Michael Madsen
Rooms: 3 (PB) $65-85 Canadian
Full Breakfast
Credit Cards: A, B
Notes: 2, 5, 7, 9, 12, 13, 14

DRUMHELLER

The Victorian House

541 Riverside Drive West, T0J 0Y3
(403) 823-3535

Nonsmoking, pet-free accommodation. Quiet scenic location with balcony and veranda overlooking river and badlands. Close to all amenities. Queen-size, double, and single beds. Private and shared bathrooms. Guest lounge with TV. Full breakfast. Open year-round.

Hosts: Jack and Florence Barnes
Rates: $55-65
Full Breakfast
Credit Cards: A, B
Notes: 5, 7, 8, 9, 10, 11, 12, 13

EDMONTON

Alberta's Gem Bed and Breakfast

11216-48 Avenue, T6H 0C7
(403) 434-6098 (phone/FAX)
www.bbcanada.com/1301.html

Great western hospitality at its best in a tastefully decorated home with friendly atmosphere in quiet park setting. Close to university, West Edmonton Mall, international airport, and city center. There is office equipment for business travelers. Enjoy "all-you-can-eat" breakfast in dining area overlooking flowering garden. Hosts have many years of experience in travel industry and can help with entire travel itin-

NOTES: Credit cards accepted: A MasterCard; B Visa; C American Express; D Discover; E Diner's Club; F Other; 2 Personal checks accepted; 3 Lunch available; 4 Dinner available; 5 Open all year; 6 Pets welcome;

erary in Canada (including national parks) and USA.

Hosts: Gordon and Betty Mitchell
Rooms: 2 (PB) $55-75
Full Breakfast
Credit Cards: A, B, F
Notes: 5, 7, 10, 11,12, 13

Barratt House Bed and Breakfast

4204-115 Street, T6J 1P4
(780) 437-2568; www.bbcanada.com/1349.html

Canada Select three stars. Member Alberta Bed and Breakfast Association. In quiet residential area of southwest Edmonton, 20 minutes from airport and downtown, 10 minutes to famous West Edmonton Mall. Parks and walking trails nearby. Beautifully appointed upstairs bedrooms with ceiling fans. Relax and unwind with cool drink and homebaking in family room with TV, VCR, or on flower-filled deck. Beverage trays in rooms. Delicious, gourmet-style breakfast served in sunny dining room. Laundry facilities available. Cat in residence.

Hosts: Doug and Joan Longley
Rooms: 2 (PB) $60-70
Full Breakfast
Credit Cards: A
Notes: 2, 5, 7, 11, 12

Brooks Place Bed and Breakfast

3230-104 A Street, T6J 2Z6
(780) 438-6048; (800) 599-7770
FAX (780) 437-7889
e-mail: brookspl@connect.ab.ca

"Come be our guest" at this modern family home in a quiet residential area with easy 15-minute access to West Edmonton Mall and other attractions; just 20 minutes from the airport. Comfortable queen-size beds and tastefully decorated rooms with the comfort of guests in mind. Guests will be treated to great hospitality and a delicious gourmet-style breakfast in the dining room. Special diets are catered to with advance notice.

Hosts: Ernie and Ethel Brooks
Rooms: 2 (PB) $60-65
Full Breakfast
Credit Cards: B
Notes: 5, 7, 8, 12

HINTON

Black Cat Guest Ranch

Box 6267, T7V 1X6
(403) 865-3084; FAX (403) 865-1924

Historic Albertan guest ranch celebrated its 60th anniversary in 1995. Guests are offered guided trail rides, hiking, line dancing, rafting in the summer, and cross-country skiing in the winter. Relaxation year-round. Home-style meals and sociable surroundings in a beautiful mountain setting one hour's drive from Jasper townsite.

Hosts: Amber and Perry Hayward
Rooms: 16 (PB) $73-119 Canadian
Full Breakfast
Credit Cards: A, B
Notes: 2, 3, 4, 5, 8, 9, 13, 14

Black Cat Guest Ranch

MOUNTAIN VIEW

Mountain View Bed and Breakfast

Box 82, T0K 1N0
(403) 653-1882; FAX (403) 653-1895
e-mail: mtnvubnb@telusplanet.net

Come experience the untouched corner of Alberta, where the prairies meet the

7 No smoking; 8 Children welcome; 9 Social drinking allowed; 10 Tennis nearby; 11 Swimming nearby; 12 Golf nearby; 13 Skiing nearby; 14 May be booked through a travel agent; 15 Handicapped accessible.

mountains, two national parks, surrounded by Waterton Lakes and Glacier; therefore there is lots to do. Come hike, bird watch, bike, horseback ride, or just relax and enjoy the scenery. The day, of course, starts off with a large breakfast with a wide variety of items—ranging from the traditional western breakfast to crêpes and any dietary preferences or needs are available on request.

Hosts: Shereen Fard and Tina Lung
Rooms: 3 (3 SB) $45-55
Full Breakfast
Credit Cards: B
Notes: 2, 3, 4, 5, 6, 8, 9, 11, 12, 13, 14, 15

NANTON

Timber Ridge Homestead

P.O. Box 94, T0L 1R0
(403) 646-5683; (403) 646-2480 (winter)

Timber Ridge Homestead is a rustic establishment in the beautiful foothills of ranching country, lying about 70 miles southwest of Calgary. There are good, quiet horses to help guests explore the abundant wildflowers, wildlife, and wonderful views of the Rockies. Good, plain cooking.

Hosts: Bridget Jones and Family
Rooms: 3 (SB) $25-50
Full Breakfast
Credit Cards: None
Notes: 2, 3, 4, 7, 8, 9

TURNER VALLEY

Nature's Nook

687 Royalite Way Southeast,
    P.O. Box 471, T0L 2A0
(403) 933-4756 (phone/FAX)
www.canadian-cowboy.com/nature's/nook.htm

Nestled in foothills of Canadian Rockies is this piece of heaven and tranquility. Views from front and back decks span immaculate golf course framed by mountains. Not only a bed and breakfast but also wellness-health retreat, spa where body, mind, and soul are made whole. The flower garden has gazebo, fire pit, swing, hot tub, delightful nooks. Guest living/dining rooms; exercise, therapy rooms. Programs, therapies available. Abundant trails, restaurants, activities. Open year-round.

Rooms: 3 (1/2 PB; 2 SB) $60-70
Full Breakfast
Credit Cards: B
Notes: 2, 3, 4, 5, 7, 8, 9, 10, 11, 12, 13, 14

NOTES: Credit cards accepted: A MasterCard; B Visa; C American Express; D Discover; E Diner's Club; F Other; 2 Personal checks accepted; 3 Lunch available; 4 Dinner available; 5 Open all year; 6 Pets welcome;

British Columbia

Sea S Cape Oceanfront Bed and Breakfast

740 Sea Drive, V8M 1B1
(250) 652-9628 (phone/FAX); (888) 791-1192
e-mail: seascape@bctravel.com

Contemporary waterfront home in a country setting only three minutes from Butchart Gardens. Private baths, queen-size beds, antique furnishings, outstanding views from every room, private decks, guest lounges, hearty breakfasts (muffins, scones, marvelous breads, preserves—all homemade). Government-approved luxurious accommodations. Relax on dock, swim, boat, and fish. Watch seals, otters, bird life, and sunsets. Deep-water moorage availabe. Close to fine dining. Twenty minutes to Victoria.

Hosts: Ray and Judith Sam
Rooms: 3 (2 PB; 1 SB) $95-150 Canadian
Full Breakfast
Credit Cards: A, B
Notes: 2, 5, 7, 11, 12

Arbour's Guest House

375 South Murphy Street, V9W 1Y8
(604) 287-9873; FAX (604) 287-2353

Reservations suggested, seasonal, five minutes from downtown and all amenities. Complimentary glass of wine on arrival, antique decor, with spectacular view of the mountains, ocean, and fishing grounds from large treed property. TV room, bicycle rentals available. Golf course close by. Boat rental arrangements made and experienced guides available for saltwater salmon fishing. No smoking or pets, please. Adult oriented. "Hospitality is our business, in the sport fishing capital of the world." Weekly rates available.

Hosts: Sharon and Ted Arbour
Rooms: 2 (1 PB; 1 SB) $70-95
Continental Breakfast
Credit Cards: A, B
Notes: 2, 5, 7, 9, 12, 13, 14

Campbell River Lodge and Fishing Resort

1760 Island Highway, V9W 2E7
(250) 287-7446; (800) 663-7212
e-mail: crlodge@oberon.ark.com
www.vquest.com/crlodge/

Small, intimate fishing lodge on the banks of the famous Campbell River. Originally constructed of logs in 1948, the lodge is the oldest and most unique in the area. Offers Old World charm and modern conveniences. Dine in the Riverside Cafe or English-style pub. Relaxing outdoor hot tub overlooking Campbell River. Light Continental breakfast served daily.

Rooms: 28 (PB) $50-94
Continental Breakfast
Credit Cards: A, B
Notes: 3, 4, 5, 6, 7, 8, 9, 10 ,11, 12, 14

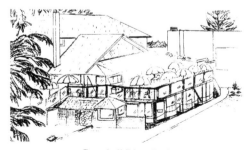

Campbell River Lodge

7 No smoking; 8 Children welcome; 9 Social drinking allowed; 10 Tennis nearby; 11 Swimming nearby; 12 Golf nearby; 13 Skiing nearby; 14 May be booked through a travel agent; 15 Handicapped accessible.

Campbell River
Courtenay
Qualicum Beach
Lighthouse Country
Nanoose Bay
Nanaimo
Chemainus
Ladysmith
Tofino
Ucluelet
Port Alberni
Parksville
Duncan
Mill Bay
Shawnigan Lake
Sooke
Metchosin
Brentwood Bay
Sidney
Victoria

Heffley Creek
North Vancouver
Whistler
Vancouver
West Vancouver
Westbank
Penticton
Fort Steele
Nelson

Surrey
White Rock
Tawassen
Mayne Island
Saturna Island
Salt Spring Island
Pender Island

British Columbia

CHEMAINUS

Sea-Breeze Tourist Home

2912 Esplanade Street, P.O. Box 1362, V0R 1K0
(250) 246-4593 (phone/FAX)

Turn-of-the-century home just steps from
the beach and boat ramp in picturesque
Chemainus. Play park and picnic area at
the beach. Beautiful views from every
room. Lighthouse and island view. Full
breakfast is served on linen with silver and
candles. English and German spoken.
Smoking in designated areas only. Chemainus is on Vancouver Island, just one house
north of Victoria.

Hosts: John and Christa Stegemann
Rooms: 4 (2 PB; 2 SB) $45-55 Canadian
Full Breakfast
Credit Cards: None
Notes: 5, 8, 10, 11, 12

COURTENAY

Greystone Manor Bed and Breakfast

4014 Haas Road, Rural Route 6 Site 684-C2,
    V9N 8H9
(250) 338-1422
www.bbcanada.com/1334.html

Waterfront Heritage Home, built 1918, one
and one-half acres spectacular English
flower gardens. Two miles south of Courtenay on Vancouver Island. Hosts are from
Bath, England. Guest sitting room. British
Columbia government-approved three and
one-half stars. Ideally positioned to explore
the Comox Valley or stop off on way
to/from Port Hardy, Victoria, Sunshine
Coast. Relax in this lovely old home and
enjoy the gardens that the hosts have created. Featured on garden tours, local TV,
and magazines. Children over 12 welcome.

Hosts: Mike and Maureen Shipton
Rooms: 3 (PB) $75-80 Canadian
Full Breakfast
Credit Cards: A, B
Notes: 5, 7, 9, 12, 13, 14

DUNCAN

Garden City Bed and Breakfast Reservation Service

660 Jones Terrace, Victoria, V8Z 2L7
(250) 479-1986; FAX (250) 479-9999
e-mail: dwensley@vanisle.net
www.bctravel.com/gardencity/html

K-23. Eighteen acres with a lake that is a
bird sanctuary. The hosts take pride in offering one of the most unique bed and breakfasts on the island. Furnished with antiques
and gardens replete with swans and winding
walkways, the Tudor-style mansion
designed by architect Samuel Maclure has
two bedrooms with en suite private bathrooms, queen-size beds, and incredible
views of the lake. These world-wide travelers are splendid host and hostess and invite
guests also to enjoy their TV sitting room
with billiards, games, piano, etc. Everything
guests could possibly hope for. From $185.

FORT STEELE

Emery's Mountain View Bed and Breakfast

183 Wardner Fort Steele Road, P.O. Box 60,
    V0B 1N0
(250) 426-4756 (phone/FAX)

Three hours from Banff, Alberta; four hours
from Spokane, Washington; and five minutes from Fort Steele historic town. On 37
scenic acres above a creek and a marsh
where wild animals and birds live and feed.
This new home and cabins have porches
and patios where guests can relax and enjoy
views of the Rocky Mountains. Enjoy
mountain hiking trails, hot springs, historic
sites, golf courses, and ski hills. Smoking
permitted on porches only.

Hosts: John and Joanna Emery
Rooms: 3 (PB) $60-110 Canadian
Full Breakfast
Credit Cards: B
Notes: 5, 7, 8, 9, 11, 12, 13, 14

NOTES: Credit cards accepted: A MasterCard; B Visa; C American Express; D Discover; E Diner's Club;
F Other; 2 Personal checks accepted; 3 Lunch available; 4 Dinner available; 5 Open all year; 6 Pets welcome;
7 No smoking; 8 Children welcome; 9 Social drinking allowed; 10 Tennis nearby; 11 Swimming nearby;
12 Golf nearby; 13 Skiing nearby; 14 May be booked through a travel agent; 15 Handicapped accessible.

HEFFLEY CREEK

Father's Country Inn

McGilliviray Creek Road, c/o Box 152, V0E 1Z0
(250) 578-7308; (800) 578-7322
FAX (250) 578-7334
www.mwsolutions.comfathersbb

Quiet, spacious home nestled in the mountains with breathtaking view of farm lands below and the snow-covered mountains. Relax in the indoor pool and hot tub surrounded by tropical plants. In-room fireplaces, candlelit Jacuzzi tubs, four-poster beds, guest slippers and robes are provided. Guest lounges, two fireside; ski room. Ski packages available. In-summer guided trail ride, fishing. Forty minutes' drive north of Kamloops. Very close to Sun Peaks Resort at Tod Mountain.

Hosts: Brenda Doppert; David Conover
Rooms: 5 (PB) $65-120
Full Breakfast
Credit Cards: A, B
Notes: 4, 5, 7, 9, 10, 12, 13, 14

LADYSMITH

Yellow Point Lodge

Rural Route 3, 3700 Yellow Point Road, V0R 2E0
(250) 245-7422

Enjoy 180 acres of forested parkland surrounded by the Gulf Islands of Canada's west coast. Accommodations range from comfortable, well-appointed yet casual cabins and lodge rooms to rustic little shacks dotted along the shoreline and mead-

Yellow Point Lodge

ows. All rates include three ample meals per day, extra tea times, and all recreational facilities. An elegantly rustic favorite for nearly 60 years.

Hosts: Richard and Sandi Hill; Millie Hogg
Rooms: 53 (23 PB; 30 SB) $110-177 Canadian
Continental Breakfast
Credit Cards: A, B, C
Notes: 2, 3, 4, 5, 9, 10, 11, 12

LIGHTHOUSE COUNTRY

Garden City Bed and Breakfast Reservation Service

660 Jones Terrace, Victoria, V8Z 2L7
(250) 479-1986; FAX (250) 479-9999
e-mail: dwensley@vanisle.net
www.bctravel.com/gardencity/html

K-Bowser. The hosts welcome guests to a very special place in Lighthouse Country, just halfway between Parksville and Courtenay. An attractive self-contained suite, set away from the highway, offers peaceful, quiet living quarters with private entrance and large sun deck overlooking a brook with mini-waterfall. The bright living room has a skylight and fully equipped kitchenette with deluxe range and fridge. Bedroom has a luxurious queen-size bed and en suite bathroom. Laundry facilities available. Every activity imaginable is within a short drive and a sandy beach, stores, shops, post office, restaurants, and service station only a few minutes away. Sorry—no smoking, no children, no pets. From $70.

MAYNE ISLAND

Oceanwood Country Inn

630 Dinner Bay Road, V0N 2J0
(250) 539-5074; FAX (250) 539-3002
e-mail: oceanwood@gulfislands.com
www.gulfislands.com/mayne/oceanwood

Overlooking the water, Oceanwood has 12 charming guest rooms, most with fireplaces and soaking tubs, plus a comfortable living room, well-stocked library, and cozy games

Oceanwood Country Inn

room. The intimate 30-seat waterfront restaurant, open for dinner every day, serves Pacific northwestern cuisine. The extensive wine list features the best from British Columbia, Washington, Oregon, and California. Large outdoor hot tub and sauna are available. Breakfast and afternoon tea included. Closed December to February. Limited smoking allowed. Golf available on the adjacent island.

Hosts: Marilyn and Jonathan Chilvers
Rooms: 12 (PB) $120-295
Full Breakfast
Credit Cards: A, B
Notes: 4, 9, 10, 11, 12, 14

METCHOSIN

Garden City Bed and Breakfast Reservation Service

660 Jones Terrace, Victoria, V8Z 2L7
(250) 479-1986; FAX (250) 479-9999
e-mail: dwensley@vanisle.net
www.bctravel.com/gardencity/html

L-8. Victoria's countryside home. Exquisite log home, built by the owners, features cozy dining room, friendly informative hosts, and beautiful guest's quarters. Queen-size beds, en suite private bathroom, on-going beverage bar, and own private hot tub. Guests' comfort, privacy, enjoyment are the major concerns in this home. Only 30 minutes drive to city center or in 20 minutes in the opposite direction, guests can enjoy the

amenities of Sooke with world-class fishing, museum, and Sooke Harbor House with its wonderful herb gardens. From $110.

MILL BAY (VANCOUVER ISLAND)

Garden City Bed and Breakfast Reservation Service

660 Jones Terrace, Victoria, V8Z 2L7
(250) 479-1986; FAX (250) 479-9999
e-mail: dwensley@vanisle.net
www.bctravel.com/gardencity/html

K-3. Oceanfront, country home on 2.5 acres, 35 minutes north of Victoria, 50 minutes south of Nanaimo. All guests are special—they will have been "spoiled" by the time they leave. Beachcombing, boating, canoeing, tea-for-two in the gazebo or by the fireplace, or ocean-gazing from the swimming pool. Dot's breakfasts include garden-fresh fruits. Activities include Farmgate Winery, cidery tours. Specialty shopping Mill Bay, Shawnigan Lake, Cobble Hill. Nearby are Duncan and the Native Heritage Centre, Cowichan Bay and the Marine Ecology Station, Chemainus, and possibility of a fishing trip with Jim. Accommodations include a suite: lounge (refrigerator, kettle, microwave), queen-size bedroom, private bath, and a room with a twin bed with private bath. Excellent for families. From $80.

NANAIMO

Garden City Bed and Breakfast Reservation Service

660 Jones Terrace, Victoria, V8Z 2L7
(250) 479-1986; FAX (250) 479-9999
e-mail: dwensley@vanisle.net
www.bctravel.com/gardencity/html

K-31. Majestic panoramic view of Strait of Georgia and snowcapped mountains with a bonus of fantastic sunsets—all this awaits guests in this lovely, peaceful, home five-minute's drive from Nanaimo city center. Simmons mattresses, on king- or queen-size

7 No smoking; 8 Children welcome; 9 Social drinking allowed; 10 Tennis nearby; 11 Swimming nearby; 12 Golf nearby; 13 Skiing nearby; 14 May be booked through a travel agent; 15 Handicapped accessible.

beds. Families welcome and spacious rooms equipped for children. From $55.

NANOOSE BAY

Garden City Bed and Breakfast Reservation Service

660 Jones Terrace, Victoria, V8Z 2L7
(250) 479-1986; FAX (250) 479-9999
e-mail: dwensley@vanisle.net
www.bctravel.com/gardencity/html

K-1. Charming contemporary West Coast-style home on two acres of quiet paradise just 20 minutes from Nanaimo's Departure Bay ferry terminal. This is a beautifully unique setting where sunsets color the mountains and sparkle on the ocean below. Only minutes from golfing, boating, strolling nature trails. One guest room has a private en suite bathroom plus a fireplace and sun deck. The other guest room has a private bathroom and sun deck. $75-85.

K- (Keith and Jan's). Fairwinds Golf Course and Schooner Cove Marina and Pub. The suite in this home has a private entrance, en suite bathroom, cable TV, mini-refrigerator, coffee maker, and private balcony with ocean view. A full breakfast is served to guests in their suite. From $90.

The Lookout at Schooner Cove

3381 Dolphin Drive, V9P 9H7
(250) 468-9796 (phone/FAX)
www.islandnet.com/~pixsell/bcbbd/i/1000169.htm

A great base for touring Vancouver Island, this contemporary cedar home is about two hours from Victoria and Tofino. It is in a quiet parklike setting with an awesome view of Georgia Strait and the mountains beyond. The challenging Fairwinds Golf Course is one-half mile away—just one of many 18-hole courses in the area. Schooner Cove Resort and Marina is 500 yards away. Fishing, sailing, kayaking, swimming, riding stables, tennis, and hiking nearby.

Hosts: Marj and Herb Wilkie
Rooms: 3 (2 PB; 1 SB) $60-90
Full Breakfast
Credit Cards: None
Notes: 2, 7, 9, 10, 11, 12, 14

NELSON

Willow Point Lodge

Rural Route 1, S21 C31, 2211 Taylor Drive,
V1L 5P4
(250) 825-9411; (800) 949-2211

A 1920 elegant country inn on the mountainside overlooking the west arm of Kootenay Lake. There is an inviting hot tub in the garden and walking trails lead to creek and forest glades. Abundance of wildlife activity in the forest. Nelson, the tour guide (and golden retriever), is always happy to stroll the trails with guests.

Hosts: Florent and Anni
Rooms: 6 (5 PB) $75-150
Full Breakfast
Credit Cards: A, B
Notes: 5, 7, 8, 9, 11, 12, 13

NORTH VANCOUVER

Grand Manor Guest House Bed and Breakfast

1617 Grand Boulevard, V7L 3Y2
(604) 988-6082; FAX (604) 988-4596

Grand Manor was built during 1911-1912 for the Gill family. James Gill was councillor and reeve of the district. This four-story stone Edwardian home is one of the original mansions of the Grand Boulevard, the widest in Canada. In the heart of North Vancouver, five blocks from Lonsdale Avenue and 20 minutes from downtown Vancouver. Rooms are available in the main house and there is a cozy two-bedroom suite in the back.

Host: Donna Patrick
Rooms: 3 (1 PB; 2SB) $60-130
Full or Continental Breakfast
Credit Cards: B
Notes: 5, 7, 8, 9, 10, 11, 13

NOTES: Credit cards accepted: A MasterCard; B Visa; C American Express; D Discover; E Diner's Club; F Other; 2 Personal checks accepted; 3 Lunch available; 4 Dinner available; 5 Open all year; 6 Pets welcome;

Norgate Parkhouse

Norgate Parkhouse Bed and Breakfast

1226 Silverwood Crescent V7P 1J3
(604) 986-5069; FAX (604) 986-8810

Gardeners' delight. Relax in the large, lush, green West Coast garden. Experience hospitality Vancouver style. Have a quiet sleep and enjoy delicious breakfasts in the morning. Telephones in guest rooms. Guest lounge with TV, books, and fireplace. Close to public transit. Only 12 minutes to Vancouver center. Near British Columbia Rail Station and all amenities.

Host: Vicki Tyndall
Rooms: 3 (1 PB; 2 SB) $95-115
Full Breakfast
Credit Cards: A, B
Notes: 5, 7, 9, 10, 11, 12, 13, 14

Old English Bed and Breakfast Registry

1226 Silverwood Crescent, V7P 1J3
(604) 986-5069; FAX (604) 986-8810

Ambleside Beach in West Vancouver is a traditional gabled home. This bed and breakfast is surrounded by a rambling English garden. The accommodation is a very large self-contained bed/sitting room. It has a small cooking area for light meals, private bath, private entrance with sliding glass doors that open to a patio deck overlooking the garden. This is a terrific location, near to all amenities, great restaurants, buses to downtown, ocean beachfront, golfing, boat-

ing, upscale shopping, etc. Minutes to downtown Vancouver. $95-125.

Deep Cove with a view. Guests will love the ocean and mountain views from the sun deck and garden patio of this contemporary coach house. Fully self-contained and very private. Minutes from the beach, parks, skiing, and restaurants. Twenty minutes to downtown Vancouver. $85.

Deep Cove II. This large, deluxe Victorian Manor is set on the side of the North Shore Mountains. It has a terrific ocean view of Burrard Inlet including Simon Fraser University on the far side. Twenty-five minutes from downtown Vancouver in a very quiet residential area, close to restaurants, mountain trails, beach walks, canoeing, kayaking, and golf and country club. Room one has a large bed/sitting room with TV and fireplace. Private patio deck with ocean view. The large bathroom has a shower and Jacuzzi tub for two. Rooms two and three share a four-piece bathroom. These rooms look out over the forest. The hosts will rent out one of these rooms with a private bath, if requested. There is a guest TV available for use. $95-125.

Deep Cove III is the ideal getaway weekend for two. The unbelievable view from this oceanfront property will have guests wanting to put their feet up and stay awhile. The accommodation is a one-bedroom suite, complete with en suite shower, a sitting room comfortably furnished and with a color TV. French doors open onto private waterfront patio. This modern home is on the side of a mountain. This is an adult-oriented, non-smoking home. Deep Cover offers guests peace, tranquility, beautiful scenery, salmon fishing, canoeing, kayaking, hiking, and fine dining. Yet guests are only 20 minutes to downtown Vancouver.

Lonsdale Quay. A Victorian-style home beautifully furnished with antiques. Each

7 No smoking; 8 Children welcome; 9 Social drinking allowed; 10 Tennis nearby; 11 Swimming nearby; 12 Golf nearby; 13 Skiing nearby; 14 May be booked through a travel agent; 15 Handicapped accessible.

room features a harbor view of Vancouver. Two rooms share a bathroom and one room has a private en suite bath. Close to all amenities and a short walk to the Lonsdale Quay. $95-105.

Norgate Park. Relax in a lush, quiet garden. This bed and breakfast has intriguing nooks and crannies that are filled with interesting items from around the world. Three guest rooms, one with private en suite bath. There is a guest sitting room with TV and fireplace. Twelve minutes to downtown and close to public transit. $95-115.

Ocean Front. An outstanding view awaits guests at this accommodation. It is an ideal getaway spot for two. The one-bedroom suite has a private en suite shower and a bright, comfortable sitting room that opens to the private waterfront deck. Restaurants, hiking, canoeing, and even salmon fishing nearby. Twenty minutes to downtown Vancouver. $125-150.

Pemberton Heights. A wonderful old English-style garden surrounds this bed and breakfast. The accommodation is comfy, casual, and relaxing. The guest area centers around the sitting room and sunroom that open directly to the garden. The sitting room is equipped with a very large TV, piano, fireplace, a juice bar, and a telephone. Close to public transit and 12 minutes to Vancouver center. $65-95.

Sue's Victorian Guest House—Circa 1904

152 East Third, V7L 1E6
(604) 985-1523

This lovely nonsmoking home just four blocks from the harbor, SeaBus terminal, and Lonsdale Quay market is close to restaurants, shops, and transportation. Featuring Victorian soaker baths (no showers).

Sue's Victorian

Each room is individually keyed and offers a TV, a local-call telephone, fan, and video player. Long-term stays encouraged. Visa accepted for deposit only. Guest refrigerator, shared kitchen available from 4:00 P.M. until 10:00 A.M. Make own food or eat out.

Hosts: Gail Fowler and Sue Chalmers
Rooms: 3 (1 PB; 2 SB) $50-75 Canadian
No Breakfast
Credit Cards: None
Notes: 5, 7

PARKSVILLE

Garden City Bed and Breakfast Reservation Service

660 Jones Terrace, Victoria, V8Z 2L7
(250) 479-1986; FAX (250) 479-9999
e-mail: dwensley@vanisle.net
www.bctravel.com/gardencity/html

K-2. Welcome to a cozy, midisland home. Relax and enjoy (seasonally) heated pool, or slate-bed pool table. Get into comfortable shoes and stroll the many nature trails along the Nature Trust Estuary. It is a beautiful, easy trip to the west coast and Tofino area. Five golf courses within a 15-minute drive. A few minute's walk to shops, beach, tennis, miniature golf, and restaurants. Two guest rooms, both with private baths, one en suite.

NOTES: Credit cards accepted: A MasterCard; B Visa; C American Express; D Discover; E Diner's Club; F Other; 2 Personal checks accepted; 3 Lunch available; 4 Dinner available; 5 Open all year; 6 Pets welcome;

Full breakfast served. Adult-oriented home where small pets are welcome with prior arrangement. $60-70.

PENDER ISLAND

The Cliffside Inn

4230 Armadale Road, Box 50, V0N 2M0
(604) 629-6691; www.penderisland.com

Cliffside Inn offering affordable tranquility, is nestled on a Heritage estate setting on three acres of secluded oceanfront on Pender Island, in the heart of the Canadian Gulf Islands. Cliffside is the perfect hideaway for a romantic interlude, or to escape the sounds of silence from pressures of city life.

Rooms: 4 (PB) $129-229 Canadian ($99-149 U.S.)
Full Breakfast
Credit Cards: B
Notes: 3, 4, 5, 7, 9, 11, 12

PENTICTON

Paradise Cove Bed and Breakfast

3129 Hayman Road, RR 1 52 C31,
   Naramata, V2A 6P1
(604) 496-5896

Deluxe adult-oriented accommodations in this modern home in rolling orchard country overlooking Lake Okanagan. Panoramic lake, orchard, and beach views. Clean, very quiet, friendly, and comfortable. One full suite with kitchen, laundry, full bath, hot tub room, fireplace. Three queen-size rooms, two with private baths and lake-view decks. All rooms have their own telephones and cable TV. There is complimentary beverage service in each room. No pets are allowed. Smoking permitted outside only.

Host: Ruth Buchanan
Rooms: 4 (3 PB; 1 SB) $75+
Suite: $115+
Full Breakfast
Credit Cards: A, B
Notes: 5, 7, 9, 11, 15

PORT ALBERNI

Lakewoods Bed and Breakfast

9778 Stirling Arm Crescent, Site 339 C5,
   Rural Route 3, V9Y 7L7
(250) 723-2310; FAX (250) 723-2310

This bed and breakfast overlooks beautiful Sproat Lake and welcomes adult travelers to a peaceful waterfront home in a garden setting. Have a swim before turning in or before the hosts serve a homemade  breakfast. The hosts enjoy having coffee with their guests in the evenings. Dutch as well as English is spoken here.

Hosts: Dick and Jane Visee
Rooms: 3 (1 PB; 2 SB) $55-80
Full Breakfast
Credit Cards: None
Notes: 2, 5, 7, 9, 10, 11, 12, 13, 14

QUALICUM BEACH

Bahari Bed and Breakfast

5101 Island Highway West, V9K 1Z1
(250) 752-9278; FAX (250) 752-9038
e-mail: lhooper@macn.bc.ca
www.npsnet.com/bahari

Rest and repast overlooking Strait of Georgia, watching sea lions cavort and seals bask, shucking oysters on the accessible beach, strolling the philosopher's path, or soaking in the outdoor hot tub—that's Bahari. Conveniently mid-Vancouver Island, making all the island's attractions a day trip or less away. Each room is a calm oasis where guests will luxuriate under eiderdown and wake to enjoy a gourmet's breakfast. The freedom of a two-bedroom self-catered apartment is also available.

Rooms: 4 (PB) $125-250 Canadian
Full Breakfast
Credit Cards: A, B, C
Notes: 7, 9, 10, 11, 12, 14

7 No smoking; 8 Children welcome; 9 Social drinking allowed; 10 Tennis nearby; 11 Swimming nearby; 12 Golf nearby; 13 Skiing nearby; 14 May be booked through a travel agent; 15 Handicapped accessible.

SALT SPRING ISLAND

Cranberry Ridge Bed and Breakfast

269 Don Ore Drive, V8K 2H5
(250) 537-4854; (888) 537-4854 (reservations only)
FAX (250) 537-4854
www.cranberryridge.com

Two kilometers south of Ganges, the main village on the island, on the route to Mount Maxwell Park. Fantastic view of the Gulf Islands and Strait of Georgia from the Sunshine Coast of British Columbia to Mount Vernon in Washington State. Three bed and breakfast rooms with private entrance to each room. The Twig Room has a fireplace. Two rooms have Jacuzzi baths and showers. Large hot tub on the deck overlooking the view. All rooms have feather beds and face the view. "The Best of the Best on Salt Spring." Two-night minimum stay. Small dogs welcome with prior approval. Children over 16 welcome. Canadian personal checks accepted.

Hosts: Gloria and Rodger Lutz
Rooms: 3 (PB) $100-150 Canadian
Full Breakfast
Credit Cards: A, B
Notes: 5, 7, 9, 12, 14

Hastings House

160 Upper Ganges Road, V8K 2S2
(250) 537-2362; (800) 661-9255
FAX (250) 537-5333
e-mail: hasthouse@saltspring.com

In a uniquely pastoral setting, Hastings House is a tranquil retreat for the discriminating guest who seeks and appreciates a tasteful difference in resort destinations. Enjoy a five-course dinner in the dining room prepared by Hastings House's award-wining chef. The dining room is recognized as one of the top 10 inn dining rooms in North America. Dining at the table in the kitchen is a real culinary experience. Nearby activities, such as golf, sea-kayaking, bird watching, and fishing, round out a perfect vacation.

Hosts: Mark Gottaas and Judith Hart
Rooms: 10 (PB) $285-520 Canadian
Full Breakfast
Credit Cards: A, B, C
Notes: 4, 9, 10, 11, 12, 14

Weston Lake Inn Bed and Breakfast

813 Beaver Point Road, V8K 1X9
(250) 653-4311; FAX (250) 653-4340
www./bbcanada.com/172.html

Nestled on a knoll of flowering trees and shrubs overlooking beautiful Weston Lake, this exquisite country bed and breakfast is a serene adult getaway. Down quilts, fresh bouquets, a fireside lounge, hot tub, wonderful breakfasts, and warm hospitality. Recommended in *Northwest Best Places* and *Best Places to Kiss*. Salt Spring Island, near Victoria, has a mild climate, exceptional beauty, and a large population of artists and artisans. Hosts also offer skippered sailing charters in the beautiful waters of the Gulf Islands on a 36-foot boat.

Hosts: Susan Evans and Ted Harrison
Rooms: 3 (PB) $100-125
Full Breakfast
Credit Cards: A, B
Notes: 2, 5, 7, 9, 10, 11, 12, 14

SATURNA ISLAND

Breezy Bay Bed and Breakfast

Box 40, V0N 2Y0
(250) 539-5957; (250) 539-3339
e-mail: breezybay@gulfislands.com
www.gulfislands.com/saturna/breezybay

This 1890s house is nestled amongst orchards, flower gardens, and west coast forest on a 50-acre farm. Its eclectic architecture combines Victorian wainscoting, period wood paneling, and stone fireplace. A spacious library on the second floor and a large lounge with a piano on the first floor are available for guests' use. A wide veranda for relaxing, reading, and bird watching stretches the length of the house overlooking the orchard and pond. Private beach suitable for

Breezy Bay

kayak launching. Wholesome breakfasts and catering to special diets are the host's forte. Families are welcome and the facilities and setting are suitable for groups.

Host: Renie Muir
Rooms: 4 (SB) $75 Canadian
Full Breakfast
Credit Cards: None
Notes: 2, 7, 8, 9, 10, 11

SHAWNIGAN LAKE (VANCOUVER ISLAND)

Garden City Bed and Breakfast Reservation Service

660 Jones Terrace, Victoria, V8Z 2L7
(250) 479-1986; FAX (250) 479-9999
e-mail: dwensley@vanisle.net
www.bctravel.com/gardencity/html

K-30. Homey, comfortable, spacious guest rooms feature many touches to make guests' stay restful and relaxing. Breakfast entrées change daily and include only the freshest ingredients. Dietary restrictions and requests carefully considered. Enjoy a favorite beverage in the garden, relax with a good book. Five-minute walk to a public beach with swimming in clean, fresh water. Shawnigan Lake is enjoyed by adults and children. Three public beaches, boat and water sport rentals, boat launching facilities, trout fishing, and a float plane available for magnificent air tours of Vancouver Island. Central

to four estate wineries, restaurants, golf courses, hiking, artisans, and four private boarding schools. From $60.

SIDNEY

Borthwick Country Manor Bed and Breakfast

9750 Ardmore Drive, V8L 5H5
(250) 656-9498; FAX (250) 655-0715

An English Tudor country manor set on an acre of gorgeous landscaped gardens in the quiet countryside area of Patricia Bay on Vancouver Island. Relax in the outdoor hot tub or walk to the nearby beach. Enjoy a delicious gourmet breakfast on the patio. Minutes from Butchart Gardens, Victoria, airport, British Columbia and Washington State ferries, golf, fishing, boating, and beaches.

Host: Susan
Rooms: 4 (PB) $89-150 Canadian
Full Breakfast
Credit Cards: A, B, C, D, E
Notes: 5, 7, 9, 12, 14

Garden City Bed and Breakfast Reservation Service

660 Jones Terrace, Victoria, V8Z 2L7
(250) 479-1986; FAX (250) 479-9999
e-mail: dwensley@vanisle.net
www.bctravel.com/gardencity/html

A-1. On the shores of Cordova Channel, about 35 minutes north of Victoria city center, overlooking a panorama of islands, mountains, and ocean. Minutes from the airport, ferries, Sidney, and Butchart Gardens. One acre of sandy beach and oriental gardens offers peace, quiet, and privacy. Guest room one has two bedrooms, private entrance, patio, and hot tub. Large sitting room has a wet bar. En suite bathroom features large Jacuzzi tub. Guest room two is a beach house on the ocean. It has a private hot tub, a bed/sitting room with TV, VCR, movies, slippers and housecoat, plus toiletries. Beverages in refrigerator, coffee maker, tea, etc.

7 No smoking; 8 Children welcome; 9 Social drinking allowed; 10 Tennis nearby; 11 Swimming nearby; 12 Golf nearby; 13 Skiing nearby; 14 May be booked through a travel agent; 15 Handicapped accessible.

A-2. One acre of incredible forest, lawns, gardens plus a picturesque Tudor-style home with the most beautiful ocean views with a pathway to the beach. Two suites, each with private entrance and en suite private bathroom with tub and shower. Spacious bedrooms. Sitting room with cable TV. The Tudor Suite has a kitchenette and double sofa bed in the sitting room. Ocean View Suite has additional single bed and private patio adjoing the garden. From $95.

A-4. Only five minutes to parks and seaside town of Sidney. The hosts offer a beautifully decorated private suite with kitchen (includes microwave, etc.), sitting room with TV, bedroom, and en suite private full bathroom. This suite is ideal for the longer stay where guests do their own breakfast. Hot tub. For a family, there is a sofa bed in the sitting room. From $115.

A-6. A beautiful Tudor-style home, nestled in beautiful gardens, only a 20-minute walk to downtown Sidney. After a sumptuous breakfast, meander out the back door to the ocean beach. The queen-size bedroom has an en suite private bathroom with large Jacuzzi tub and ocean view. The other two rooms share a bathroom. From $65-95.

A-7. This incredible executive-style home on the waterfront in a quiet area of Brentwood Bay is only five minutes from Butchart Gardens. After a relaxing sleep in one of the three guest rooms, enjoy a superlative breakfast. Views of ocean and small islands. Guests' sitting room has private entrance, TV, stereo, etc. From $90.

A-15. Drift to sleep to the sound of gently lapping waves in this beautiful seaside home. Step out the back door to a beautiful stretch of clean, sandy beach with incredible views of the gulf and San Juan Islands. Cordova Bay is just a 20-minute drive to Victoria; within walking distance of golf, tennis, shopping, and a wonderful variety of dining places. Room one (honeymoon suite) has an en suite bathroom with extra-large airjet tub and shower, sitting area—all with ocean view. Room two has sweeping ocean views from sun deck and en suite private bathroom. Room three has private bathroom with sunken tub.

SOOKE (VANCOUVER ISLAND)

Garden City Bed and Breakfast Reservation Service

660 Jones Terrace, Victoria, V8Z 2L7
(250) 479-1986; FAX (250) 479-9999
e-mail: dwensley@vanisle.net
www.bctravel.com/gardencity/html

L-3. Two beautifully appointed guest rooms in this lovely country home. The hosts offer true English hospitality in their two large rooms with en suite private bathrooms as well as private deck overlooking forest and distant ocean view. Guests' lounge and breakfast room features a large fireplace and just outside the glass doors is a deck with hot tub for guests' relaxation and pleasure. Wild flowers, deer, squirrels abound. From $95.

Ocean Wilderness Inn and Spa Retreat

109 West Coast Road, Rural Route 2, V0S 1N0
(250) 646-2116; (800) 323-2116
FAX (250) 646-2317

Ocean Wilderness offers five peaceful, forested acres with beach, a natural haven for romantics. Watch for whales and eagles from the hot tub tucked in the Japanese gazebo. The large, luxurious rooms with private entrances are furnished with antiques and canopied beds. Plant a "memory tree" after a multicourse breakfast served in the rustic log dining room. Relax, renew, revitalize in the spa facilities in the peaceful surroundings of

NOTES: Credit cards accepted: A MasterCard; B Visa; C American Express; D Discover; E Diner's Club; F Other; 2 Personal checks accepted; 3 Lunch available; 4 Dinner available; 5 Open all year; 6 Pets welcome;

Ocean Wilderness Inn

an ancient coastal rain forest. Pets welcome by prior arrangements.

Host: Marion Rolston
Rooms: 9 (PB) $75-175 Canadian
Full Breakfast
Credit Cards: A, B, C
Notes: 2, 5, 7, 8, 9, 11, 14, 15

SOUTH SURREY

Crescent Green

3467-141st Street, V4P 1L7
(604) 538-2935; (888) 972-9333
FAX (604) 538-2987; e-mail: surges@direct.ca

Exceptional Canada Select four-star accredited accommodations with an extensive range of facilities, guest amenities, and services. Sprawling rancher on show garden and mature evergreen-forested acreage. Swimming pool, sauna, hot tub. Gourmet breakfast freshly prepared. Near beaches, fine restaurants, and golf. Minutes to U.S. border and 30 minutes to Vancouver. Pamper yourself! Skiing within one hour.

Hosts: Louisa and Keith Surges
Rooms: 4 (PB) $75-120
Full Breakfast
Credit Cards: A, B, C
Notes: 5, 6, 7, 8, 9, 10, 11, 12, 14

TOFINO

Silver Cloud

Box 188, V0R 2Z0
(250) 725-3998; FAX (250) 725-3908
e-mail: silvercloud@mail.Tofino-BC.com
www.tofino-bc.com/silvercloud

Waterfront with quiet privacy and spectacular gardens. View rooms, private baths, one with hot tub. Restful lounge areas; gazebo, waterside decks. Elegant full breakfast served in solarium over the water. Self-contained apartment also available. Silver Cloud is as unique and delightfully surprising as the sea itself. Serving discerning guests for 19 years.

Host: Olivia A. Mae
Rooms: 3 (PB) $95-195
Full Breakfast
Credit Cards: A, B
Notes: 5, 8, 9, 10, 11, 12

Wilp Gybuu (Wolf House) Bed and Breakfast

311 Leighton Way, P.O. Box 396, V0R 2Z0
(250) 725-2330; FAX (250) 725-1205
e-mail: wilpgybu@island.net
www.vancouverisland-bc.com/wilpgybuubb

Adult guests warmly welcomed to this contemporary west coast cedar home. Watch boats travel through beautiful Duffin Passage while enjoying a delicious full breakfast. Walk to Tonquin Beach, galleries, and restaurants. Golf, Pacific Rim National Park's beaches, and rain forest are minutes away by car. Tastefully decorated guest rooms with twin or queen-size beds have private en suite bathrooms. Two rooms with fireplace. Cat in residence. Airport/bus pickup. Recommended by *Northwest Best Places*. Children over 12 welcome.

Hosts: Wendy and Ralph Burgess
Rooms: 3 (PB) $80-95 Canadian
Full Breakfast
Credit Cards: A, B
Notes: 5, 7, 9, 10, 12

7 No smoking; 8 Children welcome; 9 Social drinking allowed; 10 Tennis nearby; 11 Swimming nearby; 12 Golf nearby; 13 Skiing nearby; 14 May be booked through a travel agent; 15 Handicapped accessible.

UCLUELET

Burley's
1073 Helen Road, P.O. Box 550, V0R 3A0
(604) 726-4444

A waterfront home on a small drive-to island at the harbor mouth, offering single, double, and queen-size water- and regular beds, and TV in friendly Ucluelet. Enjoy the open ocean, sandy beaches, lighthouse lookout, nature walks, charter fishing, diving, fisherman's wharves, whale watching and sightseeing cruises, or later, the exhilarating winter storms. A view from every window. Breakfast is buffet style; help yourself to selections of juices, cereal, muffins, toast, spreads, tea, coffee, milk, and chocolate. No pets; no smoking. Adult- oriented. French spoken.

Hosts: Ron and Micheline Burley
Rooms: 6 (S4B) $45-65
Continental Breakfast
Credit Cards: A, B
Notes: 7, 9, 10, 11, 12

VANCOUVER

Albion Guest House Bed and Breakfast
592 West 19th Avenue, V5Z-1W6
(604) 873-2287

This restored 1906 character home is on a quiet, tree-lined residential street in the city. Within walking distance of restaurants, speciality coffee shops, delicatessens, parks, theaters, shopping, a gambling casino, beaches, boating, parasailing, and windsurfing activities. Free bicycle rentals. Hot tub. The four guest rooms have thick feather mattresses, fine cotton linens, and down-filled duvets. The guests enjoy complimentary apéritifs, refreshments, and a gourmet breakfast. Nonsmoking establishment. Reservations recommended. AAA-approved. Listed in *Best Places to Stay in the Pacific Northwest*.

Hosts: Lise and Richard
Rooms: 4 (2 PB; 2 SB) $110-170
Full Breakfast

Credit Cards: A, B, C
Notes: 5, 7, 8, 9, 10, 11, 12, 13, 14

Beautiful Bed and Breakfast
428 West 40th Avenue, V5Y 2R4
(604) 327-1102

Relax in this elegant, clean, new Colonial home with antiques, fresh flowers, views, and quiet. Minutes from downtown. Walk to tennis, golf, Queen Elizabeth Park, Van-Dusen Gardens, YMCA/YWCA, three cinemas, shopping center, and fine restaurants. Three-quarters of a block from bus to downtown, airport, ferries, and UBC. Breakfast in formal dining room with linens, silver, and fresh flowers. Friendly hosts will assist with travel plans. Children over 14 welcome.

Hosts: Ian and Corinne Sanderson
Rates: $85-150 U. S.
Full Breakfast
Credit Cards: None
Notes: 5, 7, 9, 10, 11, 12, 14

Johnson Heritage House Bed and Breakfast
2278 West 34th Avenue, V6M 1G6
(604) 266-4175 (phone/FAX)
e-mail: fun@johnsons-inn-vancouver.com
www.johnsons-inn-vancouver.com

Wonderful restored Craftsman-style home is furnished with Canadiana antique furniture, carousel horses, and comfy brass and iron beds. Full breakfasts include a main course, fresh fruit, and homemade muffins and jams. The friendly hosts invite guests to stay in

Johnson Heritage House

NOTES: Credit cards accepted: A MasterCard; B Visa; C American Express; D Discover; E Diner's Club; F Other; 2 Personal checks accepted; 3 Lunch available; 4 Dinner available; 5 Open all year; 6 Pets welcome;

one of Vancouver's finest and safest city neighborhoods. The house is a six-minute drive to downtown or the university and is close to fine restaurants, services, and tourist attractions. Fifteen minutes from the airport.

Hosts: Sandy and Ron Johnson
Rooms: 3 (2 PB; 1 SB) $75-155 Canadian
Full Breakfast
Credit Cards: None
Notes: 2, 7, 9, 10, 11, 12, 13, 14

Kenya Court
Ocean Front Guest House

2230 Cornwall Avenue, V6K 1B5
(604) 738-7085

Ocean-view suites on the waterfront in a gracious Heritage building minutes from downtown Vancouver. Across the street are tennis courts, a large heated saltwater pool, and walking and jogging paths along the water's edge. It is an easy walk to Granville Island, the planetarium, and interesting shops and restaurants. All of the guest suites are spacious and tastefully furnished. The delicious full breakfast is served in a glass solarium with a spectacular view of English Bay. Children over eight are welcome.

Host: D. M. Williams
Suites: 4 (PB) From $85
Full Breakfast
Credit Cards: F
Notes: 2, 5, 7, 9, 10, 11, 12, 13

Laburnum Cottage
Bed and Breakfast

1388 Terrace Avenue, North Vancouver, V7R 1B4
(604) 988-4877; FAX (604) 988-4877

Restful, peaceful seclusion at this English country home with leaded-pane windows. Set on one-half acre of award-winning English garden, nestled against a forest, yet only 15 minutes from downtown. Each of the guest rooms in the main house has its own decor, complemented by magnificent garden views. Also two cottages in the garden with remodeled bathrooms with soaking tubs, and new kitchen in larger carriage house cottage.

Antiques in main house. Breakfasts are jolly occasions in the big country-house-style kitchen near the cozy AGA cooker or in the breakfast room, where all can enjoy a full three- or four-course meal. May be booked through a travel agent, but not encouraged.

Hosts: Delphine Masterton and
    Karin Essinger (chef/manager)
Rooms: 4 (PB) $125-175 U.S.
Cottages: 2
Full Breakfast
Credit Cards: A, B
Notes: 2, 5, 7, 8, 9, 10, 11, 12, 13, 14

The Manor Guest House

345 West 13th Avenue, V5Y 1W2
(604) 876-8494; FAX (604) 876-5763

The Manor Guest House is an Edwardian Heritage mansion in the heart of the city. Choose from nine spacious rooms, most with king-size or twin beds and private bath. The self-contained penthouse suite has a loft, kitchen, and private deck, which offers a spectacular view of the city. A generous and delicious healthful breakfast is served, featuring fresh daily baking.

Host: Brenda Yablon
Rooms: 10 (6 PB; 4 SB) $65-125
Full Breakfast
Credit Cards: A, B
Notes: 5, 7, 8, 9, 10, 11, 12, 13, 14

Old English Bed
and Breakfast Registry

1226 Silverwood Crescent, North Vancouver,
    V7P 1J3
(604) 986-5069; FAX (604) 986-8810

This **Kitsilano** bed and breakfast has one of the best locations in Vancouver. Within walking distance of downtown, just steps away from cafés, bistros, and restaurants, one block from Kitsilano Beach, one-half block to the bus stop, and a 10-minute walk to Granville Market. The bed and breakfast is a restored circa 1900 Heritage home. There are five guest rooms in all. One has a private en suite bath. The other rooms share two, four-piece bathrooms. $100-125.

7 No smoking; 8 Children welcome; 9 Social drinking allowed; 10 Tennis nearby; 11 Swimming nearby; 12 Golf nearby; 13 Skiing nearby; 14 May be booked through a travel agent; 15 Handicapped accessible.

Shaughnessy. The Canadian Pacific Railway built this Georgian manor in 1913 for its executives. Minutes to the center of the city. The inn has 12 rooms, some with private baths, some with kitchenettes. Each room has its own unique color and design. The inn is set in a wonderful large garden with paths leading to the gazebo. The whole setting is reminiscent of a bygone era. $85-160.

South Vancouver. A warm welcome awaits guests at this budget/backpackers-style bed and breakfast. The hostess provides down-home comfort and big breakfasts. It is in a quiet residential area close to the airport and just a few steps to the busloop to downtown Vancouver. Children are welcome and so are pets. $55-85.

Vancouver Arbutus. The accommodation consists of two good-sized bedrooms. The rooms share a bathroom as well as a very large sitting room. The sitting room is equipped with a wet bar, large TV with VCR, and a library of videos. Fifteen minutes from the airport and downtown Vancouver. Public transit is nearby with two buses going into downtown on a regular basis. A short walk to a unique shopping area of Kerrisdale.

West End. The Langtry is a small deluxe apartment in the much sought after area of the city. Each of the large one bedroom apartments has been beautifully decorated with a mix of Edwardian, Victorian, and Georgian furniture. Great attention to detail. The units are fully furnished and equipped with a business area. Included in the room rate are guests' first morning's breakfast food, free parking, and free local telephone/fax calls. $175-225.

West End II. This one-bedroom fully furnished self-contained suite is a half-block away from Denman Street, a few short blocks from English Bay Beach and Stanley Park, and minutes to the center of downtown Vancouver on foot. Underground parking is provided. The apartment is on the 11th floor of an older high-rise apartment building. There is a bedroom, a bath with a shower and tub, a living room with stereo system, TV, and VCR. The kitchen is completely stocked. The apartment also comes with a telephone/fax for guests' convenience. $145.

Pacific Bed and Breakfast Agency

P.O. Box 46894, Seattle, WA 98146
(206) 439-7677; FAX (206) 431-0932
e-mail: pacificb@nwlink.com
www.seattlebedandbreakfast.com

084. Gourmet Cook. With 100 cookbooks as a source for breakfast ideas, this gourmet cook will make guests' breakfast a special occasion. The private suite with full bath can accommodate four people and has a fireplace, TV, stereo, and is furnished with lovely antiques. Eight miles from downtown Vancouver, this bed and breakfast is convenient to all sections of the city. $110 Canadian.

085. Tudor. This warm and friendly executive Tudor home is in a natural park setting and has easy access to the city center. Two rooms each with private bath share a wing of this lovely home and the hostess will serve a gourmet breakfast. Two-night minimum stay. $80 U.S.

086. Cottage. Restful, peaceful seclusion is what this charming home with a Victorian air suggests to guests. Set in a half-acre of beautifully kept garden, surrounded by virgin forest yet 15 minutes from the city center. Two cottages plus rooms in the main house all have private baths and all are decorated to make guests' stay comfortable. The hostess serves a full breakfast with homemade jams. Relax on the patio and enjoy the stream and fountain. Prices vary for each room up to $175 U.S.

NOTES: Credit cards accepted: A MasterCard; B Visa; C American Express; D Discover; E Diner's Club; F Other; 2 Personal checks accepted; 3 Lunch available; 4 Dinner available; 5 Open all year; 6 Pets welcome;

087. A cedar-sided rancher with designer nooks and crannies holds intriguing statues and knickknacks from around the world. More than 1,000 square feet of decking opens onto lush gardens. Three guest rooms all share bath accommodations. $65-70 U.S.

088. 1912. In a pretty residential area just minutes to downtown, this 1912 Craftsman-style home offers guests four rooms with either private or shared bath accommodations. It is furnished with antiques brought from England and the stained-glass windows, inlaid oak floors, and wood paneling give this home a warm and cozy ambiance. $75-115 U.S.

089. Neo-Victorian. A bed and breakfast newly built in the traditional Victorian style is near Kitsilano Point just five minutes to downtown. Two enchanting guest bedrooms wrap guests in luxury and have romantic balconies that overlook the beach and secluded garden. Breakfasts are gourmet and served on the antique dining table by the fireplace. Enjoy the private guest library. $100 U.S.

090. Kits. Inn designed in the ski chalet style. The hostess has made two suites available for her guests. With queen-size or twin/king-size beds and private or shared bath and private patio and fireplace guests have many choices for their stay at this host home. The Continental self-serve breakfast may include homemade muffins. $75-95 Canadian.

091. Chef. Breakfast will be prepared by a gourmet chef at this Victorian home just minutes away from the heart of the city. One unit with queen-size bed and private bath, TV, and telephone give guests privacy as well as comfort. $90 U.S.

092. 1920. The hostess warmly welcomes guests to her 1920s-style Tudor cottage

where they will enjoy gracious hospitality. Five rooms all with private baths and king-, queen-size, or full beds give guests a wide variety of choices. A gourmet breakfast starts the day. $120-155 Canadian.

095. Tudor-style. Tudor-style home with two lovely guest rooms with private baths. Full breakfast is served in the dining room overlooking the garden where afternoon tea is also served. Open for the summer seasons only. $110-125 Canadian.

Town and Country Bed and Breakfast Reservation Service

P.O. Box 74542, 2803 West Fourth Avenue, V6K 1K2
(604) 731-5942 (phone/FAX)

Offering bed and breakfast homes in residential areas of Vancouver and Victoria, the listings include some small inns. A few of the listings have waterfront or special views. Private and shared baths available. Some have from one to three guest rooms. Some character homes, some West Coast-style homes or townhouse accommodations. Usually within 15-20 minutes to city center. Booking service only, no lists mailed.

2. This one-of-a-kind home nestles near the banks of the Capilano River on Vancouver's North Shore. Guests have their choice of staying in a one-bedroom suite, a two-bedroom suite, or one-bedroom cottage, each with a private bath, entrance, sitting room, and balcony. One of the suites contains a refrigerator, microwave, electric kettle, and hot plate. The cottage contains a full kitchen.

3. This lovely contemporary home has two guest rooms with private baths, one with queen-size bed and patio on the ground level. Excellent location for walking to Kitsilano Beach and park, Granville Island with its market, shops, galleries,

7 No smoking; 8 Children welcome; 9 Social drinking allowed; 10 Tennis nearby; 11 Swimming nearby; 12 Golf nearby; 13 Skiing nearby; 14 May be booked through a travel agent; 15 Handicapped accessible.

restaurants, and live theater, all on the waterfront. Bus within one block. Downtown five minutes. $95-125.

5. Vancouver. Not the usual bed and breakfast, this is a private suite one block from bus line, terrific view of mountains, sea, city. Fifteen minutes to downtown. Bedroom with queen-size bed, sitting room with queen-size sofa bed, TV, also kitchen facilities. Suitable for three or four traveling together. No children. Twenty-five dollars for additional persons. $125.

6. North Vancouver. A contemporary home with a view of the city. Nutritious and delicious breakfast. Mountain-view spa. Families welcome, but children should be over eight years old. Walk to Grouse Mountain Skyride. Fifteen minutes to downtown and Stanley Park. Smoking is not permitted. Seasonal rates available. $85-135.

7. West Vancouver. From this bed and breakfast, guests can see Stanley Park, downtown city lights, the Lions Gate Bridge, the mountains, and the cruise ships on their way to Alaska. Queen-size beds and private baths. All the suites overlook the beautiful, secluded gardens. Guests can sit in the gazebo and enjoy the flowers, the birds, the views, and the serenity of this peaceful setting. $150-190.

8. In Kitsilano, one of Vancouver's most popular and safe neighborhoods, a few blocks to first-class beaches and parks; downtown is a 5- to 10-minute drive. This beautifully restored and renovated 1912 home has a sophisticated contemporary interior. Dining/living room for guests on second floor with ocean, city, mountain views. Three bedrooms on second floor share a bath and the honeymoon suite has a fireplace, double Jacuzzi bath, and en suite bathroom with shower. $115-165.

9. Perfect location for those without a car and like to walk to local buses, shops, restaurants, and cafes, Kitsilano Beach and Park, Granville Island, 5 to 10 minutes to downtown by bus/car. Popular Fourth Avenue area. Heritage-style home with three bedrooms upstairs; two sharing one bath and one with private bath. $75-115.

10. This lovely restored and updated Heritage home has four guest rooms and suite, all with private baths. On a quiet tree-lined street in popular Kitsilano area, walk to shops, cafés, fine restaurants. Garden level suites suitable for family. $135-165.

11. In the Vancouver General Hospital area, this private suite with bedroom, sitting room with TV, balcony, and private bath is just a few blocks from several bus lines, 15 minutes to downtown. Full breakfast is served. $115.

12. In a quiet part of Kitsilano, this new four-room bed and breakfast has all the features to make a stay an enjoyable one. Private and shared baths, TV, and telephones. Within walking distance of shops, restaurants, buses. Ten to 15 minutes by car/bus to downtown. $95-140.

The West End Guest House

1362 Hard Street, V6E 1G2
(604) 681-2889; FAX (604) 688-8812

Built in 1906 for the Edwards family, the West End Guest House is constructed entirely of straight-grain cedar (meaning it has no knots). The young Edwards men operated the first photography shop in Vancouver, and many of their pictures hang in the inn. In 1985 it was restored as a bed and breakfast, complete with a "painted lady" pink-and-white exterior. Its new owner has furnished the rooms with Victorian antiques and reproductions, keeping the style elegant and interesting

NOTES: Credit cards accepted: A MasterCard; B Visa; C American Express; D Discover; E Diner's Club; F Other; 2 Personal checks accepted; 3 Lunch available; 4 Dinner available; 5 Open all year; 6 Pets welcome;

with memorabilia. Rooms include bathroom, TV, telephone, bathrobes and slippers; sun deck has wicker furniture. Sherry served year-round by the fireplace.

Rooms: 7 (PB) $110-210
Full Breakfast
Credit Cards: A, B, C, D
Notes: 2, 5, 7, 9, 10, 11, 12, 13, 14

VICTORIA

Abbey Rose Bed and Breakfast

3960 Cedar Hill X Road, V8P 2N7
(800) 307-7561; FAX (250) 479-5422

Abbey Rose is near Victoria's downtown Inner Harbour, Butchart Gardens, beautiful beaches, and the University of Victoria. Hike at Mount Doug Provincial Park, bike for miles on the Galloping Goose Trail, golf at Cedar Hill Golf Course. Relax in one's own private room with en suite bath and balcony or join the other guests in the sitting room with a cozy warm fireplace. All-you-can-eat delicious home-baked breakfast. Eat delicious strawberries from the Vancouver Island strawberry fields. Stroll down the long and winding road to view the octopus rose garden.

Hosts: Joanne and Arnie Davis
Rooms: 2 (PB) $60-80 U.S.
Full Breakfast
Credit Cards: B
Notes: 2, 5, 7, 8, 9, 10, 11, 12, 14

Abigail's Hotel

906 McClure Street, V8V 3E7
(250) 388-5363; (800) 561-6565
FAX (250) 388-7787
e-mail: innkeeper@abigailshotel.com
www.abigailshotel.com

In the tradition of European-style inns, Abigail's has been marvelously transformed into a small luxurious hotel. Exquisite antique furnishings, crystal chandeliers, crackling fireplace, and fresh flowers provide the romantic ambiance. All guest rooms have private baths, fluffy goose down comforters. Many rooms have Jacuzzis and wood-burning fireplaces. The famous gourmet breakfast is included with every stay. Complimentary sherry served in the cozy library. Just three blocks to Victoria's Inner Harbour, downtown shops, restaurants, museums, parks, and ocean. Children over 10 welcome.

Hosts: Daniel and Frauke Behune
Rooms: 22 (PB) $149-299 Canadian
Full Breakfast
Credit Cards: A, B, C
Notes: 5, 7, 9, 10, 11, 12, 14

Ambleside Bed and Breakfast

1121 Faithful Street, V8V 2R5
(250) 383-9948; FAX (250) 383-9317
e-mail:hosts@amblesidebb.com
amblesidebb.com

Discover Victoria's charms right from the doorstep. Delightful 1919 Arts and Craft home in downtown Victoria's most scenic, tranquil, and walkable Heritage neighborhood. Stroll to all the attractions through lovely Beacon Hill Park or along irresistible oceanside paths. Spacious, elegant guest rooms offer the comfort and pleasure of fine antique beds, cozy goose-down comforters, deluxe en suite baths. Balconied honeymoon suite with fireplace and TV/VCR. Enjoy convivial gourmet breakfasts and gracious, helpful hospitality. Adult-oriented. Canada Select four stars.

Hosts: Marilyn Jessen and Gordon Banta
Rooms: 3 (PB) $85-170 Canadian
 (approx. $60-120 U.S.)

Ambleside

---

7 No smoking; 8 Children welcome; 9 Social drinking allowed; 10 Tennis nearby; 11 Swimming nearby; 12 Golf nearby; 13 Skiing nearby; 14 May be booked through a travel agent; 15 Handicapped accessible.

Full Breakfast
Credit Cards: A, B
Notes: 5, 7, 9, 10, 11, 12, 14

AnnaLea's

856 Wollaston, V9A 5A8
(250) 381-1195 (phone/FAX)
e-mail: snyder@islandnet.com
www.travel.bc.ca

Built in 1906, this house offers spacious
rooms furnished with era antiques, art,
brass beds, lace, and fresh flowers. The two
top rooms on the third floor have sitting
alcoves and private baths, the Alexandra
Room with queen-size bed and the Floren-
tine with double bed. The second floor
Princess Room has double bed and a grand
Victorian bathroom across the hall. All nonsmokers are welcome and for animal lovers,
a cat is a permanent resident. French and
Hungarian spoken.

Hosts: Anna and Lea Snyder
Rooms: 3 (PB) $85-125 Canadian
Full Breakfast
Credit Cards: B
Notes: 2, 7, 10, 12, 14

Arundel Manor

980 Arundel Drive, V9A 2C3
(250) 385-5442 (phone/FAX)
www.victoria-bc.com/arundelmanor/

Arundel Manor, a 1912 Heritage waterfront
home on one-half acre of bird sanctuary
with stunning sunset views. Large bedrooms, reminiscent of a grand past yet with
comforts of today, have king- and queen-
size beds and en suite bathrooms, two
having spacious balconies overlooking the
water. Old-fashioned appointments, an
eclectic mix of antiques, collectibles, and
family heirlooms fill the entire home with
warmth and beauty. A creative home-
cooked breakfast is served in the elegant
dining room.

Host: June Earl
Rooms: 3 (PB) $135-150
Full Breakfast
Credit Cards: B
Notes: 7, 9, 12

A B& B at Swallow Hill Farm

A B & B at Swallow Hill Farm

4910 William Head Road, V9C 3Y8
(250) 474-4042 (phone/FAX)
e-mail: swallowhill@pacificcoast.net
www.pacificcoast.net/~swallowhill

Apple farm in peaceful country setting a
short drive from the heart of Victoria. Spectacular ocean and mountain view. Wildlife
includes deer, eagles, seals, otters, birds.
Queen-size and twin beds, down duvets and
feather beds, private decks. Inspected and
approved accommodation. Delicious breakfasts and friendly conversation. Enjoy whale
watching, hiking, swimming, golfing, fishing, diving. See the sights, curl up with a
book, or just sit and watch nature unfolding.
So peaceful guests never want to leave.

Hosts: Gini and Peter Walsh
Rooms: 2 (PB) $65-95 Canadian
    (approx $45-70 U.S.)
Full and Continental Breakfast
Credit Cards: A, B, C, F
Notes: 5, 7, 11, 12, 14

Battery Street Guest House

670 Battery Street, V8V 1E5
(250) 385-4632

Comfortable guest house (circa 1898) in
downtown Victoria. Beacon Hill Park and the
ocean are only one block away. An ample
breakfast is served and the hostess speaks
Dutch as a first language. Nonsmokers only.

Host: Pamela Verduyn
Rooms: 6 (2 PB; 4 SB) $65-95

NOTES: Credit cards accepted: A MasterCard; B Visa; C American Express; D Discover; E Diner's Club;
F Other; 2 Personal checks accepted; 3 Lunch available; 4 Dinner available; 5 Open all year; 6 Pets welcome;

Full Breakfast
Credit Cards: B
Notes: 2, 5, 7, 9, 10

Beaconsfield Inn

998 Humboldt Street, V8V 2Z8
(250) 384-4044; FAX (250) 384-4052
www.islandnet.com/beaconsfield

The 1995 International Bed and Breakfast winner, this Heritage 1905 English manor with award-winning restoration has nine guest rooms and suites with private bathrooms. Three blocks to downtown and the waterfront. Adult-oriented. Complimentary parking. Highly rated by *Best Places to Kiss in the Northwest,* Fodor's, AAA, *Special Places, Northwest Best Places, Unique NW Country Inns,* and special award-winner: 1995 Bed and Breakfast of the Year by Andrew Harper's *Hideaway Report.* An oceanfront cottage for the ultimate romantic hideaway has two fireplaces, a Jacuzzi for two, hot tub under the stars, self-catering kitchen, TV, and VCR.

Hosts: Con and Judi Sollid
Rooms: 6 (PB) $165-350
Suites: 3 (PB)
Full Breakfast
Credit Cards: A, B
Notes: 5, 7, 10, 11, 12, 14

Dashwood Seaside Manor

One Cook Street, V8V 3W6
(800) 667-5517

Victoria's Edwardian inn by the sea welcomes guests warmly. This 1912 Heritage mansion has 14 elegant suites. Close to town, next to lovely Beacon Hill Park, on Victoria's enchanting Marine Drive. Breathtaking views, Old World charm. Some fireplaces, balconies, Jacuzzis. Each suite is complete with private bath and kitchenette. Breakfast supplies are provided for guests to prepare breakfast at their leisure.

Hosts: Derek Dashwood, Family, and Staff
Rooms: 14 (PB) $63-218
Full Breakfast
Credit Cards: A, B, C, D, E
Notes: 2, 5, 6, 7, 8, 10, 11, 12, 14

Elk Lake Lodge Bed and Breakfast

5259 Pat Bay Highway (Route 17), V8Y 1S8
(250) 658-8879 (phone/FAX); (800) 811-5188

Delightful Heritage home built in 1910. Just 15 minutes from downtown Victoria, 10 minutes from Butchart Gardens, 20 minutes from airport. Grand guest living room, outdoor hot tub, across from Elk Lake Park. Generous delicious breakfasts, comfortable rooms and spacious suites, all with private baths.

Hosts: Marty and Ivan Musar
Rooms: 4 (PB) $80-115 Canadian
Full Breakfast
Credit Cards: A, B
Notes: 2, 5, 7, 9, 10, 11, 12, 14

Garden City Bed and Breakfast Reservation Service

660 Jones Terrace, Victoria, V8Z 2L7
(250) 479-1986; FAX (250) 479-9999
e-mail: dwensley@vanisle.net
www.bctravel.com/gardencity/html

F-1. Only five blocks from city center Inner Harbour, the hosts provide two beautiful suites in their 1912 Maclure-built home. Each suite has bathroom, queen-size bedroom, sitting room with fireplace, and discreetly positioned kitchen—appropriately furnished with antiques and memorabilia. Breakfast is served to guests' suite each morning. A grand entrance hall with original wood and stained-glass windows plus beautiful gardens add to luxurious surroundings. From $125.

F-2. Two spacious suites, each with en suite private bathroom and a sofa bed for an extra person. Breakfast is served in guests' suite. Within easy walking distance of shopping plaza, lieutenant governor's residence, and bus service to city center. Twenty-five dollar for extra persons. From $110-125.

F-5. A private, fully furnished suite, about 30-minute walk to city center and on

---

7 No smoking; 8 Children welcome; 9 Social drinking allowed; 10 Tennis nearby; 11 Swimming nearby; 12 Golf nearby; 13 Skiing nearby; 14 May be booked through a travel agent; 15 Handicapped accessible.

excellent bus route. The hosts provide excellent choice of food and guests prepare it at their leisure. Queen-size bed, sitting room with cable TV, CD, stereo, sofa bed, and local telephone. Full kitchen and full bathroom. Laundry facilities available. From $115.

F-9. Be lulled to sleep by lapping waves in this 1908 character home, which has wonderful views of ocean and is also close to city center and Beacon Hill Park. Old-fashioned claw-foot tub plus many antiques, with beautifully restored hardwood floors and 11-foot ceilings. Ocean and park just across the street. $80.

F-10. Quietly elegant home built in 1915. Impressive open staircase, stained-glass windows, beautiful antiques, and friendly atmosphere. Bright and cheerful dining room. Informed host and hostess assist with itineraries, local sightseeing, etc. Excellent bus service or 25-minute walk to city center. Also a new suite fully furnished with all the comforts and necessities. From $85-90.

I-1. This truly is a gem! A fabulous 1912 Heritage home on one-half acre of ocean inlet. Entering from a large veranda which faces the salt-water bird sanctuary, guests will immediately feel comfortable and relaxed. Spacious rooms have en suite private bathrooms. Many beautiful antiques but all the modern day comforts. From $110.

I-3. This home reflects the beauty and serenity of the Hawaiian Islands. On a salt-water inlet, this bird sanctuary is only 15 minutes from city center. Rooms have water views. Guest sitting area with TV. Extra space for large groups. From $65.

J-1. Elegance and comfort tucked into historic area. Down comforters, bathrobes, Casablanca fans, en suite private bathrooms

in each room. Guests' lounge with fireplace. Early morning "silver tray service" of coffee or tea. Also English-style cottage with two bedrooms, bathroom, sitting room, eating area, kitchen, laundry facilities, and private patio/garden. $95-125.

S-1. This is truly guests' home away from home. The hostess welcomes guests with true West-Coast hospitality with warmth and generosity. The beautiful gardens are waiting for guests and their books. Three guest rooms. One with private en suite bath. The other two share a bath. From $40-75.

S-3. A lovely modern chalet across from Swan Lake and only three miles to city center. Stroll around the lake or marvel at views from atop Christmas Hill. En suite private bathrooms. Breakfast served on the deck or in formal dining room. Excellent menu. From $70.

S-6. Only 10-minute's drive to city center, this cozy, welcoming home has two rooms, shared bath. Breakfast to suite guests wishes. Excellent bus service to university, Royal Oak, and downtown. From $70.

S-7. A working Norwegian fjord horse farm. Only 20 minutes from city center. Guests are invited to use the living room, dining room, patio, and all outside areas. Families are welcome in the large room with queen-size beds and are very well fed with fresh local produce used in the country breakfasts. Hospitality and peace featured in rural setting of this Christian home. From $95.

S-10. Oak trees and ivy setting off beautiful flower gardens provide a warm welcome to this 1930s home about five-minute's drive from city center. The hosts provide great hospitality and delicious breakfast. Private bath. From $75.

NOTES: Credit cards accepted: A MasterCard; B Visa; C American Express; D Discover; E Diner's Club; F Other; 2 Personal checks accepted; 3 Lunch available; 4 Dinner available; 5 Open all year; 6 Pets welcome;

The Gatsby Mansion

309 Belleville Street, V8V 1X2
(250) 388-9191; (800) 563-9656
FAX (250) 920-5651

The mansion is poised overlooking the Inner Harbour. Its twinkling crystal chandeliers, stained-glass windows, and hand-frescoed ceilings extend an invitation for guests to come experience this taste from the past. Conveniently across the street  from the ferry and custom facilities and next to the legislative buildings. Twenty guest rooms available with full breakfast, restaurant, and martini lounge. Come share the experience.

Host: Rita A. Roy-Wilson
Rooms: 20 (PB) $105-303
Full Breakfast
Credit Cards: A, B, C, E
Notes: 3, 4, 5, 8, 9, 10, 11, 12, 14

Gregory's Guest House

5373 Patricia Bay Highway, V8Y 2N9
(250) 658-8404; (888) 658-8404
FAX (250) 658-4604; e-mail: gregorys@direct.ca

Circa 1919. This English country restored farmstead with two acres overlooks Elk Lake enjoy the water gardens, farm animals, and convenient location only 10 kilometers from Victoria and Butchard Gardens. Included are bountiful complimentary English breakfasts, a cozy parlor with fireplace, and guest rooms with antique furnishings. Children welcome. Nonsmoking. No pets. Cancellation policy of three days. Fax and library on premises. Antiques, fishing, parks, sporting events, theater, and water sports nearby.

Hosts: Paul and Elizabeth Gregory
Rooms: 3 (2 PB; 1 SB) $70-85
Full Breakfast
Credit Cards: A, B, F
Notes: 2, 5, 7, 8, 9, 10, 11, 12, 14

Heathergate House Bed and Breakfast

122 Simcoe Street, V8V 1K4
(250) 383-0068; (888) 683-0068
FAX (250) 383-4320

Casual elegance in the heart of Victoria, close to the Inner Harbour and Parliament buildings. Guest rooms have private baths, bathrobes, down comforters, and Casablanca fans. Guest lounge with fireplace, books, telephone, and TV. Silver tray service for early morning coffee or tea in rooms. Full breakfast served in the dining room in the English tradition. Private two-bedroom cottage also available at the same location with Continental breakfast brought each morning. Enjoy the hospitality of a friendly Canadian home with many of the comforts and antiques of a small English inn. Off-season discount rates available.

Hosts: Ann and Ned Easton
Rooms: 3 (PB) $70-100 U.S.
Full Breakfast
Credit Cards: A, B
Notes: 2, 5, 7, 10, 11, 12, 14

Heritage House Bed and Breakfast

3808 Heritage Lane, V8Z 7A7
(250) 479-0892; FAX (250) 479-0812
www.victoriabc.com/accom/heritage.html

Beautiful 1910 registered Heritage home on three-quarters of an acre in a country setting. Quiet and secluded with a lounging veranda. Large rooms, guest parlor with fireplace, and library/den. Gourmet breakfasts. Private parking. Convenient to ferries, downtown, and all highways. Reservations recommended. Two-day minimum stay. No pets. Inquire about accommodations for children. Cancellation policy of five-day notice. Check-in hours are 4:30-6:30 P.M.

Hosts: Larry and Sandra Gray
Rooms: (PB) $115-125 Canadian
Full Breakfast
Credit Cards: A, B
Notes: 5, 7, 9, 10, 11, 12

7 No smoking; 8 Children welcome; 9 Social drinking allowed; 10 Tennis nearby; 11 Swimming nearby; 12 Golf nearby; 13 Skiing nearby; 14 May be booked through a travel agent; 15 Handicapped accessible.

Humboldt House Bed and Breakfast

867 Humboldt Street, V8V 2Z6
(250) 383-0152; (888) 383-0327
FAX (250) 383-6402
e-mail: rooms@humboldthouse.com
www.humboldthouse.com

Relax in the romantic luxury of Victoria's most beautiful and private bed and breakfast, built in 1893. Each guest room now features its own unique decor, Jacuzzi, and fireplace. Downtown on a quiet, historic tree-lined street, this splendid Victorian home is just steps away from the Inner Harbour. Highest rating of four kisses by *Best Places to Kiss in the Northwest*. Also featured in *Country Inns* and *Weekends for Two in the Pacific Northwest*.

Host: Mila Werbik
Rooms: 5 (PB) $85-205 U.S.
Full and Continental Breakfast
Credit Cards: A, B
Notes: 5, 7, 9, 10, 11, 14

Markham House Bed and Breakfast

1853 Connie Road, V9C 4C2
(604) 642-7542; (888) 256-6888
FAX (604) 642-7538
e-mail: markhamhouse@victoria.net
www/sookenet.com/markham

Stroll the gardens and dream; sink into the feather beds and sleep till tomorrow; sip tea on the lawns and dine by the pond or luxuriate in the romantic cottage in the woods featuring private spa and wood stove. The Tudor home is set on 10 truly picturesque acres near the rural village of Sooke, 25 minutes west of Victoria on the way to the spectacular west coast beaches. Excellent bike and hiking trails are nearby and the fishing is superb. Private baths, guest lounge with fireplace, comfortably elegant decor, imaginative breakfasts, and true west coast hospitality will complete a visit. AAA three-diamond-approved. *Best Places to Kiss* 1996/1997. Canada Select four stars.

Rooms: 4 (PB) $95-175 Canadian
Full Breakfast
Credit Cards: A, B, C, F
Notes: 2, 5, 7, 9, 10, 11, 12, 14

Mulberry Manor

Mulberry Manor

611 Foul Bay Road, V8S 1H2
(250) 370-1918

In almost an acre of beautifully landscaped gardens, Mulberry Manor was the last mansion designed by Samuel Maclure. The ambiance of each room is enhanced by elegant decor and complemented by luxurious furnishings to create the idyllic retreat for the discerning traveler. Sumptuous breakfasts served in the formal dining room provide the perfect start for a day's sightseeing around the provincial capital.

Host: Susan Temple
Rooms: 4 (PB) $90-150
Full Breakfast
Credit Cards: A, B
Notes: 2, 5, 7, 9, 10, 11, 12, 14

Mylfford Haven House

1239 Pandora Avenue, V8V 3R3
(250) 0699; (888) 811-3755
FAX (250) 383-0699

Quietly elegant home, built in 1915, with charming features, including an impressive open staircase, and a friendly atmosphere. Breakfast is served in a bright and cheerful dining room. Well-informed hosts will gladly assist guests with their itineraries. Garden level self-contained suite available for longer term stays.

Hosts: Harold and Elizabeth Thomas
Rooms: 2 (PB) $85-95

NOTES: Credit cards accepted: A MasterCard; B Visa; C American Express; D Discover; E Diner's Club; F Other; 2 Personal checks accepted; 3 Lunch available; 4 Dinner available; 5 Open all year; 6 Pets welcome;

Full Breakfast
Credit Cards: A, B
Notes: 5, 7, 9, 10, 11, 12, 14

Pacific Bed and Breakfast Agency

P.O. Box 46894, Seattle, WA 98146
(206) 439-7677; FAX (206) 431-0932
e-mail: pacificb@nwlink.com
www.seattlebedandbreakfast.com

069. On the National Registry. Step back in time to the warmth of the late 1800s and in the morning wake to the aroma of fresh coffee and a gourmet breakfast. Three rooms with private baths. Turndown service and sweet-dream chocolates bring a pleasant close to a memorable day of sightseeing or shopping. $100-150 U.S.

070. Water Views. The property slopes to a bird sanctuary with stunning sunset views from a private balcony. Each large room is reminiscent of a grand past and is uniquely decorated. Full breakfast. No detail is overlooked. Choose from five rooms, all with private baths. $95-125 Canadian.

071. On Antique Row. Built by a prominent local architect, this 1901 Heritage home is within a 15-minute walk to the Inner Harbour. With handicapped accessibility, the hosts can accommodate most special needs requests. The stained-glass windows and many antiques welcome guests for a comfortable stay. Two rooms are available with shared bath (private can be arranged). Full breakfast. $60-80 U.S.

072. Edwardian Mansion. Enjoy the splendor of this grand home and be treated to a sumptuous breakfast served in the elegant dining room. The mansion features rich oak paneling, stained-glass windows, antique furnishings, and a carved-stone terrace overlooking a lovely garden. A variety of accommodations are offered. The Royal

Suite with fireplace, canopied bed, Jacuzzi, wet bar, and a bathroom with onyx tub and gold fixtures. Goose down comforters and pillows, fresh flowers, and afternoon tea. $80-200 U.S.

073. Circa 1899. Filled with antiques, this guest house has the atmosphere of genteel hospitality. All woodwork, fireplaces, and floors are restored originals, and wainscoting, pedestal sink, and soaking tub are in keeping with the period. Three rooms on the second floor have private baths. Full breakfast. $125 Canadian.

074. 1908 Character Home. Just one-half block from the ocean and a 20-minute walk to the Inner Harbour, this host home offers three rooms with queen- or king-size beds and all have private baths. The king-size room has a fireplace, lots of windows, and a big claw-foot tub. Breakfasts are creative and served with warm hospitality. $80-130 Canadian.

075. Near the Inner Harbour. This 1907 historic home has three suites to choose from. Old World charm with New World comfort pampers guests at this guest house. A Continental breakfast is brought to the suite on a tray and special breakfasts can be ordered at the time of booking. $95-105.

076. Near Butchart Gardens. Enjoy the quiet along with a cedar-shaded pond, terrace, and patio. Breakfast can be served on the patio and guests may choose either vegetarian or Continental fare with fresh coffee and country-fresh baked treats. The hostess offers organic products and chemical-free cleaning agents. Shared or private bath accommodations. $55-65 U.S.

077. 1912 Edwardian. A honeymoon suite with a fireplace and kitchen, queen-size bed, and private bath can be guests' for that

7 No smoking; 8 Children welcome; 9 Social drinking allowed; 10 Tennis nearby; 11 Swimming nearby; 12 Golf nearby; 13 Skiing nearby; 14 May be booked through a travel agent; 15 Handicapped accessible.

special trip to the island. Three other rooms with queen-size or double beds and private baths are also available. Just two blocks from ocean beachfront, guests are just four blocks from the heart of Victoria. A gourmet breakfast to start the day of sightseeing or shopping. Open for summer seasons only. $95-115 U.S.

078. Rockland District. Beamed ceilings, seven fireplaces, and elegantly furnished rooms will take guests back to a life of high society of the late 1800s. All rooms are generously proportioned in the grand style with simple touches such as handmade quilts and antique furnishings. Breakfast is served in the dining room. Guests are welcome to enjoy the den and browse the hundreds of books. A number of rooms are offered with shared or private baths and rates vary with each accommodation.

079. Waterfront Views. This guest house has views of the water and the snowcapped Olympic Mountains. Seabirds are at the front door and guests might see a whale swimming in the strait. On a bus route, these suites with private baths and private entrances include a full breakfast. All suites have TVs. $80-105 U.S.

080. Cordova Bay. This contemporary lodge features oversized rooms with private baths, refrigerators, and TVs and some rooms have kitchenettes. The guest lounge and dining room have a fireplace, coffee machine, and microwave oven for heating snacks. Cordova Bay has lovely water views to the east and is in a country-like setting but is just 15-minute's drive from the heart of Victoria and near the ferries, Butchart Gardens, and ocean beaches. Rates vary with accommodations.

082. Heart of the City Hotel. An elegant small hotel in the heart of the city with 40 charming rooms with extra touches including

fireplaces, Jacuzzi tubs, and down comforters. A morning paper, coffee, or tea is delivered to guests' room. Breakfast is served in the dining room. Seasonal rates. $79-150.

184. Tudor House and Romantic Cottage. Imagine a charming Tudor house in a setting of landscaped gardens surrounded by tall trees just a 30-minute drive from Victoria. The main house offers three guest rooms with private baths, feather beds, and down comforters. Breakfast is deliciously designed especially to please each guest. If guests prefer seclusion, the cottage may be their choice with a hot tub and barbecue on the deck. Entering the cottage guests will discover a feeling of space and coziness with a vaulted ceiling, woodstove, and a tiny kitchen concealed in an antique pine wardrobe. The bedroom has a queen-size bed and private bath en suite. Rates depend on choice of accommodation and season.

190. Manor House. A dramatic curved oak staircase welcomes guests to this traditional Tudor-style home. Three guest rooms on the first and second floors have private baths. Enjoy an elegantly served home-cooked breakfast in the beautiful classical dining room. Relax on the spacious sun deck and enjoy the fresh country air or walk to the beach where there is a lounge with a fireplace and ocean views. From $55 U.S.

191. Tudor-style European Inn. Experience the charm and hospitality of this unique bed and breakfast hotel just a few blocks from the Inner Harbour. There are 16 unique rooms individually decorated and offering Jacuzzi baths and wood-burning fireplaces. Sherry and hors d'oeuvres are served each evening in the library, and in the morning join the other guests for the famous gourmet breakfast in the dining room. Please call for seasonal rates.

192. Turn-of-the-century Manor. Secluded on a quiet, tree-lined residential street near

---

NOTES: Credit cards accepted: A MasterCard; B Visa; C American Express; D Discover; E Diner's Club; F Other; 2 Personal checks accepted; 3 Lunch available; 4 Dinner available; 5 Open all year; 6 Pets welcome;

the heart of the city, this registered designated Heritage building was named after a luxurious London hotel. Guests will feel surrounded with Old World charm and turn-of-the-century refinements of period furniture, high-beamed ceilings, and oriental carpets. Enjoy goose-down comforters, wood-burning fireplaces, claw-foot and Jacuzzi tubs, sherry served in the afternoon, and a full breakfast elegantly served. Choose from a wide range of prices.

Prior House
Bed and Breakfast Inn

620 St. Charles, V8S 3N7
(250) 592-8847; FAX (250) 592-8223
e-mail: innkeeper@priorhouse.com
www.priorhouse.com

Prior House is a five-star gracious Edwardian mansion once a private residence for the English crown. Circa 1912. All rooms have cozy fireplaces, some with marble whirlpool tubs. Olympic Mountain views or the beautiful English gardens. A sumptuous full breakfast is served in the elegant dining room or in the privacy of guests' room. Enjoy delicious high tea served daily 4:00-6:00 P.M. in the many comfortable common areas. Children 10 and older welcome.

Rooms: 6 (PB) $125-275 Canadian
    (approx. $90-199 U.S.)
Full Breakfast
Credit Cards: A, B
Notes: 5, 7, 9, 11, 12, 14

The Red Door
Bed and Breakfast

1618 Rockland Avenue, V8S 1W7
(250) 595-6715; FAX (250) 595-3714
www.cityofgardens.com/business/reddoor

The Red Door Bed and Breakfast sits among mansions, gardens, and tree-lined streets in Old Victoria. Built in the 1920s with formal drawing room with marble fireplace and grand piano. Rooms are spacious and comfortable. A hearty and varied breakfast is served. Walks take guests to Government House, Craigdarroch Castle, art gallery, or the ocean. Four-minute's drive to downtown. Off-street parking. Open June 1 through September 30. The hosts are Irish and Scottish.

Hosts: Rhya and Bill Lornie
Rooms: 4 (PB) $95-165 Canadian
Full Breakfast
Credit Cards: None
Notes: 2, 7, 8, 9, 10, 12, 14

Ryan's Bed and Breakfast

224 Superior Street, V8V 1T3
(250) 389-0012; FAX (250) 389-2857
e-mail: ryans@bc.1.com
www.bc1.com/users/ryans

Ryan's is one of Victoria's landmark bed and breakfasts. A unique Victorian home built in 1892. Lovingly restored as a City of Victoria Heritage property, Ryan's exudes an atmosphere of a bygone era. Ryan's is in the heart of Victoria, only a short stroll to the beautiful Inner Harbour and major attractions. CAA/AAA-rated three diamonds. Inquire about accommodations for pets and children.

Hosts: Kathy and Tom Jensen
Rooms: 6 (PB) $59-125 U.S.
Full Breakfast
Credit Cards: A, B
Notes: 2, 5, 7, 9, 10, 11, 12, 14

Sonia's Bed and
Breakfast by the Sea

175 Bushby Street, V8S 1B5
(250) 385-2700; (800) 667-4489
FAX (250) 385-2702

Walk along the ocean to the Inner Harbour. Guest rooms have king- and queen-size beds. Also available is the Penthouse overlooking the ocean with king-size bed, marble bathroom, and sitting room. The hosts were both born in Victoria and like to lay a map out to show their guests what to see and do. They have owned and operated Sonia's Bed and Breakfast for 14 years. Large hot breakfast. Open April 1 through October 1.

7 No smoking; 8 Children welcome; 9 Social drinking allowed; 10 Tennis nearby; 11 Swimming nearby; 12 Golf nearby; 13 Skiing nearby; 14 May be booked through a travel agent; 15 Handicapped accessible.

Hosts: Sonia and Brian McMillan
Rooms: 3 (PB) $55-85 U.S.
Penthouse: $130 U.S.
Full Breakfast
Credit Cards: None
Notes: 2, 7, 9, 10, 11, 12, 14

Sunnymeade House Inn

Sunnymeade House Inn

1002 Fenn Avenue, V8Y 1P3
(250) 658-1414

Take the scenic route into Victoria to discover this custom-designed, beautifully
decorated, English-style country inn in a
village setting by the sea. Steps to beach,
shopping, golf, and tennis courts. Pub and
restaurants. New special occasion suite with
view, whirlpool bath, private dining and sitting room. Lovely English garden. Delicious breakfasts.

Hosts: Jim and Ginny Flanigan
Rooms: 6 (PB) $89-169
Full and Continental Breakfast
Credit Cards: F
Notes: 2, 5, 7, 9, 11, 12, 14

Top O' Triangle Mountain

3442 Karger Terrace, V9C 3K5
(250) 478-7853; (800) 870-2255 (Canada only)
FAX (250) 478-2245

As guests arrive, the panoramic view of
the Olympic Mountains, Juan de Fuca
Strait, and the city of Victoria will take
one's breath away. Enter into the solid
cedar log home and immediately be "at
home" in the warm and relaxing atmosphere. Add to this sincere hospitality and

full, home-cooked breakfasts, lovingly
prepared, and one will have the "complete
bed and breakfast experience."

Rooms: 3 (PB) $70-90
Full Breakfast
Credit Cards: A, B
Notes: 5, 7, 8, 9, 10, 11, 12, 14

Town and Country Bed and Breakfast in British Columbia

2803 West Fourth Avenue, P.O. Box 74542,
    V6K 1K2
(604) 731-5942 (phone/FAX)

1. Beautiful Edwardian home one block to
waterfront road, 10-minute drive to city
center. Three rooms, one with private bath
and two that share a bathroom. Furnished
with antiques and other special touches.
Some sea views. $110-135.

2. The guests are special at Arundel Manor, a
1912 Heritage home on a half-acre of land
sloping to Portage Inlet, a bird sanctuary
with stunning sunset views. The four large
bedrooms have private en suite bathrooms,
and two have spacious balconies overlooking the water. The fifth room has twin beds
and a private bathroom. A full home-cooked
breakfast is served in the elegant dining
room. A cheerful, welcoming lounge with
fireplace awaits the guests. Check in between
2:00 and 4:00 P.M.; check out 11:00 A.M. No
smoking. Not suitable for pets. $145-160.

3. Relax in this beach home with incredible
views over the Haro Strait to the San Juan
Islands and Mount Baker. Each room has a
queen-size bed and private bath. A delicious hearty breakfast is served in the
ocean-view dining room. Within walking
distance to restaurants, shopping, golfing,
and tennis. From $145.

4. This friendly family home, just two
blocks to park, beach, buses, country
bakery, and restaurant is just a short drive to

NOTES: Credit cards accepted: A MasterCard; B Visa; C American Express; D Discover; E Diner's Club;
F Other; 2 Personal checks accepted; 3 Lunch available; 4 Dinner available; 5 Open all year; 6 Pets welcome;

downtown Victoria. Charming rooms, lovely garden, two rooms in main house plus separate cottage for families. $95-125.

5. Heritage house on historic street, large nicely furnished rooms with private baths, queen- and king-size beds, TV. Within walking distance to Victoria city center, Beaconhill Park, waterfront. $98-135.

6. This Edwardian-style Heritage home is furnished with antiques and has all the comforts of home. Quiet, yet within easy walking distance to downtown Victoria. $95-115.

A View to Sea Bed and Breakfast

626 Fernhill Road, V9A 4Y9
(250) 388-6669; FAX (250) 382-5108
e-mail: rosenbry@ii.ca
www.victoria-bc.com/ViewToSea

British hospitality awaits guests at this California-style home, which is set on half an acre of parklike seclusion and offers many luxuries. Enjoy a relaxing retreat with mountain and sea views; five minutes from downtown Victoria, close to buses, shops, and a recreation center. King- or queen-size beds, en suite bathrooms, down duvets, terry robes, beverage trays, hair dryers, reading lofts, sumptuous breakfasts, and a hot tub for further relaxation. Canada Select four-star.

Hosts: Bryan and Rose Wagstaff
Rooms: 3 (PB) $95-150 Canadian
Full Breakfast
Credit Cards: A, B
Notes: 2, 5, 7, 9, 11, 12

Wooded Acres Bed and Breakfast

4907 Rocky Point Road, V9C 4G2
(250) 478-8172

Unique countryside log home is secluded in a parklike setting on three acres of forest.

Wooded Acres

Together, the hosts built their log home and have created an authentic old-fashioned bed and breakfast. Suites provide complete privacy, queen-size beds, and sheltered hot tubs to relax amidst the pleasures and relics of bygone times. Breakfast is a feast of specialties baked daily and served at guests' convenience. The elegance of candlelight, lace, and fine china help to provide lasting memories for all special occasions. Adult oriented.

Hosts: Elva and Skip Kennedy
Rooms: 2 (PB) $110
Full Breakfast
Credit Cards: None
Notes: 2, 5, 7, 9, 10, 11, 12, 14

WESTBANK (KELOWNA)

Lakeview Mansion

3858 Harding Road, V4T 2J9
(250) 768-2205 (phone/FAX)

Okawagan Valley. Guests are welcomed to warm German hospitality in superlarge, elegant home on private, spacious, parklike grounds just above Okanagan Lake. Comfortable, large, beautiful rooms with cable TV and direct access to 2,000 square feet of open and covered sun decks. Air conditioning. Breathtaking panoramic view of lake. Relax in chlorine-free six-jet Jacuzzi. Cozy guest library with TV/VCR/movies.

7 No smoking; 8 Children welcome; 9 Social drinking allowed; 10 Tennis nearby; 11 Swimming nearby; 12 Golf nearby; 13 Skiing nearby; 14 May be booked through a travel agent; 15 Handicapped accessible.

Delicious gourmet breakfast with fruit from own trees. Close to downtown Kelowna. Five-minute walk to beaches.

Rooms: 3 (2 PB; 1 SB) $70-80
Full Breakfast
Credit Cards: A, B
Notes: 2, 5, 7, 8, 9, 10, 11, 12, 13, 14

WEST VANCOUVER

Beachside Bed and Breakfast

4208 Evergreen Avenue, V7V 1H1
(604) 922-7773; (800) 563-3311
FAX (604) 926-8073

Stay in a quiet, beautiful waterfront home in one of the finest areas in Vancouver. A lovely beach is at the doorstep. Minutes from downtown, Stanley Park, Horseshoe Bay ferries, and north shore attractions. Its southern exposure affords a panoramic view of the city, harbor, and Alaska cruise ships. A hearty home-baked breakfast is served in the seaside dining room. Close to fishing, sailing, wilderness hiking, skiing, antiques, shopping, and great restaurants. Children over 10 welcome.

Hosts: Gordon and Joan Gibbs
Rooms: 3 (PB) $145-225 Canadian
    (approx. $100-155 U.S.)
Full Breakfast
Credit Cards: A, B
Notes: 2, 5, 7, 9, 10, 11, 12, 13, 14

Beachside

Creekside Bed and Breakfast

1515 Palmerston Avenue, V7V 4S9
(604) 926-1861; (604) 328-9400 (cellular)
FAX (604) 926-7545

Quiet, romantic, parklike, casual setting with a creek flowing through this natural garden property. All-you-can-eat home-baked breakfast. Luxurious en suite bath with two-person Jacuzzi in a glass-roofed bathroom. The second bath also has a Jacuzzi tub and skylights. In-room TVs with remotes, stocked mini-refrigerators, and coffee makers. Complimentary wines, beverages, snacks, toiletries, and robes. Ideal honeymoon setting. Commissionable. Fifty percent deposit required. Half-price coupons available for entertainment and dining. Two-day minimum stay. Pets welcome by prior arrangements. Smoking not permitted indoors.

Hosts: John Boden and Donna Hawrelko
Rooms: 2 (PB) $100-145
Full Breakfast
Credit Cards: A, B
Notes: 5, 7, 9, 10, 11, 12, 13, 14

Lighthouse Retreat Bed and Breakfast

4875 Water Lane, V7W 1K4
(604) 926-5959; FAX (604) 926-5755
e-mail: 70401.3313@compuserve.com
www.vancouver-bc.lighthouseretreat/

Private romantic suites. An escapist's delight! Yet convenient to downtown Vancouver. This tranquil, secluded glade is a stone's throw from the bustle of downtown Vancouver. Elegance and creature comforts await, as do the most romantic of private garden terraces. A short and beautiful scenic coastal drive from the city brings one to this home on the edge of the rain forest and just minutes from 185-acre Lighthouse Park. A scenic, restful haven for weekend getaways, vacation, skiing, or golfing holidays or for any special occasion.

NOTES: Credit cards accepted: A MasterCard; B Visa; C American Express; D Discover; E Diner's Club; F Other; 2 Personal checks accepted; 3 Lunch available; 4 Dinner available; 5 Open all year; 6 Pets welcome;

Hosts: Hanna and Ron Pankow
Suites: 2 (PB) $95-125 Canadian
   (approx. $75-95 U.S.)
Full Breakfast
Credit Cards: None
Notes: 5, 7, 10, 11, 12, 13, 14

Hosts: Ann and Terry Spence
Rooms: 3 (1 PB; 2 SB) $65-125 Canadian
   ($45-85 U.S.)
Full Breakfast
Credit Cards: A, B
Notes: 2, 5, 7, 8, 9, 10, 11, 12, 13, 14

WHISTLER

Golden Dreams Bed and Breakfast

6412 Easy Street, V0N 1B6
(604) 932-2667; (800) 668-7055
FAX (604) 932-7055; e-mail: golden@whistler.net

Enjoy this world-class year-round resort just two hours from Vancouver. Be surrounded by nature's beauty and pampered with a wholesome breakfast, homemade jams, and fresh breads. Unique theme rooms feature cozy duvets, sherry decanter. Relax in outdoor hot tub with mountain views. Family room with wood fireplace. Full guest kitchen. Just one mile to village express gondolas. Valley trail system and bus route at doorstep. On-site bike rentals. Many seasonal activities. Now in two locations. Whistler Town Plaza is within walking distance to the express ski lifts, fabulous restaurants, and new shops. These new condos feature gas fireplace, entertainment center, full kitchen, spa access, and underground parking.

WHITE ROCK

Dorrington Bed and Breakfast

13851 19A Avenue, V4A 9M2
(604) 535-4408; FAX (604) 535-4409
www.bbcanada.com/508.html

Dorrington is a magnificent brick-and-stone estate set on one-half acre featuring themed rooms with private bathrooms, outdoor hot tub, tennis court, pond, and gardens. A four-poster double bed graces the Victorian Room, and a unique queen-size bed hewn from maple branches themes the St. Andrews Room. Full breakfast is served in the Hunt Salon or on the patio overlooking the peaceful gardens. Dorrington is close to the border or ferry terminal to Victoria and 45 minutes from Vancouver.

Rooms: 2 (PB) $90 Canadian
Full Breakfast
Credit Cards: A, B
Notes: 2, 5, 7, 9, 10, 11, 12, 13, 14

7 No smoking; 8 Children welcome; 9 Social drinking allowed; 10 Tennis nearby; 11 Swimming nearby; 12 Golf nearby; 13 Skiing nearby; 14 May be booked through a travel agent; 15 Handicapped accessible.

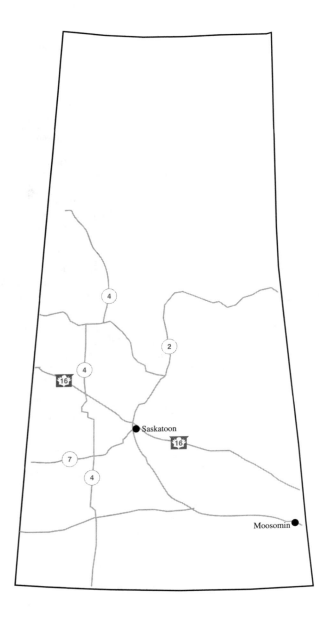

Saskatchewan

Saskatchewan

Windover Guest House

902 Windover Avenue, P.O. Box 1204, S0G 3N0
(306) 435-4336; (800) 252-1746
FAX (306) 435-3821

Private home built in 1890 by a pioneer builder as his personal residence. Many original features—handcarved front door, original hardward, and doorbell. Hosts invite guests to share their enjoyment in this little piece of history. Both rooms are on the second floor and feature double beds. House specialty is Victorian jams. By reservation only. Check-in is 5:00 to 9:00 P.M.

Hosts: Peter and Joy Rousay
Rooms: 2 (PB) $40
Full Breakfast
Credit Cards: None
Notes: 5, 7, 12

Brighton House Bed and Breakfast

1308 5th Avenue North, S7K 2S2
(306) 664-3278; FAX (306) 664-6822

A gracious character home with the warmth of country, furnished with antiques, beautifully renovated to preserve its atmosphere of a bygone era. Ideal spot for honeymoons or anniversaries. Complimentary use of bicycles for exploring the scenic river bank. Relax in an outdoor hot tub after a long, busy day. Continental plus breakfast served. May be booked through CRS at 1-800-667-7191.

Host: Barb
Rooms: 4 (2 PB; 2 SB) $45-55 Canadian

Brighton House

Continental Breakfast
Credit Cards: A, B
Notes: 2, 5, 7, 8, 9, 10, 11, 12, 13

Chaplin's Country Bed and Breakfast

Rural Route 5, Box 43, S7K 3J8
(306) 931-3353 (phone/FAX)
e-mail: chaplinr@duke.usask.ca
www.dbs2.com/chaplins

The hosts offer warm hospitality and comfortable accommodation in their country home decorated with prairie antiques. For privacy, guest quarters and lounge are on the second floor. Friendly barnyard animals, awesome sunsets, lovely gardens, bird watching, quiet.

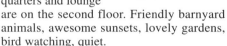

Hosts: Ron and Kathy Chaplin
Rooms: 3 (3 SB) $50
Full Breakfast
Credit Cards: F
Notes: 2, 5, 7, 12

NOTES: Credit cards accepted: A MasterCard; B Visa; C American Express; D Discover; E Diner's Club; F Other; 2 Personal checks accepted; 3 Lunch available; 4 Dinner available; 5 Open all year; 6 Pets welcome; 7 No smoking; 8 Children welcome; 9 Social drinking allowed; 10 Tennis nearby; 11 Swimming nearby; 12 Golf nearby; 13 Skiing nearby; 14 May be booked through a travel agent; 15 Handicapped accessible.